FRANK AND JESSE JAMES

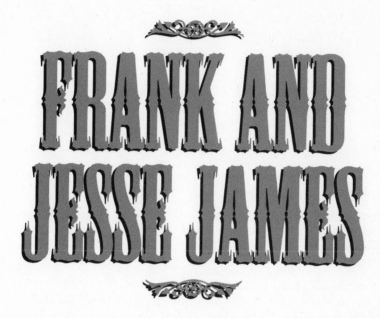

FRANK AND JESSE JAMES

THE STORY BEHIND THE LEGEND

TED P. YEATMAN

CUMBERLAND HOUSE
NASHVILLE, TENNESSEE

PUBLISHED BY
CUMBERLAND HOUSE PUBLISHING, INC.
431 Harding Industrial Drive
Nashville, Tennessee 37211

Cover design by Gore Studio, Nashville, Tennessee.
Maps by Hearthside Design, Nashville, Tennessee.

Library of Congress Cataloging-in-Publication Data

Yeatman, Ted P.
Frank and Jesse James : the story behind the legend / Ted P. Yeatman.
p. cm.
Includes bibliographical references and index.
ISBN 1-58182-080-1 (hardcover; alk. paper)
ISBN 1-58182-325-8 (trade paper; alk. paper)
1. James, Jesse, 1847–1882. 2. James, Frank, 1844–1915. 3. Outlaws—West (U.S.)—Biography. 4. Frontier and pioneer life—West (U.S.) 5. West (U.S.)—History—1860–1890. 6. West (U.S.)—Biography. I. Title.
F594.J27 Y43 2000
364.15'52'0922—dc21
[B]   00-26750

Printed in Canada
1 2 3 4 5 6 7 8 9 10 — 07 06 05 04 03

To the memory of two pioneers in the quest for
the truth behind the James legend:

Dr. William A. Settle Jr.,
1915–88,
Professor Emeritus of History,
University of Tulsa,
and author of Jesse James Was His Name

and

Milton F. Perry,
1926–91,
Director of Clay County Historic Sites
and restorer of the James farm

By some intelligent people they are regarded as myths; by others they are in league with the devil. They are neither, but they are uncommon men.

John Newman Edwards

If the incidents seem to the reader at all marvelous or improbable, I can but remind him, in the words of the old adage, that "Truth is stranger than fiction."

Allan Pinkerton

Contents

Preface

We do not object to criticism; and we do not expect that the critic will read the book before writing a notice of it. We do not even expect the reviewer to say that he has not read it.

Mark Twain and Charles D. Warner, The Gilded Age (1873)

I FIRST BEGAN THIS study of the story of Frank and Jesse James in January 1975 to track down all the information I could find on the outlaw brothers' residence in Middle Tennessee from 1877 to 1881. I planned simply to take a year, dig up all that I could, and bury it all in a nice, neat feature article. But accounts of the James brothers' Tennessee years, I found, were often vague and were jumbled chronologically, not to mention contradictory. It was difficult to tell what happened when, and questionable accounts sometimes crept into the story. My curiosity was piqued, and what started as a yearlong project eventually spread over nearly two and a half decades to include much more than just the James brothers' years in Tennessee.

With the exception of a handful of works (the most notable being the late William A. Settle's *Jesse James Was His Name*), accurate, well-documented accounts of the James story were not the norm. In the thirty years since Settle's book appeared in 1966, a considerable body of new information has come to light that has significantly altered what is known. Examples include the correspondence of Detective Allan Pinkerton concerning the controversial raid on the James-Samuel farm in January 1875, which has been overlooked in earlier works, and the forensic work of the 1995–96 James Scientific Project led by Prof. James Starrs. Therefore this book is intended as a supplement to Settle's impressive and pioneering volume. Settle encouraged my work on the Tennessee years of the James brothers, and but for his untimely death in 1988, he was to have written an introduction to the present book. It was my privilege to have known and consulted with him during the last ten years of his life.

11

Adding some details lacking in Settle's work, I have decided to write this as a narrative, telling what I believe probably occurred based on a variety of sources. I hope other scholars will excuse me for taking this route. While it was not my original intent to give a detailed, blow-by-blow account of the James brothers' lives, I have tried to provide a reasonable background of interesting new or obscure material relating to their lives and the lives of those associated with them.

While it is possible to get a fairly good picture of the James brothers' activities during the Civil War, their postwar years are harder to pin down. Only after their marriages, sometime around 1874, is it possible to document their activities with some regularity and to sort some of the facts from the fog of legend. The Pinkerton letters, mentioned earlier, provided hitherto unknown details of that famous detective agency's work involving the Jameses in 1874–75. Under aliases, Frank and Jesse James lived openly in Tennessee in 1875 and from 1877 to 1881, and they were known to many individuals. Recollections by those who knew them as ostensibly "law-abiding citizens" provide some most interesting primary-source accounts, often given under oath in court testimony. For many decades these Tennessee years were largely ignored by authors who preferred to dwell on the blood-and-thunder aspects of the James brothers' lives. Usually they were depicted either as "American Robin Hoods" or simply as "hoods," depending on the source. I have attempted to provide a truer, more rounded picture somewhere between these extremes, utilizing sources that are uncolored by the often partisan contemporary politics of late-nineteenth-century Missouri.

The truth is that although the James brothers had reputations as bandits of the Old West, a surprising amount of their time was spent east of the Mississippi, and a sizable amount of my research has been centered in this area. Records at the National Archives and the Library of Congress proved to be an untapped mine of information about this part of their lives, as were numerous sources in Tennessee, Kentucky, and West Virginia. Modern-day researchers would not think of the rural areas west of the Appalachians and east of the Mississippi as being "the West," but during the James brothers' lifetimes, this part of the country was often not much different from states we today think of as "western." This area had more in common with the states west of the Mississippi than it did with the southern states east of the Appalachians. Even during the Civil War the area was known as the "western theater" of military operations. It is my hope that, with this work, historians and scholars will reconsider some of the arbitrary boundaries that have been placed on "the West."

In the years following the Civil War, the Trans-Appalachian West, an area east of the Mississippi and both north and south of the Ohio, had its own share of bank, stagecoach, and train robberies, and many residents still alive in the 1870s and 1880s could recall when Indian tribes, prior to their removal, still held a sizable portion of the land. While perhaps less wild than the Trans-Mississippi West, it still retained a frontier quality. In one case the James gang slipped into and out of a robbery site by using the Natchez Trace, a pioneer landmark of the area, long after it had fallen into general disuse.

In most books about the James brothers, short shrift is given to events that happened after Frank James's surrender and trials. But this period turned out to be, in its own way, at least as interesting as the period of outlawry. The story of the Younger-James Wild West Show is certainly one of the oddest in the annals of show business. Until his death in 1915, Frank James led an often obscure but nevertheless interesting life. Jesse's son, Jesse Edwards James, lived in the shadow of his outlaw father. His widow's published memoir gives an interesting account of his life. However, she omitted certain important episodes she probably wanted to forget.

In writing this account, I have tried to strike a balance between the scholarly and what some might term the popular. For those who care to look, I have expanded on some points in the endnotes. I have preferred to consider accounts of some individuals as oral history rather than as "folklore," which, in its technical definition, should not be ascribable to a single historically identifiable source. Nevertheless, I have tried to use only those oral history accounts that I can link to persons who were historically associated with the James story and thus have some validity.

Just who were Frank and Jesse James? While all the pieces of the puzzle may never be found, my hope is that this research will shed new historical light on one of the great American legends. In this volume, characters who often have been portrayed as larger than life are presented in a more realistic perspective against a backdrop of the times in which they lived. The James story has a certain timeless quality, with timeless lessons, for those who care to study it.

Acknowledgments

THE WORK OF PUTTING together this book took nearly twenty-five years, more than five of which were spent in the writing. I had no idea when I started collecting this material what a daunting task it would be. I would like to thank those who have assisted me in some notable way in getting at "the story behind the legend."

The staff of the Military Reference Branch, National Archives, notably Deanne Blanton, Michael Musick, Mike Meier, Mike Pilgrim, and Tod Butler, as well as the Civil Reference Branch; the staffs of the Law Library and Manuscript Collection at the Library of Congress; Lee Pollock of Princeton, Illinois, who was invaluable in pointing out and supplying me with hitherto unknown James material that came into his collection; George Warfel of Venice, Florida, who was of great assistance over the years in matters concerning James photographs and James history; Patrick Brophy of Nevada, Missouri, the Vernon County Historical Society, and curator of the Bushwhacker Museum in Nevada, Missouri; Mrs. Nina Johnson, Cabell County Public Library, Huntington, West Virginia; Prof. James Starrs of the department of forensic science at George Washington University, Washington, D.C.; Wayne Barnes of the University of Missouri Library in Columbia, who went above and beyond in helping me research early Missouri newspapers; Fred Egloff of Wilmette, Illinois, of the Chicago Corral of Westerners, particularly for his assistance with sources in the Chicago area relating to the Pinkertons and their connections with the Rock Island arsenal; Judge James Ross, great-grandson of Jesse James, for information on his family; Walt Mathers of Glen Burnie, Maryland, for his help in detecting

James sites in Baltimore; Mary Glenn Hearne of the Nashville Room at the Public Library of Nashville and Davidson County; Marley Brant of Marietta, Georgia, author of *The Outlaw Youngers*.

In addition to those above, there are other individuals who have helped make this book a reality through their support in various ways, particularly during the final year of work on the manuscript. I would like to thank my cousin Ruth Kriz and her husband, Stan; Fred Thornton and Jack Raun; Dave Torzillo of Mason's Books in Chambersburg, Pennsylvania; Dr. Robert Ogles, William Pepper Bruce, Mike and Dona Bennett, Ed Masuoka, Peter Ansoff, Larry Guthrie, and John Kohl.

I would also like to thank Ron Pitkin, president and publisher of Cumberland House Publishing, for his confidence in this project, and my editor, Ed Curtis, for his guidance in bringing the ship into port.

FRANK AND JESSE JAMES

1

Gads Hill

Impetuosity and audacity often achieve what ordinary means fail to achieve.

Niccolo Machiavelli, Discourses (1531)

IT WAS A CRISP Saturday morning, about 10:10, when train No. 7 of the Saint Louis, Iron Mountain and Southern—the *Little Rock Express*, as it was known—pulled out of the Plum Street station in Saint Louis and headed south. Despite its nickname, the *Express* might as well have been a slow freight.

Although it pulled only a combination mail-baggage car, two passenger coaches, and a Pullman sleeper car, it was running an hour behind schedule. On board were twenty-five passengers: twelve men, five women, and eight children. The date was January 31, 1874.[1]

About 3 P.M. five men, dressed in plain, homespun clothing and "cavalry leggings" of a style worn during the Civil War, entered the tiny whistlestop of Gads Hill, a remote community on the Iron Mountain line about one hundred miles south of Saint Louis. Gads Hill was not much of a place. Three houses, an abandoned sawmill, and a railroad platform were all that comprised this hamlet in the middle of nowhere, which now merely served as a local collection point for mail and some occasional freight. Founded in 1871 by George W. Creath, Gads Hill was named for the estate of British author Charles Dickens. But the name Gads Hill had another significance that Creath may not have been aware of. For several centuries the English landmark for which Dickens had christened his home was a popular resort for highwaymen. No doubt the men on horseback that day in 1874 were aware of this fact. Armed with Navy revolvers and shotguns, they rounded up Gads Hill's fifteen inhabitants and herded them to an area near the train platform, where a bonfire was soon roaring to brush off the cold. In the course of the roundup, a merchant named McMillen was robbed of a rifle and between $700 and $800; quick thinking allowed him to hide another $450 in the lining of his coat. The locals, huddling next to the fire, could only imagine what was to follow.[2]

About 5:15 P.M. a train whistle signaled from afar. By now the good citizens had, according to one account, been locked in one of the houses (another account has them still by the fire), under guard. Conductor C. A. Alford, on the approaching train, noticed a man violently waving a red "danger" flag up the track. The engineer slowed, and the locomotive screeched to a halt onto a siding, the intruders having thrown the switch. As the puzzled conductor leaped to the platform to investigate he was collared by a man wearing a dirty cloth mask that covered his whole face, with holes for both the eyes and mouth. "Stand still, or I'll blow the top of your damned head off," he ordered, shoving a revolver in the stunned conductor's face.[3] Three other men crawled out from under the platform, and another appeared on the other side of the train. The engineer and fireman were hustled off the locomotive, then one of the bandits shouted to the frightened passengers that they had the conductor and engineer as prisoners but that the men wouldn't be harmed if the passengers behaved. The trainmen were hustled onto the platform and guarded by two of the gunmen while the other three men boarded and got down to business.[4]

Business, in this case, was very good. The first stop was the baggage car, where three of the bandits seized the express messenger, the mail agent, and the baggage master, putting them in one corner of the car "with one of the robbers to guard them at the point of a frightful looking pistol," by one account. They demanded that the mail agent show them the registered letters and parcels, but he refused. The masked men then rifled the car and found one parcel that reportedly contained four thousand dollars.

The Adams Express clerk was next. After he delivered up the keys to the safe, nearly $1,080 in money parcels found its way into the plunderers' sack. For some reason they neglected to snatch a silver watch that was also there. Before moving on, they lifted a revolver and some tobacco from the conductor's valise.[5]

After hustling the men from the baggage car to join their companions outside, the three bandits proceeded to the passenger-smoking car, brandishing their pistols at the travelers. "They weren't careful with the passengers," conductor Alford recalled. "They punched them in the ribs with pistols and pointed their shooting-irons into their faces." According to a later Saint Louis newspaper account that soon became incorporated into legend, the gunmen reportedly examined each man's hands to see if he was a "workingman." If this deed of outlaw chivalry happened, there were probably few of the laboring masses on board (at least by definition of the bandits). In a later interview, Alford failed to mention the fabled palm-reading exercise. "Not a man escaped," he recalled. "Everyone was robbed, though they took only one gold watch. Several had fine watches, but the thieves passed them over." John F. Lincoln, the superintendent of the Saint Paul and Sioux City Railroad, forfeited two hundred dollars.

Also among those robbed were the sleeping car porter, James Johnson, who lost two dollars, and an unidentified "train boy" (possibly selling dime novels and other reading matter), who coughed up forty dollars. The conductor, Alford, was relieved of fifty dollars but was spared his watch on the protest of baggage master Louis Constant. "For God's sake, don't take his watch. It was presented to him," he argued. They also spared the Reverend T. A. Hagbritt, who was asked to pray for the bandits in return.

One of the masked men recited lines from Shakespeare. There were other theatrical flourishes as well. Earlier, one of the bandits had asked the express agent for his receipt book and then wrote in the amount taken with the notation, "Robbed at Gads Hill." Another member of the gang exchanged hats with a passenger. "They were very jocular in transacting their business," Alford remembered. They also made repeated inquiries about Pinkerton detectives.[6]

A Mrs. Scott, traveling with her son from Saint Louis to Hot Springs, was relieved of four hundred dollars and left with only a dime. Curiously, another woman lost only three handkerchiefs, although she wore a fine gold watch.[7]

The heist took around forty minutes to complete, with around $1,000 in money and valuables taken from the passengers and a total haul, including the express and mail loot, of perhaps as much as $6,080. It was the first peacetime train robbery to take place in Missouri. It wouldn't be the last.[8]

As a final touch, one of the passengers was left with a telegram to send to the *Saint Louis Dispatch*, as it "had misrepresented them on one occasion." The telegram read:

The most daring train robbery on record. The southbound train on the
Iron Mountain Railroad was robbed here this evening by five heavily armed
men, and robbed of . . . dollars. The robbers arrived at the station a few minutes before the arrival of the train, and arrested the Agent, put him under
guard, and then threw the train on the switch. The robbers are all large men,
none of them under six feet tall. They were all masked, and started in a
southerly direction after they had robbed the train, all mounted on fine
blooded horses. There is a hell of excitement in this part of the country.
(signed) Ira A. Merrill[9]

As they departed, the bandits shook hands with the bewildered engineer, William Wetton, reminding him "to always stop when you see a red
flag." As the conductor related, "When I thought they were through, I
asked them if I might go. They said yes," and Alford sent a man to shut the
northern switch while he went to close the one on the south end. "They
had bent the rod so that I had to get a board and straighten it," he said. The
robbers then moved off to their horses "in a westerly direction" and rode off
"as fast as they could." Soon the train was on its way to Piedmont, a village
some seven miles south, where Alford telegraphed the desperadoes' message to the railroad office in Saint Louis.[10]

The sheriff at Piedmont reportedly formed a posse of twenty-five men,
but due to a light snowstorm, they waited until the next morning and thus
were of little use. The robbers, meanwhile, had pushed some sixty miles west
to Carpentersville, staying with a "Widow Cork" and then heading southwest to Bentonville in northwest Arkansas. There they reportedly robbed
the store of Craig and Son of two hundred dollars and assorted merchandise.
From there their trail went north to Saint Clair and Jackson Counties in
Missouri. The *Saint Louis Daily Globe* sighed in exasperation:

And so these bands of thieves seem to make Missouri their home;
intend to stay here; get their money here, and spend it here. Perhaps some
effort will be made to catch and punish them, and perhaps not. In the
meantime the traveling public are to rejoice at the prospect of some
enlivenment of an otherwise monotonous railroad trip.[11]

Just who had pulled the heist was open to strong speculation, and that
speculation was fueled by the telegram to the *Saint Louis Dispatch*. The newspaper was the home of former Confederate major John Newman Edwards,
known as "the Victor Hugo of the West" for his florid editorial prose. Two
and a half months earlier, Edwards had come to the defense of the James and
Younger brothers in "A Terrible Quintette," a special supplement to the

"Friendship is born at that moment when one person says to another:
What! You too? I thought I was the only one." —C.S. Lewis

Delight your friends. Hand them 60 million books in a single bookmark.

www.alibris.com

paper. Frank and Jesse James and Cole and John Younger had been accused of assorted crimes (including a train robbery in Iowa) since the late 1860s, and now the finger of suspicion was pointing at them again.

On February 10, 1874, *Dispatch* city editor Walter B. Stevens gave the James and Younger brothers more credit than they might have wished, running a feature implicating them by name in crimes as far back as 1866, something Edwards had been scrupulously careful to avoid. Curiously, the same edition carried Edwards's own editorial, "The Gads Hill Train Robbery," in somewhat jarring contrast to Stevens's feature:

> There cannot be a doubt of the boldness and heaviness of the blow struck at this now historic spot on the Iron Mountain railroad, nor of the fact that the work done was the work of hands well-skilled in the dangerous part of such performances; but were it worth while to retain and collate from all the newspapers all the events of a similar character that have taken place in the country for the past year, it would be found that the civilization, as it is called, of Missouri, was about on par with the balance of the states—neither better nor worse, neither producing more reverence for the criminal and less respect for the law than the rest. True, the Western highwayman is more courageous than the Eastern, he has more prowess, more qualities that attract admiration and win respect; but this comes of the locality, and that familiarity with danger which breeds strong, hardy men—men who risk much, who have friends in high places, and who go riding over the land, taking all the chances that come in the way, spending lavishly to-morrow what is won today at the muzzle of a revolver. . . . Is it hard to discriminate between the men of Gads Hill and the men of the iron clad oath and the registration law? . . . The men at Gads Hill swooped down and took a few thousand dollars of surplus money, and were gone again like the wind, the tale of their exploits a nine-day's wonder. . . . Such performances as these of late years, were unknown in Missouri in the days of old time Democracy. Murder was then murder, and hanging, hanging. . . . Since 1862, the government has been robbing, so has its officers of high and low degree, so has every administration in every Southern State, so did the administration in Missouri, so have the national banks, the tariff, the custom houses, the Indian agents, the railroads, the cabinet officers, [President] Grant himself, the Senate—society, the churches—everybody and everything that had agents or volition. To stop it—to break up private and official robbery of all kinds—it is only necessary to break up the Radical [i.e., Republican] party.
>
> For this Augean stable there must be another Euphrates.[12]

Such was John Newman Edwards's exercise in editorial rhetoric: an evocation of popular myth mixed with hyperbole, partisan politics, outright balderdash—and, interestingly enough, some significant fact. In Jefferson City, the state capital, at the time the paper went to press, Edwards was flabbergasted when he read the account and wired Stevens to "put nothing more in about Gads Hill. The report of yesterday was remarkable for two things, utter stupidity and total untruth."[13]

In actuality, the story of the Missouri outlaws was too complex to be fully understood by Edwards or other writers of his day. Indeed, what can now be ascertained in this case is perhaps more interesting and incredible than fiction *or* legend.

2

Background to Banditry

Sing, bird, on green Missouri's plain,
The saddest song of sorrow.

Henry Peterson, Lyon

I N THE SPRING OF 1842, Robert Sallee James, a twenty-four-year-old student at Georgetown College, a Baptist-affiliated institution in Kentucky, came to Clay County, Missouri, with his wife, Zerelda. They had only been married since the previous December, and Robert was there to meet his mother-in-law, who was living in the area with her second husband, Robert Thomason. The young couple were taken with the locality, which bore a striking resemblance to central Kentucky; they decided this was where they would eventually settle.[1]

Meanwhile Robert's studies at Georgetown had yet to be completed, and he left his bride with the in-laws, returning to Kentucky to finish his courses in the classical program. He graduated on June 23, 1843, with a bachelor of arts degree, a substantial education for those days. The required curriculum for the degree included courses in Latin and Greek language and literature (including reading, in Greek, some eighteen hundred lines of Homer's *Iliad*) and courses in geometry and trigonometry. Robert James, or "Bob Jim," as he was nicknamed by his classmates, was looked upon as "a high-minded, honest fellow . . . a general favorite and much esteemed," according to Basil

25

Duke, a fellow classmate and later a colonel under Brig. Gen. John Hunt Morgan, the famed Confederate raider of Kentucky.[2]

Soon Robert had a family as well as a degree. On January 10, 1843, Alexander Franklin James was born at the old Thomason place, about a mile and a half from what would later be called the James farm. On his return to Missouri in 1843, Robert, a licensed Baptist preacher since 1839, became pastor at New Hope Baptist Church. He purchased a farm of 275 acres a few miles west of present-day Kearney. New Hope Church had a membership of twenty when Robert became pastor in August, and by the end of the first year the congregation had grown to ninety-four. The family grew as well. Jesse Woodson James was born September 27, 1847. Another child, Robert R. James, had died about a month after his birth in July 1845.[3]

In 1848 Robert James was awarded a master of arts degree from George-town, and in February 1849 he was one of twenty-six charter trustees of William Jewell College near Liberty, Missouri. A daughter, Susan Lavinia, was born on November 29 of that year.[4]

Early in 1850 Robert James left with a party for the gold fields of California. His congregation at New Hope Baptist Church had grown to some 280 members. Just why he left has been a matter of speculation. His brother William thought that Robert's wife, Zerelda, had complained once too often about his being away on ministerial duties. Perhaps her nagging drove him to leave, although he planned to return. Another possibility was that he wanted to save souls in California or make a rich strike in the gold fields while visiting another brother, Drury James, who was already out there.

It was said that young Jesse, crying and clinging to his father's leg, begged him not to leave, but Robert had made a promise, and with much regret, he departed. His letter of April 14 to Zerelda ended with, "Give my love to all inquiring friends and keep a portion of it to yourself and kiss Jesse for me and tell Franklin to be a good boy and learn fast."

On August 18, 1850, Robert James died of fever. His place of death is given as the gold camp at Hangtown (now Placerville), California. He was only thirty-two years old, but his life was full of accomplishment. As the *Liberty Tribune* summed it up:

> He was a man much liked by all who enjoyed his acquaintance; and as a revivalist he had but few equals in this country. We think within the bounds of reason when we affirm that more additions have been made to the Baptist Church, in Clay County, under his preaching (length of time considered) than under that of any other person. . . . Peace to his ashes.[5]

The now widowed Zerelda Cole James had been known as a tomboy in her girlhood. A neighbor remembered her as "a buxom country lass, with no over-nice sense of delicacy, brimming full of fun, a daring horsewoman, a good dancer, and not afraid of the devil himself." Indeed, her background was something at counterpoint with that of her evangelist husband. The Coles had maintained a tavern, referred to variously as the Black Horse Tavern or Cole's Tavern, near Midway, Kentucky, on the Lexington-Frankfort Road. It was a popular stopping point, and its clientele ranged from politicians Henry Clay and John J. Crittenden to local troublemakers who were responsible for the death of Zerelda's uncle, Amos Cole, in a fight at the tavern when she was only two. Some locals dubbed the tavern Sodom for its sometimes rowdy patrons.

Zerelda's father, James Cole, died in a fall from a horse the same year his brother was killed, and her mother, Sallie Lindsay Cole, lived at the tavern until she remarried Robert Thomason and relocated to Clay County, Missouri, in 1839. Although she was a Protestant, Zerelda stayed behind and attended Saint Catherine's Female School in Lexington, where Robert James was called to preach in one of the neighborhood churches. It was here that Zerelda met him in the summer of 1841. According to Basil Duke, she had been left with an estate of ten thousand dollars (other sources say only six thousand dollars) and "was looked upon as a good catch for anyone. James proved the lucky suitor, married her quietly, and a little later announced the fact to his classmates" at Georgetown College. They were married on Christmas Eve at the home of Zerelda's uncle, James M. Lindsay, near the community of Stomping Ground, with "a large crowd in attendance," as one guest recalled.[6]

The death of Robert James in 1850 left a void that was briefly filled by Benjamin Simms, who married Zerelda on September 30, 1852. Simms, who was a good bit older than his new wife, reportedly did not get along with his stepchildren, and the marriage was headed for divorce when Simms died from, by one account, a fall from a horse.

On September 26, 1855, Zerelda married for a third and final time. Her new husband was Dr. Reuben Samuel, another native of Kentucky. Samuel had come to Missouri in 1849 with his father but had returned to the East to attend the Ohio Medical College from 1850 to 1851. From 1852 to 1854, Samuel practiced in Liberty. In 1854 he moved to Greenville, three miles from the James farm, and opened his office in a store operated by William James, brother of Robert.

Zerelda took no chances this time around. A prenuptial agreement was signed, giving her ownership of six slaves and two hundred acres should the marriage dissolve. It didn't. As a matter of fact, Samuel eventually left his medical practice for farming, probably due to Zerelda's domineering personality.[7]

Very little is known of the early years of the James brothers, although some later writers have attempted to portray them both as sadistic monsters in their youth. Prior to the Civil War, their boyhood was probably no different from that of other boys growing up in rural Missouri at that time. The James boys attended a local subscription school taught by Bird Smith, and obtained at least an elementary education. They played with local children and fished and swam in a nearby creek.

In many ways the James boys' youth was probably not unlike the childhoods described in Mark Twain's books *Tom Sawyer* and *Huckleberry Finn*. But there was an indication of something in Frank's early years that might be termed sociopathic. According to one playmate, Lambertine Hudspeth, "Frank was a bad boy; he liked to get others in a fight, but then keep out himself." According to Hudspeth, "Jesse was a boy of better turn; he preferred to do a little fighting himself." Such was boyhood in rough-and-tumble Missouri.

There was also another influence on the James boys at this time, "Wild Bill" Thomason. Thomason was the brother of Robert Thomason, their mother Zerelda's stepfather. Wild Bill had served as a lieutenant in the Mexican War, and after that conflict, in which he was cited for combat bravery, he returned to his earlier occupation as a "mountain man."

Thomason came to Clay County in the mid-1850s, and his imposing frame, nearly six feet tall and often covered in beaded buckskin garments, must have been both intimidating and fascinating to the James boys. According to playmate Jim Cummins, "He was sturdily built . . . his hair was black . . . thick and heavy as the mane of a mustang, and hung below his belt. He often wore his hair inside his belt," and with his Indian finery he had "a wild yet fascinating appearance." He told the boys about his adventures in the mountains, of bear and buffalo hunts. Thomason taught Frank to ride like the Comanche Indians and how to shoot a rifle, pistol, and bow on horseback. Presumably he also taught young Jesse a few tricks. The lessons he gave Frank in his youth would come in handy for the deadly trial the 1860s would provide.

Although Clay County was not directly on the Kansas-Missouri line, it was filled with rumblings of the conflict to come in "Bleeding Kansas." During the late 1850s proslavery "Border Ruffians" clashed with abolitionist "jayhawkers" in a quasi-war over the Kansas Territory's admission to the Union as a slave or free state.[8]

The year 1860 found Missouri and the United States nearing the abyss of civil war. Missouri was a border state with a population made up of emigrants from both the South and the North, along with a large sprinkling of foreigners, especially Germans, who had come to America in the wake of the unsuccessful Revolution of 1848 in their homeland. Clay County was largely settled by Kentuckians, Virginians, Tennesseans, and North Carolinians, and in that year most sought to avoid what some considered an "irrepressible conflict."

In the 1860 presidential campaign there were four candidates: Stephen Douglas, the Northern Democratic contender who had debated the Republican candidate, Abraham Lincoln, in an earlier Illinois election; Southern Democrat John C. Breckinridge; and the Constitutional Union candidate, John Bell.

A moderate who appealed mainly to the population of the border states, Bell carried Clay County, receiving more than a thousand votes out of nearly fourteen hundred cast. Not one vote went for Lincoln, whose Republican Party was linked with the abolition movement and the Kansas "Free Staters." Douglas carried Missouri by a slim margin in the election, although Kentucky, Tennessee, and Virginia all went for Bell. Lincoln was ultimately the winner of the badly split electoral vote, although his popular vote was less than a national majority. Lincoln did not advocate the abolition of slavery; he merely wanted to curtail its expansion into the western territories. The *Liberty Tribune* attempted to put a good face to things with an editorial stating, "It may turn out in the end that Lincoln's election will prove a blessing to the country."[9]

In the long term, that prediction probably was true, but in the short run, Lincoln's election sent a shock wave through the South and brought to the fore the Secessionist movement, particularly in the slave states of the Deep South. Clay County, with a population of 13,037, of whom 26.5 percent were slaves, was certain to be a volatile area. Led by South Carolina, seven states left the Union one by one in the months prior to the firing on Fort Sumter on April 12, 1861. The Upper South and Border States sought to remain neutral, but the clash over the fort in Charleston Harbor and Lincoln's subsequent call for troops on April 15 forced many conditional Unionists to side with their Southern brethren, albeit reluctantly. Most realized that if war came it would be fought in the Border States and the Upper South first. Few Missourians had any concept of the devastation that would soon be wrought upon their state.

When Lincoln issued his call for seventy-five thousand troops to put down what was termed a rebellion, four regiments eventually came from

Missouri, even though Gov. Claiborne F. Jackson refused to honor Lincoln's request, which he termed "illegal, unconstitutional, and revolutionary in its object, inhuman and diabolical." He declared that Missouri would not furnish a man for what he termed "an unholy crusade." Something of a closet Secessionist at heart, Jackson secretly sent agents, one being Robert James's former classmate Basil Duke, to confer with the Confederate government about obtaining artillery.

At the same time emotions were brewing in Clay County. On April 17 the headlines of the *Clay County Flag* broadcast "War Inaugurated by the Abolitionist—The Soil of the South Invaded!!!" The citizens of the county were invited to a mass meeting in Liberty on April 22. The announcement advised, "There Will Be a Southern Flag Raised."

On April 20, some two hundred Confederate sympathizers in Jackson and Clay Counties, led by Liberty attorney Henry L. Routt, raided the small U.S. arsenal at Liberty, one of two such arsenals in the state. The Liberty arsenal was a brick structure covering roughly two acres. Its only garrison consisted of caretaker Nathaniel Grant and two civilian employees. Grant surrendered the facility and its contents without resistance. For the next week, Routt and his men hauled munitions out of the structure, including close to fifteen hundred small arms and "a few cannon," which were taken by wagon and hidden in the countryside. Two of the cannon taken at the arsenal were fired at the secession meeting at Liberty on April 22. Meanwhile, Missouri Unionists, mainly in the Saint Louis area, began raising their own forces.[10]

Frank James was a recruit to the pro-Southern Missouri State Guard. He joined a company that organized on May 4, 1861, possibly at the home of George Claybrook, which was across the road from the James-Samuel farm. Among the members were men who would figure prominently in the later story of the James gang: Doniphan "Donny" Pence, Oliver Shepherd, and two brothers, J. H. and Brantley Bond.[11]

⚜

HOSTILITIES ESCALATED in Missouri when Federal command in the state was given to Capt. (later Brig. Gen.) Nathaniel Lyon. In command of a force made up of regulars at the Saint Louis arsenal as well as volunteers, many of foreign birth, Lyon captured a state guard detachment at Camp Jackson, near the arsenal, on May 11. Lyon found the streets of the camp named for Jefferson Davis and Gen. P. G. T. Beauregard, who had commanded the attack on Fort Sumter. Reportedly, there was also artillery, recently arrived from the Baton Rouge arsenal, that had been shipped to

Saint Louis in crates marked "marble." While marching his prisoners back to the arsenal, a riot ensued, resulting, by one account, in the deaths of twenty-eight civilians and many more wounded.

Col. M. Jeff Thompson of the Missouri State Guard later criticized the Clay Countians for raiding the Liberty arsenal, suggesting that the raid had precipitated the action by Lyon and other Unionists in Saint Louis. He added that the Saint Louis arsenal had held far more guns and ammunition and was thus the bigger potential prize—and greater loss.[12]

The Missouri legislature swung into action, formally organizing the State Guard and enacting funding for it. Sterling Price, former governor and Mexican War hero, was named to command. In a chain of events, Governor Jackson and the legislature were driven out of the capital at Jefferson City and replaced by a Unionist provisional government with Hamilton Gamble as governor. The pro-Southern Jackson, Price, and the motley State Guard soon found themselves independently taking on the U.S. Army without formally having joined the Confederacy.

At Wilson's Creek, outside Springfield in southwest Missouri, Frank James saw his first action with the State Guard, which had temporarily joined forces with Confederate troops under Brig. Gen. Ben McCulloch, a former Texas Ranger. On August 10, 1861, Brig. Gen. Nathaniel Lyon led his Federal army of fifty-four hundred men to defeat in an attack on a force of ten thousand Confederates and Missouri militia encamped by the creek. As part of Col. John T. Hughes's regiment, Frank James fought what he termed "a very slow fight" up and around what came to be known as "Bloody Hill." In the course of the five-hour seesaw battle, Lyon was slain and the Union army retreated to Springfield and then to Rolla in central Missouri.

Price moved north, minus his Confederate ally, laying siege to the Federal garrison of Lexington, a town on the Missouri River, in the northwest quarter of the state. It became known as the "battle of the hemp bales," for the State Guard's novel use of baled hemp. The Union force, with 2,780 to 3,600 men (by various accounts) and seven 6-pounder smoothbore cannon commanded by Col. James A. Mulligan, was pitted against 12,000 to 18,000 Missouri State Guardsmen. The guardsmen were a motley group, with all but a few of them in civilian clothing; they were armed with everything from aged flintlock muskets and rifles to the latest Sharps breechloading carbines and Colt percussion six-shooters. Anything that could kill was pressed into service and carried into the fray, including at least one grain-cutting scythe. Some sixteen cannon of various types completed the arsenal, firing a variety of captured and homemade ammunition (at Wilson's Creek some guns even fired sacks loaded with pieces of scrap iron).

Mulligan had thrown up a high fortresslike breastwork (the imposing remains of which can be seen to this day) around the local Masonic College, and behind these fortifications he held out for days, despite shortages of water and ammunition. The siege lasted from September 12 to September 20. Col. John T. Hughes, commander of the militia regiment in which Frank James served, wrote of the encounter as follows:

> On the morning of the 19th we arose from our bivouac upon the hills to renew the attack. This day we continued the fighting vigorously all day, holding possession of the hospital buildings [the Anderson House and outbuildings], and throwing large wings from both sides of the [Anderson] house, built up of bales of hemp saturated with water, to keep them from taking fire. These portable hemp-bales were extended, like the wings of a partridge net, so as to cover and protect several hundred men at a time, and a most terrible and galling and deadly fire was kept up from them upon the works of the enemy by my men. I divided my forces into reliefs and kept some three hundred of them pouring in a heavy fire incessantly upon the enemy, supplying the places of the weary with fresh troops. On the night of the 19th we enlarged and advanced our defensive works very near to the enemy's intrenchments, and at daybreak opened upon their lines with a most fatal effect.[13]

On September 20, with the hemp bales almost up against his works, and with ammunition and water nearly exhausted, Mulligan surrendered. The men of the Irish Brigade, mainly from Illinois, marched out and were paroled, promising not to fight until properly exchanged. Governor Jackson, who had, on his own initiative, proclaimed Missouri a "Sovereign, Free and Independent Republic" prior to Wilson's Creek, gave the Irishmen a political harangue before they were marched off. Mulligan, accompanied by his wife, was kept prisoner until his release on October 30.

When a new Federal force moved from Saint Louis toward Springfield, on September 29, Price abandoned Lexington and retreated to the south.[14] Just a few days prior to this, on September 22, a brigade of Kansas jayhawkers under Col. James H. Lane looted and burned the town of Osceola, Missouri, in a harbinger of the ugly war that was to follow. In December, after Price's army had left, a pro-Southern guerrilla band began to take shape under William Clarke Quantrill in the Jackson County–Independence, Missouri, area.

Frank James reportedly followed the State Guard south, and in the winter of 1861–62 contracted measles and was captured and paroled by Union authorities occupying Springfield. He was later allowed to return to Clay County.[15]

In October, a rump session of the Missouri legislature began meeting in Neosho, in the southwest corner of the state. Later it moved to several other locales and organized a Secessionist government for the state nearly two months after Governor Jackson's rather unorthodox proclamation. On November 28, 1861, Missouri was formally admitted to the Confederate States of America, although the provisional government remained in the Jefferson City capital and most of the state was in Union hands. One of the leaders of the Secession movement, in fact the man who introduced the "Provisional Act of Secession," was Rep. George Graham Vest of Cooper County, who would have later connections to the James story.[16]

Confederate and Union forces faced off again in a bloody and decisive two-day battle at Pea Ridge in northwest Arkansas. The battle culminated on March 8, 1862, with the withdrawal of Confederate forces, in great part due to the lack of ammunition. The supply wagon train somehow became separated from the army and was directed by an incompetent officer down the wrong road. Such are the fortunes of war. Colonel Hughes commanded the last Southern unit to retreat. Maj. Gen. Earl Van Dorn's Confederate Army of the West, including Price's Missourians, were subsequently ordered to Mississippi, leaving Missouri under Union control.[17]

⁂

JUST SIX days after Pea Ridge, forty mounted Confederates under a Colonel Parker raided Liberty and tore down the U.S. flag. In late April, Frank, now living at home, took the Oath of Allegiance to support and defend the Constitution of the United States of America and posted a one-thousand-dollar bond for good behavior with Col. William R. Penick of the Fifth Missouri State Militia Cavalry, a unit referred to by some as "Penick's thieves." While at home, possibly after Parker's raid, Frank had gone "wild, shooting his pistol and halloing for Jeff Davis," according to one account. Somehow word of this eventually reached Penick, and he had Frank jailed in Liberty, but Frank's mother, Zerelda, begged the colonel to parole him.[18]

Conditions in Missouri began a downward spiral as the war within the state evolved into a guerrilla conflict, the large armies having moved south and east. Missouri was of vital strategic importance to the Union in the days before the railroad joined the East and West. Sitting at the head of the Santa Fe and Oregon Trails and in the middle of the transcontinental telegraph lines, the loss of Missouri might well mean the loss of the West itself.

Many Union army units that were sent to Missouri looked upon the inhabitants as Southerners and enemies. When units such as William

Quantrill's band carried out guerrilla activities within a given locale, the reprisals that followed—often in the form of heavy fines, arbitrary imprisonment without due process, destruction of property, or outright theft—alienated the populace and further fueled the conflict. Taxes in Clay County, as well as others, increased in order to fund the pro-Union Missouri State Militia and Enrolled Missouri Militia. In 1862 a stiff "military assessment" was imposed on most of the county's citizens. In response, individuals "took to the bush" for personal safety or revenge.

Federal militia units within the state were sometimes out for loot or to settle old personal scores against individuals or families, the blue uniform giving them, in effect, a license to kill if the proper excuse could be found. An order that no guerrillas were to be taken prisoner further added to the shredding of the social fabric. Captured guerrillas taken "in arms" against the Union (or even suspected of being in arms against the North) were summarily executed, often without trial. The guerrillas adopted a similar policy, and the war became a civil bloodbath, neighbor against neighbor, brother against brother.

A Unionist resident of Smithfield, in northwest Clay County, described the conditions:

> This part of the county is truly in a deplorable condition . . . we are continually annoyed by "bushwhackers" who are prowling thro the country, annoying and plundering the citizens, without respect to party, and on the other hand, by our own troops, who are sent out as scouts under non-commissioned officers and irresponsible attachees of the army, and who are continually committing deeds of outrage upon the citizens, without respect to party or authority of law, that every Union man should be ashamed of. . . .
>
> If there are bushwhackers in the country, the soldiers should go where they will be most apt to find them, instead of drinking and loitering about the towns and public roads of the neighborhood,—where they are sure not to find them,—insulting and retaliating upon the citizens, and in many instances upon those who are as innocent of the presence of bushwhackers as they are themselves. . . .
>
> Pillage and plunder and unrestricted cruelty will degrade and render ineffective the best army in the world.[19]

During this discordant and dangerous time, Frank was legally bound by parole and oath to abstain from fighting against the Union. There was a further problem: Starting in 1863 Missourians of military age, both "disloyal" and loyal alike, were required to sign up for the Enrolled Missouri

Militia. Some viewed this as being coerced into serving two masters. Unionists sometimes viewed what was called the "Paw Paw Militia" with suspicion, as the ranks of some companies were filled with Southern sympathizers. The term "paw paw" sarcastically referred to a tree that was common to the brushy areas, where those evading enrollment often hid. If a person wished to remain neutral he encountered problems by failing to enroll. Frank no doubt discovered this in the spring of 1863, when he was reportedly arrested again; he escaped from the Liberty calaboose with aid from outside. Although it would be claimed that Frank served at the battle of Prairie Grove, Arkansas, on December 7, 1862, with a group of guerrillas who saved Gen. Joseph O. Shelby from capture, this probably was not the case. The first solid documentation of his joining the guerrillas points to a later period.[20]

Frank James was back at home near Centreville (near the later town of Kearney) when he learned that William Quantrill was in Jackson County, recruiting for his guerrilla command. As Frank later recalled:

> I met Bill Gregg, Quantrill's First Lieutenant, in Clay County and with him rowed across the Missouri River to this county [Jackson] and joined Quantrill at the Webb place on Blackwater ford of the Sni just a few miles from here [Blue Springs, Missouri]. This was in May 1863. I will never forget the first time I ever saw Quantrill. He was nearly six feet in height, rather thin, his hair and moustache was sandy and he was full of life and a jolly fellow. He had none of the air of the bravado or the desperado about him . . . he was a demon in battle.[21]

Quantrill had a questionable past and character, and unknown to Frank and others of his command, had actually ridden with the abolitionist jayhawkers from Kansas before the war. He was a native of Canal Dover (now called Dover), Ohio, not Hagerstown, Maryland (where his father hailed from), as he told his followers. Quantrill apparently felt there were better opportunities to be had with the Missourians. A rank opportunist, he led a group of abolitionists on a slave-stealing raid into Missouri and into the jaws of a preplanned ambush at the Morgan Walker farm in December 1860. He told the Missourians he was acting in revenge for a brother who had been killed by the Kansans, which was an outright lie, but it served to ingratiate him to people in Missouri, and his natural ability as a guerrilla leader gained him numerous followers after raising the nucleus of his band in December 1861. By 1863 he had a fearsome reputation among the Federal forces and was likewise admired among those with pro-Confederate leanings.[22]

Frank's first action with the guerrillas was to be at the town of Richfield (now Missouri City) under the command of Lt. Fernando Scott. Mrs. Lurena (Lou) McCoy, who was suspected, among other things, of having aided Frank and others in escaping from the Clay County jail, had been arrested by the Federals on Friday, May 15. Her husband, Capt. Moses McCoy, then recruiting Confederate troops in the area, called on Quantrill for help. A party of twelve to eighteen volunteers, including Frank James, was raised, to be led by Scott.

Crossing the Missouri, Scott made for Richfield. The guerrillas called at the home of a friend, who said rather tongue-in-cheek, "Boys, I shall have to report on you." That was just what they wanted—to lure the Federals into an ambush. It was just a two-mile ride to town, and the militia captain, Darius Sessions, who had arrested Mrs. McCoy, soon took the bait.

Scott and his men had hidden near a bridge, with four mounted men nearby to pursue any Federals who escaped the ambush. Thudding across the wooden bridge planks came Sessions along with 2d Lt. Louis Graffenstein and three privates of the Twenty-fifth Missouri Infantry, a unit that had fought at Shiloh but was now serving partly as mounted infantry, chasing bushwhackers in northwest Missouri. As the Federals neared the bridge, the guerrillas, including Frank James, were hidden in the brush on both sides of the road. They opened fire, dropping Captain Sessions and a Private Rapp, then Lieutenant Graffenstein. The two other soldiers skedaddled as the mounted bushwhackers charged. Rapp was robbed and left for dead. Sessions was shot again two or three times through the head, and Graffenstein, after surrendering, was shot twice through the head. A woman nearby begged for his life to no avail, according to a later Federal report. Rapp somehow escaped, feigning death, and was later carted to town for medical attention. Somehow the guerrillas learned of this, found the wounded private, and shot him three more times. Amazingly, Rapp survived.[23]

Reportedly, the guerrillas then robbed a store where the owner, a Confederate sympathizer, told them, "Boys, you are welcome, but I can't be supposed to give you anything. If I should I would be arrested. Take what you want." Scott's men loaded up on cigars and tobacco before their departure.

Federal troops, learning of the ambush, arrived on the scene the next day, May 20, and began to scour the country. "The citizens around that country are all sympathizers, with very few exceptions, and it is hard to get information from them," wrote a weary Capt. Joseph Schmitz of the Twenty-fifth Missouri Infantry, in charge of the pursuit. "Frank James" was one of the men named by Schmitz as being recognized by local unionists, along with Captain McCoy.[24] James H. Griffith, a neighbor of Frank's, reported meeting up with him "on the 25th day of May . . . in company with other bushwhackers on the road near Mount Gilead Church." According to Griffith, "They were in the act of robbing me of my horse and saddle when Frank James intervened for me and prevailed on his companions not to take my property and they did not interrupt me further." Nevertheless, the attention drawn to Frank's guerrilla association cost his family the one-thousand-dollar bond posted for his good behavior on parole.[25]

However, Frank was not the only person in the family actively involved in "the cause." Two nights after the Richfield raid the guerrillas were at it again, this time descending on the town of Plattsburg in Clinton County, north of Clay. They were acting on information Frank had obtained from his mother about the weakening of the garrison there, which was reportedly hunting Scott and his raiders. By one account, the guerrillas rushed into town, expecting the place to be vacant of troops but finding the courthouse occupied by militia. A nasty little fight ensued. The raiders captured Col. James H. Birch, an aide to Union Gov. Hamilton Gamble; Birch was taken at gunpoint in front of the courthouse, where a deal was struck to parole the militia inside if they would surrender. Allegedly some forty-six men gave up and stacked their arms. Some two hundred muskets were captured and destroyed in the raid, and a payroll of around ten thousand dollars was appropriated by Scott's men, who also enjoyed a fancy meal with Colonel Birch at a local hotel before leaving town around sunset. Another version of the story has the town guarded by only a handful of men, who gave up when their ammunition was exhausted.[26]

As to the fate of Lurena McCoy, May 22 found her in Federal custody at Saint Joseph, Missouri, charged with giving aid and comfort to the enemy "by feeding, sheltering and otherwise harboring brigands . . . disloyal conduct by repeatedly using violent language in favor of persons engaged in the present rebellion, and of the rebellion itself, to wit; 'I have fed Hart [a guerrilla] and will feed him again and if . . . I had no children I would turn out in the brush myself.'" She was also charged with "using and having in her possession certain wearing apparel fashioned after the manner of the colors of the Rebels" at the time of her arrest. There was an affidavit, apparently by her sister, Miss L. A. Aulden, regarding her having a tailor named James Moffat take the measurements of Joe Hart and Louis Vandiver for "clothing [uniforms]."[27]

In her defense, she made the following statement, which must have caused incredulous eyes to roll after the Richfield affair involving her husband:

> I do not know what I was arrested for, but was told it was for feeding bushwhackers, but I do not believe I have ever been guilty of that. I have

fed both parties. No union man ever came to my house and asked for some thing to eat but what he got it. It made no difference whether they were union men or rebels. I fed them. I never turned off any one who was hungry. I will take the oath willingly and live up to it. I would not take the oath unless I intended to live up to it. When the war first broke out I was for the union. Shortly after the Lexington battle I changed. I then began to sympathise with the other party, and my sympathies grew [stronger and stronger] as the [decision?] of parties was made. It cannot be proved that I ever done any disloyal act. I do not know what a disloyal act is. They say it is feeding rebels. . . . My enemies have said a great many things of me which are not so. I acknowledged to Col. Harding that I had fed rebels. I only meant then that they came to my house and asked for something to eat and I gave it to them. I did not think I was doing any-thing wrong. I supposed the federals would be mad about. I have asked for the federals a great many times. I have two children. That is one adopted five years old and one of my own two years old. I have one brother in the federal army, or rather half brother . . . and the most of my relatives are in the federal army, some are in the secession army.[28]

Lurena McCoy would be anything but contrite in two articles she wrote for the *Confederate Veteran* in May and September 1912. In the Sep-tember issue she would claim her release was due to a prisoner exchange that Quantrill allegedly engineered, swapping a captured provost marshal for her release.

She also stated that "our people were in the right. We had justice on our side; and though defeated, we gained an imperishable heritage worth more than silver and gold." Although she failed to mention her preceding statement or that she took the Oath of Allegiance to the Union on May 22, she closed her homily by saying, "Let us teach our children that their fathers were not traitors but patriots." Such was the war in Missouri.[29]

Frank and the other raiders under Scott dodged about Clay County for several days, encountering James Griffith, as mentioned earlier, and stop-ping at the James-Samuel farm the evening after their Mount Gilead encounter with Griffith. "Ma" Samuel had learned that the fords across the Missouri, which Scott intended to cross, were now well guarded. Young Jesse was active in gathering information as well and served as a messenger between his mother and the guerrillas. This "espionage" would soon catch up with the family.[30] The next morning they were visited by a patrol of the Fifty-first Enrolled Missouri Militia under Lt. H. C. Culver, a group belong-ing to the command of Capt. John Turney of Clinton County. Accompany-ing the Clinton County patrol were members of the Forty-eighth EMM from Clay County, reportedly under Lt. John W. Younger. The events that followed would become central to the story of the James brothers, although somewhat twisted through the years by various writers and by Mrs. Samuel herself until they became enshrined in legend—and accepted as history.

John Samuel gave the following account after his mother's death:

> Jesse was out plowing in a field . . . when some Northern soldiers came to the place to look for Frank. Jesse was only sixteen [actually only fifteen]. They beat him up. Then they went to the house and asked where Frank was. Mother and father didn't know [or pretended not to], but the soldiers wouldn't believe them. They took father out and hung him by the neck to a tree. After a while they took him down and gave him another chance to tell. Of course he couldn't. So they hung him up again. They did that three times. Then they took him back to the house and told my mother they were going to shoot him. She begged them not to do it, but they took him off in the woods [north of the house] and fired off their guns . . . but they didn't shoot him. They just took him over to another town and put him in jail. My mother didn't know until the next day that he hadn't been shot because the soldiers ordered her to remain in the house if she didn't want to be shot too.[31]

The official legendary version, given out by Mrs. Samuel to tourists and writers in later years, had her cutting down her poor husband after the militia had left, with Dr. Reuben Samuel becoming something of a latter-day Nathan Hale, who in this case lived to tell about his brush with death. In fact he had broken and talked, actually leading the Federals to the guerrilla camp in the woods north of the house. The shooting that erupted when they attacked was what young John Samuel had heard as a child.

Among those in the hanging party were Brantley Bond, the same neighbor who had served with Frank in the Missouri State Guard, and Alvis Dagley. Bond and Dagley were reportedly responsible for hoisting Samuel during the interrogation. Hangings like this were not an uncommon means of extracting information in what had become a vicious war. Sometimes Penick's militia simply let their victims hang. One such victim was Samuel Ramberlin, who was left dangling from the rafters of his barn on November 28, 1862. Penick once bragged that "if hemp, fire, and gunpowder were freely used" he could wipe out the guerrilla menace in the area.

Rev. William James, brother of Robert and uncle of the James brothers, dropped by the farm just as things were well under way. "In the center of a group [of militia]," he recalled, "was Mrs. Samuel, making such an outcry and giving them such a tongue-lashing as only she could give." William advised her to stop. "How can I be still when they are hanging my husband?" she retorted.

According to an interview with a Lieutenant Rogers, of Turney's command, published in the *Saint Joseph Morning Herald* several days later:

> The old gentleman [Dr. Samuel] protested that he knew of no armed men in the vicinity, but the Militia judged him to be speaking falsely, and at once procured a rope, placed it about his neck, gave him one good swing, and by that time his memory brightened up, and he concluded to reveal the hiding place of the rebels. He led the boys into the woods a short distance, and there, squatted upon the ground in a dense thicket, was discovered the whole band.

The militia, according to the account, caught the guerrillas off guard, in the middle of a poker game, with the booty taken in their recent raids spread on blankets, serving as the pot. "The boys 'went for them,'" according to Rogers, "captured the 'stakes' on the blankets, amounting to near seven dollars; five excellent horses; three guns, and quite a quantity of clothing." Frank James and companions scattered, leaving two dead comrades behind. The guerrillas later regrouped and were attacked again, this time with three more of the band reported killed, by Lieutenant Rogers's account, and several more wounded. They had a narrow escape across the Missouri, either swimming their horses across or using a hastily built raft, with the militia and a detachment of the Twenty-fifth Missouri blazing away at them from the Clay County shoreline.[32]

Dr. Reuben Samuel was taken to Liberty and lodged in the jail there then transferred to Saint Joseph via Plattsburg. On June 24, 1863, he was paroled. "The treatment [hanging] so affected his throat that he has not spoken plainly since," according to an account written more than thirty years later. His wife, Zerelda, was, according to provost marshal records, both paroled *and* given the Oath of Allegiance on June 5, 1863, also at Saint Joseph. Allegedly Zerelda was imprisoned for several weeks in Saint Joe, but unless there was a clerical error with the month, this could be another embellished story or was perhaps confused with the imprisonment of her husband.[33]

An interesting letter is to be found in Dr. Samuel's provost marshal file, signed by three neighbors and sent to the provost at Saint Joseph. Dated July 6, 1863, at Liberty, Missouri, it reads:

> In the case of Dr. Reuben Samuel, held as prisoner by the military, to report at Saint Joseph, we, his neighbors desire to state that we regard

him as a peaceable, quiet and inoffensive man, who would harm no one. He is, we hesitate not to state, under the control of his wife [and] step-son, and is really afraid to act contrary to their wishes, on any thing. This fear, we believe, caused him to make a false statement which he would not, otherwise have done. We know no man who is more peacefully inclined and who is more inoffensive. We therefore request you to dis-charge him.

> very respectfully,
> A. C. Courtney
> D. J. Larkin
> Alvah [March?]

The note also had the endorsement of one E. M. Samuel (who claimed no relation to Reuben) of Liberty, of whom more will be said later. He attested that the signers were "men of the highest character, and occupy a position to know whereof they affirm, and their loyalty cannot be doubted." One signer was even a county judge. "So far as I know Mr. Samuel is a man as they describe him," concluded the endorsement.[34]

"Franklin James" appeared in print in the August 7, 1863, *Liberty Trib-une*. The report said that the previous day Frank, with two other guerrillas, had waylaid a man named David Mitchell six miles west of Liberty on the road to Leavenworth, Kansas, relieving him of a pocketknife, some money, and a pass from the local provost marshal. "This is one of the 'rights' these men are fighting for," the *Tribune* acidly commented, adding that "James sent his compliments to Major Green [the provost marshal], and said he would like to see him." It was Frank's first "stickup" of note, and it was done with a panache that would become something of a trademark in later years.[35]

Meanwhile, brother Jesse chafed at home, "and with the assistance of a negro man raised a considerable crop of tobacco." He was reportedly turned away by the guerrillas as too young. It was possibly in 1863 that Jesse blew off the tip of the middle finger of his left hand while cleaning a pistol left at the farm, according to the family. It may well have occurred while the guer-rillas were hiding at the farm following Plattsburg, the gun being part of the booty. Jesse's "expertise" with the gun may have been a further reason for his being turned away. Jim Cummins's version of the story has the wound happening while Jesse loaded a pistol in June 1864, just after joining the guerrillas. Jesse was nicknamed "Dingus" by the guerrillas after an exclama-tion he made from the pain of his injury.

In any event, young Jesse had other pressing responsibilities, looking after his younger siblings and the farm and tending the tobacco while his mother and stepfather had their provost problems.[36]

THINGS WERE brewing on the border that August, and Frank would find himself in the thick of the raid on Lawrence, Kansas, an event that had been building since Bleeding Kansas days of the late 1850s. During the time of the "popular sovereignty" question, whereby Kansas would enter the Union as either a slave or free state, depending on the popular vote, Lawrence served as a magnet for abolitionist emigrants from New England, and also a headquarters of the violent abolitionist jayhawkers headed by Jim Lane, Charles "Doc" Jennison, and James Montgomery. Lane even made his home in Lawrence. In 1856 Lawrence had been raided by a band of proslavery Border Ruffians operating out of Missouri.

Eventually a certain criminal element drifted to the Missouri-Kansas border, taking advantage of the situation. With the outbreak of the Civil War, the jayhawkers, clothed in the uniform of the Union army, staged numerous raids across the border. Ostensibly they were liberating slaves (more than a year before the Emancipation Proclamation in a state where it didn't apply) and also "liberating" livestock, furniture, and anything else that took their fancy. It mattered not whether the Missouri victims were Unionist or Secessionist (or whether they even owned slaves); all were equal prey. Sometimes the jayhawkers destroyed what they couldn't cart away.[37]

On September 22, 1861, two days after Maj. Gen. Sterling Price captured the Federal garrison at Lexington, the town of Osceola, where a third of the residents were pro-Union, was sacked and burned by jayhawkers. After a drumhead court-martial, nine civilians were shot by Jim Lane's Kansans. The home of U.S. Sen. Waldo P. Johnson, a Democrat, was one of over a hundred houses torched. The raiders even burned the local courthouse before departing, although, oddly, the court records were hauled back to Kansas. Many of the raiders were so drunk they had to ride back to Kansas in wagons—stolen wagons at that. Not even the churches were spared plundering. Lane was said to have stolen thirteen thousand dollars in cash from an Osceola widow, and a local bank was robbed of around eight thousand dollars. Although condemned by Union authorities and even by the governor of Kansas, the raids went unpunished, and the loot was taken to Lawrence and sold.[38]

Gov. Charles Robinson of Kansas, a voice of moderation among the "free soilers," was publicly smeared by the demagogue Lane, who had once claimed he would "just as soon buy a nigger as a mule." Robinson left his first term in office amid a politically engineered scandal over state bonds involving two members of his cabinet. Lane, as both a U.S. senator and commander of a brigade of jayhawkers, was as much an opportunist as Quantrill was.

In 1862 Quantrill staged several retaliatory raids into Kansas towns such as Aubrey, Olathe, Gardner, and even Diamond Springs—one hundred miles west of the state line. Lawrence probably would have joined the list of sacked towns sooner but for the vigilance of its local militia, which previously had sounded numerous alerts for raids that never materialized.[39]

The raids on Kansas put pressure on the new Federal commander on the border, Brig. Gen. Thomas Ewing Jr., who had served as private secretary to President Zachary Taylor during his brief term in office eleven years before the war. In 1856 Ewing had moved to Leavenworth, Kansas, where he served as a member to the state's constitutional convention two years later. In early 1861 he attended a peace convention in Washington, D.C., and for the next year served as chief justice of the supreme court of Kansas. In September 1862 Ewing was commissioned colonel of the Eleventh Kansas Cavalry and was promoted to brigadier general the following March.

Ewing's military philosophy was akin to that of his brother-in-law, William Tecumseh Sherman. In General Orders No. 10, he ordered the roundup and deportation of Confederate sympathizers from the Missouri border counties. Some families, such as Reuben Samuel and his wife, were able to forestall exile by taking the Oath of Allegiance and/or parole. Others were more outspoken and landed in confinement. On August 14, 1863, the very day Order No. 10 was formally approved, a warehouse in Kansas City—where political prisoners were confined on the second floor—collapsed. Four women were killed outright. Another woman died later, and two others were permanently crippled. Two sisters of William Anderson, a bloodthirsty follower of Quantrill, were among the victims. One sister, Josephine, died, and the other, sixteen-year-old Mary, was crippled. Also in the building were two cousins of Thomas Coleman Younger. His father, Henry Washington Younger, an avowed Unionist and Cass County judge, had been murdered in July 1862 by Federal militia outside Kansas City.

For years a popular story was spread that the building had been deliberately undermined by an unofficial order from Ewing. Neglected in the storytelling was the fact that the cellar had been used to confine certain "women of the evening" infected with venereal disease. Soldiers posted in an adjoining building had tunneled into the basement, accidentally cutting through the supports. The local post surgeon had become alarmed and reported the problem, but by the time his report went through military channels the warehouse-prison was rubble.[40]

General Orders No. 10 was officially announced on August 18, four days after the collapse. Taken in conjunction with the building disaster and the rumor that the structure had been deliberately undermined by the Federals, the announcement was too much for many to tolerate without retribution. Quantrill apparently had been planning to raid Lawrence for some time, both for his own personal glory and for revenge against individuals in Lawrence. The general order and the building's collapse may have been the sparks that made him act.

In the early morning of Friday, August 21, 1863, a band of around 450 guerrillas swooped into Lawrence, a town of 2,000 to 3,000 inhabitants. The militia was caught off guard, and those recruits unlucky enough to be caught in uniform were gunned down.

The raiders carried lists of those marked for death, and high on the list was Jim Lane, who escaped from his house in a nightshirt, hiding in a nearby field. A number of those targeted in the raid, although certainly not all those killed, were thought to have jayhawker ties. The raiders planned to take Lane back to Missouri, according to some accounts, to be tried and either burned at the stake or hanged. Many of Quantrill's men shouted "Osceola!" as they rode through the town. Ultimately the foray turned into a carnival of looting, burning, and random killing, with 150 to 200 men and boys slain (depending on the account) over a four-hour span.[41] Incredibly, most of the 450 or so raiders killed *no one*, although they may have done their share of looting and burning.

Frank James's role in this affair is difficult to determine. Latter-day Quantrill hater and biographer William E. Connelley claimed that Frank "was as ferocious and merciless as a hyena" that day, but Connelley failed to explain any particulars. Connelley also claimed that "the Youngers did bloody work," although Cole was the only one present. In fact, Cole was credited with saving the lives of at least a dozen citizens at Lawrence.[42]

The raiders escaped from Lawrence, but not without some belated pursuit. Union forces in Missouri had obtained intelligence of the guerrilla concentration but were slow to pull their own scattered forces together. Kansas forces, spread along the border, likewise took time to rendezvous after Quantrill had crossed the state line. Jim Lane managed to put together some 150 men from Lawrence, who were joined by 50 volunteers collected from the Kansas City area and another 180 men from the Kansas border garrisons. They caught up with Quantrill at the settlement of Brooklyn, fought a minor skirmish, and then continued the chase to within two or three miles of Paola, Kansas. Quantrill's band then turned northeast, and early the next morning they crossed back into Missouri. They headed for the brush around Grand River, splitting into smaller bands and going in different directions along the way. Five miles west of Pleasant Hill, Col. Bazel Lazear, with part of the First Missouri State Militia Cavalry, engaged the raiders in a sharp fight, eventually killing sixteen guerrillas and wounding a number more. The area of the fight was strewn with part of the booty taken at Lawrence, by one account.

Afterward some one hundred or more individuals were killed inside Missouri as guerrillas. Some of them may have been hapless civilians unluckily caught by undiscriminating Federal patrols or jayhawkers. One supposed spy was even lynched in Lawrence following the raid.[43] The cry of outrage was such that General Orders No. 11 was issued (see Appendix A) on August 25. Drawn up by Ewing, with "help" from Jim Lane, it largely depopulated Cass, Bates, and Jackson Counties and half of Vernon County, Missouri. All those living farther than a mile from military posts in the named counties were to be removed within fifteen days. Doc Jennison's Fifteenth Kansas Cavalry had a major role in the arson, theft, and murder that accompanied enforcement of the order in what would be known for generations as the "Burnt District." Painter George Caleb Bingham, an ardent Missouri Unionist, whose wife owned the prison-warehouse building that had recently collapsed, was so moved by the brutality of Order No. 11 that he created a painting with the same name. It was exhibited in Ohio in 1879 when Ewing unsuccessfully sought the governorship of that state.[44]

⚜

MAJ. GEN. James G. Blunt, commander of the District of the Frontier and a crony of Jim Lane, had just finished a successful summer campaign against Confederate forces in the central part of what was then known as the Indian Territory (now Oklahoma). His major victory over Texas and Confederate Indian regiments at the battle of Honey Springs on July 17 was largely due to the shoddy gunpowder the Confederates had imported from Mexico, "the cartridges becoming worthless even upon exposure to damp atmosphere," by one report. By late September Blunt had cleared the area, driving the Confederates south toward the Texas border, and had captured Fort Smith, Arkansas. He then returned to Fort Scott, Kansas, a post about 110 miles south of Kansas City. Blunt was preparing to move his headquarters south to Fort Smith, where it would be closer to the action in the months ahead.[45]

About the same time, Quantrill sent word to his scattered band to gather in Lafayette County (where Lexington was the county seat). Order No. 11, brutal as it was, had the desired effect of drying up supplies, shelter, and aid along the border. Quantrill knew that the leaves soon would be off the trees, denying his men cover from Federal patrols. So on October 2, with some three hundred to four hundred men, Quantrill headed south for Texas, marching his men through the "Burnt District," where solitary blackened chimneys stood in mute testimony to the ravages of this peculiar and savage guerrilla war.

For the next four days they moved south without detection and soon were in Vernon County, across the state line from Fort Scott, Kansas. Word reached the fort of the presence of hundreds of guerrillas on the evening of October 4, and the garrison was put on the alert. In all the excitement, apparently no one thought to send a messenger out to warn General Blunt, who had left the post that afternoon with an escort of around one hundred men, including the headquarters band.[46]

Fort Blair was a hastily built military post of sod and wood situated in the southeastern tip of Kansas at Baxter Springs, a popular stopping point for troops and supply trains. The site was almost at the halfway point on the trail between Fort Scott and Fort Gibson in the Indian Territory. On the morning of Tuesday, October 6, 1863, the garrison consisted of Company A, Second Kansas Colored Infantry, and Companies C and D of the Third Wisconsin Cavalry under 1st Lt. James G. Pond of Company C. That morning Pond had sent sixty mounted troopers from the Third on a foraging expedition with eight wagons, leaving forty-five dismounted troopers and fifty infantry at the post.[47]

The cavalry camp was just south of the fort, and the men were eating lunch under a nearby brush arbor when Quantrill's men burst from the woods east of camp. Under the command of Dave Pool, a portion of the guerrillas charged between the Federals and the fort. Most of the garrison managed to make it to the sod breastwork and their weapons, but it was close. The post was only walled-in on three sides, and the raiders were soon inside the perimeter but then were forced back out by heavy fire from the defenders. Lieutenant Pond managed to make his way to a 12-pounder mountain howitzer, which he fired and loaded three times, with devastating effect on the guerrilla ranks.[48]

As this fight was under way, Quantrill, with another portion of his band, noticed a blue column approaching from the north. It was General Blunt and his escort. Many of Quantrill's men were garbed in captured Federal uniforms and were in the line of battle just north of the fort. Blunt wondered if the men in front of him were part of the garrison out on drill or perhaps had been sent as an honor guard. It was surely strange, hearing the popping of small-arms fire and the occasional *whump* of a cannon in the direction of the post. With the brass band playing and flags flying, the escort moved into formation in front of the wagons.

Then Blunt realized something was wrong. There shouldn't be gunfire. Capt. W. S. Tough, Blunt's chief of scouts, rode forward and came to the conclusion Blunt was already reaching—*bushwhackers!* Quantrill's men, about 150 in number, fired and charged with a blood-curdling yell about two hundred yards from Blunt's line. The escort broke, a portion making a brief stand before they were overwhelmed and the rest cut down as they fled across the prairie.

Blunt and about fifteen men managed to escape, but the rest, including his musicians, were not as lucky. The dead "were scattered and strewn over the ground for over a mile or two, most with balls through their heads." A number were apparently shot after surrendering. The musicians attempted to escape to the southwest in a wagon but were cut off. All fourteen were slaughtered, "their bodies thrown in or under the wagon and it fired . . . all were more or less burned and [the wagon] almost entirely consumed . . . a number of the bodies were brutally mutilated and indecently treated," according to one Union officer who survived.[49]

About 4 P.M. Quantrill's men moved off to the south, and that evening Blunt and what survivors he gathered about him doubled back to the fort. Eighty Federal soldiers were killed and eighteen wounded. Among those killed were Blunt's staff member, Maj. H. Z. Curtis, son of Maj. Gen. Samuel R. Curtis, the victor at Pea Ridge. Also killed was Lt. A. W. Farr of Massachusetts, a prewar law partner of Maj. Gen. Benjamin "Beast" Butler (one of the few Union generals having the distinction of being officially "outlawed" by the Confederacy). Also among the slain was James O'Neal, an artist from *Frank Leslie's Illustrated Newspaper,* who certainly would have had something different to sketch for the readers, had he survived.

Some twenty or thirty of Quantrill's men were left dead on the field, many with passes signed by commanders of the Union posts in Sedalia, Springfield, and Kansas City, and permits to carry arms and other papers indicating that some were deserters from the Missouri militia.

Blunt sent one member of his staff with an escort of five men back to Fort Scott for reinforcements. He would soon return to the fort himself. The Baxter Springs debacle gave Maj. Gen. John M. Schofield, Blunt's superior and political enemy, the excuse he needed to sack the Kansas general, and Blunt was relieved of command on October 19. For the next year he would be in charge of the District of the Upper Arkansas, a backwater jurisdiction embracing part of Colorado and southwest Kansas, where he kept busy chasing Plains Indians with an "army" of six hundred men.[50]

Quantrill had seen Fort Blair as too costly to storm and had backed off to the south, crossing the Arkansas River eighteen miles above Fort Gibson, capturing and gunning down a Federal scouting party of a dozen Indians. The guerrilla leader claimed he had actually killed Blunt (having captured

his sword, commissions, and baggage) in his official report of the affair to
Maj. Gen. Sterling Price, written October 13 while encamped with the
Confederate-Indian forces of Brig. Gen. Douglas Cooper on the Canadian
River. Signing himself "Colonel" Quantrill (he was only commissioned a
captain), he announced his arrival to Confederate authorities. Soon the
news was spread, via general orders, making known to the troops in Texas
"with much pleasure" the "cheery intelligence from northern Texas."[51]

WHILE QUANTRILL'S exaggerated and somewhat sanitized victory was lauded
before the troops, the Confederate authorities had mixed feelings.
"Quantrill has arrived in north Texas like an 'elephant won at a raffle' and
we are sorely puzzled to know what to do with him and his men," wrote Gov.
Thomas C. Reynolds, who had succeeded Claiborne Jackson as Confederate
governor of Missouri after Jackson's death in December 1862. Reynolds suggested that Quantrill and his followers be put to work rounding up Confederate deserters for the present but questioned their continued use as
guerrillas in Missouri.[52] "Colonel Quantrill has now with him 350 men of
that dashing and daring character . . . so feared by our enemies, and have
aided so much to keep Missouri, although overrun by Federals, identified
with the Confederacy," wrote Maj. Gen. Sterling Price to Governor
Reynolds. He noted "with much regret . . . a disposition with these men to
avoid coming into the service of the Confederacy," yet he reported that they
desired to come under Price "as partisans."

Price contended that the guerrillas had "been outlawed by the Federal
authorities, and expect no mercy or clemency at their hands, not even the
chances of prisoners of war," and felt safer protecting themselves rather
than submitting to possible surrender by some potentially incompetent
officers—or so their story ran.[53]

"I do not know as much about his mode of warfare as others seem to
know," wrote Brig. Gen. Henry McCulloch from his headquarters at
Bonham, Texas. "But from all I can hear, it is but little, if at all, removed from
that of the wildest savage, so much so, that I do not . . . believe that our government can sanction it in one of her officers." McCulloch, commander of
the Northern Sub-District of Texas, had earlier written of the "very good
news from our front," concerning General Blunt's alleged death. Now he felt
that "we cannot, as a Christian people, sanction a savage, inhuman warfare,
in which men are to be shot down like dogs" after surrendering. "I have but
little confidence in men who fight for booty," he added in another letter on
the subject.[54]

Gen. Edmund Kirby-Smith, commander of the Trans-Mississippi Department, told McCulloch, in gushing terms, to use Quantrill's men to hunt deserters. "They are bold, fearless men . . . from all representations under fair discipline . . . composed . . . in a measure of the very best class of Missourians." He also noted that warfare in Missouri was one of "no quarter" on all sides.[55]

Quantrill's band settled into a camp of hastily built huts at Mineral Creek, fifteen miles northwest of Sherman, Texas. There, in the winter of 1863–64, whatever cohesion the group had began to come apart. The break came with a man now known as "Bloody Bill" Anderson, whose sisters were in the warehouse-prison that collapsed. Anderson was a remorseless psychopath who took scalps and reportedly carried a silk cord in which he tied a knot for every man he killed. His right-hand man was Archie "Little Arch" Clement, an eighteen-year-old punk killer. Anderson and his followers split with Quantrill and moved into Sherman, where the guerrilla chieftain took quarters with a woman of easy virtue. It was during that winter when many of Quantrill's men either went into regular Confederate service, as was the case with Cole Younger, or went over to Anderson.

Sherman soon became a classic frontier "helldorado," with Anderson's men regularly shooting up the town and terrorizing the locals. Riding horses into the local stores or hotel seems to have been a favorite pastime. On Christmas Eve (some accounts say Christmas Day) several members of the band became tanked on some very potent eggnog and rode into the lobby of Christian's Hotel, shooting up the place and breaking the furniture and lobby flooring. A classic photograph of three members of this group was taken by a Sherman photographer whose equipment was smashed by the trio. Apparently they didn't like the way the photo turned out.[56]

In January, Quantrill was ordered to join Gen. John B. Magruder on the Texas coast. "Quantrill has not moved a peg," McCulloch later complained to Kirby-Smith, "and I have ordered him and his command arrested." This was easier said than done. McCulloch had ordered Col. Stand Watie and his regiment of Confederate Cherokees to do the job, but the Indian leader probably knew better and seems to have kept his distance. McCulloch was apprehensive. "They will not obey orders and I don't know what else to do," he wrote in exasperation. It was suggested later that Quantrill be ordered west of Corpus Christi, probably to fight Indians on the plains.

By late March the bushwhackers were still in the Sherman environs, orders or not. "The Major General commanding is informed that all kinds of outrages are being committed by the devils in the northern districts," read a letter to McCulloch. The guerrillas had long since worn out their welcome, as witnessed by McCulloch's reply of April 6, 1864: "Many robberies, thefts, and murders have been committed in the country, principally by men with Federal overcoats on, some of which have been traced to Captain Quantrill's company proper, and others to some of the men who came with him last fall. . . . I assure you the Captain Quantrill command has been a terror to the country and a curse to our land and cause in this section, and I never have been able to control them."

McCulloch had tried to arrest Quantrill, but the guerrilla chief escaped with part of his band to the Indian Territory, just across the nearby Red River, where Cooper, not McCulloch, had jurisdiction. The guerrillas had already started to quarrel among themselves and the command had fragmented into factions. Anderson and some of the wilder element went their way, including Fletch Taylor, who had been accused of murdering a civilian. Meanwhile, in an apparent attempt to save political face, McCulloch "requested" Cooper to send Quantrill north into Kansas, ostensibly to fight Unionist Indians. Anything to get them out of the region, where his own men were afraid to confront them.[57]

SHORTLY AFTER returning to Missouri in the spring of 1864, Quantrill, for all intents, was deposed as leader of the guerrillas following a poker game with George Todd. Quantrill accused Todd of cheating, and the latter quickly whipped out a revolver and made the guerrilla leader admit that he was afraid of him. Quantrill rode away from the camp and remained largely inactive for the rest of the year. Anderson and Todd would be the key guerrilla leaders that summer and fall, staining the Missouri landscape with some of the most violent bloodshed yet. In this both Frank and Jesse James would play a visible role.[58]

Jesse James probably joined the guerrillas in the spring of 1864 when a recruiting party under Lt. Charles F. "Fletch" Taylor, who had taken part in the Richfield affair and the Plattsburg raid (where some claimed he'd taken the bulk of the money captured), came to Clay County. It probably was not until early June that he would see any real "action." There were a few scores to settle from the year before. One was with Brantley Bond, Frank's former comrade in the State Guard who had gone over to the Federals. With Alvis Dagley, Bond had hoisted Dr. Samuel with a rope the year before when the Federals came to the James-Samuel farm looking for Frank and his comrades. Bond, in one account, was reportedly cornered at his home, near Claytonsville, by Jesse James and a party of bushwhackers. Jesse reportedly told Bond to "pray if you ever prayed in your life, because you've only got about a minute to live." Bond begged for his life but was shot dead. Differing versions of the story credit the deed to Fletch Taylor, Arch Clement, Peyton Long, Jim Bissett, or to Jesse himself. In all likelihood it was Long who killed Bond, though. In 1897 Jesse's mother recalled that "Peyton Long shot old Bond, and left him in the road."

Next came Alvis Dagley, who may have been a schoolmate of the James boys. There were a number of guerrillas eager to get Dagley, who worked for Travis Finley not far from the James-Samuel farm. Both Frank James and Jim Bissett later claimed to have killed Dagley. In reprisal for the Bond slaying, two houses in the nearby town of Centreville were burned by Federals.[59]

There would be numerous collisions with the Federals that summer. Jesse James was probably present at the siege of the home of militiamen Simeon and John Bigelow during the last week in June. Both Bigelows were killed after a desperate fight. Running out of ammunition, they fought with pieces of furniture until they were shot down. On July 4, Fletch Taylor's men ambushed a patrol of thirty troopers of the Ninth Missouri State Militia Cavalry near Centreville (Kearney) at a ford on Fishing River, killing two and wounding three.

On July 7 Taylor joined forces with Col. John C. Calhoun "Coon" Thornton, a veteran of the Liberty arsenal raid, to capture Parksville, on the Missouri River. He successfully recruited some officers and men of the "Paw Paw" Militia into the guerrilla ranks with the somewhat premature notice that Price was about to invade. The guerrillas' July 10 raid on Platte City in Platte County near the Kansas border, however, netted some three hundred Enrolled Missouri Militia, when the militiamen staged a prearranged mutiny and changed sides, hauling down the American flag and tying it to a horse's tail. A Confederate banner was hoisted in its place. The businesses of local Unionists were plundered. On July 15 Doc Jennison and his jayhawkers repeated their performance of the previous fall. In reprisal they burned a large portion of the town, including the Methodist and Presbyterian churches, and took more than one hundred horses and a variety of loot, killing six civilians in the process.[60]

After leaving Platte City, Taylor and his band paid a visit to Charles Morris, a Northern Methodist minister and outspoken abolitionist, cornering him in his home with two other men. The house was set afire and the occupants gunned down as they attempted to escape. The question of slavery had taken on religious overtones even before the war, splitting some denominations and creating a quasi-religious war in some areas like the Kansas-Missouri border. In Union-occupied Kansas City one could expect to hear sermons such as "The Sin of Rebellion," which was preached in a

Baptist church nearly two weeks before the Lawrence raid and reprinted in local newspapers. No doubt at least some Missourians also had been exposed to books such as Josiah Priest's *Bible Defense of Slavery*, which went through at least five editions of its 1852 Glasgow, Kentucky, printing. Priest's book included the dubious argument that the Canaanites (ancestors of the present-day Palestinians) of the Old Testament were black. To the contrary, Theodore D. Weld's *The Bible Against Slavery* would deny, with equally questionable logic, that actual slavery existed among the ancient Israelites. In the ensuing strife there was a collective ignorance regarding the Ten Commandments on both sides.[61]

Late in July, the crazed Bloody Bill Anderson demanded the surrender of Lexington, Missouri. In one of three incoherent and demented letters to two newspapers and Union officers there (see Appendix A) he claimed, "I am a guerrilla. I have never belonged to the Confederate Army, nor do my men." Indeed, there is no apparent record of Anderson having formally enlisted or holding an official Confederate or Missouri state commission of any type. Quantrill, who once styled himself "Colonel," probably through an election by guerrillas just prior to Baxter Springs, actually held a commission as a captain under the Partisan Ranger Act of 1862, as Confederate authorities in Texas eventually learned.

While Frank was enlisted by Quantrill, Jesse and others who joined that spring were, officially at least, more freelance raiders than not, although they would have a role in Confederate army strategy that fall. At the same time that Anderson was threatening Lexington, a Federal demi-brigade under Col. James H. Ford, containing detachments of the Ninth Missouri State Militia, Ford's Second Colorado Cavalry, and Doc Jennison's Sixteenth Kansas Cavalry—some three hundred troops in all—descended upon Liberty. The Kansan raiders were in true form, robbing local merchants and looting nearby farms until Ford reined them in. Their three-day occupation outstripped anything the guerrillas had delivered and was partly responsible for a mass meeting in Liberty on July 20. Some fifteen hundred residents attended to protest both bushwhacker and jayhawker incursions.

Taylor was seriously wounded in a fight with militia four miles outside of Independence on August 8. A load of buckshot resulted in the amputation of his right arm. He had reportedly been planning a grandiose, long-range raid on the Iowa state capital of Des Moines with either George Todd or Quantrill commanding. Instead, Taylor was briefly out of the war, as rumors spread that his wound had been mortal. He returned to action later, but was accidentally shot in his good arm by one of his men. While another rumor spread that he was dead this time, Taylor slipped out of the war.

Around August 10 Anderson arrived in Clay County, and it was then that many of Taylor's men joined up with Bloody Bill.[62]

Jesse's activity with the guerrillas also came to a brief halt sometime in July or August following an incident he related to Thomas R. Shouse after the war: "We were passing through a Dutch settlement in the southern part of Ray County," Jesse told Shouse. "In passing a house I saw a saddle on the fence in front of the house that I needed. I was in the act of picking it up when a [fifty-four-year-old] Dutchman [named George Heisenger] came to the door and shot me through the breast and escaped through the cornfield. I was able to sit on my horse for about four miles by Frank holding me in the saddle. Then they secured a wagon and placed me in it. They were driving fast and I was suffering so intensely that I wished every minute the soldiers would overtake and kill me."

Later accounts by various writers, starting with John Newman Edwards's *Noted Guerrillas* (1877), embellished the story, claiming Jesse was wounded August 12 in a standup fight with Federal cavalry at Flat Rock Ford. It certainly sounded more heroic.[63]

Jesse was taken across the Missouri River to a small wayside inn opposite Kansas City. The place was owned by his uncle by marriage, John Mimms. He was hidden in a garret room and cared for by his first cousin Zee (short for Zerelda) Mimms. Dr. J. M. Ridge of Kansas City visited Jesse there after he was contacted by Thomas James, Jesse's uncle. Dr. Ridge recalled:

> I was shown to a room in the second story and then into a clothes closet, from the floor of which a small movable ladder reached to a trap door opening into the loft. There lay Jesse in great pain and in a very dangerous condition, for he had received no medical attention. A minie ball the size of my thumb had entered his right breast above the nipple and passed clear through his body. I visited him clandestinely for two months, and as soon as he was able to sit steadily in the saddle he mounted his horse and rode to war again.[64]

Meanwhile, Jesse's stepfather was being pressured to help the Federal authorities. In a letter to the provost marshal's department from E. M. Samuel (the supposedly unrelated supporter who had endorsed the letter for Reuben Samuel's prison release a year before) on August 7, 1864, the local Unionist explained: "I told him [Dr. Reuben Samuel] very bluntly that it was his *duty* to help the military authorities in finding out his step sons and bringing them to justice. He is no kinsman of mine, thank God; yet I think he is an easy, good natured, good for nothing fellow, who is completely under the control of his wife."

E. M. Samuel was apparently the local informant for the Union provost marshal in the area, and his letters, written on the stationery of the Farmers Bank of Missouri branch in Liberty, of which he was president, turn up in the provost files of local civilians with more than passing frequency.[65]

Jesse rejoined his brother Frank around September 20, in time to serve only briefly under the demented Bloody Bill. The guerrillas had shifted their activities into north-central Missouri, mainly in the counties bordering the Missouri River. The citizens of Lawrence, Kansas, had fortified their town since the raid a year earlier, and the Burnt District offered few pickings.

On the morning of September 24, Anderson and Todd, accompanied by Quantrill and a handful of men who still followed him, rode into the town of Fayette in the central part of Howard County. The night before, Anderson and Todd, full of bluster, had proposed a raid into the town. Quantrill protested that the garrison held a fortified wooden blockhouse on the northern edge of town and to try to attack it would invite disaster. His warning was brushed aside. Quantrill could either come along or hide with his men like cowards. In the end he came along.

The guerrillas, dressed in Federal uniforms, rode into town and were not given away until one of the men began shooting at a black man in a blue uniform. Then all hell broke loose, with men, women, and children screaming, yelling, and running to escape.

The bushwhackers headed for the blockhouse. "We charged up against a blockhouse made of railroad ties filled with port holes and then charged back again," recalled Frank James. "The blockhouse was filled with Federal troops and it was like charging a stone wall only this stone wall belched forth lead." Oliver ("Oll") Johnson was wounded on a rise a short distance from the blockhouse. When Frank's commander asked for men to go after the body, Frank, Sim Whitsett, and Dick Kinney volunteered and made it to the rise but were pinned down.

"We were in plain view of the Federals and they simply peppered us with bullets," Frank related. "We got as close to the ground as we could. I was mightily scared. It was the worst fight I ever had. I knew if we raised up we would expose ourselves to the fire of the Yankees and we couldn't stay still."

Finally they pulled Johnson's body out, wrapped in a blanket. As Frank related years later, "I tell you, pride makes most of us do many things we wouldn't do otherwise. Many men would run away in a battle if the army wasn't watching them."

Likewise, Jesse was credited with dragging out wounded comrade Lee McMurtry, who had fallen near the blockhouse. Quantrill, who had advised caution, left at the tail end of the debacle, not even waiting to see it end. Todd, enraged, blamed the disaster on his former chieftain and called for men to go after him. The guerrillas refused, and Todd wisely chose not to press the matter further.[66]

It was in Boone County, about fifteen miles northeast of Columbia, that the notorious Centralia affair would take place several days later. On the morning of Tuesday, September 27, Bloody Bill Anderson and about eighty men took over the railroad village of Centralia. They looted the two stores in town, one of which held a barrel of whiskey, which was rolled into the street and opened. It was not long before the guerrillas, wild enough when sober, were roaring drunk.

About 11 A.M. they robbed the passengers of an incoming stage-coach—Union and Confederate sympathizers alike. About half an hour later the bandits stopped an express of the North Missouri Railroad, coming out of Saint Charles. On board were around 125 passengers and 25 Union soldiers, most on furlough from Sherman's army, which had recently taken Atlanta. The passengers were robbed, and the soldiers were brutally gunned down with the exception of one sergeant, whom Anderson decided by quirk to spare. Arch Clement was given the order to "parole" them as they stood in their longjohns, stripped of their uniforms. Some of the stunned passengers then asked if they could continue their trip to Sturgeon, just up the line. "You can go to hell for all I care," retorted Anderson.

The intoxicated bushwhackers torched the train without going through the express car. Consequently they lost several thousand dollars to the flames. The burning train, with the whistle tied down, was sent racing down the tracks to the west. The depot and another train parked nearby were also fired.[67]

About 4 P.M. a detachment of around 147 men drawn from Companies A, G, and H of the newly raised Thirty-ninth Missouri Infantry arrived at Centralia, which by then had been abandoned by Anderson. Led by Maj. A. V. E. Johnson, the soldiers were mounted on horses confiscated from "disloyal persons." The Federals, minus some 36 men left to police the scene at Centralia, were lured away from the town by Dave Pool and a small decoy party, who led them toward the guerrilla camp about three miles to the southeast. The bluecoats rode across a stretch of prairie till they came to a depression in front of the woods where Anderson and Todd's men were camped.

One account reported that Frank James participated in the Centralia raid, but Frank himself said that he had not gone with Anderson. Frank was in the guerrilla camp when Johnson's force approached, and he related what happened next:

The yankees stopped near the rise of the hill. Both sides were in full view of each other, though nearly a half a mile distant. The yankees dismounted, gave their horses to a detail of men, and prepared to fight.

John Koger, a funny fellow in our ranks, watched the yankees get down from their horses and said: "why, the fools are going to fight us on foot!" and then added seriously: "God help 'em!"

We dismounted to tighten the belts [saddle girths] on our horses, and then at the word of command started on our charge. The ground . . . rises sharply and we had to charge up hill. For a moment we moved slowly. Our line was nearly a quarter mile long, theirs much closer together. We were some six hundred yards away, our speed increasing and our ranks closing up, when they fired [at a reported range of 150 yards] their first and only time. They nearly all fired over our heads. We were laying low on our horses, a trick the Comanche Indians practice and which saved our lives many a time. Only two of our men were killed . . . a third . . . was shot and died three or four days later from lockjaw . . . we couldn't stop that terrible charge for anything. Up the hill we went, yelling like wild Indians. . . . Almost in the twinkling of an eye we were on the yankee line. They seemed terrorized. Hypnotized might be a better word. . . . Some . . . were at "fix bayonets," some were biting off their cartridges, preparing to reload. Yelling, shooting our pistols, upon them we went. Not a man of the line [save three] escaped. They were shot through the head. The few who attempted to escape we followed into Centralia and on to Sturgeon. There a Federal blockhouse stopped further pursuit. All along the road we killed them.[68]

The men of the Thirty-ninth were armed only with muzzleloading Enfield rifles, and the roughly 225 guerrillas had at least a pair of revolvers each. Major Johnson was reportedly shot down in the onslaught by Jesse James, at least according to brother Frank. Fellow guerrilla Jim Cummins stated that he had "heard of several parties having boasted of killing Major Johnson." He further said that it was "very difficult to know in such a general mixup who did the killing."

Dave Pool would tally the bodies afterward by walking across the corpses, an effective way to check if any were still alive. A Federal officer who arrived thirty hours after the fight described what he found at the site of what would later be called the "Centralia massacre": "a scene of murder and outrage at which the heart sickens. Most of them were beaten over the head [with rifle butts?], seventeen of them were scalped and one man had his privates cut off and placed in his mouth. Every man was shot in the head. One man had his nose cut off. One hundred and fifty [actually 149] dead bodies have been found, including twenty-four taken from the train."[69]

On October 11, Anderson, Todd, and Quantrill met with Gen. Sterling Price at Boonville. The bushwhackers had learned of Price's invasion via a newspaper found on the train at Centralia. Price was aiming to repeat his 1861 victories, hoping for a reconquest of Missouri. It turned out to be merely a large-scale raid. With some fourteen cannon and around twelve thousand men, half cavalry and half mounted infantry, Price's army was not on its best behavior this time, and some of the troops had resorted to plundering their way across the state. According to Gov. Thomas Reynolds, Price's column resembled a "Calmuck horde" accompanied by a "rabble of deadheads, stragglers and stolen negroes on stolen horses." As Reynolds later stated, "The hotel occupied by General Price's own staff was the scene of drunken revelry by night."

Regardless, Price refused to speak to Anderson until he and his men had removed the scalps that decorated their horses' bridles. The guerrilla chieftain complied and smoothed his way into Price's good graces with a pair of silver-mounted pistols he had "acquired." The guerrillas under Anderson then were ordered to destroy the North Missouri Railroad while Quantrill and his men were assigned the Hannibal and Saint Joseph Railroad. Todd was to operate against the Pacific Railroad. The orders were largely ignored, although Anderson did burn a couple of railroad depots. Price later reported some damage "but none of any material advantage." The guerrillas "totally failed in the main object . . . to destroy the large railroad bridge that was in the end of St. Charles County." On October 14 Quantrill is said to have relieved a banker in Glasgow of twenty-one thousand dollars before he temporarily vanished from the bushwhacker scene again.[70]

On October 21, Todd, by one account, was killed along the Little Blue River, near Independence, in a fight against a Federal army led by Maj. Gen. Samuel R. Curtis, whose son had been slain at Baxter Springs over a year earlier. Another account has Todd killed in an ambush just north of Independence. Regardless, on learning the news the following day, Curtis wired his wife relaying news of the bushwhacker's confirmed death. Dave Pool took over Todd's command and took part in the battle of Westport on October 22 and 23. The conflict was a resounding defeat for Price, every bit as disastrous as Pea Ridge.[71]

Maj. Samuel P. Cox, a Gallatin, Missouri, native who had seen service on the Oregon Trail in 1847–48, took it upon himself (he had no formal commission at this time) to track down the notorious Bloody Bill with a detachment consisting of members of the First Missouri State Militia Cavalry and portions of the Thirty-third and Fifty-first Enrolled Missouri Militia. Although poorly armed, with single-shot muzzleloaders even older than the

arms of the troops slaughtered at Centralia, plus only a few privately purchased revolvers, Cox thought he saw a way for his three hundred men to
defeat the deranged Anderson. Learning from a woman in the neighborhood
of Orrick, in Ray County, that Anderson's band had gone into camp nearby,
he decided to fight fire with fire and set up a classic guerrilla-style ambush.

Cox positioned his men in some woods on both sides of a road, with a
bridge over a ravine to their rear. He then sent ahead a mounted decoy
party of thirty men, who were to retreat through the jaws of the trap.
Bloody Bill and about twenty of his men took the bait. According to Cox,
"Anderson and two of his men went right through the [Federal] line shooting and yelling . . . as Anderson and one of his men turned back . . . both of
them were killed."

Arch Clement rode across the bridge, stampeding the supply wagons
on the other side, yelling that the command had been cut to pieces. Several
were wounded, including Clell Miller, who was taken prisoner. "It was with
difficulty I restrained my men and the citizens from lynching him," Cox
recalled. Clell Miller was reportedly "kidnapped" while going to a neighbor's house on October 22, just four days prior to Anderson's death. "I have
always been a loyal boy and never sympathized with the south," he is said
to have stated after his capture. He was only about fourteen or fifteen years
old at the time. His father, Moses Miller, swore that Clell had been at home
throughout the war. Moses himself had taken the oath and was reportedly a
Unionist. Several neighbors swore that Clell was loyal, and even that
noted provost informant E. M. Samuel wrote authorities in his behalf. It
was easy to be mistaken; such were the times. Clell was released in April
1865, but this would not be the end of the tragedy.

On the bridle of the guerrilla leader's horse were two more scalps, additions since Anderson's visit with Price. Bloody Bill's corpse was taken to
Richmond, the county seat, and photographed. Later Anderson's head was
cut off and mounted on a telegraph pole, and the headless corpse was
dragged through the streets. The remains were later collected and buried in
a shallow grave. Only William Quantrill would remain to be reckoned with
as Sterling Price's battered army retreated back to Texas.[72]

3

Long Ride to Destiny

This little band—scarcely a fragment of that terrible organization
known so well to the border—was the last of the guerrilla race. . . .
It was the offspring of the fury and the agony of invasion.

John Newman Edwards, Noted Guerrillas (1877)

I N LATE NOVEMBER AND early December 1864, William Quantrill began
to gather what remained of his old band. He sent Kate King (known to
the guerrillas as Kate Clarke; accounts differ as to whether she was his
mistress or his wife) to Saint Louis, probably with some or all of the loot he
had taken from a Glasgow bank the previous month. While Quantrill had
been largely on the sidelines for a while, he had apparently been planning
what could be his most ambitious escapade yet.

On June 2, 1864, a detective for the Union army in central Kentucky
reported to his superior in Cincinnati about "an old lady" from Buchanan or
Platte County, Missouri. The woman, who had returned to Missouri after
visiting Kentucky that spring, "gives Quantrill most of his information, and
brags that she has enabled him to kill many Federal officers and men," the
detective related. She may well have been practicing her avocation that
very trip.[1]

According to Jim Cummins, he and the James brothers were in Clay
County, visiting with their relatives, when word came via Allen Parmer (who
was attracted to the James brothers' sister, Susan) that Quantrill was seeking

to put the old band back together and the rendezvous would be somewhere between the towns of Dover and Waverly, in northeast Lafayette County near the Missouri River. By one account they gathered at the home of a Mrs. Wigginton five miles west of Waverly. Sometime on or about December 4, the guerrillas, numbering between forty-two and fifty, headed east then south, passing through Saline, Cooper, and Moniteau Counties until they reached the Osage River at Tuscumbia in Miller County.[2]

The weather was intensely cold, and the bushwhackers had taken the precaution of wearing Federal uniforms, in this case the ubiquitous sky-blue overcoat. They were passing themselves off, at this juncture, as members of the Second Colorado Cavalry. The guerrillas had tangled with the Coloradans on several occasions, and Quantrill carried a captured commission and wore the uniform of one of the unit's officers. Tuscumbia itself was garrisoned by a force of twenty-five men of Capt. Sayles Brown's company of the First Battalion, Provisional Enrolled Missouri Militia Infantry. According to John McCorkle, Quantrill's men rode into town as though they were just another Federal unit on a scouting patrol.

It was around 9 A.M. on December 8 when they arrived. Quantrill asked for the commander, saluted, and introduced himself as Capt. W. C. Clark. He requested feed for the horses and permission for his men to warm themselves inside the hotel where the militia was quartered. According to McCorkle:

> The commander had a fire built in their headquarters and invited us in. The Federals were standing around the room and we circled between them and the fire and also got between them and their arms, which were stacked in a corner of the room and, when we heard Quantrill, who had remained outside with the commander, tell him to surrender, we drew our revolvers and told the Federals that they were mistaken in their men, that we were Confederate soldiers and they were under arrest. They all promptly obeyed, except one man, who attempted to get out of a window, when Frank James gently tapped him on the head with his pistol and told him to get back in line or he might be seriously hurt. We marched the militia out into the street and, placing a guard over them, the rest of us proceeded to take their guns, break the stocks off of them and throw them into the river.
>
> Seeing us do this, one of the militiamen exclaimed, "Why, what in the world are they throwing our guns in the river for; we are Union men as they are?" to which his commander replied, "Why, you damned fool, they are Southern men and we are all prisoners."[3]

Quantrill's men were ferried across the Osage River in a flatboat propelled by a rope-and-pulley system. The militiamen were paroled and agreed not to take arms against the Confederacy until properly exchanged—quite a change from Anderson's method (or madness) at Centralia. Then holes were cut in the hull, and the ferry was sunk. Two militiamen were taken along as guides and kept for the next three days as the band marched southeast, past Rolla, until they entered unfamiliar country, at which point the prisoners were released. The guerrillas had reached the wilds of the Missouri Ozarks, a sparsely settled, heavily timbered region with few towns of any consequence—and most of those burned and/or abandoned as a consequence of the war.

According to McCorkle, the guerrillas moved through the largely barren forests to the southeast, following a path along the Current River until they reached Pocahontas, Arkansas. Another account has them marching by way of present-day Mountain View and Thomasville, Missouri. They then pushed east, through what was then swampland, probably over what was called the Pocahontas Trail to Crowley's Ridge, an upland area some fifteen miles wide that runs through the Missouri "bootheel" and well into Arkansas, paralleling the Mississippi River. Here they probably struck the Military Road and headed south.[4]

Just what were Quantrill's plans? According to some historians of the war, Quantrill had said he saw the war winding down and wanted to get his men out of the area where they had become notorious and move them east of the Mississippi, where they might be granted better surrender terms. To others he revealed a more sinister plan: moving east via Tennessee and/or Kentucky into Virginia and north into the mountains of western Maryland, where he would stage a raid into Washington with the intent of capturing or killing President Lincoln. According to this theory, Quantrill then planned to wage a guerrilla war into Pennsylvania, using the same mountains that abolitionist John Brown had sought a base for his planned slave uprising, which was to have followed his ill-fated raid on the U.S. arsenal at Harpers Ferry in 1859.

In all probability Quantrill was telling his men what he thought they wanted to hear in order to get them to follow him. Perhaps a few picked up on their leader's double talk or felt that any guerrilla operations should continue in Missouri. There were doubtless other personality conflicts as well. At any rate, somewhere in the vicinity of Pocahontas or Crowley's Ridge around six of the bushwhackers had second thoughts. Led by George Shepherd and including Jim Cummins and Jesse James, they said their good-byes and headed west to join some of Anderson's command who had gone back to their old haunts in Texas.[5]

With his group posing as Federal soldiers, Quantrill tried to cross the Mississippi at Memphis but was unsuccessful. A similar attempt to hail a passing transport upriver was met with failure. Quantrill then found a man, identified by McCorkle as Murray Boswell, a former resident of Lafayette County, Missouri, who had a yawl hidden in a swamp. They repaired the boat and used it to cross the Mississippi at a place called Devil's Elbow (or Bend, in some accounts) fifteen or so miles above Memphis. They crossed the river on New Year's Day 1865, swimming the horses alongside the yawl.

According to McCorkle, it took all night to ferry the command across. Among those crossing were Frank James, Jim Younger (brother of Cole), Allen Parmer, Donny Pence, and Tyler Burns. Quantrill passed through West Tennessee by way of Brownsville and arrived in the town of Paris. It was here that McCorkle met his uncle, Capt. Robert H. Fristoe of Company C, Eighth Kentucky Mounted Infantry, who had been wounded in the thigh at Harrisburg, Mississippi, on July 14, 1864. Fristoe had lost his right leg and was reported as being on recruiting service in the area. McCorkle also met his aunt for the first time at Paris, as did his cousins, Tom Harris and George Wigginton. It was an odd place for a family reunion, but the boys visited with their relatives for about two hours and then moved on with the command, apparently heading north into Kentucky after crossing the Tennessee River at Birmingham in Marshall County, northeast of Benton.[6]

⁂

MEANWHILE, BACK in Missouri, trouble was brewing for the James family. On January 29, in Liberty, Missouri, Reuben and Zerelda Samuel, and Susan James, sister of Frank and Jesse, were read Special Orders No. 9 from the Headquarters of the Department of the Missouri, which had been issued on January 9, 1865, from Saint Louis. Item number 12, in particular, related specifically to the family:

> The following named persons having forfeited their rights as citizens by flagrant acts of disloyalty in denouncing the Federal Government, aiding and assisting [Sterling] Price during the late raid into the state, uniformly aiding and giving comfort to the rebel enemies of the United States, feeding, harboring and encouraging bushwhackers and guerrilla bands to which members of their families are now and have been attached and failing and refusing to report said outlaws to the Federal authorities, are hereby with their families banished from this Depmt. Within twenty (20) days from the receipt of this order they will be sent under guard via Quincy and Cairo, Ills. to Memphis, Tenn. or Little Rock, Arkansas (as they may . . . elect) there in accordance with instructions received from Maj. Gen. Canby, Comdg. Mil. Division of West. Miss. to be turned over to the Dept. commander, to be sent by him through the rebel lines there to be removed to wit.[7]

Third down on the list of names was "Mr. Reuben Samuel of Clay Co., Mo." Also listed were the Samuels' neighbors, including a Mrs. Cummings and Mrs. Moses McCoy, among seven others. The order stipulated that all were "expressly forbidden under penalty of death from returning within the limits of this department during the war." They were "permitted to take with them such articles of household goods and clothing as is absolutely necessary for their comfort."[8]

Instead of being shipped south, however, the family actually went north—to Richardson County, Nebraska. The town of Rulo, on the Missouri River in the extreme southeast corner of the state, was their ultimate destination. Just how this came about may never be known, but what is known is that Zerelda Samuel had relatives in the Cole family who had settled in Nemaha County, Nebraska, around the town of Brownsville, in 1852. Some of her relatives may have influenced Union authorities to modify the banishment order. Zerelda, after all, had taken the Oath of Allegiance in 1863, and Nebraska was outside the Missouri combat zone. Reportedly, the James brothers had visited relatives, including their uncle, Jesse Cole, in the Nebraska City area just prior to the war. At that time a photo was rumored to have been made of Jesse and perhaps one of Frank as well. Zerelda is said to have taught school in Rulo for a term while her husband, Reuben, tried to resurrect his dormant medical practice.[9]

Oddly enough, the banishment may have saved the family from significant financial grief. General Orders No. 7 from the same commander, Maj. Gen. Grenville Dodge, stipulated that in the future even having knowledge of guerrillas in the area and failing to report them, family members or not, would result in the confiscation of the individuals' property as well as banishment: "It is time that the people who have been allowed to live peaceably, enjoy protection, and grow rich under our government, while they have given aid and comfort to the enemy, either directly or indirectly, or by a non-committal course of conduct, should be made to show their hands and once and for all to place themselves either in support of the Government or with its avowed enemies."[10]

❧❦❧

QUANTRILL'S GROUP headed southeast, across the land between the Tennessee and Cumberland Rivers, which is now the Land Between the Lakes Recreation Area. By one account the band crossed the Cumberland in the vicinity of Eddyville, Kentucky, where they skirmished with an unnamed guerrilla band. According to John McCorkle's account, they crossed somewhere near Canton, and it was here that "Old Charley," the horse Quantrill had ridden through most of the war, severed a tendon while being shod. "Quantrill was terribly worried and said that he had lost his luck," McCorkle recalled. He also suggested that the unit be disbanded and that the men who wanted to could go back to Paris. Then Quantrill found another horse and decided to "go through to Virginia." This incident with the horse may have happened at a later date, but regardless of when it occurred there may have been some demoralization within the unit at this time with many guerrillas questioning the need to push forward.[11]

Kentucky had been in a state of quasi-anarchy since at least the previous summer. Early in 1864 the War Department had authorized the recruitment of black regiments within this Union slave state, setting off a furor among antiabolition Unionists, who saw this action as a plot to extend emancipation. Bvt. Maj. Gen. Stephen G. Burbridge was given command of the Military District of Kentucky on February 15. Just three years prior he had been a farmer in Logan County, Kentucky, where the James boys' father hailed from, and now Burbridge had climbed the political-military ladder to his level of incompetence. On July 2, 1864, Congress passed an act giving military courts authority over guerrillas. Lincoln invoked martial law in Kentucky just three days later, also suspending the writ of habeas corpus. The act was probably intended to discourage Confederate Gen. John Hunt Morgan from paying further visits to the Bluegrass State as he had done every year previous, bringing destruction to Union property in his wake. The same practices that had been at work in Missouri were about to be applied to Kentucky. Home Guard–State Guard units were raised, the members receiving certification from local county judges, which gave them a political tinge. Furthermore, Burbridge ordered a tax levied to support these new state troops without even consulting Gov. Thomas E. Bramlette.[12]

Civil liberty, as many saw it, was under attack. Burbridge instituted a policy whereby four prisoners, chosen at random by lot for every Unionist killed, were to be taken to the site of the slaughter and shot. Some of these prisoners had been detained on flimsy, perhaps political, charges and were in fact innocent. Then, in mid-July came the notorious order for the banishment of what were deemed "Confederate sympathizers" living within five miles of the site of a guerrilla attack. On October 26 came an order that no guerrilla prisoners were to be taken. In the November 1864 presidential election, despite the presence of Federal troops at the polls, Kentucky went two-and-a-half-to-one for Lincoln's Democratic challenger, Gen. George B. McClellan. It was into this caldron that Quantrill's men marched a few weeks later.[13]

"The country around is pretty clear of Guerillas and I think with the present disposition of the command I can keep them out," wrote Col. H. M.

Buckley of the Fifty-fourth Kentucky Mounted Infantry to his superior, Brig. Gen. Edward Hobson. Buckley proposed sending one hundred men through Spencer, Nelson, Bullitt, and Washington Counties "to take Horses from disloyal citizens."[14]

Quantrill's group went through Cadiz to the area around Hopkinsville, where they discovered the trail of Federal cavalry and followed them in order to obtain fresh mounts. Near sundown on January 17, 1865, Quantrill cornered the horsemen at a house and, after a brief gun battle in which one guerrilla was mortally wounded, threatened to set fire to the building. According to McCorkle, six men surrendered and were paroled. With fresh mounts, the guerrillas moved on to Greenville in Muhlenburg County.

The band passed through the town posing as Federals and, according to McCorkle, hosted the Union commander for dinner at a local hotel, paying for the meal with a forged voucher.[15]

On January 22 they reached Hartford, in Ohio County, putting up the usual false front. According to one account they arranged for a guide here who was identified as a Lieutenant Barnett and said to be a white recruiting officer for the 125th U.S. Colored Regiment. They were also joined by W. B. Lawton, a furloughed Indiana soldier, and W. Lownsley, allegedly a discharged veteran of the Third Kentucky Cavalry. All three men were later killed. According to Edwards, Frank James shot Barnett on Quantrill's order.[16]

The next day the guerrillas moved on to Litchfield, in Grayson County, and crossed the Louisville and Nashville Railroad at Upton Station in Larue County. According to Edwards, their route led them near Marion County, entering the Lebanon-Campbellsville turnpike at Rolling Fork and going north from there to New Market. Then they headed east to Bradfordsville and arrived in Houstonville on January 28. In a Houstonville livery stable they found four horses belonging to a Union officer. Seeing his mounts being stolen, the officer was shot by Allen Parmer when he attempted to stop the horse thieves. Word of the killing soon spread, however, and the gang's trail became more dangerous.[17]

Around 9 A.M. on January 29, "Captain Clark" and the Fourth Missouri Cavalry entered the town of Danville; Quantrill's people continued to charade as Federal troopers. When Quantrill reached the town his men dismounted before the courthouse. According to the *Louisville Daily Democrat*, "They took possession of the place and swapped a few horses. Some of them helped themselves to boots at one of the shoe stores and left money in part pay of what they took. They then proceeded to shoe several of their horses and departed. No citizen was hurt and one Federal soldier who fell into their hands was subsequently released."

Union army reports added that they robbed the store and civilians and gutted the telegraph office. Whatever else happened, their disguise was seen through, and soon there was hell to pay. They moved out around 11:15 A.M. on the Perryville pike.[18]

Capt. James H. Bridgewater was one of those rare individuals, like Maj. Samuel P. Cox of Missouri, whom Quantrill would have done better to avoid. Bridgewater's Scouts, as they were sometimes called in lieu of their official designation—Company A, Hall's Gap Battalion, Kentucky State Guard—already had something of a reputation for their work in the summer of 1864 against John Hunt Morgan's command. The company had been raised in the area between Stanford and Hall's Gap. Men who were handy with both horses and rifles, they knew the territory better than Quantrill and were more than a match for any Missouri militia in a fight.[19]

Bridgewater's force had been alerted at nearby Stanford and soon trailed behind Quantrill's band after it left Danville. In the Oakland community two or three miles west of Harrodsburg that evening, they caught up. Quantrill's men had broken into squads of around a dozen or so men and had stopped at three houses along the road for dinner. The last squad along the road was under the command of Sgt. John Barker. Surrounding the house, Bridgewater's men took position behind what cover they could find, took aim at the doors and windows, and opened fire. No attempt was made to rush the house, but the steady fire soon killed three men, including Barker. The guardsmen were apparently armed with muskets or rifles while the guerrillas had only revolvers, almost useless at such range and at night. The militia only had to wait and blast them out.

The survivors, reportedly running low on ammunition, tried to make a run for it but didn't get far. The remainder were wounded and/or captured including, by John McCorkle's account, Jim Younger. Allen Parmer and Frank James were said to have rushed from the next house up the road but saw the situation was hopeless. Quantrill's second lieutenant, Chatham "Chad" Renick, in charge of the next squad, was killed by a minié ball as he rode to investigate. Parmer, James, and the rest rode back to find Quantrill and eventually retreated west toward Chaplin, in Nelson County.

The prisoners were taken to Lexington and when questioned said they had "intended to go to Virginia." Five of the guerrillas, probably including Jim Younger, reportedly escaped from the military prison in Louisville and eventually made their way to the Nelson-Spencer County area, where they rejoined Quantrill.[20]

The next day there was a running fight near Chaplin, along the road to Bloomfield. It was somewhere in the Nelson-Spencer County area, possibly in or near Taylorsville, that Quantrill met Capt. Bill Marion, leader of a band of Kentucky guerrillas. Nearly a third of Quantrill's command had been taken, and the survivors were probably in need of supplies and fresh horses after the fights they'd come through. Marion was at first suspicious of Quantrill, according to Edwards, but agreed to take what men Quantrill had for a raid with his own men, with Marion in charge. Quantrill reportedly stayed behind in Taylorsville because of Marion's suspicions about him and the reliability of his men. In Midway on February 2 the joint guerrilla band burned the depot, cut down telegraph poles, and robbed stores, then a squad, reportedly including Frank James, even made it as far as Georgetown that evening, where the guerrillas were repulsed. They returned to the Nelson-Spencer County area via Lawrenceburg.[21]

The band spread out for the next few days. They were taken in and hidden by the area's numerous Confederate sympathizers, including some relatives of the members of Quantrill's group, as well as some refugees from Missouri, evicted under Order No. 11. Soon a new raid was afoot. Quantrill's men, reportedly acting in cooperation with another group under Henry Magruder and possibly Jerome Clarke, around forty-five riders in all, headed south. At New Market on the Lebanon-Campbellsville pike, they ambushed and destroyed nine supply wagons at 11 A.M. on February 8. "Three of the train guards were killed and four captured and taken to Bradfordsville, where they were murdered," read a Federal report. Maj. Thomas Mahoney, with thirty-five partly disabled men of the Veterans Reserve Corps from Lebanon, followed the raiders and attacked them as they moved out of New Market and engaged them in a running fight. "They fought [us] desperately," said Mahoney, "charged us at Bradfordsville." The disabled troops "could not master their horses and load their long guns," according to the major, so he dismounted them at Bradfordsville. Some of the horses got away and raced toward the guerrillas and were captured. Things became confused, and the Federals broke off the fight, leaving the bushwhackers to head east toward Houstonville with their four-legged booty.[22]

Word was out by telegraph that the raiders were headed toward Houstonville. Headed toward them from Danville was the company of their nemesis, Capt. James H. Bridgewater. There was snow on the ground, and that evening the guerrillas sought shelter near the Little South Fork, west of Houstonville. At 2 A.M. on February 9, Bridgewater struck, killing four men and capturing thirty-five horses along with their saddles and other tack. The Federal force "ran thirty or thirty-five of their men into the woods, most of whom were barefooted . . . only six or seven escaped mounted." Quantrill was reported as among the unhorsed and barefooted escapees. Bridgewater was ordered to scour the country south of Parksville. For the guerrillas it was a defeat that rivaled the fight near Harrodsburg. Over the next two days four more guerrillas were captured while the rest escaped on foot (at least partway) to rendezvous in Nelson County.[23]

Over the next week or two the remaining guerrillas made their way back to Nelson County, appropriating horses or mules en route. They remained undercover and largely inactive over the next two months. There were reports of Quantrill's men raiding Hickman, Kentucky, on the Mississippi, on February 28. Just one day earlier Union Secretary of War Edwin M. Stanton had warned Maj. Gen. Winfield Scott Hancock, then at Winchester, Virginia, that he had received word that Quantrill and other guerrillas under the command of recently captured Henry Gilmore were preparing to raid nearby Martinsburg in the lower Shenandoah Valley. Curiously, this was the same area that Quantrill had hoped to reach. Perhaps there was a garbled Confederate rumor based on his predicted arrival. As late as April 18 Quantrill would be reported operating on the Hatchie River in West Tennessee. This was probably someone impersonating the guerrilla leader or a wild rumor that somehow started. Some of the raiders could well have been former members of Quantrill's band, but at the end of February the guerrilla leader was in Spencer County, where on April 26 he wrote a poem, a bastardized copy of one by Byron, for Nannie Dawson, the daughter of a man who was hiding him.[24]

On the Federal side, General Burbridge was finally removed and, on February 18, Maj. Gen. John M. Palmer took command of the Military Department of Kentucky. A skillful Illinois politician, Palmer was a pragmatist. Instead of cracking down on guerrilla sympathizers, he, in his own words, "made war on the guerrillas personally." He also issued an order for the protection of any Confederate deserter who would surrender. In early March he started to take what would be decisive action to clean up the guerrilla bands in the department, holding a secret meeting with Maj. Cyrus J. Wilson, a retired officer of the Twenty-sixth Kentucky Infantry. Although now a civilian, Wilson would take on the role of directing counterguerrilla operations, with Palmer placing what troops he had at Wilson's disposal for the task ahead.

On March 12 Wilson bagged Jerome Clarke–Sue Mundy and Henry Magruder near Brandenburg, on the Ohio River. Clarke was shipped to Louisville by steamboat, then tried and hanged before a crowd of around twelve thousand people on the afternoon of March 15. The wounded Magruder met a similar fate in October. But there were still other guerrillas to deal with, among them Quantrill.[25]

Cyrus J. Wilson had worked as a miller before the war, an odd trade for someone who would become the premier guerrilla hunter of Kentucky. In mid-September 1862, while serving as an officer with the Thirty-third Kentucky Infantry, a unit still in its formative stage, he was captured with several companies of his unit at Munfordville, Kentucky, after a brisk battle with and brief siege by Braxton Bragg's Army of Tennessee. The troops were paroled, promising not to fight until exchanged; they spent several months waiting for exchange at Camp Chase, Ohio, before being returned to Munfordville.

It was probably while guarding the Louisville and Nashville Railroad in the months ahead that Wilson picked up whatever experience he had in fighting guerrillas. The Thirty-third never completed its organization, though, and was consolidated with the Twenty-sixth Kentucky Infantry on April 1, 1864, with Wilson reduced in rank from a newly promoted lieutenant colonel to major. Perhaps this and/or personality clashes in the new unit led to his resignation on May 14. When called to serve as a civilian guerrilla hunter he would more than make up for his time on the sidelines.[26]

Ed Terrell was another unique byproduct of the war in Kentucky. He may have begun his checkered military career as a member of Company G, First Kentucky Infantry, a unit that served for a year, mostly in northern Virginia. Terrell spent much of this term "in arrest near Centerville" and later in Chimborazo Hospital No. 3 in Richmond. When his enlistment expired in May 1862 he went back to Kentucky and served briefly in John Hunt Morgan's cavalry before he deserted from the Confederate ranks.

According to an acquaintance, "His reputation was the worst imaginable and his fighting qualities were only developed when under the influence of whiskey." Terrell apparently was enlisted in Company D, Thirty-seventh Kentucky Mounted Infantry, on October 7, 1863, but was put under arrest seven weeks afterward and was kept in the guardhouse at Bowling Green, Kentucky, until sometime in March 1864. Basically on garrison service, he and other members of the unit were mustered out at Louisville on December 29, 1864.

Terrell and several companions were hired by the Louisville commandant, Col. L. B. Fairleigh, on January 2, 1865, as civilian "guerrilla hunters." His entrance into this vocation was inauspicious. On January 6 he and some of his men were captured by a Capt. John Smith, who commanded an independent Unionist unit nicknamed Company Q. Thought to be other guerrillas (they sometimes dressed in Confederate garb), Terrell and his compadres were lodged in the Springfield, Kentucky, calaboose until it was established that they were who they claimed to be. Their release was a mixed blessing, to put it mildly. According to a contemporary account, "He soon became a terror to the population of Washington, Marion, Shelby and Anderson counties, shooting down and plundering indiscriminately wherever his lawless horsemen rode."

On January 28, the day before Quantrill's encounter with the Bridgewater Scouts, Terrell and his self-styled "Home Guards" moved through northern Nelson County, "robbing citizens as they went." At the store of A. J. Langford they "relieved him of a quantity of bed clothing and other articles." Next they moved on to Chaplin and robbed several citizens of money "and other articles," and from there rode to Bloomfield, where they robbed the local post office. Afterward they lined up the citizens and robbed them, saying they were acting under orders of the Federal authorities in Louisville. Ironically, the timely arrival of guerrilla bands saved the day for the citizens, and the "Home Guards," although not attributed to Terrell by name, retreated in the direction of Mount Eden, where Terrell came from. In an article entitled "Thieving Home Guards," the *Louisville Daily Democrat* lamented that it was "a sad commentary upon the state of affairs in the country." In another irony, the paper also ran a feature in which Terrell's command dispatched a guerrilla named Coulter in a fight two days later.[27]

April 1865 found "Capt." Ed Terrell on the payroll of the U.S. Quartermaster's Department for "Secret Service" work and commanding around thirty scouts. They had been hunting Marion's Kentucky guerrillas, the same ones who had participated with Quantrill's men in the Midway-Georgetown raid, but apparently they hadn't been too successful. Terrell even had to remind the Kentucky adjutant general that he and his men were acting under orders of Palmer's headquarters, "belonging to the police force of the Department." This assertion must have raised more than a few eyebrows. On April 11 Terrell was ordered to proceed from Eminence to Taylorsville, in Spencer County, and to report to Maj. Cyrus J. Wilson. Palmer went to Eminence to meet with Terrell and make sure he meant business. "Terrell was an exceedingly dangerous man," recalled Palmer. "I never let him enter my quarters without keeping a revolver at hand."[28]

On the evening of April 13, Terrell's men and a company of State Guard cavalry under Capt. George W. Penn, all apparently under the direction of Wilson, attacked guerrillas belonging to Quantrill's and Marion's bands near Bloomfield, killing two and wounding three. They pursued the guerrillas south into Marion County, and on April 15, Bill Marion was killed by a State Guard carbine ball. Terrell, although his men were only armed with revolvers, tried to take credit and probably tried to claim any reward money.

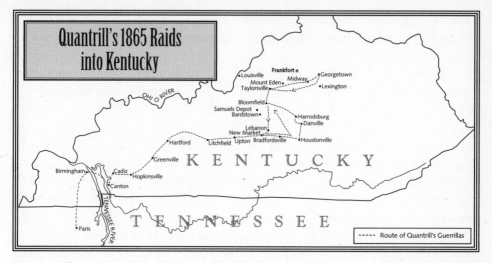

Quantrill may not have been with Marion at that time, as he turned up in Spencer County on April 16 at the home of Judge Jonathan Davis. They were celebrating the death of Abraham Lincoln the night before.

Terrell and company continued to ride roughshod over the surrounding area. On April 27 they spotted Hercules Walker plowing a field at the home of his father-in-law, a man named Montgomery, ten miles from Louisville. Walker was shot within sight of his wife, and his two mules, a horse, and clothing were taken by Terrell, who later alleged that the man had been supplying area guerrillas.

On May 10, Terrell and twenty-five or thirty men were scouting near the farm of James Wakefield between Taylorsville and Bloomfield. It was raining hard as Terrell's band followed a fresh trail into the farm. The guerrillas, numbering somewhere between eleven and twenty-one by differing accounts, were lounging in the barn, the rain pounding outside, when a lookout spotted Terrell's men cresting the hill above the barn. There was a mad scramble to escape, and at least two guerrillas were killed attempting to get away.

During the melee, Quantrill was mortally wounded, a bullet striking his spine as he attempted to flee on a gunshy horse borrowed from Betsy Russell. By another account Quantrill's horse, Old Charley, had been injured a few days prior and had been put out of its misery. Quantrill was not immediately recognized and was left, paralyzed from the waist down, at the Wakefield house. Frank James was staying at the farm of Judge Alex Sayer about fifteen miles away near Samuels Depot, in Nelson County. He was probably notified of the attack by Allen Parmer and two other guerrillas who escaped from Terrell's men. Although reportedly wounded, Frank claimed to have ridden to the Wakefield place with his comrades that evening. Quantrill's advice to the survivors of his band was to make Henry Porter the new commander and attempt to surrender, a task that would be easier said than done.

The next day Terrell returned, and Quantrill was taken by wagon to a military prison hospital at Broadway and Tenth Street in Louisville.[29]

※◇◈◆◇※

SOMETIME IN March or early April the remains of Anderson's and Todd's old bands began to stir from their bivouac in the vicinity of Sherman, Texas, to a rendezvous at Mount Pleasant. Little is known of the events of that winter, but they doubtless mirrored the previous year. Three new companies were organized, around 144 men. One was commanded by Archie "Little Arch" Clement as captain, with Jim Anderson, the brother of Bloody Bill, as his lieutenant. Dave Pool commanded the other company as captain, and Martin Ridder was elected captain of "a few boys" in the third. They left for Missouri sometime in the first half of April.

Jesse James belonged to Clement's group, and on the way north, while passing through Benton or Cass County, Missouri, he assisted Little Arch in avenging himself against a militiaman who reportedly had killed a brother of the guerrilla leader and had burned their mother's home in neighboring Johnson County. By Edwards's account, Jesse and two other bushwhackers held the militiaman while Clement slit his throat and scalped him.[30] Bracing for the coming guerrilla offensive was Col. Chester Harding, commander of the District of Central Missouri, with headquarters in Warrensburg. Harding expected he would "have the worst elements of the disbanding armies of the rebels to deal with" in the weeks ahead. Nevertheless, on May 1 he asked the assistant adjutant general of the Department of the Missouri if some provision could be made "by which repentant rebels may have at least the benefit of becoming prisoners of war."[31]

Harding also began to position what forces he had in the district, mainly Missouri State Militia and some volunteer regiments. Among the volunteers was a detachment of eighty-five men of the Third Wisconsin Cavalry, a pickup command taken from Companies F, H, I, and K, stationed in Vernon County, Missouri, in small outpost garrisons east of Fort Scott, Kansas. Their commander was Capt. John M. Bernard, who had risen from sergeant to commander of Company M since enlisting in 1862. Company M had been mustered out in the winter of 1865, but Bernard was given the detachment in late April and sent from Fort Scott to Lexington, Missouri.[32]

The new provost marshal at Lexington was thirty-two-year-old Capt. Clayton E. Rogers, on detached service since early April from Company B of the Fiftieth Wisconsin Infantry, a new regiment that had been mustered into service in March. Rogers, however, was an old veteran. A former sawmill owner from a Quaker family, Rogers had enlisted as a private in Company I of the Sixth Wisconsin Infantry, part of the famed black-hatted Iron Brigade of the Army of the Potomac. He was eventually promoted and transferred to the staffs of Gens. Abner Doubleday and James Wadsworth.

As a first lieutenant and as provost marshal of Wadsworth's First Division, First Corps, Rogers earned a footnote in history—and found himself in trouble—when he arrested an apparently intoxicated Brig. Gen. William Rowley on Cemetery Hill following the Union withdrawal on the first day of the battle of Gettysburg. It was Rogers's feeling that Rowley's raving was only making a bad situation more chaotic, and he had the irate general marched from the scene at bayonet point. According to Col. Rufus Dawes of the Sixth Wisconsin, it was "perhaps the only instance in the war where a First Lieutenant forcibly arrested a Brigadier General on the field of battle." Possibly due to this brazen act, as well as army politics, Rogers resigned his commission two weeks after the incident and returned to his sawmill. He was recommissioned, with higher rank, when the Fiftieth Wisconsin was formed.[33]

At 2 A.M. on Sunday, May 7, a band of twenty-five to forty guerrillas raided the town of Holden, in Johnson County, Missouri, robbing two stores and killing a man, Bill Rose. Holden was the terminus of the Pacific Railroad, which was under construction toward Kansas City, to the northwest.

Then, just before dawn that day, around one hundred guerrillas, including Arch Clement and Jesse James, struck the town of Kingsville. The town had been raided previously by jayhawkers, and most of the Southern sympathizers had been driven out and their homes and businesses looted and burned. All that remained were Unionists and their families. Postmaster Leroy Duncan, the leading Unionist in the area, had written an officer in Warrensburg sometime earlier that "we should have troops here in case of attack." The officer returned the letter with this notation on the back: "I feel you are unduly concerned, and see no need for such action at the present time, I feel everything will soon quiet down." In all probability his men were stretched to the limit already, and there were none to send.

Duncan apparently tried to make something of a fight when the guerrillas attacked. He was badly wounded but managed to escape. The attackers entered Duncan's house and found his son, William, and his two nephews, Walter and Wyatt Burris. Wyatt accidentally fell through the seat of a bottomless cane chair. Seeing the boy's plight, the bandits had a moment of mercy. "No, he's only a boy, come on," one of the raiders remarked. Instead they went after Walter and William, but the latter's shoe unluckily came untied and slowed him down as they raced from the scene. Walter and William were shot down; Wyatt was passed over.

The raiders burned five houses and sacked the town, killing eight men and boys and wounding two more. Four of the dead were railroad teamsters. The wounded Leroy Duncan was taken across the fields by neighbors to another house and from there by wagon to Warrensburg, some twenty-two miles away, after the raiders had left. His wounds proved mortal, and he died on May 18. He was interred in the Duncan Cemetery along with the others killed in the massacre. In *Noted Guerrillas*, Edwards credited Jesse James with killing Duncan, "a highwayman and a house burner," whom he also described as "fifty-five years old and gray headed." Jesse shot "three times before he knocked him . . . to his knees." A fourth shot in the forehead finished him off, Edwards claimed. Very possibly Jesse mortally wounded Duncan, but the report of the postmaster's immediate death was an exaggeration.

The telegraph wires to Warrensburg were cut, and it was not until later that a pursuit was organized. "The villains are . . . well armed and mounted, and very abusive and defiant," reported a Kansas City newspaper. The raiders narrowly missed the president and two commissioners of the infant Union Pacific Railroad, who got as far as Holden before news of the guerrilla presence in the area forced them to turn back to Jefferson City. Almost exactly four years later the line would join with the Central Pacific in linking a continent.[34]

It was about the time of these raids in May that the guerrillas first learned of Robert E. Lee's April 9 surrender at Appomattox Court House and that of other troops east of the Mississippi, which they termed a "damned Yankee lie." Eventually the truth of the reports must have become obvious, but the guerrilla war went on, and troops pursuing the band that attacked Holden killed three bushwhackers. Noting that "the militia [were] too poorly armed to put any confidence in themselves. The volunteer cavalry . . . too weak to do much good," Colonel Harding ordered his troops on the alert, guarding the Missouri River's fords, which was about all he could do.[35]

On May 9, Maj. B. K. Davis, commanding at Lexington, reported that Arch Clement's band was ten miles from the post, on the Columbus Road. Davis added that Clement had sent him a note "making threats of retaliation if his friends were hurt" and vowing to treat all militiamen as "public enemies." On May 11, Little Arch wrote:

Major Davis:
    Sir; This is to notify you that I will give you until Friday morning, 10 A.M., May 12, 1865, to surrender the town of Lexington. If you surrender

we will treat you and all taken as prisoners of war. If we have to take it by storm we will burn the town and kill the soldiers. We have the force and are determined to have it.

I am, sir, your most obedient servant.

A. Clement[36]

Davis had only 180 men in the garrison and asked to call out more militiamen. The major, however, wasn't easily taken in. He believed the letter was a bluff aimed at swaying him to call in the guards from the fords along the Missouri. Davis reported all boats across the Missouri secure, and May 12 passed without an attack.[37]

On the day of the threatened assault, Capt. Clayton Rogers wired Colonel Harding that around one hundred guerrillas wanted to surrender but needed assurances that they would be "treated as citizens" and not punished. Harding told Rogers to accept the surrender. He advised, "For their own protection they should be kept together for a few days until terms are made known through the country."

Each man was to take the oath and sign it in duplicate. The person surrendering would keep one copy; the office of the provost marshal general would receive the other. Until the guerrillas actually came in, however, they were to be considered legitimate prey. Harding ordered Col. Leonard Martin, the commander of Union forces in Johnson County, where Kingsville lay, "to hunt up and exterminate those already in your district."[38]

According to Edwards, the guerrillas held a meeting. Some favored surrender while some wanted to head south for Mexico. Edwards claimed that both Jesse James and Arch Clement opposed surrender. Meanwhile, according to Major Davis, Dave Pool was to gather his men and come in on May 20. Pool's first lieutenant, William Greenwood, was reportedly in the county, south of Lexington, collecting the scattered men.[39]

The complete story of the events of May 15 may never be fully known. It is certain that a Union force consisting of at least part of the Third Wisconsin and possibly some Johnson County militia, collided with guerrillas southeast of Lexington, in the lane south of the old Burns school. On May 16, Davis reported to Harding, "I am almost certain that Clement was on the [Missouri] river yesterday . . . prospecting for crossing the river. He talked with persons [near Berlin] and declared his [intentions]. I am confident that he and his party were fired upon yesterday, six miles out on the Salt Pond road on the return from the river." Clement had sent Davis a letter on May 14, proposing to send five men to meet an equal party at "the mound, on the Warrensburg road, on May 17 instant to learn particulars."[40]

Jesse James later offered his own version of events to Thomas R. Shouse. He said that he and a handful of guerrillas were headed for Lexington to surrender when they ran into some drunken soldiers.

"My horse was killed and I was shot through the breast," Jesse told Shouse. "I was running through the woods pursued by two men on horseback, one of them riding a black horse, and they were pressing me hard, every jump that I made the blood would spurt out of my wound. . . . That ended the fight. I was near a creek. I lay in the water all night, it seemed that my body was on fire. The next morning I crawled up the bank and a man was plowing nearby and he helped me get to my friends."[41]

The Third Wisconsin Cavalry (often misidentified as the Second in older accounts) was the same unit that had seen its members slaughtered at Baxter Springs, Kansas, in the fall of 1863. Pvt. John J. Jones, a twenty-one-year-old Welshman serving in Company I (called Company D before regimental reorganization in early 1865), is probably the same John Jones credited with shooting Jesse James in various accounts, although who shot Jesse in May 1865 is in fact uncertain. Jones's company had served at Fort Blair the day of Quantrill's attack and had defended the enclosure there. By now they knew that the safest policy when dealing with bushwhackers was to shoot first and ask questions later, especially when dealing with Clement's outfit. In this case Jesse apparently caught a .36-caliber revolver ball, either from Jones, another member of the Third, or perhaps even from a militiaman. Jesse would carry this slug to his grave. It would be excavated from his remains in the summer of 1995, more than 130 years later.

In all probability the guerrillas were indeed looking for an unguarded ford. Jim Cummins would later relate, "We had a fight with some Federal troops at the Missouri river," never mentioning a surrender party and tending to support Davis's account. It is entirely possible that some guerrillas were perhaps waiting for a reply to Clement's note of May 14, but the record is unclear.[42]

If Jesse had intended to flee to Mexico, he was no longer in any shape to ride. His old friend Jim Cummins related that "a good farmer found him and carried him up to Mr. Bradley's home on Tabo Creek, where he was nursed back to life by Mrs. Bradley." Cummins, who in later years resided at the nearby Confederate Soldiers Home at Higginsville, recalled that it was "right down there . . . that we put Jesse James in a wagon and started to Lexington to surrender . . . Jesse was wounded—shot in the right breast . . . I put Jesse in the wagon and we drove to Lexington, nine miles away and surrendered." Jesse James would relate to John Newman Edwards that "on the 21st [of May] . . . I surrendered at Lexington." Another account, apparently by some guerrilla comrades added, "He put up at the Virginia Hotel, and there, lying in a bed, wounded, he, with uplifted hand, took the oath and subscribed to the parole." A roster of the guerrillas surrendering at Lexington seems to back up the story, as it lists "James, J. M." as surrendering on May 21, 1865, and taking the Oath of Allegiance. On the roster the guerrillas listed their unit as "Shelby's Brigade," a deception the authorities, anxious to go home, probably winked at.

Several newspapers were quick to report the surrenders. "Dave Pool and forty bushwhackers came into Lexington last Saturday," read a *Kansas City Daily Journal* feature on May 23 titled "Bushwhackers Surrendered." Despite this verification, hastily written pseudo-histories of the James brothers later either omitted the surrender, implying that Jesse never came in, or claimed outright that there was no surrender. It became a legend that refused to die and was repeated into the 1990s in popular articles and documentary interviews.[43]

Jesse James reportedly met John Jones, the man who shot him, before leaving Lexington. The wound was serious, and it was nearly a month before Jesse could travel. Captain Rogers is said to have learned of the exile of the family and helped Jesse procure steamboat passage to Kansas City and some money for expenses. Jesse left on June 18 to stay with his uncle and aunt, John and Mary James Mimms, in whose care he had recovered from a similar wound in 1864.[44]

The war was virtually over in the Trans-Mississippi West at the time of Jesse's surrender. Shortly after his surrender the Third Wisconsin was ordered to rendezvous at Fort Leavenworth, Kansas, prior to mustering out. There one officer found the company of (now) Capt. James G. Pond, the hero of Baxter Springs, near mutiny. They had shaved the tail and mane of Pond's horse, destroyed his saddle and bridle, broken his saber, stolen his ivory-handled revolvers, and threatened him with death, for good measure. Times were changing fast. Arch Clement and Jim Anderson would make belated overtures to surrender, but, suspicious of Union authorities, they would exasperate local military officials. "If they are found, kill them at once. Hold no further parley with them under any pretext, but destroy them wherever found," read an order of June 13. As a result, the bushwhacker leaders beat a hasty retreat for Texas. For the remaining guerrilla holdouts these last days of the war would hold additional peril.[45]

⚬⚬⚬

BACK IN Kentucky, the fate of the guerrillas who had served under Quantrill was open to serious question. Circular No. 3, issued from Maj.

Gen. John M. Palmer's headquarters on April 29, 1865, indicated: "There is no longer in this department, hostile to the government, an organization which deserves to be characterized as military. The bands now prowling through the country are simple guerrillas and robbers and are to be treated as such. They will be allowed to surrender for trial."[46]

On May 1, 1865, another order was received from Palmer's superior, Maj. Gen. George H. Thomas, commander of the Army of the Cumberland, headquartered in Nashville. Thomas ordered Palmer to summon under a flag of truce "any band of armed men in your vicinity of which you may know of," calling upon them to surrender under the same terms offered to Robert E. Lee at Appomattox. However, "if they disregard your summons and continue acts of hostility, they will hereafter be regarded as outlaws and be proceeded against, pursued and when captured, be treated as outlaws."

The order was passed to the various posts and commanders in the Department of Kentucky on May 2, at least to those who could be reached. Terrell's command apparently was missed by this order. The same day Thomas's order went out by telegraph, Terrell was wired at Shelbyville, Kentucky, to "report with your command at these Head Qrs. as soon as practicable." On May 10, the day he attacked and wounded Quantrill, another telegram went out from Palmer for Terrell "to report at these Hd. qtrs. with his men bringing all his private and public property." An exasperated Palmer may have felt it was time to rein in Terrell and his band, but the capture of Quantrill may have bought Terrell extra time in which to further redeem himself.[47]

On May 18, a little over a week after the fight at the Wakefield farm, General Palmer, then staying at the Capitol Hotel in Frankfort, received a telegram from his assistant adjutant general, Capt. E. B. Harlan. It said: "E. L. Bradshaw, Esq. from Nelson Co., who is vouched for Ver[y] Highley, says if you will give safe conduct for ten Rebel soldiers through the limits of Nelson Co. that they will bring in the perpetrators of the outrage on the Lady near Bardstown. They do this to enable them to surrender."

Palmer shot back in reply: "Give the rebel soldiers safe conduct through for the purposes mentioned." The events that followed would be shrouded in obscurity for more than 130 years, constituting one of the strangest episodes in the James story.[48]

Sometime in late April or early May, a Mrs. Clark, a resident of Bardstown in Nelson County, was traveling through the countryside and reportedly was raped by two guerrillas. This was Victorian America, and unlike other wars in other eras and countries, rape was a rather uncommon occurrence and was looked upon as a particularly atrocious crime against noncombatants. Thomas Kirk, a farmer from Taylorsville, in Spencer County, came to General Palmer as a go-between for Samuel "One-Arm" Berry, a guerrilla of somewhat notorious repute who now wanted to surrender. Kirk was told there would be no surrenders in the area "until the surrender of the guilty party who committed the offense upon the person of Mistress Clark."

Palmer had issued Special Orders No. 64 stipulating:

> Satisfactory evidence having been furnished the general commanding that an infamous outrage was committed on the person of a lady living near Bardstown by certain scoundrels who profess to be rebel soldiers, notice is given to all concerned, that no guerrilla, or Rebel soldier, who now is or has been in Nelson County within the ten days past, will be allowed to surrender himself otherwise than for trial, until the perpetrators of this crime are arrested; they are guerrillas, and are known to the people of that county, and a reward of five hundred dollars is offered to any person who shall arrest or kill either of the men engaged in the commission of this outrage.

As Palmer later recalled, "It is a fact that there were some ten or more men [Quantrill's] who were anxious to come in. . . . I refused to accept the surrender unless they killed or captured those men. I recollect of making a distinct agreement with them, that they should be pardoned."[49]

The names of the men thought to be guilty were "Brothers" and "Texas," whose last name was probably Haskins or Hoskins. Brothers was from Kentucky, and Texas was presumably from the state of his nickname. A group of Quantrill's old command went after the two, and by Edwards's account came up with Brothers and Texas near Chaplin. They killed Brothers, but Texas escaped. Frank James would later take credit for killing both Brothers and Texas, and guerrilla Allen Parmer, in the Edwards account, is accorded the honors for killing the fleeing Texas in a blood-and-thunder story worthy of a dime novel. In a story Frank James related to John McCorkle, both guerrillas were captured, taken before Mrs. Clark, and later killed.

In fact only Brothers was killed. "I do not remember now the persons who killed him, or the commanding officer," Palmer recounted at the trial of local bushwhacker "One-Arm" Berry in January 1866. "Texas made his escape while Quantrill's band killed Brothers."[50]

Texas later took refuge with "One-Arm" Berry and was surrendered by him to the ubiquitous Major Wilson in exchange for Berry's own surrender and parole, and what he thought might be a pardon. "Will be down with Texas on Evening train," Wilson wired Palmer from New Haven, Kentucky, on June 5. "Major Wilson reported to me, and Texas was brought to town here and kept in jail here until Col. Coyle [judge advocate for the department] reported to me that there was not sufficient evidence of his connection with the rape," Palmer related.

Texas was apparently released four or five months after his capture. "Well, we thought, and everybody else thought, he was the man," Wilson commented later. Palmer would later admit that "it turned out afterwards that Texas was in great danger of being killed for an offense of which he was not guilty: we could not prove it on him." Nor was Brothers necessarily guilty. "I learned from Mrs. Clark, by the description, that it was not Haskins ['Texas'] or Brothers," recalled Thomas Kirk.[51]

Palmer had struck his deal with Quantrill's men, but they were not formally accepted for surrender until July 26, 1865. Palmer recalled that "the general course has been, that, when the men come in, and surrendered, and evinced a desire to return to the peaceable walks of life, I have given them the benefit of every available presumption, and left their sins, to be pursued by the civil courts. I have the case of each one investigated . . . and then turned them loose, unless evidence would occur against them of flagrant crime." This may account, in part, for the delay in processing the surrender, coupled with having an army of thousands of men to disband at the same time. As was the case in Missouri, the war was winding down, and the Union soldiers in Kentucky were anxious to go home. It is also possible that Palmer held the guerrillas in reserve to run down anyone who might cause trouble in the area.[52]

On July 26, 1865, fourteen to nineteen survivors of Quantrill's band, including "Alex. James," came in and surrendered to Capt. Robert H. Young of Company B, Fifty-fourth Kentucky Mounted Infantry. They surrendered as members of "Company E, Third Missouri Cavalry," at Samuels Depot in Nelson County. For their work in running down and killing Brothers, although he was apparently innocent, they were allowed to keep their horses, equipment, and side arms, the latter a highly unusual feature normally accorded only to officers. Each man signed a parole not to take up arms against the United States until formally exchanged.

"Captain Young—I think it was—sent me a list of names," Palmer later testified, "and I am pretty sure that I forwarded the list of names to the President, with the recommendation that he pardon the whole of them." Palmer was uncertain whether anyone was eventually pardoned when he testified at the trial of "One-Armed" Berry in January 1866.

Palmer, a Democratic presidential candidate in 1896 on a ticket with former Confederate Gen. Simon Bolivar Buckner, would quote verbatim the romanticized Edwards version of the surrender story in his posthumously published autobiography, curiously titled, *The Story of an Earnest*

Life. "I limited my order to Nelson county," he wrote, "in order that the innocent might not be punished, but I determined that the guilty men should be captured or killed, and the guerrillas did the work, as has been stated by Edwards, for me." By the turn of the century the legend had become "history," and Palmer either wouldn't admit or had forgotten what actually occurred.[53]

On the afternoon of June 6, 1865, the day after Cyrus Wilson telegraphed about the capture of Texas, William Clarke Quantrill died. Mrs. Harriet Ross, formerly of Independence, Missouri, visited him and reported his death to his followers. It was said that neglect hastened his demise. He was buried in an unmarked grave in Portland (now Saint John's) Catholic Cemetery in Louisville, where dishwater and chamber pots were emptied in later years on orders of a Father Powers, who had been given money for a tombstone. The priest said he was afraid grave robbers would steal the body. In 1887 part of Quantrill's remains were disinterred and shipped to Dover, Ohio, by W. W. Scott for reburial beside Quantrill's mother.[54]

It was perhaps the threat of another deadly run-in with Ed Terrell that made the hunt for Brothers and Texas all the more necessary to Quantrill's veterans. A Spencer repeating carbine could "kick hell" out of the pistol-wielding guerrillas, even at long range. On May 19, Terrell and his men went to the United States Saloon in Louisville. By one account Terrell "deliberately rode through the saloon, flourishing his pistol, and creating a general stampede of parties about the bar." Another account has Terrell ordering drinks for everyone, after which the guerrilla hunters smashed their glasses and left without paying the bartender. The next evening they captured a gang of seven guerrillas led by a man named Froman. According to a newspaper account, one of this captured band was believed to have been responsible for the Bardstown rape, although it's uncertain if he was.

Terrell's "independent company of scouts" was ordered to disband on May 24, just as the hunt was under way for Brothers and Texas. Palmer already had Quantrill's men working for him for their freedom, and Terrell's boys were now an unnecessary expense and embarrassment. To the locals Quantrill's men looked like choirboys compared with Terrell's ruffians.

The man who was responsible for William Quantrill's demise and who belonged "to the police force of the Department" had a curious future ahead. On September 8, 1865, the *Louisville Daily Democrat* reported "that Capt. Terrell was held to answer a charge of murder. He was tried before Judge Caldwell, in Shelbyville . . . for the murder of a man supposed to be Mr. Johnson of Sangamon County, Illinois. . . . The judge sustained the warrant, and held Terrell for further trial." Johnson was found about a mile from

Shelbyville in Clear Creek on August 27, "shot through the head and sunk to the bottom of the creek by rocks." Johnson was "believed to have had several thousand dollars on his person when killed."[55]

Terrell and Harry Thompson were up for trial on March 12, 1866, but the result was a hung jury. Terrell was then taken into custody by Spencer County authorities and taken to Taylorsville, where he was charged with the murder of blacksmith Ennis Wooten. At 2 A.M. on April 13, 1866, some of his old comrades broke him and codefendant John L. Wethers out of the Taylorsville jail. On May 26, 1866, a year and two days after mustering his "scouts" out of service, Terrell rode into Shelbyville, armed with a Henry repeating rifle and five revolvers. He was accompanied by Wethers and John R. Baker, and the three men proceeded to the Armstrong Hotel, presumably for a few drinks. Word arrived that a posse was coming, and Wethers took off. Baker and Terrell started east, but Terrell stopped briefly to talk with the owner of the Redding Hotel, Merritt Redding. When someone nearby yelled for Terrell to halt, he drew his six-gun and fired into the shadows. His shot was answered with a barrage of gunfire. Terrell, like Quantrill a little over a year earlier, was hit in the spine, this time with a load of large-caliber buckshot.

Baker's corpse was found later with eight or nine bullet wounds. Redding was accidentally wounded in the crossfire and died on August 23. Left paralyzed, like Quantrill, Terrell was taken to the jail in Louisville where Dr. T. W. Knight was unsuccessful in removing all the buckshot. Terrell was released on bond after several months in the Louisville lockup and was taken back to Mount Eden to live with his brother-in-law. He was brought to the City Hospital in Louisville on November 4, 1868, and after further unsuccessful surgery, died there on December 13, at the age of twenty-three. His remains were buried in obscurity.

The postwar world was full of such ironic twists and turns of fate, as others would discover.[56]

4

The Outlaws of Missouri

The Rebellion had also given birth to a horde of adventurers, who for years afterward infested the country, and preyed with systematic rigor and success upon the honest industry and frugal enterprise.

Allan Pinkerton, Thirty Years a Detective (1884)

JESSE JAMES SPENT THE latter part of June and the first half of July 1865 in Harlem (now North Kansas City) in the care of his aunt and uncle Mimms and their daughter Zerelda, called Zee for short. According to Jesse, "Dr. Johnson Lykins . . . visited me daily and did everything for my wound possible. . . . So did Dr. Jo Wood . . . on the 15th of July, 1865, I went up the [Missouri] river to Rulo, in Nebraska, where my family were."[1]

Dr. Samuel had attempted a return to medical practice while in Rulo, and Jesse was probably under his stepfather's care at that place. Jesse's mother, Zerelda, recalled the situation:

> Jesse was often so near death in the eight weeks he was with me in Nebraska that I would bend over his bed and put my ear to his breast to see if he was breathing or his heart was beating. One day at the end of the eight weeks he drew my face down to his and whispered:
> "Ma, I don't want to be buried here in a northern state."
> "My son, you shall not be buried here," I told him.
> "But, ma, I don't want to die here."

83

"If you don't wish to you shall not," I told him, and we started the next day [August 26 by Jesse's account]. Jesse was so weak and sick that we laid him on a sofa and four men carried him to the steamboat landing and put him aboard the boat. He fainted while they were carrying him to the boat and the people in Rulo tried to dissuade me from moving him. After the steamboat had been going down stream awhile Jesse recovered enough to ask me where he was. I told him that he was on the boat going home.

"Thank the Lord," he said.[2]

The family landed with Jesse at Harlem, and he was again taken to his relatives. According to his mother, "He was wounded so badly he could not sit up in bed." From late August until the latter part of October he was nursed by his cousin Zee. It was during this time that Jesse and Zee were secretly engaged to be married. Jesse was taken back to the farm in a wagon, and it was only after a week or two that he was able to walk again.[3]

FRANK JAMES lingered in Kentucky following his surrender. By one account he was worried about possible reprisals for his killing of Alvis Dagley the year before. Frank reportedly stayed in the Nelson County area for a while. He may well have visited his uncle and aunt, George and Nancy James Hite, and his first cousins at Adairville in Logan County, not far from the Tennessee-Kentucky line, during this time. The county seat, Russellville, was in an unsettled state in the fall of 1865. U.S. Detective J. A. Murray described the situation in a report dated October 30, 1865:

Since the removal of Martial Law in Kentucky [October 12, 1865], there have been three (3) negroes shot (one dangerously) in Russellville, without cause or provocation, by some persons in Confederate uniforms, supposed to be returned Rebel soldiers attending school at Russellville, Ky. There are from sixty (60) to seventy five (75) of these returned and pardoned Rebels attending the school, who part of the time dress and parade the streets in their Confederate uniforms, fully armed with revolvers. . . . At night it is not safe for a person to be in the Streets, as the firing of Revolvers etc., is kept up constantly, from fifty (50) to one hundred (100) shots being fired every night—*Loyal* men & returned Federal soldiers feel no security, and are completely cowed men by the Rebel Element. There is no protection in the civil courts for colored persons. . . . There is almost a reign of terror there now and matters are daily growing worse. All of the pent up bitterness of their Rebel natures seems to belch forth in redoubled fury, against the poor negro and now that Martial

Law is removed they make bold to express their real sentiments which they dared not before—Loyal citizens of the place are anxious to have something done.[4]

The situation, as will be seen, was apparently common to certain counties and communities in the Border States and also had ramifications for Unionists in certain localities. Gen. Stephen Burbridge, a resident of Logan County before the war who resigned from the army in December 1865, found that his policies in Kentucky had not endeared him to the locals when he returned to farming. By 1867 he complained that he wasn't "able to live in safety or do business in Kentucky . . . my services to my country have caused me to be exiled from my home." In other counties where Unionist sentiment was ascendant, the reverse could be true, and former Confederates were persecuted. It was an uneasy peace, to be sure, that settled in after the war.[5]

﹏﹏

ON FEBRUARY 13, 1866, a group of some ten or thirteen horsemen clad in sky-blue army overcoats approached the town of Liberty, Missouri. Three members of the band took positions outside of town, acting as lookouts, while the remainder rode into town. A few were disguised with wigs, false whiskers, and beards. The local court of the Justice of the Peace was in session that afternoon, providing local entertainment and occupying those who might have otherwise noticed the party gathered in front of the Clay County Savings Association Bank. Two of the men dismounted and entered the bank. They were about to make a major withdrawal.[6]

The bank itself had been chartered in 1859 as the Farmers Bank of Missouri and had been operated by Southern sympathizers at that time. In the summer of 1864 the president of the bank, E. M. Samuel, was writing letters on bank stationery concerning the loyalty of certain Clay County citizens, including Reuben Samuel, to the Federal provost marshal. Greenup Bird had been listed as cashier on the letterhead of the Farmers Bank with Samuel.[7]

Greenup Bird was still working as cashier at the bank that afternoon in 1866 when the men entered. One approached the counter, ostensibly to get change for a ten-dollar bill. Bird's son, William, working the counter, suddenly found himself staring down the barrel of a gun. The robbers escorted the two Birds into the vault, which they commenced to clean out. Then they shut the cashier and his son in the vault, by one account with the comment that "all Birds should be caged." The cashier soon discovered that the robbers had failed to lock the door, and the Birds made their way to a window where they shouted the alarm just as the bandits were about to ride off.

Nineteen-year-old George Wymore, a student at William Jewell College, was standing across the street as the riders pulled their revolvers to fire at the bank. Wymore repeated the alarm and was gunned down as the bandits escaped down Franklin Street, firing their guns and heading east, then south for the Missouri River. Ironically Wymore's father, William, had been an ardent Secessionist during the war, and his mother, Elizabeth, worked with the Southern Relief Association to aid war-stricken Southern families after the conflict ended. Such were the fortunes of peace. The robbers were eventually followed by two posses of thirty and fifty men each led by a Captain Garth and Capt. John S. Thomason, respectively, who lost the trail in a snowstorm near Sibley.[8]

From the Sibley area the bandits went north to Mount Gilead Church, where the gang stopped to split the loot. Something over $57,000 in assets had been taken, the bulk of which was in government bonds. Perhaps around $18,000 was in currency or gold and silver coin. The bonds would later turn up in a variety of locations—one at Frankfort, Kentucky, for $500 at the end of the month, another $1,200 worth in early March in Columbus, Ohio. A number were reportedly fenced in Howard County, Missouri, by former guerrillas of Bloody Bill Anderson's old band. Former guerrilla George Shepherd is said to have had a bond for $1,000 in Memphis, Tennessee.

In those days banks were not covered by deposit insurance, but the Clay County Savings Bank paid depositors sixty cents on the dollar in settlement. Given E. M. Samuel's work with the Federal provost and Bird's work as county tax assessor during the war and the probability that the bulk of the accounts there were those of Unionist depositors (who likely were the only ones with any real money after the war), it's not hard to figure why this particular bank, one of two in Liberty, was targeted.[9]

It is difficult to determine the identity of the robbers in what has been called the first daylight bank robbery committed in peacetime in American history. One authority on the early robberies attributed to the James gang has even gone so far as to say, probably with some justification, that those named as suspects over the years would probably form the basis of a modest guerrilla band. Most named, perhaps not coincidentally, did have earlier service under Quantrill, Todd, or Anderson. Some of those who were initially identified merit mention: Bud and Donny Pence, Oliver ("Oll") Shepherd (brother of George, holder of the Memphis bond noted earlier), and one Joab Perry. In time Frank and Jesse James would be added to the list, although Jesse was still probably recovering from wounds. Eventually Cole Younger would also join the roster.[10]

On the evening of Monday, June 14, 1866, a group of six or seven men rode up to the jail in Independence and demanded the release of Joab Perry, then incarcerated for horse stealing. They claimed to be backed up by another five hundred men, but this was a ruse and Marshal Henry Bugler called the riders' bluff, refusing to surrender Perry.

Bugler was in the process of closing the door when he was gunned down. A stray bullet also entered the window and wounded the wrist of the marshal's seven-year-old son, John, then lying in bed. A posse soon formed but had no luck in tracking down the culprits.

Word of the marshal's death and his son's wounding set off mass meetings, and the mayor issued a public proclamation denouncing "fiends in human form" and praising the late marshal as "one of the best and most respected citizens and efficient officers of this city." Resolutions were adopted "prohibiting rebels and bushwhackers coming into the city, armed, under penalty of condign punishment, declaring that no man should be permitted to make a speech or publication in the city inciting resistance to the laws of the State, and that every rebel or supposed bushwhacker, having no visible means of support should be notified to leave the city within twenty four hours."

A committee of a dozen men was formed to put teeth in the resolutions; they were backed by "a company of 100 loyal men" to serve as a posse in case of trouble "and bring those of the murderous crew to punishment who dare to remain."[11]

Jim Lane, at the apex of his political career, had backed President Andrew Johnson's veto of the Civil Rights Bill and the Freedman's Bureau Bill and was under attack on the home front, branded as a "Republican Judas." He was also under investigation in the press for certain questionable financial dealings in contracting supplies for Indian tribes in the region. The real Jim Lane had shown his face, and his constituents didn't like what they saw. Neither, apparently, did Lane. While on a wagon ride with some friends on Sunday, July 1, he dismounted, yelled "Good-bye, gentlemen!" shoved a revolver in his mouth, and pulled the trigger.

Lane lingered in a coma for ten days and died on July 11. A friend, writing to former Gov. Charles Robinson, Lane's political rival, commented that "his suicide was his own verdict on his life & actions."

Meanwhile, in Lawrence, Kansas, a flurry of outrageous rumors had been afloat that a force of a thousand former bushwhackers and Confederates might attempt to repeat their raid of August 1863. A company of infantry was sent to Lawrence, attempting to soothe the anxiety of the residents, if nothing else.[12]

It was not until October 30, 1866, that another bank would be robbed. Alexander Mitchell and Company of Lexington, Missouri, was relieved of $2,011.50 by four men who were chased by a posse headed by Dave Pool, the guerrilla leader who had counted the dead with his boots at Centralia and who had brought the bushwhackers in to final surrender. It was suspected by many that Pool had merely run interference between the posse and the bandits, some noting that he had not visited his usual drinking haunts that day. Again, the identity of the robbers remained a mystery.[13]

Election day in Clay County would provide the next incident and underscore a basic sore point in Missouri society during the late 1860s. Since June 1865 the so-called Drake Constitution of Missouri had forced voters to swear that they had not taken up arms against the Federal government or that they had not given "aid, comfort, countenance or support to persons engaged in such hostility." There was a further clause that required members of the clergy, educators, corporate officers, and lawyers to take the same oath or be barred from these positions. This latter clause was to be struck down by the U.S. Supreme Court in 1867, but the former was to remain in effect until December 1870.

The ideology behind what was known as the "Test Oath" was to use disfranchisement to drive Southern sympathizers out of the state and have their places taken by Northern and European immigrants. Why should the former Rebels stay in Missouri and literally be taxed without representation, some Radical Republicans postulated, when they could move elsewhere and regain suffrage? Meanwhile, the new immigrants would shift the political power base away from the agrarian Democrats, molding the state more along the industrial lines of the Northeast—or so it ran in theory. In practice the Test Oath was to have unexpected consequences that would haunt Missouri for more than a decade beyond 1870.[14]

"Many outrages have been practiced by registering officers over the State," commented the *Liberty Tribune* on the eve of the election, "but the acts of the registers of Clay county stand out without parallel in dark and damning villainy. Talk about the deeds of Jennison and Bill Anderson, terrible and revolting as they are, they sink into insignificance in comparison with the deeds of the Clay County registering officers—The crime of willfully and corruptly defrauding 1,600 men of their franchise, is worse than murder."

Clay County, it might be noted, was a Democratic Party stronghold and had voted overwhelmingly for McClellan over Lincoln, 777 to 216, in the 1864 presidential election. It also voted a whopping 890 over 90 against the Drake Constitution of 1865 with its Test Oath.[15]

There would be trouble at the polls when election day rolled around, although the Republicans carried the election for state superintendent of schools by a narrow 121-to-114 margin in Clay County. Statewide, the Republicans gained a lopsided majority in the Missouri legislature. Writing the commander at Fort Leavenworth were Sheriff James M. Jones and Deputy Sheriff Joseph H. Rickards, as well as County Court Clerk William Brinny and Supervisor of Registration Anthony Harsel:

> We the undersigned citizens of Clay County would respectfully represent that we deem the lives of Union men in great danger at the present time in this county. several of the most respectable citizens have been ordered to leave and many others have been publicly insulted and their lives threatened. An armed mob consisting of the most dangerous men in the county numbering more than a hundred men resisted the sheriff of the county on yesterday the 6th inst. while attempting to arrest a man for breach of the peace, the Sheriff having a Justice's warrant in proper form at the time and he was obliged to call on the soldiers stationed here to assist him in making the arrest. . . .
>
> We would earnestly request that a smaller number of troops be stationed in this county for a few weeks until the excitement has in some measure subsided. We believe unless this is done every Union man will be driven out of the county or murdered.[16]

November 6 fell on a Tuesday in 1866 and was probably election day. The incident alluded to, with the unusually large crowd or "mob," was probably related in some way to the troops' guarding the polls, if one reads between these not-so-candid lines. The *Liberty Tribune* had more fat for the fire on November 9.

> A Radical "let the cat out of the wallet" the other day, as regards one of the reasons for the very unfair registration in Clay county. He said: "Disqualify them from voting and they will sell off and leave the county, and men of *our own class* will be able to buy their farms for little or nothing." There is in our mind no doubt that the above is literally true as regards the wholesale murder of the rights of this people; but we are greatly deceived in the spirit of our citizens if they don't "stand their ground" and fight for their rights under the law here; and hold on to their farms no difference how bad radicals may covet them—Stand firm! justice will triumph.[17]

What little can be gleaned from individuals who knew the James brothers during this period and later spoke of them indicates little in the way of actual

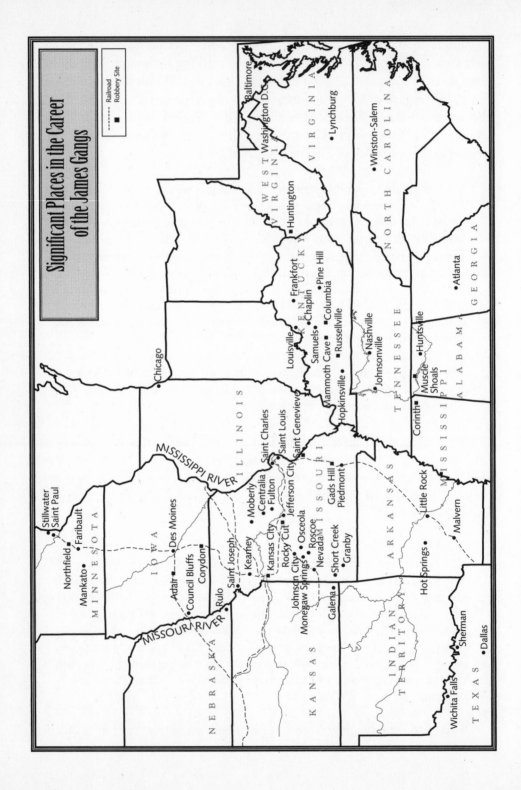

Significant Places in the Career
of the James Gangs

Railroad
Robbery Site

outlawry. Dr. W. H. Price, a resident of what in 1868 became Kearney, Missouri, recalled that "Jesse joined the Baptist church in this place, after he came out of the army, in 1866. I think he was baptized, and for a year or two acted as if he was a sincere and true Christian. In his early years, and after he came out of the army, he was quiet, affable, and gentle in his actions. He was liked by every one who knew him."

Frank James may have led a somewhat wilder life. In the wake of the war, "Frank used to visit old Centerville and go on a tear [drinking spree] now and then, and several times was arrested and bailed out by the old lady [his mother]."[18]

William Pinkerton, son of detective agency founder Allan Pinkerton, would later relate a story that Judge Philander Lucas reportedly made the acquaintance of both the James boys (or at least of Frank, in all likelihood) as well as Clell Miller, Jim Poole, and George White. They met one morning after the men arrived in Liberty, "firing off their revolvers and acting like a lot of Indians . . . they entered Meffert's saloon, had drinks, and as they left the saloon [Deputy Sheriff or] Sheriff [Joseph] Rickards arrested and disarmed the James boys, marched them into the Court House, arraigned them before him [Lucas] and then he committed them to the County jail." Pinkerton mentioned that at the time (probably 1867–68 although he says 1865–66) there were no other outstanding charges pending against them.[19]

At 3:30 on the afternoon of Friday, May 23, 1867, another group of bandits, estimated by differing accounts at from eleven to twenty men, entered the town of Richmond, Missouri, where Bloody Bill Anderson's remains had received such rough treatment in 1864. This time the target was the Hughes and Wasson Bank, which was relieved of about thirty-five hundred dollars before the locals were alerted and a gunfight ensued. Three citizens were killed: Mayor John B. Shaw, jailer Berry Griffin, and his son Frank. The robbers escaped toward Liberty, changing direction to Elkhorn, and were chased by a posse that managed to fire a few parting shots before darkness closed in.[20]

It was the bloodiest robbery to date, and the situation would become increasingly tense as time went on. One of seven men initially accused was Allen Parmer. He, however, had an alibi. Parmer claimed he was working for J. E. Shawhan and Company at the time of the holdup, and his employers backed him up. Others were not so lucky. Tom Little and Fred Meyers were arrested in Johnson County and became guests at the county jail in Warrensburg. They were lynched by a mob, although there were affidavits that both were in Dover, in Lafayette County, at the time of the robbery. One of the signatories may actually have been the head of the bank robbed in Lexington, Alexander Mitchell. That didn't mean anything in Johnson

County, which was Republican turf, having voted overwhelmingly for the Drake Constitution by 592 to 67.

Felix Bradley was taken from the jail at Richmond, in Ray County, and likewise strung up by vigilantes supposedly from Lafayette and Johnson Counties. Bradley's implication in the Richmond robbery was uncertain, but where "Judge Lynch" was concerned, no one cared.

Dick Burns, also implicated, was found three miles south of Independence in November with his skull crushed by the back of an ax. Payne Jones, another one of the accused, was killed in a shooting about the same time.

About midnight on the evening of March 17, 1868, Andy McGuire and James M. Devers also were taken from the Richmond jail and strung up. Both had been implicated in the robbery.[21] Devers had been extradited from Kentucky, and his death at the hands of a mob provoked a bit of a backlash there. Deputy Sheriff John W. Francis of Ray County, who had arrested Devers and who had been present at the lynching, attempted to arrest Bud Pence in Nelson County, Kentucky, thinking Bud was his brother Donny. Bud had married the daughter of a Judge Samuels of Samuels Depot, Kentucky. Francis had all but arrested Pence when a "Sheriff Samuels," presumably of the same clan, took Bud Pence in hand. Shortly afterward Pence "escaped." Brother Donny Pence soon married another daughter of Judge Samuels and spent the rest of his life in Kentucky. The chagrined Deputy Francis, who had reportedly boasted that Pence would share the same fate as Devers, returned to Richmond angry and empty-handed. Aside from the Samuels connection, Nelson County was a Democratic Party stronghold.[22]

⁂

JESSE JAMES still had problems as the result of the wound he received in 1865. "Being recommended to consult the celebrated Confederate surgeon, Dr. Paul Eve, of Nashville, Tennessee, I went there in June, 1867 and remained under his care for three weeks," Jesse recalled.

Eve, born outside of Augusta, Georgia, in 1806, had a life and career in medicine as interesting as the James brothers were to have as outlaws. In 1829 he traveled to Paris to study surgery under Dominique Jean Larrey, who had been Napoleon's personal physician. When the Revolution of 1830 ousted Charles X of France, Eve took care of the casualties of the street fighting. In 1831 he obtained the help of the elderly Marquis de Lafayette in obtaining a commission in the Polish army as a surgeon. When Poland made a bid for independence from Russia, he held the rank of major in the Fifteenth Infantry Regiment. In Polish service he was awarded the

Gold Cross of Honor before the Russian Imperial army crushed the revolt. Eve spent some time in a prisoner of war camp, where he contracted a near fatal case of cholera before his release.

In 1846 he served as a surgeon in the Mexican War, stationed at hospitals in Monterrey and later in Veracruz, Mexico. In 1859 Eve was in Italy, treating the wounded after the battles of Magenta and Solferino.

Naturally, when the Civil War began, Eve saw considerable service in the Confederate army, eventually serving as commanding officer at the Gate City Hospital in Atlanta. By 1867 Eve was chairman of the surgery department at the University of Nashville (later Vanderbilt University) Medical School, with some private practice on the side.[23]

Jesse's prognosis from the surgeon was not good. "He told me that my lung was so badly decayed that I was bound to die and that the best thing I could do was to go home and die among my people." Coming from the surgeon who had performed the world's first successful hysterectomy, among other firsts, in addition to his war record with gunshot wounds, this was probably not encouraging. "I had been wounded . . . once [before] in this same lung; and I did not believe I was going to die," Jesse would later state. Nevertheless, he returned to his relatives in the Adairville, Kentucky, area.

On March 20, 1868, Jesse and possibly brother Frank were at the Marshall Hotel (also referred to as the Chaplin Hotel) at Chaplin, Kentucky, in Nelson County. That same day, nearly one hundred miles to the south, what was becoming an all too familiar scenario was about to be enacted, this time in the town of Russellville.[24]

The Bank of Nimrod L. Long and Company had been known before the Civil War as the Southern Bank of Kentucky. With assets before the war of around $1.5 million, it had been one of the most viable in Kentucky. As with the bank in Liberty, Missouri, the institution was reorganized in 1863, and the later deposits probably came largely, if not entirely, from local Unionists.

On Friday afternoon, March 20, 1868, around 2 P.M., three men entered the bank. One of the men went by the name of Thomas Coleman or Colburn and had been in the bank earlier, posing as a livestock dealer from Louisville. Ten days earlier he had tried to cash a five-hundred-dollar Federal note of the type taken at Liberty. Long, suspicious and suspecting it might be counterfeit, refused to buy the bond. Nearly a week later he again refused to cash another one-hundred-dollar note brought in by Coleman-Colburn.[25]

Coleman-Colburn, later thought to be Thomas Coleman ("Cole") Younger had ridden into town with four other men on March 20. Two of the men stationed themselves outside behind a row of trees along Main Street while the three others entered town. Coleman-Colburn, the leader, presented Long with a fifty-dollar note, which was again refused. In response, Coleman-Colburn drew his revolver and shoved it next to Long's head, but the bank president attempted to escape via the rear of the bank. He ran into one of the other men who had entered the bank's side door and was grazed by a pistol shot in the upper part of his head, the bullet hitting the wall and leaving a mark that is still visible there. Long was pistol-whipped into partial unconsciousness for good measure.

Coleman-Colburn and another man cleaned out the bank while two other men, Hugh Barclay and Thomas Simmons, were held at gunpoint. Long managed to stumble out to the street and yell that the bank was being robbed while the men outside shot at him to no effect with revolvers and Spencer repeating rifles or carbines. This woke up the town, and several men armed with what were termed "weapons of a very inferior character" exchanged shots with the bandits. The only one hit in the fusillade was a man named Owens who lived in the building adjacent to the bank. He was shot in the side when he went outside to see what all the commotion was.

Some of the town residents thought there was a fire in progress and brought buckets of water to the scene, only to be met with gunshots. An old man named Lawrence, probably senile, who lived near the bank, walked right into one of the mounted robbers outside. "Old man, we are having a little serenade here and there's a danger of you getting shot," he was told. "Just get behind my horse here and you'll be out of the way."

Nine-year-old Jennie Prewitt, who attended school across the street, ran over to see what was happening. Her teacher, Mrs. Lizzie Sevier, called for her to come back or she might be shot. "No, lady, we are here to get money, not shoot children," one of the horsemen shouted back.[26]

The bandits were soon done and making tracks out of town, headed east. They were followed by another slow-moving posse, which somehow missed them. The total haul was estimated at between nine thousand and fourteen thousand dollars. The robbers reportedly crossed the Louisville and Nashville Railroad between Franklin and Woodburn, Kentucky, and divided the loot that evening in a hollow near Claypool's Mill, on the Barren River. The next day they reached Gainsville, spent the day there celebrating, then split up. Two of the robbers stopped in Warren County the second evening on the way to Glasgow and Scottsville. They asked for directions to Bardstown, in Nelson County.[27]

Louisville police Detective Delos T. Bligh, better known as "Yankee" Bligh, was called in to investigate. On Thursday, March 28, acting on a tip, he arrived in Chaplin, Kentucky, with John Gallagher, also of the Louisville police, and arrested George Shepherd, who was later identified and convicted as a participant in the holdup. Shepherd was sentenced to three years in prison. Earlier, Shepherd had led the group, including Jesse James, that split from Quantrill's band and traveled from Arkansas to Texas at the end of the war. Three other men, later identified as Cole Younger, Arthur McCoy, and John Jarrette, eluded authorities. Oll Shepherd, cousin of George, was killed in Missouri while resisting arrest.[28]

The James brothers apparently left town at the same time, evidently with funds that allowed them to make a trip to California. Brother Frank either came to California with Jesse or traveled overland to meet his brother.

Ironically, it was Nimrod Long who had supplied some of the money that had sent the James boys' father to Georgetown College, although they and the participants in the robbery may not have been aware of it. Jesse reportedly went by sea from New York via Panama and arrived for a visit with his uncle, Drury Woodson James, who lived at Paso Robles and was part owner of a large ranch and the mineral springs there.

The springs at Paso Robles were noted for their curative powers in the late-nineteenth century. Although it was not known at the time, the mineral content of the waters there was the equivalent of what would later be known as a sulfur drug. Perhaps because he availed himself of the spring's soothing waters, Jesse's chronically infected lung began to heal, although he did lose the use of it, according to Cole Younger.

The James boys reportedly returned to Missouri in the fall, and for the next year Jesse appeared in public "quite dandified." By one account he "sported a plug hat and rode a fine saddle horse which took the premium at the neighboring county fairs, and was entered at the St. Louis fair."[29]

In September 1869 Jesse James requested that his name be removed from the membership of the Mount Olive Baptist Church in or near what was now the town of Kearney. Old Centerville, a short distance south, had been bypassed by the Hannibal and Saint Joseph Railroad, and the town of Kearney was laid out in the spring of 1867. The new town was named for Fort Kearney, Nebraska, which in turn had been named for Mexican War hero Stephen Watts Kearny (the fort's name was misspelled with the additional e). Jesse's withdrawal from the congregation was accepted in November "for the stated reason that he believed himself unworthy." It was almost as if Jesse sensed what was to follow.[30]

SIXTEEN-YEAR-OLD EDWARD Clingan was dismissed from class at noon on Tuesday, December 7, 1869, and was making his way to the post office in the town of Gallatin, Missouri, with mail from his family, when he heard several shots. Probably someone who was drunk, he thought as he hurried to see what the ruckus was about. He was startled to see William A. McDowell, clerk at the Daviess County Savings Association, stagger out the door of the bank just across the street. McDowell fell, then he got up and ran toward the post office, a man running to the door of the bank and firing at him as he left.

"Captain Sheets has been killed!" McDowell yelled. Under fire from some of the locals, the robber made off with around seven hundred dollars. Two, possibly three bandits were involved in the holdup. They had hidden their horses in an alley half a block south of the bank.

One thief had escaped by the time the locals reached the alley. The other man had fallen from his horse and was dragged a distance by the stir-rup. "Let's get him!" somebody shouted. But the robber drew his gun on the crowd, which immediately scattered.

Young Clingan went to druggist Chris Gilliland's shop, which had a rear door opening onto the alley. A local silversmith named Barnum arrived, and they borrowed a gun from the druggist, cautiously opening the side door to find the man escaping on the horse of his companion. Barnum fired, and one of the bandits replied with a shot that hit the wall close to the door.

A posse formed and was soon in pursuit. Along the road the bandits encountered Daniel Smoot, whom they relieved of a horse. Then they raced off in the direction of the Hannibal and Saint Joseph. Just north of Kidder, a Reverend John Helm was taken to serve as a somewhat unwilling guide. One of the men reportedly remarked that they had just killed Maj. Samuel P. Cox in retaliation for the death of Bloody Bill Anderson. As Ed Clingan could attest, his brother-in-law, cashier John W. Sheets, was *not* Major Cox, although he may have borne a resemblance.[31]

The posse lost the trail, but the last direction noted was toward Clay County. There was also the abandoned horse, a sorrel mare. On the day after the robbery, Alec Irving and Jess Donohugh, both residents of Gallatin, passed through Kearney on their way home. They rode past two men who were somehow identified as the James brothers, and one of them was reportedly riding a horse matching the description of the one taken from Dan Smoot.

By December 11 the mare left at Gallatin had been traced to "a young man named James, whose brother and stepfather live about four miles from Center-ville." One of the robbers also matched the description of Frank James.[32]

"Two of the citizens of Gallatin, thoroughly armed and mounted, rode away to Liberty" and met with Deputy Sheriff John S. Thomason. Thomason had served as captain of Company I, Eighty-second Enrolled Missouri Militia, during the war. He had largely taken over the law enforcement duties of Sheriff Moses, "who in those days devoted his time to collecting county revenue," according to Thomason's son William. Thomason was also the nephew of both Robert Thomason, stepfather of the James boys' mother, and of Wild Bill Thomason, who had taught Frank to ride and shoot before the war. Accompanied by the two riders from Gallatin, Thomason and his son Oscar mounted up and headed for the James-Samuel farm west of Kearney.[33]

Arriving close to the Samuel place, Thomason sent the Gallatin men to cut across to the woods north of the house while he and his son came through the front gate and went up to the house. A contemporary account described what happened next:

> Before reaching [the house], however, a little Negro boy ran past them and on to the stable, and just as he got there the door opened suddenly and out dashed the two brothers on splendid horses, with pistols drawn, and took the lot fence at a swinging gallop. The Gallatin party from the fence above [the house] opened fire on sight; the deputy sheriff and his son followed suit; the brothers joined in at intervals, and the chase began.
>
> Thomason mounted his horse and dashed after the James brothers, gained upon them, fired at them, but saw his aim was off and dismounted to get a better shot. The frightened horse broke away and ran toward the James boys, and got even with the other horses when one of the brothers shot the horse dead with his revolver. From there the pair escaped free.[34]

"My father went to the James's pasture, selected one of the finest horses, and rode it back to Liberty," son William related. "When my father asked Mrs. Samuel . . . for the horse, she said, 'You can't have it. I'll die first.' My father answered, 'Well, you should have died years ago,' and rode the horse away."

Thomason continued to play cat and mouse with the James boys over the next few weeks. A reward of three thousand dollars was given for their capture, largely by the outraged citizens of Daviess County. On December 24, 1869, Missouri Gov. J. W. McClurg authorized the sheriff of Jackson County to raise a posse of thirty men in his jurisdiction to aid Thomason, should the James boys scoot over the county line. The state would pay the expense and offered five hundred dollars for each man, dead or alive.[35]

Aside from Jesse and Frank, there was suspicion, because of a statement made to the Reverend Helm, that the other man involved was Jim Anderson. All of the men eluded capture, and Jesse began his own public relations counteroffensive in a series of letters printed in the *Kansas City Times* and addressed to Governor McClurg. The chief argument given in these letters, probably with some polishing by editor John Newman Edwards, was that the brothers had fled the farm, fearing that they would suffer the same fate other former guerrillas had met at the hands of a lynch mob.

Their fear was probably not without foundation, as robbery victim John Sheets had served in a number of public offices in Daviess County and was very popular. In November 1867, two years earlier, John Reno and another member of his outlaw gang from Indiana had stolen twenty-two thousand dollars in a less spectacular safe-cracking job at the Daviess County treasurer's office. When captured a few weeks later, Reno at first had claimed his innocence, but a mob of enraged taxpayers outside the jail convinced him to change his plea to "guilty," and he was sentenced to a twenty-year term in the Missouri State Penitentiary. In the case of the James boys, that sort of arrangement could mean a hangman's noose either way. It was not an inviting proposition.

"Governor, when I think I can get a fair trial I will surrender to the civil authorities of Missouri. But I will never surrender to be mobbed by a set of blood thirsty poltroons," one letter in the *Times* read. The descriptive (and not exactly endearing) term for the citizenry of Gallatin was probably the Edwards touch. More will be said about this redoubtable journalist later.[36]

Jesse claimed that he had sold the sorrel mare to another man from Kansas (perhaps Jim Anderson) and was innocent. Curiously, no mention was made of brother Frank in the letters, which appeared in June and July 1870, but Jesse did manage to marshal affidavits in his behalf from several local citizens and members of his family, sworn before Franklin Graves, justice of the Clay County Court, no less.

Zerelda Samuel claimed that Jesse had sold the horse to a man from Topeka, Kansas (again implicating Anderson), and that he was at home during the robbery. Additional affidavits from Reuben Samuel and sister Susan James stated similar facts. Another affidavit, from John S. Groom, said that Jesse had bought goods at his store at Kearney the evening before the robbery. The words are both insightful and ironic: "I have been personally acquainted with Jesse James since 1866, and I have never known him to act otherwise than respectful, and I have never known a more honest person in all his business transactions." Groom would later have a significant role in the James story. When one excludes the family testimony, there is a gap from the evening of December 6 until the afternoon of December 8, enough time to cover the ground to Gallatin, rob the bank, and return.[37]

Mrs. Samuel asked for the prayers of the congregation of the Baptist church in Kearney "for her erring boy Jesse," and sister Susan "made one of the most touching appeals to Heaven for him . . . in the New Hope Baptist Church [six miles northeast of Kearney] in 1870." Susan James would marry

Allen Parmer in November of that year. "Those who have read Jesse James' defense generally believe him innocent—at least all I have heard speak of it," reported a stringer in Kearney to the *Liberty Tribune*. Again, there was no mention of Frank James.[38]

William Thomason, whose brother and father hunted the James boys and who served six years as sheriff of Clay County in the early 1900s, had a different view of things: "They did not have to do it, although some people have asserted that they were not allowed to return home after the Civil War, they came back and lived here for more than three years. They chose the sort of life they led afterwards. . . . No one sympathized with the James boys who knew them well. Those who feared them befriended them. These people had been intimidated and were afraid to be anything else."[39]

From time to time the James boys would appear and disappear in the years leading to 1874. For the next four years their activities are difficult to pin down, but they probably drifted between Missouri, Texas, Arkansas, Nebraska, and Kentucky, and possibly as far as the East Coast. Outside a few exceptional episodes, their lives during this time frame are undocumentable. According to Jesse, he and Frank went to Texas in August 1870 and left for the Indian Territory early in 1871. It was near Perryville, around February 22, that Jesse and Frank ran into their old antagonist Oscar Thomason, who with several men was passing through the area. Brother William related that "Jesse offered him [Oscar] $50, which my brother accepted, as payment on father's horse that had been killed. Later Mrs. Samuel called to collect this $50 from my father, but did not get it."[40]

Other robberies would be attributed to the outlaw brothers too. On June 3, 1871, four bandits robbed the Obocock Brothers Bank of Corydon, Iowa, about fifty-eight miles southeast of Des Moines and about fifteen miles north of the Missouri state line. The haul this time was around six thousand dollars. At the time of the holdup, the townsfolk were in the yard of the Methodist church, listening to Missouri politician and orator Henry Clay Dean expound upon the possibility of the railroad coming to the area. There apparently was a fairly good crowd as a local paper reportedly advised its readers that there would be plenty of beer in addition to Dean's long-winded discourse on the "iron horse."

Dean was interrupted by one of the riders, who stopped to inform him and the crowd that the bank had just been robbed. The man was dismissed as a heckler, but after he rode on it was discovered that, indeed, the bank *had* been robbed. The bandits were thought to be Cole Younger, Frank and Jesse James, and Clell Miller. Dean later said he believed Frank James was the man who had interrupted him.[41]

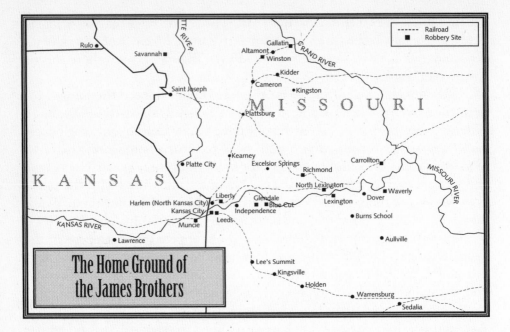

The Home Ground of
the James Brothers

There was the usual ineffective chase by a posse, but in addition the bank retained the services of the Pinkerton National Detective Agency to catch the robbers. Robert Pinkerton, son of agency founder Allan Pinkerton, was sent to Iowa to track the band. With a local posse he scoured the nearby counties then headed for Missouri, accompanied only by a sheriff from Iowa. The pair pressed on as far as Cameron Junction on the Hannibal and Saint Joseph Railroad. There Robert Pinkerton left the sheriff, who decided to look for help (apparently with little success), and continued on the trail to the Missouri River at Sibley and Blue Mill Ferry. Pinkerton was wary of continuing farther without aid and returned to Iowa.[42]

The usual denial appeared in the *Kansas City Times*: "As to Frank and I robbing a bank in Iowa or any where else, it is as base a falsehood as ever was uttered from human lips. . . . I don't care what the Radical [Republican] party thinks about me. I would just as soon they think I was a robber as not; but they don't think so, they know it is false when they say so. . . . If times ever get so in Missouri that I can get an impartial trial, I will voluntarily go to Clay County and stand my trial. But I am satisfied that if I was disarmed at present, those brave Radical heroes in Missouri would try to mob me."

Clell Miller was arrested shortly after the robbery and taken to Iowa for trial but had a convincing-enough alibi to prove his innocence. Miller was not "mobbed," it should be noted. Still, Jesse's concerns were probably not entirely unfounded, especially if he were to be placed in custody in Missouri.

Vigilante justice had not entirely left the jurisdiction of the Show-Me State. Nevertheless, Clell Miller was outraged that he had been wrongfully accused again. There is no indication that he had anything to do with the robbery, although he did know the James boys socially.

Detective R. W. Westfall was involved in the arrest and, it turned out in testimony, had a reputation for dishonesty; he associated with "scoundrels" and ladies of the evening and often failed to pay his bills. It could be argued that he needed to implicate someone—anyone—for the reward money. The arrest was a turning point in Clell's life, and he told others later that he might as well be an outlaw as everyone seemed to treat him as though he were.[43]

THERE WERE other individuals in Missouri, not to mention the United States, who made the James gang pale in comparison when it came to thievery. Although perhaps not as colorful or as spectacular a gang as that which would inform a crowd that their bank had been robbed or leave press releases in their wake, their activities often netted far more money. For example, at the same time the James gang was beating a retreat to Missouri from Iowa, the *New York Times* was busy exposing "Boss" William Tweed, head of the New York City Department of Public Works. Tweed had built a corrupt political machine based on kickbacks, fraudulent contracts, bribery, fake vouchers, and ghost employees. Some two hundred million dollars had been siphoned out of the municipal treasury over six years, bringing New York to the verge of bankruptcy before Tweed was exposed and arrested. Many of his confederates escaped the country with their share of the ill-gotten gains, never to face prosecution. One of those posting bail for Tweed was "robber baron" Jay Gould, a multimillionaire whose attempt to manipulate the gold market in 1869 created economic havoc in financial markets nationally. Gould would later gain quasi-respectability as a railroad tycoon.[44]

Missouri had similar problems in Cass County, which had been home to the Younger brothers and where their father had served as county judge before the Civil War. In 1858 the county had sought to issue some $229,000 in bonds for the construction of the Missouri Pacific Railroad, but they were never issued because difficulties arose with the railroad. Later the bonds were taken by the Union army but were eventually returned to the county. Presiding County Judge J. C. Stevenson, Judge Forsyth, and others put together a "ring" to secretly issue the bonds and illegally collect the money for their own ends.

On April 24, 1872, a mob stopped an eastbound train of the Missouri, Kansas, and Texas Railroad outside Holden. According to one account:

After the train stopped four of the mob mounted the locomotive and guarded the engineer with drawn revolvers. The train was then surrounded, and [J. R.] Cline and Stevenson called out. Cline appeared, and after some words regarding his connection with the fraudulent issue of the Cass County bonds, was riddled with bullets, and his body thrown by the side of the track. Several emptied their revolvers into the mangled body.

Stevenson was in the baggage car, and had barred the doors against the mob. They broke them in, however, with a log . . . and poured a volley into the judge, killing him instantly. They dragged the body out and threw it beside Cline. . . . [Elsewhere in Cass County] Judge Forsyth, another of the county justices, was shot today [April 25], and the body hung to a tree. Great excitement prevails throughout the county, and fears are felt that still others will be murdered.[45]

Gov. B. Gratz Brown sent militia from Kansas City to Holden. The *Louisville Courier-Journal* commented, with barely concealed disgust, on public corruption, vigilantes, and the times:

In our older cities there has been a carnival of spoilation since the war, and millionaire robbers, State, Federal, and municipal, walk the streets with the most confident assurances of safety. Not such is the case in Cass County, Missouri. . . . The statutes of mobs, like those of Draco, are writ in blood . . . this lawless combination reflects upon certain sham courts in other portions of the country the discredit of utterly failing . . . as it cut through with one rude Alexandrian stroke.[46]

THE BANDITS wisely chose to give Missouri a wide berth the next time around. On Monday, April 29, 1872, around 2 P.M., five men approached the town of Columbia, Kentucky, from Burksville. Three rode into the alley next to the Bank of Columbia and dismounted; the others stood mounted guard on the street. Three men inside the bank managed to escape and spread the alarm amid parting gunfire that wounded one. The bandits on the street began riding up and down the street, firing at anyone who was foolish enough to show themselves, yelling "Lowery's gang! Lowery's gang!" in case no one got the message. One man dared to fire two shots at the bandits from a small pistol before he was compelled to run. This was the only opposition.

The robbers retreated from the bank, leaving cashier R. A. C. Martin dead inside. He had refused to open the main vault, which had a combination lock. The loot was first estimated at seventy-five thousand dollars, but this was soon tallied downward to around fifteen hundred dollars. The gang was reported passing through Lebanon, Kentucky, the following evening, around nine o'clock, headed in the direction of Bardstown, in Nelson County. One of the bandits was reported as having a Roman nose and was thought by Detective Bligh of Louisville to be one of the men at Russellville. Frank James had a Roman nose—but so did others. Bligh felt that Cole Younger and the James brothers were involved. Men matching their description, posing as stock buyers à la Russellville, had been in the area earlier.[47]

In the wake of the robbery there were two ludicrous incidents in which the alleged bandits were supposedly apprehended. A shady character, supposedly named James Festus Dickenson, was arrested and accused of being the leader of the gang. When it was pointed out that Dickenson was bald, unlike the men in the holdup, the excuse was given by arresting lawman that he had possibly worn a wig. Also hauled in was a very disgruntled B. R. Kirkpatrick, "captured" at Bowling Green, Kentucky. There was one slight problem: Kirkpatrick was a deputy marshal from Jefferson County who had come to pick up a prisoner himself. Upon proving his identity, the lawman was released, much to the embarrassment of the arresting officer.[48]

≈≈≈≈

ON THE afternoon of Thursday, September 26, 1872, three men wearing checkered bandannas pulled over their faces rode up to the Twelfth Street ticket booth of the Kansas City Exposition. A huge crowd was surging out of the gate. One of the men dismounted, marched to the ticket office, and seized a tin box containing $978 that was lying just inside the window. Ben Wallace, in charge of the receipts, reportedly came outside and grappled with the masked man, who had already put the money in his pockets. One of the men on horseback fired at Wallace, who ducked out of the way. The robber then mounted his horse and took off with his companions.

In the confusion a little girl was either accidentally stepped on by one of the horses or was wounded by the stray bullet fired at Wallace. Even the newspapers couldn't agree. The bandits had narrowly missed taking some twelve thousand dollars in receipts that had been sent to the bank half an hour earlier, but in terms of publicity generated, they gained much more: They became legendary.

The Kansas City Times called it the "Most Desperate and Daring Robbery of the Age" and was audacious in itself by declaring that "the affair all in all surpasses anything in the criminal history of this country at least if it does not overtop the exploits of Claude Duval or Jack Shepherd [legendary eighteenth-century highwaymen in England], in the way of cool-blooded nerve and stupendously daring villainy." The article proclaimed that the perpetrators of the crime "deserve at least admiration for their bravery and nerve." Like most of the robbers' victims, Ben Wallace, the man who struggled with one of the robbers, would be forgotten over the years. However, he would have a grand-daughter, Bess Wallace, who would one day marry a man from Independence named Harry S. Truman, later president of the United States.[49]

The author of the *Kansas City Times* piece was probably John Newman Edwards, a thirty-three-year-old former adjutant to Confederate Gen. Jo Shelby. During the war Edwards had written all of Shelby's official reports, curious pieces that often lurched from a prose description of a battle into Tennysonesque verse. His poetry could turn a backwoods cavalry scrap into another "Charge of the Light Brigade." At the conclusion of the war Edwards followed Shelby and some five hundred men, all of whom refused to surren-der, in an epic march into yet another conflict in Mexico, fending off bandits and Juaristas and almost coming into conflict with the French Foreign Legion. Edwards would later chronicle these events in *Shelby and His Men* (1867), perhaps with a little poetic license, although it was an exploit worthy of Hollywood (which has somehow neglected the story). Edwards edited *The Mexican Times*, a newspaper for Confederate exiles in that country, before returning to Missouri just prior to the downfall of Emperor Maximilian.

An incurable romantic, Edwards saw in the former guerrillas a chance to create a legend. He used the former partisans to further the ends of former Confederates and the state Democratic Party over the ascendant Republi-cans. In some ways the legend would approach fact, and in others it wouldn't. To a country in the throes of changing from an agrarian to an industrial economy, with rampant public corruption, Edwards would provide a literary antidote—an American Robin Hood with a band of merry men.[50]

Edwards distilled the legend on September 29 in an editorial entitled "The Chivalry of Crime" (see Appendix B). He was a chronic alcoholic who periodically would go on binges, and the editorial's purple prose shows the influence of Edwards's potent "ninety-proof" journalistic style. Without too much imagination one can discern Edwards speaking as much of him-self, at least vicariously, as of the audacious men he describes. These were men "who learned to dare when there was no such word as quarter in the dictionary of the border. Men who have carried their lives in their hands so long they do not know how to commit them over into the keeping of the laws and regulations that exist now. And these men sometimes rob."

In fact, the men who were pulling these robberies were probably suffer-ing from post-traumatic stress disorder, although the term was not known in those days. They had gone through a horrendous guerrilla war, full of atrocities, and later were psychologically unable to adjust to life in peace-time. More than a century later a study of Vietnam veterans would indicate that nearly three-fourths of those who had engaged in exceedingly violent or criminal activity during a similar guerrilla conflict were engaged in crime after release from the service. More than half of these men had no prior history of violent antisocial behavior before their war experiences.

"These are not bad citizens," wrote Edwards, "but they are bad because they live out of their time. The nineteenth century is not the social soil for men who might have sat with Arthur at the round table, ridden at tourney with Sir Launcelot. . . . What they did we condemn. But the way they did it we cannot help admiring. It was as though three bandits had come to us from the storied Odenwald . . . and shown us how the things were done that poets sing of." Considering the rough lifestyle of the Middle Ages, which had its own robber barons, Edwards is probably not far off the mark, although he probably never intended it this way. The rival *Kansas City Daily Journal of Commerce*, in a more caustic vein, said the "villains" were "more deserving of hanging to a limb."[51]

On October 5 yet another letter appeared in the *Times*, this one signed with the names of eighteenth-century highwaymen Jack Shepherd, Dick Turpin, and Claude Duval. The author or authors offered to pay the medical expenses for the girl who had been injured and apologized to Wallace. "Just let a party of men commit a bold robbery and the cry is hang them, but Grant and his party can steal millions, and it is all right. . . . Some editors call us thieves. . . . It hurts me very much to be called a thief. It makes me feel on a par with Grant and his party. . . . We are bold robbers. . . . Please rank me with these, and not the Grantites . . . they rob the poor and give to the rich, we rob the rich and give to the poor. . . . I will close by hoping that Horace Greeley will defeat Grant, and then I can make an honest living, and then I will not have to rob." How much, if any of this, was the actual writing of one of the bandits and how much was the editorial work of Edwards will never be known. Suffice it to say the letter fit the editorial position of Edwards and the *Times*. A legend had been born.[52]

The complaints against the Grant administration came in the wake of the exposure of the Credit Mobilier scandal by the *New York Sun* a month earlier. Oakes Ames and several directors of the Union Pacific Railroad had formed a separate company, the Credit Mobilier, to handle the construction of the transcontinental railroad, which had received Federal subsidies. Construction costs were inflated some twenty-three million dollars over cost by the Credit Mobilier, and the money was siphoned off. In an attempt to avoid congressional scrutiny, Ames (also serving as a congressman from Massachusetts) distributed shares of Credit Mobilier stock to members of Grant's cabinet as well as other congressmen and to Vice President Schuyler Colfax. Although expulsion from Congress was recommended, Ames suffered nothing more than censure. As a result of the scandal, Horace Greeley, the Liberal Republican candidate in the 1872 presidential race, was also backed by the Democrats, who had failed to find an acceptable candidate of their own.[53]

Jesse James may have tried to live up to his Robin Hood image for real in the month of November 1872. A fifteen-year-old black hired hand named Joe Miller was working for Jo Shelby over in Lafayette County. Shelby's wife sent Miller to Aullville, where he was involved in an altercation with a white boy named Catron. "This boy fired at the negro three times," recalled Shelby. Catron followed Miller to the Shelby place and was reloading his shotgun when Miller pulled him from his horse. A crowd of white men followed Catron, probably with the intent of lynching Miller, who had run into the house and was seeking protection from a frantic Mrs. Shelby. Jesse James was a visitor and offered to intervene. "Jesse rode to the Davis Creek bridge, between my house and the town," recalled Shelby, "and there stationing himself . . . he told the advancing crowd that if they harmed the negro there would be enough business around there to amuse the county undertaker for several days." The mob disbanded, and Miller was saved.[54]

⚜

AT 7 P.M. on July 21, 1873, about three miles west of the station at Adair, Iowa (halfway between Des Moines and the Nebraska line), a rope pulled loose a rail on the Chicago, Rock Island and Pacific Railroad, sending the train into a ditch. Engineer John Rafferty was slammed into the side of the engine cab, fatally breaking his neck. Fireman Dennis Foley managed to open the relief valve to prevent a boiler explosion before he dragged Rafferty's corpse from the wreckage. The first train robbery attributed to the James-Younger gang had begun. The train was rounding a curve when it hit the vandalized track, and the engine, tender, baggage, and express cars slid down an embankment.

O. P. Killingsworth, the postal clerk riding in the express car, described what happened next:

> There was a violent concussion, the express-car lifted at one end, shoved forward, and then careened at an angle of forty five degrees and stopped . . . packages went pounding to the lower side of the car, and the inmates were considerably knocked about and shaken up. They had hardly recovered their uprightedness when into the door on the lower side—the one on the upper being shut—sprang a man with a revolver in each hand and a mask on his face. He was the leader of the robbers. . . . No sooner had he entered, than he tore the mask from his face. . . . Two other fellows in masks appeared at the door, with a revolver in each hand . . . leveled at the heads of the inmates. The scoundrel in the car did the talking, and he commenced as soon as he was in, shouting at the top of his voice, "Give us

those keys—give us those keys, or I'll blow your brains out! Give us the
money or I'll blow you to hell. We want money! Where's them safe keys—
quick, or some of you'll get killed."

According to some accounts the outlaws had been in Omaha when they
learned of a shipment of gold and silver being transferred east. After wrecking the train, the head robber started shouting, "Where's the bullion—give
us the bullion." He ordered his men to "rush in and help! Come on! Such a
set of robbers as you are—rush in and help!" The leader was given the key
and unlocked the safe, stuffing its contents into a satchel belonging to the
express messenger. He then complained, "Here isn't half as much as we
want; where's that bullion, give us that bullion!" Killingsworth pointed to
the gold and silver bars lying underfoot, some three and a half tons' worth!
"We don't want them things; give us the bullion or we'll blow your brains
out," the chief robber declared. The robbers had come unprepared, on
horseback, when a wagon was called for. Evidently they thought "bullion"
meant gold and silver coin. The bars scattered about the car were "nothing
better than lead," according to Killingsworth.

Meanwhile, there were confusion and pandemonium in the three passenger cars. A group of Chinese immigrants lay huddled on the floor of one.
The coaches had somehow remained on the track, the new Westinghouse
air brakes having saved them. Many passengers stuck their heads out the
windows to see what was going on, only to be greeted with gunshots and
ordered back inside. Some passengers attempted to escape out the rear but
were ordered back in and told, "We don't want to hurt you," by the bandits.
There was also "one plucky old gent" who left his car and started to walk
toward the engine. "A robber told him to go back. He told the robber to go
to the regions below, and called him a scoundrel, and cried to the passengers
to 'come out and go for the villains' . . . nobody was infected." The old man
spent the remainder of the holdup airing his lungs at the bandits, who had
better things to attend to.

After looting the express car of between seventeen hundred and three
thousand dollars, the bandits went to survey the damage to the engine.
Killingsworth recalled:

> The chief directed them around the place where the engine lay, at the
> same time expressing the hope that nobody was killed—they didn't want
> to kill anybody; all they wanted was money. He asked if anyone was
> killed—and just then . . . saw the engineer. . . . The head robber expressed
> sorrow, and really spoke as if he meant it, and repeated the remark that
> they didn't intend to hurt anybody. Then all the robbers went off towards

their horses, which were hitched about a hundred yards south of the track, and, mounting them, rode off towards the south-west.

The passengers came stumbling out of their cars. "Some of the ladies, who had been frantic with terror, came out pale as ghosts and still trembling, and several of them wept like children when they heard of the death of the engineer," Killingsworth recalled. Amazingly, no one in the passenger cars had been robbed, and even the men in the express cars retained their gold watches. The robbery took somewhere between five and ten minutes in all.

The general opinion, at first, was that the perpetrators were amateurs from the area. There were between five and seven men by varying accounts, each armed with a pair of "Navy revolvers . . . some with one or two of another kind in addition."

The railroad offered a five-thousand-dollar reward, and Governor Carpenter of Iowa offered an added five hundred dollars for each thief apprehended. Southwestern Iowa began to swarm with posses, some brought in by special trains from Council Bluffs. Later five horsemen were tracked to the Nodaway River and then south toward Missouri. It eventually was speculated, based on the description of the horses, that the bandits were the same who had pulled the Corydon robbery two years before.

The Saint Louis police, by July 25, believed the heist to be the work of "Jesse and Frank James, Bill Sheppard [George Shepherd?], Cole Younger and [Arthur] McCoy." The first train robbery attributed to the gang drew mixed reviews; "they did the track work well, but bungled terribly in their attempts to make a fortune out of the express safe alone." This was the first and last time the loose-rail tactic, commonly used by Kentucky guerrillas during the war, was employed, in what one newspaper termed "a grand scheme of audacious murder and plunder." It was perhaps the greatest potential haul the gang ever had in its clutches, but it is probable that a large portion of the bullion was actually silver, which was not necessarily worth the hazard involved to cart away. In the darkness and confusion it was probably difficult to tell which was gold and which silver. The fact that there even *was* bullion on the train would be omitted by contemporary biographers. It made for a better story. The matter would rest for well over a century. America seemed to need its Robin Hood, and this was what the reading public would get in the months and years ahead.[55]

❧⊰❧⊱❧

THAT AUGUST, Edwards moved to the *Saint Louis Dispatch*, and it was there that he would write "A Terrible Quintette," a supplement to the paper giving the apologia-biographies of Frank and Jesse James, John and Cole Younger, and Arthur McCoy. The supplement appeared in the November 22, 1873, issue. It was here that the story of the militia leaving Dr. Samuel to hang first appeared, as well as an apocryphal tale of Jesse allegedly engaging in a bloody shootout with militia at the family farm in February 1867.

The romantic image of a group of persecuted former Confederate guerrillas got a further shot in the arm just as the country began a slide into one of the deepest economic depressions in the nation's history.[56] It became known as the Panic of 1873. A rash of bank closings came in the wake of the failure of the financial house of Jay Cooke and Company in September 1873, due to its inability to sell several million dollars' worth of Northern Pacific Railroad bonds. More than five thousand businesses closed in the first year alone. Compounding the problem in the plains states was a grasshopper plague that summer, destroying crops. Many farmers lost their farms as banks foreclosed on unpaid crop debt. The displaced were often forced to return to the industrial cities farther east, their dreams shattered.

Unemployment became rife, and the "hobo" or "tramp" was a common sight as men drifted from place to place looking for work. Those small farmers who held on to their land often joined the Grange movement in an effort to have government regulate volatile railroad freight rates as wholesale prices dipped some 30 percent. Banks and railroads became despised institutions to many. For the next six years the country would struggle toward recovery. The panic would leave an indelible mark on the American psyche for the remainder of the century—and the legend of Jesse James.[57]

※⊘⊙⊘⊙⊘※

ON JANUARY 15, 1874, a stagecoach stopped at the Gaines place, five miles east of Hot Springs, Arkansas, on the road to Malvern. It was time to water the horses. Five men rode past, down the road toward Malvern. About half a mile east, beyond the Gaines place, the riders came up behind the moving stage and ordered the driver to halt if he didn't want his head blown off. It was around 3:30 P.M. Throwing up the window curtain, passenger G. R. Crump of Memphis, Tennessee, saw a pistol pointed at him and heard an order "to get out quick, accompanied by an oath." As they got out, the passengers were ordered to throw up their hands. "Three men were in front of them with cocked pistols and another with a shotgun, while on the other side of the stage was still another—all pointing their weapons towards the passenger and the driver." The passengers were bunched in a circle, and the leader of the group took all the money, jewelry, and watches that appeared to be of special value. T. A. Burbank, former governor of the Dakota Territory, was relieved of $840, a gold watch, and a diamond pin. A man named Taylor from Lowell, Massachusetts, forked over $650. Crump lost his watch and around $40 to $45. Several other passengers were relieved of varying amounts of money and valuables. An express package containing $435 was also taken. Finishing with the passengers, the highwaymen tore open several bags of mail looking for registered letters but found none.

The leader of the group, thought by many later to be Cole Younger, asked the passengers where they were from and if there were any Southern men who had served in the Confederate army. When Crump replied that he had, he was handed back his watch and money and told "they didn't want to rob Confederate soldiers; that the northern men had driven them to outlawry and they intended to make them pay for it." And so the story began that the gang never robbed Confederate veterans.

Taylor, the man from Massachusetts, claimed to be from Saint Louis, but his New England accent doubtless gave him away. "Yes, and you are a newspaper reporter from the *Saint Louis Democrat,* the vilest paper in the West," commented the bandit leader. "Go to Hot Springs and send the *Democrat* [actually a Republican paper] a telegram about this affair, and give them my compliments." The bandit with the shotgun remarked, "I'll bet I can shoot his hat off, without touching a hair of his head."

The passenger from New York asked if he could get back five dollars to send a telegram home. "Eyeing him closely, the chief responded that if he had no friends or money, he had better go and die—that he would be little loss anyway." One of the coach horses was taken by a bandit needing a remount. One passenger with rheumatism couldn't leave the coach and was not molested.

Former Governor Burbank asked for his private papers back. The leader examined them on the ground then turned and said, "Boys, I believe he is a detective—shoot him!" Three pistols were immediately pointed at him. "Stop!" barked the leader. "I guess it's all right." He handed the governor back his papers. "All of them appeared to be jolly fellows and enjoyed the fun very much," noted the *Arkansas Daily Gazette*. The bandits made off with something over two thousand dollars, excluding watches. The desperadoes would ride north to Gads Hill, Missouri. Beyond that lay a rendezvous with destiny—and the law.[58]

5

To Capture the James Boys

In those evil days bad men in bands were doing bad things
continually in the name of law, order and vigilance committees.

John Newman Edwards, Noted Guerrillas (1877)

ALLAN PINKERTON WAS A self-made detective, founder of Pinkerton's
National Detective Agency, whose symbol was the all-seeing eye and
whose motto was "We Never Sleep." Agency founder Pinkerton was
born in a Glasgow, Scotland, tenement in 1819. Twenty years later he was
working as a traveling cooper, or barrel maker, embroiled in the Chartist
movement seeking political reform in British election laws and better conditions for the laboring class. Ultimately, his involvement with the
Chartists led to an arrest warrant, and he fled to America in 1842, setting up
a cooper shop at Dundee, Illinois.

In 1847 he discovered his life's work when he accidentally stumbled upon
and exposed a counterfeiting operation near town. Moving to Chicago, in
1849 he was appointed that city's first detective, a post he held until "political
interference" led to his resignation. He then worked as special agent for the
Post Office Department, helping to solve a series of robberies and thefts in the
Chicago area and eventually going on to found his own small detective
agency. His clients eventually included several express and railroad lines. In
1858 he made the acquaintance of George B. McClellan, vice president of the
Illinois Central Railroad.

A contract with the Pennsylvania, Wilmington and Baltimore Railroad led to his guarding president-elect Abraham Lincoln during his trip to Washington, D.C., early in 1861. Pinkerton's star rose when he claimed to have uncovered a plot against Lincoln's life. The plot was not improbable but was contested by some for its alleged scope. Pinkerton uncovered Confederate spy Rose O'Neal Greenhow in August 1861 and soon was helping gather intelligence for his friend George B. McClellan when McClellan became commander of what would be known as the Army of the Potomac.

Pinkerton's inflated estimates of Confederate troop strength during the Peninsula campaign contributed to McClellan's sluggish performance against the Southern forces under Joseph E. Johnston and Robert E. Lee in the spring and summer of 1862. Similar generalship at the battle of Antietam cost McClellan his post in November 1862. Pinkerton too was soon on the train for Illinois, his espionage-counterintelligence activities in the East eventually taken over by others. But he still had friends in high places, both in politics and business, and there were always criminals to catch.[1]

In the late 1860s the Pinkerton Agency found work hunting down a variety of petty thieves, safecrackers, and even the first train robbers—the Reno gang—whose first assault on the "iron horse" occurred on October 6, 1866, near Seymour, Indiana, where an Adams Express car was robbed. The dogged pursuit of gang members, along with vigilante action (probably abetted by the Pinkertons), destroyed the Renos.[2]

The Panic of 1873 hurt the national economy and with it many of the agency's clients, but there were rumblings even earlier. A business slowdown hit Pinkerton in the pocketbook in 1872, forcing the agency to dun customers for unpaid bills. Eventually Pinkerton would be forced to borrow money from his agents, to mortgage his personal railroad stock portfolio, and to obtain a loan from the general superintendent of the Adams Express Company in order to finance detective operations. This may in part have accounted for the less than vigorous pursuit of the gang following robberies in Iowa. Pinkerton complained that his friend at Adams Express had "insulted me in every way lately," and fretted to the head of his New York office, George Bangs, that "business will be failing I fear very fast unless some way or other we can get it roused up." Thus the Gads Hill robbery and the uproar that followed would come as manna from heaven.[3]

Missouri Gov. Silas Woodson, who had served as colonel and inspector general of the Missouri State Militia during the Civil War, was offering a reward of two thousand dollars "for the bodies of each one of the robbers." Although the Pinkertons did not accept rewards for itself or its employees, it was said that the Adams Express Company and Iron Mountain Railroad had retained the agency to investigate the Gads Hill robbery. The Pinkertons, in fact, had traced the route into Arkansas from Gads Hill and were following the trail back into Missouri. Suddenly there was another contractor for the services of the Pinkertons, the U. S. Post Office, whose involvement would have deadly consequences in due course.[4]

⚜

SHORTLY AFTER the Gads Hill robbery, Jo Shelby had a visitor, George Graham Vest, a member of the Missouri bar from Cooper County. It was the same George Vest who in the fall of 1861 had introduced Missouri's "Provisional Act of Secession." Since that time he had earned some lasting fame as the result of a lawsuit he had handled in nearby Johnson County in 1870. A hound named "Old Drum" was suspected (although not proven) to have killed sheep grazing on the property of one Leonidas Hornsby, who in turn shot and killed the dog. Charles Burden, owner of "Old Drum," was so outraged that he sued Hornsby and hired Vest as his attorney. During the course of the trial, which ultimately went as far as the Missouri Supreme Court, Vest delivered an oration to the jury arguing that "the one absolutely unselfish friend that a man can have in this selfish world . . . is his dog." The speech would later be paraphrased to the effect that a dog is man's best friend, and a statue would be erected to the memory of "Old Drum" on the courthouse lawn in Warrensburg.[5]

Vest arrived on the train after dark, getting off at Page City, a mile from the Shelby place. He had brought a double-barreled shotgun with him in order to do a little hunting. About twenty paces from the house Vest was commanded to "halt!" A rifle barrel could be seen glimmering in the moonlight, pointing from an open window. "I intuitively felt that the man at the other end of the rifle had a bead drawn on me," Vest recalled, "and I halted. . . . My blood seemed to chill." Shelby called out, "Who are you?" and Vest replied with a slight stammer, "G-G-George Vest." Shelby told him, "Wait a minute," and in about five minutes locks and latches began to turn and the front door slowly opened. Vest was told to put the gun down and come toward the door. "It's all right boys, I will vouch for him," Shelby told someone inside. Vest recalled what happened next:

> I then entered and looked about me. The cosy little sitting room had been turned into a fortress. The windows were barricaded securely, and furniture moved up against the door, while on a table in the center of the room lay a collection of revolvers and repeating rifles that would have excited the admiration of a pirate. . . . The gentlemen also wore their small arms.

"These are some friends of mine," said Shelby, and I was not introduced further. I immediately knew that the visitors were the two James boys and the three Younger brothers. Shelby then indulged in conversation for some time, which the others showed no disposition to enter, and at last I was shown to bed, where I tossed until daylight in a troubled sleep. When I came down to breakfast the curtains were drawn . . . Joe was calmly smoking his pipe . . . The traveling arsenal of the night before had departed—so quietly as not to break my light sleep. . . . Shelby did not refer to the visit of the night before, nor did I. I did not know, however, whether they would return that night . . . and limited my stay. . . . And that is the only time I met the Missouri bandits.[6]

<hr/>

ALLAN PINKERTON would have relished having one of his men get as close to the gang as Shelby or George Vest. Agent Joseph W. Whicher, only twenty-six years old, with previous experience as a seaman prior to 1871, was sent to Clay County with a scheme to bring in the James boys single-handedly. There certainly was madness to his method. Robert Pinkerton, son of Allan, had prudently backed off while tracking the gang from Iowa. Now Detective Whicher planned to go straight to the James-Samuel farm, posing as a farmhand looking for work. Arriving in Liberty on Tuesday, March 10, 1874, he proceeded to the Commercial Bank and deposited fifty dollars for safekeeping, a larger amount than a typical laborer would carry. Reportedly in a hurry, Whicher spoke with bank president D. J. Adkins, revealing his purpose. Adkins called in Oliver P. Moss after warning Whicher of the danger. Moss, former sheriff of Clay County and brother-in-law of Mexican War hero Alexander Doniphan, advised him not to try it, saying the James boys were not at home, but even if they weren't, "The old woman would kill him as quick as the boys would."

The five-foot-eleven-inch detective ignored the advice then proceeded to the Arthur House. He ate a meal and departed on the train for Kearney, dressed as a common laborer sporting a three-week-old beard. Arriving there at 5:15 P.M., about sunset, Whicher set off on foot for the farm nearly three miles away.

What happened in the hours that followed is unclear, but before 3 A.M. the next morning four men on horseback were taken across the Missouri at Blue Mills Ferry. This was the same ground that Robert Pinkerton had covered in 1871. One of the men was bound and gagged, and the ferryman, a Mr. Broxey, was told that they were a posse under Deputy Sheriff Jim Baxter. They had just captured a horse thief, they said, and were taking him to Independence where they were to find and arrest his partner. The men, whose faces were covered by "mufflers" and slouched hats, were only barely recognizable. They let the prisoner down off the horse to exercise his legs as they crossed the river. Mr. Broxey noticed that Deputy Baxter was not one of the party as the men disembarked on the south bank.

Three of the men were later identified by Deputy Sheriff Thomason, based on descriptions given by the ferryman, as Jim Anderson (brother of Bloody Bill), Arthur McCoy, and Jesse James. Whicher's corpse, shot in the temple, neck, and shoulder (the first two at close range, with powder burns), was found late that morning four miles east of Independence near the forks of the road leading to both Liberty and Lexington. Reportedly, this was at or near the spot where Robert Pinkerton gave up his quest, and by one account a note was pinned to the body: "This to all detectives," a none too subtle warning about forays into James country. Whicher's body apparently bore a tattoo with his initials, "J.W.W." the same sort of tattoo that the outlaws reportedly searched for on a train passenger at Gads Hill. He was also carrying a pistol, not typical of the usual farm worker, which was probably marked "P.G.G." for Pinkerton Government Guard. Former barrel maker Allan Pinkerton still had a few lessons to learn about disguising his men and sending them out on crack-brained missions without backup. The Pinkerton agency was going up against dangerous men who had ridden with Quantrill and Anderson, not counterfeiters, safecrackers, or embezzlers. It was a different game altogether, and the Younger clan wouldn't prove any easier.[7]

THE YOUNGER brothers—Cole, Jim, John, and Bob—were the sons of Judge Henry Washington Younger and Bursheba Younger of Cass County, Missouri. Their maternal grandfather, Richard Marshall Fristoe, had also been a judge and was one of the founders of Independence, Missouri. During the course of the war Judge Younger had been murdered by Union soldiers, even though he was a Unionist, and most of the family's rather extensive property had been either destroyed or stolen by jayhawkers or other Union troops. If anyone ever had even a remote excuse for outlawry or any claim to anything close to a Robin Hood title, they did. Cole Younger probably saw himself as stealing back what had been stolen from the family by the Yankees; thus any Northerner or Unionist sympathizer was fair game.

According to an unconfirmed story, Cole took part in the Liberty robbery in 1866 that had been plotted by Jesse James from his bed, with brother Frank helping to coordinate this and other bank raids with former guerrillas before Jesse recovered. Cole at least later claimed to have helped fence the bonds taken. They were mostly war bonds issued by the federal or state government, as it turned out, an ironic twist that must have amused Cole. The banks and their customers held these bonds, the sale of which had financed the war as well as jayhawker and Missouri Militia plundering and atrocities, among other things.

Cole may well have suffered some persecution after the war. There were claims that he and the known guerrillas who had raided Lawrence were wanted for the killings there, but this is unconfirmed. Cass County was slightly tilted politically toward the Republicans, despite being situated on the Kansas border. The family ultimately moved to several locations, even staying in Texas for a spell, where John Younger became a wanted man. He shot and killed Dallas County Deputy Sheriff John McMahan in January 1871 while McMahan was attempting to arrest him over a minor shooting scrape. Before this only Cole was wanted in connection with any of the various robberies, starting in 1868 with the Russellville bank job. By early 1874 all four brothers were suspects in the Gads Hill robbery, although Bob and Jim probably had some limited activity in earlier robberies. Prior to 1874 only Cole and John had any real criminal notoriety.

Matters came to a head on March 17, 1874, at Roscoe in Saint Clair County. Earlier that week Louis J. Lull and John Boyle (also known as James Wright and Duckworth), both Pinkerton agents, had arrived in Monegaw Springs from Osceola, posing, oddly enough, as cattle buyers. On March 16 the detectives had moved on to Roscoe, registering at the Roscoe House with Edwin B. Daniels, a part-time deputy sheriff who was acting as a guide. Lull and Daniels were out scouting the area, with Boyle holding back in reserve. They stopped at the Theodorick Snuffer farm, where Jim and John Younger were staying, and inquired the direction to the home of the Widow Simms but, curiously, went in the opposite direction when they left. John Younger noted that they were too well armed to be who they claimed, and he wanted to go in pursuit. Jim Younger wanted to let the matter be but finally agreed to accompany his brother.

Just a short distance up the road they caught up with the trio. Boyle fled and had his hat shot off in the process. Lull and Daniels were ordered to drop their guns. Lull's British Tranter revolver was the giveaway. When John asked the pair if they were detectives, they denied it, sticking to the cattle-buyer story. But they were too well armed to be what they claimed, argued John, waving a double-barreled shotgun at the pair. Sensing trouble, Lull pulled a Smith and Wesson No. 2 revolver and shot John through the neck. Lull was hit in the shoulder by a blast from the shotgun. Daniels caught the other barrel and fell, dying.

Lull took off, pursued by John, who caught up with the detective after he had ridden under a low-hanging branch. John fired twice at the detective with his pistol, the second shot hitting him in the chest. John then started to ride back to his brother Jim, but fell off his horse—dead. Agent Boyle and Jim Younger were the only survivors. Boyle fled the area, although he was to work on the case for a few more weeks.

Thomas Jefferson Younger, an uncle, and by one press account a Saint Clair County judge, was invited to John Younger's funeral. The story of affairs in Missouri again made the pages of the *New York World,* which held the state up to ridicule in both the Whicher and Roscoe affairs. The blood-and-thunder exploits made better copy, although New Yorkers probably suffered worse crime daily, albeit of a sometimes wider and different variety, than the whole state of Missouri combined.[8]

Out-of-state papers were not the first to go on the attack. An editorial, "The Banditti of Missouri," appeared in the *Saint Louis Republican* on March 21. It reiterated many of the facts already given, then stuck in the knife:

> Judges, sheriffs, constables and the whole machinery of law are either set at defiance by a gang of villains, or bought or frightened into neutrality. If such a condition of affairs existed in central Africa, it might not provoke much surprise, but that it exists in Missouri is a fact as remarkable as it is outrageous. If the governor of Missouri and the legislature of Missouri are unable to devise ways and means for effectively breaking up these nests of thieves and cut-throats, then let them formally announce their inability to preserve the peace and dignity of the state, and ask assistance from the federal government [which was already involved via the Post Office, which hired the Pinkertons]. Anything is better than this tame submission to systematic brigandage.

Governor Woodson went before the legislature on March 23 and delivered a special message in which he deplored the state of affairs and absolved himself of blame. He told the legislators that he had done all he could legally do at that point in offering rewards. Something more was needed, and he suggested that a special "secret service" force be created and funded by the state to track down the bandits, and perhaps better funding could be provided for the state militia. He reiterated that "with the power to employ a secret police force, and the means to pay them provided, I can enforce the law and either arrest or exterminate the parties to whom I have been referring."

After much political jockeying, the Senate committee on criminal jurisprudence introduced a bill appropriating five thousand dollars for a "state secret service" limited to twenty-five men. Ultimately the sum was increased to ten thousand dollars, although nearly one-third of the House members abstained from voting, and no funding was given for militia.

Sheriff George E. Patton was outraged by the articles and editorials in the *Saint Louis Republican* and *Globe* that insinuated he had been "bought or frightened into neutrality." He denounced them in an open letter as "maliciously false" and eventually sued the papers for libel. Some sort of settlement was apparently reached, for the *Republican* eventually called him "a fearless and honest officer who has not flinched from the performance of his duty as sheriff." This, however, was as he was going out of office at the end of the year and probably of moot solace.

Clay Countians still nursed ill feelings dating from the war and the period of the Drake Constitution; those feelings apparently lasted for decades. Tradition has it that the statue of justice in front of the courthouse was situated so it faced south in a symbolic gesture of sympathy. Another story has it that from at least the 1870s until well into the twentieth century county officers would not fly the American flag on the courthouse grounds. It was only in 1912 that the practice resumed, and the flag was hoisted again by Will Hall, who as a student at William Jewell College had hauled down "Old Glory" in Liberty during the secession frenzy of April 1861.

The law-and-banditry issue would become a true political football for the next few years in the press and political arena. Republican newspapers both in and out of Missouri continually harped on the "bandit state of Missouri," or used similar phrases. Nationally, if not in Missouri particularly, the Republicans now wanted to link the Democratic Party with loose enforcement of the law and with banditry in general. The *Kansas City Times*, however, had a fine retort to that proposition from across the state line: "Robbers in Democratic Missouri are outlaws, with a price on their head . . . while robbers in Radical Kansas are elected to the highest offices in the State. . . . Democrats may not be good at catching fugitive thieves, but they can be counted on not to elevate such cattle to the highest offices in the State."[9]

BLOOD HAD been spilled on both sides, and in the final tally the outlaws were still at large and still on top of the score. From this point forward, an ordinary case would become a blood feud for Allan Pinkerton. On April 17, 1874, he wrote George Bangs, the superintendent of his New York office, of a telegram from Lee's Summit, Missouri, reporting that the Younger and James brothers had left Jackson County: "At least they are out of the country for the present time. I have started the men forward but will of course recall them. . . . I hear that the James and Youngers are desperate men and that when we meet it must be the death of one or both of us, they await, my blood was spilt, and they must repay. There is no use talking, they must die. . . . Mr. Horner and William [Pinkerton?] refuse to go with me to Mo. . . . I make no talk but simply say I am going myself." He went on to say that the departure of the outlaws had ended the matter for the present, but if allowed to hunt them by a "Mr. Dinsmore" he would send his men forward again: "When the time comes when we find the men can be arrested then . . . I shall be with my own men in charge. I apprehend there is no danger with the proper direction of the men, but still if the work has to be done then I shall see it done. . . . I have the men in Clay County and at Liberty and Kearney, who will know when the James' [are to] be heard of. I have taken care to have Mr. Cannon keep me posted in Jackson Co." Pinkerton told Bangs that he would inform him of further developments.[10]

Pinkerton must have been sadly misinformed about the James brothers leaving the area, and about a week later he would have a very rude shock. For nine years Jesse and his cousin Zerelda (Zee) Mimms had been engaged. Now Jesse and Zee had decided to finally tie the knot. Zee's mother and Rev. William James, uncle of both Zee and Jesse, were against it and tried to talk Zee out of the idea. Zee protested. According to Uncle William, "She said Jesse had been lied about and persecuted and that he was not half so bad as pictured." She wanted her uncle, now a Methodist minister in Platte County, to preside. So the date was set for Friday, April 24, 1874, at the home of her sister, Lucy Mimms (Mrs. Boling) Browder, at Kearney. Jesse came in about 9 P.M. for the simple ceremony. Uncle William "upbraided his nephew for his reported deeds of violence, but Jesse argued with him long and earnestly to prove he was not the marauder he was painted."

Finally, the reluctant William agreed to perform the ceremony, but there was a hitch, as someone had reportedly tipped off detectives, and two were observed by an informant as heading from Liberty to Kearney as fast as their horses would carry them. A small woman, Zee was hidden between the mattress and the feather bedding, and the bed made up around her. Jesse, in the meantime, ducked out the back door to the barn of a neighbor where he had two horses. When the detectives arrived and went into Lucy's house, Jesse rode out of the barn, making as much noise as he could, drawing the detectives off on a wild-goose chase in the dark. Jesse then doubled back, was hastily married, and left with his bride for their honeymoon. It was certainly going to be an interesting marriage.[11]

Eventually news of the wedding leaked to the press, with Edwards's *Saint Louis Dispatch* reporting a large wedding with around fifty guests at Kearney on April 23, the day before. Meanwhile, the editorials thundered away without mercy: "Where are the Pinkerton Detectives? Where are the men the Governor is authorized to employ—$10,000 appropriated—to catch these outlaws?" the *Saint Louis Democrat* would rail.[12]

Allan Pinkerton was between anguish and anger as he wrote George Bangs again on May 12:

> The business in Clay County is humbling me badly. I don't know but that I have one, if not two snakes [possible disloyal employees]. I allude to Boyle and Mizner. Boyle I feel it in my bones, and then I think that he holds the lives [of] three of my men in his hands . . . tis horrible to think that any moment will bring the news of the murder of my men. Oh God, tis awful. If necessary I am going to Cameron Junction to talk to Mr. Hardwick and a man from James' neighborhood or even into Liberty should that be necessary. I will not leave Chicago until about to morrow night and if Boyle acts rightly I will not require to go at all.[13]

What the problem was with John Boyle and Mizner we can only specu-late. Perhaps these were the two detectives that Jesse and Zee eluded at their wedding. Boyle, by some news accounts a former Confederate soldier from Saint Louis, may have been suspected of selling out. At least he was held responsible for running during the Roscoe affair. On July 2, Allan's son William Pinkerton would write Dan O'Connor, chief detective of the Saint Louis police, that "Boyle was at one time a member of this force, but he was found to be cowardly, deceitful, and utterly unreliable, therefore discharged. Had he been half a man, Captain Lull would have been living." Billy Pinker-ton, who with his brother Robert would eventually take over the family busi-ness, advised O'Connor that if Boyle was looking for work he should "have nothing to do with him, he is a dirty dog."[14]

⁂

FRANK JAMES would have a bride that summer as well—Annie (or Anna) Ralston, daughter of Samuel Ralston, a native of Ireland who moved to the area around Independence, Missouri, and became a prosperous farmer before the war. According to an 1881 newspaper account, Ralston was a Unionist. He probably sat out most of the conflict as a civilian, suffering the loss of property typical to residents of the area. Several accounts report that he was wounded on June 13, 1861, in a skirmish near his farm at Rock Creek, but it is unclear from these whether he was a spectator or a participant. His member-ship in the Masons may well have aided him in his dealings with Union army officers. Sometime during the latter half of the conflict, Ralston moved his family to Omaha, Nebraska, where he engaged in freighting, assisted by his

son John. The family lived in a small brick house near the corner of Davenport and Sixteenth Streets. After several years the freighting business dwin-
dled and he moved the family back to the farm outside Independence.[15]

Annie attended Independence Female College, graduating with a
degree in science and literature in the summer of 1872. She later went on to
teach school at Little Santa Fe, to the south of Kansas City. Apocryphal stories of how Frank and Annie met abound. However they met, during June
1874 she told her father she would be visiting friends and relatives in Kansas
City and Omaha, taking the Chicago and Alton out of Independence.
Somewhere in the Kansas City area she met Frank, and the pair eloped,
apparently going to Omaha for their wedding and honeymoon. The family
eventually received a note: "I am married and going West." It was signed
"Annie Reynolds."

The family feared Annie had run off with a gambler, but imagine their
horror when one day Annie's eldest brother, John, returned from a trip to
Kansas City with tormenting news. He had visited with a local china merchant, Thomas M. James, and was informed that his sister had eloped with
the merchant's nephew Frank James, the notorious outlaw. The family was
stunned, and patriarch Sam Ralston is said to have disowned his daughter.
Following the honeymoon Frank and Annie reportedly joined Jesse and Zee
at the home of sister Susan in Texas. But matrimony had its expenses, and
the James brothers soon laid plans that involved certain business transactions in Missouri.[16]

⁂

NORTH LEXINGTON was the link between Lexington, Missouri, and the railroad, which had located its tracks north of the Missouri River, outside and
north of town. To get from the railroad to town, one had to catch a stage.
Around 6 P.M., Sunday, August 30, three horsemen dashed out of the woods
and stopped the stage that was on its way to the ferry with nine passengers.
One stopped the horses while the other two thrust their guns inside the
windows, threatening the passengers if they resisted. One man, later
identified as one of the James brothers, dismounted and ordered the eight
male passengers to get out, hands in the air, and line up beside the road.
Another man, identified as one of the Youngers, noticed some people who
had crossed the river on an afternoon stroll and rode off to order the
bystanders into line with the stage passengers.

Among the latter was Mattie Hamlett, whose brother Jesse had served
with under Anderson and had died in 1864. Mattie was reportedly an
acquaintance of both the James and Younger boys. She had allegedly nursed

one of the James brothers, identified as Frank although it was probably Jesse, "when he was very badly wounded" in the last year of the war. It was Jesse, of course, who had spent several weeks in Lexington recovering from his wound after his 1865 surrender. As the masked man urged her on from the river she turned and said, "I know who you are in spite of that dirty old veil over your face."

He replied, "Who am I then?"

"Why, you are Will Younger, and you ought to be ashamed of yourself," Mattie replied.

"Well, you are the same saucy girl you always were," he said with a laugh.

One of the James boys was relieving W. T. Singleton, the railroad agent, of his watch as Mattie stepped up and laid a hand on his arm. "Why, Frank [Jesse], I'm astonished to see you have come down to such small work; I thought you never did anything except on a big scale."

The bandit turned and shook her hand. "Well, I am a little ashamed of it myself. It's the first time we've ever stooped to such small game. But you needn't call names quite so loud here." Mattie asked the bandit to return the watch. He asked if he was any relation and she replied that he was. James handed the watch back but started to keep the chain. "No, give back the chain too; I won't have part if you can give all." Sheepishly he returned the chain as well.

Prof. W. J. Allen, who had moved from Lexington, Kentucky, to set up a male academy, lost fifty dollars and a gold watch as well as his coat and vest. "Oh Frank, don't take that man's clothes. Your mother would be grieved to death if she knew what you are doing," Mattie interrupted. "I nursed you when you were wounded during the war; and now I believe I ought to have let you die."

With a sad tone to his voice he replied, "It's a pity you didn't. I need good clothes myself and mine will do for him to go over to town in." With that he swapped clothes.

Only the woman passenger was left, a Mrs. Graham of Bowling Green, Kentucky, visiting her uncle in Lexington. "Why Frank, you certainly would not disturb a lady?" Mattie protested.

"No, Miss Mattie, we never have done that, and we won't do it now." The robbery netted only a little over two hundred dollars in cash, with perhaps another hundred dollars or so in other booty.

Apparently the bandits were after a Parson Jennings of Mayview, who had reportedly sold a lot of hogs in Saint Louis for around five thousand dollars and was said to be returning by train. In this case he wasn't present.

"Damn it, he isn't here," one of the robbers exclaimed. Jennings had arrived home the night before.

The theatrical aspect of the whole affair was not lost on Professor Allen, who said he was "exceedingly glad . . . that it was done by first class artists . . . men of national reputation." The passengers were told that pursuit would be futile, as they would be long gone on "the finest horses in Missouri." As they left one called back, "Good-bye, Miss Mattie. You'll never see us again."

As the highwaymen rode off down the riverbank nonchalantly, numerous (some said hundreds of) spectators on the Lexington side watched in amazement.

The *Lexington Caucasian* applauded the bandits:

> Taken altogether, it was an exploit which, in cool audacity, was worthy of its distinguished perpetrators—the James boys and one of the immortal Youngers. Rob Roy and Claude Duval must hide their diminished heads abashed. Missouri is ahead in its banditti, as she is in her soil, her climate, her minerals, her women, her—everything. Big Muddy forever![17]

But others were not amused. The rival *Lexington Register* commented that its editor had forwarded to Governor Woodson an account of the robbery "and an offer to furnish . . . the proper affidavit making the formal charge. The Governor can have a chance to show his zeal in the matter if he so desires to do."[18]

Meanwhile, the bandits were spotted again in Lafayette County. A week later, around 5 A.M. on Sunday, September 6, the highwaymen ran into the Lexington brass band as it returned west from the Saline County fair at Marshall. The "members of the band, being well armed presented a bold front and were allowed to pass unmolested." Apparently they had been tipped off to a probable ambush and robbery of the money earned from playing the fair.[19] As if Governor Woodson or his acting governor, Charles P. Johnson, needed further encouragement, the story of a brass band standing off the highwaymen hovering around Lexington received statewide press notice and made a mockery of law enforcement. Mattie Hamlett was starting to have memory problems after receiving a note from the mother of the James boys. Mrs. Samuel would later visit Lexington and be interviewed by the press about her family's Civil War woes in an effort at damage control. "After mature reflection on the subject, I am prepared to doubt the accuracy of my recognition," Mattie would publicly state.[20]

Officer Flourney Yancy of the Saint Louis police was ordered to report to Acting Governor Johnson on "special duty" on September 3. C. C. Rainwater, vice president of the Saint Louis police board, told Johnson he was satisfied that a detective would accomplish little. He suggested that the sheriffs of Clay or Ray County organize posses of twenty-five men and scour the surrounding country, and that this was the way the outlaws could be killed or captured. But Yancy had trouble finding the elusive bandits as well as what he considered trustworthy sheriffs who were not afraid or sympathizing with the outlaws. The only exception was Sheriff Brown of Ray County, according to Yancy. On September 21 Yancy reportedly cornered Jim Younger and Jesse James near the Ray–Clay County line and exchanged pistol shots with them, although they ultimately slipped from the posse's grasp.[21]

THAT FALL the Missouri outlaws became an issue in the various state political campaigns. The Democrats dodged the issue, but it became a plank in the platform of the Missouri People's Party, essentially the old Liberal Republican Party plus some converts from the Democratic ranks. The Republicans, having no strong candidates, backed those of the People's Party and declined to nominate any of their own. The rationale was that old Unionist Democrats might bolt the party if the outlaw issue started to stir former animosities, with the former Confederate wing defending the James and Younger boys.

Carl Schurz, a Liberal Republican who was up for reelection as a U.S. senator, ran on the People's ticket. Schurz delivered an attack on the Democrats in a speech given in Saint Louis on September 24, only a few days after Officer Yancy's gun battle with James and Younger. He had been accused by opposition newspapers of calling Missouri "the Robber State," a point that he hotly denied. Schurz countered and accused the Democrats of waffling on the issue of banditry and the Democratic press of encouraging the bandits with their editorials. Just who was doing the most damage to the reputation of the state and retarding its development? he asked.

Schurz and other People's candidates were defeated in November. Why? The situation in Missouri was far more complex, politically, than is generally realized today, and the predicament was one of moral ambiguity more than anything.[22]

The postwar era brought to Missouri a unique situation involving the railroad. In the late 1860s the state of Missouri liquidated its railroad assets, which had cost the taxpayers some $32 million, to individuals in the private sector for a little over $6 million. The idea was that state government shouldn't be doing the work of the private sector. Railroad entrepreneurs then went a step lower on the political ladder to the county courts, the governing bodies for Missouri's counties, lobbying for local bond issues to finance the construction of their privately held railroads. The promoters were particularly successful in gaining support from individuals with property holdings in or near a railroad that might be developed into a town and from business owners who stood to profit locally. The counties would often hold a referendum on the issuance of railroad construction bonds, but the local plebiscites were not binding on the county court, particularly if court members had something to gain from the construction of the railroad line. Many county officials ignored referendums that swung against bond issues. In addition, Confederate veterans and sympathizers were shut out of the electoral process for more than five years.

Between the end of the war and 1875 nearly half of Missouri's counties subscribed to more than $18 million in public aid for railroad construction. By 1880 Missouri ranked third in the nation for local bonded debt to finance railroad building. During the same period Missourians bore triple the tax debt, on a local level, of citizens in all surrounding states, including Illinois and Iowa. Many counties were paying several times more on railroad debt than they were in support of education. Farmers caught it both ways, as wholesale prices dipped during the Panic of 1873 and freight rates to ship produce to market fluctuated upward. A railroad bond issue led to the mob-violence killings of a Cass County judge, a Harrisonville councilman, and a circuit attorney in April 1872, as related earlier.[23]

While Officer Yancy trailed the gang across several counties, the *Carrollton Journal*, about twenty miles northeast of Lexington, would ask cynically:

> The people of this part of the state, who have been so handsomely plundered by the highwaymen who have absorbed their means under the name of the B. and S. W. R.R. [Burlington and Southwestern Railroad], will ask themselves, . . . What other fresh class of tax-payers . . . have been captured, and will now be ordered to stand and deliver? What new set of victims are to be fleeced?

The *Journal* felt that the "humbler transactions" of the James-Younger gang only drew attention away from what it termed "these more gigantic scoundrels." The gang's booty, following one train robbery, would be contemptuously described by the *Lexington Caucasian* as "just as honestly earned as the riches of many a highly distinguished political leader and railroad job manipulator." The editor, no doubt, had read *The Gilded Age* by Mark Twain and Charles D. Warner, which brutally satirized the situation. The attitude of many Missourians toward the railroads and the politicians who aided them was one of distrust, if not outright bitterness.

It was only after the revision of the Missouri Constitution in 1875 that grievances began to be addressed. This document asserted the public's right to regulate and even tax the railroads. It also prohibited political subdivisions within the state from lending to private corporations and set a limit on future public debt and the tax rates. Many Missouri voters were so alienated that they failed to vote on the ratification of the new constitution, although it passed easily. But resistance to paying the bonded debt already incurred would be fought out in the courts and on a local political level for years to come. It was amid this milieu that the James legend would be fostered.[24]

AT 3:30 P.M. on December 8, 1874, two men on horseback rode up to the grocery–post office run by John Purtee at Muncie, Kansas, a whistlestop twelve miles west of Kansas City on the Kansas and Pacific Railroad. "They came in and asked me what time the train was due," recalled Purtee. "I answered, 'in twenty minutes.' One of them wanted to know if it was the train that carried the express matter, and on my answering yes, he pulled out a revolver and put it to my face saying, 'Consider yourself my prisoner—I am going to rob that train.'"

The bandit then asked if there were any guns in the store and took the one behind the counter and even a wallet containing two counterfeit two-dollar bills and twenty dollars in real currency from the cash drawer. Three more men arrived, and everyone put on masks ranging from scarves to one made from part of an old oilcloth coat with holes for the eyes and mouth.

"When they heard the train coming they made me go out and flag it," Purtee continued, "one man covering me with a revolver. They had previously made the section men put two rails across the track." The section hands and several locals, eight or ten in all, were herded into the store just before the robbery. At least one shot was fired as the eastbound express train came to a halt. The engineer was ordered out and told to uncouple the engine from the express car, but this was a mistake. The robbers wanted the engine and express uncoupled from the other coaches. Finally they got it right and pulled the express car about four hundred yards up the track.

Both sides of the train were covered as two men entered the express car. Frank D. Webster, the express messenger for Wells, Fargo and Company, heard "a loud hallooing outside, and not expecting anything wrong, walked up to a small window in between the mail room and the express room."

A revolver was thrust under his nose, and Webster was ordered to come out, a bandit threatening to shoot if he didn't. Getting off, he was told to put his hands up and to get back in the car. Two bandits followed him in. Webster recalled that "one placed a revolver to my head and the other leveled a Henry rifle on the other side, and I was told to unlock the safe. I readily obeyed, and at their order handed out the contents."

One bandit picked up a mail sack, and the contents of the safe were deposited by the other bandit in the sack. "I took out $18,000 in currency, $5,000 in gold [dust], and all the packages of money in the safe," Webster related. They refused to take the messenger's watch or a silver brick that was lying in the safe. The messenger was then ordered outside and told to get on the ground. The value of the loot aboard the express car was estimated at some thirty thousand dollars. No mail was taken.

The whole robbery lasted only twenty minutes, and as at Adair, not a passenger was robbed. However, there was quite a commotion in the passenger cars as the affair progressed. The conductor came into one car and asked if anyone had a revolver. This set off a panic. "Men commenced to get down between the seats and divest themselves of their valuables, placing them in their boots," one passenger, W. L. Kilbourn of Chicago, recalled. "Ladies hurriedly took their jewels from their ears, necks and hands, and without blushing a particle lifted their dainty skirts and shoved their valuables down under garters."

The bandits rode off over a hill to the north of the robbery site but may have doubled back and ridden south. Near Shawneetown they met a man named Boateele about 5:10 P.M. and forced him to exchange his horse for one of theirs. Boateele later followed their trail to a place near the Findley farm where they had camped and divided the loot. A quantity of papers and envelopes was scattered about, including a mortgage paper that had been left behind. Also dropped in the dark was a lump of gold, $105 in paper currency, and a pocketbook containing a Confederate $20 bill and the oilcloth mask plus the Wells, Fargo and Company express seals. It appeared that the gang was headed back to Kansas City, where authorities feared they would be hard to locate.

A company of soldiers from Fort Leavenworth was sent out to look for the bandits but had no luck, and one posse arrested "a band of sufferers from Kansas" by mistake. Some thought it was the work of the James gang, some did not. It was noted that Jesse's wife, Zee, had been in town "for a long while back, visiting her brother," but had left eight or ten days prior to the robbery. Governor Woodson telegraphed Sheriff Booth of Jackson County that the bandits should not be allowed shelter in the county or state if they had crossed back into Missouri. He cautioned Booth not to take steps "without reliable information" but offered to pay all expenses "not paid by the state of Kansas" in the apprehension of the perpetrators.

The rewards for the robbers were $2,500 from the state of Kansas for their arrest; $5,000 from the Kansas and Pacific Railroad; and $1,000 each, dead or alive, from Wells, Fargo, plus $5,000 for the recovery of the property.

It was not long before the lawmen had some luck. On the evening of December 10, William "Bud" McDaniel, a known associate of the Youngers, was arrested by Officer Callopy of the Kansas City police. McDaniel had in his possession more than one thousand dollars and some jewelry identified by Wells, Fargo as part of the loot taken from the express safe. He was placed in custody and on December 13 was packed off to the county jail at Leavenworth, Kansas. McDaniel had a five-man guard and narrowly missed being mobbed in both Kansas City, Missouri, and in Wyandotte, Kansas. In Kansas City, before his transfer, there was talk of lynching. McDaniel was described as "a very reckless man in appearance, and in conversation seems little like the gallant knight of the road that some would make him." McDaniel was also very reckless in his actions, having been initially arrested on a charge of public drunkenness. Later he was mortally wounded by a German farmer named Bierman, who got the drop on him with a heavy-caliber rifle after McDaniel escaped from the Lawrence, Kansas, jail in late June 1875.[25]

<hr />

OVER THE months since his agency's debacles in trying to apprehend the James and Younger brothers, Allan Pinkerton had been spinning a new web. Jack Ladd, a Pinkerton agent, had obtained work on a farm adjacent to the Samuel place. The property was owned by Daniel Askew, probably the "man from James' neighborhood" that Pinkerton had alluded to in his May 12 message to George Bangs. It was from this vantage point that the Pinkertons kept up surveillance.

On December 15, 1874, Pinkerton wrote to his federal employer. Marked "Personal," the letter was sent to "Mr. P.H. Woodward, Esq., Chief Special Agent P.O. Dept., Washington, D.C." It began, "Yours of the 12th inst. received. Many thanks for your kindness in this matter. I am under obligation to the Postmaster General, more than I can ever pay. We have now got inside the K[earney?]. [post?] office. Harsel the post master has appointed a deputy, and has himself gone into the country. . . . I am obliged to you for your solicitation of an agent to operate near K[earney?]. I am expecting every day to bring this thing to a climax. At least two or three of the parties are there, but they are well armed, we have all the advantages men could ask, we must be cautious and make our movement secure, and then I hope every tick of the wire will tell us we have got the men." He appended to the letter a copy of the secret telegraph cipher used by the agency (see Appendix C). "Please consider this strictly confidential and please say to the post master general that I shall ever remember his kindness," Pinkerton closed.

Apparently Pinkerton had someone operating within the local post office to monitor the mail to and from the Samuel family—the nineteenth-century equivalent of a wiretap. At some point word of this situation leaked back, and the James brothers sent letters to members of their family in code.[26]

The next letter from Pinkerton was sent to "Samuel Hardwick Esq., Liberty, Clay Co. Mo." from Chicago, dated December 28, 1874. Hardwicke was an interesting, and for well over a century a somewhat enigmatic, character in the James story. He was born in Clay County in 1833; his mother, Margaret, was the sister of Josiah Gregg, a noted explorer-scientist and author of the classic *Commerce of the Prairies*. Hardwicke had obtained what was known as a classical education, perhaps not unlike that of the father of the James boys. He then read law under Judge Norton and was admitted to the bar in 1857. "Close habits of studiousness have always been one of his marked characteristics," one biography noted.

> He has become one of the best read lawyers in this part of the State . . . His knowledge of the law and his judgement upon legal questions command respectful consideration from the court and bar wherever his duties as a lawyer call him, whilst his culture, eloquence and ability as an advocate and his integrity, professionally and in private life, are recognized by all. Though an active, successful lawyer, Mr. Hardwicke is a man of retiring disposition, more given to the study of his books and reflection than to the enjoyment of society or the pleasures of conversation.

It was noted that he had one of the best law libraries on the circuit. But there was another aspect of Sam Hardwicke's personality that went unnoticed. His association with Pinkerton was about to take him on a trip to the wild side, not unlike his illustrious uncle's adventures with the Comanches.[27]

Pinkerton had apparently been in contact with Hardwicke since May, when he mentioned Hardwicke in his letter to George Bangs. Apparently Hardwicke had been acting as something of a point man for Pinkerton, whose letter to Hardwicke gives a chilling glimpse at what was to follow:

> Yours of the 25th inst. from Hannibal is received. I have given it serious thought. Have had Robert with me at the time and we had to accord you credit in taking care of everything you had to do in meeting Mr. Towne.
>
> I thank you for what you have done, would I could say to you in person, all I feel in regard to you. With regard to Mr. Towne he has done

well if his men will only do as he requires, all is well. I would not ask much more than Mr. Towne has given us. I am grateful for all he has done. Now for the battle, it makes me feel almost like laughing at the great preparations we are making to tackle 2 or 3 men. Still they have many friends, we may set them down as legion.

I will go to an officer of the C. B. and Q. RR [Chicago, Burlington, and Quincy Railroad] and see Mr. Robert Harris, as soon as possible. I shall at all events get the ammunition into a car, of this I am confident. Whether he will be willing to pass us through the same as Towne, I will be able to tell you before I mail this letter. You have seen the letter previous to this, and will see the necessity of Robert going to Rock Island to see Col. Gallagger [Bvt. Lt. Col. Daniel W. Flagler]. This will be due in 2 or 3 more days. Will you see that the guns are in good order. I will buy 2 or 3 additional guns. The men will bring them along.

I will now definitely say that Robert will go to Rock Island, the ammunition will be brought from there to Chicago, kept here until the men are going away then slipped on board the baggage car, by order of Mr. Harris, the balance of the road is fixed by order of the agent.

Robert has had the recruiting of the men he assures me.

We can rely on six anyway and himself, making seven, we may be able to get another man.

With regard to yourself, you and Robert can arrange that matter, when you meet at Cameron, where, the men, of course, will take supper, it would be as well to get Davis' wife get some lunch ready to eat in the morning, it could be left somewhere for Jack [Ladd?] to pick up, but great care must be taken to excite no suspicions, and have no clue behind.

There is one thing of vital importance, how are we to know positively when the peas [probably code term for the James brothers] are there. it won't do for us to take chances how are you to devise a plan write or telegraph without fail.

I have been thinking of sending a surgeon along with the party for fear of accident. or do you know some one whom you could implicitly trust and pay him to accompany you, at least to Cameron, or other points where surgical help could be obtained.

Please instruct your guides not to be too far from the depot, because if they are a number of miles away, the men will be tired in getting through the woods. You must remember the men are not woodsmen.

Jack [Ladd] will be the guide on the return, Please to instruct him, if any men are wounded, to take as smooth and speedy a road as possible, remember this particularly.

It will be as well for you to hold the freight train long enough, say until 6 A.M., as necessary, but as soon as all are on board, go ahead, rapidly, no danger, it will all be over before that time. Robert will count noses, if all are on board, he will let you know.

Above every thing destroy the house, blot it from the face of the earth. Here the logs will burn, let the men run no risk, burn the house down. Robert has charge of the ammunition in the shape of Greek fire, etc., etc.

The State of Mo. and Clay Co. in particular remind one of Seymour, Ind. It was partially run down. People were leaving instead of coming to it. They were seriously thinking of moving the track of the O. And M. R.R. [Ohio and Mobile Railroad] away from Seymour because the murderers, thieves and robbers [of the Frank and John Reno gang] had taken possession of it.

The robbers had robbed the express company for the 5th time. They were in Seymour, but I had not the evidence to take them. They left and went to Canada, where they defied me. Soon I followed them to Detroit and commenced operations across the river in Windsor. I need not tell you the delays of the law, but all the Canadian courts were in my favor. I brought them back and soon after 6 of them were swinging on the square tree [i.e., lynched]. What is the consequence. Seymour is improving rapidly, three banks where one was before and everything peaceful and happy. I trust Clay will become as prosperous.

I shall expect you to meet Robert with the surgeon if possible, at Cameron.

I have sent and seen Mr. Harris. He at once said he would refund the fares and give me an order to carry the box.

> Yours Truly,
> Allan [Pinkerton]
> E. J. Rob[28]

Towne was probably someone connected with the Hannibal and Saint Joseph Railroad, just as Harris was with the Chicago, Burlington, and Quincy. But just who was "Robert," and what are the references to Rock Island and the "ammunition" and the mysterious "box"? An entry from the Rock Island (Illinois) arsenal's "Register of Letters Received" for 1874 provides an intriguing clue. Dated December 30, 1874, it records the receipt of a letter of introduction, dated December 24, from Lt. Gen. Philip H. Sheridan, for Robert J. Linden, "one of Pinkerton's National Detective Police, who wishes to obtain certain materials from Rock Island Arsenal, to aid him in arresting certain Railroad robbers."[29]

Robert J. Linden had started with the agency sometime after the Civil War, serving briefly in the Philadelphia branch before transferring to Chicago, where he was eventually promoted to assistant superintendent in 1871. Linden would have one of the key roles, if not *the* key roll, in what was to follow. He was Pinkerton's right-hand man in the James-Younger case and was sent to the side of the mortally wounded Louis Lull after Lull's fight with John Younger. Linden later accompanied Lull's body back to Chicago, with Lull's widow, for burial in the Pinkerton plot.[30]

The letter of introduction to Lt. Col. Daniel W. Flagler, ordnance officer in charge at Rock Island, from Sheridan, commander of the Military Division of the Missouri, was probably obtained as the result of the Pinkerton Agency's work on the James case for the Post Office Department. Sheridan's headquarters in Chicago was only about two blocks from the Pinkerton office there. The Union army's hero of the Shenandoah Valley was noted for his destruction of that area in the latter half of 1864 in what would afterward be known as "the Burning." He was similarly ruthless in his pursuit of Confederate partisan ranger leader John Singleton Mosby, using tactics similar to those employed by Ewing in Missouri. As a military observer during the Franco-Prussian War of 1870–71 he had again encountered partisan activity, by the French this time, and advised his host, German Prince Otto Von Bismarck, to take strong action against civilians in like manner. "The people must be left nothing but their eyes to weep with over the war," Sheridan told the "Iron Chancellor." Shortly afterward Bismarck instituted a policy of burning villages near the sites of guerrilla forays and of hanging all adult male residents thereof, a practice that would see its culmination some seventy to seventy-five years later in the atrocities of World War II.

We will never know the circumstances by which Sheridan's December 1874 letter was obtained, but Allan Pinkerton had somehow taken on a similar mindset in his agency's pursuit of the James boys. He apparently had a willing, although silent, ally in the person of Philip H. Sheridan.[31]

6

The Hunters and the Hunted

And I looked, and behold a pale horse: and his name that sat on him was Death, and Hell followed with him.

Revelation 6:8

OUTGOING GOV. SILAS WOODSON had some few words about banditry in the state of Missouri in his final message to the General Assembly on January 6, 1875. "The prevention of crime and the arrest and punishment of violators of our criminal code, are subjects of the highest importance," he told the representatives, pointing out that "despotic governments" had large standing armies and police forces to enforce "obedience to law." But in a "free state" such matters were "dependent on popular support," although he excoriated mobs and the protection of hardened criminals by those who held "popular sympathy with them."

It was at best a homily not unlike the one the year previous. With a tone of irony, he quoted Bacon's abridgement of an Elizabethan-era English law that punished "the hundred of Gravesend for a robbery on Gads-hill." The inhabitants pleaded that there were too many robberies, and that they would "be undone" if forced to answer for all of them. Woodson darkly hinted at a similar law for Missouri, although this smacked of the old Unionist levy against Southern sympathizers during the war. Former Confederates would have none of this, and many former Unionists probably didn't care to see a return to those days either.

133

Woodson appealed for the organization and funding of a "well organized militia," which he felt was "the chief reliance of all republican and
free governments." Those who recalled the depredations of the old Missouri State Militia and the EMM during the war must have rolled their eyes
at this statement. Woodson argued that there was no force to stop mobs
from going on the rampage in central Missouri.

Although not mentioned specifically, it was generally known that the
militia unit that had been sent to Cass County in 1872 had been turned
back by county lawmen who said their arrival would set off more bloodshed. Mobs could burn Saint Louis, and large outlaw gangs sweep into the
state from Indian Territory, Woodson contended.

His warning fell on deaf ears, as militia units might also be used to force
counties into railroad bond payments, which some were now balking at,
since county judges were now elected on the premise, or the threat, that
they avoid taxation and payment. The General Assembly knew the way the
local electoral winds were blowing too. And so went yet another governor
who had to cope with well-publicized and highly theatrical outlawry.[1]

Incoming governor Charles Hardin had campaigned that he was a "safe
man with an iron will." During the election, one Missouri newspaper had
interpreted that he was "'safe,' because there was no danger of extricating
himself once the robbers encircle him. 'With an iron will' because it
seemed to be his will to support the roads of iron rail." Hardin would soon
have his turn in the hot seat.[2]

On January 12 the new governor gave his inaugural address, stating that
lawmen and citizens should cooperate to enforce the law. There was no
mention of a militia panacea. "No compromise should be made with or
quarter given to crime," Hardin told his audience. "Officers should be held
to strict accountability for failure to arrest offenders. . . . Uncertainty and
feeble execution of the laws not only promote crime, but give excuse to the
formation of mobs. . . . Whilst you ought to provide a reasonable secret service fund . . . in the case of unusual acts of brigandage and outlawry, yet I
would attach more value to the vigorous cooperation of officers and citizens
for the general repression of crime, than to the limited benefits that may
result from the employment of such a fund," the new governor declared.
The "limited benefits" Hardin alluded to were about to turn into liabilities.[3]

AROUND 7:30 P.M. on Monday, January 25, 1875, a train approached the
town of Kearney on the Hannibal and Saint Joseph Railroad line. It was
unusual in that it consisted of only an engine, a tender, and a caboose. Its

destination was strange as well, a wooded area two miles north of town, out in the middle of nowhere. When the train stopped, a party of men, variously estimated at between four and eight in number, left the caboose and headed south through the newly fallen snow, cutting across toward the James-Samuel farm after apparently joining other men who had brought horses.[4]

What happened next is perhaps best described first in a January 27 letter sent by Allan Pinkerton to Patrick Henry Woodward, chief special agent for the U.S. Post Office Department:

> After great precautions and being positively assured, that the James boys and other of their friends, were at home in their mother's house, near Kearney, Clay Co., Mo. Then having failed so many times, but this time every thing appeared perfectious, for we were sure they were in the house, on Monday, Jan. 25th at 5 P.M.
>
> I today send a newspaper to Mr. Jewell Postmaster General, Mr. Corchrane [Charles J. Corchrane, division superintendent of Special Agents, Mail Depredations], and yourself, containing exaggerated details of what has taken place, all of which comes through Kansas City, a bitterly conservative state.
>
> On Monday night every thing was ready. We were well supplied with Greek Fire, balls of cotton well saturated with combustible material.
>
> After getting things ready we advanced on the house, not a word was spoken, and about half past twelve mid-night we commenced firing the buildings. but judge of our dismay, when we found every window fastened on the inside with wooden boards. although so concealed by a curtain that they could not be seen from the outside. When we threw the fire balls in, they fell harmless. such is the manner in which the house is kept, it is a perfect citadel, however my men were equal to the occasion and soon battered in the windows, then flung the fire balls into the house, wild crys of dismay were heard from the inside, and soon the residents ran from the inside, which was lit up as light as day.
>
> Mrs. James, or as she is better known by her present name Mrs. Samuels, was bitter in her denunciations, and used any-thing but polite language. I had given positive orders that no harm was to be done to the women or Dr. Samuels, and no one else was there. We stopped half an hour and saw everything plainly, so the men we were in search of must have left the house after dark. I am informed by telegraph that there is great feeling in regard to this business. one thing I am certain of, that is the same house, about one year ago, poor [Joseph] Whicher, my detective, was bound and gagged, then taken to Independence, or near that place, and foully murdered.

I do not know what I will do next, I shall have to take time to consider my men in Louisiana and Texas. I shall continue for a short time, but I must say that I am considerably disheartened.

It is rather hard on me spending money continually, and then not finding them. It's too much for me, and I may probably withdraw, but I have not yet decided.

I hasten to lay the matter before you, and you will please consider it as strictly confidential.

> In haste Yours Truly,
> Allan Pinkerton[5]

The story was not quite as simple as Pinkerton explained it. Pinkerton's men had taken position around the outbuildings near the house, the barn to the northwest, and the icehouse or smokehouse to the west of the house. Using "hollow tubes shaped like a Roman candle, and filled with combustible material," the detectives first attempted to set fire to three or four places on the weatherboarded northwest side of the house, which served as the kitchen and servants quarters. The tubes probably contained Levi Short's 1863 patented solid Greek fire. However, there were thick logs underneath, which the fire only scorched before Dr. Samuel, awakened by the cries of the black cook and her children, managed to extinguish the blaze by tearing off the boards. Mrs. Samuel was aroused by then and made her way around the house, the west section being locked from the inside. Entering the door on the north side, she found "something like a bowl of fire in the middle of the floor," along with a burning quilt on the bed. She tossed the quilt outside and tried to remove the flaming fireball, some seven and one-half inches in diameter, but it was too heavy. Then her husband came in and tossed it in the fireplace with a shovel. Next there was an explosion, and a portion of the shell struck Mrs. Samuel in the right wrist, shattering the bone. Another fragment hit thirteen-year-old Archie Peyton Samuel in the midsection. Another piece reportedly struck Dr. Samuel in the head, but only stunned him. Archie later died of his injuries, and Mrs. Samuel had the lower portion of her right arm amputated.[6]

The coroner's inquest the next day found that Archie's wound, in his right side, was "inflicted by the bursting of a shell thrown in the house . . . by some unknown person or persons." Tracks in the snow led to the point where the train had stopped. Before leaving the farm, the detectives had also fired around five shots. There was at first speculation that there had been a gun battle between a bandit and the detectives, but most likely these were only parting shots to keep those in the house at a distance. Blood was found along the trail and was later determined to have been the result of a possible cut or nosebleed, not a gunshot wound.[7]

Another train from the south, identical to the one that had stopped earlier, arrived in the same general location about 2 or 3 A.M. When the Pinkerton men returned to the train, the conductor asked, "What success?"

A weary detective replied, "Don't ask us; don't say anything about it."

The train, heading east, was spotted at several locations with around eight men on board as passengers. Around 2 P.M. on January 26, it was reported to be at Ottumwa, Illinois, where the express "special" pulling the caboose was last seen, carrying men ranging in age from thirty to forty-five. A large crowd was kept at a distance as four of the men from the caboose obtained provisions. It was noted that the train was kept "fired up" all the time and sped rapidly out of the station.[8]

Some days later the *Saint Louis Republican* noted the legal ramifications of the situation. Capturing or killing one of the outlaws on the James property would have established that the Samuel family had harbored fugitives of the law, and the family would have been "without the pale of legal protection." But failing to establish that the outlaws had been harbored by the family meant "the detectives would become subject to prosecution for homicide." However, Pinkerton's earlier letter stating that it had been his intention to "burn the house down" indicated his apparent plan to mix business with revenge. But the former barrel maker had miscalculated, and now he and his men were viewed by many as murderers and arsonists.[9] It all played quite well into the hands of John Newman Edwards of the *Saint Louis Dispatch*, who rose to the occasion with one of the classic "ninety-proof" editorials of his career:

> If, as the telegraph reports this morning, Chicago detectives or any other detectives surrounded and set fire to the house of Mrs. Samuels, the mother of Jesse and Frank James, threw a hand grenade through the window and into the midst of a family of helpless and innocent children, the citizens of Clay county owe it to their self-protection and manhood to rise up and hunt the midnight cowards and assassins to their death. Such a species of warfare is worse than any yet painted of savage nature of the dastardly dogs who were hunting human flesh for hire, and who, although the men they sought were only two, even if they were at home, dared not meet them six to one and kill them in an open fight or bring them in as prisoners for a mob to hang or a fanatical public opinion to condemn and execute without trial. Men of Missouri, you who fought under Anderson, Quantrill, Todd, Poole, and the balance of the borderers and guerrillas—you who live in Clay county, and Jackson, and wherever these detectives have dared to

leave the railroad to go into the country, recall your woodcraft and give up
these scoundrels to the Henry rifle and Colt's revolver. It is not for the robberies that Pinkerton hates the James brothers. It is because like you they
were at Lawrence, Centralia, and Fort Lincoln [Baxter Springs], and upon
the Canadian, and wherever the black flag floated and men neither knew or
wanted quarter. The monstrous crime of attempting to destroy a whole
family in the heart of Missouri because two members of it have been
accused of acts believed by half the state to be false and slanderous, is something that calls for redress. To set on fire a house in which women and children are sleeping, to throw a bomb-shell into it in order that through
ignorance it may be permitted to explode amid a group of innocent boys
and girls, are things too horrible to be tolerated. Surely none of Mrs.
Samuels' neighbors were there and in the midst of the assassins who had
surrounded the house. If they were and the names of them are ever known,
the devil will help them all and save them from the vengeance of the sons.
Meanwhile we await further particulars before we can understand fully the
diabolical nature of the plot or who were engaged in it.[10]

Edwards brings up the interesting point of culpability.

On August 6, 1874, James R. "Jim" Reed, a former Clay County native
who had served under Quantrill and later turned to postwar outlawry, confessed on his deathbed that he had led the gang that robbed the train at
Gads Hill and that the James brothers and Arthur McCoy had nothing to
do with it. Reed had been shot in Texas by Deputy Sheriff John Morris.
While Reed's confession may be open to debate, it is almost never mentioned in regard to the Gads Hill affair.

The killing of Detective Joseph Whicher is another matter, however,
and the evidence here pointed very strongly in the direction of at least one
of the James boys and their confederates.[11]

Jesse James had been reported in the vicinity, perhaps even at the Samuel
house the night before the Pinkerton raid and was suspected to be lurking
somewhere nearby. On August 29 a new figure, or rather a bit of an old one,
entered the picture: the newly elected sheriff of Clay County, John S. Groom.
This was the same John Groom who had attested in an affidavit that Jesse had
purchased items from his store at Kearney on the evening before the Gallatin
robbery in which John Sheets had been killed. In his affidavit Groom had
called Jesse one of the most honest persons he had ever dealt with.

Groom was not someone to be trifled with, though. Born in Clay County
in 1828, he had served in the Mexican War as a corporal in O. P. Moss's
Company C, First Missouri Mounted Volunteers, taking part in Alexander
Doniphan's epic campaign through New Mexico and into northern Mexico

itself. During the Civil War he had sided with the South, raising a State Guard company and rising to the rank of captain. Just prior to the battle of Lexington, the company had joined Sterling Price for that engagement and the battle of Pea Ridge. Groom returned to Missouri in the summer of 1862 and took part in small battles at Independence and Lone Jack. He was wounded in the ferocious fighting during the latter engagement and barely escaped with his life. Groom tried to raise troops after his recovery then wisely decided to sit out the rest of the war in Colorado and Nebraska, engaging in mercantile pursuits there. Perhaps two wars were enough for him; he left when the conflict was starting to get extremely nasty.[12]

Groom was apparently serious about his job as sheriff, however, and on Friday afternoon, August 29, he staged his own raid on the Samuel place. A posse of forty-six men had been scouring the county ever since the raid by the Pinkertons. On Friday morning the posse split up, half going into the western portion of the county and the rest heading to the Samuel place. Groom further divided his segment into three parts on reaching the farm. His party covered the outbuildings, another under J. W. Courtney watched the house itself, and the third group under Capt. Oscar Thomason, whose horse had been shot by Jesse in 1869, entered the house to search it.

It had been rumored that an underground tunnel or hiding place existed at the house, but nothing of the sort was found. "The family seemed to be not in the least concerned during the search," by one account. However, a search of the barn turned up a very fine-blooded mare that was said to belong to Jesse. The animal was presumably confiscated. Several individuals also were taken into custody at the farm, including Ed Miller, the younger brother of Clell; George James, a cousin of the James brothers and son of the Reverend William James, who had married Jesse and Zee; Ed M. Samuel, nephew of Dr. Reuben Samuel, and William Fox, whose brother Dory was a notorious character who would later be arrested for the murder of Whicher. From her bed Mrs. Samuel told the boys, "They're just taking you down there to pump you: keep your mouths shut and don't tell anything you don't know."

The boys were eventually released, except for Fox, who had an arrest warrant pending for stealing the horse of a Dr. Scruggs, the Kearney physician who had treated Mrs. Samuel's arm and whose horse disappeared at that time. Ed Samuel had had enough of the hounding. "I am past 22 years old, I ain't married but if I get out of this I am going to be. . . . If I get out of this I am going to get the hell out of Missouri," he told a reporter shortly before his release. True to his word, he left the state, married, and settled near Clifty, Arkansas.[13]

Responding to public outrage, the Missouri legislature, after lengthy and rather rancorous partisan debate, voted to authorize further investigation of the incident at the James-Samuel farm.

Stilson Hutchins, who introduced the resolution, was the key owner of the *Saint Louis Dispatch* and later in his career founded the *Washington Post*. One of the main points at issue was the sovereignty of the state, as it was reported that prisoners had possibly been spirited out of Missouri without proper extradition proceedings, something that could create a dangerous precedent if ignored. Governor Hardin assigned the investigation to Adj. Gen. George Caleb Bingham, better known for his paintings of Early American subjects such as county elections, boatmen on the Missouri, and Daniel Boone crossing through Cumberland Gap.

Bingham reported (see Appendix D) that the inability to compel witnesses to testify under oath hampered his efforts. He also said that he tried to cooperate "with the proper authorities . . . in . . . effort to bring the perpetrators to justice," but that he had no idea who they were. Investigators found a pistol (which subsequently disappeared). It had "the marks upon it . . . which I have been credibly informed, are identically such as are known to be on the pistols of a well known band of detectives," Bingham reported, but he failed to specifically name the Pinkertons or others, at least officially.

Bingham commanded a virtually nonexistent state militia. His appointment was a matter of political patronage. He obviously knew more than he was willing to state officially, because the newspapers had already reported that the pistol in question bore the initials "P.G.G.," which purportedly stood for Pinkerton Government Guard. Bingham, however, suggested that a grand jury investigation might be appropriate in a matter such as this.[14]

Journalistic probing brought forth new information on the raid as Bingham conducted his ceremonial inquiry. First, the *Chicago Tribune* reported that "for several months Samuel Hardwicke, a man well known here and well acquainted with the country, has been making Liberty . . . his headquarters, and carrying on a cypher correspondence by telegraph with Pinkerton in Chicago, keeping him posted as to movements." It was further noted in covering one of the legislative debates that "a body of men had, by authority of a former governor [i.e., Woodson] attempted or succeeded in capturing them [the James brothers]." The *Saint Louis Republican* reported, "It will probably be established that the attacking party belonged to, or was employed by [the] Pinkerton agency, and that the raid was made under the auspices of the federal government, and with warrants for murder and highway robbery of the United States mails." Journalists were no slouches at sleuthing on the sleuths.[15]

Governor Hardin released a censored version of the Bingham report (see Appendix D). The original disappeared like the "P.G.G." revolver. He also promised "to use all the power I possess to bring the offenders to trial . . . requisitions for the return of such parties will be made as soon as developments shall establish . . . the names of the parties."[16]

The February 11 *Liberty Advance* contained an intriguing letter, cryptically signed "W.J.C." explaining the workings of the shell thrown into the house. It has been speculated by western historian Fred Egloff that this might have been sent by someone to deflect any suspicion of military involvement. As Egloff pointed out, whoever wrote the letter apparently had more than passing knowledge of incendiary devices:

> The hand grenade seemed to me to be what I call a home-made concern—not made in any regular armory—of very rough and ordinary workmanship, one half being wrought, the other half cast, and connected by an iron band, with a fuse hole to ignite it. My impression is that it was charged with "Grecian fire," and saturated with turpentine for the purpose of preventing it from being handled and thrown out of doors, thereby rendering it harmless. The fuse being set on fire would burn in causing heat to generate, the two pieces to expand and separate, let out the Grecian fire all over the house, and envelop the building in flames at once. The iron band around the instrument was too tight to give, thereby causing the explosion which was not what the attacking party expected—and they fled to the silent train that wafted them away. Being a beautiful moonlit night if they had wanted to kill any one they could have killed Dr. Samuel while he was putting out the fire.

Murder may not have been the original intent, but destruction of the house certainly was. Egloff speculated that the shell was probably an experimental hybrid of two Civil War–era designs that had been invented and patented by Alfred Berney of New Jersey and Levi Short of Philadelphia, a combination of both liquid and solid incendiary material, respectively, possibly with a bursting charge of powder. The explosion was reportedly heard two or three miles away. "Greek fire" was, however, a rather temperamental substance. It was sometimes known to simply sputter and fizzle on wooden surfaces, failing to ignite. It is probable that the explosion and fire consumed whatever was in the shell before it could do any damage to the house.[17]

Pinkerton was aware of the trouble he faced. Those involved in the raid were probably guilty, at the very least, of arson and manslaughter. A letter dated February 16, 1875, to attorney Sam Hardwicke and signed "George McQueen," found in Pinkerton's letter book (see Appendix C), mentions a desire to meet with him in Quincy, Springfield, Joliet, or Chicago—all in Illinois. "The evidence is plain and clear where I was all the time. Any of our courts, or any court in Christendom must take a truthful view of such a situation. . . . Gen. [John L.] Beveridge, the Governor of Ill. has been informed and is prepared. I rather think it would be troublesome for them to get any of the men from Illinois."[18]

"McQueen" speculated that he would be slapped with a civil damage suit by the Samuel family. "Well, if they want to try that . . . take it to a United States court and I am ready." He said he was simply waiting and saying nothing to the newspapers. He also apologized for any blame that Hardwicke might be getting for his association with the agency and said he was glad to hear "that you got along so well at the Capitol." It would appear that Hardwicke had made a trip to Jefferson City, probably lobbying certain influential politicians and perhaps even Governor Hardin or one of his assistants on Pinkerton's behalf. The agency had, after all, apparently been retained by the previous administration, and there were surely a few matters in this regard that could prove politically damaging to certain individuals if the raid received further scrutiny. In smoke-filled rooms deals could be cut, and Hardwicke had Masonic connections that probably proved valuable as well.

"McQueen" offered to send Hardwicke law books citing "rulings in such a court as will be strongly in our favor." He also mentioned that one of the men, identified only as "J.A." had "taken some money, is badly scared and says he will burrow himself, as that he won't be seen for a long time."

A professional rivalry resulted from the raid. "I rather think the Saint Louis Police are enemies of ours, as I have been informed how their chief has been talking, however he cannot hurt me or mine."

Hardwicke was told to send correspondence in cover envelopes, the outer one to a "D. Robertson" and the inner to "Mrs. Hattie Smith," at 2809 South Morgan Street, Saint Louis. In a postscript, McQueen told the attorney that he was in receipt of his most recent letter and agreed to meet him at Macomb, Illinois, if he would set the time and place.

The letter is written in the paternal tone of, and in a similar hand to Pinkerton's other letters. Very likely McQueen was an alias that the detective was using, lest this letter somehow fall into the wrong hands. The complex system of mail drops was also arranged to evade scrutiny. Obviously someone felt the agency had something to hide.[19]

Another partly legible letter (see Appendix C), dated February 26, 1875, to an unnamed individual, probably Dan Askew or another agent who had participated in the raid, discusses the revolver Bingham alluded to in his report. "The Pistol which they said they found marked 'P.G.G.' is not mine,

and never was mine. we know too much. don't be afraid, that's another game
to make you afraid, if they found any pistol it was after they had left it . . . all
this is a game of theirs, simply stating the story to see how it would effect
you." The writer, using only the initials "E.J.A." was possibly Pinkerton using
his old Civil War undercover alias, E. J. Allen. He reported that "Jack [possi-
bly Jack Ladd, the undercover agent at the Askew place] is down in La. . . .
He was sort of weak kneed and appeared to think he has been doing a great
deal of service and that his services could never be paid. but Bob told him
that was all nonsense, that what he had done was for the good of all."

The mysterious "Jack" was paid some money and put back to work. "I
think he is a bad egg, but we dare not move in the matter," the writer said.

Cole Younger was reported to have been at Delhi, Louisiana, on January 25 or 26, and there was speculation that he might have gone to Independence, Missouri, by train. The correspondent reported a letter from
"Sam," probably Hardwicke, three days earlier and said he would be meeting with him shortly and would relay what he learned. "Keep cool and let
me hear from you by St. Louis," the letter closed.[20]

There were jittery nerves aplenty in the Pinkerton ranks, and perhaps for
good reason. The March term of the Clay County Circuit Court returned a
grand jury indictment against "Robert J. King, Allan Pinkerton, Jack Ladd,
and five other persons whose names are to the Grand Jurors unknown,"
charging that they "feloniously, wilfully deliberately Premeditatedly and of
their malice aforethought, did kill and murder said Archie Samuel." Regretfully, no record of testimony is known to exist, but the list of those called as
witnesses contains some intriguing names: Oscar Thomason, Daniel and
Adeline Askew, Samuel Hardwicke, and former Gov. Silas Woodson, among
others. Dr. and Mrs. Samuel were also called.[21]

Most of the indictment was concerned with the actions of "Robert J.
King," probably Robert J. Linden, the Pinkerton agent who had picked up
the "ammunition" at the Rock Island arsenal and had charge of it. "King"
may have been an alias Linden used in the field, or it may have been a "mistake" by one of several witnesses who had something to lose. Neither Sam
Hardwicke nor Dan Askew was implicated in the indictment, although a
letter reportedly exists from Jesse James to his stepfather arguing that Hardwicke should be indicted as well. Hardwicke, who claimed to represent the
Pinkertons in only a legal capacity, probably used the argument of attorney-
client privilege to bypass incriminating testimony on his part. Despite his
earlier public pledge to extradite, Governor Hardin apparently chose to look
the other way after the indictment, and requisitions to the governor of Illinois for Pinkerton and his men were apparently never made.[22]

At the same time as the grand jury probe and indictment, a move was under way in the Missouri legislature to offer a limited amnesty (see Appendix E) to the James and Younger brothers for any alleged crimes committed during the Civil War. It was a token gesture at best. For the James brothers, at least, it would have meant very little, because they apparently had no charges pending from this period. The media played up the offer anyway. On February 22, 1875, a requisition was made by the governor of Kansas to Governor Hardin for the arrest of Jesse James, charged with "robbery in the first degree" for the Muncie railroad heist. Hardin obligingly issued a warrant for Jesse's arrest two days later, on January 24. This was on top of other pending warrants dating back to 1869. It was not an unlikely prospect that lawmen would have to stand in line to get at the James boys, even if they came home.

On March 20 the amnesty bill, which required a two-thirds majority, was defeated in the Missouri legislature with fifty-eight voting for and thirty-nine against. Oddly enough, the defeat of the amnesty bill only served to fuel the legend of the James brothers' being persecuted for their Civil War guerrilla activities. Had the bill passed, it probably would have deflated the myth as the James brothers failed to take advantage of its provisions. Meanwhile, yet another bloody episode was in the making.[23]

⚜

ALMOST A week later, on March 26, "three detectives, supposed to be of Pinkerton's gang," arrived at Carrollton, Missouri, with an arrest order for gang member Clell Miller in connection with the Muncie robbery. Sheriff John Clinkscales accompanied the detectives to the farm of Sharpe Whitsett, six miles west of town, where Miller was allegedly holed up. The sheriff approached Whitsett at his house and asked if Miller, alias Hines, was there. Learning that he was, Clinkscales tried to arrest him. When Miller refused to budge from the house, the detectives threatened to burn the place down. Clinkscales went back to the house to try to reason with Miller, but the outlaw took him hostage and escaped. Whitsett was reportedly unaware of any pending charges, or so he said. Miller was reportedly an uncle of Whitsett's wife.

The *Carrollton Journal* commented later:

> These Pinkerton men were ready for arson. They had determined on going out, it seems, if they would not get the accused out of the house to fire it and burn the whole family out! It strikes us that this is a bold move for men who profess to act under law and for the ends of jus-

tice. But there is no doubt upon the point. They intended to fire Mr.
Whitsett's house and burn out his family, in order to capture a prisoner
and get a reward. Of course they meant to pay for the house. Still, that
renders the act no less arsonous. If these Pinkerton Volunteer officers of
the law purpose to practice the hand grenade and torch, it is about time
that the Missouri homes were fortified against their appearance in the
state with rope guards.[24]

No doubt word reached the James boys about the other threatened
burning. The *Saint Louis Republican* ran the story on April 8. Four days later,
about eight o'clock on the evening of Monday, April 12, Dan Askew, a
neighbor of the Samuel family, started to fetch some water at a spring on his
property. Askew was the erstwhile employer of "field hand" Jack Ladd, the
Pinkerton agent who had been on the stakeout for the James boys and one
of the men charged in the murder indictment. The following story was
passed down to John Nicholson, grandson of Sarah (Sallie) Samuel Nicholson, the James brothers' half sister:

> They [the James brothers visiting their family] heard old Dan Askew
> over there whistling. He always whistled, so he said, while getting a bucket
> of water. So they walked over there and told him this deal about notifying
> the Pinkertons and everything and he tried to deny it. And he said he could
> prove it if they'd go in the house where these women was. Frank knew that
> if he got in the house . . . he would talk him out of shooting, but he didn't
> go in the house and told him to set his bucket down and they killed him
> right there. I heard my grandad [William Nicholson, husband of Sarah
> Samuel] say that Frank was the cold-bloodedest one of the two. If he said he
> was going to kill ya, he would kill you, but you could talk Jesse out of it.[25]

Daniel Askew had been shot three times in the head. Shortly afterward
another neighbor, Henry Sears, was called to his door and was told by one
of the men outside, "We have killed Dan Askew tonight, and if anyone
wishes to know who did it say the detectives did it. Tell his friends to go
and bury the damned son of a bitch tomorrow. Will you do it?"[26]
Only a few die-hard James adherents bought the story Sears was told to
spread, and public opinion began to swing against the James brothers. For
more than 117 years a debate has raged as to whether Askew was indeed
working with the Pinkertons. At the time he was slain some were openly
speculating that the raid on the James-Samuel farm was actually the work of
Clay County vigilantes and that the Pinkertons had nothing to do with it.
(Apparently more than one side could play the disinformation game.) The

killing of Dan Askew probably had roots going all the way back to the Civil War, however. According to one newspaper account, Askew was "an old and respected citizen of Clay County . . . a Union man. . . . During the war he was in the state militia and ever since has been a Radical in politics." The Pinkerton incident may simply have been the last straw in a chain of events going as far back as the hanging of Dr. Samuel in 1863.[27]

≈≈≈

ON APRIL 16, 1875, Allan Pinkerton sent a letter to Dr. J. C. Bernard of Haynesville in Clinton County, Missouri:

> I have heard of the murder of Daniel Askew. He was an honest man; God help his family. The blow must have been tremendous. I would like to speak to his wife, but I cannot; a reign of terror prevails all through Clay County at the present time. Could I ask a favor of you, to go and see Mrs. Askew, and say to her that I commiserate with her in her deep and grave affliction. Say to her that he did no more than right [and?] that will be shown when the years have rolled away. . . . He was an enemy to murderers, thieves and assassins.[28]

Dr. Bernard apparently delivered the message indirectly. On May 11, Pinkerton somehow managed to get a letter directly to Adeline Askew:

> I have not seen you, but yet I cannot help calling you a friend, and one of those dear friends, whom, one can never have but once in life.
> I have received your letter of the 7th inst. and was glad indeed to see it. Oh, how my heart bled, as I read in Dr. Bernard's letter to me, of the great thoughtfulness of a woman, and when you first heard the shot which told of your husband's death, you sent your daughters out of the room and destroyed the letters of mine, it showed careful forethought when it occurred to you that none other should know what your husband held in life, in death the proof died with him. . . .
> Oh! how I've thought over Daniel Askew's murder, and hope the time will come when both you and I shall seek the same revenge, my own men have been slaughtered, as you know, both in Clay Co. and Monegau [Monegaw] Springs; those men the Younger's and James' are red with my men's blood. I want to impress upon all the men in my company that they shall be avenged.

Often maudlin and redundant, the letter (see Appendix C) thanks Adeline Askew for her kindness to "Rob" (probably Robert J. Linden) and to "Sam" (probably Hardwicke). "I think H[ardwicke?]. shall come out all right in the end, and has to be pretty quiet for a little time yet. H. speaks to me of the noble traits that your husband had." Pinkerton asked Mrs. Askew to "look out for yourself, and the sake of your children." He also mentioned that he wanted to purchase a tombstone for her husband. "I know what will suit a man who died a martyr . . . have it put in the graveyard . . . and I shall go there and mix my tears in the ground in which your martyred husband lies."[29]

Shortly after the Askew killing, Sam Hardwicke moved to Saint Paul, Minnesota, but his role in the James story was far from over, because he was reportedly being pressured to testify before the Clay County grand jury about the Pinkerton involvement. In an effort to stymie any attempt to extradite himself and his men to face charges in Missouri, Pinkerton wrote a letter to Governor Beveridge of Illinois (see Appendix C). Robert J. Linden, the man who probably tossed the bomb into the Samuel farmhouse, was transferred east to work on the Molly Maguire case in the Pennsylvania coal fields. He was inducted as a captain in the controversial Coal and Iron Police and had a major role in breaking up the group, which was allegedly terrorizing the coal fields. An awkward moment came during the trial of several of the "Mollies" in August 1876, when a defense attorney asked Linden if he was somehow involved in the raid on the Samuel place. The detective dodged the question, but his heart must have skipped a beat.[30]

Allan Pinkerton would never catch up with the James brothers. The murder case against him and others never came to trial. According to Missouri law, prosecutors were allowed only two continuances or postponements of trial. On the third motion the defendant was entitled to an acquittal without trial. Such occurred on September 13, 1877, when the case against Pinkerton came to the bar.[31]

The Hannibal and Saint Joseph Railroad, which carried the detectives on the raid, would have seemed a likely target for the gang later on. Realizing this vulnerability, someone in the administrative offices had the shrewd forethought to give Mrs. Samuel a free lifetime pass for herself and family members. For decades Zerelda would take both real and "adopted" relations on numerous train excursions to Kansas City. The line was never molested by the James gang.[32]

7

The Huntington Raid

What else could Jesse James have done? . . . He could not be
frightened out from his native county; he could neither be
intimidated or robbed.

John Newman Edwards, Noted Guerrillas (1877)

T HE EDITORIAL OUTPOURING FOLLOWING the slaying of Daniel Askew was
a predictable babel. One Chicago newspaper, obviously either not on
good terms with the Pinkertons or seeking controversy, speculated that
the detectives had perhaps killed Askew after he had threatened to expose
them (not likely, in view of the revelation of John Nicholson and the
Pinkerton correspondence). The Republican press in Missouri went about
its usual attacks on the Democratic Party and its journalistic following. The
Saint Louis Republican called the situation in Clay County "disgraceful and
intolerable." The county was home and rendezvous of the James brothers, it
said, "and a free fighting ground for them and their enemies."

There was also the usual attack on local law enforcement: "The bandits
come and go through Clay and Jackson counties at their pleasure." Sheriff
John S. Groom exasperatedly wrote Governor Hardin that Clay County
was in a state of terror unseen since the war and that the James brothers
and their friends had threatened others. Groom felt that Hardin should
publicly assure the James brothers of a fair trial if they surrendered and offer
a bounty for them, "dead or alive," if they didn't. Even the Samuel family,

149

tired of the situation and, in the midst of a grasshopper plague, put the farm up for sale. But there were no takers for this controversial piece of real estate, and the idea was eventually dropped.[1]

The press harangue began to wane with the revelation in early May of the notorious "Whiskey Ring" in Saint Louis, a web of corruption involving Treasury Department officials and lower-level employees (all Republican political appointees), distillers, and even Orville Babcock, the secretary to President U. S. Grant. In exchange for his assistance in censoring the incoming mail, keeping the president in the dark, and warning the ring of impending Treasury inspections, the presidential secretary received "gifts" ranging from thousands of dollars tucked in boxes of cigars to the services of a Saint Louis prostitute known as "Sylph." The James-Younger gang looked penny-ante in comparison to the nationwide whiskey ring that extended over several states and cost the U.S. Treasury around two-thirds of its liquor tax revenues in Saint Louis alone.[2]

Sometime during the first month or two of 1875, Jesse and his now pregnant wife, Zee, moved to Nashville, Tennessee. The city had the advantages of being safely out of the area of major Pinkerton investigations, was only about forty miles south of Uncle George Hite's place (west of Adairville, Kentucky), and had good medical facilities. Furthermore, it was a relatively large city, a place where one could blend into the crowd easily. Here Jesse James first took on the alias of John Davis (Dave) Howard, with Zee going by the name Josie. The Howards settled into a small wooden frame house at 606 Boscobel Street in what was then the independent city of Edgefield, north of the Cumberland River from Nashville proper. According to a later account by Zee, the proceeds from the Muncie robbery paid the expenses, just as the Hot Springs and/or Gads Hill affair had paid for their honeymoon in Sherman, Texas, the year before. Zee had lived with relatives in the Kansas City area during the time of the Muncie affair and even perhaps up until the time of the Pinkerton raid. It was her presence that had served as a red flag for detectives staking the area, in fact. In the immediate Nashville and Edgefield areas there were no family ties to lure the detectives, and it would prove to be a perfect hideout.[3]

"Mr. Howard" claimed to be a wheat speculator and was looked on as a "quiet, unassuming man" by his neighbors. But they noticed odd things as well. Howard was away from home for weeks at a time, and while away he would get John Vertrees, the young son of his wife's physician, Dr. W. M. Vertrees, to stay at the house. John was paid for his trouble. Josie Howard would be told by her husband when he planned to return, and if for some reason he failed to show up by that date she would "weep bitterly," John

Vertrees recalled. He would hear the neighbors talk about a diamond necklace worth fifteen hundred dollars that Mrs. Howard's uncle had allegedly bought for her in Illinois at an estate sale. The young man would also recall the rolls of money Howard would deliver to his wife on his return, along with other valuables. Every time he left Howard would fire the servant he'd previously hired for his wife and get a new one. Mrs. Howard kept a brace of fine pistols in the house, commenting frequently that if anyone came to molest her or her family she intended to use them. It was a knee-jerk comment after the Pinkerton raid on the James-Samuel farm but not what one would have expected from the wife of an ordinary commodity speculator off on lawful business.[4]

Jesse was probably up to other things at this time, and it's entirely possible that he was involved in the Askew killing in Missouri at the time of his residence in Tennessee. He also appears to have been stalking the Pinkertons for a while during this time. "He went to Chicago once to kill Allan Pinkerton," recalled cousin George Hite, "and staid there four months, but never had a chance to do it like he wanted to. . . . He said he could have killed the younger one [William or Robert], but didn't care to do it. 'I wanted him to know who did it,' he [Jesse] said; 'it would do me no good if I couldn't tell him about it before he died. I had a dozen chances to shoot him when he didn't know it. I wanted to give him a fair chance, but the opportunity never came.'" Jesse finally gave up and left Chicago but would often say, "I know God will some day deliver Allan Pinkerton into my hands."[5]

Even if Jesse couldn't duel with one of the Pinkertons in the flesh there was always the newspaper medium. It was in the Nashville press, over the summer of 1875, that the war of words would come to a boiling point. The first shot was fired in a letter by Jesse that was published in the July 11 *Nashville Republican Banner*. Allegedly sent from Raytown, in Jackson County, Missouri, just south of Independence, it was without the grammatical corrections and flourishes that accompanied the earlier letters and hinted of the editorial handiwork of John Newman Edwards.

There had been reports in the press that the James and Younger brothers had been seen on the Bardstown Road near Louisville, as well as in Taylor and Spencer Counties in Kentucky. Ostensibly, Jesse James was writing to deny this:

> I would treat those reports with silent contempt but I, have many friends in Ky. and Nashville that I wish to know are falce. . . . I have never been out of Missouri since the Amnesty bill was introduced into the Mo. Legislatur . . . I am in constant communication. with Gov Hardin [and] Sheriff Groom . . . & several other honorable county and State Officials, and they are hundreds of people in Mo. who will swear I have no. been in Ky, and it is probily

very important for the Officials of Ky to be very vigilant. if a robbery were committed in Ky. to day Detective Blyths of, Louisville, would telegraph all over that the James & Younger did it . . . I am satisfied some of the informers is conserned in many robberys charged to the James & Youngers [.] for 10 years the Radical papers . . . have charged nearly every darring robbery in America to the James and Youngers [.] it is enough persecution in the northern papers to persecute us without the papers in the South, persecuting us, the land we fought for four years to save from northern tyranny, to be persecuted by papers claiming to be Democratic, is against reason. the people of the south have heard only one side of the report.

Jesse repeated his version of the detective raid story: "Nine Chicago assassins and Sherman bummers led by Billie Pinkerton Jr. crep up to my mothers house and hurled a misle of war (a 32 pound shell) in a room among a family of innocent women and cheldren." He also denied connection to the Russellville robbery for both Frank and himself and promised to write more later. "I will close by sending my kindest regards to old Dr. Eve and many thanks to him for his kindness to me when I was wounded and under his care." He added in a P.S., "I have never had an opportunity of receiving an education, which you will see by my composition." He asked that a copy of the newspaper be sent to his mother in Clay County.[6]

Almost three weeks later, on July 28, there was a response from William Pinkerton, son of Allan, in the same paper, sent from New York and dated July 24:

> My attention has been called to an article in the Chicago Tribune, clipped from the *Banner,* in which Jesse James says that I led eight men who hurled a 32 pound shell into his mothers house . . . Personally I do not think anything a murderer and thief, like Jesse James, says worth replying to, but his statement is made in such unqualified terms that, to set myself right before the public, I concluded to write a brief card.
>
> On the very day he says I led the party who stormed his mother's house I was in Chicago attending the session of the Criminal Court as a witness. . . . The fact is I have not been in Clay County, Missouri, for four years, and there is about as much truth in the last statement of Jesse James as there was in any other which has emanated from him or any member of his cut-throat gang.[7]

On August 8 the *Banner* published two more James letters. The first, allegedly written in Clay County, was dated August 4. Marked as "Confidential" to the editor, it bore the same poor grammar as the earlier note: "They is no doubt about Pinkerton's force committing the crime & it is the duty of the press to denounce him." Jesse commented that there was a further move afoot to push an amnesty bill in the winter session of the Missouri legislature, and he further excoriated Pinkerton, who "has got his best men killed by him sending them after us."

The other letter, published in the same issue, was supposedly written from Kansas City on the same date. It called Pinkerton's note "a pack of falsehoods." As with William Pinkerton, he was condescending to write, "altho I consider it the greatest stains ever thrown on my character to notice an article written by him." He publicly doubted Billy Pinkerton's assertion that he was in court, although it was probably the case. Then Jesse again resorted to the tactic of "waving the bloody shirt," so popular in both North and South during the Reconstruction era, making further allusions to Chicago being the home of "Sherman bummers" who had burned and looted their way across Georgia and South Carolina during the march to the sea ten years before. He also referred to Chicago as the home of Philip H. Sheridan. (If he had only known of the general's actual role in obtaining incendiary material for the raid, which he again described!) Pinkerton "better never dare to show his Scottish face again in western Mo. again and let me know he is here, or he will meet the fate of his comrades, Capt. Lull & Wicher. . . . Pinkerton, I hope and pray that our Heavenly father may deliver you into my hands." Jesse's letter is rambling, damning the Pinkertons, all but confessing the murder of Whicher (an amazing action for someone seeking amnesty), and playing on lingering sympathy for the Confederacy. It was as if Jesse's mind had somehow slipped into reverse, and he was still fighting the war. Perhaps he felt that he was.[8]

The letters apparently had been forwarded to Jesse's sister-in-law and cousin in Kansas City, Nannie McBride, and mailed from that point. A private letter from Jesse to "My Dear Friend," that was apparently written in late May 1875 but was not published until 1882, mentions letters being received and forwarded. "You say you was greatly surprised, you supposed I was in Texas or Mexico. I am generaly where people least expect me to be." Jesse expressed concern that he would be unable to afford his defense in case he surrendered for trial, "and besides, a requisition would be issued for me from Iowa and how long do you suppose I would be spared a MOB in that radical State." Jesse tried to pin the blame for the Muncie robbery on Clell Miller, Tom and "Bud" McDaniel, Sol Reed, and a fellow called "Jack Keene" (who also gave his name as Thomas J. Webb). He warned of an impending robbery, as yet uncertain, claiming that Miller, Tom McDaniel, "Keene," and perhaps Reed would be involved. Jesse claimed to have penetrated the Pinkerton detective force, allegedly having men "who keep me fully posted." This may have been in hopes that word would somehow leak to Pinkerton and make him more suspicious of his own men and thus defeat his own purpose. "Pinkerton is suspicious of every one."

Jesse wrote to his "friend," who may have been Sheriff Groom of Clay County, "If you believe me guilty I honor you for hunting me. It is your duty to put down crime, but I solemnly assure you that Clay Co. is [in] no danger from the James boys." Jesse claimed that if the men he named were caught then the robberies in Missouri would cease, and he gave directions as to where the individuals might be found. He also mentioned being in contact with Governor Hardin, although no correspondence between Jesse and the governor is known to exist, at least in his official papers. The whole business apparently was some sort of ploy, with Miller, McDaniel, Webb-Keene, and perhaps Reed, being set up as expendable.[9]

THOMAS J. WEBB was reportedly something of a drifter, and his drifting had taken him across Kentucky and West Virginia; he was allegedly a native of Pike County, Illinois. Webb, who used the alias of Jack Keene or Rogers, may actually have been Sol Reed's brother-in-law (possibly named Matt Brock), whose family lived in Clay County. By some accounts the twenty-six-year-old Webb met Cole Younger in Cincinnati or somewhere else in Ohio. Younger and Webb were joined by Tom McDaniel, brother of the late Bud McDaniel, and probably by Frank James (although Frank later claimed it was Clell Miller) before heading to West Virginia by rail to scout possible robbery sites.

They had first planned to rob a train on either the Baltimore and Ohio or the Chesapeake and Ohio, but after scouting it decided there appeared to be little potential money in it. A bank at Wheeling was the next possibility, but the getaway would be difficult. The bank at Grafton didn't have much money, and the Parkersburg bank had the same escape problem as the one at Wheeling. At Parkersburg the gang purchased horses and rode to Charleston, the state capital, but banks there were not suitable either. Then they came to the town of Huntington.[10]

Huntington had perhaps more going for it than simply location. The town was named for Collis P. Huntington, a railroad "robber baron" who was one of the "big four" partners of the Central Pacific Railroad, which was constructed east from California to join the Union Pacific in 1869 as the first transcontinental railroad. In that year Huntington, operating out of New York as eastern agent of the Central Pacific, had personally acquired the ailing Chesapeake and Ohio. His idea was to build a line from the Atlantic Ocean to the Ohio River, and to this end he founded both Newport News, Virginia, and Huntington. A scant five years previous, the site of Huntington had been five thousand acres of farmland along the Ohio. Huntington's brother-in-law, Delos W. Emmons, had acted as his personal agent, buying the land and, with help of survey and construction crews, laying out and building the rail yards. The excess land was transferred to the Central Land Company, owned by Huntington and managed by Emmons, and laid out in town lots.

In 1871 Huntington received its town charter and post office, and in the next year there was an influx of emigrants to the area from New York and New England. The town was hit hard during the Panic of 1873, and for nearly six months during the worst of the crisis, workers on the Chesapeake and Ohio were paid in railroad script in lieu of money. In 1872 the Bank of Huntington was chartered with Delos Emmons on its board of directors. Its closest competitors were located in the Ohio towns of Ironton and Gallipolis, and it was said to be "one of the most substantial banking concerns in the Ohio valley." In all probability the Central Land Company and the Chesapeake and Ohio had money on deposit there.[11]

Collis P. Huntington himself would have been an inviting target to rob, if only indirectly. A native of Connecticut, he had followed the gold rush to California, where he made a small fortune selling supplies to the miners for exorbitant prices. Huntington was said to have visited the town named for him occasionally. Those who knew him could have described him as profane, cynical, and vindictive, with a touch of dishonesty thrown in. Over the years he spent a good amount of time in Washington lobbying (and perhaps bribing) senators and congressmen to do his bidding and to vote his way on bills affecting the railroad business, notably against the funding of rival railroad construction and postponing, or even forgiving, the repayment of government loans for the construction of the transcontinental railroad.

It was suspected that Huntington and others of the "big four" had siphoned off funds of the Construction and Finance Company in an operation similar to the infamous Credit Mobilier. In the Central Pacific case, the accounting books for the construction work were mysteriously destroyed. Years later author Ambrose Bierce would coin the term "railrogue" to describe Huntington and his Central Pacific colleagues.

From newspaper accounts circa 1873, Cole Younger was probably familiar with Collis Huntington's phenomenal memory loss before congressional investigators. All this aside, it was said that, during a scout of the area preceding their arrival in town, the gang had learned of an Adams Express package containing one hundred thousand dollars, which reportedly was to arrive around September 3 or 4.[12]

The gang arrived sometime around September 3, greeted by Father Quirk of Saint Joseph's Catholic Church, who thought they had arrived to take part in a Methodist conference. Father Quirk, by one account, suggested that the men seek lodging in the home of Isaac Crump some distance east of town. Another account has them directed to the home of Rev. Calvin Reese, a Baptist minister, who directed them to Crump, his neighbor. Two of the men, probably Cole Younger and Frank James, found lodging with Crump. One of the men obtained a room at the Huntington House, registering as J. C. Johnson from Tennessee. The fourth man stayed at an unknown location. They gathered at the Crump place on Saturday, and by one account, the two other men were allowed to room there also. On Sunday the new guests reportedly spent the day reading the Bible (obviously not the Ten Commandments!) and were presumed by the Crumps to be very pious men.

On Monday, September 6, at the magic hour of 2 P.M. (bank jobs almost always occurred at 2 P.M.), the four bandits rode into Huntington and tied their horses near a local blacksmith shop at Tenth Street and Fourth Avenue, with one man left to watch them. The three remaining bandits proceeded to Laidley and Johnson's Grocery, near the bank, and procured a grain bag. Two men, identified later as Tom Webb and Younger, went into the Bank of Huntington, then located at 1208 Third Avenue, while the other man remained at the grocery store across the street.

Webb leaped over the counter, and Younger followed him through an opening in the counter. Robert T. Oney, the cashier, found himself staring at the muzzles of at least two revolvers, after having made an ineffectual attempt to grab a nearby revolver in the bank. Oney was ordered to open the safe, and he replied that it was open. He was then ordered, guns at his forehead, to open the cash drawer inside. Oney stalled for ten minutes, but the men threatened to shoot him, claiming to be former members of Mosby's partisan rangers during the war. Oney pulled out two packages of money, but the bandits suspected something was wrong, and he soon pulled out a third. In all, some $9,000 in cash and a $5,000 certificate of deposit were taken from the safe along with around $1,500 from the bank counter.

The robbers were chagrined to learn that the Adams Express delivery they had heard about had been shipped ahead to Cincinnati prior to their arrival. They forced the cashier to show them the express receipt to prove what he'd said. Oney was asked if he had any deposits in the bank; he said no, but on examining the books they noticed that he had deposited $7.50. "We don't want this little scrape to cost you anything," they told him.

During the heist, a black bank messenger named Jim returned to the bank from the post office and was taken prisoner. The two bank employees

then were marched toward the blacksmith shop and the horses. The fourth
bandit emerged from the grocery store, where he had been entertaining the
owner, or one of the employees, since he'd seen his two comrades vault
over the bank counter. The man told the grocer that the "men in the bank
were going to take what change there was there, and that if he understood
to raise an alarm or escape, they would kill him." He also told the grocer
that he had "a real hankerin' for one of your cigars." He paid for it with a
five-dollar bill and nonchalantly talked with him about the weather until
the others came out of the bank.[13]

As they started to ride away, Oney yelled to bank president John H.
Russel, just returning from lunch, that the bank had been robbed. Soon a
posse of at least a dozen men, including Russel, Emmons (Huntington's
brother-in-law), and Sheriff D. I. Smith, was in pursuit. They followed the
outlaws out of town and to the south down Wayne and McCoy Roads toward
Hodge. The bandits tossed aside a thirty-two-dollar bag of nickels and the
five-thousand-dollar certificate of deposit, hoping to slow the pursuit.

Another posse of around fifteen men headed out of Barboursville under
George F. Miller, executive vice president of the bank and a former Confederate cavalryman. This second posse pushed at least as far as West Liberty,

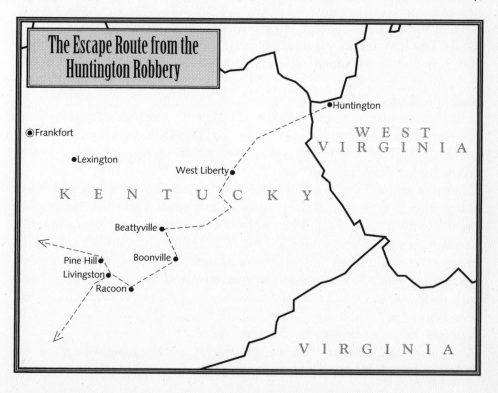

The Escape Route from the Huntington Robbery

Kentucky, four days after the holdup. The word was telegraphed across neighboring counties in West Virginia and Kentucky, and soon the man-hunt was on in force.

The bandits reportedly crossed the Big Sandy River into Kentucky at Bear's Creek, traveling through Elliott County, then Hazel Green in Morgan County, to Beattiesville in Lee County. They continued through Clay and Jackson Counties and into Laurel County, where speculation ran that they were heading for Livingston and the railroad. On September 10 in Owsley County, the bandits had a run-in with a fifteen-man posse headed by Capt. Harrison Litteral of Carter County, Kentucky, and armed with shot-guns and Spencer rifles. If Frank James was indeed there, the experience must have brought back not-so-fond memories of the last months of the war. Litteral was, in fact, a veteran guerrilla chaser. Around eighty shots were fired at the bandits, who returned fire before taking to the brush. That evening the gang reentered Lee County and stole fresh horses.

The outlaws then fled through Owsley and cut through southern Jack-son County, where they had a short gun battle with Deputy Sheriff Bowling and his posse, who crept up on them as the bandits were feeding their horses that morning. Again, the gang took to the brush, leaving their horses behind. Eventually they again stole fresh mounts and made for the town of Raccoon, in Laurel County, where they were fired on by a band of locals. The bandits hit the Rockcastle River and began to follow it north-east, into Rockcastle County. Bowling had a hunch that the robbers might make Livingston, where they could hop a freight of the Louisville and Nashville Railroad.[14]

Just five miles up the railroad, near Pine Hill, Kentucky, lived William R. Dillon, his wife, and his brother James. The Dillons, who were in the coal business, had heard reports that the bandits were in the area and were on the lookout for strangers.

About midnight on September 14–15 they saw four men approach their house. Two disappeared off the road about fifty yards from the house, arous-ing the Dillons' suspicions. The brothers were wearing revolvers when the two men in sight came up to the door. "Gentlemen, you are up rather late tonight," remarked one of the Dillons. There was no reply, and a similar remark was made. The strangers opened fire, and the brothers shot back with their pistols. One of the bandits was hit by a shot from William Dillon's revolver, crying "Oh, Lordy!" He ran about two hundred yards before he fell, crying for help. Meanwhile his companion fled.

One of the Dillon brothers went to the back of the house where a noise had been heard. He soon had emptied his revolver at the other two men, driving them off. The Dillons locked themselves in the house until morning. Then, venturing out to a nearby cornfield, they found the injured robber, a bullet wound in his chest. He was carried to the house and later identified as Tom McDaniel.

Mrs. Dillon told him that his wound was fatal and that if he had anything to say to his friends he should say it. "I don't care a damn whether I die or not; I won't tell anything," he answered.

McDaniel was taken to the home of a man named Woodson and examined by physicians. He allegedly asked, "Did they get Bud, my partner?"

Cole Younger was called Bud, and it is probable that he was the other man at the door. As fate would have it, William Dillon was, by one account, a former member of Bridgewater's Scouts who had given Quantrill such a drubbing ten years before.

The three remaining bandits were later seen by a watchman at a coal mine about three miles from the Dillon house, but the men disappeared after questioning him about any guns he might have.

McDaniel was found to have only seventeen dollars in fractional currency, maps of Kentucky and Tennessee, a compass, three photos, and two letters to "dear brother" from "Anna."

Cashier Oney soon arrived by train and identified the man as one of the robbers before McDaniel died on Sunday morning, September 20. That afternoon three men came to view the body. It was at first reported that these men were the robbers, but a later account said they were simply curious citizens. The bandits, who had been initially pursued by a posse of around sixty men, had vanished.

There was much speculation about the identity of the fatally wounded robber. Some press accounts claimed it was Cole Younger, and others claimed it was Jesse James. McDaniel had told those attending him that his name was Hutchinson, and on another occasion he said he was Charley Chance.

On September 25 a letter was published in the *Nashville Daily American*, reportedly from Jesse James. It was dated September 21 and came from Saint Louis. Curiously, the grammar and spelling of this letter were much improved over that of the earlier *Banner* letters, but of course Saint Louis was where Edwards worked on the *Dispatch*. The letter castigated Detective Delos T. Bligh, "the incompetent detective of Louisville." The letter writer commented that he was glad that the captured man was neither one of the James or Younger brothers: "Every bold robbery in the world is laid on us . . . and when it is seen . . . that other people are robbing banks, we may get fair play in the newspapers. In a few days it will be seen how the James and Youngers have been lied on by such men as Pinkerton and Bligh. . . . I think the public will justify me in denouncing Bligh, and I now do, as an unnecessary liar, a scoundrel and a poltroon."[15]

DELOS THURMAN BLIGH, better known as Yankee Bligh, was born in Franklin, New York, on March 19, 1823. His family later moved to Meadville, Pennsylvania, where Bligh learned the bricklaying trade. In 1842, at the age of nineteen, he headed west, down the Ohio, to seek his fortune as a fur trapper. At Louisville the boat was delayed due to low water and Bligh obtained work as a hod carrier and later as a bricklayer in the construction of the Louisville Theater. He eventually became night watchman there. During the Mexican War, Bligh served with the Louisville Legion and was wounded in service with Zachary Taylor's army in northern Mexico. He returned to Louisville and by 1858 was a member of the city's "day watch," a forerunner of the Louisville police. When a formal police force was established in 1861, Bligh became one of its first members.

Like Allan Pinkerton, Bligh specialized in investigating con artists and forgers, and he bagged a number of them during his early years on the force. One was the Spanish counterfeiter La Trenga, who had spread hundreds of thousands of bogus dollars; another was a crooked gambler named Devol. Bligh had first encountered the Missouri outlaws in 1868 in the Russellville bank robbery, where he was responsible for the capture and incarceration of George Shepherd. Shepherd had been kept in the Nashville, Tennessee, jail for security reasons prior to his trial in Russellville. When the time came to remove him, Bligh and his assistant, John Gallagher, had accompanied the Logan County sheriff. Word was out that a rescue might be attempted, and Shepherd's "brother," probably cousin Oll Shepherd, was seen in Nashville with some suspicious characters. Bligh and the sheriff took George Shepherd to the Louisville and Nashville Station off Broadway (across from the later Union Station) while Gallagher kept an eye on the "brother." Longinotti's Saloon at the corner of Ninth and Broadway was near the depot, and it was here that Gallagher found Shepherd's relative accompanied by two men. Gallagher, with the help of Nashville officer Enlow, arrested the two accomplices, who gave their names as Charles E. Cahill and Richard Haddocks. In their horses' saddlebags were five Navy revolvers. The "brother" escaped down Broadway and was not seen in the city again.

In 1870 Bligh was made chief of detectives in Louisville, and three years later he established an international reputation after arresting J. M. McDonald, a British subject wanted in a three-million-dollar forgery case on the

Robert Sallee James (*left*) was a pioneer minister and the father of Frank and Jesse James. He left the family in Missouri for the gold fields of California, allegedly to minister to the miners and do a little mining himself. Others say that he needed the time away from his temperamental wife, Zerelda. He never saw his family again, dying of a fever in August 1850 in Placerville, California. Many contended that Frank bore a strong resemblance to his father.

This painting of Jesse James (*right*) is based on a July 10, 1864, photograph, which was taken during a guerrilla raid on Platte City, Missouri. Jesse wears a "guerrilla shirt," a sort of heavy cloth smock with large pockets, which was usually made by one's mother, wife, or sister. He carries several Colt revolvers, which in the days of single-shot rifles and muskets gave one an edge in firepower, particularly in close-range engagements.

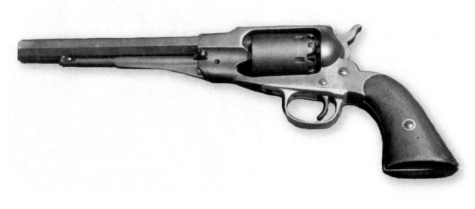

The surrender papers of Frank James (*above*) included the unusual instruction, "This man, A. James, is allowed to retain his horse, arms and equipment by order of Maj. Gen. J. M. Palmer." The arrangement was part of an agreement between Palmer and former guerrillas who helped to hunt down other bushwhackers who were wanted for various alleged crimes. Using his legal name, Alexander Franklin James, Frank was paroled on July 26, 1865, at Samuels Depot, near Bardstown, Kentucky. The Remington .36-caliber revolver (*below*) was one of the weapons he was permitted to keep.

On the facing page, the photograph of (*from left to right*) former guerrilla leader Fletch Taylor, Frank James, and Jesse James was taken in the C. C. Giers studio in Nashville, probably in June 1867 when Jesse was examined by Dr. Paul Eve. Frank wears a studio-prop Confederate officer's uniform and checkered trousers. This image is often erroneously dated as 1864 or 1865.

The photograph of Jesse James above was taken in 1874 or 1875 in Nebraska City, Nebraska. Three major events occurred during these years: Jesse married his cousin Zerelda "Zee" Mimms (*right*), his mother's farm was fire-bombed by Pinkerton detectives, and Daniel Askew was murdered.

Zee's likeness is based on a photograph. She and Jesse were married in 1874. Prowling lawmen interrupted the wedding ceremony. Jesse escaped, and Zee hid under a mattress.

This previously unpublished photograph (*above*) is of Annie Ralston, wife of Frank James, and her family. From left to right they are Annie, brother Harry M. Ralston, sister Margaret Ralston, and brother Samuel Ralston Jr. Margaret was briefly courted by train robber John "Quail Hunter" Kennedy. The image was taken in 1893 in Kansas City at the studio of D. R. Thomson.

The photograph to the left is of Annie Ralston at approximately sixteen years old, a few years before she eloped with Frank James in 1874. Her father temporarily disowned her when he learned who she had married.

Jesse Edwards James (*above*) and his sister, Mary, were photographed in Saint Joseph, Missouri, in April 1882. Jesse was known as Tim Howard and only learned his real name after his father's death. He was, however, known as Tim to family members for the rest of his life.

Frank's son, Robert Franklin James (*facing page, top*), was born in Nashville in 1878 and was usually dressed in skirts, a not uncommon practice with infants of both genders.

A boulder (*right*) marks the grave of one of the James twins, Gould or Montgomery, who both died at the Link place in Humphreys County, Tennessee, in early 1878. According to Banks Link, field rocks were used to mark the graves. The use of boulders as grave markers was a common practice in the area in the 1870s. Sometime after 1963 the area is believed to have been salted with carved stones, visible to the left of the photograph, to support the story that Jesse had carved grave markers. One stone bears the date 1842 and may have come from a nearby cemetery.

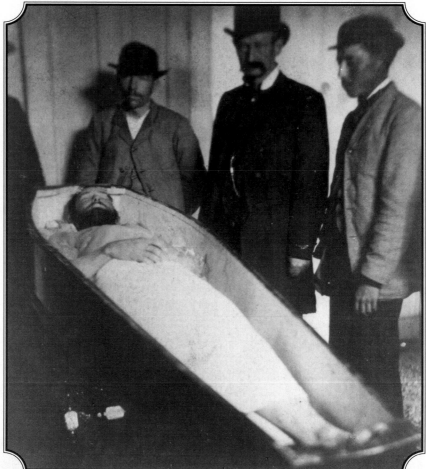

The body of Jesse James (*above*) was packed in ice and displayed inside Sidenfaden's Funeral Parlor in Saint Joseph, Missouri. The scars on his right side are from two wounds during the Civil War. The second wound was caused by a .36-caliber bullet that never exited the body; it was recovered from his chest area during the 1995 exhumation.

One of the photographs of Jesse's body was used for a front-page illustration for *Leslie's* (*left*). Only then did former neighbors in Nashville realize that the man they knew as John Davis Howard was actually the famed outlaw.

Zerelda Samuel (*facing page*), Jesse's mother, stands beside his grave on the James-Samuel farm outside Kearney, Missouri. She gave tours of the farm to the curious and sold pebbles from the grave to them for twenty-five cents. The supply of stones was regularly replenished from a nearby creek bed.

This engraving of Frank James was based on a photograph probably made in Lynchburg, Virginia, in March 1882, shortly before Jesse's death. Both Frank and Jesse had grown beards following the publication in May 1880 of their likenesses based on photographs in the *Illustrated Police News*.

The wallet below belonged to Jesse at the time of his death. The two pockets were for railroad tickets and stamps. Despite the popular impression of Frank and Jesse as enemies of the railroad in general, the brothers were some of the best paying customers the railroads ever had, although they often traveled in disguise.

The James brothers sold well in print, whether the subject was social commentary or entertainment. To the left, the satirical magazine *The Judge* spoofed Frank's treatment as a prisoner of the state during the series of trials that followed his surrender to the authorities. The sign posted in the hallway reads, "Visitors will please not annoy Mr. James." The one placed next to his room indicates, "Mr. James desires privacy—by order of the sheriff." The editors added the caption, "A Western Hero—Make way for the champion murderer."

Shortly before Frank James surrendered in 1882, this dime novel (and in some places it was a nickel) appeared. The list of James brothers titles is quite lengthy; only Buffalo Bill Cody was the subject of more of these fictional adventure stories.

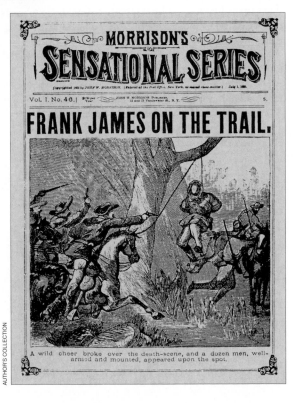

The James-Samuel home was photographed in 1877 (*above*), two years after the fire-bomb raid that crippled Frank and Jesse's mother, Zerelda Samuel, and killed Archie Samuel. The front portion of the cabin was removed sometime and replaced in 1893. It was later exhibited elsewhere in the early 1900s.

Although the letter book entry from the Rock Island Arsenal (*below*) refers to letters of introduction from Lt. Gen. Philip H. Sheridan for R. J. Linden, a Pinkerton agent, there are no copies of the letter in either Sheridan's correspondence or the archives of the arsenal. Interestingly, there is no correspondence in the arsenal's files that makes any mention of the Pinkerton Agency. Yet it appears that the fire bomb used in the raid on the James-Samuel farm was among the "certain materials" obtained there "to aid [Linden] in arresting certain Railroad robbers," according to other Pinkerton correspondence.

Frank James (*above*) was photographed in November 1914, three months before his death. The "Kodaks Bared" sign had long been notorious. Tourists would tell Frank that the sign should read "Barred," and he would bet them five dollars that it did. Many visitors lost their money to the old bandit when they saw that the second *r* had been penciled in on the sign.

Annie James and her son, Robert, were photographed (*below*) in the late 1920s. Annie usually avoided having her picture taken, and it is likely that this image was captured by a family member, possibly Robert's wife.

Jesse Edwards James (*left*) played his father in the 1920 silent film *Jesse James Under the Black Flag*. His childhood friend Harry C. Hoffman (*right*) played Cole Younger. The floral vests and ten-gallon hats were anachronistic, but Jesse Jr. claimed that the guns he carried had belonged to his father. The film was a financial disaster.

Most of the family was involved in the film and posed (*below*) next to the Plattsburg, Missouri, county courthouse. From left to right, they are (*back row*) Joe Hall (husband of Fannie Samuel, the half sister of the James brothers), Belle Nicholson (wife of Arch), Effie Nicholson (wife of Frank), Mary James Barr (daughter of Jesse James), Jesse Jr. (son of Jesse James), Stella James (wife of Jesse Jr.), Norma Samuel (wife of John), John Samuel (half brother of the James brothers), (*second row*) Harry Nicholson (great-grandson of Zerelda), Addie Hall (wife of George), Arch Nicholson (grandson of Zerelda Samuel), George Hall (great-grandson of Zerelda), Frank Nicholson (grandson of Zerelda), Leda Nicholson (great-granddaughter of Zerelda), (*front row*) Nadine Nicholson (great-granddaughter of Zerelda), Perry Samuel (possibly illegitimate son of Reuben Samuel), Josephine Hall Monkers (great-great-granddaughter of Zerelda), and John Nicholson (great-grandson of Zerelda).

In 1933 Jesse's daughter, Mary James Barr (*above*), was photographed in front of her birthplace, the Felix Smith house, near Nashville on the fifty-first anniversary of her father's death.

Of the two weapons below, the bone-handled Colt .45 (*top*) was probably taken by Jesse during the Muscle Shoals robbery that preceeded his flight from Nashville. The Merwin and Hulbert 44/40 Army revolver (*below*) was one of the weapons seized from Jesse Edwards James in 1924 following a traffic accident.

The great impostors: The photograph to the right is one of several bogus Jesse James images to surface during the J. Frank Dalton hoax. The picture was taken in Davenport, Iowa, in the winter of 1901, using studio props and a quartet of former soldiers, recently mustered out of the army. Newspapers and magazines have used this image innumerable times as "the James-Younger gang," and it continues to turn up like a bad penny in books and feature articles.

John James (*below left*) was the first Jesse James impostor of national note. Many of his yarns were repeated by his successor, J. Frank Dalton (*below right*), who was probably the most ubiquitous of at least twenty-six Jesse James pretenders. Dalton and associates spawned one of the longest running hoaxes in American history.

Bank of England. Bligh received a five-thousand-dollar reward and the praises of the English press. It is said that Queen Victoria commissioned an oil portrait of the now famous sleuth.

The Huntington robbery brought the Missouri outlaws once more into Bligh's turf.

Called Yankee because of his New York origin (and perhaps his accent), Bligh stood six feet one inch tall and weighed a hefty 240 to 250 pounds. He was said to have a remarkable memory for the faces and characteristics of criminals. One underworld figure put it bluntly: "Stay away from Louisville. Bligh is the toughest 'fly cop' in the country and there ain't money enough to 'square' [bribe] him."[16]

⁂

ON SEPTEMBER 27, Tom Webb was captured in Fentress County, Tennessee, his horse having thrown a shoe. Some four thousand dollars, part of it bloodstained, was found in his possession. Webb offered the local sheriff the money as a bribe for his release, but he was shipped back to stand trial in Huntington. In December he would be convicted and sentenced to fourteen years in the West Virginia Penitentiary at Moundsville. The other bandits either made for the old Walton Road and escaped to Nashville, or they managed to double back at Pine Hill and escape into their old haunts in Spencer or Nelson County, Kentucky.[17]

Jesse must have been in a dither when Webb was caught about a hundred miles northeast of Nashville. He reportedly had been uneasy about the rumors that Webb was a gambler. On August 31, Zee had given birth to Jesse Edwards James, named for Major Edwards. Jesse was in Nashville at the time of the Huntington robbery, by Zee's account.

Moving was an inconvenience, but Jesse, Zee, and the baby moved anyway. In November they relocated to Baltimore, Maryland. It was possibly during this move that Bligh encountered a bearded man at the Jeffersonville, Madison and Indianapolis Railroad depot at Fourteenth and Main in Louisville. According to one account, the stranger recognized Bligh, claimed to be a tombstone salesman, and asked the detective if he was still after the James brothers. Bligh replied that he was indeed. A few days later Bligh received a post card from Indianapolis or Baltimore (by different accounts), signed Jesse James and expressing his regrets at not having revealed his identity at the depot. One version of the story has James asking Bligh if he was still hunting Jesse James and Bligh replying that he wanted to catch up with the bandit before he died. The post card, in this case, told him he had met Jesse James, so now he could die.

Very little is known of the Baltimore residence of the James clan beyond some statements by Zee James in 1882 and by Frank James around the turn of the century. They probably arrived by train, and the Baltimore and Ohio route would have been the most logical. The line ran through Parkersburg, West Virginia, past Harpers Ferry, the scene of John Brown's raid, which had stirred pro-secession passions only fifteen years before. The line terminated at Camden Station in Baltimore, not far from the present-day Orioles Stadium. For this year alone the 1876 *Baltimore City Directory* lists a John Howard, laborer, at 3 Burrows Court. It is probable that Jesse and his family occupied a row house at this address just off Fort Street, now part of the Key Highway as it runs past the present-day Chesapeake Paperboard Company. According to Zee, she remained in Baltimore one year, although Jesse was away much of the time. He reportedly visited the Centennial Exposition in Philadelphia.

Frank and Annie also lived in Baltimore, perhaps at the same address as Jesse and Zee, or nearby, as was often their fashion later. In later years Frank would relate a story of a close call with the Baltimore police, probably in the winter of 1875–76. One night Frank had gone out to an all-night market in town for some food. When he returned he found a number of policemen walking around in front of the row house. Frank suspected that someone had learned where he lived and that the police were lying in wait. He decided to brazen it out and walk past the officers. If they tried to capture him he would attempt to get to a nearby horse and buggy, shooting it out with the officers if necessary. Frank was clutching his revolver, under his left arm, when a policeman tried to stop him. Frank backed off, warily, toward the buggy. The policeman told Frank not to be so edgy. A man had died in the row house next door, he said, and they were trying to get men to serve on the coroner's jury. Relieved, Frank told the police that he was a resident of Washington, D.C., just visiting, and went on to his home. It was a close call, but there would be closer calls in the months ahead. The year 1876 would prove to be something of a turning point in the lives of Frank and Jesse James.[18]

8

The Road to Northfield

The demoralizing influences of the war upon humanity has long
been felt . . . and the crimes that have been engendered by its
influence would appall the casual reader or the indifferent observer.

Allan Pinkerton, Thirty Years a Detective (1884)

O N MAY 9, 1876, the Centennial Exposition opened in Philadelphia. It
is entirely possible that Jesse James (possibly accompanied by brother
Frank) was on hand for the inaugural ceremonies. As his wife, Zee,
recalled, he was away for a week in Philadelphia and "saw a great many
people from Missouri whom he knew [of] very well, but who did not know
[i.e., recognize] him" at the exposition.

The exposition was a celebration of America's entry into the industrial
revolution, with its Machinery Hall and giant Corliss engine powering
other machines over a thirteen-acre area. Demonstrations showed that
machines could do almost anything from spinning cloth to manufacturing
shoes to printing newspapers in bulk. Many craftsmen would be economi-
cally displaced by the machinery on display in the hall, but not all inven-
tions would be so menacing. A little device run by something called
electricity would get scant attention in all the hum and clatter of the other
machinery. It was called the telephone.

"The first day crowds come like sheep," recalled a Japanese visitor, "run
here, run there, run everywhere. One man start, one thousand follow. Nobody

can see anything, nobody can do anything. All rush, push, tear, shout, make plenty noise, say damn many times, get very tired, and go home."

The hubbub of the exposition was exhausting as well as exhilarating. Perhaps as he made his way through the crowds Jesse had in the back of his mind a quip that was making the rounds in Philadelphia. It speculated that the only man to get rich off the Centennial was Benjamin F. Butler, whose company reportedly was the country's largest manufacturer of bunting (the red, white, and blue cloth that decorated just about everything in sight). Where, Jesse may have wondered, would a man like that keep his money?[1]

※※◎※※

JESSE WOULD ultimately get tired of the East and decide to return to Missouri, although he apparently left his wife and son in Baltimore. He and Frank returned to Missouri sometime in late May or June. Frank faced a peculiarly difficult task—to meet his father-in-law, Sam Ralston. According to the *Kansas City Times*, Ralston was sitting in the yard, reading, around sunset (another account has Frank arriving in time for breakfast), when a rider approached the gate. One account states that Frank was reluctant to dismount. "The interview was brief, and on the part of the father angry and the mother tearful. The father demanded the whereabouts of his daughter. James replied carelessly that she was all right." Ralston demanded to see his daughter. "You cannot see her," Frank answered. "She is far away." Ralston asked where they had been married and was told it had been in Omaha. One report said "the conversation closed in anger." Then Frank, who had finally mustered the courage to dismount, got back on his horse and rode away, leaving the sixty-six-year-old Irishman to fume.[2]

※※◎※※

HOBBS KERRY had wintered in the Joplin area of southwest Missouri, where he had met Bruce Younger, an uncle of the Younger brothers, and two other associates: Sam Wells, alias Charlie Pitts, the son of Washington Wells, a neighbor of the Younger family in Lee's Summit, Missouri; and Bill Stiles, alias Bill Chadwell, from Minnesota. Kerry was a laborer in the local coal mines, and Younger was an associate, but Younger didn't care for the work, and Kerry moved across the state line to another mine near Coalville, Kansas, south of Fort Scott.

Sometime in May or early June, Kerry and Wells-Pitts started kicking around the idea for a bank robbery somewhere around Granby, Missouri, a lead- and zinc-mining center south of Joplin. Perhaps Pitts (as he will be referred to here) had gotten the idea from the exploits of, or his association with, the Younger brothers. Apparently Pitts had approached the Younger boys about the potential robbery by early June, but the Youngers were cautious. "They are afraid of everybody," wrote Kerry on June 9 to his Granby saloon-keeper friend Richard Stapp. Kerry proposed that Pitts and one of the "'Y' boys" would come in and case the area. "Bill says they are red hot to do something, and you bet when I get to see them I will convince them that Granby is the best place and the easiest to get at. . . . Charlie [Pitts] is getting wild and so am I . . . but we want to get them boys with us before we start," Kerry wrote.

There was too much loose talk about the proposed bank heist, and word somehow reached Saint Louis police chief James McDonough. The chief sent six handpicked officers to the Granby area disguised as miners prospecting for ore. After several weeks in the area it became apparent that the bank job had been abandoned, and the men, under the command of a Sergeant Boland, were ordered back to Saint Louis. The Youngers had apparently become suspicious and had something else in mind.

Bill Stiles, alias Chadwell, delivered the message that the Youngers were coming, but when they hadn't shown up by late June, Pitts and Kerry decided to go north and find them. At Monegaw Springs they learned that the brothers had not been in the area for some time. They proceeded to Jackson County and made contact with Dr. Lydell(?) Twyman, who was related by marriage to the Youngers.

Somehow word got back to the outlaws that Pitts, Stiles, and Kerry were looking for them. On the way back to Independence from a trip to the Twyman place, just east of the town, the trio ran into a man who acted suspiciously. Stiles believed it was Cole Younger at first, but it proved to be Frank James. Frank was wary, and when Stiles rode up to him, Frank pulled a gun on the Minnesotan and asked who he was.

"It's me, Bill Chadwell," he answered, using his alias. Frank asked who was with him, and he replied Charlie Pitts, not naming Kerry. Frank told Stiles, who had been ordered to raise his hands, "that he thought [he] was a damned detective and that he had a notion to kill him." He said he wanted to speak to Pitts, and ordered Stiles away.

Pitts spoke with Frank, who told him to go to Dick Tyler's place in Jackson County. Evidently it was a long ride, for Kerry, Stiles, and Pitts spent the night in a schoolhouse to escape a rainstorm. The next morning they rode in to Tyler's and met Jesse James and Cole Younger, who knew Stiles and Pitts. That evening, July 1, around five or six o'clock, the group started off and were met by Bob Younger and Clell Miller along the way. The gang made rather slow progress east, eventually splitting into two groups of four and then meeting again near California, Missouri, on July 4. It appeared to

Kerry that the James boys were behind whatever was going on. "You fellows suggested this," Cole told the James brothers, "and I'm just going with you."[3]

Jesse had apparently sold Bob Younger on a plan to rob a bank in Minnesota, and Bob, in turn, brought his brothers, Cole and Jim, into the scheme. Bob had reportedly settled on a farm in Missouri with a common-law wife and was planning to give up the robbery business. It was the old story of "one last score," but in this case money would be needed for expenses to carry off the long-range operation. Cole was skeptical and perhaps had unpleasant memories of the aftermath of Huntington, but he reluctantly agreed after Bob said he would go with or without him and after Frank James entered the picture. The robbery that was planned would raise the money needed for the Minnesota raid.[4]

On July 6 the gang proceeded west from California, Missouri, in groups of two, meeting around 2 P.M. about two miles east of a bridge where the Missouri Pacific Railroad crossed the Lamine River. Around sunset the bandits approached the bridge, and Bob Younger, Charlie Pitts, and Clell Miller captured the watchman. "You ain't going to hurt me," he said as he was hustled away. "What would we want to hurt you for?" replied one of the gang. "We want that money, that is all we care for."

Hobbs Kerry and Bill Stiles stayed behind as the others headed in the direction of a railroad cut.[5]

Around 4:45 P.M. the Missouri Pacific's No. 4 express left the station at Kansas City, bound for Saint Louis. Comprised of two sleepers, three coaches, and two baggage cars, the train reached a spot known locally as Rocky Cut around 10:30 P.M. The captive watchman flagged down the train. Just to make sure it stopped, the bandits had piled ties on the track ahead. Some of the gang members were posted on the banks of the cut. It was such a short distance that the "engine climbed up on the ties, rising fully ten inches off the track, and then stopped and of its own weight settled back on the track," according to one witness. Kerry and Stiles quickly brought up the rear, placing an obstruction there. The outlaws began yelling and whooping, firing shots. "The scene was wild," a baggage master named Conkling recalled. "Women shrieked, some fainted, and many of the men crawled down under the seats of the cars. Some began to take out their money and jewelry for the purpose of hiding it under the seats, but others, seeming utterly paralyzed, remained in their seats blanched and trembling. Meanwhile the yells and pistol shots continued . . . and the passengers had every reason to believe that a massacre was in progress."

Two men boarded the engine while three others entered the side door of the express car, left open due to the summer heat. Baggage master Conkling was captured in the car, but the express agent had fled to a rear car with the key. The bandits took Conkling through the train, past rows of trembling passengers, until the express man was pointed out. "Give us the keys, my Christian friend, and be damned quick about it," one of the gang ordered. According to one account, a minister on board prayed loudly that the passengers' lives would be spared, exhorting them to repent, and leading some of the pilgrims in hymns to the Almighty. If this indeed occurred it must have made for an unusual scene.

The robbers, all but one of whom wore a mask, proceeded back to the express car, unlocked the Adams Express safe, and dumped the contents into a wheat sack. Another strongbox was on the train, but none of the keys fit it. It eventually had a large hole knocked in its side with a pick, and one of the men with small hands pulled the contents out and dumped them in the sack. They next proceeded to rob the newsboy's concession chest. By one account, "One big fellow created considerable amusement among his comrades by the way in which he demolished a pie, making a crescent of it in two bites, and smearing his face till he looked ridiculous." They rifled a Missouri, Kansas, and Texas Railway letter box, scattering its contents but finding nothing of interest. They went on to the Adams Express freight car but found nothing worth looting there either. Someone finally suggested they rob the passengers, but the leader of the group said they had taken enough and none of the passengers were to be touched.

Only the newsboy attempted to fire at them with a small pistol, but the robbers only laughed. "Hear that little son of a bitch bark," one declared. Finally, the gang bid "good-bye boys" to the trainmen, warning of the obstruction to their rear. The bandits could be heard talking and laughing as they left the scene.

The bridge watchman, bound and gagged beside the track during the holdup, was released just before they left. It was estimated that something over fifteen thousand dollars was taken in the heist.[6] The gang proceeded in a southerly direction, riding through Florence about 2 A.M. According to Kerry they made about twenty miles by dawn and divided the loot at a site seventeen miles southeast of Sedalia.

"Frank James counted the money and gave each one his share," Kerry recalled. He remembered receiving around twelve hundred dollars. The gang broke into groups of three, crossing the Osage River west of Warsaw.[7]

Posses were soon in the field, including one led by the sheriff of Pettis County and another by Bacon Montgomery, the former militia officer responsible for the death of Archie Clement in 1866. This second group operated out of Sedalia and would end up chasing its tail across central Missouri for around a month.

The posses ultimately caused more trouble than they solved. At dawn on July 25, a posse of eight men, led by Deputy Sheriff Homars of Pettis County, surrounded the house of Albert Harris on the McKean (or McKeehan in some accounts) farm, six miles southwest of Lamonte. It was supposed that Sam McKean, reportedly a brother of Jack Keene (also known as Tom Webb) of Huntington infamy, was at the place and might have had something to do with the Rocky Cut affair.

Harris and his wife, Margaret, McKean's sister, were talking at the front door when a shotgun blast tore through the rear of the house. Four of the nine buckshot killed Margaret. According to the coroner's report, a shotgun held by A. M. Aimes of Otterville, Cooper County, had discharged by accident. Less than a month later, on August 18, Harris filed a lawsuit against the Missouri Pacific Railroad, Adams Express, and United States Express for five thousand dollars plus the cost of litigation in the wrongful death of his wife.[8]

Meanwhile, Hobbs Kerry made his way south, boarding a train at Montrose, Missouri, and proceeding south to Fort Scott, Kansas, and from there to Granby and Joplin, Missouri. On July 31, following a quick trip to the nearby Indian Territory (now Oklahoma) to visit his brother, he was apprehended near Granby by Saint Louis detectives along with Bruce Younger, uncle of the Younger boys. Kerry had lost most of his money gambling and had only twenty dollars at the time of his arrest.

Both Kerry and Younger were hauled off to Saint Louis and questioned for several days before news of their capture was made public. On August 4, Kerry confessed in Sedalia, gave a very detailed account of the robbery, and was jailed in nearby Boonville to await trial. He guided a group of lawmen to the site where the gang had divided its spoils. Payroll checks, bank drafts, and bond coupons, damaged by rain, were found scattered about the site, along with some stray pieces of gold jewelry.

Bruce Younger was eventually released. In 1880 he would be briefly married to Myra Belle Shirley, better known as Belle Starr, a fact that has caused Bruce to be confused with his nephew Cole by some authors. Kerry eventually received four years in prison for his role in the Rocky Cut affair.[9]

In the month following the Rocky Cut robbery the usual back-and-forth editorials appeared in the press. A letter, allegedly from Jesse but with the suspicious touch of Edwards's style, appeared in the *Kansas City Times*, accusing Unionist Bacon Montgomery of the robbery and denouncing Kerry as a "notorious liar and poltroon." Sam Ralston's farm, to his undoubted indignation, was raided and searched on August 11. There was also a wild report of Clell Miller's capture in Kansas. In fact, the Adams Express Company had seized two wagons at Fort Scott, Kansas, that were being used by C. E. Wells, younger brother of Sam Wells (alias Charlie Pitts). The company claimed the wagons were purchased with the stolen loot. On Friday, August 11, Pitts and Stiles left their wives three miles east of Godfrey, Kansas, at the home of Stiles's father-in-law, a man named Robinson. Another raid, perhaps the most ambitious yet, was already in motion.[10]

DURING AUGUST 1876 the hunt for the James and Younger brothers shared the headlines with the death of Wild Bill Hickok in Deadwood, Dakota Territory, and a war between Christians and Muslims and Turks and Serbs in Bosnia-Herzegovina (the latter subject to international peace mediation). There was also a presidential campaign pitting Democrat Samuel J. Tilden of New York against Republican Rutherford B. Hayes of Ohio in what would turn out to be one of the most controversial elections in American history. Tilden, who had a major role in breaking up the Tweed ring in New York, would campaign on the issues of government corruption under the Grant administration and the ongoing depression. Hayes's supporters countered with their own promises to clean up politics and by "waving the bloody shirt," tarring the Democrats as collaborators with the former Confederacy. The Republicans also included a plank in the party platform to end immigration from Asia. Such was the world situation as the gang prepared to steal more dollars, if not headlines in "Yankee" Minnesota.[11]

Bill Stiles was a convicted horse thief and a native of Minnesota. Following his release from jail, he drifted south to the Missouri-Kansas border area under the alias of Bill Chadwell. Sometime after Jesse returned to Missouri, Stiles appears to have encountered the now famous outlaw and piqued Jesse's attention about the various banks in the North Star State.

Events were in motion for a Minnesota raid by at least August 11, when Stiles and Charlie Pitts left Kansas. Essentially the gang was the same as at Rocky Cut, with the substitution of Jim Younger for the now traitorous Hobbs Kerry. Just how the gang got to Minnesota is described in conflicting accounts saying they rode north on horseback, traveled in a covered wagon together, or even moved by train from Missouri. Cole Younger himself would later give different stories. What actually happened may never be known with any certainty. The same goes for the date of their arrival in Minnesota. It can only be said that they arrived sometime during the last two weeks of August.[12]

As they did before the Huntington raid, the gang apparently did a survey of several banks between Mankato, in south-central Minnesota, and Red Wing, southeast of Saint Paul along the Upper Mississippi. Mankato, the most westerly, may have been on the short list for robbery. However, western Minnesota had been hard hit by the Rocky Mountain locust, which in the spring of 1876 was "making a clean sweep of the grain and shrubbery of all kinds" for the fourth consecutive year. According to Cole Younger, "We came to the conclusion that they [the banks] had enough to do to take care of the farmers . . . to be suffered by us; therefore we went to Northfield."[13]

Northfield, about thirty miles south of Saint Paul, was a small farming community and college town. It was first settled in the late 1850s by New Englanders, and by the 1870s it was seeing an influx of Scandinavians. There was a certain New England native whose connection to the town, and the First National Bank there, attracted the attention of the gang. His name was Adelbert Ames.

Ames's father, Jesse, a former sea captain from Maine, was owner of a flour mill in Northfield. Adelbert Ames had graduated from West Point on the eve of hostilities in 1861 and was seriously wounded at First Manassas in July 1861, earning the Medal of Honor in the process. In the summer of 1862 he was commissioned as colonel of the Twentieth Maine Infantry, a unit that was to have a peculiar destiny.

The Twentieth Maine was in a sad state of disarray when Ames took command, snarling in disgust, "This is a hell of a regiment!" He set about kicking the regiment into shape.

"I swear they will shoot him in the first battle he is in," wrote Sgt. Thomas Chamberlain. But the regiment slowly came around and on December 13, 1862, acquitted itself well under fire in the foolish slaughter at Fredericksburg.

Ames would eventually be promoted to brigadier general in the Eleventh Corps of the Army of the Potomac, leaving command of the regiment to a precocious newcomer at arms, a former professor at Bowdoin College named Joshua Lawrence Chamberlain, older brother of Thomas (now a lieutenant). Under Chamberlain the Twentieth Maine played a crucial role in the defense of Little Round Top at the battle of Gettysburg.[14]

It was in the latter part of the war that Ames assumed command of a division in Maj. Gen. Benjamin F. Butler's Army of the James in southeast Virginia. Butler was a political general from neighboring Massachusetts and controversial, to say the least. He earned his commission in a smoke-filled room and was called a "notorious demagogue and political scoundrel" by one Massachusetts newspaper. At the 1860 Democratic Party convention, Butler supported Jefferson Davis on fifty-seven ballots for the presidential nomination. But in 1861 he was a Union general supporting Lincoln. Butler carried considerable clout among Unionist Democrats in the North, which the Lincoln administration prized—at least until the 1864 presidential race was over.

In late 1864 Butler came up with a cracked-brain plan to destroy Confederate Fort Fisher, which guarded the remaining Southern port open to blockade-runners in Wilmington, North Carolina. He schemed to take the USS *Louisiana*, an aging blockader, fill her hold with two hundred tons of gunpowder, run her up near the walls of the fort, and blow her up. He believed the concussion would blast down the sand parapets and kill or disable the fort's garrison. But one general of engineers scoffed that the proposed detonation would have "about the same effect on the fort that firing feathers from a musket would have on the enemy." A naval officer suggested that "it has about as much chance of blowing up the fort as I have of flying."

Despite such predictions, on the early morning of Christmas Eve 1864, the plan was executed. The explosion was heard more than seventy miles away in Beaufort, North Carolina, but was mistaken by the garrison for the scuttling of a blockader that had run aground. Fort Fisher survived the blast unscathed. The futile explosion, however, demolished Butler's career in the army. Ames survived his superior and took part in the campaign that eventually stormed the blockade bastion.[15]

Butler's infamy in the South rested largely on his occupation of New Orleans in 1862. It was reported that Union officers, and even Butler himself, had shipped out large quantities of fine furniture and silverware seized from the Crescent City. Then after Flag Officer David Glasgow Farragut had a chamber pot emptied on him by a New Orleans matron, Butler published his notorious Woman Order, which stipulated that any woman displaying similar discourtesy to the occupying forces would be treated as a "lady of the evening." The Confederate government promptly outlawed Butler for this unchivalrous act, and chamber pots with "Beast" Butler's face painted on the bottom became the rage in some cities of the South.

In the summer of 1870 Adelbert Ames, now a "carpetbag" senator from Mississippi, married Butler's daughter Blanche. In 1873 he was elected governor and overall seems to have done a creditable job in office, given the turbulent situation. However, he was still a Yankee and was probably a century ahead of his time in terms of civil rights for blacks. In addition, his connection with the detested Beast of New Orleans and his apparent high-strung manner fed into redemptionist propaganda. In 1876 he resigned amid trumped-up allegations of misconduct in office. Ames simply had had his fill of Mississippi politics and moved to Northfield, where the family flour mill was located.[16]

"General Benjamin F. Butler, whom we preferred to call 'Silver Spoons' Butler from his New Orleans experiences during the war, had a lot of money invested, we were told, in the First National Bank at Northfield," Cole Younger later wrote, "as had J. T. Ames, Butler's son-in-law . . . we felt little compunction, under the circumstances, about raiding him or his." This was the same Benjamin F. Butler who was jokingly said to be the only person getting wealthy off the Centennial Exposition in Philadelphia.[17]

One day in the last week of August, two strangers in linen dusters (Bob Younger and Bill Stiles, according to Cole Younger; the James brothers by another account) rode into Northfield. Hitching their horses near the bank, they inquired about the roads and left after about half an hour. According to most accounts the gang rendezvoused at Mankato, Minnesota, on Saturday, September 2. It was probably there that the various options were weighed over the weekend and a decision was made to hit the bank at Northfield.

On Monday the gang proceeded to Janesville, about eighteen miles east of Mankato. Tuesday evening found them at Cordova, where on the following day the gang reportedly split, half going to Millersburg and the others to Cannon City. They reunited at Dundas, five miles west of their target, on the morning of Thursday, September 7.

About 11 A.M. five of the band rode into Northfield and after looking the place over, they went into a restaurant owned by J. G. Jeft and ordered ham and eggs for lunch. "During their stay in the restaurant they discussed politics," it was later recalled, "several of them desiring to bet one thousand dollars that the state would go Democratic." The owner was not a betting man, however. The men paid for their meal and left.

Around 2 P.M., three men—later identified as Pitts, Bob Younger, and one of the James boys—rode back into town and dismounted in front of the bank. Somewhere near the bridge they had chanced to pass Adelbert Ames and his brother John, who were headed back to the mill after a meeting at the bank.

"There is Governor Ames himself," one of the men remarked.

"Those men are from the South and here for no good purpose," commented the former Union general to his brother. "No one here calls me Governor."

Hitching their horses, the men in the dusters loitered about some boxes of dry goods in front of Lee and Hitchcock's store. Shortly afterward two other riders, Cole Younger and Clell Miller, rode up. As Younger and Miller approached, the trio in front of the store crossed the street and entered the bank. Miller dismounted briefly, walked to the door, and looked in, then positioned himself in front. Cole dismounted in the middle of the street and attempted to adjust his saddle girth.

J. S. Allen tried to enter the bank just then but was collared by Miller and ordered at gunpoint not to say a word. Allen broke free and dodged around the corner, yelling, "Get your guns boys! They're robbing the bank!"

Henry Wheeler, a young medical student, took up the alarm. Miller mounted his horse and he and Younger ordered Wheeler back, firing a shot or two over his head to make their point. The pair then began riding up and down the street, shooting in the air and ordering everyone to "get in."

Things were not running smoothly inside the bank either. Frank J. Wilcox, assistant bookkeeper at the bank, recalled glancing up from his work to see three men pointing their revolvers at him as well as at bank teller Alonzo Bunker and assistant cashier Joseph Lee Heywood. "Throw up your hands. We are going to rob the bank," ordered one of the men. "Don't any of you holler. We've got forty men outside."

The robbers sprang over the counter. Heywood rose from his desk but was ordered to his knees. "Are you the cashier?" one asked. Heywood replied that he wasn't, and the others were asked if they were.

"You are the cashier," one said, turning to Heywood. "Open that safe damned quick or I'll blow your head off."

Pitts ran to the vault and was inside the outer door when Heywood tried to shut him in. He was yanked back and ordered to open the safe or be killed.

"There's a time lock on it, and it cannot be opened," Heywood answered.

"That's a lie!" one of the outlaws shot back. Continued threats and rough treatment failed to work.

"Murder! Murder! Murder!" Heywood shouted.

Pitts, now out of the vault, drew a pocket knife. "Let's cut his damned throat," he said, slightly cutting Heywood's neck. Pitts then fired off a shot close to Heywood's head, but their scare tactics didn't work.

Wilcox and Bunker were ordered to unlock the safe, but they backed Heywood's story. Indeed, they couldn't unlock a safe that wasn't locked to begin with. The bandits were too slow to figure that out, however.

"It was very evident that they had been drinking, as the smell of liquor was very strong," Wilcox recalled later. The bandits contented themselves with some fractional currency and coins, which went in the grain sack. When Pitts was ordered to go back and try his hand at the safe, Bunker recalled a small gun he'd kept under the teller's window. Pitts detected Bunker's plan and grabbed the gun before he could reach it. "You needn't try to get hold of that. You couldn't do anything with that little derringer anyway," he declared.

Bob Younger also threatened Bunker when Younger couldn't find the main cash drawer, which was sitting in front of them with three thousand dollars in it.

As the robbers became preoccupied, Bunker made a dash for freedom, heading toward the rear door. Pitts was after him, firing his pistol as Bunker crashed through some outside shutters to the alley. Bunker was almost inside the rear entrance to a nearby building when he was hit in the right shoulder. He mustered enough strength to make his way to the office of a Dr. Coons. Pitts gave up and went back inside the bank.[18]

Meanwhile, things had started to warm up out on the street. Cole Younger recalled later that "Miller was shot . . . by a man named Stacy and his face was filled full of bird shot . . . the street was full of flying lead, coming from every direction." At least two citizens even resorted to throwing large rocks at the bandits, one of them crying "Stone 'em! Stone 'em!" amid the gunfire. Another man drunkenly waved an old rusty gun at the bandits but was ignored by them.

Despite being shot at by Miller and Younger, Henry Wheeler had made his way to the Dampier Hotel. There he found a .52-caliber Smith carbine, an early breechloading, single-shot weapon left over from the Civil War that used a separate foil-and-paper cartridge and a percussion cap. The hotel clerk was only able to find four cartridges, and with these Wheeler ran up the stairs to a third-floor room facing the bank

"As I approached the window, three . . . men on horseback came riding up across the bridge square, shooting," Wheeler related. "I shot at one of them, but missed him."

A. R. Manning, who ran a hardware store next to the bank, at first thought the gunplay in the street was an advertising stunt by the Forbes Dramatic Company, which had just arrived in town. When he caught the words "robbing the bank," he realized it was for real. Manning grabbed a single-shot Remington rolling-block rifle from the store window and a handful of cartridges, which he threw in his pocket. Soon he was taking potshots at the bandits around the corner. He shot a horse belonging to Charley Pitts, then wounded Cole in the hip, and finally picked off Bill Stiles with a shot through the chest.

It was a cat-and-mouse gun battle. Wheeler, who had now reloaded, said, "The man who had fired at me before [Clell Miller], had gotten into the saddle and was bending down. . . . I got a rest for the gun in a corner of the window, aimed low and shot him through the chest."

"Come out of the bank! For God's sake come out, they are shooting us all to pieces!" cried one of the bandits. "Bob [Younger] came out in a hurry and started down the street towards Manning, who ran into a store, hoping he would get a shot at Bob from under cover," Cole Younger recalled later. "Bob ran on but didn't notice . . . Wheeler, who was upstairs in the hotel, behind him. Wheeler's third shot smashed Bob's right arm."

Exiting the bank, one of the bandits, thought to be one of the James brothers, turned and fired at Heywood, who dodged behind his desk. "As the robber made over the desk railing, he turned, and placing his revolver to Heywood's head, fired, shooting him dead," according to bookkeeper Wilcox.

"Bob switched his gun to his left [hand]," recalled Cole, "and got on [Miller's] horse, thinking that Miller was dead. By this time [James] and Pitts were out of the bank, and I told them that Miller was still alive and we'd have to save him. I told Pitts to put Miller on my horse, but when we lifted him I saw he was dead, so I told Pitts I would hold off the crowd while he got away, as his horse had been killed. While Pitts ran, less than ten yards, I stood with my pistol pointed at anyone who showed his head, and then I galloped off and overtook him and took him up behind me."

Cole would later tell a similar story with Bob Younger riding behind him in the place of Pitts. According to another account, Pitts covered Cole as he took Bob up behind him.

The surviving members of the gang scurried out of town amid gun-shots, the clanging of church bells, and the barking of dogs. The whole affair had lasted around seven minutes and netted the gang a grand total of $26.70.[19]

In the streets of Northfield lay Bill Stiles, the expedition's guide, and Clell Miller. Inside the bank lay the body of Heywood. Mortally wounded was a thirty-year-old Swedish immigrant named Nicholas Gustavson, who reportedly had been warned to get out of the way and was shot when he didn't. It was said that he didn't understand English and/or was drunk. Gustavson, who received a head wound, lingered for four days as the bandits made their way across the Minnesota countryside with a small army at their heels.[20]

9

The Getaway

At last accounts there was hope that the entire gang would be exterminated. Good for Minnesota.

New York Express editorial, September 14, 1876

ADELBERT AMES HAD WITNESSED part of the Northfield shootout but had gotten out of the way. He recounted the story of the raid in a letter to his wife, Blanche, then visiting in Lowell, Massachusetts, commenting about the bodies of the outlaws, which were put in a wagon and displayed for gawkers. An immediate effort to raise a posse had been stymied due to lack of arms and horses. The robbers had taken the Dundas road southwest out of Northfield. Ames and his brother John were concerned, because this road passed near John's home. Adelbert sent John back to town to take charge of matters there and went out to check on his nieces, who had no idea what had been going on in Northfield. "The time yesterday reminded me of an election in Mississippi," Ames wrote Blanche. John and his father gathered a dozen or so men and pursued the robbers. John also telegraphed to the state capital for aid and then stationed some armed men at his home for the remainder of the day.

About halfway to Dundas the gang stopped and took a horse from a farmer's team to replace the one shot in Northfield. The use of plow horses as remounts would slow the gang down in the days ahead. A little later, representing themselves as lawmen in pursuit of horse thieves, they absconded with a saddle from yet another farmer.

News of the robbery had been telegraphed to Faribault, and a party of four men from there reached Shieldsville, about fifteen miles from Northfield, ahead of the gang. The posse headed for the local saloon for a round of liquid courage, leaving their guns outside with the horses.

The gang rode into town later and headed for the town water pump, where they soaked rags to wash their wounds. One of the bandits, thought by some to be Bob Younger, passed out from loss of blood and fell off his horse. When an old man in front of the saloon became suspicious, one of the gang explained that he was a captured horse thief.

The man went into the saloon and a few moments later the posse came to the doorway but found themselves staring at drawn revolvers. After warning the men to stay clear, they shot up the water pump and rode off. About five minutes later another posse of around ten to twelve men rode into town, and the whole lot went into pursuit. For reasons unknown, the gang had not taken the guns or horses of the men they stood off.

At a ravine about four miles west of town the posse caught up with the bandits and exchanged a few shots before the gang escaped into the woods. By the time the sun went down that evening at least two hundred men were in the field. Most of them were armed with old shotguns, muskets, and revolvers.

On Friday, September 8, a drizzling rain set in; the inclement weather continued for the next two weeks. The gang moved west-southwest toward Waterville, where they forded the Little Cannon River, after being fired upon by three men guarding the crossing. Then they pushed on to Elysian, taking three worn-out horses nearby before camping in some woods between Elysian and German Lake. There a fateful decision was made to turn the stolen horses loose, leave the others tied, and escape on foot. On Sunday morning the gang creeped around the outskirts of Marysburg. They only made four miles by evening. The next day they made nine miles then hid until Wednesday at an abandoned farmhouse two or three miles from Mankato.[1]

Meanwhile, the manhunt had turned into something of a circus. On September 9, a schoolteacher named E. B. Tull from Meeker County had been arrested near Norseland as one of the robbers. At Faribault the same day, a reporter found several hundred people crowding the center of town:

> The number of volunteers was larger than could be armed readily, and delay was caused by a search through the city for weapons. Everybody seemed willing and anxious to go to the front, and they came armed and mounted in every conceivable manner. A lad with a decrepit wooden leg

came mounted on a bad-looking nag, and having a double-barrelled fowling piece full of buckshot nearly to the muzzle, strapped on his back, while a horse-pistol stock peeped from his side pocket, He was accepted promptly, as his pluck was unquestionable.

The manhunt was criticized for its lack of organization, and there were other problems. "The St. Paul boys are often mistaken for bandits, and the people run like mad," one Minnesota newspaper reported. Some members of the posses were equally spooked and were "scared at the sight of a stump. One squad ran from Cannon River Ford. One man lost his false teeth. Another threw away his gun."

The national press was quick to pick up on the defeat of the outlaws at Northfield, though. "Minnesota is not a healthy state for bank robbers," declared the *New York Evening Mail*. "Happily the spirit of such resistance does not seem to be wanting in the town of Northfield," wrote the *Baltimore Gazette*. "The pluck displayed by the citizens of that little town was most commendable," stated the *Indianapolis News*. On September 12 Gov. John S. Pillsbury of Minnesota added an additional $1,000 to the $1,500 already offered by the state and the $500 reward for each robber offered by the Bank of Northfield. Little wonder so many were eager to join in the hunt.[2]

On Wednesday the gang captured a man named Thomas "Jeff" Dunning, who worked on a farm three miles north of Mankato. At first Dunning was told that the men were in search of the robbers, but this guise was soon dropped. Dunning remained in their custody for about an hour, during which time they made only half a mile. Apparently they hoped to use him as a guide but then became apprehensive. Some wanted to kill him, but he was forced to promise he would tell no one, instead, and released. Dunning, badly shaken, reported the incident three hours after his return to the farm, and the posse was back on their trail.

It was decided that the best thing to do was to split into two groups, hoping at least one group stood a chance of escape and that group might take the attention away from the other. The Youngers and Pitts (and the James brothers, as well, in some accounts) crossed Blue Earth River that evening on foot.

The next evening the James brothers, who finally had split from the others, stole a horse; about midnight they had reached a fork in the road some two miles from Lake Crystal village. One branch ran to Garden City, about six miles away, the other to Crystal Lake Station. The road intersection was wooded, and a strong guard force was posted nearby. The road itself was sandy, and the riders hoped they could slip past the pickets without making much noise.

The brothers made their way past several groups but were spotted before they made it to the road fork. They were challenged by Richard Roberts, a native of Wales, who fired a load of buckshot at the pair. The boys slipped off the horse, leaving it to run past the guards. They were able to tell from all the commotion where the pickets were. Then they slipped off the roadway into the woods, making their way past the guards to a point past the road fork, where they crossed the Lake Crystal road, jumped over a fence into a cornfield, and headed due west.

About 3 A.M. Jesse and Frank reached the farm of a man named Seymour about four miles from the road fork. A Methodist minister from Garden City, whose name was given as George Rockwood or Rockwell, had been helping Seymour with his haying and had brought over a team of "large iron grays." The farmers had been notified to guard their livestock, and the good minister was standing watch at the barn when a man slipped through the door, knocked the musket out of his hands, and pistol-whipped him. The outlaws then constructed makeshift saddles out of grain sacks stuffed with hay and tied them with rope to the horses' backs. Rope stirrups were also improvised. The brothers then slipped into the night, leading another horse away with them. It was let loose about a mile or two from the barn.

By 7 A.M. they had made it twenty-four miles farther west, where they had breakfast. One of the brothers bought a hat off a farmer for $1.50 to replace one lost during the escape at the road fork. The rest of the day was spent riding at a trot of about six miles an hour, according to a member of the party that was trailing them from Mankato. They secured lodging with a German farmer that evening, and the farmer's wife helped dress the wound of one of them. "It was only a flesh wound, and extended from near the hip on the outside of the leg, to near the knee, making an ugly gash or furrow." It was later thought to have been from a shot fired from an upstairs window in Northfield, although it is hard to say.

By 2 P.M. the following day the brothers had crossed the Des Moines River at Swan's Ford; they bought milk and bread from Swan and consumed it on horseback in the yard. "They were gentlemanly in their address, and asked questions about the distances to different railroads. They stated that they had lived in Rock County, Minnesota, and had purchased the team on account of their size and beauty," and were taking them home overland. According to Swan, "They looked like brothers." The fugitives then rode southwest from Swan's place all that night, headed toward Rock County.[3]

The Younger boys and Pitts continued to make their way on foot in the direction of Madelia, twenty-four miles southwest of Mankato. Over the next few days the Younger party altered their route, heading due west, north of Madelia. Near Linden they had a close call with a posse and abandoned their scavenged meal of chicken, turkey, and watermelon, as well as some blood-soaked clothing and two bridles. As they suspected, much of the attention was turned in the direction of the escaping James brothers, but would it take the pressure off enough to allow them to escape?

T. L. Voight ran the Flanders Hotel at Madelia. When news of the robbery at Northfield flashed across the state he recalled two men who had stayed at the hotel in late August under the names J. C. King and Jack Ward. Reportedly, he thought they might have been involved. King and Ward had been interested in the roads of the area, in particular an intersection of roads near Lakes Hanska and Linden. According to the hotelkeeper's son, Voight and others kept a watch on the area for several days but then figured the men had either escaped or gone in a different direction, and gave up.

Seventeen-year-old Axle Oscar Sorbel lived on a farm between Lakes Linden and Hanska, north of Madelia. Just a little after sunrise, on Thursday, September 21, he was helping his father, Ole, who was milking the cows. Oscar recalled, "It had rained for two weeks; it was a kind of drizzling rain, falling night and day, and it was terribly muddy." The Sorbels kept the cattle in the road to the north of Lake Linden. Oscar had gone to the barn with a milk pail when Jim Younger and Pitts came along. The men stopped to stroke the cow and chat briefly with Sorbel. Oscar stood by the gate until they were gone and then went to his father:

> I said to father they were the two robbers. Father said he did not think so, as they looked like "nice" men. I went out in the road and there toe prints showed in the mud, they having worn out their boots. I showed that to father and said "Look here. I will show you how 'nice' they are."
>
> "Well," he said, "never mind; tend to your business."
>
> I milked one cow. Then I set one pail inside the fence, and started after them, and, 60 rods west of our place, I saw where they had walked into the timber. I walked slow till I knew I was out of sight of them. Then I went to Anton Owen's house, and notified him, and also to Mads Owen's farm; and then I went west one mile to Gutterson Grove's house, where I went on top of the roof to see if they left the timber.

Oscar could not get a good view of the three nearby roads that ran to Madelia, New Ulm, and Lockstock. He set off to the east where a big hill gave him a clear view. The two men had not left the woods. Oscar rushed to Anton Owen's house and told three neighbors gathered there—Anton

Anderson, Jens Nillson, and Amund Brustingen—to get up on the hill and watch the roads while he rode to Madelia and alerted the men there.

Arriving back home, Oscar learned that two more men (Cole and Bob Younger) had come by, and they had bought bread and butter for breakfast. He sent his sister Mary to warn Owen and the others that there were two more men. Then he headed along a roundabout route that led to the eastern road to Madelia, some three miles away, east of the lakes.

About two miles from town his horse fell down in the road. Covered head to foot in mud, Oscar told his story, but the first man he talked to didn't believe him. Oscar told the man to find John Owen, who would vouch for his honesty. "Well, in less than half an hour the whole people of Madelia were in the road," Sorbel recalled.

Back at the hill, the men who were watching the gang spotted them making for a threshing machine. One jumped on a horse, and the others headed for three other horses in a prairie nearby but found the horses' hobbles locked. Meanwhile, as Oscar and others made their way north from Madelia, they were met by a neighbor who told them to head west, as the robbers were moving in a southwesterly direction. They arrived at the timber about three miles from Saint James, "just as the robbers got there." Sorbel described what happened next:

> Capt. W. W. Murphy stationed us around the timber, which was on the north side, and we were all shooting into the woods about one hour when the robbers quit shooting. Then it was that seven men went into the woods and we got orders to quit shooting. When the seven men got near the place, Bob Younger held up his left hand and said, "I give up," as the others were all shot to pieces. . . . Cole Younger had one bullet and some buckshot received at Northfield, besides ten fresh buckshot in his body, but he did not pray. He offered to fight two of our best men at once. He said he had been dogged for two weeks in the rain with no food, but that he could lick two of our best men. Bob slung his left arm around him and said, "Come, or we will be hanged." But Cole said that he didn't care, that he would just as soon hang today as tomorrow. Jim Younger had been shot in the mouth and five of his teeth knocked out, and Charley Pitts had been killed. I helped lift him in the wagon myself. Bob Younger asked for a chew of tobacco, and some of the boys swore he would not get any. I went over to Ole Wisty and got a ten-cent plug and handed it to Bob, who took about half of it in one chew, and was going to hand it back. But I told him to keep it. Two days after we caught them, . . . I had to go up. Bob said, "Why that's the boy that gave me the tobacco." Cole made quite a speech to me and saying I did my duty, but, that if they had suspected me they would have shot me or taken me along.

Oscar Sorbel, the seven men who went into the timber, and the people who had kept a watch on the robbers for Sorbel shared the rewards for the capture of the outlaws, and it has been generally assumed that only seven men took part in the brief gun battle with the Younger party before the outlaws surrendered. According to Cole Younger, however, "A party of forty men soon surrounded us and opened fire. We were cut off from our horses and our case was hopeless." Between the accounts of Sorbel and Younger it appears that the fight near Hanska Slough was probably longer and involved more people than has generally been thought.[4]

But what had become of the James boys? They crossed Rock River at the C. B. Rolfe ranch eight miles northeast of Luverne on the morning of September 17, and one appeared to walk with a limp. The horses still had their makeshift saddles and were "badly roweled" by long spurs. Rolfe's wife was asked if being away from the telegraph and near Indians wasn't a problem. She told them about the locality, and they were able to figure the way to the border via a route where they probably wouldn't run into more posses. But there would be another posse on their tail when Rolfe's brother-in-law came by after the men had left. The posse was the usual assortment of indifferently armed farmers. They chased the band to Split Rock River, where they exchanged a few shots. "One of the horsemen turned and fired at the posse, hitting the mule ridden by Jack Dement, as I remember it, in the neck," recalled Martin Webber, "but doing no serious damage. This, as I remember it, ended the pursuit," and the posse returned to Luverne.

The next pair of horses stolen was strictly by the luck of the draw, and it was a bad draw at that. The animals were a pair of black mares taken from Andrew Nelson, who lived in a sod house on Split Rock River below the Palisades. The horses were nice looking, but one was totally blind and the other was blind in one eye. They were abandoned after about ten miles, and a pair of grays was stolen about five miles north of Sioux Falls, South Dakota [then Dakota Territory], reportedly from a man named Burgeson. When a young man tried to ride for help, the James brothers shot his horse.

About 5 A.M. Frank and Jesse passed through Sioux Falls and ran into the Yankton stage south of that place, where they exchanged greetings with the driver but left the stage unscathed. The bandits spent a rainy evening on September 18 at Ole Rongstad's place, seven miles northeast of Canton, South Dakota; they crossed the Sioux River into Iowa the next morning. Rongstad and two friends, all unarmed, attempted to follow, but the brothers shot Rongstad's horse in the neck, as they had several others previously. The pair then headed southeast. The rain washed out their tracks, and it was impossible for a twenty-five-man posse from Canton to follow.

The next night, September 19, the James brothers landed at the farm of Rev. S. M. Krogness, a Norwegian Lutheran minister who lived in Iowa, two miles east of Canton. "They were well armed, but looked very much fatigued and played out. We knew at once who they were, as we had heard lots about the Northfield robbery. . . . My father did not know what to do, but allowed them to stay," recalled his son, A. D. Krogness. "The next morning they took one of our horses, and said, 'We are sorry, but we have to have this horse.' They put the saddle over him and went. . . . Mother, when she went to make the bed, said there were blood stains on the sheets . . . father went to Beloit to give the alarm." The horse later turned up at Calliope, about a mile or so north of present-day Hawarden, Iowa, near the Sioux River, and about thirty-five miles north of Sioux City, Iowa.

On Wednesday, September 25, Dr. Sydney P. Mosher of Sioux City was on his way to visit a patient, Mrs. Robert Mann, who lived in the area of James City, on the Illinois Central Railroad, about eight miles northeast of Sioux City. Seeing two horsemen and not being sure of his own direction, the doctor hailed them and rode up to the pair, only to find himself a prisoner at gunpoint. "You are the man we want," they told him. Apparently they suspected that Mosher was a detective, but they eventually were convinced that he was indeed a doctor and forced him to accompany them for some distance. About 7 P.M. Frank exchanged clothing, horses, and saddles with Mosher, and the outlaws told the doctor to walk away and not look back or they would shoot him.

Next the boys reportedly went into or near Sioux City, but where they went from there is a matter of conjecture. Some claim they crossed into Nebraska, and others say they floated down the Missouri River on a boat or raft, heading back to their old stomping grounds. The successful escape of the James brothers added to their legend. As the *Sedalia (Mo.) Bazoo* would later note, "They ran the gauntlet of Minnesota and Dakota for a distance of 490 miles, and the wildest exploits in the romance of Dick Turpin [an eighteenth-century English highwayman] will not compare with this bold ride for life."[5]

THE CAPTURE of the Youngers was greeted with jubilation in Northfield. Crank letters threatening to burn the town had arrived from Saint Paul, and guards had been posted about town, if for no other reason than to reassure the community. "I saw a great bonfire in Mill Square," wrote Adelbert Ames to his wife, "and saw and heard the flash and report of guns, pistols, and Anvil Artillery [anvils fired in the air with gunpowder]. Everybody talks and laughs with everybody else."

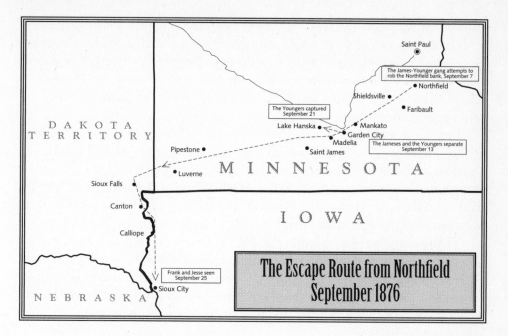

The Escape Route from Northfield
September 1876

Ames noted that the bank had held on to around $15,000 after the raid and had paid $500 to Heywood's widow and would be paying $500 each for the four captured bandits. These payouts amounted to almost half of what had been in the vault, but apparently the bank and townspeople felt it was worth it. The gang had suffered its first major defeat, and the elusive Youngers were behind bars. The wounded Youngers were taken to the Flanders House in Madelia and briefly kept there under heavy guard. Soon they were shipped to the jail at Faribault, where they became a major attraction for the curious. Guards were issued with .58-caliber muzzleloading rifle-muskets left over from the Civil War and were posted to prevent any escape or lynching.

Meanwhile, another story would provide a rather odd twist to the Northfield saga. In those days cadavers were highly prized items needed for anatomical dissections in medical schools. Exhuming bodies was a crime, so medical schools often turned to "resurrectionists," who resorted to grave robbery to obtain specimens for the schools. These "sack-em-up-men" or "grabs," as they were known in the trade, operated far afield of the respective schools, dealing in corpses on a "cash-and-snatch" basis with no questions asked. One medical instructor at the University of Michigan, when asked where he obtained his cadavers, replied, "We raise 'em." There was a saying that "a medic is never happier than when he finds a fellow man in a pickle."

Indeed, many barrels labeled "pickles" arrived at the Ann Arbor school over the course of a year. Sometime in late September 1876 two barrels marked "fresh paint" arrived. Henry Wheeler, the young medical student who had fired at the Northfield robbers from a window of the Dampier Hotel, had his friends and fellow medical students Clarence Edward Persons and Edward Dampier (son of the hotel owner) "procure" the bodies of Clell Miller and Bill Stiles while Wheeler rode with the posse in search of other potential cadavers.

But the story of Miller's and Stiles's corpses did not end in the medical school anatomy lab. Sometime during the last quarter of 1876, Samuel Hardwicke, by then an attorney in Saint Paul, tracked the bodies—apparently now skeletons—to Ann Arbor. He had one of the skeletons shipped back to Missouri. It was thought to be Miller's, but it is possible that Wheeler may have pulled a switch.

The remains were interred in the Muddy Fork Cemetery in Clay County. Out of gratitude (and apparently not aware of his full role in the Pinkerton raid) Zerelda Samuel is said to have thanked Hardwicke and invited him to return to Liberty, promising that her "boys" would not bother him. Hardwicke eventually did return, assured that the mother of the James boys would keep them off his back.

The other skeleton remained with Wheeler, who displayed it like some kind of big-game trophy in his medical office at Grand Forks, North Dakota, until a fire destroyed it in the early part of the twentieth century. Wheeler apparently told others, in later years, that the skeleton in his office was that of Miller, the bandit he'd shot at Northfield.

The remains of Charlie Pitts were given to Dr. Frank Murphy, surgeon general of Minnesota. Dr. Henry Hoyt obtained the remains from him and put them in a box that was sunk in Lake Como, outside the city, to decompose. Saint Paul police found the rotting remains of Pitts in the lake after they were discovered by a muskrat hunter and reported sometime in March 1877. Hoyt, who was living in New Mexico at the time, returned to clear up the mystery and reportedly took the bones to Chicago. What happened to the skeleton later on is not known. It was a sorry end to a story that began in the summer of 1862 when Pitts, running errands with the wife of his employer, had discovered the body of Cole Younger's father. Pitts again encountered the Youngers in southwest Missouri around 1874 and eventually joined the gang.[6]

⁂

BACK IN Missouri, authorities were not taking the situation lightly. The day after the capture of the Youngers, Gov. John S. Pillsbury of Minnesota wired Gov. Charles H. Hardin of Missouri that three of the bandits had been captured. Pillsbury asked Hardin to "send some reliable persons acquainted with them at once to identify them." Hardin wired back that Capt. James McDonough, the Saint Louis chief of police, would go with others to Minnesota. Hardin added that he trusted that "they will be convicted and subjected to the severest punishment, which their conduct so richly deserves."

Using descriptions given by Hobbs Kerry, McDonough and another officer, along with United Express Company superintendent C. B. Hunn, identified Stiles, Miller, and Pitts from photos of their corpses. By the time the men visited the Youngers in the Faribault jail they had been joined by two Gads Hill victims, Col. John Merriam (founder of the Merchants Bank of Saint Paul), his son, and John F. Lincoln (superintendent of the Saint Paul and Sioux City Railroad). Bob and Cole Younger were identified, but Jim was thought to be "Al" or "Cal Carter," a notorious outlaw from Texas who was rumored to have been a new recruit. Jim apparently had not been present at Gads Hill.

McDonough had thought he had Bob Younger back in Missouri under watch but soon was apprised of his mistake. Nevertheless, he returned to Missouri and reported in a letter to Hardin that "Cal Carter" was being held in jail at Faribault.

Meanwhile, plans were being laid to intercept the James boys as they returned to Missouri. "I have now posted Capt. [he was actually a sergeant] Boland and his force, who are now in the north western portion of the state, guarding the crossings and their haunts," wrote McDonough to the governor on September 29. "I feel assured of their capture, should they make for the state, and from information received, believe they will, after making a very circuitous route, and doubling on their pursuers."

On October 12 McDonough received word through an informant that one of the James boys was receiving medical treatment for a wound and staying at the home of a Dr. Noland on the Harrisonville road in Jackson County, about five miles from Independence via the Missouri Pacific Railroad. The wounded outlaw was reportedly guarded by "four Texas desperadoes."

Boland telegraphed in cipher that he would need additional men, and four more men (he already had three) were sent from Saint Louis. The force was apparently underwritten by a state appropriation administered by Governor Hardin.

The next afternoon, about four o'clock, the reinforcements left a train at the Little Blue River. The men took off through the brush, avoiding the roads, until they reached the Noland house and surrounded it. The *Saint Louis Globe-Democrat* reported that when the lawmen entered the house,

"Frank James was found in bed, suffering from a wound in the knee, and the detectives making a rough litter, removed him from the house." The Saint Louis officers also raided the home of Dick Talley, about a half-mile away, expecting to find Jesse. The home of the widow of Bill Pettis, a former bushwhacker who had been hanged after the war, was raided as well. Still no Jesse. The officers took their prisoner to a special train, which hustled them via Olathe, Kansas, to Kansas City, Missouri, and later back to Saint Louis.

"Frank James—the Notorious Outlaw in the St. Louis Calaboose," read the *Globe-Democrat* front-page headline of October 15. But there was one little hitch: Some people claimed they had the wrong man!

The matter first came up when the prisoner was taken. Both the captive and the wife of Noland claimed he was actually John Goodwin of Louisiana. During the stop in Kansas City, Deputy Marshal Hope of Independence, who claimed to know Goodwin, attempted to visit the prisoner but was turned away by the Saint Louis police. Earlier Goodwin had said he knew only one other man in Jackson County, and his name was Doyle, so Hope was not allowed to visit. "He is one of the Northfield bank robbers beyond a doubt, Chief McDonough claims, because all the circumstances go to establish that fact, and he must be either Cal Carter or Frank James," the newspaper reported.

Over the next day or so several individuals were allowed to see the prisoner, but while some said he bore a striking resemblance in various ways, he was not Frank James. One former bushwhacker attempted to see "Frank" but was told that he would have to wait for Chief McDonough, who was at dinner. The man was dressed in the coarse jeans-cloth (a mixture of wool and cotton) clothing of a farmer, and his face bore the scars of saber and knife wounds. Asked whether he knew the James boys, he spat tobacco juice on the carpet of the chief's office and replied, "Wa'al, I reckon."

How long? he was asked. "Long enough to get to know each other. We bushwhacked together during the war."

When told by an officer that he'd better wait, he turned to leave instead. "I know them boys, you see, and I don't believe you've got Frank James, no how," he said.

The *Kansas City Times* began lashing out:

> Jackson County is angry, and well it may be. . . . The old folks are mad, and the boys are brightening up their shooting irons for work; and when Jackson County boys settle down to business, they mean it. There is no foolishness about this thing this time, as the Chicago and St. Louis police-

men will find out the next time they attempt to invade and kidnap and carry away, without due process of law, peaceable and innocent citizens. . . . *The Missouri Pacific should take note of this.* Three times have peaceable farmers of Jackson and Clay Counties been raided by illegal and unauthorized bodies of armed men. Farm houses have been broken open and robbed. . . . If the James boys are here, or come here, there is a proper way to take them, and all the good people of this county of Jackson are willing to aid and assist in their capture. Let the railroad and express companies cease their lawless raids upon the peaceable people of Clay and Jackson Counties and join with the sheriffs, marshals and police authorities of these counties, and they will be able to capture their men, and perhaps save their emissaries from the fate which awaits them at the hands of an outraged people.

The mother of the James boys, Zerelda Samuel, had her two cents to add when questioned by a reporter from the *Times*:

"Do you think I would be here laughing and talking with you, if my boy was in jail?" Zerelda recalled how, after Northfield, the town of Kearney was invaded by six or eight detectives who posed as sewing machine or lightning rod salesmen. "I went up to them and told them I wanted three lightning rod put up. Offered to pay them well to come out. . . . But the villains had no lightning rods to put up."[7]

By October 18 the police had finally decided that their prisoner was neither Frank James nor the elusive Cal Carter but John Goodwin of Cheneyville, Louisiana, a cattle trader and former member of Gen. Sterling Price's bodyguard during the war (identified as such by Price's son, Celsus). Several doctors also stated that the wound was several months old and could not have dated from the Northfield raid. One of them, Dr. J. C. Nedlet, was vice president of the board of police commissioners, and he ordered the prisoner to be released. "The whole affair has a farcical phase about it, and there is evidently ample room for Carter, the Jameses and their friends to laugh at the expense of the people and the papers," commented the *Globe-Democrat*. The detectives were again forced to eat crow, and Chief McDonough "was disgusted . . . and there is no getting over it."[8]

The same day that Goodwin was released newspapers reported an incident illustrating just how partisan Missouri politics could get. An excursion train from Springfield, loaded with two hundred Republicans, was leaving a rally at Marshfield when a shot was fired at the train and stones soon began to pelt the cars. The local Republicans fired back, but the train soon sped out of range. "Blood and Politics—Lawless Democrats Maintain Their Reputation in Missouri—They Shoot at and Set Fire to a Railroad Train" read one headline. "To complete the true inwardness of democracy, and to sustain the reputation Missouri has already acquired for firing into and stopping trains, this exhibition of partyism was necessary," the *Globe-Democrat* jibed.[9]

Soon national politics of an equally questionable and partisan nature would be snatching the headlines.

ON TUESDAY, November 7, 1876, voters went to the polls to elect a new president of the United States. Three days later the country was still wondering who had won. Samuel J. Tilden, a New York Democrat, was running against Ohio Republican Rutherford B. Hayes. Many press pundits were of the opinion that Tilden had won, but elections in three southern states—Louisiana, Florida, and South Carolina—were in dispute. It also happened that these three states were still under military occupation. In South Carolina a special Canvassing Board was established to decide who had won. All five members were Republican, and three of them were running for local office and thus had a conflict of interest. Louisiana had a board made up of four Republicans and one Democrat. In Florida, as in the other two states, there were reports of widespread voter fraud. "Vote early and vote often" apparently was more than just a jest.

On Wednesday, November 22, the *New York World* called the decision of the South Carolina Canvassing Board to hand the vote to Hayes "the foulest outrage yet. . . . The robbery was brazen and shameless. It rests with the American people to decide whether they will surrender the control of their Government into such hands, or maintain their liberties, their self-respect and prosperity by enforcing the remedies of the law against a lawless conspiracy without parallel in our annals."

Gen. Lew Wallace, later to author the novel *Ben-Hur,* was sent to Florida as an observer for the Republicans. He commented, "It is terrible to see the extent to which all classes go in their determination to win. Conscience offers no restraint. Nothing is so common as the resort to perjury, unless it is violence—in short, I do not know who to believe." Candidate Tilden would claim that the Florida delegation had offered to sell their vote for two hundred thousand dollars.[10]

On the same day that the *World* was crying foul over the election, Sheriff John S. Groom of Clay County, Missouri, tipped off to a visit by the James boys, was headed for the Samuel place outside Kearney, accompanied by a four-man posse. Arriving after dark on what was apparently the proverbial dark and stormy night, the men had trouble finding their way and getting into position.

"Frank was seen and saw the posse about the same time. He fired a shot in the air, as a signal for Jesse. Sheriff Groom and one man fired at Frank, without effect, when he fired at them, hitting the tree behind which Groom was concealed. The boys then mounted their horses and got away, halloing, 'Come on you cowardly sons of bitches.'"

The following day Groom trailed the brothers to the "Cummings [perhaps Jim Cummins's] place" about a mile outside of Liberty, but they again gave him the slip. For several days the posse combed the back roads of Clay County. Ed Miller, the brother of Clell, "and a man named Hoffman," were said to have been watching the movements of Groom as spies for the James brothers. The brothers' old haunts were becoming too hot, and in the wake of the Northfield defeat it was noted that the people of the county were "at last determined to rid the country of the bandits."[11]

On Sunday, November 26, Rice County, Minnesota, Sheriff Barton and three deputies took the Younger brothers, shackled together, by wagon from Saint Paul to the Minnesota State Penitentiary at Stillwater. On December 9 the Youngers had been arraigned at Faribault and had pleaded guilty on December 11 to robbery, attacking Alonzo Bunker, and being an accessory to the murder of Joseph Lee Heywood at the bank in Northfield. Cole was charged with the murder of Nicholas Gustavson in the streets of Northfield, and Bob and Jim were charged as accessories. By pleading guilty, under Minnesota law, they avoided hanging and were subsequently sentenced to prison for the rest of their natural lives.

Earlier, Sheriff Barton had attempted to get Cole to reveal the identity of the man who killed Heywood in exchange for consideration at the trial. "Be true to your friends if the Heavens fall," was a message Cole scrawled on a scrap of paper for the sheriff. That was all he would say.

"So the romance is knocked out of all this murderous and horrible business," commented the *Saint Paul Pioneer-Press*, as the Younger brothers departed for the Stillwater prison.

On December 28 the sheriff of Leavenworth County, Kansas, received a report that the James brothers had been spotted on a Chicago, Rock Island and Alton train heading for the city of Leavenworth. He went to the commander of Fort Leavenworth and obtained troops, which he posted along the line around the station. The train was searched on arrival, but the James boys were not to be found. Sheriff Groom, who may have sent the warning, telegraphed a description of the brothers. A man answering the description of Jesse James was reportedly spotted along the iron bridge across the Missouri, and railroad detective Jack Bridges of the Kansas Pacific, along with four other detectives, attempted to find him, but were unsuccessful.[12] As the year 1876 drew to a close, important changes were in the offing for the nation—and for Frank and Jesse James.

10

Alias Woodson and Howard

If you write a novel that's laid east of the Mississippi, it's an "historical." Set your story west of the river, and it's just a "Western." Basically it's a distinction engendered by "snobbishness."

Louis L'Amour, The Roundup, July 1975

B ELLICOSE UTTERANCES" READ THE headline over an article in the *New York Herald* on December 19, 1876. Gen. Jo Shelby had dropped a political bombshell amid rumors of impending civil conflict over the presidential election results. "If the Democrats determine upon an active opposition it will be necessary to inaugurate Tilden in some sort of fashion, give him a cabinet and establish a separate seat of government. . . . Then the issue will be reduced to a question of force. I for one will go with General Grant in whatever decision he may make," Shelby stated.

The former Confederate brigadier, who had led his men into Mexico at the end of the war to serve under Emperor Maximilian, must have either been "in his cups" or just plain confused about the situation. He was giving President Grant virtual dictatorial power in selecting his successor. The Twelfth Amendment of the Constitution spelled out that the vice president, presently a Republican, would open the ballots, but it didn't say who would count them. In any event, there were two sets of ballots from the disputed states of Florida, Louisiana, and South Carolina, and who knew what would happen in this highly charged political atmosphere? Jo Shelby,

193

friend of the James boys, had his own opinion on the matter: "If actual war should occur between the political parties, and President Grant should find it necessary to call for volunteers to sustain him, I should not lose two hours in responding."

Shelby, who had seen what the internecine war had done to Missouri, was backed by Col. Clay King of Lafayette County and by Col. Alonzo Slayback, both former Confederates. Shelby felt that the northern Democrats would sell out their southern brethren and leave them to fight it out alone. However, former Confederate Governor Reynolds "stated . . . that there was no doubt of Tilden's election, and if he was not sustained by those who elected him it would be a clear surrender of constitutional liberty." Allegedly former Confederate Gen. John S. Marmaduke of Missouri was then in New York conferring with Tilden on a military course. Perhaps Shelby was also trying to rein in the former bushwhackers, fearing that some latter-day Quantrill, possibly in the form of Jesse James, soon would be leading armed bands across the state (or even farther afield) again. Although not outwardly stated, this thought must have been on the minds of many that winter.

Early in 1877 Congress passed the Electoral Count Act, setting up an electoral commission of fifteen members, five each from the House, Senate, and Supreme Court (the president had no formal part in the proceedings). When the commission was called upon to decide the Florida vote in February 1877, the Republicans, who outnumbered the Democrats on the commission by eight to seven, tipped the scales in favor of their party's set of returns. The Democrats were furious. However, a deal was struck that, in exchange for recognizing Hayes as the winner of the presidential race, placed some Democrats in public office under the Republicans and withdrew federal troops from Louisiana and South Carolina, formally ending what was left of Reconstruction. There were rumors that a subsidy for the Texas and Pacific Railroad project, a southern transcontinental line, was part of the bargain too. Thomas Scott, president of the Pennsylvania Railroad, had been lobbying southern congressmen for some time on the project.

Perhaps memories of "the late unpleasantness" were too fresh. Tilden, in any event, did not dispute the election results, and Hayes was sworn in as president in March 1877, three days after the issue was settled. Federal troops began withdrawing from their old garrisons shortly afterward.

Just what was going on in the minds of Frank and Jesse James during the winter of 1876–77 will probably never be known. Even their whereabouts is a matter of question. By one account they spent at least part of the time in Adairville, Kentucky, with Uncle George Hite and family; another story has Jesse in northern Arkansas. Wherever they were, the sudden end of Reconstruction removed whatever excuse they had used for their outlaw escapades. Henceforth, there would be even less sympathy for them than there had been before. The word *carpetbagger* had about as much emotional impact in the post-1876 American South as the word *communist* would have in the United States following the 1991 collapse of communism in Eastern Europe. A new day was dawning. The James brothers' escape after the Northfield fiasco was no doubt still fresh in their memories. The controversy over Clay County's refusal to pay Sheriff Groom's posse may have struck them as humorous, but there would be other posses to contend with if they continued their banditry. They knew it, and perhaps more important, so did their wives.[1]

Not only was the Clay County posse having trouble collecting, but also the individuals who had had a hand in capturing or killing members of the gang in Minnesota were having a difficult time claiming what they believed should be their reward from Missouri. While attorney Samuel Hardwicke was visiting Northfield on other business at the end of 1876, the cashier of the bank mentioned to him that the bank was planning to withdraw its reward offer for the James brothers. "They showed me Gov. Hardin's letter in which the rewards were for 'arrest and conviction' whereas these parties [Stiles, Miller, and Pitts] were killed and technically, this may be a good objection," Hardwicke wrote a friend in Missouri. "But men like the James' who boast they will never be taken alive, if that construction is put on the rewards offered, they might as well not be offered at all."

Noting that the bank's reward of five hundred dollars each was still outstanding for the "capture" of the James boys, Hardwicke had further revelations. The offer was being made "because a client in the bank says, as he told me yesterday, that he was just as certain that Jesse James (or the one whose photograph he had) was one of the robbers who entered the bank as he is of anything. I saw the photograph. It is a good likeness of Jesse." Apparently the authorities had somehow obtained a photograph of Jesse and perhaps of Frank as well. At any rate, the brothers' hiding had just become a shade more difficult.

Hardwicke told the cashier that if the bank would postpone its decision to withhold the reward money he would write Judge E. H. Norton of Platte City, Missouri, to whom his letter quoted above was addressed. He was suggesting to Norton that for the good name of the state Hardin should take the matter to the legislature and ask it to authorize payment. He recalled overhearing, on his return to Saint Paul, two ladies talking about Missouri and the James brothers. "'Do all the people there sympathize with them?' asked one. 'No, only about two-thirds of them,' the other answered. . . . Hers is about the general impression that prevails with regard to Missouri," Hardwicke told Judge Norton.[2]

⚜

WHILE THE country failed to explode as the result of the election of 1876, yet another crisis loomed on the horizon. An economic depression, which had lasted since 1873, was being felt hard, and major "distress and suffering among the laboring classes" was reported by the British consul at Baltimore, where Frank and Jesse had left their families. Baltimore had fifteen trade unions at the start of the 1870s, but by 1876–77 only four or five remained.

At some point, Zee, Annie, and young Jesse Jr. left the city on the Chesapeake and headed back to Missouri. Apparently their plan was to relocate in Tennessee, perhaps around Nashville. The city was within a fairly easy ride of Uncle George Hite's place just across the state line in Adairville, Kentucky, and was a southern community that had withstood a harsh Union occupation during the war, something the James boys could identify with.

Ordinarily, the James families probably would have gone to Nashville by rail that summer of 1877, but fate prevented it. On June 1 the Pennsylvania Railroad had cut employee wages by 10 percent. Earlier, during a May meeting in Chicago, the Pennsylvania, Baltimore and Ohio Railroad and the Erie and New York Central and Hudson Railroads had met and agreed, as part of a pooling arrangement, to cut wages. On June 2, longshoremen working for the Pennsylvania Railroad in New York City walked off the job in protest. A month later most of the leading railroads—except the Baltimore and Ohio—followed suit and cut wages. On July 11, that line also announced cuts starting on Monday, July 16. On that date a strike began at Camden Junction, two miles from Baltimore, and at Martinsburg, West Virginia.

Militiamen were sent to Martinsburg, and a striker was fatally wounded. By the end of the week Federal troops had quashed the strike at Martinsburg, but the militia had been attacked outside Camden Depot. Rolling stock and buildings at nearby Camden Yards were burned by a mob. More troops and some marines were ordered to Baltimore. Violence also flared in Pittsburgh, where a battle developed between the militia and a mob at a Pennsylvania roundhouse.

By Sunday, July 22, the strike had spread as far as Saint Louis, and the next day railroad workers held a giant meeting in Kansas City, declaring a general strike to start on July 24 unless wage cuts were rescinded. Strikers in Saint Louis demanded such radical propositions as an eight-hour work-day and an end to child labor. A full-blown general strike failed to materi-alize in Kansas City. Troops and two Gatling guns were sent to Saint Louis from Fort Leavenworth.

The story of the strike of 1877 has been the focus of several books. In the words of historian David T. Burbank, "Only the element of indignation at cor-ruption in high places, added to the economic pressure of four years of indus-trial stagnation, can account for the explosive quality of the Great Strike." As Mark Twain put it, "Pittsburgh and the riots neither surprised nor disturbed me; for where the government is a sham, one must expect such things."

It was in this milieu that bandits could become folk heroes, at least when their enemies represented the side of oppression. In the aftermath of the strike came another ghostwritten tome under the name of Allan Pinker-ton, *Strikers, Communists, Tramps and Detectives*, a work that preyed on the fears and pandered to the prejudices of many of the well-to-do. It doubtless won the agency future business in antilabor spying and strike-breaking.[3]

Meanwhile, the James brothers and their families made their way to Tennessee. Tyler Burns, a former guerrilla who had gone to Kentucky with Quantrill in 1865, related how it happened: "I took Frank James and his wife away in a wagon. . . . While we were on our way in the wagon, when-ever we came to a town, Frank would ride around, joining us as soon as we passed the town. Johnnie Samuel [half brother of the James boys] was driv-ing Jesse James and his wife, who joined us, and all went together until they had a quarrel and separated, each saying to the other that they never wanted to see one another again."

The brothers apparently parted company somewhere near the Kentucky-Tennessee state line. Frank headed to Nashville while Jesse sought a more remote location in Humphreys County, not far from the Tennessee River, about seventy-five miles west of Nashville by rail.[4]

Jesse and his family probably arrived at the county seat of Waverly in August 1877. They came from the north, the direction of Clarksville. Whether Johnnie Samuel was with them is uncertain. Jesse lodged his wife and son at the Nolan Hotel and proceeded to check the lay of the land. Sizing things up, Humphreys County appeared to be good cattle country.

In the southwestern part of the county, about ten miles from Waverly, was an area known as Big Bottom. The Big Bottom was actually the flood-plain of the Duck River near its confluence with the Tennessee. It was in this area that most of the planting was done by local farmers, who lived on less fertile land farther to the north, near the community of Plant.

Using the name John Davis (Dave) Howard, Jesse rented some property owned by W. H. Link north of the bottomland. When the James family
moved in, there was only a small cabin on the place, although in later years
post cards claiming to show the home of Jesse James would picture another
house that was built on the property after their departure.[5]

Before moving to the Link place, there were a few loose ends to be
taken care of. Jesse bought some items at a store owned by Dan Goodrich,
who in later years remembered "Mr. Howard" as a rather agreeable fellow.
Jesse also made the acquaintance of Henry Warren at Box's Station (now
called Denver), a short distance from the town of Johnsonville on the railroad line to Nashville. Jesse had ordered two carloads of goods, apparently
from Nashville, and when he lacked the money to pay the freight, Warren
offered to loan the amount to him. Jesse never forgot this, and soon the
railroad agent and the outlaw were close friends.

Apparently, Jesse, alias Dave Howard, was trying to downplay his image
in public. The Mr. Howard of Humphreys County behaved quite differently from the Mr. Howard who had lived in Nashville two years before. A
number of stories were related in later years about the Howards and provide
a closer glimpse of Jesse, although it is impossible to say with accuracy
when these events occurred.

During the stay in Humphreys County Jesse assumed the role of gentleman farmer and grain speculator, at least as far as his means allowed. He and
Zee were known to give a number of parties, and they attended church
socials, always bringing plenty of food to the latter. According to Waverly
merchant Dan Goodrich, "There was no nicer family anywhere. Mrs.
Howard or Mrs. James . . . was an excellent lady, friendly to everyone and
especially attentive to the sick." No doubt Zee was tired of running and
wanted to live some sort of normal life for a change. Frank's wife doubtless
felt the same. The Northfield affair had been too close a call for all concerned. Despite their bravado, the James brothers probably considered
themselves lucky to have escaped.

Jesse is said to have laid off a race course on the Link property where he
showed off his prize possession, a racehorse named Red Fox. The horse was
admitted by all to be the fastest in the county and one of the fastest in the
state. Few realized that there was a better reason for owning such an animal
than everyday racing. Whenever he rode into Waverly, Jesse kept Red Fox
close at hand. The story also went that Jesse would sleep in the barn at the
Nolan Hotel if a single room was unavailable. Supposedly Jesse always tried to
keep people from coming up behind him and sat or stood with his back to a
wall whenever possible.

Like a number of people living in rural Tennessee, Jesse carried a pistol, usually concealed in a shoulder holster or saddlebag. Rural areas in the eastern half of the country, and particularly in the South, were in many ways similar to Jesse's stomping ground in Missouri. Both had their share of violence.

On a few occasions Jesse was reported to have displayed his marksmanship with a revolver. Once during a barbecue at the Humphreys County Fairground, a dog managed to filch some meat. Someone said the dog should be killed, and Jesse obliged. Taking a pistol from his saddlebag (in this case), Jesse killed the marauder with one shot, to the surprise of everyone. Another time a contest was held at the county fair in which a candle was placed on an upturned barrel, and the locals tried to shoot it out. Jesse was apparently rather exasperated with the display and is said to have snuffed the candle with one shot, again to the amazement of onlookers. "Light it again," he said, and shifted the gun to his left hand and repeated the feat.

There were other episodes as well. One day while racing horses at the Link place an argument over a bet developed between Jesse and another racer, Jim Ward. Ward began to curse out "Mr. Howard," using language that was anything but sacred, and it appeared that he wanted to fight. Jesse got his saddlebags, tossed them over his left shoulder, and slipped his hand under the flap of one of them. He walked up to Ward and said: "Jim, when I came up here I had my mind made up to kill you, but I've changed my notion. You can call me anything you want, but if you hit me I'm going to shoot you. Now what are you going to do?"

Ward resumed telling Howard off, but he never struck Jesse.

The outlaw listened with a grin on his face and then mounted his horse and rode away laughing. It was only years later that the impact of what had happened dawned on those present.

Jesse had a similar run-in with D. B. Thomas, described by his neighbors as "a very fractious man." Without obtaining a waiver, apparently a customary practice in the 1870s, Thomas had hired one of Jesse's black field hands out from under him. When Jesse told Thomas he wanted his man back, Thomas lost his temper. Jesse reached for his gun then stopped, suddenly turned his horse, and again rode off laughing.

Jesse may have realized that his Howard character was acting a bit out of character after word spread about his skill with a six-shooter. To rectify this situation, Jesse began to feign cowardice, or so the story goes. One evening he appeared in front of the Nolan Hotel in a frightened state, claiming he had been "set upon by ruffians" at a nearby bridge. Several men at the hotel, including station agent Warren, gathered an assortment

Nashville Sites Related to the James Brothers

1. Earthman's Store
2. Felix Smith Place
3. Josiah Walton Farm
4. Nashville Blood Horse Association Racetrack
5. Jeff Hyde Place
6. Mrs. Kent's Boarding House
7. 903 Woodland Street
8. 711 Fatherland Street
9. 814 Fatherland Street
10. 606 Boscobel Street

of firearms and moved on the bridge, only to find two other locals, Pat Halpin and Cul Fortner, who were drunk. The two had stumbled across Jesse while entering town and had tried to assure Howard of their undying friendship by hanging on to his neck and shoulders. Jesse asked the erstwhile posse to forgive him for becoming so alarmed and implored them not to mention the incident.[6]

Early in 1878 a rather unusual event transpired when Howard was sued by Steve Johnson of Nashville, supposedly to collect a debt. It is not known whether the money owed was a loan given to Howard or a gambling debt. Certainly Jesse required capital to get set up at the Link place, and he was also known to gamble on the side.

James Koger recalled that Jesse-Howard "associated with some gamblers of notorious reputation" who frequented the Nashville racetrack. On one occasion Jesse had even pulled a pistol on a man who tried to cheat him out of a five-hundred-dollar wager in a horse race. Still, Jesse hung around with what Koger called the "crooked gambling fraternity" in Nashville, something Koger objected to about his boss.

Steve Johnson, possibly one of the gamblers, brought suit against Howard. Although the date this grievance began is uncertain, Jesse was in contact with John P. Helms, his attorney in the matter, by at least January 17, 1878. Howard wrote Helms, in Nashville, from Johnsonville, Tennessee:

> Please let me know about my suit; has Johnson gave bond, etc. Fully investigate the law and see what can be done with Johnson. He is trying to get money under false pretenses and has testified to things he knows are false. If there is any show to receive damages, I want to recover something, as I have been put to considerable expense. If Johnson could be arrested and sent to jail, his friends, the gamblers of Nashville, would pay us for our trouble to get him out of jail. . . . First and last he has caused me $56 expense and has acted so as to injure my credit unless I prosecute him.

On January 24 Jesse wrote again to Helms, speaking of being needed at home and not being able to travel. His wife was sick, he said, and he was busy. He asked Helms if Johnson would drop his suit and let him have some money owed him by a third party. If he did he would not "prosecute" (file a countersuit?); otherwise he would "prosecute him with a vengeance."[7]

Jesse's wife was pregnant and in February gave birth to twins named Gould and Montgomery after the two attending doctors. The twins lived only a short while, a week by one account, and were buried in a grave behind the Link place at the bottom of a hill. The graves were marked with plain boulders. A popular story grew later that Jesse had carved headstones with his own hands and placed them over the graves, but such was probably not the case.[8]

The Johnson case carried on into the spring. On April 5, a motion was overruled in court "to dismiss the appeal because the appeal bond was given after the time proscribed by law." A letter to Helms from Howard dated April 20 tells of the twins' deaths and his wife's fragile health. He asked that the matter be brought to trial as he feared Johnson would try to delay the matter.

On May 12 Jesse sent yet another letter to Helms, asking that B. J. Woodson of "Eaton's Creek, Davidson County, Tennessee" serve as a witness for him. Woodson was Jesse's brother Frank. "Let him know and he will be present," the letter said.

All correspondence mentions a May 30 court date, but when the date rolled around, Howard failed to appear. On June 10, however, Jesse sent a letter indicating that he had been surprised to learn of the date. Earlier he had asked that Helms write him ten days in advance. "I am so busy I only go to the post office on Saturdays." In addition to work, Jesse may have had recurring problems with malaria, of which more will be said later.

Jesse's main concern in the letters seems to have been obtaining access to some money that may have been in contention. "Has Mr. P. K. Rhea got possession of the money, or has he turned it over to the Circuit Court Clerk? Please let me know, for I want to get possession of the money, so I can use it, for there is no telling when it [the case] will be decided," Jesse wrote Helms. On June 14 Helms received his last written communication in the case via post card. "Mr. Rhea does not want to give up the money until he is released from the bond is why I want to give a new bond." Presumably other contacts with Helms were in person after this.[9]

Meanwhile, after leaving Jesse and Zee near the Kentucky line, Frank and Annie had gone to Nashville, arriving sometime in August 1877. Posing as a farmer from Indiana, Frank resumed the alias of Ben J. Woodson while Annie added an F to her name and became Fannie. Frank may have been suffering from a bout of malaria when he stopped at the home of Ben Drake, who lived several miles northwest of Nashville on Hydes Ferry Pike. Drake, noting Woodson's illness, asked Frank and his wife to stay until they could find quarters elsewhere. A week later Frank and Annie moved in with Drake's sister, a Mrs. Ledbetter.

Frank began to recover and soon rented some land along nearby Whites Creek from Josiah Walton. The Woodsons would live in a cabin near the Walton house (near the intersection of present-day Kings Lane and Drakes Branch Road) west of the Clarksville Pike. Frank engaged in sharecropping while living at the Walton farm, "seldom failing to put in ten hours a day in the field," by his own account.

Yet there was something odd about the Woodsons. One day a son of Josiah Walton decided to visit with Mr. Woodson in the field while he was planting corn. He called out to Frank, who in turn yelled back asking who it was. Walton failed to respond and soon found himself looking down the barrels of two loaded six-shooters. Lowering his guns, a much relieved Frank told the boy to answer the next time.

At another time Annie offered a startled Mrs. Walton, who was about to attend a party, her pick from a box of jewelry. Mrs. Walton had none, yet the tenant wife did—and in some quantity. The James women were noted for having committed several good deeds while in Tennessee, which doubtless only later served to enhance the Robin Hood image of their spouses.[10]

In the Nashville area Mr. Woodson earned the reputation of an honest, hardworking citizen. He also claimed to be a "good Republican" from Indiana, which on at least one occasion caused him some trouble. Frank was having some horses shod by blacksmith Dan "Dude" Young. Young was a former Confederate soldier and had reportedly been drinking rather freely prior to Frank's arrival. Frank supposedly had stung Young earlier in a horse swap, which didn't help matters. When Frank made a suggestion about shoeing the horses, Young's rage exploded. The black-smith, "a great double-fisted fellow," as Frank later described him, began airing his lungs, calling Frank a "carpetbagger and a damn yankee," among other things. It looked for a time like Young planned to rough Frank up, and of course Frank would have shot him before that happened, although Young wasn't aware of that danger. Frank tried to reason with Young and eventually slipped away after he quieted down. Normally Frank was on good terms with Young and his brother, a Davidson County constable.[11]

Frank apparently had some contact with Jesse following their parting, but when and under what circumstances they got together is uncertain. Frank was certainly in contact with Jesse by early 1878, when Robert Franklin James was born at the Walton place on February 6. In an effort to confuse others about his identity, Robert was reportedly called Mary. It was common practice in those days to dress infants of both sexes in skirts until they were toilet trained.[12]

James Koger recalled introducing Woodson and Howard to each other. He was a bit puzzled when the newly introduced men went behind some stacks of grain and had a private conversation that lasted at least an hour. Later Woodson would be known in Humphreys County as Dave Howard's brother-in-law. He visited Jesse at the Link place, possibly with Jonas Taylor, a blacksmith whose shop was at 9 South College Street (present-day Third Avenue South, just off Broadway). Jesse and Taylor were part owners of several racehorses, Jim Scott and Colonel Hull. Taylor also reportedly visited Jesse at Big Bottom and had both Jim Scott and Colonel Hull down there, too. "We went to Waverly, to the fair . . . on account of the Yellow Fever didn't go any further," he later recalled, possibly referring to Jesse's bout with malaria in 1878. "I ate dinner with Howard several times; they lived common, like poor folks, his wife doing the cooking."

Apparently Jesse's investments in horseflesh could partly account for his straightened-out financial circumstances.

In Humphreys County as well as in Nashville, Howard was known to gamble, which may have caused some of his problems with other residents there. "Although Frank looked like a preacher he played poker like a politician," according to one account, and many Humphreys County wallets left the game a little lighter in consequence. Jesse, by contrast, had a terrible reputation at poker and often lost.[13]

There were numerous stories of Howard's racehorse, Red Fox, which he raced locally. One story passed down in the Link family claimed that Jesse would sometimes disguise a horse with shoe polish and enter it in a race under an alias. Jesse also reportedly threw a race while riding Red Fox against a horse from another county. Red Fox stumbled, and rumors afterward suggested that Howard had bet heavily on his competitor. On another occasion, Jesse contested a race in which his horse fell, and the race was run again. It was also said that during the times of the county fair, Jesse would stay with his horses at night.[14]

Jesse's days in Humphreys County were numbered as the result of the very complex financial house of cards he was living in. The catalyst was likely the Johnson lawsuit. Sometime, possibly in the summer of 1878, Jesse learned that Ennis Morrow Cooley had a herd of cattle for sale. Cooley had served in T. A. Napier's battalion of Nathan Bedford Forrest's cavalry during the war. The man was trying to send his son, James T. Cooley, to medical school at the Nashville College of Surgeons and needed the money for tuition.

Howard came to Cooley, offering to buy the cattle and pay with a bank draft. "Don't sell that man anything without cash," Cooley's wife advised. But Cooley went ahead and sold Howard the cattle in exchange for a check (reportedly between five hundred and one thousand dollars). Jesse had the cattle shipped to the Wade and Kessler Stockyard in Nashville, where they were sold.

Meanwhile, Howard's check bounced. Cooley was furious, and according to one story he set out to get payment armed with a double-barreled shotgun. During the confrontation Howard nervously paced back and forth, keeping an eye on the shotgun. "All I ask is that you do not shoot me in the back," he reportedly told Cooley.

Howard may have offered to mortgage his horses to settle the debt. Whatever happened, Cooley appears to have left empty-handed. His son, later to become the "baby doctor of Humphreys County," would have his schooling delayed that fall and for some time after.

Jesse set off for the state fair in Nashville. Ironically, the earlier legal problem was coming to a head at the same time. The Johnson suit was set for trial the same day as the horse race, September 11, but Jesse apparently used some of the proceeds from the cattle sale to settle with Johnson and cover his legal expenses. The circuit court docket for September 11, 1878, records the case as being dismissed: "It appearing to the Court that this cause has this day been compromised, the same is thereupon dismissed at the cost of the defendant, which has this day been paid."

Meanwhile, back at the fairgrounds, right under the eyes of the police and detectives, was Jesse, alias Howard, one of about thirty contestants vying for the prize being offered to the most graceful horseback rider. If he had been Robin Hood, he would have won, but Jesse lost the competition to one of the local "dudes," as he put it. Under their aliases, both Jesse and Frank entered horses in the various races. Ben Woodson's horse Rebel finished last in a race on September 11. On September 13 Woodson's Jewell Maxey won the first race and Colonel Hull (who may then have been owned in partnership with W. H. Cheatham) won the second race's purse of two hundred dollars. Woodson's Rebel, entered in the same race, came in third, earning a forty-dollar prize, and Howard's Rio Grande finished last.[15]

Time, however, was running out for John Davis Howard at Big Bottom. Sometime earlier Howard had accompanied Sheriff J. P. White while riding through the Big Bottom country. That night he had shown White some rather fine watches and jewelry, probably from the Hot Springs and Gads Hill affairs. White was surprised, and Jesse realized that the next time he saw Sheriff White he might be bearing a warrant or a summons. Arriving back from a trip by rail in December, Jesse packed his family and belongings in wagons and left for Nashville.[16]

Just what was going through Jesse's mind at that time has remained a mystery for more than a century, but a recently discovered letter from John Davis Howard to Henry Warren, sent from Nashville on January 12, 1879, explains much:

Friend Henry,
    I know you will be surprised to hear from me but I hope it will be an agreeable surprise. I understand that most people in the Bottom are giving me the *Devil*. Talk is cheap & dont *hurt me*. I did not *leave* the Bottom to *defraud* any one. I am *broke* and left there to avoid lawsuits. I am *broke* but as soon as I am able I expect to pay every dollar I owe except what I owe M.M. Box & Sam *Larkin*. I will see them in *Hell* before I will ever pay *them* one *cent*. I fully intended to pay Box, but he came here & had Mr. Woodson's *corn Attached* and *swore* to knowing & *malicious Lies*. but Mr. Woodson [replaced?] the *corn* & *mark it* Henry. Box has come in contact with men he can't bluff—and he will have to spend several hundred dollars to

fight the *law Suit* and he will be sure to *meet with* a defeat in the *end*. Box's *knowed* I had sold the corn to Mr. Woodson & it layed in the Depot several days & was on the track several days & box knowed all about it & when it goes to a *Jury* & the rulings of the Supreme Court are read to the Jury, Box will get beat sure. If Box had acted a man & come to me I would have borrowed the money & payed him but he acted a *damd wolf* & proved him self not to be a through*bred* & you ask Jack [King?] what I told Box to his *face* & he took it like a child. Henry I owe *Hearne* four dollars. Tell him to rest easy I will pay him *sure*. Also, tell W. K. Jackson to rest easy about the note he has against me for the S[ewing] *machine*. I will pay him every dollar of it as soon as I can and I will be able to pay him soon.

Henry I have been Box's friend & have made a desperate fight for him in the *Depot matter* but he is a damned wolf & I am at *war* with him and I will do all in my power to defeat his Depot & I think I can do it & some of our friends will call on major Thomas tomorrow & give him some [choir music] about Stock yards at Box's depot *&c.&c.* any thing I can do to defeat *Box* I will do. *Please* tell Frank Haggner to forward all my mail to Nashville . . . Your friend, J. D. Howard

Please let me know where Jno. [Hagley?] colored is & if you see him tell him I want him to come & live with me . . . let me know what he says about it. JDH

Henry I am anxious to see you & will meet you at Depot any day you will come here [if you will write me?] in time. JDH[17]

Before he left Big Bottom, Jesse reportedly paid Henry Jackson sixty dollars he owed him from an earlier loan, but he did not attempt to pay back Ennis Cooley, who was also on his hate list. Cooley reportedly filed a lawsuit against Jesse-Howard, apparently in Humphreys County, but the case met with various legal tangles and was reportedly still before the Tennessee Supreme Court in 1882, long after Jesse had left the state. According to one story, Jesse challenged Cooley's attorney to a duel. He apparently declined, perhaps because dueling had been illegal in Tennessee since the days of Andrew Jackson. Jesse's letter gives us a fleeting glimpse of his dealings with others, including his "bantering insults and challenges."

Sam Larkins may have been the man Jesse accused of selling him a blind mule. Jesse refused to pay for the animal, claiming Larkins was a cheat. The *Waverly Journal* termed his dealings with "Mr. L." as "unique and decisive," brushing away "the annoyance, trouble, expense and delay of a 'horse law suit.' He just leveled his double barreled shot gun at L. and told him if he wanted any thing for that mule to talk to that shot gun. This was, and doubtless wisely, taken by L. as the decision of the court of last resort."[18]

11

Back on the Outlaw Trail

The New South was a notoriously violent place. . . . Lethal weapons
seemed everywhere. Guns as well as life were cheap.

Edward L. Ayer, The Promise of the New South (1992)

SOMETIME IN LATE 1878 or early 1879 Frank rented a farm known as the
Felix Smith place, to the east of the Clarksville Pike, not far from the
Walton farm. It was a good location. The house stood on a knoll overlooking the pike, and one could see anyone coming for a good distance. It was to
the Smith place that Jesse and family came next.

On March 17, 1879, Dr. W. A. Hamilton diagnosed "Mr. Howard" as
having malaria. Just when he began having problems with his health is
uncertain, but he seemingly was laid up for quite a while.

The next glimpse we have of Jesse is in a letter he wrote to Henry Warren
on April 24, 1879:

Friend Henry,

Your welcome letter of the 19th to hand and note Henry, I hope you will
be sure to come up the 29th and Stay all week as the races will be very interesting, I am sure you can make more than your expenses.

If my creditors will compromise me at .50 on the dollar the prospects
are very flattering for me to get money enough to pay all my debts off,
bring up the Larkins note and probably we can trade on it, also bring up

the following acts that I owe, Amos Corbitt, $12; Harve Warren, $4; Robert Clark, $15; Linzy Warren $2.25; McLey, $4; Joe McKelvy, $1.70 and I will try to pay those small debts [off] in full get those gentlemen to permit you to give me [their] receipts.

As some things have transpired recently, I do not promise to pay Mr. Jackson until after the Cooley law suit is decided. I will explain fully to you be sure to come up Tuesday the 29th I will be at the race track write aonce on the arival of this letter and let me know if you will be up, Address to

John D. Howard
Nashville, Tenn

I will get your letter sooner as I am in the city every day.

your friend,
J.D.H.

Jesse apparently had come to terms with Larkins, probably through the intercession of Warren. It is likely that there was an earlier meeting or an exchange of correspondence that has since been lost.

Many of the debts are small and possibly were gambling debts.

The race mentioned on April 29 was at the Nashville Blood-Horse Association racetrack, sometimes called "the Flats" (in an area of present-day north Nashville occupied by the Metro Center complex). There were at least three races that day, including the Young America Stakes No. 1, a half-mile run for two-year-old horses, which had an entry from "B. J. Woodson." Frank's horse, Jim Scott, finished dead last. The horse would run again on May 3, and would come in next to last of seven horses running.

Jesse wrote Warren again on May 18. From the sound of the note Warren had come up as invited, earlier:

I felt very bad all day yesterday after drinking so much beer, but am OK today. I expect to attend the faul races at Nashville this week and invest on the Louisville events and hope you will attend if we will be prudent I think we can win some money if you come up bring up those claims you had at the races against me and first winnings I will pay you, also bring the $40 note Jackson holds against me and if I ever win I will pay them off, What does Morry say about getting his foot in for the cost here and getting beat, if you are not coming up please write me at once and address Nashville.

Your Friend,
J. D. Howard[1]

Jesse had settled down to something of a sporting life. Aleck Ament, a bartender at the Crockford Saloon in Nashville, had a very clear recollection of both Frank and Jesse at this time:

They were very quiet men. They spoke very little and attended their own business. . . . Frank was the quieter of the two, though Jesse never talked a great deal. They were the greenest looking fellows I ever saw, but I never heard of anybody's getting the better of them. Frank used to sit off by himself on the track and whittle a stick, and seemed to think a great deal. Neither of the men ever joked and they laughed but little. They both gambled a great deal. They were said to play poker right smart and play all sorts of games big and little. They used to own two or three quarter horses and loved to run quarter races. They were very successful at these. The horses heads are turned away before the start and at the signal they turn around and the whips are used freely till they run the quarter of a mile. The James boys used to have a little mare that was the most successful quarter runner I ever saw.[2]

Jesse once was playing a game of poker at a faro parlor in the Colonnade Building on the corner of Deadrick and Cherry (now Fourth Avenue North) Streets. Someone ran in a "cold deck," and Jesse, ever so calmly, drew a revolver from his shoulder holster and placed it in his lap with the remark, "Nothing like that goes." Apparently it didn't.[3]

In the summer of 1879, Jesse very likely made a trip west of the Mississippi that took him as far as the railhead of the new Santa Fe line at Las Vegas in northern New Mexico. He probably was investigating the prospects in New Mexico Territory, either to relocate there and escape creditors, as he attempted to "go straight," or to operate in the area with a new gang. He was at least sizing it up as he visited with an old friend from Missouri, Scott Moore, who with his wife ran a hotel and bathhouse at the hot springs about six miles from town. It was here that a rather remarkable meeting probably took place between two of the most legendary American outlaws of all time.

Dr. Henry Hoyt, the same man who had left Charlie Pitts's corpse to rot in a Minnesota lake, was a witness to this unique event. As fate would have it, after leaving medical school he had drifted first to Deadwood, Dakota Territory, in 1877, then to the Texas Panhandle, where he lived and worked out of Tascosa, patching up cowhands and brawlers in the local saloons. It was during his stay there that he made the acquaintance of William McCarty, alias Bonney, known as "the Kid"—Billy the Kid. Hoyt eventually drifted to Las Vegas, where he also worked as a bartender.

On Sunday, July 27, 1877, Hoyt went out to the hot springs hotel run by Moore. The room was crowded, but Hoyt managed to find the last vacant seat, at a corner table with three other men. One was Billy, uncharacteristically dressed in a suit. The doctor and he were chatting away about Texas when a man on the Kid's left made a comment. Billy introduced the stranger:

"Hoyt, meet my friend Mr. Howard from Tennessee." Hoyt sized up Howard initially as a "railroad man," noticing his "piercing steely blue eyes with a peculiar blink" and a missing fingertip on his left hand.

Howard was "most congenial, a good talker," and appeared to have traveled a good bit over the years. After dinner Billy took the doctor to his room at the hotel, and then, after pledging him to secrecy, revealed that Howard was none other than Jesse James. Hoyt was at first skeptical.

According to Hoyt, Jesse had made a tentative proposition "that they join forces and hit the trail together." But Billy was not a bank or train robber. His specialty was the somewhat less controversial although still illegal practice of rounding up livestock owned by others. Rustling was held in about the same category as bootlegging and was not as serious an offense. This, and the fact that teaming up with Jesse would pull him away from the Fort Sumner area (about ninety miles away from Las Vegas), caused Billy to reject the proposition. That evening, Hoyt and Jesse met again. Hoyt couldn't resist, during a conversation about different areas of the country, asking if Howard had ever been to Saint Paul, Minnesota. "He replied in the negative, in the most nonchalant manner, and changed the subject."[4]

At least one other man claimed to have met Jesse at the same time. Miguel Ortero, later to serve as territorial governor of New Mexico from 1897 to 1906, was working for his father's commission house and bank in Las Vegas when Jesse visited there. He too frequented the hotel dining hall, having known Moore in Kansas when Moore was working as a freight conductor there. Ortero met Howard in the dining room the day before Hoyt met him there. Moore had tipped him off about the stranger's identity but had sworn him to secrecy. Ortero recalled Jesse as "noticeably quiet and reserved," with "piercing" blue eyes. He wore a short, full beard at the time and was dressed in a short brown frock coat "on the order of a short Prince Albert" and a black felt hat with a low crown and moderately wide brim.

During the conversation Jesse asked a few questions about stock raising in the area. Moore apparently told Ortero that his guest was there for a little rest and to explore the possibility of relocating in either the Southwest or in Mexico as a rancher. He reportedly stayed in the area only a few days. The *Las Vegas Optic* for December 6, 1879, reported, "Jessie James was a guest at the Las Vegas Hot Springs, July 26th to 29th. Of course it was not generally known."[5]

If Jesse had any intent on possibly coming to the Las Vegas area he undoubtedly learned that a crowd of "bad hombres" had been lured to the area by the railroad. John Henry "Doc" Holliday had arrived just prior and was operating a saloon and gambling hall in East Las Vegas when Jesse arrived. On his heels came Hyman G. Neill, alias Hoodoo Brown, and other members of what became known as the Dodge City gang. Brown started out as a gambler and confidence man, but after settling in East Las Vegas was elected justice of the peace! Brown even managed to place cronies, including gunman "Mysterious Dave" Mather and train robber Dave Rudabaugh, in positions as policemen. Jesse may have figured that the fox would be running the hen house here and that there would be trouble, either from outside lawmen or in a turf battle between the flotsam.

Between August and October the Dodge City boys robbed one or two Santa Fe trains and a couple of stagecoaches. When Jesse eventually put together a gang in Missouri and began operations against the Chicago and Alton, he was at first suspected of having a hand in the robberies around Las Vegas, so much so that detectives were sent east to Missouri to investigate a possible link. In all probability those holdups were the work of Rudabaugh and company, aided and abetted by Brown. There are numerous tales of the James brothers' allegedly holding up stagecoaches in Colorado in the same general time frame, but these robberies were apparently the work of two men known as the Thompson brothers, who either posed as Frank and Jesse or were mistaken by others for them.[6]

Jesse was indeed set on starting up a new gang, though. Certainly he had more legal bills to cover in his life as "Mr. Howard" back in Tennessee. He also had another mouth to feed after a daughter, Mary, was born at the Smith place on July 17. Jesse may well have returned to Nashville by September before heading back to his old stomping grounds in Missouri. Trying to establish a reputation for honest work, Frank refused to have any part in the schemes his brother was dreaming up.

In addition to farming, there is a chance that Frank and Jesse may have been connected with the Lambert Mocker barrel factory in the fall of 1879, if not before. A photo showing Mocker and his employees, possibly taken in September 1879, is linked by oral history and photo analysis to the brothers' likenesses in other photos.[7]

Jesse apparently was making plans for a new gang as early as the spring of 1879. In April of that year Daniel Bassham, who went by the nickname "Tucker," had been approached by Bill Ryan, an Irishman who lived in the "Crackerneck" area south of Independence, Missouri. Ryan, who appears to have had no criminal activity up to this point in his life (he was about twenty-eight years old) and who was better known as a boozer who frequented Independence's saloons, somehow hooked up with Jesse and was helping him recruit. It was to prove a strange and fateful collaboration.

Another recruit was James A. "Dick" Liddil, a rather dapper-looking young man from Vernon County, Missouri, who had recently been released from the penitentiary after serving three and a half years for horse stealing. Liddil met Jesse at the farm of Ben Morrow in Jackson County. Morrow was a former Quantrillan who had harbored the James boys on numerous occasions. One day in late September 1879, Morrow told Liddil that Jesse wanted to see him. "About 2 o'clock I went to Ben's and found Jesse in the yard," Liddil later recalled. "We had a chat, and went out where his horse was tied in the woods. He said he was broke and wanted to make a raise, and wanted me to help him. I agreed."

The new gang would consist of Tucker Bassham, Bill Ryan, Dick Liddil, Jesse's cousin Wood Hite, and Ed Miller, brother of Clell Miller, who had been killed in the Northfield raid. The band gathered at the Seever schoolhouse about sundown on October 8. Jesse was armed with two Colt .45s, and Miller had a breechloading shotgun, a Smith and Wesson .44, and a Colt Navy cap-and-ball revolver. Liddil had a pair of Smith and Wessons. Bassham didn't have a gun, so he was given a revolver from Miller and Hite, type uncertain, and Jesse gave him a shotgun, probably a double-barreled muzzleloader, "and a supply of cartridges, buckshot, powder and caps." He also read them a dispatch he'd prepared to give out after the robbery was done. Jesse finally pulled out a watch, glanced at it, and said, "Boys, it's time to go." With that they took the main road to the little station of Glendale, just south of Independence, riding two abreast.

Around 1877 the railroad had begun doing surveys for a line into Kansas City that took it through the Crackerneck. As Phil McCarty recalled, "There was a lot of opposition by the farmers to having the road run through their farms and as a compromise the railroad company agreed to a depot at that point [Glendale] with a nice depot, telegraph accommodations, stock pens and loading platforms where freight could be loaded and received."

About seventy-five feet from the depot was a small store run by Joe Matts. "Joe's stock in trade consisted of cigars, plug tobacco, a few canned goods and a barrel of whiskey at the back end of the room," recalled McCarty, who was only fourteen years old in October 1879.

"It had a wooden faucet and a tin cup on the barrel. All you had to do was give Joe a dime, walk back and wait on yourself and Joe would look the other way while you drank from the tin cup."

McCarty and his brother loitered about the area that day until, by one account, they were chased off by the telegraph operator, who didn't like their looks. They were about three hundred yards from a bridge that crossed the Little Blue River when they heard six horses "trotting fast over the bridge, coming directly towards us." McCarty recalled that "as they neared us they motioned for us to open the gate [leading to the road from the station]. As the first pair, Bill Ryan and Jesse, rode through, Ryan recognized my brother. Ryan had a large handkerchief around his neck. He pulled it up partly over his face and told Jesse to order us to come back to the depot. My brother almost asked 'Bill, don't you know us?' but he didn't and it was well he kept still."

McCarty and his family did know the Ryans. When Bill Ryan's older brother, Ed, had struck his head on a low-hanging tree limb while returning from Independence, McCarty's oldest brother had been one of the first on the scene. Years later the story of Ed Ryan's death would be muddled by a reporter named Duke with the *Kansas City Star,* who would claim that Bill Ryan, not Ed, met his end this way. The tale would be repeated by author Carl Breihan in his books about the James gang.

Tucker Bassham explained what happened next at the Glendale station.

> When we reached the gate [on the county road near the station] Jesse James called a halt, and said he wanted Ryan, Underwood [Liddil] and "Arkansas," as he called me, to take possession of Joe Matt's store and let no one come out. We did so while he, Miller and "Bob" [Wood Hite] went to the depot. We stayed at the store for ten minutes and drove back all who attempted to come outside. Ed Miller and "Bob" then came over and we, together compelled the men in the store to go to the depot. There were eight or ten of them.

The bandits entered the telegraph office, took the operator, named Andrews, prisoner, and smashed his telegraph. Upstairs in the living quarters they captured W. E. Bridges, auditor for the railroad, and robbed him. Mrs. Andrews, mother of the telegrapher, was also upstairs. Bassham continued the story:

> The first thing I heard after reaching the depot was a lady crying and saying "Don't kill my son." Jesse James told her he would not hurt her boy if he would do what was wanted of him. He then ordered the young man, who was the station agent, to bring out a signal to stop the train. The agent told Jesse he had no red light, when Jesse said he could use a white one.

The agent got a green light, which was turned over to Ryan with instructions to go down the track and stop the train. Ryan was disguised with a winter cap, similar to a modern ski mask, drawn down over his face. Jesse and Hite wore no disguise, but Bassham, Liddil, and Miller "had handkerchiefs tied over [their] faces with mouth and eye holes cut in them."

The nervous agent asked Ryan if they were going to kill him. "No, it's the money we want." The agent then said he'd heard about train robberies and the James gang and was curious about them. "You see them tonight," Ryan replied. "We are the James gang."

Jesse asked the agent if there were any rails about with which they could block the track, but there weren't any. Jesse and Miller walked down the track and found a boulder that they rolled onto the track.

About five minutes later the eastbound train came along. Ryan and Liddil took the engineer and brakeman prisoner and stopped the train. Bassham and Hite were on the platform; their prisoners were locked in the depot shed. Jesse and Miller approached the express car, and there was inter-mittent shooting throughout the next few minutes. Miller began beating in the door until the messenger yelled, "Don't break it down, I'll open it."

Jesse and Miller entered the car with a sack. They demanded the keys to the safe. Express messenger William R. Grimes was a little slow and was pistol-whipped. "You hadn't ought to strike an old man that way. I used to be a gray myself," Grimes retorted.

The men busied themselves in emptying the safe and were told that the packages contained $60,000. "That tickled them and they danced around the car for joy," Grimes recalled.

Jesse and Miller overlooked one package containing $180 for a station down the line. According to one version of the story there was reportedly a bullion shipment coming out of Leadville, Colorado, which they thought was aboard, but apparently the safe held only paper money. Nevertheless, "They gave a whoop and disappeared into the darkness," Grimes related later.

"Boys, we had better get away," Jesse yelled and told the railroad men that they'd better remove the rock from the track.

"We are the lucky men; we have got $50,000," Bassham recalled Jesse saying. Aside from the money taken, the bandits took two revolvers and a shotgun, which they threw into a nearby stream.

Inside the passenger cars folks had scrambled to hide their valuables anywhere—curtains, spitoons, seat cushions, and so forth. According to a railroad porter, "They just lay quietly on their stomachs" until the robbers rode off. One man told the porter to give his family in Wisconsin his prayers in case he was killed. Another, after the shooting had stopped, was indignant because the porter would not go outside and see what was hap-pening. But the porter told him that he could go himself, that he wasn't going to risk his life to satisfy the passenger's curiosity. Outraged, the man called the porter a coward and threatened to report him to the company.[8]

The gang rode south down the Harrisonville road, right through the heart of the Crackerneck. Traveling several miles, they eventually stopped at an unoccupied house known as the McPhereson place. Jesse broke in the door, and one of the gang produced a lamp with no chimney, which was lit. "Miller turned the contents of the sack out on a table in the room," Bassham recalled. "He and Jesse James then counted out the money and divided it around; I got about $800 or $900 [Liddil said he got $1,025]; Jesse then told Ryan to burn the papers in the stove." They discovered that the $60,000 had turned into roughly $6,000, with most of the packages containing nonnegotiable securities, if anything of remote value. After this the men split up. Jesse advised Bassham to go home and go back to work as though nothing had happened. He told him to be careful how he spent his money and not to carry more than $15 with him at any one time.

Jesse headed off with Ed Miller to the "Six-Mile" country, where they hid for several days in the thick woods that had sheltered the guerrillas during the war. Liddil, staying nearby with Lamartine Hudspeth, brought them food until they headed off to Kansas City. Ryan and Bassham, meanwhile, went back home, and Hite went to Kansas City, staying with Charlie McBride. Posse members, many armed with old Springfield rifles from the Craig Rifles armory in Kansas City, scoured the area around the robbery but came back empty-handed. Eventually someone stumbled onto the trash at the McPhereson house, but this was a long time after the bandits had departed.[9]

Sometime in late October or early September, a story began circulating about an alleged attempt on Jesse's life by George Shepherd, the former guerrilla who had been captured after the Russellville robbery and had served time for his marauding. Reportedly he was in the employ of Marshal James Liggett of Kansas City, who had led one of the first posses to the scene at Glendale.

The bandit leader had given the telegrapher a note that had appeared in the press:

GLENDALE, October 8—We are the boys who are hard to handle, and will make it hot for the party who tries to take us.

> James Brothers
> Jim Connor
> Cal Carter
> Underwood
> Jackson
> Flinn
> Jack Bishop

[reverse read]
Adams Express Co. has no charter, there fore can not convict guilty men.

> Cal Worner
> Frank Jackson

The United States Express Company, the primary victim of the Glendale robbery, was not amused. It offered a twenty-five-thousand-dollar reward, and the Chicago and Alton Railroad put up an additional fifteen thousand dollars. Each bandit had more money on his head than in his pocket. The reward offer might be tempting to a former cohort of Jesse.

Shepherd claimed he made a successful attempt on Jesse's life in an ambush at Short Creek outside of Joplin, Missouri. Jesse, according to Shepherd, planned to rob the bank but had seen one of Marshal Liggett's men and took off for the Kansas line. Some, including the Pinkertons, were skeptical. It was suspected that Shepherd, and possibly Liggett, had cooked up the tale to get the reward money and allow the James brothers to get off the hook.

Shepherd was reportedly being paid one hundred dollars a month, plus expenses, to catch Jesse and others in the gang. So was Tyler Burns, who was sent to Kentucky, and ran up quite a tab (much of it for whiskey) aiding Louisville detective Delos T. Bligh to run down false leads. Apparently the railroad and the express company were bankrolling Liggett. Shepherd was also claiming that Frank had died of tuberculosis. Not quite.[10]

⁂

BACK IN Nashville, Frank James was probably chagrined to learn that the "James Brothers" were suspected of being at it again. Up until this point the brothers could claim that mistreatment during Reconstruction had led to their life on the run. Jesse's return to outlawry caused a number of people, even former Confederates, to look upon any new gang activity as a menace. Many of the new recruits had been only children during the war.

On October 4, 1879, four days prior to the Glendale holdup, Frank's horse, Jewell Maxey, had finished second in that day's race at the Tennessee State Fair, winning a twenty-five-dollar prize. "I entered my horse Jewel Maxey for the gents riding stakes at Nashville two successive years," Frank recalled later, "winning . . . second money the second year. I rode myself the second time and would have . . . received first money I think, had not the starter, Ben Cockrell, ruled me down a bit unfairly at the start."

It's a safe bet that Frank was at the track on October 8 and as often as he could be at other times during the fall races the Nashville Blood-Horse Association scheduled at the Flats, which continued through October 11. Twelve days of races, no posse to contend with, a family to come home to, and sleeping in a bed rather than out in the woods must have made Frank wonder about his little brother.

When the prodigal brother eventually showed up in late October or early November, he likely had a little explaining to do to both Frank and

Zee. Jesse's wife had already admonished him because of some of his gambling, by one account. Nevertheless, the account of Frank's death apparently caused a different reaction in the James household. "I am sure I don't know the details, all I know is that it was a great hoax," Frank recalled. "Jesse was down at Nashville at the time, and my wife read him the telegraphic account of it from the newspapers the morning after it occurred. We laughed a good deal over it but never learned what it all meant."[11]

Frank had pretty much fit himself into the groove in his role as Ben J. Woodson. "I exhibited and took the premium for Poland China hogs at the Nashville and Jackson fairs," Frank would remember. He was apparently looking ahead to the day when his life in Nashville could be used to advantage if he ever had to surface and surrender himself. For the present he was content to play Ben Woodson. "Among my intimate acquaintances I numbered Charles H. Eastman, County Clerk; J. W. Shute, member of the Legislature; Dr. Jourdan, Dr. Manlove, Dr. Wm. Hamilton, Sheriff Tim Johnson, Rev. Dr. Wall, Clint Cantwell, Wm. Bryan Jr. and others. These men knew me only as B. J. Woodson," he recalled.

Around the end of the year Frank "engaged to team for one year on Jeff Hyde's place, for the Indiana Lumber Company, and I carried out my agreement to the letter, driving a four mule team every day, taking my meals in the woods with the darkies, and never doing less than a full hand's work. Our boss in that work was T. J. Jefferson, an Ohio Republican of the most pronounced views, and I was as good a Republican as any of them." When Frank moved to a cottage off present-day Hydes Ferry Road, just uphill from the ferry on the north side of the Cumberland River, Jesse and family followed—and so did some of the new gang.

Jesse had returned from Missouri with Ed Miller, and together they pooled their resources to buy a racehorse named Jim Malone in Sumner County. William A. Guild, son of the original owner, recalled the sale:

> One day a man who said his name was Howard came to the farm to buy a horse. My father took him out and showed him "Jim Malone," as fine a colt as lived in those days. Mr. Howard was well pleased with him. As he climbed over the fence to get a better look his coattails flew up and I saw two pistols, one in each hip pocket. I didn't think much of it, because it was a general thing for men to go armed then. He liked the horse and paid $500 for him. Mr. Howard was so pleased with his purchase that he gave me and my brother, Joe C. Guild, a quarter each.

Out of twenty-six starts in 1880–81, the horse won nine races, came in second in four, and finished third seven times, winning a total of five thousand dollars by the time of his death in July 1881. Of course only part of this was under Jesse's ownership. Jim Cummins, the Quantrill veteran who had brought Jesse in to surrender in 1865 and a friend of the Miller family, related that Ed and Jesse "gambled frequently and lost considerable money. After this they went to Atlanta, Ga., where the horse was badly beaten. This left them broke." Jesse and Miller finally sold the horse for three hundred dollars and were able to get back home.[12]

When the two returned to Nashville they discovered that Tucker Bassham had been taken into custody after flashing around a wad of cash, and he was apparently in the process of telling authorities in Missouri what he knew. Jesse and Miller set off on horseback to check up on other gang members and perhaps to silence Bassham, if they could. Somewhere in the vicinity of Norbourne, Missouri, Ed Miller disappeared while riding a horse that had been loaned to him by Jim Cummins. A few weeks later a decomposed body, at first thought to be Cummins, was found in the area. Jesse's cousin, Clarence Hite, later claimed that Miller got into an argument with Jesse over stopping for some tobacco. Miller reportedly shot at Jesse, missing him but hitting his hat. Jesse didn't miss. Another story that was handed down in the Miller clan and was perhaps more plausible, had Ed Miller coming into an inheritance and telling Jesse that he wanted out of the group—no more robberies. Jesse and Ed argued, and Jesse shot and killed him. Or perhaps Jesse, aware that Miller knew where he and Frank were hiding, and not trusting him to keep the secret, shot him down. Whatever the case, Jesse's action would have serious repercussions in the future.[13]

In July Jesse returned to Tennessee, accompanied by gang members Dick Liddil and Bill Ryan. The trip took three weeks on horseback. For Ryan, the trip ended at the Hite place, near Adairville, Kentucky, where he would stay for a while. After a couple of days, Liddil and Jesse continued on to Nashville and then home to the Hyde place. After about two weeks in Nashville, the pair headed back to Adairville and trouble.

Clarence Rutherford, who lived in the vicinity of the Hites, had been arrested on a murder charge and was in jail at Russellville awaiting trial. His brother, James O. Rutherford, appealed to Jesse to help him break Clarence out of jail. Somehow word leaked that an attempt would be made, and the guard at the jail was increased. Two of the guards, armed with shotguns, spotted two heavily armed members of the gang in a saloon. Supposedly, seven men were ready to help with the escape. About a half-dozen men were inside the jail, a large brick-and-stone structure built like a fortress. Some of these men were friends of Jim Rutherford, who eventually had second thoughts and begged Jesse to call off the attack. Jesse slapped him in the face and berated him, scolding: "You've fooled me. I never go into anything until I am ready. I was ready for this and could have carried that jail like it were a chicken-coop." Clarence Rutherford was sentenced to life imprisonment but was pardoned on August 4, 1883.[14]

During the day Jesse and his gang stayed in the woods and then slept at the Hite place at night. One evening Liddil, Jesse, and Ryan started off to rob a sightseeing stage near Mammoth Cave. But "it rained so hard that we gave up the idea after getting within one mile and a half of the place," according to Liddil, who decided to go back to Nashville while Jesse and Ryan continued to search for a target.

On the morning of September 3, 1880, ten-year-old August Vial and his mother were driving from the direction of Mammoth Cave toward Cave City with a load of peaches for market. Just after turning a bend in the road, two horsemen rode out of the woods and asked the woman for some peaches. She told them to help themselves. They filled their pockets, eating one or two and offering to pay for the fruit. The woman said no charge. The men then asked about two stages.

That afternoon, about five o'clock, the stage called the "Florida" pulled away from the Cave Hotel. The passengers were mostly from out of state, coming to see the cave, which even then was a tourist attraction of some note. Eight passengers were crowded inside the coach, one of whom, J. E. Craig of Lawrenceville, Georgia, noticed something odd. As the stage neared Little Hope Baptist Church, he remarked, "I see two men on the road behind us taking a drink out of a bottle."

One of the men rode up to the stage and ordered the driver, Hiram Hawkins, to stop. "Come out of the stage please," he ordered as the other bandit covered the group with his pistol.

Phil Rowntree, editor of the *Milwaukee Evening Wisconsin*, hid his watch and wallet under the seat cushions. His cousin Lizzie did likewise with three rings. "The lady can keep her seat; she need not be alarmed, we will not disturb her," one of the robbers announced.

The woman's father, Rutherford H. Rowntree, who was a clerk of Marion County and president of the Marion National Bank, was allowed to stay as well. The other men were ordered out of the coach and formed in a line where they were searched for valuables. One of the robbers threatened to shoot any of the passengers who held anything back. Jesse took from "Judge" Rowntree, as he was called, $30, a $150 gold watch, and a watch key or letter seal of gold. The watch was engraved with a presentation from U.S. Congressman James Proctor Knott. The congressman had served under Gov. Claiborne Jackson as attorney general of Missouri at the start of the Civil War and had earned a reputation as a reformer while in Congress in the 1870s.

The bandit also searched under the seat cushions and found the valuables hidden there. Jesse asked the passengers for their names and addresses, which he wrote down, promising to return their losses at a later time. He told Craig, the Georgian, that he hated to take his money because he had fought in a Georgia regiment during the war. He and his partner were poor moonshiners, pursued by revenue officers, and needed the money in order to leave the area. Their situation was desperate and they were forced to rob the stage.

When Jesse came to take down Judge Rowntree's name, he recognized it. "Oh yes, I know the Rowntrees," he said, pulling the handkerchief up over his face.

Then Jesse produced a quart bottle of whiskey. "As I have done pretty well, I feel I ought to treat. To show that it is not poison, I will drink first." Having taken a pull at the bottle, he placed it on the ground, and pointing his pistol at the nearest man, ordered, "Take a drink!" All the passengers except Judge and Lizzie Rowntree took a swallow. Craig asked for another pull. They told him he could keep the bottle. The robber who took the inscribed watch had earlier promised to return it if he made a good haul. Now he had reservations and decided to keep it and the rings. "This is one watch I'll always be proud to wear," he said. There would be yet another ironic twist to the James story that indirectly involved Proctor Knott some months later.

Lizzie Rowntree asked for her diamond ring back, but the bandit said it would look good on his wife. "I told you I wouldn't disturb you, but you chose to hide your rings, so I will keep them." As he left, Jesse told Lizzie to "give my respects to the Gray girls in Lebanon. They know me."

Jesse claimed he had earlier robbed another stage, the "Jumper," which had been headed for the cave. Two of those passengers—Newton Gassaway, an elderly preacher, and George Crogan, nephew of one of the cave owners—were robbed of twenty-five dollars and a bottle of whiskey, possibly the one now left behind.

The robbers, in fact, may have been after some money that was to be sent to the heirs to the cave property. Each year six letters containing around one thousand dollars each went out to each of the nieces and nephews. Crogan was suspected of carrying the money, but the letters were sent another way.

R. L. Jolly, town marshal of Cave City, formed a posse and went after the culprits, but they had little luck. Jesse and Ryan were back in Logan County, and the Louisville Courier-Journal soon was wrong-headedly singing praises for the outlaws: "So dashing and yet so cool were the performances that they would have reflected credit upon the taste of that prince of romantic freebooters, the well known Claude Duval, of last century." By one account, the holdup men made off with between eight hundred and twelve hundred dollars in loot.[15]

Judge Rowntree was outraged, not so much at having lost his money and his watch, but that seven men were so easily robbed. Rowntree offered a $500 reward for the apprehension of the culprits. The cave proprietors offered an additional $250, and the state added another $500 on top of that. As could be expected, there was a roundup of undeserving suspects. The first was reported by the *Glasgow Weekly Times* on September 23, 1880. This individual luckily escaped. A paper in Lebanon reported on October 13 that a man from Wayne County had been unjustly accused. Undaunted, Rowntree hired Detective William Cutliff to track down the man who stole his watch.

Ultimately, Cutliff's search led him to an itinerant schoolteacher–coal miner named Thomas J. Hunt, who lived in Ohio County. Cutliff built what seemed to be a good circumstantial case against Hunt. But on November 1, just as Cutliff was about to bring in his man, both he and Hunt were arrested by G. W. Bunger, a deputy sheriff from Hartford. Bunger, one out-of-county newspaper claimed, had gotten the drop on Cutliff so that he instead might claim the reward. Hunt was lodged in the Barren County jail.[16]

Meanwhile, Jesse continued his crime spree in the Bluegrass State. With Ryan and Liddil, he set off for Muhlenberg County, some sixty-odd miles northwest of Adairville. Near the town of Mercer were the Dovey Coal mines, operated by John Dovey and his sons William and George. One of the outlaws arrived and acted as if he were seeking work. He asked casually when the railroad pay train came through and learned it had already come the morning before. John Dovey remarked that it would be payday for the miners the next day, October 15, and that his son William had gone for the money and would be back that night.

The next morning after the miners had gone to work, the three bandits went to Dovey's store. Liddil and perhaps Ryan guarded the front door while Jesse went inside to rob the safe. George Dovey opened the safe and handed the thief the contents—thirteen dollars and a gold watch. William Dovey had been delayed.

Meanwhile, two men and a woman entered the store. One of the outlaws followed them inside and, drawing his pistol, told them to sit down and be quiet as "young Mr. Dovey was transacting business with his friend."

It was a dismal haul, hardly the sort of robbery to get newspaper accolades. The bandits departed quickly, heading toward Pond Creek and then to Rosewood and on to Logan County. Somewhere along the line the trail was lost. As a final gesture, Liddil left near Adairville a horse that he had stolen to use in the raid. Soon the men would head back to Nashville.[17]

12

Last Highwaymen of the Natchez Trace

The unchecked career of the James Boys had run so long that there is no wonder that many believed them to have a charmed life. . . . They lived on defiantly, as if they dared Fate to the utmost. . . . But Fate or Fortune is a fickle goddess.

The James Boys (1890)

THE IMAGE OF FRANK and Jesse James was based on the popular media's rather shrewd manipulation of late-nineteenth-century America. It was undoubtedly with a mind to creating a sensation in the press that Jesse left the telegram behind after the Glendale robbery and that he attempted to play the role of the dashing eighteenth-century highwayman in the Mammoth Cave stage robbery. While the James boys had gained some notoriety in the papers, by 1880 they were becoming the subjects of books.

This trend had actually started in 1877 with the release of John Newman Edwards's rambling *Noted Guerrillas*, which gave some attention to the alleged wartime exploits of Frank and Jesse as well as others who had served under the various guerrilla chieftains in northwest Missouri. Edwards's accounts, which appear to be the war stories of sundry Quantrill vets related over a bottle, were only the beginning. In the early months of 1880 *The Life and Adventures of Frank and Jesse James and the Younger Brothers*, by J. A. Dacus, appeared from the press of W. S. Bryan in Saint Louis, with some twenty-one thousand copies allegedly sold the first four months. Dacus, interestingly, had been on the editorial staff of the *Saint Louis Republican* and was

223

author of *Annals of the Great Strikes in the United States*, which appeared following the strike of 1877 and tended to argue the case of the strikers.

As 1880 wound to a close, yet another literary work was nearing completion. It was actually two books bound in one volume. *The Border Outlaws* and *The Border Bandits*, by James William Buel, another Missouri newspaperman, was published in early 1881, with reported sales of sixty-five thousand copies in the first six months. As if this weren't enough, R. T. Bradley's *The Outlaws of the Border* was released in 1880 bound with a reprint of Edwards's *Noted Guerrillas*.

These books would all go through various updates and revisions as new events happened. Most were pulp histories, hastily written and generally based on a mix of old news clippings and the writers' imaginations, the first of a long line of endeavors by journalists to tell the James story. Unfortunately, when these writers ran out of facts, they would often spin yarns, and thus there were stories of the James boys cavorting out in the far West or in Mexico when in fact they were living in Tennessee.

To Buel, however, must go the prize for either creating or repeating the first story of an alleged Jesse James cave. Buel related that he was told about a cave that reportedly existed in Jackson County, Missouri. His informant was a fellow who supposedly had stumbled upon Frank while out riding. In Buel's account, "Frank" greets the man cordially and then tells him, "I have every confidence in you and I know you would not betray us to save your right arm," and invites him to the gang's lair. (Obviously someone had been reading the story of Ali Baba and the Forty Thieves and had given it an industrial revolution spin.) The cavern has a nice stove with a series of pipes that disguise the smoke. The roof of the cave is paneled with wood, and there are a dozen neatly made beds as well as twenty-one stalls for horses. As if that were not enough, the cave also held "an arsenal of firearms and a magazine for ammunition, while the approach to the cave was commanded by a fierce, breech-loading ten-pound cannon, which was kept constantly loaded with buckshot."

In later years Frank would brush aside such tales as hogwash, saying he never stayed in a place that didn't have a good rear exit. Nevertheless, the public bought the books and believed the stories they contained. In later years variations of the cave yarn would be incorporated into the stories of at least one James impostor and would become a "fakelore" staple across several states.

The James brothers' larger-than-life legend was created on both sides of the law. Over the years many books appeared under the name of Allan Pinkerton, actually ghostwritten "memoirs" of earlier adventures and cases.

Pinkerton would hire a hack writer at "so much" per week ("and the 'so much' doesn't represent a very large sum either," commented the *New York Times*). He would meet with a shorthand writer for most of a day, relating events as he recalled them (he'd had at least one stroke by then). The material would be written out and handed over to the writer, "generally some young Bohemian who has worked on the daily press in the capacity of a reporter, and he works the matter up in as good shape as possible." The manuscript then would be sent to Pinkerton for his comments and revisions, and this version would go to the publisher-printer. "Pinkerton makes a pretty good thing on sales," the *Times* commented in 1875, "as they are pushed extensively, particularly by the news-fiends of railway trains." Pinkerton would use the publicity to project the image of his agency as "getting their man," and gain new clients in the process.

However, as the story of the raid on the James-Samuel farm in an earlier chapter illustrates, reality sometimes conflicted with the image various writers created. This was not necessarily a bad thing. As western historian Fred Egloff points out, "An inflated reputation was undoubtedly a key weapon in the arsenal of a frontier lawman . . . intimidation by reputation was certainly an asset." The same could be said of those operating on the other side of the law as well, and this factor would help the James brothers in their brushes with the law in the months ahead. Propaganda can be a double-edged sword, though, when its own creators begin to believe it.[1]

Frank was busy in his role as Ben J. Woodson, teamster for the Indiana Lumber Company, and certainly had little recourse to the old ways in the year 1880. Obviously his wife, Annie, had a part in his coming back down to earth and living a peaceful life. It was said that Woodson "was accustomed to swear like a sailor" when he first came to the area but later "reformed and joined the Methodist church."

County clerk Charles Eastman lived near Frank at a house called Cedarwold and became acquainted with both the Woodsons and the Howards when one of the James children became ill:

> They and their families were very grateful to us for the assistance rendered while the child was sick. We visited back and forth across the road and Frank would often come and sit with us on our porch of evenings. He was fond of Shakespeare and the drama and could quote extensively from the great play writer, and poet. Jesse seemed ill at ease and talked but little, but the fact that Frank and I had congenial literary tastes brought us closer together. He often rode to town with me in my buggy, and on one occasion went with us to see a noted actor play. He dressed neatly and did not have the appearance of a common laborer. He looked more like a

prosperous farmer. . . . When I was candidate for County Court Clerk, Frank was one of my active supporters.

Eastman's wife recalled that the James women were "polite, neat and evidently possessed some refinement":

> They often came over to our house, and as we had a large garden we offered them all the vegetables they needed, as they had no garden. In fact they never even had a chicken, and while the house was well kept and clean, there was not in it a piece of surplus furniture.

The Eastmans had an orchard that yielded more fruit than they could use, and they recalled how the James women availed themselves of the offer to help themselves. During the year when the women of the area got together and made apple butter, the James women were there. "Those . . . years of quiet, upright life were . . . the happiest I have spent since my boyhood, notwithstanding the hard labor attending them," Frank would later recall. "My old life grew more detestable the further I got away from it."

Jesse, Dick Liddil, and Bill Ryan returned to Nashville in late September and remained in the area about two weeks, for the October races, then went to the races in Atlanta. While members of the gang were at the Hyde place, Frank would often put them to work with him and his teams, hauling logs for the lumber company. This, however, apparently didn't keep them out of mischief. "One night someone attempted to rob our house," recalled Charles Eastman, "and Frank said the next day: 'I will see that this does not occur again. There are three or four of us and we will guard your house.' We were not suspicious at the time, but later on we thought perhaps it was one of the men with James who attempted the robbery."

Jesse and gang were soon to head back to Missouri. The object was probably to intimidate Tucker Bassham, who went on trial for his part in the Glendale affair on November 6, as well as possibly to commit another robbery. Jesse and Ed Miller were the only members of the gang implicated by Bassham at this point. Word probably had gotten to Bassham through third parties that Jesse and his pals were not happy with the confession he'd made and that he'd better not say more. He apparently started to implicate Jim Cummins, of whom more will be said, perhaps at the gang's suggestion. Bassham was ultimately sentenced to ten years in prison. He initially confessed in writing, then retracted the confession and pleaded not guilty. Then he changed his plea to guilty and threw himself on the mercy of the court. Apparently he was pressured heavily for both his silence and his testimony in the Glendale affair. He would have plenty of time to think about it in the penitentiary in Jefferson City.[2]

Jesse would have plenty of other things to worry about. The disappearance and probable death of Ed Miller had caused some concern among Miller's friends, including Jim Cummins. Cummins was a former guerrilla and had helped get Jesse to Lexington, Missouri, to surrender and get help for his lung wound in May 1865. Since the mid-1870s Cummins had been wanted for allegedly stealing a horse from a neighbor, Joe Pettigrew, a charge Cummins denied. Instead he fixed the blame on Ed Miller and an unnamed man.

Cummins left the area, and for several years he drifted around Texas and the Southwest, where he claimed to have used the alias James Johnson while serving as a teamster and a scout for the army. He had come back to Missouri just in time to be considered a suspect in the Glendale robbery and had skipped around Arkansas and Missouri for several more months, dodging the law. Cummins had either sold or given Ed Miller the horse Miller was riding at the time he was killed by Jesse, and thus Cummins had been confused with Miller. When the corpse was found, some thought they'd seen Cummins riding with Jesse instead of Miller, and the rumor began to circulate that Cummins was dead.

Meanwhile, Jesse had one horse too many, and as fate would have it, he temporarily left the one Miller had been riding with a young fellow named Charlie Ford. Ford asked what had happened to Miller, and Jesse told him that Ed was seriously ill and had decided to go to Hot Springs, Arkansas, for his health. Jesse later picked up the horse and rode it back to Nashville in the summer of 1880. In November 1880 Cummins hooked up with Jesse and Dick Liddil while Jesse was on a visit back to Missouri to see his mother. "I asked Jesse James several times on this trip what had become of Ed Miller," Cummins recalled. "Jesse said that Ed was in East Tennessee and that he did not think Ed would ever get well."

When he arrived in Nashville, Cummins stayed out at the Hyde place with Frank. The James brothers had apparently had another falling out, this time over Bill Ryan and probably related to the attempted burglary at the Eastman home and/or Ryan's drinking. "Are you fellows going to bring that damned Irishman, Bill Ryan, down here to give us all away?" Frank asked in exasperation. "Jim, you are welcome at my house any time, but will you be so kind as to go over to Nashville and tell 'Dingus' [Jesse] not to bring that damned Irishman to my house." Cummins did so, and "Jesse raved and swore and said he believed Frank would like to see [Jesse] dead, and see his family suffer."

Jesse and his family had relocated to a boarding house run by a Mrs. Kent on Summer Street (now Fifth Avenue North) near the Tennessee State Capitol. The site of this abode of the supposedly law-abiding John Davis Howard is now, perhaps fittingly, the Tennessee Performing Arts Center.

T. W. Killough, a railway mail clerk, and his wife also boarded at Mrs. Kent's. Mrs. Killough later described the Howards as "refined people who lived a quiet unassuming life." They apparently had enough money, and Mr. Howard was interested in racing. The mail clerk and the bandit apparently spent a good bit of time together. The Howards only boarded a short while at Mrs. Kent's before moving in December 1880 or January 1881 to a house across the river in Edgefield, probably at 903 Woodland Street.

Frank James and family, meanwhile, had Christmas dinner with county clerk Eastman. It was all part of a plan that Frank had carried out since he'd settled in the Nashville area. According to Frank, he was deliberately "seeking the acquaintance of prominent men and officers of the law," setting about "with the determination of winning their high regard and good will. . . . Why, I made my headquarters in the sheriff's office with Tim Johnson, I could go into Charlie Eastman's office, ask him to cash a check, and he would do so without even looking to see if it was correct." Frank said he had "been around hundreds of times and heard . . . officers talk about the reward for me and how they would like to make the capture. They have even joked with me about it." This familiarity with officers of the law allowed Frank to have a little fun at Jim Cummins's expense during the latter part of 1889 or early 1890. Two of "Ben Woodson's" friends were city police detectives Fletch Horn and William P. Watson. Watson was a man of few words, "rather morose," according to Frank, who recalled that he "went around staring hard at everything and everybody."

Cummins and Frank were at a restaurant one day, and Frank saw Detective Watson through the window. He asked Cummins, who was "an apprehensive, nervous sort of chap, who always feared the worst," to come outside and be introduced to a detective. "He paled and grew very fidgity as he backed off and drawled out 'Not by a damned sight. Do you think I'm a damned fool?' He got as far back in the restaurant as he could, and the most I could elicit from him was 'You ain't got a damn bit of sense. You'll get pulled in one of these days with your brashness.' I explained to him that the safest course was in 'cheeking it out,' and that the man most liable to be pulled in was the man who sneaked."

Cummins still wanted to know about Ed Miller. "I remarked on several occasions to Frank and Jesse that I believed that Ed Miller had been foully dealt with, and if I ever found it to be fact, that I intended to avenge his death," he said. In talking with Zee and Annie James, Jim became even more suspicious "that there was something dark between Jesse James and Ed Miller."

On the day Jim delivered Frank's message about Bill Ryan to Jesse, Jim suspected there would be trouble between the brothers. The next day Jesse hired a carriage and drove out with Zee and Ryan to see Frank. Zee managed to pull Jim into the kitchen and confided in him that Jesse was mad and she was afraid there would be a row. Indeed, Jesse baited Frank all day, trying to pull him into an argument, but from long experience Frank knew how to deal with his younger brother. Jesse then started an argument with Dick Liddil, pulling a pistol on him. Jim reportedly stepped in between them, telling Jesse that if this was the way it was going to be he wouldn't stay with anyone and certainly not Ryan, "as he was always getting drunk." This was apparently just before Jesse moved to Edgefield again. Cummins eventually went to Kentucky, where he noticed Miller's horse at the Hite place. He then went to see Donny Pence at Bardstown, Kentucky. Cummins told Pence that he suspected Jesse had killed Miller.

The situation with Cummins was working toward a potentially violent climax. It was Jesse's opinion that Cummins was about to go to the law. In fact Cummins was probably more afraid of Jesse at this juncture than he was of the law. According to Dick Liddil, Jesse tried to get the other members of the gang to agree to have Cummins killed. Sometime in late January 1881 or early February the heat became too great, and Cummins, who was reportedly staying with Jesse and family, took off for parts unknown, leaving most of his clothing behind.[3]

Jim Cummins's hasty departure sent Frank and Jesse into something short of a panic. Jesse rode over to the Hyde place and compared notes with Frank. Both worried that Cummins might have gone to the Nashville police. As a precaution they packed their gear and spent a wintry evening some distance from the house, watching for a posse that never came.

The next day, satisfied that Cummins probably hadn't gone to the authorities but unsure if he might not be headed for a rendezvous with those from Missouri, Frank, Jesse, and Ryan decided to get out of the Nashville area for a while, leaving Zee and the children behind at the cottage on Woodland Street with Liddil. One account has the brothers going as far south as New Orleans. Ryan's whereabouts and activities are unknown, but it is probable that he was sent by Jesse to scout a possible target for the gang. Frank and Jesse did spend some time in Selma, Alabama, visiting with boyhood friend John Green Norris. Norris had become a well-known contractor in Selma during the postwar years and must have been surprised when two of the most wanted men in America turned up at his door, registered as the "Williams" brothers at the Saint James Hotel on Water Street. When not visiting Norris at his home at the corner of Washington Street and Jeff Davis Avenue, Frank and Jesse were in the billiard room at the Saint James. It probably became apparent pretty soon that the coast was reasonably clear for their return. Norris was presented with a photo and a pair of autographed shirt cuffs for his hospitality.[4]

Meanwhile, in Nashville, a strange incident had occurred at Jesse's residence on Woodland Street. Jesse Edwards James, then known as Tim Howard, recalled the incident of February 14, 1881, as one of his first memories:

> There was a sound as if someone was throwing rocks at the front door. Dick [Liddil] started to open the door, but mother suspected it was someone who had discovered who we were and were trying to entice Dick out to capture or kill him. She would not allow him to open the door. Dick then got my father's shotgun from the closet. Both of its barrels were loaded heavily with buckshot. Before my mother could interfere to prevent it, Dick aimed at the door and fired a charge of buckshot, tearing a great hole in the door panel and splintering it. Dick rushed to the door and threw it open and ran out on the porch. In the darkness he saw a man running around the corner. Dick fired the second barrel straight at him, barely missing him, the charge rattling against a lamp post on the street . . . a great crowd that had heard the shots gathered to see what was the matter. Dick told them simply that he had shot at a burglar.

They never were able to discover who the person was, but they figured it was a friend of Jesse's who was trying to play a joke. The man who was suspected of the prank showed up at the house the next day with a long and solemn face. A little bit later the James brothers were back in Nashville. Perhaps news of the shooting convinced them that the situation was not as bad as they'd feared.

At some point Frank moved his family from the Hyde place to a small one-story brown frame house at 814 Fatherland Street. Jesse also moved his family at about the same time, probably to a nearby two-story brick house at 711 Fatherland. One Sunday while Mrs. Killough, who knew the Howards from Mrs. Kent's, was visiting "Josie Howard," "three horsemen, roughly attired and drinking, rode up to the front gate, dismounted, and strode into the house without the formality of a knock, greeted Mrs. Howard by her first name and went into the kitchen, where they spread a meal for themselves and pulled out a bottle of whiskey. . . . Mrs. Howard was very agitated at the appearance of the men . . . [and] attempted to allay suspicions that might have been aroused by the sudden appearance of the rough characters . . . by explaining that they were westerners whom they had known for a number of years." Mrs. Killough left in a hurry, forgetting an umbrella. The following Sunday she returned and found the house vacant. The umbrella had been left behind with a neighbor.[5]

ON THE morning of March 6, 1881, three men left Jesse's house in Nashville before daylight. Their idea was to cross the suspension bridge and be out of the city before anyone was up. The men probably proceeded out the Harding Pike, past Belle Meade Mansion, and out the Centerville Pike (now Tennessee Highway 100). At some point they would have veered off to the south, perhaps taking the road to Union Valley in northwestern Williamson County. Just where they spent the night is uncertain.

On the afternoon of March 7 they stopped at the tiny hamlet of Kinderhook, in northwest Maury County, and bought some whiskey at the town's only store. A few hours later they crossed the Duck River at Gordon's Ferry and asked a black man, Moses Jones, who operated the ferry, if they could

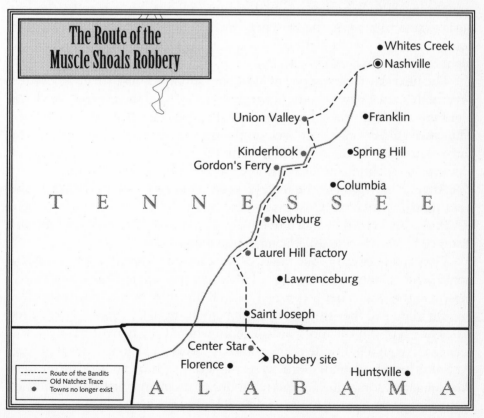

The Route of the Muscle Shoals Robbery

Whites Creek
Nashville
Union Valley
Franklin
Kinderhook
Spring Hill
Gordon's Ferry
Columbia
TENNESSEE
Newburg
Laurel Hill Factory
Lawrenceburg
Saint Joseph
Center Star
Robbery site
Florence
Huntsville
ALABAMA

- - - - - Route of the Bandits
·············· Old Natchez Trace
  ⊛   Towns no longer exist

get a ferry across at night. The band had been following the Old Natchez Trace for some time by the time they crossed the river. By 1881 much of the old trace had fallen into disuse or had been incorporated into little-used farming roads. Connecting Nashville and Natchez, the trace passed through areas that were still sparsely populated. There were no towns of any real size, no telegraph, and on certain stretches of the trace a person could go for miles without encountering a house or people. After the advent of the steamboat in the years following the War of 1812, time and civilization seemed to have bypassed the historic road.

Originally it had served as one of the main roads of the infant United States, carrying settlers, flatboatmen, and the army of Andrew Jackson. Highwaymen including the Harpe brothers, the Murrell gang, and others had lurked along the trace in the past when Natchez-Under-the-Hill was the "Wild West." Perhaps it was this romantic aura as much as the secluded nature of the trace that drew Jesse there. The gang may have ridden past the stone shaft that marked the grave of Meriwether Lewis, head of the Lewis and Clark Expedition, who died along the trace under mysterious circumstances in 1809. Whether or not Jesse intended it, his was to be the last outlaw band to traverse the Natchez Trace on horseback with the intent to commit robbery. About eight miles south of the ferry the gang halted for the night at the house of Ab Weatherly.

The next day they stopped at William Lindsey's house six miles beyond Weatherly's, the halfway point between that place and the town of Newburg. Here the old trace crossed a creek, and apparently a newer road took over. They asked directions to get back on the trace farther on. That evening the three men came to Laurel Hill Factory, in the northwest portion of Lawrence County, and spent the night at a house owned by E. A. "Buck" Jones.

After an early supper the men locked themselves in their room and the next morning had breakfast and were gone before Jones could see them again. At breakfast they had a lively discussion with Mrs. Jones, asking the distance to Muscle Shoals, Alabama. She didn't know.

They made twenty-four miles down the trace that day, reaching the home of J. L. Golihan, where the old trace met the road to Waynesboro, Tennessee, to the west. They proceeded south from Golihan's the next day.

On March 10 they stopped in the late morning at Chinubee Store, three miles north of the town of Saint Joseph, where they bought whiskey and tobacco. About a half-mile farther on they stopped to eat at Tidwell's Store. At Saint Joseph, a small German settlement just north of the Tennessee-Alabama line, sometime around noon one of the men bought a whip. They spent the evening at the house of Alfred Hill in the Green Hill community.

The men claimed to have traveled from Robertson County and asked questions about the canal being built at Muscle Shoals. One of the men commented that it must take a lot of money to pay so many workers. Just when did these men get paid?

Hill never thought anything of their questions. Many travelers were interested in this canal, and the curious would sometimes stop at his place on their way to see it.

The Muscle Shoals Canal was a project of the U.S. Army Corps of Engineers that was begun in the mid-1870s to improve river traffic along the Tennessee River in this area of northern Alabama. In all probability, Jesse had picked up on Muscle Shoals as a target during his trip to Alabama the month before. Someone, possibly Ryan, had apparently scouted the project, which had numerous workers on its payroll. All they had to do was find out when that payroll came through and who handled it.

"On the 11th day of March 1881, about the hour of 10 A.M. I saw three men ride up to my saloon, which is located about one hundred yards above Lock No. 7, Muscle Shoals Canal," Thomas Peden recollected. The men dismounted, tied their horses, and then went inside for a couple of drinks. They asked about the canal and made some small talk about the new president, James Garfield. The leader of the group was described by Peden as "very correct and intelligent in conversation, quick spoken . . . he talked politics most of the time, remarking he was well acquainted with secretarys [William] Windom and [Robert Todd] Lincoln." Windom was secretary of the Treasury; Lincoln was Abraham Lincoln's son and the secretary of war. Jesse was trying to put on the appearance of a politically well-heeled individual who had somehow landed a job as a Treasury Department revenue agent via political patronage. Throughout the trip, Jesse and his cohorts were mistaken for revenue officers hunting illegal stills.

In Jesse's own mind a strike against a Corps of Engineers payroll might well have been a strike against the army he had fought against in the war—and against the son of Lincoln in the bargain. But times had changed somewhat. Robert Lincoln was in many ways very different from his father. Prior to becoming secretary of war he had earned a reputation, and a good bit of money, as a railroad lawyer.

The men stayed at Peden's for about two hours, eating a snack of cheese and crackers—and waiting.[6]

⁂

ON THURSDAY, March 10, Alexander G. Smith was ordered by assistant engineer Henry J. Gielow to go into Florence and get the payroll for the workers in the Bluewater Division of the canal project. This was part of Smith's duties as receiver of materials as well as working in the office for Gielow. Smith was given a Treasury Department check for $5,290.18. He left Bluewater Camp, as it was known, about 2 or 3 P.M., and reached Florence by about 6:30 in the evening.

The next morning Smith went to the bank of W. P. Campbell and Company and spent about two hours there, leaving with $500 in gold, $419.18 in silver and nickels, and $4,371 in paper currency. He took out fifty dollars to pay two workers in Florence. The paper money was in a package in an inside pocket of his inside coat, and the gold and silver were in a bag attached to his saddle and covered with his overcoat.

Smith reached Harkin's Quarry, along the canal, around 3 P.M. He crossed Four Mile Branch and for the first time noticed three men about a quarter of a mile behind him. He looked back occasionally, but the men remained a safe distance away.

On reaching the commissary building near Lock No. 5, Smith stopped and waited until the men passed him. They stopped, however, to ask him the way to Fish Creek and then went on their way. "I had concluded they were U.S. Revenue Officials; deputy marshals on duty frequently passing along the line of the canal," Smith recalled.

> I came up with them on the east side of Douglas Branch; the men stopped, appearing to hesitate, so I caught up with them. We rode along, they making inquiries about the canal, for about two hundred yards, until we reached the railroad track. When we reached the trestle I was about a horses length ahead of them, I crossed the track and got down in the bed of the canal first, I went along the canal trunk about twenty-five or thirty feet, until I came opposite the gate in the fence. I went up the bank to the fence, when I heard a peculiar noise behind me. I turned and saw each of the three men with a pistol pointed at me, they forming a kind of semi-circle around me, and the fence barring my way in front, the gate not being opened. They ordered me to throw up my hands, threatening to kill me, if I hesitated. This demand being several times repeated, and evidently by desperate men, I had no alternative but to comply. . . . After throwing up my hands, they disarmed me, taking my pistol: ordering me to dismount, they searched me, taking the paper package containing the money from my inside coat pocket, and taking the bag of coin from my saddle and transferring it to one of their saddles.

While searching Smith the outlaws found the money left from the fifty dollars he had put aside in his vest pocket after paying the men in Florence.

"The robber inquired if . . . the money was Government money or my own money. I told them it was mine, meaning it would form a part of my salary. The robber told me he did not want it, neither did he take my watch, they said they only wanted government money."

The robbers ordered Smith to remount, threatening to kill him if he gave them away. They rode back down the canal and over Douglas Branch. At the top of a hill they struck a path leading to the Bellview Road. The three continued on the Bellview Road until they reached the Huntsville Road, going east on this road until they were within a quarter-mile of Center Star, in Lauderdale County, Alabama. At this point the band struck due north, through some woods, along a bridle path. Apparently someone, perhaps Ryan, had scouted the area in advance the month previous.

"The robbers kept me under close armed watch the entire distance, one riding in front, one behind, and one alongside," Smith later told authorities.

About four miles north of Center Star, atop a high ridge, the gang halted, dismounted, and divided the loot. They then proceeded north, through the woods, until it was quite dark. It was also raining. In a hollow they told Smith he was free to go, but he was confused about where he was. One of the men apparently swapped overcoats with him and told him to wait until daylight. Smith took the coat and left, making his way out of the woods to a house occupied by John Berendsen, a German immigrant whom Smith "understood with great difficulty." He obtained some food for himself and feed for his horse, then headed off in the middle of a heavy thunderstorm, guided by the German to the home of John Springer.

"About two hours and a half after dark," Springer related, "a man calling himself Smith called at my gate and asked to be permitted to remain all night. His appearance and actions caused me to doubt his sanity and made me hesitate before granting his request. He stated that he had been robbed, as a consequence was a ruined man, and asked my advice as to what course to pursue." Springer recalled hearing the dogs barking about sunset and figured that must have been the party passing nearby.

Smith discovered that he was eighteen to twenty miles from Bluewater Creek and at least fourteen miles from Center Star. "My horse was used up . . . so I rested my horse until daylight, and started for Camp, reaching Center Star about 9:30 A.M., having lost my way three different times," Smith recalled.

He made it to Bluewater Camp and reported to Gielow, who was in the process of organizing a search party. Smith passed along to his supervisor a card that had been given to him by one of the robbers "with an name, etc. pencilled thereon," the old overcoat, and the rawhide whip that had been bought at Saint Joseph.

Smith described the bandits to the engineer. One was about thirty to thirty-five years old, five feet eight inches tall, broad face, scar on the upper lip, near the middle. He had a dirty, sandy-colored beard, "general respectable appearance," carried a gold watch, and wore dark pants and a slouch hat. His horse was a dark bay with a white star or spot on the face. This was probably Jesse. Smith described the next as being five feet ten inches tall, pale and thin, about thirty-five years old with a light, sandy mustache and chin whiskers. Smith described the man as being "sallow looking and consumptive," or sickly and with a cough like a man with tuberculosis. This was probably Wood Hite (his brother Clarence would die of tuberculosis in 1883, and he may have had the disease too). This man wore a dark overcoat and slouch hat and rode a sorrel horse with four white feet. The last bandit was described as about twenty-eight years old, five feet ten inches tall, dark eyes, dark brown mustache, and chin whiskers. He wore a "full suit of dark brown clothes, a sack coat and slouch hat." The third man's horse was a dapple gray with a Texas saddle, and the man "talked with a kind of brogue, like an Irishman." This was, of course, Bill Ryan.[7]

Gielow was not content just to sit there. He had a man working for the engineers, probably a former Confederate cavalryman, named Daniel Comer. He sent Comer north to track the robbers, alone. What is known of the route they took, going and coming, is his work. Apparently the three bandits made fairly quick time on a portion of their return leg, although Comer lost their trail at one point and headed off to Perryville, Linden, and the Clifton and Waynesboro area before discovering his mistake around March 28. When he picked up the trail again the men were long gone, but their itinerary shows how fast they were traveling. By 7 A.M. on March 12 they had passed through Newburg, stopping again at William Lindsey's cabin for bread for themselves and corn for their mounts. Lindsey noticed the horses were "badly jaded." The men told Lindsey "that they were Revenue Officers and had been down in a country where they could get nothing to eat for man or beast." They stopped about two miles north of his cabin to eat before proceeding on north.

The party passed Ab Weatherly's about dusk, going for Gordon's Ferry at "a slow gait." They crossed the ferry about 9 P.M.

The next morning about sunrise the three riders stopped at the home of William Rails, about three miles northwest of Kinderhook, near the head of Turnbull Creek in Maury County. Each man rode up a few minutes apart. The first to arrive asked for "feed for three horses, and six cups of coffee for three men." Two of the men went into the house and ate breakfast, while one stayed outside. He went in when they were done. The men remained at

Rails's place for about an hour "and were on the lookout, keeping their pistols in readiness." Rails noticed their horses were so worn out that they only ate a little. The men asked directions to the road leading to Union Valley, wanting to know if it was a seldom-traveled route. They also asked directions to Kingston Springs and to "Old Well." They were about twenty-three miles due south of Kingston Springs, a community along the railroad from Nashville to Johnsonville.

Jesse and his companions passed a church in Union Valley about 11 A.M. on March 13; four miles north of the valley they struck the road between Centerville and Nashville. One of the men, probably Ryan, headed straight to Nashville while the other two roamed a ten-square-mile area off the pike until March 17. It was in this vicinity that their trail came to an end.

Daniel Comer checked Kingston Springs, Bellview, Ashland City, and other communities, but no one there had seen the three men. The report of Comer's trip would be filed away in Washington, D.C., for well over a century before coming to light.

There were reports that one or more of the robbers had been in the vicinity before the robbery. One of the bandits had told Smith that "they were old hands at the business from Texas." Maj. W. R. King, who commanded the engineer office in Chattanooga, speculated that a local man might be involved. And there was the predictable rounding up of suspects. The Memphis chief of police already had a man in custody there by March 14, just three days after the Muscle Shoals holdup. The distance was about 125 miles there as the crow flies, which would have required some fast riding, to be sure! King sent Smith to Memphis to identify the would-be outlaw (and probably have him released).[8]

⁂

DICK LIDDIL would later claim he was in Kentucky while all this was happening. And what of Frank James? For well over a century various writers have been quick to place Frank at Muscle Shoals as one of the participants, when he was in fact in and around Nashville. Sam Fields, a Nashville city detective, would later testify under oath that he had seen "Woodson" on March 11 on several occasions, the first at the office of Justice J. B. Brown, where the suit of *Stevens v. Chickering* was being settled. He later saw Woodson and walked with him to the corner of Cherry Street (now Fourth Avenue North) and Deaderick, accompanied by David Pitman and Deputy Marshal Theodore Willard. Frank later ran into Fields at Jonas Taylor's blacksmith shop at 9 South College Street (Third Avenue South) having a horse shod. Frank was also seen by others in town between March 8 and 14.[9]

ON FRIDAY, March 25, 1881, some two weeks after the robbery at Muscle
Shoals, Bill Ryan, alias "Tom Hill," set out for Adairville, Kentucky. Ryan
started north in the afternoon, eventually hitting the Whites Creek Pike.
The weather began to get nasty, erupting into a thunderstorm with high
winds. Around 7:30 P.M. Ryan reached the shelter of a store run by W. R.
Maddux in the Whites Creek community, seven and a half miles north of
Nashville. It was another combination mercantile and saloon, not unlike
Peden's in Alabama.

As a fish takes to water, so Ryan took to liquor. Throwing some money
on the bar, he asked for a bottle of whiskey and a can of cove oysters, certainly a strange combination. Soon he was gloriously drunk and making a
nuisance of himself. He claimed to be Tom Hill, "outlaw against State,
County, and the United States Government," and a "Government detective" to boot! To make his point he pulled a pistol on one of the patrons,
James McGinnis. It was a bad mistake, for the storeowner, W. L. Earthman,
who happened to be a Davidson County constable, was also in the store
that night.

Ryan was humored to put away his hogleg and then sat back down at a
table and had another snort. The other men had a rather hasty conference
and then pounced on the desperado, pinning him in his chair and tying his
arms. A quick search revealed two nickel-plated revolvers, a Colt Navy
and a Smith and Wesson, plus about seventy-five cartridges. Not exactly
the typical rig for a farmer in those parts. He also wore a rather expensive-
looking diamond ring.

Trussed up in the chair, Ryan was hauled outside, hoisted into the back
of a wagon, and driven to Nashville, where he was locked up in the local
jail about 10 P.M. One can imagine Ryan cursing his lungs out amid the
driving thunderstorm, lightning crashing in the distance as the wagon rat-
tled along the dirt road to the Cumberland River and across by ferry.

More discoveries were made once they reached the jail. Some $1,400
was found on Ryan: $400 in gold, $980 in paper, and $20.45 in other coin.
His saddlebags contained maps of most of the United States as well as bits
of poetry, some original doggerel included. This, in addition to the guns
and jewelry that included a fine gold watch, caused the authorities to look
further into the case. Just who really was this man? For the moment at least,
he wasn't talking.[10]

13

The James Boys on the Run

The Jameses trust very few people—probably two out of every ten thousand.

John Newman Edwards, Noted Guerrillas (1877)

THE DAY FOLLOWING THE arrest of "Tom Hill," Dick Liddil went into Nashville to collect some money owed on the sale of some furniture. While there he read of Hill's arrest in the *Nashville Banner* and realized Tom Hill was actually Bill Ryan. The Nashville police were still puzzled about his identity, but there was no telling how long Ryan might remain silent. Captain Yater, the chief of police, had already confronted Ryan with a photo of a man known as Obediah Ross, who was wanted for the murder of a man named Cornwell in Georgia. The man in the photo and Ryan bore some resemblance to one another. Perhaps the possibility of going to the gallows would loosen his tongue.

Liddil headed for Edgefield, where he spoke with both Jesse and Frank about the situation. There was no speculation as there had been with Cummins. All agreed that the matter was serious and that they must leave Nashville at once to avoid capture. Kentucky seemed the most logical place to go for the short run.[1]

Frank and Jesse may have learned of Ryan's capture during visits to Jonas Taylor's shop that day. "Dave Howard" was there, discussing the capture of "Tom Hill," and "Ben Woodson" paid Taylor a visit that day as well. Frank

239

said he was there to say good-bye because he was leaving for Florida. W. R. Spann also saw Frank on March 26. Woodson withdrew some money on that date, reportedly to send his cousin away. Attorney Raymond Sloan was the last person to see Frank in Nashville. First running into him at Taylor's shop, Sloan later saw him at the Louisville and Nashville depot, where he had probably bought tickets for the James families. Sloan stated that he saw Frank on horseback, telling another man, "Good-bye. I may never see you again."[2]

About dark, Jesse, Frank, and Liddil left Nashville. "It was with despair that I drove away from our little home," Frank related, "and again became a wanderer." Frank rode his own horse. Jesse and Liddil had no horses. "We had to borrow the horses on which we made this trip," Liddil recalled. "We didn't ask their owners' permission to use them, they being asleep."

The first pair gave out about twenty miles north of Nashville, and another pair were requisitioned by Jesse and Dick. Silas Norris, who was George Hite's new father-in-law, noted their arrival at the Hite place the next morning. Jesse was riding a horse while Frank and Liddil were said to be on foot. Presumably the extra horses were let loose somewhere along the way. Frank and Dick were armed with pistols, and Jesse had a pistol and a shotgun. They would remain there at least a week.[3]

Back in Nashville Ryan was sticking to his "Tom Hill" story and saying nothing more. When accosted by a reporter from the *Banner,* Hill said he had "an aversion to lawyers and reporters, and if turned loose among about a hundred of the latter, for ten minutes . . . would give the newspapers something to write about." For the moment Nashville authorities were convinced Hill was Obediah Ross. They also had strong suspicions, which were later confirmed, that he was in some way connected with the Muscle Shoals robbery as well. On Wednesday, March 30, Hill was identified out of a group of nineteen other prisoners by Alex G. Smith. An item still puzzling authorities was a note found on Hill during the initial search. It read, "Clawson, 3½ miles on Gallatin Pike" and "Dear Uncle, Take Care of my horse and get his back well, Dave."[4]

On March 31, Hill was arraigned before U.S. Commissioner (the federal equivalent of a justice of the peace) Lewis T. Baxter on a charge of robbery in the Muscle Shoals case. He was to be held for trial by the U.S. Court in northern Alabama. The same day, Smith, accompanied by Deputy U.S. Marshal W. S. Overton, identified the horse as the dapple gray the outlaw had ridden in the robbery.[5]

On April 14, 1881, a hastily scribbled telegram was delivered to the office of the chief of engineers at the War Department in Washington, D.C., from Maj. W. R. King in Chattanooga:

Two of the muscle shoals robbers have been tracked to Adairville Kentucky by Deputy Marshal Overton I have authorized him to employ a
number of scouts and U.S. Marshal Wheat has furnish arms for them Overton reports that U.S. Commissioner at Russellville refuses to issue a warrant
for fear of assassination by the desperadoes. sheriff of Logan County refuses
to act for same reason I am in communication with marshal Crittenden at
Louisville but fear that the robbers may be allowed to escape or defiantly
remain quietly in their stronghold the robbers are reported to be the notorious James and Hite outlaws & the local authorities are afraid to oppose
them is it practicable to get a detachment of soldiers to assist the marshal.

In Washington the matter had been referred up the chain of command
to President James Garfield himself. Garfield was dealing with the opening
stages of an investigation of what would come to be known as the Star
Route Frauds, in which the Post Office Department had been bilked of
nearly half a million dollars by a ring of influential people involved in rural
mail delivery. The robbery of a $5,200 payroll was a pittance by compari-
son. Acting as special agent for the Post Office Department, as fate would
have it, was none other than Patrick Henry Woodward, who had been
involved in the Pinkerton affair in 1874 and 1875. "The corruption and
wrong has been of a very gross and extensive kind. I am surprised that it
could have so long escaped the notice of Pres. Hayes's Administration,"
Garfield wrote of the Star Route case in his diary. The matter of the James
brothers was turned over to Attorney General Wayne MacVeagh, who
delivered the following official opinion on April 16, 1881:

> In reply to the inquiry of the Adjutant General this day referred to me
> by your direction, as to whether it would be proper, in view of the provisions
> of section 15 of the act of June 18, 1878, chap. 263, to furnish a detachment
> of troops to aid the civil authorities in arresting certain persons in the
> State of Kentucky who are charged with the recent robbery of the clerk of
> the Engineer office superintending the government works on the Tennessee
> river, I have the honor to state that in my opinion the civil authorities
> referred to (the marshal and his deputies) cannot, without violating the pro-
> visions of that section, be thus aided by the military forces of the United
> States as a *posse comitatus*, and that it would therefore not be proper to fur-
> nish a detachment of troops to be employed by those authorities as a *posse* in
> the case mentioned. . . . The papers referred to me are herewith returned.

The law to which the attorney general referred had been adopted as a
rider to an army appropriations bill on June 18, 1878, and was know thereafter as the "Posse Comitatus Act." Except in certain specified cases, such as

enforcing civil rights provisions of the Constitution or by a specifically excepted act of Congress, it was illegal for the army to have anything to do with civil law enforcement. This law was the result of a backlash against the use of troops during Reconstruction (notably in installing and removing certain state governments and during the presidential election of 1876), heavy-handed use in the Great Strike of 1877, and even back to the Civil War era, when martial law had been brought to bear against the Democratic Party in the North. There also had been abuse in the use of troops on the side of the Murphy-Dolan faction in New Mexico's Lincoln County War (involving Billy the Kid on the opposite side) even while the bill was in congressional debate.

The House of Representatives had fallen back into the hands of the Democrats in 1874 for the first time since before the Civil War. As the party regained congressional power there was a movement to ensure that the army stayed out of the civil-political arena in the future. Ironically, one of the key proponents of the Posse Comitatus bill in the House was James Proctor Knott, the same man whose gift of an engraved watch to Judge Rutherford H. Rowntree had been stolen by Jesse James! Knott probably had memories of his own 1862 arrest and imprisonment by military authorities in mind as he pushed the legislation through the House.[6]

The James boys left the Hite place and stayed about a week at the home of Uncle George Hite's nephew approximately three miles away. They spent one more day back at the Hite place and then departed for Nelson County, Kentucky. The Hite home had been a refuge for the James boys since just after the Civil War. It was here in 1870 that Jesse had overdosed on laudanum in what was later termed a suicide attempt (but probably wasn't). Jesse and Frank had hidden out at the Hites' following the Northfield raid, by at least one account. Now it wasn't even safe to stay there. Surely word had filtered back to them about the deputy U.S. marshal who was poking around in response to the Corps of Engineers payroll theft. They had been saved this time largely through the intimidating factor of their reputation, plus an unwitting act of Congress. Fate, however, plays many tricks, and the story was far from over.

<hr>

ON MAY 23, 1881, a letter was received by Major King from the Nashville police. It was a May 19 letter from Bardstown, Kentucky, to Detective William P. Watson of Nashville. The writer was George W. Hunter, a former city marshal of Bardstown turned detective–bounty hunter. Hunter introduced himself to Watson, saying he had been referred by city marshal Sam Adams of Bowling Green, Kentucky:

What I was after him to find out, was about some strange men (three in number) passing through this county at night just one month ago to day—April 19, they inquired the way to a certain place which was a great place for the James boys to harbor at and a place where three of their old army comrades are now living, which is eight miles only from this place, and about four miles from where the men stopped and inquired in the night from an old black man & woman to this point above mentioned. Soon after leaving this place that night they shot a very fine sorrel horse long mane & tail rather silver or flax colored showed me he was a good horse and what their object could have been was a mystery to me, it was I suppose to cover up some tracks. the horse was shot square in the forehead & died instantly from the appearances. they hid their saddle near bye, which was a regular Texas Ranger saddle made in Dallas Texas, with the makers name on it. the saddle is a little worn from having a gun near the pummel. Mr. Adams told me their had been some robbing done at Mussell Sholes on Tenn. river and that one of the party had been captured with some of the money. may be if you could see this captured man he would tell you about this sorrel horse, &c. I had a letter from D.T. Bligh of Louisville, and he said he had heard it was an Irishman which had been captured with $1,400 on him of the money. I wish you would give me the particulars of the whole thing. I have good reason to think they are in this county yet. I learn in making inquiry of stolen horses that their is a good sorrel horse but thin in flesh at the house of one of those harborers. these men harbored at this place when the Russellville Bank & Columbia Bank was robbed. I came very near getting them on the Columbia Bank robbery. . . . If you can give me any clue to these men may be we can make it pay. I can refer you to Bligh who will tell you who I am I have been an officer ever since the war pretty much . . . wont captured man reveal nothing, may be some one saw them before the robbery who could describe horses saddle & men.

On receipt of a copy of Hunter's note, King fired off a letter to R. H. Crittenden, the U.S. marshal in Louisville. "Would it not be well to send a detective with the necessary authority to make arrests to Bardstown at once?" he asked. "Even if the men have left, some information may very likely be obtained from Mr. Hunter."

Marshal Crittenden replied, "I would willingly send a detective, as you suggest, to ferret out the robbers had I the necessary authority or funds out of which he could be paid. I have recently asked the Department of Justice to allow me to employ a detective—my request was denied—will refer your communication to the local officers. Is there a reward offered—if so, how much?"

Crittenden's letter underscored one of the big problems that hamstrung federal law enforcement in the late nineteenth century—money. Until 1896, the U.S. Marshals Service was run on a fee basis within a very tight budget.

Marshals usually made about $200 a year plus 2 percent of all funds of the courts they served; Congress placed a $6,000 cap on this total to be sure the marshals didn't drum up unnecessary work. Much of a marshal's earnings came from the deputies who worked for him. Marshals could keep up to a quarter of the fees the deputies earned while the deputies kept about three-fourths of their fees. For example, for a trip to make an arrest where the party was not apprehended, the deputy would get $2 a day, or $1.50 after the marshal's cut. When transporting a prisoner, deputies would be allowed up to $3 a day for food and ten cents a mile, one-way only. Marshals and deputies had to submit their accounts to audit by Justice Department examiners, and accounts could be and were sometimes disallowed.

Even that fabled symbol of authority, the badge itself, was not an issued or regulated item. Marshals and deputies received a printed commission signed by the president (usually by proxy even then), and that was it. If a deputy wanted a badge he could have one made to his own design and budget—anything from cheap sheet metal to fancy cast or engraved silver.

Adding to the problem, the post of U.S. marshal was one of political patronage, the job often going to presidential electors or those who were owed a political favor by the machinery of the party that occupied the White House. As a result the marshals and their deputies were a mixed bag. Amazingly, some performed quite well in their jobs. Many others were mediocre.

This system explains why U.S. Marshal Crittenden would ask about a reward (there was none at this point for the Muscle Shoals robbers) and why the marshal was loath to take on the James gang at the Hite place unaided by a large posse. It was easier just to let the matter pass and go on serving writs, delivering prisoners, etc., than to stick one's neck out.[7]

It is possible that Marshal Crittenden did notify the Louisville police about the possibility that the James boys were in the Bardstown area. In his later years, Ben Johnson, a former Kentucky legislator and U.S. congressman from Bardstown, related a story of an incident involving George Hunter and Louisville Detective Delos T. "Yankee" Bligh that possibly could have happened about this time or in mid-October 1881. Johnson had become acquainted with Sheriff Donny Pence, a former Quantrill gang member, when Johnson's father had served as an attorney for the sheriff. One day Pence told Johnson, who was then twenty-three years old, that Frank and Jesse James were in town having dinner at what was then the Ellis or Central Hotel. Pence asked Johnson if he wanted to meet them. The two were within sight of the hotel when Pence suddenly grabbed young Johnson and came to a dead halt. "There's Yankee Bligh and George Hunter," he said. "They must know the boys are here."

Johnson suggested that Pence go in the back way and warn the James boys so they could escape. Pence did just that while Johnson entered the hotel lobby. A door off the lobby led to the dining room, and Pence slid through it. The James brothers apparently said they were not going out the back way for Hunter, Bligh, or anyone.

Pence asked Johnson if he would get into the fray if shooting started. Johnson said he would, even though it wasn't his fight.

Bligh and Hunter, meanwhile, had entered the lobby, accompanied by two other local men, Bill McAtee and a relative of Hunter's named Edson. Bligh and McAtee positioned themselves on the north side of the lobby near the windows, while Hunter and Edson took the south side. Pence and Johnson went to the area near the dining room. Three or four people were lounging in the lobby, oblivious to the potential explosion about to take place. The hotel clerk, however, was ready to dive under the counter.

Five minutes later Jesse James came out the dining room door, his hands crossed and reaching into his coat for his pistols. He glanced at the men in the lobby, they looked at him, and then Jesse walked to the front door, turned around, and faced the room. The dining room door opened again, and Frank James appeared, also with crossed arms, clutching a pair of 1875 Remington .44s under his coat. The detectives stood petrified. Frank made his way to the door and turned. The door opened again, and another man, probably Dick Liddil or one of the Hites, came through the lobby and went out the door, hurrying to the nearby livery stable. Then the last man came out of the dining room and proceeded to the door. The outlaws then backed out to the street to their horses, which had been brought up. The gang quickly mounted and then gave a yell and rode off. Years later Hunter explained to Johnson that both he and Edson were good shots, "But if Yankee Bligh ever shot at anybody in his life, I didn't know it, and Bill McAtee was in the same class." Against him were arrayed the James brothers, two other gang members, and James crony Donny Pence, "all probably crack shots." Hunter guessed that Johnson would side with Pence. Thus he realized they were seriously outgunned, "six against about two and a half." And the way the detectives were positioned for a crossfire, with the James men lurking behind the dining room door, made it worse. It wasn't worth the risk.[8]

The James wives and children had been sent to Nelson County from Nashville and probably were staying with Donny Pence. Frank stayed at Aleck Sears's house, and Jesse and Liddil were at Bob Hall's. The gunfight that nearly occurred at Bardstown underscored the other serious stumbling block encountered by law enforcement. It had only been sixteen years since Ed Terrell and his "scouts," among others, had ridden roughshod over the folks in and around Nelson County, Kentucky, in the name of the U.S. government. Many people had long memories, and the hatred was still there. Marshal Crittenden may well have been aware of the strong antigovernment sentiment in those parts. It was not unusual for federal officers to face resistance from local law enforcement in various parts of the South. Jesse and Frank knew the score. But even with the local sheriff on their side, it would not be safe to stay around. So the James boys, their families, and the gang once again headed back to Missouri.

And so did Bill Ryan. On June 4, 1881, Gov. Thomas Crittenden of Missouri issued a requisition for Bill Ryan in the matter of the Glendale train robbery of 1879. Ryan had been identified as one of the Glendale culprits by Deputy Sheriff W. G. Keslear of Jackson County, Missouri, Chief of Police Thomas Spears of Kansas City, and operatives of the Pinkerton Detective Agency. But earlier in May, Ryan also had been indicted in Davidson County, Tennessee, Criminal Court on charges of "assault upon the body of one Jas. McGinnis with a pistol" and "carrying weapons." Ryan was also suspected of involvement in the Corps of Engineers payroll robbery in Muscle Shoals, Alabama, but had not yet been formally charged. On June 2, two days before Governor Crittenden requested Ryan's extradition, Major King had complained from Chattanooga to the chief of engineers:

> The robber at Nashville was still in jail last account, and the money that was under attachment, but not withstanding the positive proof that this is Government money, and that the prisoner is the man who committed the robbery, the State authorities still hold him on a trifling charge, and the Government appears to be powerless to either recover its money or to punish the robber.[9]

King's letter, with enclosures, made its way up the chain of command to Secretary of War Lincoln, who forwarded the package to Attorney General MacVeagh on June 14, requesting that the U.S. attorneys in Tennessee and Kentucky be instructed "to render Major King such assistance as may be necessary in the apprehension and prosecution of the parties guilty of the robbery." It was a bit late, considering that Ryan had been requisitioned for extradition to Missouri and the gang had already fled both Tennessee and Kentucky, but the process inexorably ground forward. It was an interesting clash of state and local vs. federal law enforcement. A week later, Lincoln received an acknowledgment from acting Attorney General S. F. Phillips, saying that instructions had been sent out that very day "to the Attorneys in the Eastern and Middle District of Tennessee and for the District of Kentucky to consult with the Marshals for their respective Districts and with Major King and to take whatever steps may seem expedient and likely to be successful for the arrest and conviction of the guilty parties and secure possession of the money belonging to the government."

In a letter to U.S. Attorney James Warder in Nashville, Phillips spelled out that Ryan was liable to indictment, even citing the statute. He ordered Warder to "take such steps as may be necessary for his delivery to the Marshal, and to recover the money belonging to the United States." Warder replied on June 26, informing MacVeagh that since the crime had been committed just over the state line in northern Alabama, Ryan would first have to be charged in that district. Warder said he would do all in his power to apprehend the other robbers (within his district) and reminded the attorney general that one of the deputy marshals for his district had tracked them to Adairville. "He was compelled, as I understand it, to give the matter up because the local authorities in Kentucky were afraid to move in the matter," Warder said. He mentioned that his assistant had placed a warrant on "Hill" and had attached, or seized, the money taken from him. "The State authorities in Tennessee thought best to let him be delivered to the State authorities in Missouri," Warder said, but he hoped to get a judgment in favor of the U.S. government at the next federal court session to get the money back. When this occurred he would see it transferred to the U.S. Treasury.

On July 6, MacVeagh wrote William H. Smith, the U.S. attorney in Montgomery, Alabama, ordering him to consult with King about the case and to arrest those responsible. MacVeagh received a telegram from the U.S. marshal in Huntsville, Alabama, on July 15, informing him that a warrant had been issued "for William Ryan alias Thomas Hill," charging him with robbery. He noted that Ryan had been removed to Missouri and asked if he should "send after him" there. The attorney general replied on July 18 that he couldn't be taken from the custody of the state officers in Missouri but asked that a copy of the warrant be forwarded to the U.S. marshal in Jefferson City for service, in case he was acquitted of charges in the Glendale robbery.[10]

⁂

WHAT HAPPENED to the James brothers for a month or so after leaving Kentucky is still a matter of some question and contention. Frank would try to obscure his movements following his departure from the Bluegrass State, and so would others connected with the gang. Frank was without regular work once more, so it was probably necessary to bring in cash, and that probably meant getting sucked back into the gang one last time, at least until he could get the money he needed to settle elsewhere. He would claim otherwise in later years. Jesse and Zee returned to Kansas City. Frank later claimed he went to Texas to visit his sister, Susan, and brother-in-law, Allen Parmer, who lived eighteen miles outside Henrietta. Frank's wife and son went to Gen. Jo Shelby's, then to her father's, and then on to visit her brother, Sam Ralston, who lived in Sonora, California.

Jesse stopped at the home of Zee's sister, Mrs. Charlie McBride, in Kansas City. Then he moved to a rented room at the Doggett Hotel, telling his son, "Tim," that they were moving to another town when in fact they were still in Kansas City. A few days later, when young Tim was playing outside the hotel, he spotted Charlie McBride, his uncle, and wondered how he had gotten there. A nervous Jesse then moved the family to a rented four-room cottage on Woodland Avenue between Eleventh and Twelfth Streets. Little did Jesse's landlord, former newsman D. R. Abdeel, know that "J. T. Jackson" was the most wanted man in the state, perhaps in the nation. Jesse was probably somewhat perplexed to learn that a neighbor, John Murphy, was the father of Cornelius Murphy, the marshal of Jackson County. Oh well, they'd brassed it out before in Nashville. They did have to keep a watch on the children, though, and Jesse and Zee discouraged Jesse Jr. from playing with kids in the neighborhood, saying the family would be moving soon, so it was best not to get attached to friends there. Nevertheless, the boy did make friends with a young fellow about the same age named Harry Hoffman.

"We played together most every day," Hoffman later recalled.

One day Harry and "Tim" got into an argument while Jesse was sitting outside on the porch. "He came to the side door and called us in," Hoffman recalled. "'Now you boys shouldn't quarrel, you are good friends and good friends should not quarrel.' He lectured us in a kindly way. He told us some stories and we left him, having forgotten our quarrel."

As in Nashville, the Kansas City neighbors soon began to think "Jackson" was a gambler who was away from home for long periods of time. If the confessions of Clarence Hite and Dick Liddil are valid, a good bit of Jesse's time during this period went into laying careful plans for robberies that were later scrubbed. In one case Jesse reportedly had a toothache, and in another rain and mud would have hampered their escape from the area around Chillicothe, Missouri. Finally a target was selected, the Chicago, Rock Island and Pacific Railroad, somewhere around Gallatin, Missouri. Twice each week trains brought several thousand dollars in cash to the Farmers' Exchange Bank there.

The gang had cased the locale for about a week when, on the evening of July 15, four or five of them boarded a northbound train at either Cameron or Winston, Missouri. Two of the bandits, Clarence Hite and Dick Liddil, positioned themselves on the platform outside the baggage car. The others, Jesse, Wood Hite, and possibly Frank, went to the smoking car.

Conductor William Westfall gave the signal to proceed, waving a red lantern to the engineer, then went into the smoking car to take tickets. Suddenly there was a commotion at the front of the car as three bandits knocked out the glass windows around the door and entered with drawn pistols.

"Hands up!" they yelled. One man took a position at the front of the car while at least one man went down the aisle. Suddenly one of the bandits, probably Jesse, fired at Westfall. According to Clarence Hite, Jesse later explained that he thought Westfall was going for a pistol. Another story later circulated that Westfall had been on the train that carried the Pinkertons to and from their 1875 raid on the James-Samuel farm, but Hite said this revenge was not planned.

The body of the conductor was hauled out to the platform, and later it fell off the moving train. But it wasn't moving for long. By accident or design, the bandit in the front of the car cut the brake-alarm cord with his knife, and engineer Addison E. Walcott applied the air brakes.

Walcott suddenly heard a voice behind him from the tender yelling, "Go ahead!" He tried to speed up, but the brakes had been set and the train began to slow. When he was told to go ahead again, the engineer turned to find two men who were pointing their guns in his face.

The brakes were down, he explained. But one of the robbers hit him in the head with a lump of coal and told him to start the train or they would kill him. The brakes were released, and the train surged forward.

Back in the smoking car, two passengers, John Penn and Frank McMillan, had slipped out the back door of the car. The robbers fired after them, shouting "Down! Down!" to the passengers. There was a commotion inside the car, and McMillan thought he heard his father crying out. Quickly he glanced up and while looking through the window was struck by a bullet above the eye. He tumbled off the platform, dead.

One of the bandits, identified by Clarence Hite as Frank, made his way to the engine and put the brakes on again. The robbers had positioned their horses in the woods up the track and were in danger of overshooting the spot if the train kept moving. After the train ground to a halt, baggage master Frank Stumper curiously leaned out the door to the express car with a lantern. He was yanked to the ground by his legs, reportedly by Frank. Shots were fired into the car, and U.S. Express Company agent Charles N.

Murray came out from behind some trunks. The robbers demanded the keys to the safe, and Murray nervously opened it.

It was the wrong train. The safe held less than seven hundred dollars. The bandits repeatedly asked if that was all then knocked Murray senseless with a pistol.

In all, the robbery lasted between fifteen and thirty minutes. The bandits escaped down the track to find their horses, but the story wasn't quite over.

About midnight the train reached Gallatin, and a posse was formed to hunt down the marauders. It seems that the local post office, a white frame house on the square, was used by the express companies to house late-night deliveries in its safe. On duty that night was the assistant to the postmaster, seventeen-year-old Webster Davis, who was waiting for a late shipment of cash coming in on a Wabash-line train.

After the posse left, three strangers, all heavily armed, rode into town. They stopped in front of the post office while one man dismounted and walked to the door. The man had just put his hand on the door handle when there were hoofbeats. The men outside exchanged nervous words, and the man at the door quickly mounted. The trio were off as fast as their horses would take them.

Earlier, it seems, Jesse and Liddil had cased the post office. Somehow they learned about the express shipment and came back.

Two years later Davis was introduced to Liddil, who told him it was Jesse who had dismounted and was about to try the door to the post office when the posse appeared, having trailed the gang back to town. "And it was a good thing for Jesse," Davis told Liddil, "for I was inside with a double-barreled shotgun, and in all probability I would have killed him if he had tried to get in!"[11]

There was the usual consternation in the press at this latest robbery. At first some doubted that the James boys were involved. It was as if some people just didn't want to believe it was so. This consternation was doubtlessly shared by the members of the gang when the loot was divvied up: $126 plus change per person involved. For that measly amount two men had been killed and some or all of the gang members would possibly face charges of murder and a hangman's noose.

"The train robbery in Northwest Missouri was despicable," thundered the *Saint Louis Republican*. "Everyone except the driveling enemies of the state does deplore it. It will, however, be the occasion of endless inane, nauseating demagoguery about crime in Missouri, and will elicit as much unrelieved asininity as the attempt to assassinate the president." (Garfield had been shot on July 2 by Charles Guiteau, an insane man who had been rejected for a political spoils job with the new administration. The president would die on September 19.) There were the usual accusations that the Democratic Party was shielding the James gang. Joseph Pulitzer's *Saint Louis Post-Dispatch*, although a Democratic paper, was highly critical of certain Democrats for failing to round up the gang. It was political season in the press once again.

There were suggestions to put armed guards on all trains and time locks on safes and to offer a huge reward for apprehending those responsible for the robbery. John Newman Edwards came out, as usual, in defense of the James boys, stating, no doubt from experience, that "the average newspaper would sell its soul for a sensation" and that stories claiming the James gang was responsible simply were written to sell papers.

Not only were newspapers trying to cash in on the gang's notoriety, but so were the fiction factories of New York. In June 1881 *The Five Cent Wide Awake Library*, published by Frank Tousey, issued the *The Train Robbers: Or, A Story of the James Boys*. It was the first of many junk-fiction accounts, dubbed "nickel" or "dime novels" according to their price. These works generally were printed in an 8½" x 11" format and usually contained sixteen to thirty-two pages of dreadful fiction. Often (although not always) the plot was framed around newspaper accounts of a robbery, with lots of wooden dialogue and trite, hackneyed plot devices; often a gushing Victorian romance was thrown in for good measure. Dime novels were, in fact, the ancestors of numerous traveling plays, B westerns, and television shows. Only Buffalo Bill Cody had more of these yarns written about him than did the James brothers.

In the midst of the furor, Zerelda Samuel, mother of the James boys, made her customary appearance and was stalked by the press during a trip to Kansas City. Both of her sons were dead, she claimed. In fact, they had been hiding on the family farm following the robbery, and according to one gang member had actually planned the caper there.

That the gang's reappearance got under the skin of Gov. Thomas T. Crittenden cannot be understated. Crittenden, a distant cousin of the U.S. marshal of the same name, had been elected governor of Missouri in 1880 on the Democratic ticket after campaigning on the promise to rid the state of the James gang. He had served as lieutenant colonel of the Seventh Missouri State Militia Cavalry during the war and had fought in the final battles against Sterling Price around Kansas City in the fall of 1864. After the war he had gone into law partnership with Confederate Brig. Gen. Francis M. Cockrell in Warrensburg.

Crittenden had been chosen by the Democrats in part because, as a former Union officer, he couldn't be charged by the Republicans with having sympathy for the James brothers; yet his association with former Confederates like

Cockrell would get him support from that quarter. The burly and genial Crittenden was a skilled political operator and served several terms in Congress during the 1870s. There he made important contacts with the railroad lobby, notably with railroad mogul Collis P. Huntington, for whom the town in West Virginia was named. It was said that the railroads had been particularly generous in their support during Crittenden's gubernatorial campaign.

Responding to the hue and cry going on in the press, Governor Crittenden swung into action. He was prohibited by Missouri law from offering a large reward for the capture and conviction of the outlaws. So with the assistance of Col. Wells H. Blodgett, a Wabash Railroad attorney, Crittenden brought together representatives of the railroad and the express companies that operated in the state. The group met in Saint Louis, in the gentleman's parlor of the Southern Hotel. "There was no chance to mistake the temper of that meeting," a participant later told a reporter. "It was a gathering of men terribly in earnest, and they showed that they were determined to stop at nothing, but to push forward the movement that has been inaugurated by the governor until the state has not only been rid of every desperado and outlaw, but has established such a reputation that that class of ruffians abroad would as soon think of committing suicide as to undertake such an outrageous crime as that recently perpetrated."

The governor gave quite a sales pitch, and in turn the railroads anteed up $50,000. The money would be turned over to Crittenden and offered by him. Two days later the governor issued a reward proclamation offering $5,000 for each of the perpetrators of the Glendale or Winston robberies, the James brothers excepted. "For the arrest and delivery of said Frank and Jesse W. James, and each or either of them, to the sheriff of said Daviess county," would earn the captors $5,000 along with a bonus of another $5,000 each on conviction. The James boys were now worth more money than the take in most of their robberies. It is worth noting, however, that the reward offer was for bringing them in alive. The proclamation was printed up on small handbills and distributed across Missouri.

A little over two weeks later a letter, ostensibly from Kansas City, was received at the offices of the *Cincinnati Commercial*, which was in the middle of a charity fundraising drive:

To the Editor of the *Commercial*:
    Although detested and despised and feared by a good many, and only $20,000 of a reward offered for us, dead or otherwise, and for all of the above we honor and respect our president, and stand ready not only to

slap, but to shoot, if need be, for him. Sorry it is not dollars instead of
cents that is rolling in to the honorable and patriotic old Capt. Cook.

FRANK AND JESSE JAMES
Missouri's Awful Outlaws

Please copy it for all Missouri's Governor's sake. I have not seen his name
in your paper yet. Frank

Whether this was the work of a prankster or the real James brothers will
never be known.

There was a certain grim irony to Jesse's predicament, his son later
recalled. "At that time Marshall Murphy was very anxious to capture my
father and nearly every night a posse would gather at Murphy's house [actu-
ally Murphy's father's house, next to Jesse's] and start out for the country
around Independence and in the 'Cracker Neck' district in search of members of the James band. My father used to walk over to Murphy's house in the
evening when the posse would be starting out to talk with them about their
plans, and wish them luck on their trip." At the end of August Jesse would
rent another white house with four rooms from H. C. Sailers on East Ninth
Street, in the first block east of Woodland. He had other plans brewing.[12]

⁂

THE GANG had another train robbery in the works by early September 1881.
They struck on Wednesday night, September 7, five years to the day after
the Northfield disaster. The site they picked was a good one for this sort of
work, a spot known as Blue Cut on the Chicago and Alton line about three
miles from Independence, and just a mile or so from the site of the robbery
at Glendale. The target was probably no accident, as employees of the line
were slated to testify in the trial of Bill Ryan later in the month. Blue Cut
was, as the name implies, a thirty-foot cut, on a curve, where trains were in a
habit of slowing down. Earlier that evening the gang had almost hit one of
two eastbound trains, but couldn't decide whether those trains had any
money. Finally it was decided to hit the train headed west.

"Chappy" Foote was the engineer that night when the train came around
the curve at about twenty-five miles an hour. Freight trains often stalled in
the area, so it was no surprise to Foote to see a figure waving a red lantern in
the distance. "I began to slack up and soon saw that the man who was
flagging the train was masked, and I also saw him set the lantern on a pile of
stone between the rails," Foote recalled. He turned to his fireman and said
they were about to be robbed.

The outlaws had positioned themselves well. According to Clarence Hite, he and Jesse were on the north bank of the cut and Frank James and Dick Liddil were on the south. Wood Hite and a new recruit, Charlie Ford, were to take the engine and the express car. The gang had brought along quite an arsenal to do the job. Four of the six men were armed with rifles or shotguns in addition to a pair of revolvers that each man carried. The close-in work would preclude the use of long arms, which would be used by the men on the bank to provide cover.

"Don't shoot, boys," Foote told the robbers.

"All right, we won't hurt you if you get down and out of that right lively," one man responded.

The engineer was ordered to bring a coal pick or hammer from the tender. He tried to stall, hoping the express messenger might use the time to get away. But the robbers threatened to shoot Foote's head off if he didn't get on with it. One of them came up and introduced himself as Jesse James, and then, curiously, introduced Liddil. It may have been a bad attempt at a joke on the part of Wood Hite or Jesse, for reasons that will be explained later.

The engineer was taken to the express car and told to bash in the door. A few blows did the job. The messenger and baggage master had slipped out and were on the other side of the car. One of the robbers told Foote to get the messenger back or he would be shot. Foote called out, telling H. A. Fox, of the U.S. Express Company, to come back and open the safe.

"The messenger was very slow in opening the safe, and they struck him over the head with a revolver," the engineer recalled. When little money was found in the safe, he was struck over the head again. According to both Liddil and Clarence Hite, Charlie Ford hit the messenger. Less than four hundred dollars was reportedly found in the safe. Little did the robbers know that nearby, under a pile of chicken coops slated for delivery farther west, lay an Adams Express safe containing much more money. Frustrated, Jesse ordered them to rob the passengers.

Conductor J. N. Hazelbaker had already warned the passengers to hide their valuables. The conductor hid seventy-five dollars and his watch in a water tank in one of the cars, reserving another fifty dollars as a "contribution." One woman tucked fifteen hundred dollars in her stockings, offering the robbers a gold watch and chain and her pocketbook. "We don't want it," she was told. Another robber commented, "The next time we undertake a job of this kind we will have a lady to search the lady passengers."

A woman begged to differ: "No sir, you will never have a lady. You may have a woman, or a man dressed as one, but never a lady."

Another passenger, John O'Brien of New York, who was traveling with his wife and daughter, had one thousand dollars. He put seven hundred dollars in his pants, giving the bandits three hundred dollars. Somehow the money slipped out onto the floor. "There's some money, Papa," his daughter said. The robbers had sharp ears and took the balance.

Another passenger was a German immigrant. He was asleep when the robbers came along asking for his money. "Vat for?" he asked. "I bays my fare already."

"Gimme yer money, you Dutch fool, or I'll blow a hole through you," the bandit ordered.

"You rob me, hay?"

"Yes, you, I'm Jesse James. Give it up quick."

"All I've got?"

"Yes, every damned cent of it."

"But I goes to Joplin to buy a farm. Vat will I do?"

"Beat your way there, and hire yourself out when you get there," the bandit told him.

The outlaws took a number of silver and gold watches from the men. As the conductor recalled, "They gave one silver watch back to a boy that was going out West, telling him it wasn't worth enough to steal." Not all the passengers were robbed, and at least one man with eighteen hundred dollars, in the middle of one car, was overlooked. They also overlooked the spitoons, which had been crammed with cash.

In the course of the robbery the brakeman ran out to the rear of the train to flag down a freight that was scheduled to be following. The outlaws thought he was trying to escape or summon help, firing about forty shots his way. The engineer finally explained the situation to Jesse, who ordered the shooting to stop. In all, the holdup lasted roughly half an hour. Jesse shook hands with Foote and gave him two dollars.

"You're a good one," he told Foote. "Take this and spend it on the boys." And then he added, "You'd better quit running this road. We're going to make it so hot for this damned Alton road they can't run." The bandits disappeared into the underbrush and apparently made their escape on foot after squaring up. Each man reportedly got between $140 and $160 plus some jewelry, by the accounts of Clarence Hite and Liddil. It's possible that they minimized the reported take, fearing they might have to pay the money back. The total amount is uncertain.[13]

"A more thoroughly frightened and disgusted lot of people were never seen," wrote a reporter for the *Saint Louis Republican*, "than the passengers who left the Alton train at the Union depot last night, and some of them were indeed to be pitied as they had lost every cent of their money and were left stranded here in a strange city. . . . Some passengers were tender-feet . . . and with voices choked with emotion . . . they asked if it was safe to go further West." Others took the matter more stoically and were simply glad to be alive. "Some ladies, after the first excitement was over, went into hysterical fits and wept the greater part of the night." Those who had the means continued their journeys while others, who were able to do so, tele-graphed relatives or friends for help.

Marshal Cornelius Murphy and a posse went out to the robbery site on a special train and were soon combing the area. They were joined by Chief Speers and men from Kansas City as well as a posse under Sheriff Casin from Saline County. Some of the lawmen were apparently a bit overzealous and scooped up the wrong people again, something that would have a neg-ative impact later.

The fact that the robbers had fled on foot led officers to believe that this was a job pulled by some of the locals and *not* the work of the James gang. One of those arrested was John Bugler, whose father, Marshal Henry Bugler, had been gunned down in front of the old jail at Independence in June 1866 when he refused to surrender Joab Perry. Young John, then seven, had been wounded in the wrist by a stray bullet during the incident. Another suspect wrongly arrested was William Murray, son of John Murray, a former treasurer of Jackson County. In all, about eleven young men were brought in. Only Andy Ryan, brother of Bill Ryan, was even remotely con-nected. But eventually he and seven others were released while three of the suspects, including Bugler, were set for trial. In the eyes of the law and of the press, Bugler and the others were guilty until proven innocent.

The *Saint Louis Republican* and a few other papers were quick to assume that the guilty parties had been caught and published stories that tended to reinforce the claims of the lawmen. Comments such as those of the *Republi-can* must have caused Bugler to shake his head in bewilderment, saying, "The success of the James boys, their gods, inspired them with a desire to become as noted and feared and they but lack a leader in the midst of such temptation to do any crime on the calendar."

Fortunately, there were some doubters. It just so happened that one of the passengers on the train had also been present at the Winston robbery in July. He noticed that the leader of the group on both occasions had a par-ticularly cool manner in which he went about things. There was "also the peculiarity of his walk and the general build of his person." The witness "said that the walk once seen could never be forgotten, yet he could not describe it." The witness was probably describing Jesse James, who was bowlegged and walked with a quick step.[14]

⁂

WILLIAM WALLACE, prosecuting attorney for Jackson County, had an uphill battle. In 1880 he had run for the job as an independent candidate, stumping the county amid threats, campaigning to bring to justice the culprits responsible for the Glendale robbery. At the end of September 1881 he faced his first task, the trial of Bill Ryan for robbery in the first degree.

Born in Clark County, Kentucky, in 1848, Wallace had moved with his family to a Jackson County farm near Lee's Summit, when he was eight. The family farm was ransacked by Jennison's jayhawkers during the war, and following Order No. 11 the family was forced to move to Independence. Eventually his father, Joseph Wallace, a graduate of Princeton's Theological College, obtained a teaching position at Westminster College in Fulton. Young William was allowed to attend classes there, and returning to Jackson County after the war, he taught in a one-room schoolhouse before going back to Fulton to read law. He was eventually admitted to the bar and practiced in Kansas City.

From his writings it is apparent that Wallace was irritated by attempts to politicize the James situation. Wallace believed that, despite the press blather, a majority of Jackson County's citizens were against the lawlessness.

Nevertheless, many of Bill Ryan's friends, fully armed ruffians from the Crackerneck area, hovered around the courthouse during the course of the trial. There were also anonymous letters threatening death to Wallace and his assistant, John Southern, a former Confederate soldier who had been wounded during the war. Potential witnesses were intimidated as well. An official of the Chicago and Alton Railroad informed Wallace that other officials, after consultation, had requested that he refrain from dragging the railroad and its employees into the trial. The official explained that his superiors believed no member of the gang could be convicted in Missouri, and that if the railroad were a party to a conviction the gang might single out the line for further robberies in the future.

Wallace insisted that the trainmen come as witnesses. However, on their arrival they told him they could swear to nothing and could identify no one, and they were subsequently released from testifying.

The prosecution now rested its case on the testimony of Tucker Bassham, who had been serving a ten-year sentence in Jefferson City when offered a full pardon in exchange for his cooperation. He was more than willing to oblige, and gave Wallace and the jury a detailed account that pinned Ryan to the robbery. Bassham recited how Ryan had asked him back in April 1879, "What are you plowing there for?" Bassham had responded that he was supporting his family.

"Damn it, why do you do that? Let's go knock a train off the Pacific track," Ryan urged him. It was glaringly obvious that some sentimental attachment to the Lost Cause was not the central motivation behind the outlawry.

In retaliation, Ryan's cronies tried to burn Bassham's home, an old cabin in the Crackerneck, but the oak floor wouldn't catch fire. So the men piled his belongings in the yard and torched them. Understandably, Bassham reportedly fled the area after his release.

"There is a desperate organization in the county banded for to prevent the arrest, trial and conviction of the train robbers," stated the *Independence Sentinel*, "or, failing in this, to rescue them from the officers in case of conviction."

Both Frank Miller and William Grisham had recognized Ryan and had been forced to flee the area. The *Sentinel* strongly hinted that vigilante action might come into play if lawful means could not bring an end to the situation, "for sure as there is a God in heaven the honest men in this county are going to rule it, and in ruling it, rigidly enforce the laws. If they cannot do this through the courts then they are going beyond the courts."

The situation was very tense as the Ryan trial came toward its finish. Governor Crittenden went to Independence in person to assess the situation and asked Chief Speers to bring a posse from Kansas City to that place. Ten men from the Kansas City police and ten from the local Craig Rifles militia company left for Independence by rail. Crittenden ordered two crates of rifles shipped to the city along with ammunition, but they were never unboxed.

"From what I can see," the governor told a reporter, "there is a settled determination . . . that the laws must be upheld and lawlessness suppressed. . . . The people are fully aroused and have arrived at that state of mind in which it will be very dangerous indeed for the desperadoes to undertake the liberation of their friends or the commission of another robbery. . . . Should Ryan be acquitted, thousands would despair of being able to bring the guilty to justice or of reforming the bad people of the county, and then Judge Lynch would try his bloody hand against not only the suspected robbers but their friends also, and there would be a grand cleaning out. This cleaning out I would prefer to see accomplished by the courts."

On the morning of September 28 the jury found Ryan guilty and fixed his sentence at twenty-five years in prison. Ryan's lawyers entered a motion for a new trial, claiming that the governor had overawed the jury by shipping arms to Independence. On October 15, Judge White overruled the motion and then officially passed the twenty-five-year sentence. According to a witness, "Ryan turned very pale and was so much affected that it was necessary to allow him to support himself with a chair."

A rescue attempt never materialized. Dick Liddil later stated that a rescue effort was considered until it was learned that Capt. M. M. Langhorne, "one of the coolest, gamest men in Shelby's Brigade," during the war and afterward in Mexico, had charge of the prisoner. Bassham, the star witness, was guarded by Amazon Hays, brother of Col. Upton Hays, who had commanded some of the men at Lawrence. There would have been hell to pay if any attempt had been made to get at either of the two men.[15]

According to Wallace, "The jury which convicted Ryan broke the backbone of outlawry in the state of Missouri. Thousands of mouths that had been locked by fear were opened, and the denunciation of train robbery was open and unstinted." Just as the Ryan trial came to a conclusion, Confederate veterans attending a reunion in Moberly, Missouri, passed a resolution condemning train robbery and extending approval to "all efforts of the governor of the state for the suppression of highwaymen and murderers," asserting that they would be "content with nothing less than the extermination of this class of enemies of society." As an editorial in the *Saint Louis Republican* so aptly observed, "It begins to look as if the day of reckoning with these villains [has] come at last."

Things were certainly not looking bright from the viewpoint of the James gang. The Missouri Pacific had converted a baggage car "into a regular armory," with "sixteen men each provided with Winchester repeating rifles inside."

Prosecutor Wallace learned of a plan, after the Ryan trial, in which vigilantes and/or railroad gunmen would make up a special train at Saint Louis, transporting men and horses to the Little Blue River in Jackson County under cover of darkness. The men were to go after and kill certain men, known to Wallace, who had given shelter to the gang. But Wallace, strenuously disapproving, would not turn over the names either to a former Jackson County deputy or to a railroad man from Saint Louis, and the plan was abandoned.

Frank could probably see that there was little reason to stay around in Missouri. Officially, he never admitted being anywhere west of Saint Louis during the fall of 1881. He would claim to have met his wife there after visiting his sister in Texas. He would at least stay around Kansas City long enough to help Jesse move to a house at 1017 Troost Avenue in early October. In April 1882, Zee James would tell a reporter that she had not seen Frank "since last September," when he met his wife at their home on Troost.

After visiting with his mother, Frank, Clarence Hite, and Charlie Ford "took a Wabash train at Richmond and Lexington Junction," for Danville, Illinois, and on to Indianapolis. From there they went to Cincinnati, where they parted. This at least was what Clarence Hite later contended. Frank said that he had met his wife in Nelson County, Kentucky, in the latter part of October. He claimed to have stayed at Rufer's Hotel in Louisville the week of October 10–15, registered under the name of Fred Thorn. Just what was going on during this time will probably never be fully known. There are allegations that Jesse wanted to rob a train on the Louisville and Nashville Railroad and that he too may have been in Nelson County at this time. Other accounts say he never left Missouri. Whatever the case, there was trouble waiting in Kentucky—woman trouble.[16]

≈≈☙❦☙☙≈≈

SARAH NORRIS PECK HITE was the daughter of a slave catcher. In 1864, long before Jesse's rise to notoriety, her father had earned an illustrated chapter titled "Norris the Kidnapper" in John Fitch's *Annals of the Army of the Cumberland*. The chapter related how Norris, a carpenter and former constable in Edgefield, had engaged to capture and transport to Alabama several abandoned slaves belonging to a local minister who had sought refuge inside Confederate lines after Nashville fell to Union forces in 1862. Norris accomplished his task but was arrested and sent to Alton Military Prison after his return, charged with kidnapping. Fitch termed Norris "a man who will do anything for pay, however dirty the job."

In 1880, following the death of Nancy James Hite, aunt of the James boys, Sarah Norris Peck, then a young widow, became the second wife of George Hite. "She was a fine looking woman, and she led the old man a dance that was rapid," as one account put it. The Hite family was against the marriage, and most of the children moved out. Indeed, it was about this time that Wood Hite joined the James gang. Wood and his stepmother did not get along. He suspected her of being a loose woman. Dick Liddil was suspected of being one of her paramours, as was another man in the neighborhood named Hicks, to whom she reportedly passed notes.

Sarah also reportedly passed letters along to the law. Possibly her father saw a potential reward in the proposition, and it may well have been that one or the other tipped off authorities earlier in the spring. Apparently in October 1881 she had alerted Detective George Hunter, who with City Marshal Sam Adams of Bowling Green put together a posse of seventeen men, including Detective Rosenheim of Cincinnati and Sheriff Plummer of Simpson County. There had apparently been reports that the James gang

planned to rob a Louisville and Nashville train at Muldraugh's Hill, south
of Louisville, but details surrounding this plan are uncertain. The posse met
around 10 P.M. at the Russellville law office of William F. Browder, then
they rode out to raid the Hite farm. The party divided in two, one covering
the front of the house and the other the back. But only Wood and Clarence
Hite were there, and Wood wasn't recognized as a wanted man and was
released. Clarence managed to hide, according to one account. Reportedly
the James boys were there but were warned and hid nearby—at least that's
how one story went.[17]

Wood and Dick Liddil had an argument at the Hite place, which probably occurred sometime in October 1881. Wood's brother, George T. Hite,
later claimed that Wood accused Liddil of stealing money from him and
Jesse during the split after Blue Cut.

"Let's shoot it out," suggested one of them. Strapping on their six-guns,
they went out to the barn to have a duel. The two stood back to back and
then stepped toward the place where they would turn and fire. But before
Hite had time to reach his position, Liddil turned and fired. Wood ducked
behind a tree, and so did Liddil. Dick emptied his pistol at Hite, who held
his fire. Hite then returned fire, and Dick broke and ran for the house with
Wood following and shooting at his opponent. No one was hurt, and members of the family stopped any further gunplay. Liddil reportedly beat a
hasty retreat from the area, leaving a gun belt and other belongings behind.

In all likelihood there was more to it than just an argument over
money, if this was the case. There may have been words between Hite and
Liddil over a rumored affair with Sarah Hite. Jesse may have had a hand in
stoking the controversy, probably seeing Liddil as a potential rival for gang
leadership or a potential traitor in the vein of Jim Cummins. Earlier in the
summer, between the Winston and the Blue Cut robberies, Liddil and
Charlie Ford reportedly robbed a stage that ran between Excelsior Springs
and Vibbard, netting a whopping thirty dollars. About a week later, Liddil,
Charlie and Bob Ford, and Wood Hite robbed a stage in Ray County, netting around two hundred dollars, three watches, and a pocketknife. They
also robbed a man in a wagon of twenty dollars. Jesse was not present and
probably was unaware of those plans before they happened.

A few weeks after the shooting, Wood Hite shot and killed John Tabor,
a black laborer on the Hite place, who was perhaps passing another letter
from Hite's stepmother and/or talking a bit too freely. A few days later
Sarah Hite swore out a warrant, and Wood was arrested by Marshal Jeter
and taken to Adairville. Wood was sequestered in a store on the square,
and a guard was posted over him. But Hite slipped out the back way and

managed to find a horse, which he rode around town an hour later, offering a reward of one hundred dollars for the return of his guard. The man couldn't be found, and the rumor was that the guard had been bribed to let Hite escape. Afterward Jeter was threatened by friends of the gang, and subsequently he moved to Kansas City, where he was given a job on the police force by Commissioner Henry H. Craig.

One evening during the first week in December, Dick Liddil arrived at the Harbison place, home of Charlie and Bob Ford and their sister Martha Bolton, a few miles outside Richmond, Missouri. "Next morning I came down to breakfast, and Wood Hite who had come from Kentucky three or four days before, was there," Liddil recalled. "When he first came in he spoke to me, and I told him I did not want him to speak to me as he had accused me of stealing $100 at the divide in the Blue Cut robbery."

Liddil said Hite had lied and that he could prove it by Martha Bolton, and then wanted Hite to prove it. "He then denied saying anything of the kind. I told him he did and we both commenced drawing our pistols."

Hite fired four shots, and Liddil fired five shots back. Hite was wounded in the right arm and Liddil in the right thigh. Liddil was in the process of pulling his other revolver when Hite started to fall. Bob Ford had rushed to Dick's defense and fired one shot at Hite, which he would claim was the fatal bullet. Whoever did it, Hite had been shot in the head and lingered for about twenty minutes before he died. The body was taken upstairs, wrapped in an old horse blanket after any usable clothing had been removed, and then hastily buried in a shallow grave near an old spring some distance from the house.

The gunfight at the Harbison place marked the end of the James gang. Liddil had distrusted Jesse earlier, and Hite's belligerence only tended to confirm his suspicions. Now both Liddil and the Fords had reason to fear if Jesse ever learned the fate of his cousin Wood Hite.[18]

14

An End and a Beginning

The best energies of the intelligent criminal are devoted to the achievement of success in such a manner as to baffle the detective and secure immunity from punishment.

Allan Pinkerton, *Thirty Years a Detective* (1884)

SOMETIME IN LATE OCTOBER 1881, Frank James, his wife, and his son left Nelson County for Georgetown, Kentucky, where they caught the Cincinnati Southern train for Chattanooga. Frank was finally putting some distance between himself, Jesse, and the gang. At Chattanooga, Frank registered at the Stanton House as "J. Ed. Warren and wife." They then took the East Tennessee, Virginia, and Georgia Railroad to Bristol, catching the Norfolk and Northwestern bound for Lynchburg.

"I remained there a couple of weeks, detained by the miscarriage of a trunk which I had expressed from Louisville to Georgetown when I had gone across country in a buggy," Frank recalled. He stayed at the Arlington Hotel in Lynchburg for about two weeks. "My intention was to go into North Carolina somewhere, and remain there."

Frank took his family via the Virginia Midland to Danville, Virginia, then to Jonesboro, North Carolina, a town near Sanford and southwest of Raleigh on the Richmond and Danville line. Here he put his family up at the McAdoo house, probably a boarding house, using the same alias he'd used in Chattanooga.

263

Frank thought about settling in the town of Salem, now part of Winston-Salem, as there were a number of mills there. However, there was a diphtheria outbreak in that area, and rather than risk the lives of himself and his family, he went back to Jonesboro, and from there to Raleigh. The town, as Frank sized it up, "was dead. There wasn't a manufacturing establishment in it to amount to anything." They continued on to Norfolk, Virginia, staying at Purcell's, another boarding house, registered as before. Frank didn't like Norfolk, so at Annie's suggestion, they went up the James River, on the steamboat *Ariel*, to Richmond. "I found the town all yellow flagged for the small-pox, which scared me, as I didn't want to lose my wife and child."

In the end they went back to Lynchburg and rented a frame house from C. V. Winfree on Wise Street, between Sixth and Seventh, near the College Hill reservoir. Frank went under the alias of James Warren, and would later claim that a reason for choosing Lynchburg was its proximity to the mountains, allowing for escape if someone happened to catch on to who he was. Frank was noted as being uneasy, but never in a way that would arouse suspicion. He and his family would live a very low-profile life in Lynchburg for several months as events ran their course elsewhere.[1]

Back in Kansas City, Jesse moved from the Troost Avenue house during the first week of November 1881. He went to Atcheson, Kansas, then, on November 9, to Saint Joseph, Missouri. With him was Charlie Ford.

⁂

THE FORDS were a roving family. In the early 1800s, Austin Ford, the grandfather of Charlie and Bob, reportedly lived for a time on the grounds of Mount Vernon, George Washington's home near Alexandria, Virginia. Some of the stone masonry that was completed there after Washington's death was done by Ford. Later Ford lived in Fauquier County, Virginia, where his son, James Thomas Ford, was born in 1820. The Fords moved to Missouri and back to Virginia several times. James Ford worked as a tenant farmer at Mount Vernon from 1841 to 1843 then returned to Missouri. He came back to Virginia in 1862, shortly after his son Bob's birth in Missouri, where things were starting to take a nasty turn in terms of guerrilla warfare.

According to Ford family tradition, James rented rooms and acreage at Mount Vernon in 1862 and then eventually moved to Fauquier County, near present-day Marshall, where Bob later attended school. During their brief time at Mount Vernon the Ford children are said to have sneaked to the attic where furniture and artifacts such as the Bastille key given to Washington by Lafayette and Nellie Custis's piano were stored.

Apparently the Fords tried to stay out of the Civil War as long as possible. They escaped the worst of the guerrilla war in Missouri, but another was brewing in northern Virginia under Maj. (later Col.) John Singleton Mosby. Raids by the "Gray Ghost" ultimately contributed to Union Gen. Philip H. Sheridan's ravaging a portion of Fauquier County. John T. Ford, brother of Charlie and Bob, probably with their father, James, joined Company C of Mosby's Forty-third Virginia Partisan Rangers in the latter part of 1864, following the "Burning" (the local term for Sheridan's campaign of retribution in the Shenandoah Valley in 1864). Jesse and the Fords would later swap guerrilla yarns, which perhaps attracted him later to the family.

Following the war, around 1869, the Fords again relocated in Missouri, eventually settling outside Richmond. Jesse and Frank James had already become living legends by the summer of 1879 when the Fords were introduced to Jesse.

"He came over with Ed Miller," Bob later testified. "He was acquainted with Ed Miller and he and Jesse came to our house one night in August. . . . He was then planning a robbery." The Fords also knew Jim Cummins, whose sister Artella married Bill Ford, uncle of Bob and Charlie. After killing Miller in 1880, Jesse took his horse and Ed's to the Harbison place and left them there while he was out on other business. He told Charlie that Ed had been seriously ill and had gone to Hot Springs, Arkansas, for his health. Cummins heard about the horse and tracked it to Kentucky.

Doubtless, somewhere along the line the Fords heard about Cummins's suspicions regarding Jesse's involvement in the death of Miller. For a while they were perhaps content to ignore it, until Jesse began to act in a similarly hostile manner toward Dick Liddil. It was beginning to look like an old story, and Jesse was probably viewed more and more as a loose cannon by other members of the gang. "Jesse . . . had outlived his greatness as a bandit, though not as an individual robber," Bob Ford related. "As a leader he was dead. There were few who would place themselves in his clutches. . . . It was his tyranny among his fellows that wrecked his empire." With the killing of Wood Hite at their hands, the Fords could see that sooner or later Jesse would discover their role in Hite's death and come gunning for them. For the time being, however, Jesse was ignorant.

Meanwhile, Charlie Ford had been hiding out with Jesse in Saint Joseph at a house on the corner of Lafayette and Twenty-first Streets. As in Kansas City earlier, Jesse would spend most of his time at home during the day and go out at night, often to get a newspaper. On Christmas Eve, Jesse and his family moved to another house, this one being at 1318 Lafayette Street, atop a hill with an excellent view.

That evening Jesse decided to play Santa Claus for his children. He borrowed a costume from a nearby Presbyterian church and obtained some small toys and candy. Somehow he managed to don his costume and slip out of the house unobserved by Jesse Jr. and Mary. Then there was a loud banging at the door, and Santa appeared and asked the kids if they had been good all year. The two little ones vouched that they had indeed been virtuous, and the jolly old elf produced his bag of presents. As Jesse Jr. searched the bag for goodies he felt something odd under the cloth, something that felt like his father's Smith and Wesson. The young lad exclaimed that the guest was not really Santa, but his father. Jesse and Zee then fell back on the story that Jesse had volunteered to help Santa, as he was so busy that night.

A few days later, around December 29, Jesse and Charlie Ford left Saint Joe for the Harbison place, where they tried to convince Dick Liddil to join them. They told him they had just returned from Nebraska.

"I mistrusted that Jesse intended to kill me and so left," Liddil later confessed. This was the last he saw of Jesse, who left with Charlie the following night for the farm near Kearney.

It was shortly afterward that Bob Ford secretly met with both Governor Crittenden and Clay County Sheriff Henry Timberlake. He talked with the governor on January 13, 1882, at the Saint James Hotel in Kansas City during a ball held for the Craig Rifles. Crittenden asked Ford if he could assist the local officers in capturing the outlaws, and Ford agreed to do so. Ford also said he was seeking a pardon for Liddil. "He told me what he would give for the capture—said he would give $10,000 apiece for Jesse and Frank, dead or alive," Bob would later testify. Charlie would claim it was only for the *capture* of the outlaws, and so would Crittenden. The governor told Ford to get in touch with Timberlake and Police Commissioner Henry H. Craig in Kansas City. Bob agreed to furnish them with information.

A few days earlier Sheriff Timberlake had raided the Ford lair at the Harbison place, narrowly missing Dick Liddil, who had returned there to convalesce. Liddil eventually surrendered to authorities on January 24, 1882, but the matter was kept quiet to keep from arousing Jesse's suspicion. Apparently Jesse already had an idea of what was coming. He reportedly wrote his cousin Clarence Hite in Kentucky in early January that Liddil was about to betray him to the law. Jesse suggested that Clarence should get out of Adairville and go into hiding. But Clarence, then suffering from tuberculosis and with only a little more than a year to live, didn't budge.

About 2 A.M. on February 11, Craig, Timberlake, Liddil, and another man came to the Hite place. After searching the house, they handcuffed

Clarence Hite and took him from Adairville to Springfield, Tennessee, over the state line, literally kidnapping him without the formal niceties of extradition. From there, he was taken, presumably by rail, to Kansas City, where he was charged with robbery.

The noose was getting tighter, and Jesse was either ignorant of how things were lining up or very careless. On March 2, 1882, he wrote a letter to D. H. Calhoun in Lincoln, Nebraska, responding to an advertisement for 160 acres of land in Franklin County that Calhoun had placed in the *Lincoln Journal*. Signing his name now as Thomas Howard, he said he would be headed for northern Kansas and southern Nebraska in about eight days and if the land had good soil and suited him he would buy the property.

Despite appearances that Jesse might be planning to abandon outlawry, in all likelihood it probably would be another exercise in futility. "He said he expected to be a bandit as long as he lived," Charlie Ford later told a reporter. Cousin George T. Hite would have concurred: "He wanted to quit the business, but he said he had to make a living, and as the whole world seemed pitted against him, and he couldn't do anything else, he kept on with it. He used to tell me that if some fellow—I can't think of his name— was made Governor of Missouri he'd pardon him out, and then he'd be happy. 'They wouldn't let me stay at home, and what else can I do?'"[2]

On March 10 or 12, Jesse and Charlie departed. Jesse wanted to case the banks in northeast Kansas and said he would get the men to pull off further robberies. He asked Charlie if he knew of anyone, and Charlie suggested his brother Bob. Jesse and Charlie went through Hiawatha, Pawnee City, Forrest City, White Cloud, and then back to Forrest City.

"He said that he liked the way the bank at Forrest City was situated, and said he wanted to take that bank," Charlie recounted. "But I told him I did not want to go into that as I was sick then."

They then cased the bank at Oregon, Kansas. Charlie recalled, "He would go into a bank with a large bill or several small ones to get changed, and while the cashier was making the change he would look and see whether they were caged up, what sort of looking man it was and whether they had a time lock or not."

On their way back to Saint Joseph they apparently took a roundabout detour by way of Ray County and the farm near Kearney. They picked up Bob at the Harbison place and headed off. Bob had arranged for Sheriff Timberlake to keep a watch on the place from nearby, but the weather got bad and the sheriff had left just before Jesse arrived. So much for plans to trap Jesse in Ray County. Bob Ford left word before he left, through his sister, that if no one heard from him within ten days he would probably be dead.

Jesse wanted to visit his half brother, Johnnie Samuel at the family farm. "Young Samuels, who is about 22 years of age, is reported as being quiet and orderly when sober, but is decidedly wild when under the influence of liquor," according to an account in the *Kansas City Journal*. At a party in January, Samuel had one drink too many and had started a quarrel. He was thrown out of the house. Angry, he threw a rock through the window. The owner, George Rhodus, came out and fired a warning shot at Johnnie with a pistol. But the warning shot struck Johnnie in the right lung. He was not expected to live.

The grand jury failed to indict Rhodus. That someone would dare to shoot Jesse's half brother shows how public fear of the outlaw was waning following Bill Ryan's conviction.

Jesse and the Fords hid in the barn during part of their visit to the Samuel place while some friends and neighbors visited at the cabin. Jesse's mother told him she didn't like the looks of the Fords and to be careful.

Later the three men managed to steal a horse from a man named Robinson, in Clay County, for Bob to use. The trio spent the night inside a church some eighteen miles from Saint Joseph and slipped back into town the next evening. If they ever went out afterward, it was usually at night. Occasionally Jesse would venture out to shoot pool at a local saloon in south Saint Joseph.

Jesse liked to read the stories that were coming out as media attention focused on the gang. On Sunday, April 2, Bob Ford read Jesse an account that predicted his early capture. Jesse "laughed and remarked that he might have to go under eventually, but before he did he would shake up the country once or twice more."[3]

The next evening big things were planned. Jesse and the Fords intended to depart for Platte City, Missouri, to raid a bank there on the following day. A rather sensational trial was getting under way in Platte City, and "[Jesse] said when they was making speeches everybody would be up at the court house and we would rob the bank," Charlie Ford recounted.

That morning at breakfast Jesse noticed something in the paper about Liddil's surrender. The news had finally leaked out. "When Jesse read that Dick Liddil had surrendered he said that Dick was a traitor and ought to be hung," Zee James recalled.

The Fords were nervous at this new development, wondering whether Jesse was really going to take the bank or was just using the scheme as an excuse to get them out of the house so he could dry-gulch them on the road, as he'd apparently done with Ed Miller. There was some irony here in that Jesse had given Bob a pistol that Jesse might have taken from Miller.

After breakfast the men went out to the stable to feed and curry the horses. Charlie would later testify that Jesse "complained of being warm and pulled off his coat and threw it on the bed and opened the door and said that he guessed he would pull off his [gun] belt as someone might see it. Then he went to brush off some pictures and when he turned his back I gave my brother the wink and we both pulled our pistols but he, my brother, was a little the quickest and fired first. I had my finger on the trigger and was just going to fire but I saw his shot was a death shot and did not fire. He heard us cock our pistols and [was about] to turn his head. The ball struck him in the back of the head and he fell."

Zee recalled that they had not been in the room more than three minutes when she heard the fatal shot. She found Jesse lying on the floor where he fell. Charlie explained to her that "a pistol had accidentally gone off."

"Yes," Zee countered. "I guess it went off on purpose."

The Ford boys were soon off to the telegraph office, where they sent off wires to Governor Crittenden, Sheriff Timberlake, and Commissioner Craig. They also had a chance to use a newfangled gadget to report the shooting to City Marshal Enos Craig. It was a telephone, an invention Jesse probably saw at the 1876 Centennial.

Young Harry Hoffman, Jesse Jr.'s playmate on Woodland Street in Kansas City, was surprised to see knots of people milling about the neighborhood when he came back from school around 4 P.M. "I asked one of them, an old man what's the trouble: He said, do you remember the little boy that you used to play with named Tim Howard: I said, 'Yes, I remember Tim.' Well, the old man said, 'His father was Jesse James.' He was killed today in St. Joseph.'" About three days later Hoffman's father told him they were going to go on a trip up to Kearney. "Upon reaching the town the following day, the body of Jesse James arrived at 2:45 on the Hannibal and St. Joe Railway [by special train] and was taken to the Kearney House [a hotel]. There the casket was placed on benches, the lid was removed, and the people were permitted to pass by in a line and view the remains. There were hundreds of people there, a number of relatives, among whom were his mother, wife, two children, and the Samuel children, who were Jesse's half-brothers and sisters. There were many neighbors who knew Jesse James all his life. When we passed the casket I said to my father, 'That is Mr. Howard.' He said, 'Yes, son, that is Mr. Howard, it is also Jesse James.' The body was conveyed to the Baptist Church, the same church where Jesse had been baptised in 1866. The funeral sermon was given by the Reverend J. P. Martin, pastor of the church. He selected the text 24th chapter [verse 44] of Matthew ["Therefore be ye also ready: for in such an hour as ye think not the Son of man cometh"]. Jesse's body was taken to the old James farm where he was born, and placed in a grave in one corner of the broad lawn that surrounds the house, under a coffee bean tree."[4]

⁂

SOMETIME AROUND April 5 or 6, Frank James went out for a walk around Lynchburg, "and when I got back to the house I saw my wife was excited, and she came rushing to me with the paper [the *New York Daily Herald*] and says 'Jesse James is killed.' I says, 'My God, where and how and who killed him?'"

The first reports told how Jesse had been living in Saint Joseph with Charlie and later Bob Ford and making plans for another robbery.

"James and the two Fords were in the front room together about nine o'clock this morning. James took off his pistols and laid his pistols on the bed." The account went on to wrongly state that Jesse was starting to wash himself, "when Robert Ford sprang up behind him and sent a bullet through his brain." The Fords had given themselves up and were under guard. Jesse's body was at the undertaker's. The *Herald* article said that the Fords claimed to be detectives who had been on the trail of the gang for a long time.

From the vantage point of Lynchburg, getting thirdhand reports out of New York, Frank must have felt very uneasy. He probably had little suspected the Fords, whom the paper added were working with Police Commissioner Craig. Later reports highlighted the involvement of Timberlake, which must have caused Frank to take note. Timberlake had served under Shelby and had marched into Mexico with him. These were not Pinkerton gumshoes.

An editorial spoke of the funeral, saying the service began with the hymn "What a Friend We Have in Jesus" and went on to state, "Mr. James children, like children everywhere else, say their prayers every night, and among their petitions they always put up one that their uncle Frank, who is no slouch in the outlaw business, may be saved from the officers of the law."

There were plenty of questions about Frank—some accounts had him in the Texas Panhandle, or closer. Frank followed the matter in the *Herald* and discussed his possible surrender with his wife. "Possibly if you return to Missouri and show a willingness on my part for the past to be buried, and that I am willing to surrender myself up, and be tried, and meet every charge they can bring against me, I may have a fair and impartial trial," he told her.

She would go, and Frank would depart Lynchburg on May 10 for Nelson County, Kentucky, to await news.[5]

⁂

BACK IN MISSOURI there was a flurry of excitement following the death of Jesse James. The Ford brothers were taken into custody and charged with murder. A controversy arose over the plan to kill Jesse James, which was mentioned in the coroner's inquest by the Fords as something that Governor Crittenden had sanctioned. It is hard to say just what had been said in the back room of the Saint James Hotel. Crittenden always maintained that any reward was for the *capture* of the James boys, but Bob Ford, particularly, was facing a possible murder charge, and he dropped the term "dead or alive" in his conversation with reporters and jury testimony. Rightly or wrongly, Crittenden would be tarred with collusion in Jesse's slaying for the rest of his life. From his comments made to the press it was obvious that the governor was anything but sorry about the outcome.

"I am not regretful of his death and have no words of censure for the boys who removed him. They deserve credit is my candid, solemn opinion." he would say. Crittenden pointed out that others might have died in a holdup at Platte City had the Fords not intervened.

John Newman Edwards was in the forefront of condemnation with his editorial "The Murder of Jesse James" (see Appendix B). It is one of the grandest exercises in hyperbole in American journalism, a small sample of which will suffice here: "The whole land is filled with liars, and robbers, and assassins. Murder is easy for a hundred dollars. Nothing is safe or pure or unsuspecting or just; but it is not to be supposed that the law will become an ally and a co-worker in this sort of civilization. . . . Why, the whole State reeks to day with a double orgy, that of lust and that of murder. . . . Tear the two bears from the flag of Missouri. Put thereon in place of them as more appropriate a thief blowing out the brains of an unarmed victim, and a brazen harlot, naked to the waist and splashed to the brows with blood."

Editorial reaction to Jesse's slaying was mixed, as had been the coverage of his story all along. "The killing of Jesse James has given occasion for a not unexpected flood of mawkish sentimentality that cannot but be very disgusting to people of well ordered minds. . . . The very journals that have clamored most loudly about the failure to arrest Jesse James are now indulging in maudlin sentimentality over the manner of his death," wrote the *Saint Louis Republican*.

Outside the state the *Augusta (Ga.) Chronicle* had this to say: "Jesse James had a $500 coffin. Two preachers officiated at his funeral and the choir sang 'Oh, What a friend we have in Jesus!' And yet some people wonder that Bob Ingersoll [a noted agnostic] is a power in the land!" And in Chattanooga, the *Times* said, in response to criticism and threats against Crittenden, "If Governor Crittenden is assassinated as a result of the loud lamentations . . . it might be a wholesome exercise of popular sovereignty to hang a score or so of editors and correspondents." There was nothing like controversy to sell papers, and the death of Jesse James gave the press plenty of fodder to chew on for more than two months.

Wood Hite's corpse was disinterred at the Harbison place when someone got the idea that there was a reward for him, only to learn that it was for a *live* body. Nevertheless, there was an inquest into Hite's death, and Bob Ford was charged with his murder.

Reports coming out of Dallas, Texas, had a group of men leaving that state by rail for Independence to hunt down and kill Dick Liddil, under the impression that he had sold Jesse out. If this were actually the case they must have eventually given up—or possibly sobered up. A crank letter posted at Nashville, signed Nemo, alias Remo, was written on official stationery apparently lifted from the state legislature. The Ford boys, then cooling their heels in custody at Saint Joseph, offered to meet the sender anywhere in the country if he would supply his name.

And there were other hoaxes. A wire report out of Chicago on April 9 said that Governor Crittenden had been assassinated in Jefferson City. The report was sent to Washington, D.C., and spread from there before being debunked. That same day it was reported that Tucker Bassham, who had fled to parts unknown in Kansas after testifying against Bill Ryan, had been kidnapped and murdered. Bassham's wife generated this report, which proved to be false. And in late April and early May there were reports of an alleged bombing in Northfield, Minnesota, that was tied to the now nonexistent James gang by out-of-state newspapers thirsting for more James copy. The local Minnesota press reported it as the work of pranksters, and the explosion was far less powerful than reported from the scene.[6]

By curious coincidence an English visitor of some importance was in Saint Joseph on April 19. Poet and playwright Oscar Wilde was at the World's Hotel, not far from the house where Jesse was slain. To a friend, Norman Forbes-Robertson, he wrote, "The Americans are certainly great hero worshipers, and always take their heroes from the criminal classes." To another, Helena Sickert, he commented, "At St. Joseph the great desperado of Kansas, Jesse James, had just been killed by one of his followers, and the whole town was in mourning over him and buying relics of his house. His door knocker and dust bin went for fabulous prices, two speculators absolutely came to pistol-shots as to who was to have his hearth-brush, the unsuccessful one being, however, consoled by being allowed to purchase the water-butt for the income of an English bishop, while his sole work of art, a chromolithograph of the most dreadful kind, of course was sold at a price which in Europe only a Mantegna or an undoubted Titian can command!"[7]

Jesse's death did clear up some matters with regard to the robberies near Mammoth Cave, Kentucky, and at Blue Cut, Missouri. In both cases the legal system had gone terribly astray. Thomas J. Hunt had been rotting in jail in Kentucky for over a year awaiting trial on two counts of robbery for the Mammoth Cave stage holdup. Being poor, he had trouble paying legal fees, and his attorney did little in the way of digging up facts that would have proved his client innocent. Hunt was the victim of an overall bias against poor clients within the legal system. The arrest of Clarence Hitt and Bill Ryan, associated with the colorful James gang in Tennessee and Kentucky, not that far from the area of the Mammoth Cave crime, caused Judge Rutherford Rowntree, who had been a passenger on the robbed stagecoach, to have second thoughts as to whether Hunt was guilty. By March, Clarence Hite had received a quick trial and had been sentenced to twenty-five years in the Missouri State Penitentiary in Jefferson City. Rowntree wrote the warden, requesting that he question Hite about the Mammoth Cave robbery.

Hunt was brought before the judge on March 31, 1882. He pleaded for a continuance of the case, but got none. Then he pleaded not guilty to the charge. The following morning Hunt went to trial, with four passengers testifying that Hunt was the leader of the holdup pair. Rowntree expressed doubts, and the two stage drivers actually declared that Hunt was not the man. Hunt, unfortunately, did not present a very good picture for the jury. He was argumentative, he insulted witnesses, and he had a "sullen demeanor," by one account. His reputation was rather bad, to boot. The jury found him guilty and recommended sentencing him to three years in the Kentucky State Penitentiary in Frankfort, a hellhole so bad that the governor regularly pardoned some individuals sent there as he felt conditions too harsh.

Rowntree knew something was definitely wrong when City Marshal Enos Craig of Saint Joseph found Rowntree's gold watch among the effects of Jesse James after his death, along with the ring that belonged to his daughter. On April 12 Rowntree asked Judge C. H. Leslie to postpone formal sentencing. Rowntree then sent the information he had been given to the prosecutor and to Hunt's attorney, Harry Gorin. Gorin only then swung into action, filing a motion for a new trial and petitioning for a pardon from Gov. Luke Blackburn. The petition was signed by sixty-eight residents of the community where Hunt lived. Gorin visited Rowntree to obtain his signature on April 25. Just as he was about to sign, a parcel arrived from Saint Joseph containing his daughter's ring. In a letter to Blackburn he wrote, "The conviction with me is that he [Hunt] is innocent."

Hunt was pardoned on May 1 and went back to his family. He soon left with them for parts unknown. Deputy Sheriff G. W. Bunger, incredibly, still claimed he'd gotten the right man and threatened to sue for the reward. Rowntree eventually got his watch back, after his nephew, Jesse Rogers, paid Marshal Craig the thirty dollars he'd demanded for finding it. Rowntree was outraged but glad to get his prized timepiece back. Police Commissioner Craig sent Rowntree a photo of Jesse in death, and he recognized a strong resemblance between the dead outlaw and Hunt. Rowntree then sent a photo of Hunt to the warden at Jefferson City. Neither Ryan nor Hite recognized the man as a gang member. The watch eventually found its way to the Filson Club Museum in Louisville where it stayed in a display case for three years. On June 24, 1967, someone broke into the display case and stole the Rowntree timepiece and eleven other old watches. It has not been seen since.[8]

Meanwhile, back in Kansas City, Matt Chapman and John Bugler were also being charged for a crime they never committed. On April 5, 1882, as their trial on charges stemming from the Blue Cut robbery was entering its final phase, prosecuting attorney William Wallace abruptly dropped the case. He had just been to Saint Joe the day before and came back convinced that the two men were innocent. The court, jury, attorneys, and visitors were thunderstruck. The case had gotten a major media buildup persuading readers of their guilt. There was even a confession by another lad named John Land, who incriminated Chapman and Bugler. Wallace had questioned the Fords, Liddil, and earlier he'd questioned Clarence Hite. Wallace sent for Land, and the truth came out. Land had made the confession in part because he had hard feelings against Chapman and Bugler and had believed they were likely to be convicted even though they were innocent. He turned state's evidence in order to broker a dismissal for himself. Wallace had other plans for John Land, however; he was to be prosecuted for perjury and burglary charges. Incredibly, after Chapman and Bugler were discharged, the jury took a vote informally and came up with the verdict of guilty! Both cases in Kentucky and Missouri gained wide media coverage after the truth became know. The results of these false prosecutions would probably have serious reverberations later.[9]

The Fords' action in bringing down America's most wanted man gained them a short stint in the slammer at Saint Joseph, charged with murder. There was that little undignified point about shooting an unarmed man with his back turned. Cap Ford, brother of Bob and Charlie, was arrested in Ray County as an accessory to the murder of Wood Hite, as well. Never mind that Hite had died in a regular gun battle. For all authorities knew, foul play had been committed there, too.

In the midst of all this hullabaloo, a heist that dwarfed anything the James gang ever did occurred in Saint Joe. A broker for the city register's office and another man made off with one hundred thousand dollars in municipal bonds. The two men were arrested in New York, trying to fence their ill-gotten gains.

In Illinois, home of the Pinkertons, the state senate passed a resolution praising Bob Ford, who "has rendered valuable service to his country by killing the worst outlaw known to the history of modern times." It was resolved that Governor Crittenden should "unconditionally pardon Bob Ford, the young and noble hero."

On April 17 Charlie and Bob Ford were indicted for first-degree murder. Both pleaded guilty, and Judge Sherman grimly pronounced sentence on them, one after the other. They were to be taken to the county jail and on May 19 they were to be "taken to some convenient place and hanged by the neck until . . . dead." That afternoon Governor Crittenden issued unconditional pardons for both men.

Bob Ford would be arrested again and taken to Ray County, where he would stand trial for the murder of Wood Hite. He was released on bail after arraignment and left for the farm shortly afterward. That fall, following another rather sensational trial, he was acquitted, as was his brother Cap. Charlie Ford emerged a free man and eventually returned to Ray County as well.[10]

Jesse James became big business following his death. As mentioned, many of his family's household goods and some of his personal effects were auctioned, although the most important heirlooms would remain in the family. Photographers lucky enough to have taken pictures of Jesse's corpse had a brisk business selling copies to souvenir hunters.

Zee James, in an effort to raise money to live on, contracted to endorse Frank Triplett's *The Life, Times and Treacherous Death of Jesse James*, something she would later regret. Zee and her mother-in-law supplied certain items that were associated with the story—photographs, guns, and the piece of the infamous "bomb" thrown by the Pinkertons in the 1875 raid on the James-Samuel farm—for engravings used in the book. The book, however, implicated Frank in certain robberies (although none after 1876), and rumor had it that Frank was not at all happy about the book. Supposedly the text was dictated by Zee and Mrs. Samuel. In fact it was a whirlwind production, slapped together in a few weeks and drawing largely on old news stories about the gang without much analysis of their veracity. As was typical, the Tennessee years were largely ignored, and there were plenty of fictitious episodes south of the border when Triplett needed to fill

gaps in the narrative. The book also attacked Governor Crittenden, saying
he should be tried for murder. Somewhere along the line, most of the forty-
five hundred copies sold "vanished." It was supposed that somehow the
book was suppressed by the governor. In many ways it outdid even John
Newman Edwards in espousing sympathy for the brothers, but, written in
haste, the story became muddled and was sometimes contradictory.

Tourists started visiting the house where Jesse was shot, marveling at the
alleged bullet hole in wall. Never mind that a later autopsy removed the
bullet from Jesse's brain. The boards on the spot where Jesse hit the floor
were pulled up and replaced, and the new boards were said to have been
doused with chicken blood. Splinters from these new additions were sold to
hapless tourists for a quarter apiece.

Jesse's mother got into the same business at the farm outside Kearney.
Just a few days after Jesse's burial, the Louisville Courier-Journal reported a
gentleman souvenir hunter at the farm asking for a copy of a photo she had
on the wall. At first she would not let it go, but thinking again she offered to
sell it. Her words, overheard by a reporter, were "I must have money now.
They have killed him on whom I depended, and I have got to have money."
She first wanted to sell the picture for fifty dollars but was eventually bar-
gained down to ten dollars.

Zerelda's comments are interesting and may in part explain Jesse's turn
toward crime. After the war, money was scarce in Clay County, at least for
those on the Southern side. In all likelihood some of the money used to take
care of property taxes and farm expenses came out of the proceeds from the
various jobs the gang pulled. Charity probably began at home.[11]

Meanwhile, the newspapers were full of speculation about Frank
James's whereabouts. A purported letter signed "Frank James" from Memphis, Tennessee, dated April 4, 1882, surfaced just after Jesse's death. There
were other reports claiming Frank had been seen in Cincinnati and even
had him attending his brother's funeral in Missouri. Naturally there were
those who claimed that Frank would soon be taking to the vengeance trail,
out to get the Fords, Liddil, and possibly Governor Crittenden. Indeed,
Crittenden received some crank mail, allegedly from Frank, following
Jesse's death. Frank later expressed concern about these, thinking that if
some lunatic or political enemy of Crittenden had killed the governor and
escaped, Frank would likely become the chief suspect in the crime.

One of the more bizarre sightings of Frank occurred shortly after the
killing of Jesse and involved the mother of the Ford brothers. Traveling by rail
back to Richmond from Saint Joseph after visiting her sons in jail, she spotted
a stranger in the rear of the car who frightened her. She nervously sought out

the conductor and asked him if he knew who the man in the rear of the coach was. No, he didn't know.

"That's Frank James," Mrs. Ford nervously confided, "and he's following me; I know he is and I wish to have him arrested the minute we arrive at the next station."

The conductor told her she must be mistaken. But Mrs. Ford was adamant. "I'll never forget those whiskers or that nose if I lived a thousand years," she said.

The conductor got the man to accompany him to the next car. The man, who had been watching the conversation somewhat apprehensively, said he was Charles S. Perks, the delegate from Saint Joseph to the Catholic Knights of America convention in Saint Louis. The conductor was so amused he couldn't keep the story quiet, and it soon spread throughout the train. Mortified, Mrs. Ford maintained that it really was Frank and asked the conductor to be certain the man didn't get off the train at Richmond but continued to Saint Louis. It was yet another case of mistaken identity.

Frank's cousin George T. Hite believed Frank would try to come in and settle down, if allowed. "Frank is a fine business man and can make a living at anything," he told a reporter.

"Frank James is alone left," Governor Crittenden remarked in an interview on April 18. "If some of the persons who are so much dissatisfied at the way Jesse was 'taken off' will now enter the field and capture Frank with silken balls, I shall be much obliged and will pay them $5,000 for their bravery. . . . Frank James still remains at large. I shall not relent in his pursuit if he exhibits a disposition to continue his old pursuits." Indeed, Frank was worried that as long as he was on the run someone might impersonate him and bring on further heat. He began sending out feelers to negotiate his possible surrender.

According to articles appearing in the *New York Times* on May 31 and June 1, 1882, Frank had reportedly been in negotiation with Governor Crittenden for a pardon if he came in and surrendered. Supposedly Crittenden was willing to give the pardon and even to seek pardons for Frank from Texas and Minnesota as well. There was a public outcry as a result, notably from the area of Northfield, Minnesota, but also elsewhere. Crittenden publicly denied the stories on June 2, calling them "bosh." It was political season once more, and the governor was learning, as his predecessors had learned, what a thorny matter this James business could be.

One day two women came into the office of prosecutor William Wallace. One had an empty sleeve to her dress; the other wore a thick veil. The older lady with the missing limb said that they wished to speak with him in private. After the door was shut the younger woman removed her veil, asking if he knew her. He certainly did. It was Annie Ralston, who he knew was the wife of Frank James. He hadn't seen her in years. She and her mother-in-law had come to propose that Frank surrender to Wallace. Frank was reportedly afraid of being killed for the reward while in the act of trying to surrender. They were satisfied that Wallace had nothing to do with the killing of Jesse and felt he would protect him.

"Mrs. James, if your husband surrenders to me, if he is harmed it will be over my dead body," Wallace told her. She then asked what sort of terms he would get. Wallace said he could only answer respecting offenses charged in Jackson County and would have to consult with the governor. He immediately sent off a telegram to Jefferson City. Crittenden telegraphed back that he would let Wallace name the terms. "I sent word to Mrs. James that the State could not agree that her husband could go absolutely free, but if he would give himself up and end the whole matter the State would be satisfied with a short term in the penitentiary." This was not good enough, and the offer was refused a day or two later.

Frank asked John Newman Edwards, his newspaper mouthpiece, to work behind the scenes as well. "Things are working as fast as they can," he wrote Frank on July 17. "There has been so much hell lately all along the line about the governor that matters had to wait. Be perfectly quiet. There is nobody particularly anxious to find you, although the sooner we can settle this thing the better. . . . I know that they are anxious to withdraw the reward. . . . The work being done in your behalf is being done by others. They only consult me as your friend."

On August 1, Edwards wrote again, after admitting he'd been on a drinking binge: "I have been to the governor myself, and things are working. Lie quiet and make no stir." If ever a man could maneuver his way through the corridors of power and smoke-filled rooms in Jefferson City it was Edwards.

On October 1, Frank sent a very wordy letter to Governor Crittenden, probably ghostwritten by Edwards. It was a flowery offer to surrender, admitting he was tired of running. Some of what he had to say was rather brazen for a man in his position: "I submit that it is not a proper question for your consideration, whether it would not be better to have Frank James a hunter of fugitives than a fugitive? Whether Frank James, humbled, repented and reformed before all the world, will not be an example more frought with good to the rising generation than Frank James, a mysterious wanderer, or the occupant of a felon's cell or grave?" Frank explained that his life "has already stood the test of four years of a sober, industrious farm life." This offer was not a sudden whim, he said, but "a determination which has been forming for years."

The governor replied on October 5 that as far as any pardon went, "I cannot grant any pardon, even if inclined to, before conviction of some crime. . . . You may be innocent or you may be guilty of all the various crimes charged to you. That the courts will determine, as before said, and after the voice of the courts is heard, then, if it becomes necessary, I will decide what my action shall be."

A few hours before this letter was written, at one in the morning, two men stepped off a train and walked to the McCarty House in Jefferson City, registering as John Edwards of Sedalia and B. F. Winfrey of Marshall, Missouri. A little before 5 P.M. Edwards and "Winfrey" walked over to the capitol, where Crittenden had already gathered together some of the notables of state government. Edwards presented himself to Finis R. Farr, secretary to the governor. The two men then accompanied Farr to the governor's inner office.

"Governor Crittenden, I want to introduce you to my friend Frank James," Edwards began. James shook hands with the governor then stepped back and unbuckled his gun belt, handing it to the governor. It was only then that the other men, who were engaged in conversation, realized who the man was.

"Governor Crittenden, I want to hand over to you that which no living man except myself has been permitted to touch since 1861, and to say that I am your prisoner," said Frank. "I have taken all the cartridges out of the weapon and you can handle it in safety."

The governor, apparently with some concealed amusement, took the gun rig, remarking: "Not since 1861?"

The pistol was of course an 1875 model Remington; cap-and-ball revolvers being the norm during the war, as any veteran knew. "The cartridge belt has been mine only seventeen years," Frank replied.

Crittenden then formally introduced his guest to the others. Among the topics of conversation over the next few minutes was the crank mail allegedly sent by Frank. "I have received them not only from three or four different men on the same day but from several different states," Crittenden commented.

Adjutant General Waddell had no idea Frank was the man he had met earlier at the hotel with Edwards. State Supreme Court Justice John Ward Henry was impressed. "He has won my sympathy already. If I were Governor I would pardon him right away," Henry observed.

It came up that there was an indictment for Frank in Jackson County, so it was decided to send him there. Crittenden told Edwards he was putting Frank in Edwards's charge that night, without restraint. Edwards suggested that Crittenden's secretary, Farr, take Frank to Independence the next morning, where he would be taken into custody by Sheriff Hope. A carriage conveyed Edwards and his prisoner back to the hotel. Word spread across town, and soon the curious had gathered at the McCarty House, where Frank held court in his room with admirers and the curious until around 11 P.M.

Frank's return to Independence was more like the return of a hero than that of a felon. All along the route crowds gathered to catch a glimpse, and Frank made sure to point out to the reporters on board all the spots where he had allegedly been while serving as a guerrilla. "I know every foot of that ground; many a time I watched from these hills and seen soldiers pass up and down," he said.

At Independence the outlaw's wife, mother, son, and father-in-law came to meet the train. The touching nature of the scene was noted by the press. The crowd along the route to the courthouse made for slow going, with many reaching through the carriage window to shake the outlaw's hand. There was such a commotion that it was decided best to take Frank to the Merchants Hotel.

After registering under his real name for the first time in sixteen years, an immediate bidding war broke out among souvenir hunters for the page. The hotel owner refused to have his register torn or cut up, however. Edwards soon arrived at the hotel for a repeat of the gala held in Jefferson City the night before.

Frank was by now a celebrity in both pulp history and dime-novel fiction. A group of bankers from Independence offered to put up one hundred thousand dollars bail for the former bank robber. Edwards pulled Wallace aside to see if bail arrangements could, indeed, be made. Wallace explained that in first-degree murder cases, such as Frank was charged with in the death of Detective Whicher, there could be no bail without a court showing. Edwards told Wallace if he would consent to Frank's having bail, it would make him the most popular man in the state, perhaps a future governor, with his help. "Major, I would like to be governor, but I am on oath," Wallace replied, "and it comes too high."

Governor Crittenden even managed to put in a visit at Independence. It was a welcome antidote after the furor that had surrounded the killing of Jesse. When Frank was finally taken over to the old jail by Marshal Murphy, things started to die down. In Kansas, the *Atcheson Daily Globe* commented, "There is something strange about this. When we reflect that Frank James is the most hardened criminal in the United States, we cannot help but wondering why he is not taken out of the jail in Independence and lynched."

James stories came back into vogue in the press. The *Louisville Courier-Journal* reported the capture of Jim Cummins the day after Frank arrived at Independence. Sheriff Timberlake went down to Princeton to investigate his alleged apprehension and found that another innocent man had been scooped up in the dragnet.

In Nashville there was chagrin among some residents at Frank's recent revelation in the Saint Louis press that he had lived so close to the law for so many years. Already stories speculating about Frank's identity had circulated with the death of Jesse James when many readers recognized Jesse's death picture as John Davis Howard and wondered who his "brother-in-law" really was. The *Nashville Banner* chided:

> The Tennessee members of the James gang have all confessed since the surrender of Frank James. They evidently saw how useless it was to further attempt to conceal their identity, especially after Frank squealed on them. When Detective Watson heard that Frank had surrendered he came up like a little man and acknowledged the corn. County Court Clerk Eastman, Sheriff Tim Johnson, Detective Horn and others also surrendered and are now leading quiet peaceful lives, as they have done for many years past.

Meanwhile, Frank was now entertaining visitors at the jail, where his cell was decorated with a Brussels carpet and pictures hung on the wall. A rocking chair was even placed in the corridor for his use. The cell door remained unlocked, and he was free to walk about the jail as he pleased and could theoretically have escaped if he'd wanted to. His wife brought him the morning paper, and food was delivered to him from a local eatery. Crittenden had announced that as long as Missouri had him, there would be no extradition to other states. In fact, Frank was quite safe in jail. Any would-be bounty hunter from Minnesota would first have to deal with Missouri authorities. Frank's residence in the jail was also turning into a remarkable public relations ploy. Edwards wrote at the end of October:

> Your stay in the jail has been worth millions to you as far as public opinion is concerned. In fact, it was the best thing that could have happened. You can have no idea of the number of friends you have, nor how rapidly public sentiment is gravitating in your favor. You have borne yourself admirably, and every man who has seen you has become your friend. Do not refuse to see any body, and talk pleasantly to all. There is a great deal in diplomacy. A soft answer turns way a heap of wrath.
>
> Be patient. Make no sharp issue. Keep the Cracker Neck people as quiet as you can. Lose your identity as much as possible and so sure as you

live you will come from it all a free man. I do not believe that the Minnesota authorities will send a requisition for you. There is not one scintilla of evidence to base an indictment upon.[12]

Prosecutor Wallace found himself having to dust off an old indictment of Frank James in the murder of Joseph W. Whicher, the Pinkerton man killed in 1874 when he had tried to hire on at the James-Samuel farm. As a newspaper reporter, Wallace had covered the murder and had seen the body close-up. According to Liddil, the banker with whom Whicher had deposited funds and confided his plans had given away the man's identity to the gang. There was nothing to convict Frank with there, however. The ferryman who had taken Whicher and the outlaws across the Missouri that night said he didn't recognize them. Thus the case against Frank James effectively died, and charges in the Whicher case were dismissed on January 23, 1883.

However, at the same time Frank was charged with participating in the robbery at Blue Cut in the fall of 1881. It was more a stall for time, as Wallace was intent on building a case against Frank in the Winston robbery, where, according to Dick Liddil, Frank had killed Frank McMillan. There was one major hitch in the case, however. The chief witness, Liddil, was in federal custody following his conviction for his complicity in the Muscle Shoals robbery. But the judge in that case had suspended sentence until the next court term. A move was made by Wallace, Sheriff Timberlake, Police Commissioner Craig, U.S. Sen. Francis Marion Cockrell, and *Kansas City Journal* publisher R. T. Van Horn to have President Chester A. Arthur pardon Liddil so he could testify against Frank. Furthermore, the Alabama jury, two federal court clerks, the U.S. marshal and four deputy marshals, plus the trial judge had joined the movement to let Liddil off so he could testify. The federal attorney, however, objected, on the ground that one robber shouldn't be let off simply to testify against another. Attorney General Benjamin Brewster agreed, and there was a political tussle for some weeks in Washington, D.C., as the matter was referred to Brewster three times at Senator Cockrell's insistence. Neither he nor President Arthur would budge.

Finally, the matter was settled in a roundabout way when Judge John Bruce released Liddil without sentence, on his own recognizance, on April 10, 1883. Craig and Timberlake quickly posted bond and whisked their charge back to Missouri. Liddil would prove to be the state's best witness—and weakest link—in the trial that was to follow. Meanwhile Edwards kept up the Civil War drumbeat in his editorials: "Everybody has been forgiven and forgotten except Frank James . . . it is time to draw the veil of charity over the terrible past and deal honorably and fairly with Frank James."

The Winston robbery case went to trial on August 21, 1883, and attracted such an audience that it was moved from the courthouse to the perhaps more appropriate opera house in Gallatin, Missouri. This was going to be a show trial, and the sheriff was obliged to issue tickets for admittance. William Wallace, prosecutor for Jackson County, was the leader of the state's legal team, under whom came Daviess County Prosecutor William D. Hamilton and four other attorneys. Frank James was represented by former Lt. Gov. Charles P. Johnson, and his legal team included John F. Philips of Kansas City and six other attorneys. Both Philips and Johnson had served in the Union army during the war, and this was brought out repeatedly during the trial.

Philips had served as an elector for John Bell, Constitutional Union candidate in the 1860 presidential race, and he had commanded the Seventh Missouri State Militia Cavalry during the war. The Seventh and Philips had considerable experience in hunting guerrillas and had chased Jo Shelby's command around Missouri as well. After the war Philips was a partner in a law practice with Sen. George Vest and later served two terms in the U.S. House of Representatives. During a term in 1876 he had voted in favor of the electoral commission that decided the presidential race.

Also, something of a fifth wheel on the defense team was Henry Clay Dean, the man who had yielded his speech-in-progress to the man on horseback during the bank robbery at Corydon, Iowa, in 1871. Dean apparently had his suspicions that Frank had been involved at Corydon but said nothing publicly about it. Indeed, he claimed he had been invited by Frank to help. However, he was frozen out by the others on the defense team who probably viewed the "Sage of Rebel Cove" as a loose cannon and a potential liability.

Wallace would claim that the jury was impaneled from a list, probably supplied by one of Frank's attorneys to Sheriff Crozier. Faced with the possibility of a packed jury, Wallace was about to leave but was persuaded to stay by others on the team. Liddil gave his story, naming Frank as the gunman, and Bob Ford's sister, Martha Bolton, with her children and father, J. T. Ford, testified that Frank had indeed been in Missouri that summer while he claimed to be in Texas.

Frank's attorneys, in turn, did their best to discredit Liddil as a convicted horse thief, confessed robber, and all-around malefactor who was testifying to save his own skin. The Fords were dismissed as harboring fears of Frank and also as being undesirable consorts in crime with Liddil. Other witnesses against Frank were sometimes unclear about his identity, although at least one testified about a man who was fond of quoting Shakespeare.

The prosecution claimed that five men had taken part in the robbery, but it started to look as if this tactic could not be maintained. Frank's defense team claimed that only four men had been present, with Wood Hite being mistaken for Frank. No one but Liddil testified positively that Frank was the alleged killer.

Frank's alibi was based on the testimony of his sister, Susan, and her husband, Allen Parmer, who said that Frank had been visiting with them in Texas. Frank somehow could not recall in detail his wanderings in Indian Territory, although he could recite his travels across the Southeast later. Witnesses from Nashville testified to Frank's fine comportment there. Attorney John Philips touched on a chord that resonated back to the Bugler and Hunt cases in his address to the jury: "To convict this man because some town politician or public clamor demands it, would not only be cowardice but judicial murder." The jury was instructed to acquit Frank if there was any reasonable doubt about his having committed the murder. This they did after three and a half hours of deliberation. The trial lasted sixteen days in all.

The trial had its colorful moments. According to Wallace, "There probably never was a trial where there was so much talk about 'honor,' 'duels,' 'shooting on sight' and so forth as this one, and I seemed to be the intended victim of all the intended vengeance, although I had never done anything except look up the law and evidence and push the prosecution." In one case a man challenged Wallace to a duel but later tore up the note when his second told him that he would prosecute the man under the dueling statute if he persisted. Another challenge to Wallace, published in the *Kansas City Times*, was picked up by Liddil. The man reportedly backed down, claiming that the former outlaw was "no gentleman." There were reports that a noted gunman was hanging around Gallatin and would kill Wallace, but this never materialized. The prosecutor went armed during the trial, as did many others. When Judge Charles Goodman ordered all those entering the court to disarm themselves, Wallace reckoned that more than a hundred pistols were taken up.

An odd assortment of hucksters gathered outside the Gallatin opera house, drawn by the hordes of people who were in town for the trial. The site soon took on the atmosphere of a carnival midway. On the fifth day of the trial a snake-oil salesman known as "Wild Harry" rolled out his Indian medicine show, which featured his wife who was billed as a "real" Indian princess but who was actually an out-of-work actress from Kansas City. Wild Harry had a little too much to drink and, angered by the fact that his show was being outdrawn by a puppet show, drove a wagon through the crowd. He was promptly arrested by Sheriff Crozier and lodged in the county jail, with Frank James, to sleep it off.

Gen. Jo Shelby also put in a rather colorful appearance at the trial, testifying in Frank's behalf. He too had a little too much to drink one day and was fined by the judge for contempt of court.

A week after the close of the trial Police Commissioner Henry Craig publicly released the confessions of Liddil, given after his surrender in early 1882, and, more damning, the confession of Frank's cousin Clarence Hite shortly before his release and death from tuberculosis early in 1883. Neither confession had been used in the trial. "The acquittal of Frank James could not have caused surprise anywhere," bemoaned the *New York Tribune*. "The announcement that the jury was composed entirely of Democrats was probably enough to determine in advance the verdict that would be passed."

Interestingly, Governor Crittenden had been called as a witness to refute some of Liddil's testimony. Sentiment in the Confederate wing of the state Democratic Party aside, it would have been a blow at Republican campaign accusations had Frank been exonerated and allowed to lead the life he said he desired. With Jesse's death, the real wild card had been removed from the deck. The gang had now been broken up, and if Frank were left to retire to peaceful obscurity, the sting of Republican accusations might well be somewhat blunted while Crittenden could reconcile himself with the southern wing of the party after the killing of Jesse. A hard-line approach by Crittenden, on the other hand, might well have splintered the Democratic Party in Missouri.[13]

But the end was not yet in sight. "I need not tell you how great a joy was the verdict," Edwards wrote Frank after the trial. "The employment of Philips was an inspiration . . . what a speech he made." Edwards had left Gallatin at the suggestion of Philips, Johnson, and William Rush, of Frank's defense team. "I am now quietly watching the expressions of public opinion and building up some breastworks. Never mind what the newspapers say, the masses are for you. The backbone of the prosecution has been broken." Edwards closed by noting that he had "been through hell . . . since I last saw you [another drinking binge], but have driven out the pirates, and got the vessel again." As a parting note he added, "Remember me to Sheriff Crozier. He is a man that is everything." Crozier was the man who had picked the jurors.[14]

At the beginning of October Edwards wrote Frank again. "My own impression is that the two other cases against you in Daviess County will be dismissed," he told Frank. "However, we shall know what is what and very shortly." The other two charges were for the murders of Conductor

Westfall during the Winston robbery and John Sheets in the 1869 Gallatin bank robbery.

We get a brief glimpse of Frank from a letter he wrote to Annie from jail in Gallatin on October 19, 1883:

> My Dear Wife
> Bond has been refused and my case set for the third week in Dec.—Two long months, it is just awful but you must try and not take it too [writing unclear] heart, I will make the best of it, I will not trust all I think to paper[.] When I see you I can tell you all. I am getting thoroughly disgusted with Every Thing and Every body, Except you. When would you like to Come up and see me. . . . Darling, you need not Expect me to write any thing of interest for the reason my letters are liable to get into the papers. If you can be just as cautious as you can be, at the same time we can't tell what will happen[.]
> Love To All
Your Loving Husb
Benny

On November 5 charges were dropped in the case of the Westfall killing, and a continuance was granted in the Sheets case. Frank was handed over to Jackson County authorities and shipped back to Independence. Edwards wrote to Frank on November 10 about the situation:

> I could not see how else they could do in the matter of the Westfall indictment except to dismiss it. There is nothing whatever in the sheets case. That too will be dismissed in due time.
> I can see that you are very near the end of your imprisonment. It may have appeared a long time to you, and no doubt did; but when you take everything into consideration, it will not be so in fact. Everything in the shape of a robbery, especially if it had bold features about it, was invariably put upon the James gang. You had to bear your share of every bold piece of outlawry between the two oceans. It made no difference to you that you were innocent, or that you had nothing whatever to do with the crime. Public opinion decreed otherwise.

Frank was released on bond in Jackson County on December 13 but was promptly arrested again and sent back to Gallatin, where he was again released on bond there. Just a few days later the Missouri Supreme Court handed down a ruling in the case of *State v. Grant* in which a witness convicted of a felony was deemed not competent to testify in a case for the prosecution. The ruling virtually gutted Wallace's case against Frank in the Blue Cut affair. Dick Liddil, his star witness, had never received a full pardon from the governor for his horse thievery in 1874. On February 11, Prosecutor Wallace announced that the state was dismissing charges against Frank James and Charlie Ford for their part in Blue Cut. Ford and his brother had been touring the East and the Midwest in 1882 and 1883 with a stage version of *The Killing of Jesse James.* It was received well enough in New York, but in Louisville, Kentucky, the brothers were hissed and booed, and as the curtain hastily came down, cries of "murderers" and "robbers" filled the theater.

Shortly after the dismissal of the Blue Cut case, federal authorities arrested Frank for complicity in the Muscle Shoals affair. Actually he had been arrested by the U.S. marshal for western Missouri on December 21 on a warrant from the U.S. District Court for the Northern District of Alabama. His bondsmen in Missouri complained to the federal circuit court in Kansas City, which handed down the ruling, known as *In re James.* In a nutshell, the court found that federal authorities did not have the right to snatch Frank from his bondsmen, who were legally obliged to deliver him for trial in Independence for the Blue Cut case. Only after Missouri's jurisdiction had been exhausted for this matter could he be arrested for Muscle Shoals. The ruling set a precedent in federal case law that remains to this day.

Apparently not hampered by Missouri law concerning the testimony of felons, Liddil was again to be the star witness in a trial to be held in Huntsville, Alabama. It was to prove a waste of the taxpayers' money, though. The case against Frank was weak. In fact, when coupled with the testimony of those who had seen Frank in Nashville, some of the prosecutor's evidence, including a deposition by scout Daniel Comer, gave Frank an ironclad alibi. Frank was charged simply with conspiracy to rob Alexander Smith of the payroll. But this charge was even tougher to prove beyond a reasonable doubt. Furthermore, even if convicted, Frank would have been guilty of only a simple misdemeanor, punishable by up to two years in prison and a ten-thousand-dollar fine, or both. It seems that the Justice Department was after Frank more on principle than anything. Frank could have pleaded poverty and escaped the fine, with an added thirty days tacked on to his stay in prison.

In this trial, Frank was represented by Leroy Pope Walker, a former Confederate secretary of war, and by Raymond F. Sloan, a Nashville attorney who had known Frank as Ben Woodson and had testified on his behalf at Gallatin. James Newman of Winchester, Tennessee, completed the team.

The lead prosecutor was William H. Smith, a former Reconstruction governor of Alabama. He was a native-born "scalawag" from northern Alabama who had deserted the Confederate cause in 1862 and, through the patronage system, had managed to get an appointment as U.S. Attorney for the Northern District of Alabama. Smith faced an uphill battle, and this case proved to be not only a political popularity contest but also a struggle with a factually weak case.

The trial was essentially a rerun of the affair at Gallatin, without all the threats. Frank had this one sewed up, and he knew it. It ran for ten days, ending on April 26, when the jury, after six hours of deliberation, announced Frank not guilty to rousing cheers from the spectators. The sheriff of Cooper County, Missouri, however, immediately arrested Frank, charging him with the Rocky Cut train robbery near Otterville, Missouri. It was rumored that Minnesota officers were in Huntsville and this new charge gave Missouri authorities a chance to whisk Frank back to that state.

It was again a highly political season in Missouri, and in early September, Missouri Republicans were slated to hold their state convention at Moberly. Frank was now free on bond and coincidentally asked to serve as a race starter by the Moberly Fair Association. The fair was planned to run at the same time as the convention, and a howl of indignation went up when the Republicans learned of Frank's scheduled appearance. In protest, the state committee voted ten to seven to move the convention to Jefferson City. Naturally, the Democratic press was quick to poke fun. One reported that the Republicans had planned to move the meeting to Kansas City, but upon learning that a pair of old boots formerly belonging to Frank James were on display at a local pawn shop, the idea was canceled. The *Kansas City Times* offered to have the offending boots taken out of town, but the proposal was reportedly declined—or so the story went.

The Otterville charge would be Frank's last hurdle.

Edwards wrote Frank on October 20, crowing about the recent nominating defeat of William Wallace in his bid for a seat in Congress. Wallace's failure to win the nomination, however, was due more to a backlash from his rigorous enforcement of the laws closing Kansas City saloons on Sunday than to anything relating to his prosecution of Frank James:

> Rest quietly until after the election, and keep the Booneville matter on as long as you can—until after the new administration comes in. We will attend to the balance.
>
> *I do not believe that Minnesota will ever send a requisition down. I do not believe that the Northfield people will ever stir matters in the matter. If they do they will have their trouble for their pains.*
>
> What you need to do is get you to a place somewhere and go on a farm. Once settled down, the hue and cry will die out. It will die out anyhow after the election. To read the Republican papers & the State *it would look as though you were running for Governor. How frantically the blood shirt is*

waved again to be sure. For all that, Marmaduke's majority will be fully 50,000. The old mossbacks are getting mad once more, thank God.

The former outlaw had again become a campaign issue in the election of a new governor, the Moberly affair being but the opening round. John Sappington Marmaduke, a former Confederate general, was now running for the office, and there were charges that he was biased in Frank's favor. A few days later, Edwards wrote Frank again, telling him he thought the Otterville trial might be in November. Again, he felt there would be no requisition from Minnesota. Frank wanted to see if Edwards could get a promise out of Crittenden not to honor an extradition request. "We have never asked him to *promise* anything yet. But he would deny a requisition. I am just as well satisfied as I am of anything not yet accomplished."

On February 21, 1885, two days before the trial, the case against Frank James in the Otterville robbery was dropped. The sole witness, R. P. Sapp of Kansas, was dead, and important evidence was missing.

Marmaduke had been elected governor. On March 18, 1885, Edwards wrote to Frank of an interview he'd had with the governor. Marmaduke had said: "Tell Frank James from me to go on a farm and go immediately to work. Tell him to keep away from any sort of display, like that Moberly business. Tell him to keep out of the newspapers. Keep away from fairs and fast horses, and to keep strictly out of sight for a year." Edwards talked further with Marmaduke about Minnesota. "I here say to you *that under no circumstances in life will Gov. Marmaduke ever surrender you to the Minnesota authorities, even should they demand you, which I am equally well satisfied will never be done.*" Frank was, in effect, a free man at last.[15]

Frank moved to Nevada, Missouri, sometime in 1885, living in a house at 520 South Cedar Street that had been purchased for him by W. C. Bronough, who was lobbying to have the Youngers released from prison in Minnesota. Frank worked at McGowan and Jordan's shoe store. Robert McGowan, his employer, had served in the war under Gen. John Hunt Morgan in Kentucky. Frank James was a mild-mannered man, as recalled by Walter Wilson Mayes. Mayes noted that Frank was not a clerk by nature. Robert James, now six years old, attended Franklin School. Annie tended to be withdrawn, according to neighbors.

Frank would eventually decide to move to Dallas, Texas, in 1887. An account in the summer of that year had him working in a store owned by Worthington, Jones, and Company, selling dry goods:

> Frank is the mildest-mannered man you ever saw. You would think he was a preacher to look at him and listen to the soft cadences of his voice.

But you ought to see how the women flock about him to buy dry goods. It beats the world. It's Mr. James this and Mr. James that—a perfect love of a man some of them call him. I don't mean that all the women visit him at the store and dote upon him, but a big per cent of them do—the morbidly curious and mentally off. . . .

It is understood in Dallas that he gets $300 a month. He ought to have more, for in the past four months he has just about doubled the firm's business. It was a lucky stroke, their getting him.

Frank was now leading about as normal a life as he could expect, given the circumstances. Attorney John Philips wrote Frank in Dallas that summer. He was glad to hear that Frank was pleased with his new home:

I am well satisfied now that you will have no more trouble with the old affairs. Time is a wonder worker in the material world; and the sweet waters of oblivion run through all the pastures and woodlands of this life. It shall ever be a pleasing reflection to me that I was able, even to a small degree, to give you freedom, and place your feet in the path that leads to peace and quiet amid the shady banks of those streams.

Frank was indeed lucky. Most of the other members of the gang were either dead or behind bars. Tom Webb had been released from the West Virginia Penitentiary in Moundsville in 1883, and had vanished into oblivion. Bob Younger died of tuberculosis at Stillwater Penitentiary on September 16, 1889. Several months prior to this, Bill Ryan, who was thought to be dying of the same illness, was released by Gov. Albert P. Morehouse, in accord with the Missouri three-fourths law, which permitted commutation of sentence for good behavior. He was to be released at noon on April 16, 1889, but Tucker Bassham changed this arrangement slightly.

Following his conviction in 1881, Ryan swore that if he were ever released from prison he would "perforate Bassham's liver pad with so many bullets it could never be used again." There was a report in circulation several days prior to Ryan's scheduled release that Bassham might try to get the drop on Ryan and that he had been seen in disguise about Jefferson City. After consultation, prison authorities decided to release Ryan at midnight on April 15.

A reporter described the scene: "The night was dark and cloudy, and rain was falling in light showers. One minute after midnight the iron cage revolved, the ponderous bars were taken down, and Bill Ryan stood surrounded by his friends, a free man. After a hasty handclasp, a long Colt's revolver was handed to him and he began the walk to the railway depot.

"Every man in the party was armed," the writer continued, "and had Bassham appeared he would have been given a midnight meal of lead; the smallest measure not less than .32 caliber. The trip to the depot was accomplished without incident, and Ryan left the prison under circumstances the most peculiar of anyone who has ever been an inmate there."

Ryan apparently wandered out West, where he was recognized in California by Jim Cummins, who was still on the run. Just a few weeks after Ryan's release, on May 4, 1889, John Newman Edwards, steadfast defender of the James boys and creator of the James mystique, died of a heart attack in Jefferson City. The Missouri state senate voted a resolution of respect. Among the many death notices was that of the *Saint Louis Spectator*:

> In the sudden death of Major J. N. Edwards western journalism has certainly lost one of its most brilliant votaries. His style was at once original, unique, and frequently startling and erratic. . . . Many will, no doubt, remember his brilliant and heroic fusillade of boiling fury poured out upon the perpetrators of the death of Jesse James. . . . Noble, generous, child-like in simplicity, but great in mind, a journalist, a historian, and altogether one of Missouri's most illustrious sons.

After touring with *How I Killed Jesse James*, the Ford brothers returned to Missouri. On May 4, 1884, Charlie Ford, terminally ill with tuberculosis and now addicted to morphine, shot himself in the chest. Shortly afterward, Bob Ford and Dick Liddil went to Las Vegas, New Mexico, where they were joint owners of the Bank Saloon on Bridge Street, in West Las Vegas. The venture fell flat on its face, and by early 1885 the saloon had been sold. Next Liddil leased the bar and billiard room of the Plaza Hotel, and Bob Ford became a city policeman. The *Albuquerque Democrat* made this wry note at the end of March: "Las Vegas has morally advanced a notch. It has Bob Ford as a police officer. If any citizen of the meadow town hereafter disobeys the law, Bob will bring him a sense of his duty to good government when said citizen may be hanging a picture."

Bob's reputation as a "back shooter" did not go over well in town, and matters came to a head when Sheriff Celofas Romero maneuvered Bob into a shooting match with gunman Jose Chavez y Chavez, who had been a crony of Billy the Kid from the Lincoln County War in 1878. According to the story, Chavez shot a coin off a fencepost after Ford fired and missed. Bob claimed the match was unfair, and Chavez challenged him to a duel—twenty paces, turn, and fire.

Ford backed down and left town in a hurry. Bob later operated another saloon south of Santa Fe at the mining town of Cerrillos. He would eventually move on to Colorado, where he ran saloons in Walsenburg, Pueblo, and Creede. It was in the last place, on June 8, 1892, a little over ten years after killing Jesse, that he was gunned down by a man with a sawed-off shotgun whose first name was Ed and whose last name is variously given as Kelly or O'Kelly. Ford's killer was sentenced to life at Canon City Penitentiary but was later released, sometime around 1902. On January 13, 1904, the man who shot the man who shot Jesse James was himself gunned down by police officer Joe Burnett in Oklahoma City.

Dick Liddil had a more peaceful end, dying of a heart attack at a racetrack in July 1901. Dick was not much of a saloonkeeper, but he was certainly a good judge of horseflesh, and he spent the latter part of his life in the employ of J. W. Lynch of Las Vegas, running a string of his horses at racetracks in the East.

Frank would later turn to work with horses as well. He had been serving off and on as a race starter at county fairs, and finally went to work for Shep Williams, a livestock importer in Paris, Texas, from 1892 to 1894. The work involved a lot of travel, with trips to New Orleans and Guttenberg, New Jersey. Frank eventually quit and returned with his family to Missouri, where he worked as a doorman at the Standard Theater, a Saint Louis burlesque house, with part-time work at various racetracks. It was in the midst of working in Saint Louis that the specter of the "old days" began to appear again at the door of the James family.[16]

⁂

BEGINNING WHEN he was eleven years old, Jesse Edwards James had supported his mother and sister, working part-time in a Kansas City department store then as an office boy for the Crittenden and Phister Real Estate Company. Thomas T. Crittenden Jr., son of the governor, was one of the partners in the latter concern. In the summer of 1891, young Jesse went to work for the Armour Packing Company as a timekeeper and made enough money to purchase a cottage for his family at 2402 Tracy Avenue in Kansas City. His employers thought highly of his work, and there was no hint of possible trouble until January 1898, when he quit his job at Armour to set up a tobacco stand at the county courthouse in Kansas City. It was there that he became acquainted with some unsavory characters, chief of whom was a man named John F. Kennedy.

Born in the Crackerneck in 1868, Kennedy, as a boy, had heard the shooting that night in October 1879 when the James gang robbed the Glendale train. Around 1886 he moved to Texas and operated a saloon in Houston until his liberal credit policies and overindulgence in the company stock wrecked the business. Afterward he went to work for the Southern Pacific Railroad as a fireman and was injured in a train wreck, causing him to have a permanent limp. The company offered him a position as engineer if he would not sue them. Kennedy went on to join the Brotherhood of Locomotive Engineers in Houston, Texas, and reportedly became involved in union activity that culminated in his dismissal and blacklisting by the railroad line.

In 1896 he returned to the Crackerneck, and shortly thereafter a series of train robberies occurred in and around the former haunts of the old James gang. Jack Kennedy had found a new career. While perhaps lacking some of the cunning and polish of Jesse Edwards James's father, Kennedy put together a gang of his own, largely recruited from friends in the Crackerneck. Kennedy was apparently fascinated by the old James gang, and at different points over the next two years he courted the sister-in-law of Frank James, Margaret "Madge" Ralston, and "Rett" Rose, a niece of the Younger brothers. This courtship would backfire in an 1897 trial when the jilted Madge Ralston testified against Kennedy for his role in one of the robberies. Curiously, another person who came out of the woodwork to offer testify against Kennedy was that arch-perjurer, John Land, of Blue Cut notoriety. It turned out to be next to impossible to build a solid case against Kennedy, though, and he was quickly released on bond.

On the night of January 28, 1898, a little after Jesse Jr. had set up his cigar stand, Kennedy was out riding when his horse slipped on the pavement. Kennedy was knocked unconscious. The accident might have passed unnoticed if it weren't for the fact that Kennedy was wearing a mask and a false beard and was carrying a Colt .44 as well as a sawed-off shotgun. When questioned by police, Kennedy claimed he was simply going quail hunting. His attorney later came up with a better excuse, saying Kennedy had been on his way to a masquerade ball dressed as a train robber! He was charged with carrying concealed weapons. The story given by Kennedy was so preposterous that he was henceforth dubbed the "Quail Hunter," a nickname he carried the remainder of his life.

Jesse Jr. became acquainted with Kennedy and an associate, William W. Lowe, in between the Quail Hunter's numerous court appearances, and he even served as a witness on Kennedy's behalf in one case. Jesse Jr. had his mother, sister, and grandmother visit Kennedy in jail, a practice that County Marshal Sam Chiles tried to discourage. Kennedy would prove to be an unfortunate choice of companions for young Jesse.

On the evening of September 23, 1898, around nine or ten o'clock, a dull explosion was heard throughout the southeast area around Kansas

City. A group of bandits had dynamited the express car of a southbound Missouri Pacific train near the hamlet of Leeds, eight miles from Kansas City, causing an explosion that was heard for miles. The robbers, in attempting to open the safe, had used too much dynamite and had razed the express car totally, shattering the safe and scattering debris, which included dozens of wedding invitations, over a two-mile area. As a Jamesian touch, a card was left behind claiming responsibility by Kennedy, Bill Ryan, Bill Anderson, Sam Brown, and Jim Redmond. The text stated: "WE THE MASKED KNIGHS OF THE ROAD ROBBED THE M P AT THE X BELT Juntion To night THE SUPPLY OF QUAILS WAS gOOD." Naturally, the Quail Hunter was an instant suspect, but he claimed he had been at his parents' home in the Crackerneck at the time. Others insisted they had seen him in Kansas City, though, and the police suspected that at least he had a hand in the planning if nothing else. Kennedy's number-two man, William W. Lowe, now came under scrutiny.

At least two detective agencies, the Furlong of St. Louis and the Pinkertons (now headed by William and Robert following the death of their father in 1884), were called in to investigate. Some evidence turned up to indicate that Bill Ryan had indeed been seen in the Kansas City area about that time. He was thought to have used the name Evans during the incident. Police detectives ultimately arrested Lowe in connection with the affair and managed through repeated interrogations to extract a confession. Unfortunately, the confession named Jesse Jr. as one of the perpetrators. Andy Ryan, Bill Ryan's brother who was often suspected of criminal activity after the Blue Cut affair in 1881, was also arrested. It was an old story. The police had offered Lowe a deal to serve as a witness for the prosecution in exchange for special consideration. Jesse Jr. was at his cigar stand when detectives came to arrest him on October 11—without a warrant, as it turned out. Ironically, one of those passing by the stand at the time was attorney William Wallace.

Young Jesse was held overnight, and the next morning his attorneys—Finis C. Farr, Governor Crittenden's former secretary, and R. L. Yeager—sought their client's release. They appeared before Judge Henry, who told a reporter that he felt the manner in which Jesse had been arrested and treated was "a damnable outrage." Former Governor Crittenden called it "a greater crime than train robbery. If I were governor I would have the men who arrested him indicted." Jesse was eventually released on twenty-five hundred dollars bail.

The arrest of young Jesse soon became the center of controversy. The partisanship that had bristled in the Missouri press during the heyday of the old James gang now sprang to life once again. "Under Democratic domination in this community, train robberies and election frauds have been continued, not as occasional events, but as a regular diet," railed the *Kansas City Star*, a Republican newspaper, in a pre-November election editorial. The Democratic *Kansas City Times* rushed to the defense: "Many people argue that the police made a mistake in arresting him [Jesse Jr.], even if there was evidence enough to put a striped suit on his back." Police Chief Hayes was none too flattering in pointing out that, contrary to the Horatio Algeresque image: "Young Jesse James was not the innocent youngster many people imagined. He was arrested once for kicking in the door of a disreputable house near the corner of Seventeenth and Main streets." Hayes further alleged that Jesse had been a frequenter of the notorious North End saloons and bawdy houses. The editorial duels doubtless had a polarizing effect, but young Jesse had a strong alibi.

As fate would have it, Zerelda Samuel, grandmother of young Jesse, came to Kansas City on a visit and first learned about the arrest when a newsboy cried out, "All about the train robbery! Jesse James Arrested!" The old lady bristled and went on the attack. Reporters were soon after her for comments, and she had plenty. "It's the detectives that's done this. They're the ones. . . . They shot off my arm and killed my poor little Archie, a little child. And do you suppose they would hesitate to arrest an innocent boy?" Mrs. Samuel went on to explain how her grandson had been with her and the family that night. He had gone out to take a family friend to catch a trolley and afterward had been seen by a number of reliable witnesses. At the trial in late February these people would testify that Jesse was not at the scene of the robbery at the time Lowe gave.

The jury turned in a verdict of not guilty. One juror explained, "We simply made up our minds that the police had picked out this boy to railroad him to the penitentiary and were going to turn Lowe loose, and we wouldn't stand for it." Nonetheless, the charges were dropped against Lowe, who probably was involved in the holdup, and the others who had been accused. The trial would have a marked impact on young Jesse and his choice of a future career.[16]

Shortly after the trial, Judge John F. Philips wrote to his former client, Frank James:

It is astonishing that young Jesse submits himself to such malign influences. He is young and heady, and permits designing and selfish men to take advantage of his vanity. He seems to imagine that such notoriety and distinction as these little attentions give him magnify his importance;

and he is not old nor reflective enough to understand that the beautiful and attractive fruit they are offering him is nothing but bitterness in the eating. He does not seem to recognize the fact that some of his professed friends are using him for their gain, with no concern whatever for the effect such use may have upon the boy's future. His mind, which is bright and his spirits which are abounding, ought to be directed into channels which would carry him as far as possible from all the sad memories of the past, with their mildew and canker. The first opportunity I have I will improve it to give him a serious, but persuasive talk; and try to impress him with the necessity of setting a face of iron against the approaches and blandishments of designing, false friends.

Jesse closed his cigar stand at the courthouse and opened an ice cream–soda parlor at Ninth and Main and Delaware in Kansas City. In 1899 he wrote a book entitled *Jesse James, My Father,* which was published in Independence and later in various editions across the country. Much of the work was an account of the Leeds affair, but it also contained dim memories of his father and stories he had heard from family members. The book apparently was the work of young Jesse and not, as many speculated, ghostwritten by A. B. McDonald. Jesse had plans to go to law school, for which an ability to write was mandatory.

Immediately following the train robbery trial, Jesse was "daily besieged by hosts of girls who brought him flowers and lingered over the counter to try to make him talk." One of these young ladies, eighteen-year-old Stella Frances McGown, a descendant of Daniel Boone, caught his eye, and he asked her out, to attend a football game. Their wedding was held on January 25, 1900, at the McGown house in Kansas City and received coverage in the *New York Herald.* The ceremony was attended by Frank James and T. T. Crittenden Jr., son of the former governor. Jesse Jr. and Stella spent their honeymoon at the James-Samuel farm outside Kearney.

⚜

ZEE JAMES, in poor health at the time of her son's trial, died on November 13, 1900. She was buried next to her husband.

Zee may have been the first non-outlaw in the family to have been impersonated by an impostor. In 1885 a woman claiming to be Mrs. Jesse James, widow of the dead bandit, appeared in Nebraska giving a trick-shooting exhibition. Eight years after Zee's death, a woman attending a religious camp meeting in Ocean Grove, New Jersey, came to the assistance of a woman evangelist who had dropped dead in front of two thousand of the faithful. Word somehow leaked out that the woman was Mrs. Jesse

James, widow of the noted outlaw, who had been living for years at the religious resort in the area. This new "Zee" gave her personal testimony (which would probably have startled Lazarus) to the crowd, telling them "of the great relief her religious belief [had] brought her." Being a member of the James family, real or pretended, could grab headlines, especially on a slow news day.

※❦※

AN ONGOING factor in the James mystique was the continuing proliferation of dime-novel adventures. "Look at the stuff they print," remarked Zerelda Samuel to a reporter in 1897. "I read them all and they're awful. Why, I read only a little while ago a novel about the James boys going out to Salt Lake City to rescue two Missouri girls that had been kidnapped by Mormons. The fact is that neither of my boys was ever in Salt Lake City. And there is another story about them going up in a balloon and throwing out a detective. There ought to be a law against printing such stuff."

Authentic stories, however, could be embellished, as in *Jesse James, Gentleman; or, the Hold-up of the Mammoth Cave Stage*, in which "the notorious bandit chieftain assumes the role of detective and after a long chase recovers the famous emerald belonging to the Crown Jewels and appropriates it." Parents frowned upon this genre much as parents frown on certain entertainments in every day.

A young boy who grew up a few miles south of the Ralston place, near Independence, learned this only too well when a teacher caught him with a James dime novel hidden in one of his schoolbooks. She reported him to his father who gave him one of the "soundest lickin's" ever. The youngster's name was Harry S. Truman.

※❦※

AROUND 1894 Frank James had settled his family in Saint Louis. After briefly living off what little he could bring in as a race starter, working odd jobs at the local fairgrounds racetrack, and whatever bets he won, he found work as a doorman at the Standard Theater. The theater was owned by James J. Butler, son of Ed Butler, an Irish blacksmith who had become the political boss of the city. Although he was officially a Democrat, Ed Butler was so good at controlling elections that both parties sought his services. And on at least one occasion Frank James was brought in to assist as clerk or poll watcher at one of the wards, but he was mainly there to intimidate.

Frank's civics lessons under the Butlers unfortunately led to false expectations for his own political advancement. He continued his ward work as needed and attended various political functions, hoping to land some minor office. In late 1900 Frank was encouraged to seek the post of door-keeper to the Missouri House of Representatives. On January 2, 1901, the office came up for a vote before the Democratic caucus. But Frank gained only fifteen of the eighty-nine votes, because many of the legislators delib-erately missed the vote.

"Oh, the bosses have turned their machinery against me," Frank told a reporter. "They said it wouldn't do to elect me. There are a few men in Mis-souri who think they ought to run everything."

Undoubtedly the thought of Frank James as doorkeeper sent shudders through many, but in this instance he may have been victimized by his politi-cal associations. Incoming Democratic governor Alexander Dockery had carried virtually all of the state except for Saint Louis, and there was probably little warmth in his heart for anyone associated with the Butler machine.

Several months later Frank would have an altercation of sorts with Democratic state chairman J. M. Seibert in the lobby of the Laclede Hotel in Saint Louis. "Friends of both men gathered about them and interfered to avert a fight," the Kansas City Star reported. "James abused Seibert and cursed him savagely." By this time the new mayor, Joseph W. Folk, had turned on his former benefactor and initiated an investigation into politi-cal corruption in the city. Ed Butler was arrested in early 1902 and charged with bribery, but he was acquitted ultimately. His political machine, how-ever, was so badly ripped apart by the investigation and ensuing trials that by 1904 it was no longer a factor on the Missouri political scene.[17]

15

Outlaws of the Sawdust Trail

The playwrights mouth, the preachers jangle,
The critics challenge and defend,
And Fiction turns the Muses mangle—
of making books there is no end.

Justin Huntley McCarthy, A Ballade of Book Making

FOR ALMOST TWO DECADES since his surrender in October 1882, Frank
James had, with the exception of his work as a race starter, generally
tried to avoid the public limelight. All of that changed when he was
denied the position of doorkeeper to the lower house of the Missouri legislature. That rejection ushered in a new chapter in the life of the celebrated
Missouri outlaw—as well as one of the most curious and bizarre episodes in
American show business.

In early November 1901 word leaked to the press that Frank would be
joining a touring theatrical troupe with a small role in *Across the Desert*. He
would first appear at Zanesville, Ohio, on November 25 and would tour
several states east of Illinois, including parts of Canada. "This move marks
a radical change of purpose on my part, but the development of conditions
has been such to make my course a rational one," Frank explained.

The former outlaw observed that his conduct over the years had shown
him to be a law-abiding citizen. Unspoken, but no doubt prominent in his
mind, was his disappointment over losing the doorkeeper appointment. "I
do not expect to become an actor in the true sense of the word. I do not

delude myself with the belief that I have any talent in that direction. . . . Whatever value I may possess as a theatrical attraction comes from the limited facts and liberal fiction woven into the published stories about Quantrill's men and the James boys," he admitted. "This drama is not made up of 'blood and thunder,'" he added. "I will not have anything to do with a performance that idealizes law-breaking and makes a hero of the lawbreaker. . . . Whatever I appear in will be clean and wholesome, and my part will be a small one.

"My experience from boyhood had been such that there were few things I could do to earn a salary. I did the best I could and by close economy lived within a very small income," Frank said, revealing that he had received numerous lucrative offers to appear on stage over the years, but he had always thought the subject matter was inappropriate. Now that he was getting up in years he wanted to put aside something for his retirement.[1]

Frank's next appearance on the public scene was in Kansas City, not as actor but as censor. A play, *The James Boys of Missouri,* blew into town and was soon playing to packed houses at the Gilles Theater. It *was* a "blood-and-thunder" production having little to do with factual history. There was a "Jack Bently, captain of guerrillas," whose lieutenant was none other than Bob Ford. One "Jennie Summers" was the love interest for Jesse, and "Adee Grandly" was Frank's sweetheart. The guerrilla band contained "Jim Hite" and "Dick Cummings," as well as a chap named "Dirty Dog."

Frank returned home to Saint Louis from Shenandoah, Pennsylvania (scene of the "Molly Maguire" coal field unrest in the 1870s), after *Across the Desert* had closed for the season. Learning of the Kansas City production, he filed suit to block any future performances of *The James Boys of Missouri.* His attorney again was Finis Farr, former Governor Crittenden's secretary. The *Kansas City Star* quoted Frank as saying:

> "The dad-binged play glorifies these outlaws and makes heroes of them. That's the main thing I object to. It's injurious to the youth of the country. It's positively harmful. I am told the Gilles Theater was packed to the doors last night, and that most of those there were boys and young men. What will the effect upon these young men to see train robbers and outlaws glorified?"
>
> Frank James hit the table with his fist and anyone might have known that meant what he said, because when he is emphatic he looks it.

Frank's suit complained that "said play represents said plaintiff, Frank James, and his deceased brother, Jesse James, now deceased, as being outlaws, gamblers, fugitives from justice and as being engaged in various crimes. The plaintiffs deny that they ever engaged in gambling, outlawry and crimes, but affirm they are law abiding citizens of good repute."

"By the Eternal," Frank said, "I'm not going to permit any one, whether he calls himself an actor or not, to represent me or my family on stage." But the judge, named Teasdale, could not find a legal reason to close the show. All the publicity, however, attracted the curious, and when the play reopened it drew a packed house each night.

Frank compared the impact of the play to the silliness of the dime novels that also portrayed him as a criminal: "I always thought such publications were too silly for people to take seriously, or for anyone to believe. Some fellow in a back room in New York sits down and takes the names of Frank and Jesse James, and weaves a lot of sensational rot around them and the book is published. How could there be any truth in it?"

Frank, however, was soon plugging his own theatrical endeavors, notably an upcoming thirty-week appearance in *The Man from Missouri*, which was to pay five hundred dollars a week plus railroad fare for him and his wife. He likened the play to his own latest lifestyle—"a clean wholesome play without a revolver, a train, a bank or a bit of blood and thunder in it."[2]

Almost a year later, on February 16, 1903, Cole Younger arrived in Lee's Summit, Missouri. He had spent twenty-five years in prison; his brother Bob had died behind bars of tuberculosis in 1889. He and his brother Jim had, after monumental effort on their behalf by numerous individuals, been granted parole in July 1901 that confined them to the boundaries of Minnesota. They worked as salesmen for a tombstone company. Jim, despondent over his inability to obtain a pardon or to marry, shot himself in 1902.

In the wake of Jim's death, Cole had been granted a pardon and had returned to his old stomping grounds with new plans. He announced to reporters that he was writing his autobiography and would be involved with a "Wild West" show. He then made a well-timed telephone call to a Kansas City hotel, where Frank James just happened to be staying. The two aging outlaws lined up a rendezvous in Independence to discuss the particulars of the proposed plan.

Cole had obtained sixty-seven thousand dollars in backing from Val Hoffman, a businessman from Chicago, and also from a silent backer, probably Sen. Steve Elkins of West Virginia. Cole would use the money to purchase an interest in the Buckskin Bill Wild West Show. Cole had saved Elkins's life when Elkins was a Union soldier and a prisoner of guerrillas. Elkins had gone on to bigger, although not necessarily better, things. Some have credited him with being a founding member of the Santa Fe Ring in New Mexico in the 1870s, although he left the state before the troubles known as the Lincoln County War erupted. Back east in West Virginia he started his rise to power, both financial and political.

The Buckskin Bill show was owned by H. E. Allott, a shady individual who owned the notorious "Bucket of Blood" gambling den and saloon in Chicago. An ex-con himself, Allott was also known to friends by his alias, "Bunk Allen." Allott would serve as assistant manager of the show, with Cole as manager, receiving 25 percent of the net profits. Frank was brought on board as arena manager at three hundred dollars a week.

The name of the show was changed to "The Great Cole Younger and Frank James Historical Wild West." It began to come together in April 1903, near the Chicago Stockyards immortalized in Upton Sinclair's contemporary novel, *The Jungle*. It was to be one of the most incident-prone shows on the circuit during its brief, although colorful, existence.

The show departed Chicago by rail with some thirty cars in the train, after being delayed while Cole arranged (with a deputy sheriff in attendance) to take care of an overdue bill for more than a thousand dollars in horse tack. The May 4 show in Galesburg, Illinois, went smoothly, but by the middle of the month, when the production hit Fort Scott, Kansas, word was out that a number of con artists and toughs were following the show—cronies, as it turned out, of Bunk Allen and his brother Frank. The reports of grifters shortchanging customers scared people away from the evening show.

Another major blow to the show's reputation came when railroad cars belonging to competing Floto Shows United were burglarized at Springfield, Missouri. The culprits were thought to be a gang of toughs associated with Younger-James advance agent Frank Allott, H. E.'s brother, who would often try to bribe local lawmen to turn a blind eye to any gambling and chicanery associated with the show. Cole and Frank were now only too aware of what they'd gotten into, and they tried to make the best of it as the show headed through Arkansas for Tennessee. There would soon be some unscheduled, and very real, "blood and thunder."[3]

The Younger-James Wild West Show arrived in Memphis on Saturday, May 23, and at least a dozen of the cast members decided to celebrate since it was payday. About seven o'clock the following morning, two muscular cowboys, Eugene Scully and Charles Burrows, got into an argument, and a drunken slugfest ensued. Having exchanged a few haymakers, Scully drew his six-gun and had started to throw down on Burrows when a bystander knocked the gun aside. The pistol went off, nevertheless, wounding Burrows in the leg. The wounded man and his friends—and even his assailant—

crowded into a streetcar and headed back to the show's camp. Lawmen were soon on the trail of the band, and Scully was arrested and charged with carrying a pistol and "assault with intent to kill." Burrows was taken to the city hospital, where his injury was treated. There were no performances until Monday, so the cast at least had a chance to sober up. There would be two performances, both of which were "unique" even by Wild West standards.

Chickasaw Ball Park, the site of the performance, had been stripped bare of grass and was quite dusty. The *Memphis Commercial-Appeal* was underwhelmed: "After Chief Bad Eye and the band of cowboys had done one or two fast riding turns about the lot the grand stand was obscured in dust." With great understatement, the reporter observed that this "became a great handicap before the conclusion of the performance." The crowd was large, the show was enclosed within a large tent—and it was hot! The spectators perspired and suffered. "Collars wilted. Babies fretted. The lemonade boys plied their trade incessantly and with an insidious determination to produce congestion, if possible." The band played airs that failed to bring comfort, and the faces of fat men turned purple. The show was not exactly refreshing.

The reporter blamed the time lag in introducing the new acts to poor stage management: "This causes an interim in which the audience has time to figure out how tired it is." Although the acts were generally "creditable," the reporter noticed that Frank and Cole appeared in none of them. One of Cole's pardon stipulations barred him from an active role in any theatrical proceedings, so he merely lent his name to the show and his presence in the grandstand. He was also involved in back-stage management. In Memphis at least, Frank only rode in at the start of the show to be introduced to the crowd and flourish his hat. In later shows he appeared as the victim of a stage robbery!

According to the Memphis reporter, except for the dust and the heat and the delay between acts, "the show satisfied those who were present when they got over the disappointment in not seeing Frank James and Cole Younger hold up a train or blow a safe."[4]

On May 27 the show played Jackson, Tennessee. Robert H. Cartmell, a local farmer who had purchased a Poland China pig from Frank in his days as Ben J. Woodson, recorded in his diary what many others must have felt:

> Show in town this evening . . . have heard the band playing and considerable shooting going on. . . . This was enough to draw a considerable crowd . . . it is best to stay away from such shows, but so long as the world stands and people are in it—such things will be, and many there will be to go.[5]

By Sunday, May 31, the Wild West troupe stopped at Nashville, having played Dickson then making detours to play Bowling Green, Kentucky, and Lebanon, Tennessee. Cole and Frank were interviewed at the old Maxwell House Hotel by a reporter from the *Nashville American*, Cole doing most of the talking and plugging his book, *The Story of Cole Younger by Himself*. He emphasized his Tennessee family ties. His mother, Bursheba Fristoe, came from the McMinnville area, and his grandfather Richard Fristoe had fought at New Orleans under Andrew Jackson in the War of 1812. "I feel at home in Tennessee," he declared.

"I never wanted to be an outlaw," Younger affirmed, "for I think a man who does is either a fool or a lunatic." He said he had been driven into banditry by the war; his father had been murdered and his family persecuted. "They forced me into fighting and I kept on fighting until I landed in prison." Or so he claimed. Cole also said that the James brothers did not participate in the Northfield raid. It was a rather transparent lie; Cole insisted that the men involved were actually two other men named Woods and Howard.

Frank had little to say except how good it felt to be back in Nashville among such nice people, many of whom were his old friends. He only intended to stay with the show for one season "to feather my nest in my old age."

One season was almost one too many for this Wild West company. While the reporter was quizzing the two outlaws-turned-showmen, trouble was brewing at the show's encampment near Centennial Park. Somehow the sheriff's department had learned there was a crap game in progress, probably with one of the sideshows, and around 3 P.M. four deputies and a police officer raided the game. According to a separate article in the *American*, they had an "Exciting Time":

> When the players found themselves in the hands of the officers they raised the cry of "Hey Rube!" and the entire West aggregation of Indians, cowboys and attendants hastened to the rescue of their comrades. Things looked squally for the officers, but the bold front put up had its effect and the prisoners were taken to jail without trouble.

Ten members of the cast were arraigned on gambling charges, and according to the *American* so were Frank James and Cole Younger. At the hearing the two former bandits explained that it was not *their* show, that they were merely salaried employees of the real owners and their names headed the show for promotional purposes only. They claimed to have no prior knowledge of *any* gambling and were released with no charges filed. This had been a close call for Cole, who had a conditional pardon. His little business arrangement might well have been grounds to incarcerate and eventually ship him back to prison in Minnesota, but the Nashville authorities took him at his word. No doubt he raised some sand with the cast once he returned to the camp.[6]

This episode set the stage for what followed. Up to this point the Tennessee press had at least tolerated the show, even in Memphis with the shooting incident. But when it reached Columbia, Tennessee, on June 8, Frank, Cole, and the cast of hundreds felt the double-barreled wrath of that city's *Daily Herald* in an editorial headlined "The Moral of It":

> The James-Younger aggregation of poor horses and painted men is a bum show, according to the testimony of a large majority of those who paid their money and wasted their time going to see it. But that is not the chief objection.
>
> Its chief objection, and the one the American people should frown upon—and are frowning upon—is that the said to be reformed ex-bandits at its head, are making merchandise of their lawless, wicked and disgraceful past . . . they are parading and prostituting for sordid gain . . . to attract the morbidly curious and put money in their purses . . . they seek to turn a doubtfully honest penny now by making profit of a notoriously dishonest past.[7]

The gauntlet had been thrown! Picking it up was Columbia writer John Trotwood Moore, a romantic novelist and later state librarian and archivist. Moore, like the late John Newman Edwards, saw these former outlaws through a romantic haze. As it so happened, although it was not generally known in his lifetime, Moore was also the son-in-law of the former Lizzie Daniels of Missouri, Cole Younger's former sweetheart. The Tennessee writer had, in fact, corresponded with Cole during his Minnesota parolee days and would become his resident Tennessee apologist. On June 14 the *Nashville American* printed Moore's lengthy letter to the editor, "In Defense of Cole Younger," covering nearly half a page in small print. "Who are you and the editor of the *Herald*—being indeed men and not gods—to pose as custodians of other people's morals?" Moore righteously inquired. Amid allusions to Victor Hugo's *Les Miserables*, Sir Walter Scott, Rob Roy, Robin Hood, and Shakespeare's Falstaff, Moore brazenly stated, "The very blood of freebooting runs through the Saxon veins, our customs and our laws." The Younger-James Wild West Show was "one of the best shows that ever came to our country," he concluded.

A week later Frank James shot back a letter from Lynchburg, Virginia: "As virtue is to woman, as azure to the sky, truth and chivaldry is to Trotwood Moore."[8]

The show continued on its way through part of northern Alabama, finally reaching Chattanooga on June 11. Word of the Nashville mayhem apparently reached local authorities, possibly through a message sent by Cole. A special force of police, billy clubs at the ready, was assigned to the show grounds, "to protect patrons of the attraction from the small swindlers that usually gather where large crowds congregate." The next day, prior to the performance, Frank and Cole toured Lookout Mountain and "were greatly impressed with its beauties."[9]

Undoubtedly the presence of the local gendarmes made a deep impression on the cast and sideshow crew, and the show was well received by the press. Not so on June 13, when the show rolled into Cleveland, Tennessee. According to an article in the *Knoxville Sentinel:*

> The Frank James and Cole Younger Wild West Show . . . proved to have more gamblers and swindlers with it than have been in Cleveland in many a day. They have a regular gambling concern in their side show which swindled several parties out of from $1 to $20, and it seems to be part of the show, as none was found who would give the names of the swindlers. The sheriff of this county (Bradley) has a warrant for some of them, but as soon as they suspected trouble they closed up and secreted themselves as he could not find them. It is believed this gambling concern had taken in several hundred dollars before it closed.[10]

The Wild West show train pulled into Knoxville in the early morning hours of Sunday, June 14. Checking into the Imperial Hotel, Frank and Cole met with reporters from both the *Sentinel* and the *Daily Journal and Tribune*. Underplaying his outlaw days, Cole again recounted the story of his grandfather Richard Marshall Fristoe, who had served under Andrew Jackson and who had been born in Knoxville in 1789 and named after his great-uncle, Chief Justice John Marshall of the U.S. Supreme Court. Cole adamantly told the reporter for the *Journal and Tribune* that he was "trying to run an honest show" and would "get rid of every 'scamp'" he found and wouldn't stand for any graft.

Cole, who often carried a sawed-off billiard cue in lieu of a cane, probably laid down the law to the cast again before the show opened in Knoxville. No incidents were reported there when the show played on June 15. Interestingly, as the Younger-James actors held their mock robberies under the big top, Harvey "Kid Curry" Logan, of Butch Cassidy's Wild Bunch, was plotting his escape from jail across town. It was reported later that a member of the Wild West show's management visited Logan during the Knoxville layover.[11]

On June 16 the show played Morristown, where one week earlier, advance man D. P. Phillips had stopped by the office of the *Morristown Gazette*. Perhaps oblivious to the earlier antics of the cast, the paper nonchalantly reported, "He was glad he was coming to a 'dry town' as he regarded such as good for his company and all concerned." Indeed, no incidents were reported at Morristown, or at subsequent performances in Johnson City and Bristol on June 17 and 18.[12]

The show arrived at Lynchburg, Virginia, on June 22, having played Roanoke the day before. Lynchburg had been Frank's hideout for about six months in 1881–82. The show unloaded at the Twelfth Street depot and pitched camp "in an open field just above the station." During the morning the performers paraded through the main streets of the city, but "its appearance was not such as to encourage folks in anticipating much of a performance," observed the *Lynchburg News*. "Those who went to the performance with the expectation of seeing a good show were disappointed, while those who did not expect much got just about what they expected." Frank visited his old home near the College Hill reservoir on Sunday afternoon before the show left town.[13]

By June 28 the show had reached Newport News, Virginia, where it gave performances the following day. It was from here that Cole wrote to Trotwood Moore in Columbia, Tennessee, apologizing for having written late but thanking Moore for his defense in the Nashville press. Cole said modestly, "I must say you overrated me ever so much." He thanked Moore for having him over to visit with his family while he was in town and mentioned that he had written his in-laws about it.

The show's reception at Richmond on June 30 was somewhat chilly, to say the least. Officials of Henrico County asked the entourage to leave after only one performance, claiming that the production posed a threat to the community. The troupe played Gordonsville on July 1 and then headed for Washington, D.C.[14]

The reception in Washington more than made up for the snub it had been given in the former capital of the Confederacy. People took every opportunity to shake hands with Cole as he sauntered about the show grounds at Fifteenth and H Streets Northeast. There was some irony in the choice of the site, which must have caused some comments and joking, for just a few blocks down Fifteenth Street stands the U.S. Treasury Department! The parade through the city, although not noticed as such in the local press, was perhaps a victory parade of sorts for the James legend and the legend of the Old West. "Frank James was the most conspicuous figure in the parade," wrote a reporter for the *Washington Post*. A band of forty Indians in war paint led the procession. The parade moved along H Street to Massachusetts Avenue Northwest, then onto I Street and down to Pennsylvania Avenue, going east toward the Capitol then bearing left on Maryland Avenue to the show grounds.

The show apparently gave one of its best performances. Around two hundred horsemen rushed into the arena, "representing cavalrymen, Indians, cowboys, cowgirls, Cossacks, Russians, and Mexicans. The last to appear was Frank James on his bronco." There was a marksmanship display while the shooter rode a bicycle. "Then came massacres galore and hair raising rescue of whites from the hands of the Indians." There was also a display of cavalry drill by alleged veterans of the famous Seventh Cavalry. "Everything ended well, except in the attack on the stage coach, when a cavalryman and Yellow Legs collided, and the Indian and his horse left their imprint in the dust. Yellow Legs was slightly hurt and greatly chagrined and could not be induced to mount again." The Indians performed a sun dance, the Arabs demonstrated a polo match, and there was even a mock hanging of a horse thief! At least two thousand spectators attended the morning show, and the evening performance was jammed to capacity.[15]

The following day the show played Baltimore's Industrial Park at the corner of Pennsylvania Avenue and Cumberland Street. The parade was canceled due to extreme heat that incapacitated several horses and performers, and probably affected the spectator turnout. The *Baltimore American* said it was a good performance and the "several hundred" spectators were "well repaid" for enduring the weather.[16]

The show pushed across Pennsylvania, playing York, Lancaster, Harrisburg, and Erie, along with a number of other small towns in between. By July 30 the show reached Wheeling, West Virginia, where it gave a good performance, and the police were alert for grifters. Only ten days later they would make a stop that was unique by any Wild West show standards.[17]

On August 1 the *Huntington (W.V.) Advertiser* announced to the populace, "After 28 Years Bandit Returnes." After recounting in brief the story of the Bank of Huntington robbery, the article concluded, "Frank James has been changed into a law abiding citizen and a joint proprietor of the Great Frank James and Cole Younger Wild West Show." But the public wasn't buying it. The presence of a show run by the former bank robbers who had targeted their town rankled the sensibilities of many residents. As one citizen complained in a letter to the editor of the *Advertiser*:

> This is not a propitious time for any sort of public show in Huntington—Wild West or other—but never at any time ought the Younger and

James aggregation be tolerated. . . . In the course of their scoundrelism they came to the city of Huntington, then in the experimental struggle of its first development, and robbed the only bank there of a large sum of money. And now, after twenty-eight years, as though an illustration of how unstable and topsy turvy a thing is our American civilization, these wretches are coming back with all the tawdry trapping and humbug of circus advertisement to exhibit themselves. And just to the extent that they are admired or tolerated by the public, will they be attractive examples of human depravity for every embryo criminal here or elsewhere. Had they a spark of real manhood or contrition they would seek the deepest seclusion for such years as are yet given them and not seek to recall to the public attention a chapter of villains wherein they were the chief actors.

There were threats that the two former outlaws would be arrested if they showed themselves in Huntington, and a good coat of tar and feathers might not be out of the question for the duo, but on they came. "I was not in the gang that robbed the Bank of Huntington on the fourth of September 1875," declared Frank James on his arrival on September 10, "nor have I ever been in this town before in my life." Huntington would prove to be one of the most masterful acting performances of his life.

Incredibly, Frank admitted to the press that he had indeed led a life of crime in the past, perhaps the only such admission on public record: "While I was guilty of quite a number of bank robberies as well as several holdups of trains and stage coaches, there have been dozens of affairs which the authorities say they traced directly to me and which I not only took no part in but knew nothing of them until after the affair was over."

The performance went off peacefully, although Cole Younger was noticeably absent in any accounts of the show. Perhaps he feared being arrested in Huntington, a situation that would be grounds for shipping him back to the slammer in Minnesota for the rest of his days for violating his conditional pardon. Cole appears to have laid low during the performance, although Frank was conspicuous and even attempted to recruit a local constable, Doc Suiter, after the lawman's exhibition of horsemanship as he chased a fleeing man through the town. "A man who rides like that is too much of a horseman for a constable," Frank was heard to mutter. "Of all the riders I have ever seen he takes the medal for rough riding on paved streets. If he wants a job it is always open for him with the Younger and James Wild West show." Frank later spoke to Suiter, and the constable was heard to say rather loudly, "It is impossible." But Suiter refused to discuss the matter with the press, leaving the newspaper speculating that the county might lose an officer to the Wild West show at a future date.[18]

From Huntington the show pushed into Kentucky, playing Lexington on September 15. Frank and Cole had dinner with Capt. Oliver Redd, probably a former guerrilla from Quantrill's final days in the Bluegrass State. From Kentucky the show crossed into Indiana, playing the town of Nashville in the midst of a rainstorm. Illinois was next on the itinerary, followed by another swing through Missouri. The first three weeks of the show earlier in the season had been bogged down in rain, so another swing through this territory wasn't out of order. What *was* out of order was the show, however. Allott's grifters had returned with a vengeance.

The show hit Maryville, Missouri, in the northwest corner of the state, on August 29. "The show is generally regarded as being without exception the poorest one ever seen in this city," declared the *Nodaway Forum* the following week. "The program consisted of some fair horseback riding, robbery of a stage coach, boomerang throwing and a continual discharge of firearms." The Maryville paper added:

> The show was largely composed of toughs and jailbirds, one of their chief actors having served a term in the penitentiary for stealing horses. Gambling games were run wide open and it is said some foolish people lost many dollars. . . . The "short-change racket" was vigorously pushed . . . before leaving town the employees broke into a car of watermelons and destroyed a greater part of them. . . . Such shows should, in our opinion, be suppressed. The younger generation sees men of world wide notoriety as criminals exhibited and hailed as heros. The influence upon children is undoubtedly bad.

The end was drawing near when shortly afterward, the show arrived in Osceola, Missouri. There some of the thugs caught Frank alone and said they would teach him a lesson about trying to run them off. Frank was carrying a .38 revolver in his pocket and spotted Cole nearby, who was similarly armed. "Come in here, Cole, we've got a little cleaning up to do," Frank called out. The rabble soon scattered.

Frank was fed up with the show, and in the middle of September he left the production in Monett, Missouri. On September 21 while in Nevada, Missouri, Cole filed a twenty-five-thousand-dollar damage suit against the owners as the result of the grifters. Cole claimed they had caused his character and the show's reputation to be attacked in the press, thus scaring off customers.

The owners swore out warrants for the arrest of Cole, his nephew Harry Younger Hall, and B. F. Lindenfessler, who worked for the show as treasurer and bookkeeper, respectively, charging them with embezzlement of five thousand dollars. It turned out that Hall and Lindenfessler had given the money, in bank drafts, to Cole pending the decision of the court.

Cole won his suit on October 13, although he was ordered to pay Hoffman and Allott one thousand dollars from the drafts he held. Cole said he would use the money to reimburse some of the people swindled. More important, the three-year contracts of Frank and Cole were dissolved. Neither had been involved with the show for the last month of the season.

"Bunk Allen" Allott impersonated Cole for the last few weeks of the show's run in Kansas, claiming to be the aging outlaw. By the end of October the show had returned to winter quarters in Fort Worth, Texas, and the railroad cars would soon be getting a new coat of paint over the names and images of Cole Younger and Frank James.[19]

ON AUGUST 20, 1904, Frank James exploded a political bombshell at an annual reunion of Quantrill veterans. The reunions had started in 1898 after a glow of romantic nostalgia had descended upon the memory of the fabled Lost Cause. Frank was finally venting his spleen over the slight of being turned down for the position of doorman with the Missouri legislature. "Holding his hand high above his head yesterday, as is the custom when delivering a remark born of anger," he shouted to his old-time Quantrill followers:

> "I have been in Ohio, Pennsylvania and other states we learned to hate because they gave birth to the Federal troops we hated so well, and their people have treated me like a man. . . . Then why should I not turn to the belief of the people who have, in my declining years, proved my friends? I am an ex-Confederate, a guerrilla, boys," he shouted, "but I am no longer a Democrat. This year I vote the straight Republican ticket from Roosevelt down the line. The same as the people will vote it who have been my friends in Ohio, Pennsylvania and the other states."

Frank had mentioned that he was making only $3 a day as race starter in Missouri, whereas he could make $150 a day in the East. Interestingly, it was these states in the East and Midwest that were experiencing industrialization and real or imagined threats to the agrarian sector of the economy, as well as labor unrest.

The James boys who had pillaged the "robber baron"–owned railroads in pulp history and dime-novel fiction, who had been hunted by America's Sheriff of Nottingham, Allan Pinkerton, had become media-created icons, archetypes from a bygone era. The legend of America's Robin Hood had firmly taken root.

Theodore Roosevelt impressed Frank with his exploits in the Spanish-American War and as an individual and as an outdoorsman on the Dakota frontier, related in TR's book, *Ranch Life and Hunting Trail*. Still, Frank's comment and his switch in party allegiance caused a major stir in the ranks of the former bushwhackers. "The boys didn't like it, I can tell you," one erstwhile guerrilla told a reporter. Frank was rushed out of the yard of the courthouse in Independence before he was mobbed. In contrast, Cole Younger took center stage at his first reunion since his release and in spite of the commotion was welcomed by his former comrades.

Interestingly, the party that had been so quick to attack Frank in years past was now eager for his support. Frank asked for two Republican speakers for a meeting in Kearney; in particular he invited Herbert S. Hadley (later governor of Missouri and chancellor of Washington University). Hadley replied that he would come if Frank agreed to preside and preserve order. "I won't promise to preside, but I surely will preserve order," Frank said.

By one account, word of the former outlaw's support eventually reached the ears of Roosevelt. While he was visiting the Louisiana Purchase Exposition in Saint Louis, the president was told of Frank's conversion by George S. Johns of the *Saint Louis Post-Dispatch* at a banquet in the president's honor. Roosevelt wanted to meet Frank, but the former outlaw was in Montana at the time. Later there was almost a meeting at the White House, arranged by Johns, but it never came off. Newspaper owner Joseph Pulitzer was having something of a disagreement with the administration over certain policies at the time, and the idea for the meeting was nixed at a lower level without Pulitzer's knowledge. Some time later the newspaper mogul learned of the plan, but it was too late. He complained that it would have made a great Sunday feature.[20]

FRANK JAMES still had a career he could go back to on the theatrical circuit. In November 1904 the *Kansas City Star* announced that Frank "has a leading part in the play, 'The Fatal Scar,'" which was playing the opera house in Chillicothe, Missouri. Frank gave an address before the curtain, a highly moralistic spiel (see Appendix F) justifying his appearance on stage.

James then pointed out Cole Younger sitting in a box seat and said: "There is a man with all the goodness of an angel in his heart. If our savior was to come to earth and say to me, 'Where can I get a brave and fearless man to assist St. Peter to guard the portals of heaven?' I would say Cole Younger.'"[21]

A review in a Butte, Montana, newspaper sheds more light on the production and Frank's role in it:

> Frank James As An Actor: He does not claim to be much in that line and no one will dare dispute him. . . . It may not be charitable to say that Frank James is still engaged in the holdup business, although his show at the Broadway theater last night might justify such an observation. . . . There are four acts in "The Fatal Scar," but James does not appear upon the scene until a minute before the drop of the curtain in the third act. The heroine is in the clutches of her enemies, who enticed her into a disreputable house, where she is made a prisoner for the night for the purpose of blasting her good name. She pleads earnestly for her honor and release, but she pleads in vain.
>
> "Is there not one among you who has a sister?" she cries.
>
> Enter Frank James: "Yes, come with me," says he, tragically, as he throws his gun down on the crowd in an old familiar way. The audience cheers, and the gallery howls as the curtain goes down. That is all there is of Frank James in "The Fatal Scar," and there isn't any very good excuse offered in the plot for his butt-in even then. The play could get along fine without his "Yes, come with me" but the gallery would not be satisfied without something of the sort.

It appeared that the advance man for the play had promised "that Mr. James would come upon the scene on horseback and shoot up the den as he rescues the peroxide blonde. Well, James didn't do anything of the kind."

Actually life in Butte was proving stranger than "art," at least for Frank. A man named Charles N. Galland was making threats to kill the former outlaw before he left town. Galland had been drinking rather heavily, "some of the time in Frank James' society," but there was no indication then that he intended to kill Frank. Galland waited until Frank had gone to change for his part in the play, then started making threats out loud in the lobby of the Finlen Hotel. Galland was packing a .45, and although he was under the eye of local lawmen, he managed to slip out of the hotel unnoticed, "secured a hack, and was driven to the stage entrance of the theater at 10 o'clock. There he sat with the carriage door swung open, intent on his purpose. Detective James Murphy of the Butte police managed to disarm the man, but it turned out that the gun had been unloaded by a friend who feared the worst."

Meanwhile Frank had been tipped off that a man was gunning for him. He was prepared and since his encounter with the Wild West show toughs he had bought an automatic pistol (probably a .30-caliber Mauser broomhandle), his "Gatling gun," as he called it, "that fires nine leaden bullets with one pressure of the trigger." As Frank left the theater his right hand was across his chest, gripping the automatic pistol. It was a scene out of another time, only with greater potential firepower. When Frank learned that the man was gone there was some hint that he might seek Galland out and force him to eat his words. Detective Murphy calmed the ruffled old outlaw, asking him later to leave Butte before there was any trouble.

Galland was apparently a strange bird, claiming to be the brother of Attorney General-elect Albert Galen. When asked why he wanted to kill Frank James, he claimed that Frank had killed his brother-in-law, Albert Briggs, who allegedly had been the teller at the bank in Northfield. It turned out that Galland and Galen were not related; he was simply a traveling sales-man from a hardware company in Chicago. The Finlen Hotel and/or the Broadway theater in Butte was thus saved the notoriety of being another "death house" like the one in which Jesse was killed in Saint Joseph.[22]

⁂

IN 1907 Frank and Annie moved to Fletcher, Oklahoma. Frank had used the money he had saved from his Wild West and theatrical appearances to buy a small farm. Frank grew pears, and he and Annie attended the local Presbyterian church. It was a relatively quiet life.[23]

Cole Younger went on the road from 1905 to 1908 managing Cole Younger's Coliseum (in which Cole had on exhibit a number of saddles, spurs, and guns), with a carnival owned by Lew Nichols, who had formerly worked for the Wild West show. In June 1908, when the carnival played Richmond, Missouri, Cole learned that "Bloody Bill" Anderson had been buried in the potters field of a local cemetery without a burial service, and he resolved to do something about the matter. Cole brought the bands from the carnival out to the grave site to play some hymns. He said a few words of praise for the late demented guerrilla, then turned the matter over to a preacher named J. E. Dunn. A Missouri newspaper of the period com-mented about Cole, "He is advertised as the last of the famous Younger brothers, which, it seems to us, is going in the right direction."[24]

The ranks of those associated with the James story had thinned dramat-ically, but occasionally one of them still reappeared in newspaper accounts. On March 23, 1909, readers of the *Kansas City Times* were greeted with the headline "James Boys' Friend Kills." It was Jim Cummins, now a resident of the Confederate Soldiers Home in Higginsville, just southeast of Lexing-ton, not far from the spot where Jesse had been wounded in 1865. The paper reported that one J. R. McCormick, an eighty-five-year-old veteran of the Mexican and Civil Wars, had died "as the result of a fist blow by 'Jim

Cummings.'" These old-timers still had a lot of spirit and the previous afternoon both men had argued and then duked it out.

"McCormick applied a vile name to Cummings. . . . In the fight that followed, Cummings struck the blow that caused McCormick's death." Cummins was not charged since the other man had started the fight, but the incident was another indication that the elderly former guerrilla and James gang groupie apparently still drew trouble like a magnet and in his declining years had not mellowed much. During a Quantrill reunion at Independence on August 23, 1906, Cummins had angered another former guerrilla and resident of the home named David Edwards, who pulled a pistol and took a shot at Cummins. "The bullet missed Cummings and struck the foot of another man. The quarrel followed boasts made by Cummings after he had whipped a man in the home."

Cummins had spent almost twenty-five years on the run, living under aliases, wanted either for stealing horses or in connection with crimes committed by the James gang. During this time he reportedly served as a scout at Camp Apache, Arizona, under a Lieutenant Johnson, and in the 1890s worked as a deputy U.S. marshal out of Eureka Springs, Arkansas. He eventually surfaced under his real name in northwest Missouri around 1898. By this time the statute of limitations had expired on all charges and he was able to live in the open again.

Cummins had written two books, *Jim Cummins' Book* (1903) and *Jim Cummins the Guerrilla* (1908), and at one time had discussed writing a history of the gang with Cole Younger. "The public will not . . . be treated to a lot of spiced trash written by 'fakes' that knew no more of the 'James gang' than a Mexican greaser knows about the 'Rubiyat,'" Cummins declared at the time. Cummins, however, had only been on the fringe of the gang's activity, and his relations with Frank were often cool at best.

Cole decided to write his own apologia, and Cummins's book about the James gang never came to pass. Nevertheless, Cummins's slim volumes about himself and his guerrilla days contain some interesting, if chaotically written, information, and are more useful historically than Cole's autobiography. Cummins would live on until 1929 and is sometimes credited with being the last surviving member of the James gang.[25]

JESSE EDWARDS JAMES became an attorney, graduating with honors from the Kansas City School of Law in June 1907. Jesse Jr. then sold his tobacco-pawnshop and began practicing law, but the work began to take its toll on his family life. By 1910 domestic problems had arisen with his wife, Stella.

On November 5, 1909, the *Kansas City Post* ran a story headlined, "Jesse James, Son of Famous Bandit, Sued for Divorce." The article related how Jesse Jr. allegedly had quarreled with Stella, "and frequently remained away from home until late hours of the night, refusing to inform her of his whereabouts." Stella eventually withdrew her suit, but the problems continued to fester.

On September 20, 1910, the *Post* reported how the couple's children were praying, "God keep my papa a good man and bring him home some day." When questioned by a reporter, Jesse Jr. claimed there could be no reconciliation. "Never, never, never . . . wholly out of the question," he said. Complicating the matter was the fact that Jesse Jr. had come to the house and taken away the youngest child, Ethel Rose, and he refused to reveal where he had taken her. "It will not do any good for her mother to try to get her back. She is not in this state now, and a habeas corpus writ would not apply. I took her with me because I wanted her. I had no other motive."

Jesse filed for divorce about the same time, "alleging that his wife twice tried to kill him and left a note which he construed into a threat to take his life. . . . He accuses his wife of trying to shoot him in his offices in the Scarritt building, after she had waited all night for him in his room in the Victoria hotel." Stella denied that she tried to shoot her husband but admitted waiting for him with her other children.

"James accuses his wife of quarreling with him, nagging him and being unwantonly jealous. The petition says he spent no day at home without some row, and says that Mrs. James accused him of every known crime. It says whenever he had a woman client in his practice of the law his wife made trouble," the newspaper reported. Jesse Jr. further claimed that "his wife armed herself and went to disreputable houses to hunt him, imagining he was there . . . that she also went armed to homes of reputable people to hunt for him. . . . One time last winter . . . Mrs. James came to his office with her mother . . . armed with a 45-caliber revolver, which he had to take away from her to keep her from shooting him. . . . That Mrs. James came to the lawyer's office with a 32-caliber revolver in a hand bag." Jesse said he took this gun away from her and could produce it.

Stella supposedly left the following note for her estranged husband when he failed to show at his hotel room:

Jesse: The three children and I stayed all night here in your room last night. It is up to you to find out how we did it. There would have been a warm reception had you come last night. Well, I missed you this time, but I mean to keep right on your trail until I land you. I could have done it last night while I was pretty close behind you, but it was not just the chance I wanted.

Lovingly,
STELLA

It was a case of he-said, she-said. It also was alleged that Jesse had been having an affair with the wife of a neighbor. Stella claimed she did not have a gun when she visited his office. In the divorce that followed, Stella was granted custody of the children and one hundred dollars a month alimony.

However, Jesse Jr. was reunited with his wife a year later. He had been a regular visitor with his children every Sunday, and when Stella became ill and was hospitalized in 1911 he took the children to visit her. The couple patched things up over the following months and were remarried that fall. Stella glossed over the Jameses' domestic problems in her autobiography, which was published posthumously.[26]

Zerelda Samuel's death on February 10, 1911, while returning from a trip to see Frank in Oklahoma, brought Frank back to the James farm. Her husband, Reuben, had passed away in 1908 in a mental hospital in Saint Joseph. Some claimed that his hanging by militiamen during the war had led to his dementia, but in all probability he was suffering from what is now known as Alzheimer's disease, or a related disorder. One wonders if "Uncle Ben," as Jesse Jr. called him, might not have had a few words with his nephew on domestic matters. Frank and his family would take over the James farm and run it as a combination tourist attraction and farm.

At one point in 1912 Frank had a portion of the old cabin dismantled and the components numbered so it could be taken to Hot Springs, Arkansas, and reconstructed for display, with Frank in attendance, for about six weeks. Apparently the cabin section was left in Arkansas, and what became of it is still a matter of speculation.

In 1912 Frank was again supporting Teddy Roosevelt, this time as candidate for president on the Bull Moose, or Progressive, Party ticket. While on a speaking engagement in Milwaukee in early October 1912 Roosevelt was shot by a bartender from New York, John Shrank, who claimed that William McKinley had told him in his dreams that Roosevelt was behind his assassination and that Shrank should avenge him. Elbert Martin, TR's secretary and a former football player, tackled the would-be assassin. The feisty Roosevelt said he would "make this speech or die; one way or the other." TR appeared before the crowd where it was announced that he had been wounded. Luckily, the bullet's impact was deflected in part by the manuscript of the rather lengthy speech that the former Rough Rider had in his pocket.

"I don't know if you fully understand that I have just been shot," he told the crowd, "but it takes more than that to kill a Bull Moose." The audience cheered wildly.

Back in Kearney, when Frank learned of the affair, he sent a hasty telegram to Roosevelt, who was recuperating in Chicago:

> Offer my service as one of one hundred, or less number as you may suggest as a body guard the remainder of campaign. Choose for your self ninety nine, allow me to name myself making the one hundred. Would choose no one who is not willing to go into Eternal darkness, for you if it is necessary to do so. Will pay my own expenses.

Elbert Martin, the man who had captured Shrank, replied by mail, on October 19, from Mercy Hospital in Chicago:

> My Dear Mr. James:
> Colonel Roosevelt wishes me to express to you his hearty thanks for your kind telegram of sympathy. He will probably be able to do little or no campaigning before Election. He is feeling as hearty as a Bull Moose, he says.

Frank identified with Roosevelt as a man of action and, like Roosevelt, believed in certain progressive causes, such as women's suffrage. He reportedly used to call in the livestock at the James farm for feeding by yelling the words "Bull Moose" at the top of his lungs.[27]

Frank would give his last interview in 1914, speaking with a reporter from *Collier's Weekly*. He "lectured" on various topics, including the ongoing revolution in Mexico (involving Pancho Villa) and women's suffrage, aside from giving his usual spiel about the farm and what happened long before. "The women ought to have the vote. . . . Look what we owe to the woman," he said. "A man gets 75 per cent of what goodness is in him from his mother, and he owes at least 40 per cent of all he makes to his wife. Yes, some men owe more than that. Some of 'em owe 100 per cent to their wives."

Frank still had words about the media. Motion pictures had appeared and *The James Boys of Missouri*, the first film version depicting Frank and Jesse's pseudo-adventures, had been released by Essenay Film Company in 1908.

Whether this was based on the Kansas City play that Frank had tried to close is not known. But Frank did have this to say: "I tell you, those yellow backed books have done a lot of harm for the youth of this land—those and the moving pictures showing robberies. . . . If I had a job of censoring the moving pictures they'd say I was a regular Robespierre."

When asked about the various stories that had been told about the gang, he simply answered, "I neither affirm nor deny. . . . If I admitted that these stories were true, people would say, 'There's the greatest scoundrel unhung' and if I denied 'em they'd say: 'There's the greatest liar on earth,' so I just say nothing." Frank went to his grave saying nothing, dying at the James farm on February 18, 1915.

Possibly fearing that his bones might be stolen and put on display or sold to morbid souvenir hunters, Frank's remains were cremated, and, ironically, kept in a bank vault in Kansas City for later interment beside his widow. By request, no religious services were held at the funeral. Annie was truly saddened by his death. "No better husband ever lived," she was quoted as saying. Annie James would spend the remainder of her life at the old James homestead with her son, Robert, and his wife, May.[28]

Cole Younger was the next old outlaw to pass over the bar. He died at Lee's Summit of heart and kidney trouble on March 21, 1916. On March 19, just before his death, Cole asked to see Jesse Jr. and Harry Hoffman, now a deputy marshal in Jackson County. Cole wanted to tell them about the old days, in particular he wanted to identify the man who had shot the teller at Northfield. He had imparted the same information to his nephew Harry Younger Hall sometime earlier, swearing him not to tell anyone until after the death of Frank James and himself. For years it had been assumed the killer had been Jesse James, but Cole said it was in fact Frank, "the greatest scoundrel unhung."[29]

⁂

In 1920, Mesco Pictures, an independent motion picture company in Kansas City, made Jesse Jr. a fifty-thousand-dollar offer to play his father in *Jesse James Under the Black Flag.*

A number of friends, business associates, and even some relatives backed the project and later invested money in it. The offer was tempting as there was the college education of his daughters to think about. So Jesse accepted the role. The picture was shot on various locations using a number of actors of dubious quality, notably Jesse Jr. (by admission of his wife and relatives) and even some relatives such as John Samuel and sister Mary James Barr.

The film ran over budget, and in order to raise more money, Jesse Jr. mortgaged his house. Jesse had a hard time shooting the death of his father, which he had witnessed as a child and which still had a very traumatic resonance. He is said to have fainted twice during the shooting of the scene.

Once finished, the picture, which had a somewhat melodramatic plot and featured a wardrobe derived more from Hollywood than history, made a road-show appearance in the East in 1921. In the film, a millionaire airman just happens to land next to the James farm, the pilot falls in love with one of Jesse Jr.'s daughters, and Jesse Jr. explains to the young aviator, in flashback, the story of his father. For four months Jesse Jr. toured, but the picture was a financial bust. Jesse Jr. spent the money he earned paying back investors and ended up having to sell his house.[30]

On Sunday, May 11, 1924, a headline in the *Excelsior Springs Daily Herald* proclaimed "Jesse James Wrecked—Armed to Teeth." The evening before, Jesse's car had collided head-on with another vehicle driven by two young men from Kansas City. The boys, one reportedly seriously injured, and James, were taken to the office of Dr. J. F. Lowrey in Excelsior Springs. "Mr. James who was armed with two revolvers and a shotgun said his party was patrolling the highway on behalf of the State Highway Commission." James, whose knee was injured, was to appear before the local police court the following day to explain.

The next day further news came out in the case. Lowrey told the authorities and the press "that Mr. James is suffering from a nervous breakdown and he would recommend he be sent to a local hospital." No charges were filed, and Jesse was taken from Vineland Park Hospital "to a private sanitarium where patients are treated for nervous diseases." Lowrey said that "James had been extremely nervous some time prior to the motor wreck . . . in which he figured while acting as a self-appointed armed patrol on the new Excelsior Springs–Kansas City Highway."

Jesse was taken to the Simpson-Major Sanitarium for three to six weeks of rest and treatment. "Mr. James is suffering from grandiose hallucinations as the result of his breakdown," reported Dr. Herbert S. Major. In later decades, with advances in medical knowledge and treatments, Jesse Jr. might have resumed something of a normal life, but his illness continued until his death in 1951.

In October 1926 Jesse Jr. and family moved to Los Angeles, where he once again resumed the practice of law for two more years. In previous years he had demonstrated a remarkable legal mind. In a case involving Missouri railroad workers having rights protected under federal law, Jesse went all the way to the U.S. Supreme Court. A copy of the appellate brief was reportedly returned later with the following note written on it: "This is the best brief I have ever read. Charles Evans Hughes, Chief Justice, U.S. Supreme Court."

Jesse also served as a "technical adviser" for the 1927 Paramount production of *Jesse James*, starring silent actor Fred Thomson and his wonder horse Silver King. Although it played rather fast and loose with the facts, the film was a box office success, unlike Jesse Jr.'s earlier fiasco.[31]

John Newman Edwards was a Missouri news-paperman and the father of the James legend. He was known as "the Victor Hugo of the West" for his florid editorial prose, which was usually enhanced by heavy drinking. During the Civil War Edwards had been adjutant to Confederate Gen. Jo Shelby and had followed the general to Mexico when most Southern soldiers surrendered in 1865. Edwards and most of the expatriates reentered the United States after surviving bandits and Juaristas and a near run-in with the French Foreign Legion. The image above was made in 1868, shortly after his return. The photograph to the right shows him as he was near the end of his life, after helping to broker the surrender of Frank James.

Capt. William Clarke Quantrill (*left*), the Ohio-born Confederate partisan leader under whom Frank James served between 1863 and 1864 and during the 1865 incursion into Kentucky. Quantrill was wounded in a scrape with guerrilla hunters in May 1865 and died in Louisville, Kentucky, a month later.

On the facing page, three guerrillas—(1) Arch Clements, (2) Dave Pool, and (3) Bill Hendricks—were photographed in Sherman, Texas, during the Christmas holidays of 1863. The men were on a tear and visited a photographer's studio after shooting up a local hotel. The three were not happy with the image and destroyed the camera. After sobering up, they paid for the damages.

The body of William "Bloody Bill" Anderson (*right*) was photographed in Richmond, Missouri, on October 26, 1864. He wears an elaborate guerrilla shirt and carries two revolvers, the preferred weapon of guerrillas. The ring finger of his left hand was cut off by a militiaman to get a gold wedding ring. Anderson's head is held up by Adolph Vogel, a bugler for Maj. Samuel P. Cox, whose troops had succeeded in hunting and ambushing the guerrillas. After two photographs were taken, Anderson's head was cut off and mounted on a pole, and his headless corpse was dragged through the streets. The guerrilla chieftain's remains were later collected and buried in a shallow grave.

This fanciful engraving of the January 1874 Gads Hill robbery appeared in *Bank and Train Robbers of the West*, a pulp "history" published in 1890. In fact, Gads Hill was only a freight platform at the time of the robbery (there was no station), and there was no gun battle.

The Clay County Savings Bank (*below left*) in Liberty, Missouri, on February 13, 1866, was the scene of the first daylight bank robbery in peacetime. The bank's cashier Greenup Bird and his son, William, were "caged" in the vault (*below right*) at the conclusion of the robbery.

During the past century, the building (*right*) that housed the bank of Huntington, West Virginia, was moved to another site in town and presently houses a florist's shop. More older buildings have been saved in the United States because of a connection to Jesse James than to any other person in American history, with the exceptions of George Washington and Abraham Lincoln.

This is what the James-Younger gang would have seen (*below*) as the bandits entered Northfield, Minnesota. They crossed the bridge, heading east into Bridge Square, then turned into the street behind the building on the right side of the square. The Dampier Hotel, from which Henry Wheeler fired on the robbers, stands in the middle of the photograph.

George Shepherd (*above left*) was a one-eyed former guerrilla who was imprisoned after his capture following the Russellville bank robbery in 1868. The Younger brothers met a similar fate in 1876 after their capture and wounding at Hanska Slough, Minnesota. Bob Younger (*above right*), Thomas Coleman "Cole" Younger (*bottom left*), and Jim Younger (*below right*) were imprisoned following the Northfield, Minnesota, raid. Bob died in the Stillwater, Minnesota, penitentiary of tuberculosis in 1889. Cole and Jim were paroled in 1901 and became salesmen for a tombstone company. Jim became despondent over his failure to obtain a pardon or to marry and committed suicide in 1902. Cole was granted a conditional pardon following Jim's death and wrote his autobiography and joined a traveling Wild West show.

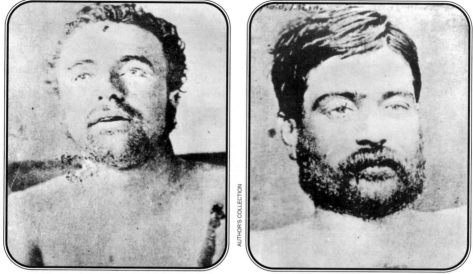

Two of the most unfortunate participants in the Northfield, Minnesota, raid were Clell Miller (*above left*) and Sam Wells, a.k.a. Charlie Pitts (*above right*). Miller was killed during the get-away by Henry Wheeler, a medical school student who reportedly managed to have friends ship the body and that of Bill Stiles (who was also killed in the shootout) to the University of Michigan Medical School for use as cadavers. Despite various efforts to claim and return the remains to Missouri, Wheeler is said to have displayed Miller's skeleton in his office at Grand Forks, North Dakota, until a fire destroyed it in the early 1900s.

Wells was killed at Hanska Slough, where the Youngers were wounded and captured. His remains were delivered to the surgeon general of Minnesota, who gave them to Dr. Henry Hoyt, who sank them in a lake outside Saint Paul to decompose. When the skeleton was discovered by a hunter in March 1877, Hoyt reclaimed it and reportedly took the bones to Chicago. Their eventual whereabouts is not known.

The Smith and Wesson "American" .44-caliber revolver below was taken from Jim Younger on September 21, 1876, at Hanska Slough by T. L. Voight, a member of the posse that captured the Youngers and killed Sam Wells. Cole Younger reportedly had a similar weapon with ivory grips, which was confiscated by Sheriff James Glispin of Madelia.

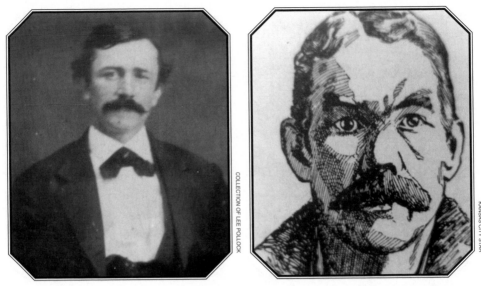

COLLECTION OF LEE POLLOCK

KANSAS CITY STAR

After the Northfield raid, the James gang was in need of new men. One of them was Bill Ryan, of whom there are no historically confirmed photographs. The image above (*left*) is from a photograph belonging to former guerrilla leader Fletch Taylor. It is believed to be Ryan based on tradition and its similarity to the sketch (*above right*) of Harry A. Glenn, an inmate at the Minnesota State Penitentiary in 1898. Pinkerton detectives believed Glenn was Ryan, and Glenn's friends noted the similarity as well.

James Andrew "Dick" Liddil (*below left*), a convicted horse thief, was a youngster during the Civil War. He joined the gang in 1879 in time for the Glendale robbery.

Former Quantrill guerrilla Jim Cummins (*below right*) was said to be a member of the gang, but there is no evidence that the accused horse thief participated in any of its robberies. This sketch was made after his return to Kansas City around the turn of the century.

COLLECTION OF LEE POLLOCK

FROM JIM CUMMINS' BOOK

James Cooley (*above left*) pursued a medical education despite the fact that Jesse had swindled his father (a Confederate veteran) out of money from the sale of some cattle that was supposed to pay for Cooley's admission to the Nashville College of Surgeons. Cooley eventually became known as "the baby doctor of Humphreys County." His wife is in the background.

Ben Morrow and his wife (*above right*) sheltered members of the James gang at times on their Sibley, Missouri, farm (*below*). Morrow was a Quantrill veteran and was allegedly the target of a vigilante lynching party until the county prosecutor, William Wallace, intervened. These previously unpublished photographs were taken in the early 1900s.

Allan Pinkerton (*above left*) dispatched agents to apprehend the James brothers. Following one foolish attempt, Joseph Whicher was slain and buried in Chicago (*above right*). In retaliation, the James-Samuel farm was fire-bombed, apparently with federal assistance.

Delos T. "Yankee" Bligh (*left*) was credited with the capture of George Shepherd in 1868 and involved in the investigation of the Huntington, West Virginia, bank robbery in 1875 after the bandits fled into Kentucky. He is sometimes erroneously identified as a Pinkerton, but his badge (*below*) attests to his association with the Louisville police.

This view of Nashville (*above*) was taken in the early 1880s from the state capitol grounds, looking north toward the Davidson County Courthouse in the square in the center. The area below was known as "the Flats" and was the site of the Nashville Blood Horse Association race-track, a favorite venue of the James brothers. Both Frank and Jesse raced horses here, and Jesse's financial losses played a significant role in his decision to return to banditry. In 1976 the area was transformed into the Metro Center complex.

To the left is the house in Nashville at 606 Boscobel Street in which Jesse Edwards James was born in 1875.

The old Walton farm (*right*) off Kings Lane, north of Nashville, near the Clarksville Pike, was photographed in the 1950s. Frank James and his family lived in a cabin on the farm in 1878. The house was demolished sometime in the 1960s or 1970s.

In late 1878 or early 1879 Frank rented a farm, known as the Felix Smith place (*left*), on West Hamilton Road, in the Bordeaux section of Nashville, east of the Clarksville Pike and not far from the Walton farm. It was a good location for a fugitive. The house had an excellent view of the pike so that one could not be easily surprised by unwanted visitors. Jesse and Zee moved in, and their daughter, Mary, was born here in 1879.

In 1880 both families moved into the Jeff Hyde place (*right*) on Hydes Ferry Road, north of Nashville. Here the brothers had a falling out over gang member Bill Ryan, whose drinking was jeopardizing Frank's attempts to maintain a low profile.

NASHVILLE BANNER

TED YEATMAN

Jesse moved his family in December 1880 or January 1881 to a house across the river in Edgefield, at 903 Woodland Street (*left*). In February 1881, Dick Liddil fired a shotgun through the door at someone sneaking around the porch. The culprit was never found, but the incident was considered a prank gone awry. The family, ever cautious, moved again. The house was lost in a fire in the 1980s.

This house (*right*) at 711 Fatherland Street was probably the last residence of Jesse James in Tennessee. Frank and his family moved into a house a block away on the same street. Neither stayed in residence long. It was here that Dick Liddil and Jesse discussed Bill Ryan's capture and it was decided to leave Nashville for Kentucky.

TED YEATMAN

Jesse James, Bill Ryan, and an unidentified gang member crossed the Cumberland River over this suspension bridge as they left Nashville en route to the Muscle Shoals robbery. This image was probably created by Otto Griers and looks toward a section of town known as Edgefield.

Following the Muscle Shoals, Alabama, robbery, gang member Bill Ryan was apprehended on the evening of March 25, 1881, at Earthman's Store at Whites Creek, Tennessee. Fearful of exposure when they learned of his capture, Frank and Jesse and their families abandoned Nashville the next day. The store is the only James site in Tennessee with a historical marker.

The house in which Jesse James was killed in Saint Joseph has been moved at least twice from the original site. The bullet hole in the wall is of questionable authenticity.

Jackson County prosecutor William H. Wallace (*above left*) was approached by Zerelda Samuels and Annie James concerning the surrender of Frank James. He passed the information on to Gov. Thomas T. Crittenden (*above right*) and was subsequently involved in the court trials of Bill Ryan and Frank James. Crittenden had gained the governor's mansion in 1880 on a pledge to purge Missouri of the outlawry that had plagued the state since the Civil War. As part of that purge, the governor enlisted the aid of Bob and Charlie Ford and later pardoned them.

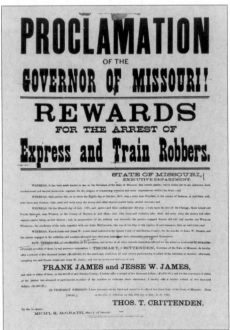

Following the train robbery at Winston, this reward proclamation was printed as a hand-bill and distributed across Missouri. The reward was carefully worded "for the arrest and delivery" of Frank and Jesse James, not "dead or alive" as the Ford brothers asserted. Engravings of photographs of Frank and Jesse were published in the *Illustrated Police News* of May 1, 1880. Although there are no images of the bandits on the handbill, the earlier published images probably influenced the brothers to grow beards as disguises.

Mary James Barr, who had appeared in the first movie with her brother, lived at Claybrook, across the road from the James farm, after her marriage to Henry Barr in 1901. On April 3, 1933, fifty-one years to the day after the death of her father, Mary visited her birthplace in Nashville, then owned by E. B. Smith. "My father was never understood," she told *Nashville Banner* reporter Ben West (later mayor of Nashville). She repeated the myth of the widow and the mortgage (in which Jesse, at his Robin Hood best, paid the mortgage on the widow's farm and then robbed the banker after the funds were collected from the widow), and she claimed that Jesse couldn't have been at Northfield.

"We never knew our real names until father was killed," Mary said. She claimed that she had no recollection of her father, having been so young at the time of his death, and merely repeated the stories told her by her mother. Mary died on March 11, 1935, and was buried near her father, whose body had been moved to Mount Olivet Cemetery in 1902 from the James farm. Mary had lived next to the cemetery for a number of years and kept an eye on his old gravestone. Souvenir hunters chipped it to pieces after her death.[32]

16

The Resurrection of Jesse James

> The history of the race, and each individual's experience, are thick with evidence that the truth is not hard to kill and that a lie well told is immortal.
>
> Mark Twain

I N THE FALL OF 1931 an old man calling himself John James arrived in the town of Excelsior Springs, Missouri, not far from the James farm, driving a horse-drawn wagon. He spent much time sitting around the police–fire station talking with other old-timers, and much of the talk, after they heard his name was James, was about the outlaw brothers and their exploits.

An elderly blind resident of the town, known as "Aunt Margaret," had known the family and was visited by the elderly drifter, who repeated many of the stories he had picked up. John James told the woman he had come back home to visit with friends and apparently somewhere in all of this he claimed to be Jesse James. The old woman, who couldn't see, at least thought he'd said so.

Word soon got out, and John James was put up in the finest hotel in town. Soon the story was appearing in the national press that Jesse James was actually alive and well. A Los Angeles newsman had called on Jesse Jr. and wife Stella, but he had done most of his talking there with the old mystery man's promoter in Missouri. Jesse Jr. was quite disturbed by the reports of his father's reappearance, but illness prevented his traveling back. He at first thought it was a publicity stunt for a motion picture. In April 1932, Stella decided to return and investigate.

John James had apparently been coached, using Jesse Jr.'s book and whatever other information he could glean. Still, it was not enough, and under questioning, the old man could not recall the name of Jesse's half brother, Archie, who had been killed in the Pinkerton raid, or which forearm Jesse's mother lost in the same affair. Stella learned that John James actually was a parolee from Menard Penitentiary in southern Illinois, where he had been sent after killing a man. She was able to convince the locals of the fraud by using a unique tactic. Stella had brought one of Jesse's old boots, along with Frank Milburn, the man who had made boots for Jesse's wedding. Jesse had small feet and wore a size 6½ boot, which wouldn't fit John James.

That was enough to convince most of those gathered at the Royal Hotel that the man was an impostor, but the story didn't end there. John James's promoters sought public engagements, including a trip to California, bearing more affidavits and a new promoter, and appearing on radio in Los Angeles and at a local beach as a curiosity. John James claimed that a man named Charlie Bigelow had been killed in Jesse's place, a story that was to become a fixture in James-impostor lore.

When he began bothering the family, Stella took the gloves off again. It seems that William John James had a sister, Dr. Bessie James Garver, who was a physician in Los Angeles. Dr. Garver gave an affidavit as to his real identity and his questionable sanity. According to her, John James was mentally unbalanced and a potential threat to society. He ultimately was to spend his last years in a Little Rock mental hospital, where he died in 1947.[1]

The impostor experience was nothing new. Women posed as Zee James before and after her death. Frank James's experience was no different. "Frank James, Once Noted Bandit, Now 70 Years Old, A Berry Picker," a headline in the *Washington Post* broadcast on July 28, 1914. A man in Tacoma, Washington, claimed to be the former outlaw. "I could not write the story of my life in five years," the aged rascal told a clueless reporter, who spent five days soaking up all the blarney the elderly man shoveled out. This "Frank" claimed that he was driven to outlawry after his father had been killed during the Civil War. According to the impostor, the James boys, "dressed as cowboys," caught up with the Pinkertons after the bombing at the farm, and "They never got back." He and "Jesse" killed thirty-one of the men responsible, and "God Almighty got the other." The James boys, according to this mountebank, used "a dark stain" on their faces instead of masks, and "Frank" lost part of his hand at Northfield, where "the two Cobb brothers and a man named Mitchell lost their lives." The old man had a good sense of just how to end his yarn. He claimed to have tracked Jesse's killer, Bob Ford, to a Kansas City dance hall, where he offered to treat the crowd and laid ten dollars on the bar. "Ford returned $2.00" when "Frank" revealed who he was. The *Post* had prefaced the story with an editorial statement, "What follows is a matter of history." Not only was it not a matter of history, it was something of a low point in journalism for the newspaper. For several days after the story appeared, the *Post* was a national laughingstock, as the Missouri press corrected the story and pointed out that Frank was alive and well on the old homestead.

In 1926 a book by Joe Vaughn appeared, titled *The Only True History of the Life of Frank James*. Vaughn, who lived in northwest Arkansas, died before the book went to press, but his children were active in promoting the story, which claimed that Frank had hired a stand-in prior to his surrender and then had faded into obscurity in the Ozarks for the last years of his life. Western bibliographer Ramon Adams called the book "one of the most brazen bits of writing it has been my experience to read." Author Burton Rascoe described it as "maudlin, illiterate, vague, confused, pathetic." It is possible that Vaughn, in his declining years, was suffering from the delusion that he was Frank James.[2]

Just prior to his death in 1931, a Colorado recluse named James Sears reportedly revealed to a friend that he was actually Jesse James. In his version of the story, a typhoid victim had been dragged into the house and shot by the Fords to give the illusion of Jesse's death. This impostor also received media ink.[3]

And then there was the notorious "skeleton of Jesse James." In 1938 a traveling carnival arrived in the small town of Trimble, in west Tennessee, proclaiming that for one dime spectators could see the skeleton of Jesse James, whose jaw was rigged to open and shut with the aid of a rope. The carnival operators' wagon broke down, and in order to pay the repair bill he left "Jesse" with Will Hamilton Parks as collateral. "He told me that he was going to Halls and would bring the money back on Monday, but he didn't say which Monday it would be, because he hasn't come back yet," Parks told a reporter decades later. The skeleton, complete with six-shooter and a (now) motorized jaw, would later make an appearance at the Kentucky State Fair in 1974.[4]

THE JAMES-SAMUEL farm, during the declining years of Frank's widow, Annie, was still run as a tourist attraction, and from the 1920s to perhaps the 1950s her son reportedly ran a small nine-hole golf course on the place.

For five dollars, a princely sum in those days, one could play a round with the son of Frank James in the field in front of the old cabin once raided by the Pinkertons; piles of cow dung and clumps of high grass substituted for water and sand traps. George Warfel, a visitor during the late 1930s and early 1940s, recalled that "during my visits . . . I never encountered any tourists at the farm. It is not at all like today, with visitors arriving at 10 A.M. and departing at 5 P.M. . . . Except for my first visit to the James farm in '37 Bob did little talking and let Mae [his wife] do the story telling to my groups. She was always very informative and enthusiastic in relating incidents. Bob and she both related the story of the bombing in explicit detail. Mae had a lot to say about the structural changes in the house from the 1860's until 1941."[5]

Robert James lived a fairly normal life with his wife and mother on the James farm. Annie usually shunned publicity and would go into a room whenever tourists dropped by the farm. When John James made his appearance in Excelsior Springs, though, Annie broke her seclusion and denounced the impostor publicly, to his face.

Annie's eyesight began to fail in the 1930s, but she would listen to the radio, and her son would read to her. During the winter months of her last years, she stayed in Texas or at the mineral baths in Excelsior Springs, when travel became difficult. She spent the rest of the year at the farm. On July 6, 1944, amid features about the Russian offensive against Hitler's armies in Poland and attacks by V1 and V2 rockets on London, the story announcing her death appeared on the front page of the *Kansas City Star*.

Over the years the media had offered Annie tens of thousands of dollars for her story, but she had vowed that it would die with her. And the ninety-one-year-old widow of Frank James took her memories with her to the grave. Frank's ashes were brought out of the bank vault and interred beside those of his wife at Hill Cemetery, now inside Jackson County's Hill Park, at Independence.[6]

THE GREAT DEPRESSION of the 1930s brought about a renewed Hollywood interest in the James story, or the legend that continued to evolve. Jo Frances James, the daughter of Jesse Jr., had written a manuscript giving her version of the James story and was trying to get it published as a book. She was contacted indirectly by Twentieth Century Fox through her good friend William S. Hart. Jo Frances met with movie mogul Darryl F. Zanuck, who offered to purchase her manuscript. Zanuck reportedly was not terribly enthusiastic about her project, but he had apparently been approached about the same time by producer-screenwriter Nunnally Johnson, who had written a James gang screenplay. Johnson's version was based in part on a James melodrama he had seen on stage as a youngster and on the writings of John Newman Edwards, various pulp histories, and another play entitled *The Purple Mask*. Henry King was to direct what later became the film *Jesse James* (1939), starring Tyrone Power and Henry Fonda as Jesse and Frank, respectively. The motion picture company rather cynically gave Jo Frances screen credit for the film treatment, which bore little resemblance to Johnson's script.

"I don't know what happened to the history part of it," Jo Frances told the press, "it seemed to me the story was fiction from beginning to end. . . . About the only connection it had with fact was that there once was a man named James and he did ride a horse." These words would echo down the decades as other James films were cranked out.

In the film the Saint Louis Midland Railroad is trying to buy the James farm in order to run its tracks across the property. (The nearest railroad, in reality, is miles away from the James farm.) Over the years countless Jesse James "Wanted" posters, offering a reward from the fictitious "Saint Louis Midland Railroad," have been sold to tourists as copies of an alleged 1870s original. The posters were probably used to promote the film.

As the story unfolds, a gang of railroad toughs headed by Brian Donlevy (who would also play an overaged William Quantrill in the equally fantastic *Kansas Raiders*) tosses a bomb into the home of the James boys, this time *killing* their mother. From there on it's the vengeance trail for the James brothers. Jesse robs trains and banks, and at Northfield he walks into a well-laid ambush planned by the railroad. Many of the action scenes were repeated in later James films, in particular one where the brothers ride through a store window to escape at Northfield and another where the brothers plunge their horses off a cliff into a lake.

Johnson probably had the pulse of the moviegoing public of 1939, for *Jesse James* did well at the box office. Coming at the end of the Great Depression, it had a particular resonance, as evidenced by a review in the Communist *Daily Worker*, which called the James brothers "victims of a social system which forced them to take up six-guns instead of plows. And for that reason alone we can thank Twentieth Century-Fox for a film of unusually high caliber and social significance." Frank James would have winced.

It had been almost a decade since the last cinematic effort, Paramount's silent *Jesse James*, but there would be a flood of other James flicks (see Appendix G) in the wake of the Power-Fonda opus. These included Roy Rogers as a singing Jesse James in *Days of Jesse James* (1939), *Jesse James at Bay* (1941), and a pre–*Lone Ranger* Clayton Moore in the 1947 Republic serial *Jesse James Rides Again*. In the latter, a true celluloid dime novel, Jesse James goes into hiding in Tennessee after being wrongfully accused of robbing the Bank of Northfield. There he battles a band of hooded raiders who are trying to take over land containing a rich oil deposit! In such a media environment, what followed should have come as no surprise.[7]

THE NEXT appearance of "Jesse James" was, fittingly, in a radio broadcast by Ray Palmer, science fiction editor for *Amazing Stories*. The publication had become somewhat notorious for a series of stories on cave monsters. Palmer claimed the thought waves from the denizens of the underworld had melted his typewriter keys when his publisher told him to nix the series. In this broadcast, the story of one J. Frank Dalton as the secretly surviving Jesse would be similarly mind bending and would result in what may well be the longest-running hoax in American history. The day after the broadcast the *Lawton (Okla.) Constitution* would announce to the world "Jesse James is Alive in Lawton!" Editor Frank O. Hall and reporter Lindsay Whitten had swallowed the story of Jesse's alleged survival, hook, line, and sinker, later producing a book titled *Jesse James Rides Again*.

Among Dalton's claims was the whopper that at age sixty-nine he had piloted an airplane in World War I. Nevertheless, some thirty thousand curious people showed up in Lawton when the old man first appeared in public. "Corroborating" the story of this aged liar was ex-outlaw Al Jennings. A former lawyer, Jennings had built a career as a western celebrity based largely on his role in a badly botched train robbery in the 1890s and a resulting stint in prison where he had met short-story writer William S. Porter, better known as O. Henry. Upon his release from prison, Jennings had written an inflated biography and worked in silent films. Now this professional western old-timer was playing rodeos with Dalton, who claimed to be Jesse. Jennings, of course, had never laid eyes on the real Jesse James and would later admit, "They paid me, why not?" to author Carl Breihan.[8]

August 1948 found Dalton and company in Chicago, where an unsuccessful attempt was made to get the town of Northfield, which had decided to celebrate the defeat of the gang, to pay one thousand dollars for a personal appearance. In Los Angeles, Stella James was thoroughly irritated at how this impostor was disrupting her family life:

> When the first story came out about this old man Dalton, the news paper of Lawton Okla. called us on the phone. Jesse became so up set that he walked the floor, and did not sleep at night—would read—books on

the History of his fathers life all night. Finally, became so bad that I had to get a nurse and doctor. He would not let the doctors in the room, and after several weeks refused to let the nurse in his rooms. He would get his fathers guns The shot Gun, rifel and the pistol [Harry Hoffman] gave me, and wanted to keep them on his bed. He seemed to think I had joined with those people, to try to put this old man over as his father. He turn[ed] against me—refused to eat. He went eight day[s] with out eating I had to put him in a private hospital where he remained for two months.

Jesse Jr. was starting to get better after the initial Dalton episode when a "crackpot preacher" named Highley, as Stella called him, approached her, offering to fly her to Chicago to meet Dalton. Stella couldn't go, much as she wanted to expose this latest impostor. "This latest incident," Stella explained to Jesse Jr.'s friend Harry Hoffman, "up set Jesse, all over again. I had to put him back in the Hospital, where they have to strap him down at times." Highley later came back to the James house with an offer from Dalton and his promoter, but was not let in the house. Stella said, "This man . . . [Dalton, masquerading as Jesse] had a hundred thousand dollars hidden a way . . . he wanted his son, [Jesse Jr.] to have, and . . . it would pay me to go and see him. I told him we wanted no part of the old man, and if he had any money he would not be appearing in cheap shows and selling his book of lies." Stella related how upset she was about her husband's condition and how she worried that he might never be well enough to come home, recalling how it took three men to strap him down and take him back to the hospital. It was indeed a sad time for the family.[9]

Dalton hit the carnival circuit in the fall of 1948 under the watchful eye of Orvus Lee Howk, who would later claim to be old man Dalton's grandson, taking the name Jesse James III. Dalton arrived by train from Chicago at Union Station in Nashville, Tennessee, on the morning of September 17, 1948, appearing as a sideshow attraction at the Tennessee State Fair.

"I could tell you things you would never believe," the elderly man told a reporter for the Clarksville Leaf-Chronicle. Some of the stories, indeed, stretched credulity. He claimed that his mother's maiden name was Dalton (not Cole) and that he had never seen his father. He said a man named "Charlie Bigelow" was shot in the house in Saint Joseph as "Jesse" while the real Jesse was in a stable nearby. Nunnally Johnson to the contrary, Dalton also claimed to have written the script for the movie Jesse James starring Tyrone Power and Henry Fonda. At this time Dalton and others apparently held some hope that the James family would take the money offered. Dalton even mentioned that he had a son in Los Angeles, Jesse James Jr., whom he planned to visit soon.

Lying in a hospital bed on a platform, surrounded by old furniture and photos, Dalton was exhibited like the proverbial two-headed calf to gawking fairgoers. J. Frank Dalton, for all his bluster, was an enigmatic figure. In the 1920s and 1930s he was involved in wildcat oil leasing and drilling in Texas. By the 1930s he was claiming to be a veteran of Quantrill's guerrillas and had published a couple of pamphlets, *Quantrill in the Civil War: Reminiscences of Civil War Days* (1935) and *The Men of Quantrill*. Both appear to have borrowed some from the yarns spun by a man calling himself Captain "Kit" Dalton in a book titled *Under the Black Flag* (1914), which J. Frank Dalton reportedly helped with. Interestingly, in *Quantrill in the Civil War*, Dalton stated: "Jesse James was killed by Robert Ford in St. Joseph, Missouri, April 3, 1882. There can be no doubt of his death, for there were too many people from all walks of life who had known him since early childhood, and who had flocked to St. Joe to identify him, for there to be any doubt about it." *The Crittenden Memoirs*, edited by H. H. Crittenden and published in 1936, contain letters from Dalton to Crittenden along with some yarns Dalton contributed about the James boys and Quantrill. Dalton again states that Jesse died in Saint Joseph in 1882, adding that he helped identify the body and that he had worked with Frank James at the Standard Theater in Saint Louis at one time. Interestingly, he lambastes an impostor, possibly John James, who was going the rounds at the time. Dalton told Crittenden, "I believe it would be a good idea to stop him."

All of these statements are telling. Dalton apparently had been studying the James story for some time, perhaps informally at first. Working with Frank at the Standard Theater would explain how he knew a number of facts. In 1947 Dalton surfaced in Austin, Texas, during an investigation by a reporter for a local radio station into the mistreatment of a number of elderly men in a local home for the aged. There Dalton repeated his claim to have served under Quantrill, for which there was dubious evidence. He applied for a Confederate pension as Frank Dalton on February 21, 1947, and was placed on the pension roll in Texas.

Dalton was not alone in his pension quest. Several so-called last surviving veterans of the Civil War were pension-hunting impostors. It apparently had been common in the 1930s, amid the economic wreck of the Great Depression, for some elderly southerners to add years to their actual age and then claim service in some unit for which records were lacking, usually state militia or guerrilla service. The practice carried on into the 1940s, as occurred in Dalton's case. Many perhaps felt sympathy with these elderly men who in their later years had fallen on hard times. These men had lived their working lives prior to Social Security, and Medicare was several decades away. Dalton found himself a relic of the Old West who had lived beyond his time, stranded like a beached whale in the middle of the twentieth century.

Also surfacing with Dalton in Nashville was "Colonel" James Russell Davis, who, it would later be claimed, was the secretly surviving Cole Younger. Davis claimed to have known Dalton-"Jesse" from youth and also claimed to be 108 years old when renewing his driver's license. Author Carl Breihan thought Davis looked around age seventy-five, however. Colonel Davis, who wore a pistol to bed at night, claimed to have served, at various times, on both sides during the Civil War and as a spy during World War I. His attempts to enlist for service in World War II were rebuffed, even though he boasted at being a crack shot.[10]

Dalton and his handlers next appeared in California, using recycled affidavits given in the case of the 1932 impostor John James. It was even claimed that Dalton and John James were the same man, even though the latter had died in an Arkansas mental hospital in 1947. Stella James again went on the offensive, threatening legal action through her attorney. A Chicago showman, John Shevlin, who was backing Dalton's tour, suddenly pulled the plug on the money, and the papers stopped running stories about "Jesse." "They gave up the fine house they were living in [and] discharged the maid," according to Harry Hoffman. Stella James reported that Orvus Lee Howk, Dalton-"Jesse's" impostor grandson, skipped town, leaving the old man to fend for himself. Police took Dalton to a nursing home, and he was later shipped back to Texas. But the amazing story of J. Frank Dalton, alias Jesse James, wasn't finished yet.[11]

Early in 1949, Dalton spent some time in a Texas hospital, until Frank Hall, one of the authors of *Jesse James Rides Again*, took over Dalton's management. Dalton was flown to Saint Joseph, Missouri, for an appearance at the Jesse James Hotel there. He repeated the Charlie Bigelow story and told a new yarn about how the Pinkertons had thrown a bomb made from a whiskey bottle into the James cabin. But too many people were still alive who remembered the real stories, and Dalton's yarns failed to hold water. In Saint Joe, Dalton was identified by Mr. and Mrs. Denny Reno as a former carnival barker who had gone by the name "Happy Jack" Dalton in the Texas Panhandle around the turn of the century. Hall apparently realized he had a white elephant on his hands, and Dalton's contract was eventually signed over to Lester Dill, owner of Meramec Caverns, where Dalton would hold court for much of what remained of his life.

On September 5, 1949, the cave management threw a media-event 102d birthday party for the old man, which included Billy the Kid impostor

Ollie "Brushy Bill" Roberts and the redoubtable James Russell Davis, among other members of what was becoming the Jesse James–impostor stock company. Also on hand was big-game hunter–novelist Robert Ruark, who had gullibly written up Dalton in three syndicated newspaper columns— another trophy for Dalton's wall. On January 13, 1950, Dalton, Davis, and Roberts appeared on NBC's *We the People*, receiving national radio airplay as well as television coverage in some broadcast areas. But Dalton's Waterloo was only two months away.[12]

On March 13, 1950, Dalton went to circuit court in Union, Missouri, to have his name changed "back" to Jesse James. On hand was Colonel Davis, whose agent was angling for a movie contract with Paramount for the film version of his alleged adventures as an Indian scout in the Apache wars under Gen. George Crook. Davis was irritated by the attorney for the James family, Edgar Eagan, whom he called a "whippersnapper." "I'm as sure of him [Dalton] as I'm sure of myself," he told the court. Dalton appeared with a wad of chewing tobacco in his mouth and a tomato can for a cuspidor.

"I want to ask you—" attorney Eagan began.

"Well do it!" snapped Dalton. "And do it in a hurry—and in a polite manner."

Six hours of testimony passed before Judge Ransom A. Brewer, an eightyyear-old Abraham Lincoln lookalike, handed down his decision:

> There is no evidence here to show that this gentleman, if he ever was Jesse James, has ever changed his name. If his name has never been changed, he is still Jesse James in name and there is nothing for this court to pass on. . . .
>
> If he isn't what he professes to be, then he is trying to perpetrate a fraud upon this court. If he is Jesse James, what he claims to be, then my suggestion would be that he retreat to his rendezvous and ask the good God to forgive him so he may pass away in peace when his time comes to go.

"There have been many famous trials in Union," the *Franklin County Tribune* summarized, "but the Dalton case Friday was the first in Union ever managed and staged as a publicity stunt."

In his testimony Davis told the court that he had "one foot in the grave and another on the brink." Two days after the court verdict his other foot followed. Davis's body was shipped back to Nashville for burial at Mount Olivet Cemetery as Davis.

Dalton returned to Texas in September 1950. A visitor to Meramec Caverns noted, just prior to his departure, that "his bed lacked the care he had formerly enjoyed" and "his long white hair was uncombed and neglected." A

United Press wire service feature dated September 6, 1950, reported Dalton's being discovered in a room in east Austin, "ill and penniless." He was taken to a local hospital as authorities worked to have his name restored to the state pension roster. He died in the town of Granbury, Texas, on August 15, 1951, and was buried under a tombstone bearing the name Jesse James. Dalton outlived Jesse Edwards James, who died in California on March 26, 1951.[13]

Over the next few decades a number of books and pamphlets, most self-published, would set forth Dalton's case. As Dalton authority Steve Eng notes, "They pose false questions, open closed issues, shift the burden of proof to others, disorient and distract the readers with post-1882 escapades, flagrantly flout logic and history, misspell basic names and botch dates, and their bad writing whines with petulance and paranoia." Some of the more noteworthy fabrications deserve mention. *Jesse James and the Lost Cause* (1961), by Jesse Lee James III, a.k.a. Orvus Lee Howk, has Dalton, a.k.a. Jesse James, stashing buried treasure all over the map, with a "Confederate Underground" plotting a second Civil War and digging a series of tunnels under Saint Louis, Nashville, Kansas City, Saint Joseph, and (incredibly) Lawrence, Kansas!

Jesse James Was One of His Names, by Del Schrader (with "Jesse James III"), is even more fantastic. In this version, John Wilkes Booth is poisoned by Jesse James in 1903, the "Confederate Underground" supplies Gatling guns and Winchesters to the Indians at Little Big Horn, and Jesse rescues Emperor Maximilian from the clutches of the Juaristas and invests in the Hughes Tool Company, from which millionaire Howard Hughes derived his fortune.

Between 1951 and 1995 Hollywood would crank out at least seventeen more James films (see Appendix G), including *Jesse James' Women* (1954), which boasts wretched acting, along with modern Coca-Cola signs and other anachronisms in the background of certain scenes. Other memorable films include *The Outlaws Is Coming* (1965), with the Three Stooges, and *Jesse James Meets Frankenstein's Daughter* (1966).[14]

Robert Franklin James, the son of Frank and Annie, died on November 18, 1959, and was buried at Kearney, Missouri. He was the last of the surviving children born in the Nashville area. The story of the James brothers was, or at least should have been, closed, but the legacy of the impostors lingered, and periodically over the years, the claims of Dalton and others would find an airing in the national media. It was always good filler on a slow news day. Occasionally sparks would fly, as when Lester Dill's son-in-law, Rudy Turilli, offered a reward to anyone who could prove that Jesse really had died in 1882. On February 27, 1967, Turilli appeared on the Joe Pyne show, which was broadcast on nationwide television. Pyne had the habit of baiting and insulting his guests, and after one swipe, Turilli said he "would pay ten thousand dollars . . . to anyone who could prove me wrong." Stella James and her daughters took Turilli to court over his offer and won the case in 1971 and the subsequent appeal in 1972.

It didn't quite end there, however. In 1978 an account of the survival story, apparently cribbed from Turilli's *I Knew Jesse James*, appeared in *The People's Almanac # 2* without mention of the 1971–72 verdict. Over the next few years there appeared a number of newspaper and tabloid features repeating the survival yarn. In March 1984 the NBC television program *Real People* broadcast a pseudo-investigative feature to further muddy the waters of history.[15]

On September 28, 1992, the *Dallas Morning News* reported an attempt to recover an alleged "Jesse James" treasure buried in Waco, Texas, in a vacant lot near the banks of the Brazos River. It was claimed that Dalton, a.k.a. Jesse James, had buried some forty million dollars' worth of silver coins and gold bars in a giant safe on the lot. As Stella James had been quick to point out in 1948, if the old man had any money stashed away there was no reason for him to have played carnival sideshows. Nevertheless, an investor reportedly spent $350,000 digging a thirty-two-foot tunnel to the water table of the Brazos. Predictably, no treasure was recovered. Jesse James IV (son of Jesse Lee James, a.k.a. Jesse James III, a.k.a. Orvus Lee Howk) was quoted as posing the possibility of exhuming the body buried in the grave at Kearney to settle the matter. By the early 1990s the James story had virtually left the realm of history for that of low comedy— and science.[16]

⁂

THE IDEA for a serious forensic study of the remains of Jesse James was first laid out by James historian Emmett C. Hoctor in an article published in *Wild West* magazine's June 1994 issue. Already DNA testing had been used in an unsuccessful attempt to locate the remains of Butch Cassidy and the Sundance Kid in Bolivia.[17]

In March 1995 I was contacted by Jay Ferguson, graduate assistant to Prof. James Starrs of the forensic science department at George Washington University in Washington, D.C. Ferguson asked me to suggest some historical questions that could be cleared up through a forensic investigation of the remains in the grave. That was easy enough. Was Jesse on opiates at the time of his death? What was the caliber of the weapon used to kill Jesse? What about the bullet that Jesse carried in him from his

1865 chest wound? These were three questions that came off the top of my head, among others.

It appeared that somehow a forensic investigation was actually taking shape, something I hadn't dreamed would ever happen. Forensic work of this type is expensive, but this was apparently going to be a volunteer effort, used to publicly showcase what forensic science could do as well as to answer the riddle of Jesse James. The next few weeks I was busy copying information relative to the 1902 reburial of Jesse, his various documented bullet wounds, and the 1882 autopsy, the official record of which had vanished. Also copied were samples of handwriting from Jesse James and from J. Frank Dalton.

The main question now was whether the court would allow an exhumation. A motion for the exhumation of the remains of Jesse James was filed on June 19, 1995. The descendants of Jesse James were in favor of the study so that scientific evidence could remove lingering doubts the public might have about the identity of the body in the grave. A pressing concern was that the court might decline to issue an exhumation order if word got out too far in advance, and the Clay County Courthouse would become the center of media attention. So everything was done without fanfare.

Then on June 27, 1995, the Associated Press ran a short feature, "Scientists Want to Dig Up Jesse James," and the phone in Professor Starrs's office started to ring.[18]

On Thursday, July 6, Clay County Circuit Judge Victor Howard issued an exhumation order based on a request by County Prosecutor Mike Reardon. Dr. Gerald B. Lee, Clay County coroner, had written to Reardon requesting the exhumation order. According to Missouri law, an exhumation can be ordered if an individual died of mysterious and/or violent circumstances and there is no autopsy *of record*. Although an autopsy was reported in the press, the records of the 1882 autopsy were missing. Judge Howard stipulated that the remains were to be reinterred on or before October 31.[19]

So it was that at eight o'clock on Monday morning, July 17, the exhumation—and media circus—began in Kearney's Mount Olivet Cemetery. Joan Lunden of ABC's *Good Morning America* and a raft of other reporters and television crews (*Washington Post, Los Angeles Times*, AP, Reuters, NBC, and others) were on hand for what was perhaps *the* Jesse James media event of the century.

Lunden interviewed Mark Nikkel, who, with his uncle Robert Jackson, would give the blood used in the DNA testing. Both Jackson and Nikkel were direct descendants from Zerelda Cole James Samuel to her daughter,

Susan James Parmer (Jesse's sister), to Susan's daughter, Feta Parmer Rose, to great-granddaughter Dorothy Rose, to great-great-grandson Robert Jackson and great-great-great-grandson Mark Nikkel. The mitochondrial DNA is only passed down in a direct, unbroken, female line. While Jackson and Nikkel have the same mitochondrial DNA pattern, it cannot be passed on by them. The same techniques have been used to identify hundreds of remains of American soldiers killed in Vietnam, as well as the remains of individuals murdered in Argentina and Bosnia.

It had been reported in 1902 that Jesse's remains were reburied in a metal coffin. But five hours into the dig and nearly seven feet down, no metal coffin had turned up. Starrs was disappointed. From here on the dig would be more of an archaeological affair, entrusted to forensic anthropologist Michael Finnegan of Kansas State University and his former student Dan Kysar.

Bits of rotten wood started to appear, then a tibia bone that was in terrible shape.

"Munge," Kysar uttered. This was bad news.

The coffin was apparently of wood and had rotted and collapsed. The soil in the area is clay, which leeches the salts from bones and holds moisture. "Munge" is slang for a mixture of remains decayed almost to dirt. Mitochondrial DNA normally no longer exists when remains get to this state.

A pall set in over the crew, and the excavation was shut down for the day. Starrs, normally a jovial punster, retreated to his hotel, despondent.

The next morning at seven Kysar returned to the grave. The media, which had been out in force the day before and had to be kept back by security provided, appropriately, by Pinkertons Incorporated, were dwindling. Now, with nothing but damp dirt to show, many had pulled out or were preparing to leave. An exception was the crew of the television tabloid A Current Affair. They were banned from the site for drinking beer in the cemetery.

Slowly, and somewhat to the surprise of everyone, it turned out that the remains were not as decayed as earlier thought. Bones in better shape were unearthed, including a piece of skull bearing the marks of a saw, the kind used by coroners in the nineteenth century. It now appeared that there were enough bones to piece together the top of the skull.

It also appeared that the remains were flipped over and the body had been buried face down. Some would suggest that ninety-three years of impostor stories, bad fiction, and movies had caused Jesse to roll over in his grave. A different theory is offered here: The 1902 reburial took place in a rainstorm, and the original coffin came apart while being raised. In all likelihood the workers simply tossed the remains into the new casket, wanting to get the job over with, and were not particular about which way the corpse landed.

Fourteen teeth were found, a major plus, as teeth are excellent repositories for DNA and last much longer than bone. A tie pin similar to one in an 1882 photo of the body turned up, as did a .36-caliber pistol ball in the area of the right rib cage, apparently fired from a cap-and-ball Colt 1851 Navy revolver.

The bones were taken by Professor Finnegan to Kansas State University in Manhattan, while other non-bone items went to George Washington University in Washington, D.C. Mark Stoneking performed DNA testing on the teeth at Penn State University.[20] A scalp sample taken from the 1978 excavation of Jesse's first grave at the James farm was sent to Dr. Bruce Goldberger at Florida State University in Tallahassee for toxicology tests.

It seems that not all of Jesse's remains had made it to the second coffin in 1902 when the original coffin collapsed. These other small bones were dug up at the James farm on September 15 and placed in the care of John Hartman, county historical sites director, to be turned over to an attorney for the James family at noon the following day and then given to Professor Starrs. But a funny thing happened on the way to this meeting at Liberty the next day. Hartman found that he had a commitment that day to drive a vehicle carrying three Clay County commissioners in the annual Jesse James Festival parade beginning at 10 A.M. Hartman took the bones with him, so that part of Jesse rode in his own parade, hiding out in the glove compartment of a Jeep.

The third and final burial of Jesse James was yet another story. Plans were originally made to hold the funeral in Liberty at William Jewell College, the school Jesse's father helped to found. The controversy that erupted was not about Jesse but rather about the display of a Confederate battle flag on his casket. The flag in question was not the familiar Saint Andrews Cross, but rather an obscure blue flag that had been carried by Missouri troops during the war. There reportedly had been a handshake deal about using the Missouri banner, but a few days later the chaplain of the college notified funeral organizers that school officials had decided that even this flag was considered "racially inflammatory," even though no complaints had been voiced to them. The First Baptist Church at Kearney also rejected a funeral, fearing a media onslaught similar to that at the exhumation.

Organizers eventually arranged to have the service at the local Knights of Columbus Hall in Kearney, complete with Confederate flags. The funeral service took place on Saturday, October 28. Jesse, who according to Starrs, had been "resting in pieces" since the exhumation, was brought back in one place for the final rites. While two uniformed reenactors of Company A, Fifth Missouri Infantry, watched over the process, the remains were placed in a new poplar casket at the Fry Funeral Homes.

The casket was then moved to the Knights of Columbus Hall, where some six hundred people gathered, including Brad English, U.S. Marshal for Western Missouri, and Jean Carnahan, wife of Missouri Gov. Mel Carnahan. The service, which included several period hymns, centered on a reading from the Book of Job: "If a man die, shall he live again?"

Only a few reporters covered the ceremony. The flag-draped casket was taken by an original 1870s horse-drawn hearse to Mount Olivet for a small graveside ceremony and interment.

"We are not here for the cardboard cutout, the character from dime novels, the Robin Hood," said funeral organizer Robert L. Hawkins III. "We are here to remember the man and to support a family protective of his memory." Asked by a reporter if this was indeed the final burial ceremony, Judge James Ross, Jesse's great-grandson, answered: "Absolutely yes . . . never again. Three times is enough."[21]

On Thursday evening, February 22, 1996, in Nashville, the former refuge of the James brothers, some fifty or more people packed into a smoke-filled suite at the Opryland Hotel to view the memorabilia recovered from Jesse's grave and parts of the casket that had collapsed, as well as a cast of Jesse's skull. The next day the final report on the exhumation would be given at the annual meeting of the American Academy of Forensic Sciences, which had made Starrs a "Distinguished Fellow." Jesse James IV was there in the room with Judge James Ross, grandson of Jesse Jr. and son of Jesse Jr.'s daughter, Jo Frances. There were bitter memories of the Dalton hoax, and Ross refused to shake hands with Dalton's reputed kin. When Ross asked Jesse IV and his attorney if they wanted to bet $150,000 whether it really was Jesse James in the grave, they walked away.

The next morning more than two hundred people gathered to hear what the experts had to say. On hand were Jesse James IV and his attorney, who backed Dalton's claim. Also on hand was Vincel Simmons, who had claimed in a book titled *Jesse James: The Real Story,* that his grandfather, Jacob Benjamin Gerlt, was actually Jesse and that he died at Sedalia, Missouri, at age 103. Also attending was Alan Crawford, a forty-eight-year-old prison guard from Ohio, who claimed in a low voice to those who would listen that his great-grandfather was the real Jesse, who had died in the Ozarks sometime in the 1930s after spending his last years as a Baptist preacher.

The report began. First, the presenters said, the remains are consistent with what is historically known about Jesse James. It turns out that the bullet hole in the skull was made by a .44- or .45-caliber revolver. While it's probable that the bullet never exited the head, there was not enough of the skull to show if it in fact did. Toxicology tests on hair taken from the original grave at the James farm in 1978 show that for the last three months of his life, Jesse James was not taking opiates. Furthermore, an examination of the hair showed that it apparently had been dyed with boot polish. An analysis of handwriting showed that J. Frank Dalton and Jesse James clearly wrote differently.

Finally the DNA results were given. DNA testing was made difficult by the deteriorated condition of the bones. Several attempts only drew skewed DNA patterns. "The eerie and unnatural elusiveness of Jesse James plainly qualifies him to be termed the Houdini of American outlaws," Starrs commented during the program. "The question for us this morning is whether Jesse has carried his elusiveness beyond the grave."

A tooth taken from the Kearney grave had produced consistent results, and the mitochondrial DNA pattern for the remains and the descendants of Susan James Parmer, Jesse's sister, matched. "I will go out on the deep end and say I feel with a reasonable degree of scientific certainty that we have the remains of Jesse James," Starrs told the gathering. (See Appendix H for the text of the press conference.)

Applause filled the auditorium and video cameras recorded the scene for local news outlets in Nashville and Missouri. It turned out that James's DNA pattern was unique and did not match any in the various DNA databases used for comparison in the study. Ross was elated, and the "James" claimants were disappointed but undeterred. There was even talk by Jesse James IV of unearthing J. Frank Dalton, and it's possible that Jacob Gerlt may be unearthed by Simmons.[22]

But the story of Jesse's alleged survival apparently doesn't end there. As this book nears completion, yet another contender has appeared for the title of being the secretly surviving Jesse James. One James Lafayette Courtney, who died in Falls County, Texas, in April 1943, reportedly left diaries and numerous photos of himself that bear a resemblance to Jesse (though the difference in noticeable, too). According to the story, it was really Wood Hite who was shot in Saint Joe and put in the grave at Kearney under the gravestone marked Jesse James. This is where the story falls apart, for Hite was a cousin of Jesse's on his father's side, and mitochondrial DNA is passed on from the maternal side only. Had it been Hite in Jesse's grave, DNA tests would not have shown a match with that of the descendants of Jesse's sister, Susan. And so it goes.[23]

It comes as no surprise that stories of Jesse's survival continue to appear. As explained by Prof. Eric Hobsbawm in his masterful book, *Bandits*, in a chapter on "The Noble Robber," the idea that the noble outlaw can't be defeated and will return one day is "the same sort of wish . . . [that] produces the perennial myths of the good king . . . who has not really died, but will come back one day to restore justice. Refusal to believe in a robber's death is a certain criterion of his 'nobility.' . . . For the bandit's defeat and death is the defeat of his people; and what is worse, of hope. Men can live without justice, and generally must, but they cannot live without hope."

So it is with legendary Robin Hoods anywhere in the world.[24] The legend of Jesse James, if not quite consistent with historical fact, brought America a populist antihero, an undefeated holdout of the Lost Cause, a Robin Hood who stole from the rich and gave to the poor in an era of corrupt politicians and robber-baron industrialists. He remains a cultural icon, a creation of the mass media, whose name and (all too often fictional) deeds are recounted in song, dozens of books, television shows, and at least thirty-six motion pictures. Well over a century after his death, his name is as familiar as those of Washington and Lincoln. Such is the power of the legend—a legend that refuses to die.

Appendix A

General Orders No. 11 and the Letter of Bloody Bill Anderson

FOLLOWING THE August 21, 1863, raid on Lawrence, Kansas, Order No. 11 was issued by Brig. Gen. Thomas Ewing, commander of the District of the Border.

General Orders No. 11, Hdqrs. District of the Border, Kansas City, Mo., August 25, 1863

I. All persons living in Jackson, Cass, and Bates Counties, Missouri, and that part of Vernon included in this district, except those living within 1 mile of the limits of Independence, Hickman Mills, Pleasant Hill, and Harrisonville, and except those in that part of Kaw township, Jackson County, north of Brush Creek and west of the Big Blue, are hereby ordered to remove from their present places of residence within fifteen days from the date hereof. Those who, within that time, establish their loyalty to the satisfaction of the military station nearest their present places of residence will receive from him certificates stating the fact of their loyalty, and the names of the witnesses by whom it can be shown. All who receive such certificates will be permitted to remove to any military station within the district, or to any part of the State of Kansas, except the counties on the eastern border of the State. All others shall remove out of this district. Officers commanding companies and detachments serving in the counties names will see that this paragraph is promptly obeyed.

II. All grain and hay in the field or under shelter in the district from which the inhabitants are required to move within reach of military stations after the 9th day of September next will be taken to such stations and turned over to the proper officers there, and report the amount so turned over made to district headquarters, specifying the names of all loyal owners and the amount of such produce taken from them. All grain and hay found in such district after the 9th day of September next not convenient to such stations will be destroyed.

III. The provisions of General Orders, No. 10, from these headquarters will be at once vigorously executed by officers commanding in the parts of the district and at the

341

stations not subject to the operation of paragraph I of this order, and especially in the towns of Independence, Westport, and Kansas City.*

IV. Paragraph II, General Orders No. 10, is revoked as to all who have borne arms against the Government in this district since the 21st day August, 1863.†

By order of Brigadier-General Ewing:

H. Hannahs,

Acting Assistant Adjutant General.

⚜

The Letter of Bloody Bill Anderson

WHAT FOLLOWS is the text of a letter to the two newspapers in Lexington, Missouri. It graphically shows Anderson's sometimes incoherent, deranged state of mind in the summer of 1864. It was forwarded to department commander Gen. William S. Rosecrans as "A curiosity." Keep in mind while reading this the trouble Confederate authorities had with the guerrillas in Texas and subsequent actions in Missouri by Anderson and his band.

To the editors of the two papers in Lexington, to the Citizens and the community at large, General Brown, and Colonel McFerran and his petty hirelings, such as Captain Burris, the friend of Anderson.

Mr. Editors:

In reading both your papers I see you urge the policy of the citizens taking up arms to defend their persons and property. You are only asking them to sign their death warrants. Do you not know, sirs, that you have some of Missouri's proudest, best, and noblest sons to cope with? Sirs, ask the people of Missouri who are acquainted with me, if Anderson ever robbed them or mistreated them in any manner. All those that speak the truth will say never. Then what protection will they want? It is from thieves, not such men as I profess to have under my command. My command can give them more protection than all the Federals in the

---

* These orders are reprinted in *Official Records*, ser. 1, vol. 22, pt. 2, 40–461, 473. Officers were to arrest and send to the district provost marshal all male and non-head-of-household females, who willfully aided and encouraged guerrillas. They were to discriminate between those who had been coerced into giving help. Wives and children of guerrillas, and women heads of families helping guerrillas willfully, were to be notified by officers to move out of both the district and the state. They would be allowed to take their stock, provisions, and household goods. If they did not remove quickly they would be escorted to Kansas City to be shipped south with whatever belongings they could carry. Officers were to aid free blacks and the slaves of disloyal persons; the latter were removed to Kansas or military stations within Missouri.

† Persons who had borne arms against the Union and had surrendered at military posts would be sent to the district provost marshal to be banished, with their families, to any state or district out of the department as the commander of the department directed. They would remain exempt from military punishment but not from civil trial for treason.

State against such enemies. There are thieves and robbers in the community, but they do not belong to any organized band; they do not fight for principles; they are for self-interest; they are just as afraid of me as they are of the Federals. I will help the citizens rid the country of them. They are not friends of mine. I have used all that language can do to stop their thefts; I will now see what I can do by force. But listen to me, fellow citizens; do not obey this last order. Do not take up arms if you value your lives and property. It is not in my power to save your lives if you do. If you proclaim to be in arms against the guerrillas I will kill you. I will hunt you down like wolves and murder you. You cannot escape. It will not be Federals after you. Your arms will be no protection to you. Twenty-five of my men can whip all that can get together. It will not be militia such as Mcferran's, but regulars that have been in the field for three years, that are armed with from two to four pistols and Sharps rifles. I commenced at the first of this war to fight for my country, not to steal from it. I have chosen guerrilla warfare to revenge myself for the wrongs that I could not honorably avenge otherwise. I lived in Kansas when this war commenced. Because I would not fight the people of Missouri, my native State, the Yankees sought my life, but failed to get me. Revenged themselves by murdering my father, destroying all my property, and having since that time murdered one of my sisters and kept the other two in jail twelve months. But I have fully glutted my vengeance. I have killed many. I am a guerrilla. I have never belonged to the Confederate Army, nor do my men. A good many of them are from Kansas. I have tried to war with the Federals honorably, but for retaliation I have done things, and am fearful will have to do that I would shrink from if possible to avoid. I have tried to teach the people of Missouri that I am their friend, but if you think that I am wrong, then it is your duty to fight. Take up arms against me and you are Federals. Your doctrine is an absurdity, and I will kill you for being fools. Beware, men, before you take this fearful leap. I feel for you. You are in a critical situation. But remember there is a Southern army, headed by the best men in the nation. Many of their homes are in Missouri, and they will have the State or die in the attempt. You that sacrifice your principles for fear of losing your property will, I fear, forfeit your right to a citizenship in Missouri. Young men, leave your mothers and fight for your principles. Let the Federals know that Missouri's sons will not be trampled on. I have no time to say anything more to you. Be careful how you act, for my eyes are upon you.

W. Anderson
Commanding Kansas First Guerrillas*

---

*This is the first section of a four-part letter sent by Anderson and is quoted from the *Official Records*, ser. 1, vol. 41, pt. 2, 75–77.

Appendix B

Two Editorials of John Newman Edwards

The Chivalry of Crime

Kansas City Times, September 29, 1872

There is a dash of tiger blood in the veins of all men; a latent disposition, even in the bosom that is a stranger to nerve and daring, to admire those qualities in other men. And this penchant is always keener if there be a dash of sin in the deed to spice the joy of its contemplation. Crime, in the ordinary sense of the term, affords nothing but disgust. It is an instinct of human nature that he who lifts his hand against his fellow man, are against the things which are his, shall be despised and ostracized. There is no palliation for crime in any shape, and especially more disgusting is it the more sordid its motive and secret its execution. Thus, the burglar who breaks a lock or a bank vault in the still hour when the honest world slumbers; the highwayman who lays in wait in lonely places to pounce upon the inoffensive and unwary; the pickpocket who pilfers the loose change and valuables of his victim in the shelter of a throng; the horse-thief who halters his prey at midnight in the still fields and hides it in the thick woods; or the murderer who steals upon his unsuspecting sacrifice in the deadly ambush or poison or when the victim sleeps; all of these are execrated of men and condemned of God and His commandments. But there are things done for money and for revenge of which the daring of the act is the picture and the crime the frame that it be set in. Crime of which daring is simply an ingredient has no palliation on earth or forgiveness anywhere. But a feat of stupendous nerve and fearlessness that makes one's hair rise to think of it, with a condiment of crime to season it, become chivalric; poetic; superb.

There are thieves and pickpockets and burglars and garroters in Kansas City, who, it were better for the city, should sleep some night under the shade of a tree with no ground for the soles of their feet to touch. But there are now men in Jackson, Cass, and Clay—a few there are left—who learned to dare when there was no such word as quarter in the dictionary of the Border. Men who have carried their lives in their hands for so long that they do not know how to commit them over into the keeping of the laws and regulations that exist now, and these men some-

344

times rob. But it is always in the glare of day and in the teeth of the multitude. With them booty is but the second thought; the wild drama of the adventure first. These men never go upon the highway in lonesome places to plunder the pilgrim. That they leave to the ignobler pack of jackals. But they ride at midday into the county seat, while court is sitting, take the cash out of the vault and put the cashier in and ride out of town to the music of cracking pistols. These men are bad citizens but they are bad because they live out of their time. The nineteenth century with its Sybaric civilization is not the social soil for men who might have sat with Arthur at the Round Table, ridden at tourney with Sir Launcelot or won the colors of Guinevere; men who might have shattered the casque of Brian de Bois Gilbert, shivered a lance with Ivanhoe or won the smile of the Hebrew maiden; and men who could have met Turpin and Duval and robbed them of their illgotten booty on Hounslow Heath.

Such as these are they who awed the multitude on Thursday while they robbed the till at the gate and got away.

What they did we condemn. But the way they did it we cannot help admiring. It was as though three bandits had come to us from the storied Odenwald, with the halo of medieval chivalry upon their garments and shown us how the things were done that the poets sing of. No where else in the United States or in the civilized world, probably, could this thing have been done. It was done here, not because the protectors of person and property were less efficient but because the bandits were more dashing and skillful; not because honest Missourians have less nerve but because freebooting Missourians have more.

⁂

The Killing of Jesse James

Sedalia Democrat, April 13, 1882

"Let not Caesar's servile minions,
Mock the lion thus laid low:
'Twas no foeman's hand that slow him,
'Twas his own that struck the blow."

No one among the hired cowards, hard on the hunt for blood-money, dared face this wonderful outlaw, one even against twenty, until he had disarmed himself and turned his back on his assassins, the first and only time in a career which has passed from the realms of an almost fabled romance into that of history.

We called him an outlaw, and he was, but fate made him so. When the war came he was just turned fifteen. The border was all aflame with steel, and fire, and ambuscade, and slaughter. He flung himself into a band which had a black flag for a banner and devils for riders. What he did, and it was fearful. But it was war. It was Missouri against Kansas. It was Jim Lane and Jennison against Quantrill, Anderson and Todd.

When the war closed Jesse James had no home. Proscribed, hunted, shot, driven away from among his people, a price put upon his head—what else could a man do, with such a nature, except what he did do? He had to live. It was his country. The graves of his kindred were there. He refused to be banished from his birthright, and when he was hunted he turned savagely about and hunted his hunters. Would to God he were alive to-day to make a righteous butchery of a few more of them.

There never was a more cowardly and unnecessary murder committed in all of America than this murder of Jesse James. It was done for money. It was done that a few men might get all the money. He had been living in St. Joseph for months. The Fords were with him. He was in the toils, for they meant to betray him. He was in the heart of a large city. One word would have summoned 500 armed men for his capture or extermination, Not a single one of the attacking party need to have been hurt. If, when his house had been surrounded, he had refused to surrender, he could have been killed on the inside of it, and at long range. The chances for him to escape were as one to 10,000, and not even that. But it was never intended that he should be captured. It was his blood the bloody wretches were after—blood that would bring money in the great official market of Missouri.

And this great commonwealth leagued with a lot of self-confessed robbers, highwaymen and prostitutes to have one of its citizens assassinated, before it was positively known he had committed a crime worthy of his death.

Of course everything that can be said about the dead man to justify the manner of his killing, will be said; but who is saying it? Those with the blood of Jesse James on their guilty souls. Those who conspired to murder him. Those who wanted the reward, and would invent any lie or concoct any diabolical story to get it. They have succeeded, but such a cry of horror and indignation at the infernal deed is even now thundering over the land that if a single one of the miserable assassins had either manhood, conscience, or courage, he would go, as another Judas, and hang himself But so sure as God reigns, there never was a dollar of blood-money obtained yet which did not bring with it perdition. Sooner or later there comes a day of vengeance. Some among the murderers are mere beasts of prey. These, of course, can only suffer through cold, or hunger or thirst; but whatever they dread most that thing will happen. Others again among the murderers are sanctimonious devils who plead the honor of the State, the value of law and order, the splendid courage required to shoot an unarmed man in the back of the head; and these will be stripped to the skin of their pretensions, and made to shiver and freeze, splotched as they are and spotted and piebald with blood, in the pitiless storm of public contempt and condemnation. This to the leaders will be worse than death.

Nor is the end yet. If Jesse James had been hunted down as any other criminal, and killed while trying to escape or in resisting arrest, not a word would have been said to the contrary. He had sin[n]ed. And he had suffered. In his death the majesty of the law would have been vindicated; but here the law itself becomes a murderer. It leagues with murderers. It hires murderers. It aids and abets murderers. It borrows money to pay and reward murderers. It promises immunity and protection to murderers. It is itself a murderer—the most abject, the most infamous, the most cowardly ever known to history. Therefore this so-called law is an outlaw, and these so-called executors of the law are outlaws. Therefore let Jesse James' comrades—and he has a few remaining worth all the Fords and Littles, that could be packed together between St. Louis and St. Joe—do unto them as they did unto him. Yes, the end is not yet, nor should it be. The man had no trial. What right had any officer of this state to put a price upon his head and hire a band of cut-throats and highwaymen to murder him for money?

Anything can be told of man. The whole land is full of liars and robbers, and assassins. Murder is easy for a hundred dollars. Nothing is safe that is pure or unsuspecting, or just, but it is not to be supposed that the law will become an ally and a co-worker in this sort of civilization. Jesse James has been murdered, first, because an immense price has been set upon his head, and there isn't a low-lived scoundrel to-day in Missouri who wouldn't kill his own father for money; and second, because he was made the scape-goat of every train robber, foot-pad and highwayman between Iowa and Texas. Worse men a thousand times than the dead man have been hired to do this thing. The very character of the instruments chosen shows the infamous nature of the work required. The hand that slew him had to be a traitor's! Into all the warp and woof of the devil's work there were threads woven by the fingers of a harlot. What a spectacle! Missouri, with splendid companies and regiments of militia. Missouri, with a hundred and seventeen sheriffs, as brave and efficient on average as any men on earth. Missouri, with every screw and cog and crank and lever and wheel of her administrative machinery in perfect working order. Missouri, with all her order, progress, and development, had yet to surrender all of these in the face of a single man—a hunted, lied-upon, proscribed and outlawed man, trapped and located in the midst of thirty-five thousand people and ally with some five or six cut-throats and prostitutes that the majesty of the law might be vindicated, and the good name of the State saved from all further reproach! Saved! Why, the whole State to-day reeks with a double orgy—that of lust and that of murder. What the men failed to do, the women accomplished.

Tear the two bears from the flag of Missouri. Put thereon, in place of them, as more appropriate, a thief blowing out the brains of an unarmed victim, and a brazen harlot, naked to the waist and splashed to the brows in blood.

Appendix C

Letters Concerning the Pinkerton Raid on the James-Samuel Farm and the Death of Daniel Askew

WHAT FOLLOWS are full and partial transcripts of letters not fully quoted in chapters 5 and 6 that relate to the raid on the James-Samuel Farm near Kearney, Missouri, in January 1875 and the subsequent killing of Daniel Askew three months later.

These were transcribed from the pages of letterpress copybooks containing the correspondence of Allan Pinkerton in the papers of Pinkerton's National Detective Agency in the Manuscript Department of the Library of Congress, Washington, D.C. The papers were donated to the library in 1956.

Some of these letters are difficult or impossible to read in portions due to the method used for copying. A page of the letter book made of a tissuelike paper was moistened and laid on top of the original ink letter, with sheets of wax paper placed on top of this and below the original. It was then squeezed in a press, which drew off a copy on the tissue sheet much like a blotter. The process was a pale forerunner of carbon paper and the photocopier. Sometimes the results were excellent, other times the image was barely legible. Unfortunately, due to the nature of the correspondence and the intervening years, none of the original letters are known to exist. In the text below, an extended space has been inserted to mark where the original was indecipherable. In a few instances I have tried to decipher a word or phrase and placed these in brackets with a question mark [?]. Occasionally I have used brackets to add a brief explanation.

※※◎※※

THE FOLLOWING letter was sent in late 1874 to Patrick Henry Woodward at the Post Office Department. Most notable is its explanation of the Pinkerton telegraphic code. It also hints that an operative, probably a Post Office Department agent, was then within the post office in Kearney, Missouri.

Chicago, Dec. 15th 1874

Private
P. H. Woodward Esq.
Chief Special Agent, P.O. Dept.
Washington, D.C.

Dear Sir,

Yours of the 12th inst. is received. Many thanks to you for your kindness in the matter. I am under obligations to the Postmaster General more than I can ever pay;

We have now got inside of the K. office. Hassel the postmaster has appointed a deputy, and has himself gone into the country; of course we will take care to keep him out, until we get through with the matter.

I am obliged to you for your selection of an agent to operate near K. [Kearney]. But if you please, let everything remain for the present. I am expecting every day to bring this thing to a climax; at least two or three of the parties are there, but they are well armed; and have all the advantages men could ask, we must be cautious and make our movement secure, and then I hope every tick of the wire will tell us we have got the men. . . .

I send you a form of "cypher" telegraphing which I sometimes use, and which I may telegraph you. I will also suppose the following to be a telegram, you will observe how I will write it out.

weather	rainy	and	probably	snow
We	shall	get	all	our
trees	in	order	and	likely
to	save	every	one	of
them	from	winters	storms	our
horses	and	mules	are	in
splendid	condition	they	will	get
along	the	sheep	are	good

The following is the form the message passes over the wires.

good get in our of likely our snow weather we trees to them horses splendid along are will are storms one and all probably rainy shall in save from and condition the sheep they mules winters every order get and

There you will see I use the words up the 5th column, down the 1st column, up the 4th column, down the 2nd column, and up the 3rd column.

Be sure you fill up your columns so that your aggregate of words will divide up by "5" without a remainder. I think you will be able to understand it.

Please consider this strictly confidential, and please say to the Post Master General that I shall ever remember his kindness.

Yours Truly,
Allan Pinkerton

USING THE alias of George McQueen, Pinkerton or one of his agents sent the following letter to Samuel Hardwicke. The detective used false identities in his correspondence so that the letter would not be traced directly to him. In February 1875 Pinkerton was anxious to learn how the Clay County Grand Jury investigation was proceeding. The writer evidently feared arrest should he travel to Missouri.

16 Feb
1875

Sam,

Your two letters are duly received. I will meet you wherever you please, say at Quincy, Springfield, Joliet or Chicago which ever one you think is best either is as good as the next to me. I should like to see you very much, you undoubtedly know much more than I know, but I am anxious to know what is going on. The reason why I was away at the last was because I had matters to attend, which had lain over for some time. Somebody has asked the question what I was doing when away, well I was on legitimate business and am prepared to prove it, where I was night and day, and as soon as I saw that Robert was in difficulty, I got on the first train from New York and came to this city. Without stopping to go home, or take a mouthful of victuals, I had an interview with Robert, and arranged for party to return, offering myself to go with them, if they wanted me, game leg and all. You know the rest.

The evidence is plain and clear where I was all the time. Any of our courts, or any court in christendom, must take a truthful view of such a situation, after the witnesses I could produce and above all Genl. Beveridge [Gov. John L. Beveridge] of Ill. has been informed and is prepared. I rather think it would be troublesome for them to get any of the men from Illinois. I suppose the only thing the parties want in taking me to Missouri, would be to hold me on a civil suit for damages, well if they want to try that, take it to a United States Court and I am ready, I am doing nothing with regard to the newspapers, nor will I do anything in fact I am simply waiting.

I am very sorry indeed about any "blame" being attributed by me to you. I never did mean any thing of the kind, and I trust you will look at the matter the same as I do.

I am very glad to hear you are getting along so well, and that you got along so well at the Capital. I have no doubt they could give you a good deal of trouble, and I assure you, I can appreciate all the difficulties and dangers you have to undergo.

I have just received a letter from Robert. J—k [Jack Ladd?] has taken some money, is badly scared, and says, he will burrow himself, as that he won't be seen for a long time.

Yesterday I had to attend the funeral of Robert's infant, he being away and not likely to return for about a month.

I cannot understand what you mean by that "infamous spirit." I should like to hear it. Cannot you let me know? I rather think the St. Louis Police are enemies of ours as I have been informed how their chief has been talking, however he cannot hurt me or mine.

I shall send you the law books tonight the rulings in such a court as that will be strongly in our favor. Let me hear from you when in your power. Mail in Kansas City or to St. Louis, the inner envelope addressed to D. Robertson, etc., the outer one to Mrs. Hattie Smith 2809 S. Morgan St., St. Louis.

I hope all will go well with you.

Geo. McQueen

[Feb. 16]

Sam,

I have received yours while attending court. Macomb [Illinois] will suit me well enough, anywhere what-ever, select the place and write or telegraph me and you may calculate I shall be there I am anxious to know what is going on; am glad to know things are quieting down.

Geo. Mc.Q.

IN ANOTHER letter, E.J.A., probably Allan Pinkerton, using his old E. J. Allen alias of Civil War days, wrote to an apparent operative on the James case who was still in the field in late February, possibly Daniel Askew, though the name is unclear. While the references in the last part of the letter to "Sarah" are uncertain, it could be a code name for Jesse James.

Feb. 26/75

I have just received your long letter. I am glad to hear from you, and I hear that you are all well. The letter that you received from Perkins, McPherson & Co. is not from me, you may rely on that. I have told you the truth, rely on this. Perkins cannot be trusted, I know of him but he blabs too much, and can't be trusted, consequently he don't belong to me.

The pistol which they said they found, marked "P.G.G." is not mine and never was mine. We know too much, don't be afraid, that's another game to make you afraid, if they found any pistol, it was after they had left it.

In regard to Perkins, or letters for you or about the revolver, let it be known right of the letter should not have been sent to you, it would never have been done by me, let the thing right out, I would not keep any secrets, show them you are all perfectly right, there is no doubt whatever neither Perkins nor the pistol are mine.

There is one thing   I would impress upon you, that is that I will make no move whatever without consulting you in regard to it, if it was 1000 miles away, all of this is a game of theirs, simply starting the storm to see how it would effect you. I say to you positively, don't be afraid of any of my men or employees or myself posting you fully. I see too well around the kind of men we have to fight. Jack [Ladd?] is down in Pa. Bob has seen him he was a   weak kneed and appeared to think he has been doing a great deal of service and had an idea that his services could never be paid, but Bob told him, that was all nonsense, that what had been done was for the good of all, that no one was paying me that I was willing to give him a little money but now he should go to work and he earned to the conclusion that it was the best thing for him to do. I think he is a bad egg, but [he, we?] dare not move in this matter.

I have not heard from Sam since three days ago, when he wrote me, and told me he would see me, and tell me how matters stood. I will meet him somewhere on the river, he will either tell you or I will, after the pow-wow.

Cole Younger was in Louisiana near Delhi on January 25th or 26th and by the train he might have got in the neighborhood at the time you say. Cole is not at Yellville [Ark.] as you will observe still he might have stopped there on his way. Bye the Bye, you heard the story that Sarah, that near Independence [Mo.], Sarah attacked the sheriff and took a prisoner from him, and rode away. I doubt the story, but the papers say it was true. I am getting pretty well acquainted with the country in and around Independence and we might make a good thing of Sarah if she's there. I still cannot think Sarah was there on that night, but he may have been. I have no doubt Z. [Jesse's wife?] was taken in the wagon to Blue Hills where she was safe. The road from Independence to Kansas City, may be safe for Sarah and his gang, but would not be for me, unless I had a sufficient number of men, what you bet I'll try it when it becomes a favorable time to do it. Keep cool. depend upon it, there will be nothing done by me without you knowing of it before hand and if you hear any thing which they swear is mine don't believe them. Keep cool, let [me?] hear from you by St. Louis

Your Friend
E.J.A.

※◎※

THE FOLLOWING letter was found in the fall of 1999. It was unreadable on the microfilm copy used for the early transcriptions in 1991–92. The portion of the letter that is readable is significant, as it implies the collaboration of Illinois Gov. John L. Beveridge in aiding Pinkerton and his agents in avoiding extradition to Missouri for trial in Clay County on charges of killing Archie Peyton Samuel, the young half-brother of Frank and Jesse James. In this letter, Pinkerton seeks the governor's continued support following the killing of agent Daniel Askew and the ongoing probe by the Clay County Grand Jury. Pinkerton tended toward literary exaggeration in his description of the James cabin as a fortress and noting that the Youngers were warned by a bugler stationed near Monegaw Springs. He apparently wished to wave the bloody shirt with the governor, making it seem like the James and Younger gangs were part of a larger conspiracy involving highly organized former Confederates. Pinkerton's suggestion that the James boys didn't suspect the detectives' use of Daniel Askew's farm is ridiculous. Interestingly, the James brothers were just as fearful of the Missouri courts as Pinkerton.

Chicago April 16th 1875

To His Excellency John L. Beveridge
Governor State of Illinois
Springfield Illinois

My Dear Sir

I have just now had an interview with my Superintendent Mr.   and heard what he had to say.

I know the position you have taken is a good one, with regard to which I have nothing to urge & am satisfied you are acting for the best of motives but will ask the privilege   don't want to go to other Judges, for so far as they are concerned, I could get the sequesture of every Judge in Chicago including the United States Judges but in some way or other it would break out, that it was done some way or other upon an [operation?] in Missouri.

May I reiterate the arguments used by Mr.   when he saw you a few days ago.

The necessity for having someone in or around Kansas City to   associate with these bad men to get all we can from them and report every thing to me;

It is not for my sake alone that I ask the pardon of villains,   there are others beside me, citizens of Illinois, who are entitled to protection. At least it will be known by the James' that a band of men seven or eight in number, was at their house that night, with a view of arresting them, but where did they come from of course the answer is obvious, they must have come from Illinois.

After hearing all the circumstances with regard to this matter is it not right and proper that those citizens of Illinois, or any other State should receive protection!

Can anyone expect that a fair and impartial trial can be had in Clay Co. No Sir! never! at least not at the present time   question   to see the time when Clay will be a law abiding county as it ought to be.

Am afraid   [my boys?]   doesn't. Samuel Hardwick, my attorney—and whom I paid liberally for his services—is working about there now, afraid of his life and well he may be.

Daniel Askew was a peaceable and law abiding citizen of Kearney Clay Co. Mo. living about a quarter of a mile from the house of the James boys. I may say from their fortress, for it is one.

Daniel Askew when he learned to know me offered his door widely for the shelter of my men, who remained there nearly three months during last summer, until the frost became so severe that they were no longer able to stay out any longer. Mr. Askew's home was their habitation, and the James nor their friends knew any thing about it and I question much if they know it at the present day so well was the secret kept. Askew was a Union Soldier during the late civil war, a volunteer leaving his farm of about 220 acres and beautifully enlisted to take action for the Union, fought for his country then returned to his farm; but what of that, there also came those accursed rebels politely styled Confederates, viz. the

James, Youngers, Maj. Edwards, Genl. Shelby and a host of others, in whose track followed robbery rapine and murders, and thus it is to the present time.

The James, Youngers and their gang committed the Russellville Bank robbery, the Columbia, Ky. Bank robbery, killing the cashier, soon followed by robberies at other Banks at St. Genevieve Mo. Liberty Mo. and Corydon Ia. These followed in quick succession the Iowa train robbery the fair grounds Kansas City and the attack on the stage at Hot Springs Ark. The Wells Fargo robbery in Montana, executed by Jesse James and Arthur McCoy, and the robbery of a store at Montgomery Co. Mo., then came the Gads Hill train robbery where I determined to follow them. After Whicher had been decoyed by the James; he was taken tied on horseback 10 or 12 miles from their house and shot on the road near Independence Mo. with not a kind word said   followed the Youngers into St. Clair Co. Mo where their fortress is. Their home as they call it, Yes! it is a house of murderers, thieves, and villains, yea; of the deepest dye and Missouri seems full of these at the present time. My men followed [them?] to Monegau Springs and whilst on a piece of rising ground in the neighborhood of the springs they heard a bugle call, sounding clear and shrill on the air, again the same bugle cadence was produced, and on looking around no one could be seen, and yet again that shrill bugle sound pierced the air, but no one was in sight. My men followed the track from the   of old Juniper's house to where they saw two men   these men followed them and the rest is known. Jim Younger killed Daniels in one instant, Lull returned to fire on John Younger shot Lull which wound ultimately ended his days. The Youngers had fiends all around   but as far   .

Do you think Governor you could have stood more than this, no no! General you have blood in your veins which could boil over and revenge would boil in your bosom, Governor. I will come to see you, to ask you again to aid me. You have seen my men butchered and such crimes shall continue.

Askew fell on Monday last Hardwick still lives; he does not leave, he knows very well his life would pay the penalty and yet   stand by and witness such horrors.

Governor, I ask you again what will be the fate of the citizens of Illinois who went for the purpose of arresting the James' who will follow in their track and follow me; my men can be seen any day and what will be the   consequence.

I am not able to protect them and myself, these, I shall ask them   I find the right   my Governor   will not believe it, I ask you in the name of Justice and right but you have not to leave it on your own shoulders, for the time being; politicians will not talk about it but good and true men never. Yet it would not do to let the matter out at the present time. Governor, I implore you, I ask you, your blood must tingle in your veins—at the rehearsal of such atrocities in a manner unknown to one who has not been on a battlefield.

I hope you will give over to easy prayer for the pardon of Forester; I don't think there is any thing bad in the man and I have faith and confidence in him.

[I] really think Governor, you mean to do right by all men, and some may be more liable to receive benefits than others.

I know of nothing more to say. I beg of you to give them a favorable consideration and please write me a reply [as?] soon as possible.

Ever and Truly Yours
Allan Pinkerton

P.S. I have just been informed by the underground railway; attorney counsel who
was retained by me for legitimate purposes has been taken by the Grand Jury of
Clay Co. and forced to answer them   consequently he is obliged to leave the
State and thinks of seeking asylum in Illinois.

A.P.

THE SAME day that Pinkerton wrote Governor Beveridge, he wrote the following note,
hoping to contact the widow of Daniel Askew, Adeline, through an intermediary.

Personal

Chicago April 16/75

Dr. J. C. Bernard
Haynesville, Clinton Co. Mo.

Dear Sir;
    I have heard of the murder of Daniel Askew. He was an honest man; God help
his family. The blow must have been tremendous. I would like to speak to his wife,
but I cannot;
    A reign of terror prevails all through Clay County at the present time. Could I
ask a favor of you, to go and see Mrs. Askew, and say to her that I commiserate
with her in her deep and grave afflictions. Say to her that he did no more than
right, that will be shown when years have rolled away; when that   doom
approaches when every man's heart shall be opened. He was an enemy to the murderers, thieves and assassins. Say to Mrs. Askew that I desire to procure a tombstone to put on his grave [with the inscription?]

Sacred to the memory of
Daniel Askew
Born ——
Murdered on the 12th of April 1875
A martyr to law, truth and justice

My heart bleeds   the condition of affairs in Missouri.

Yours Truly
Allan Pinkerton

⁂

ALMOST A month later, the following letter was sent directly to Adeline Askew. It makes reference to other correspondence with Pinkerton that is not found in the pressbooks. Apparently only a portion of the correspondence related to the case was copied. In spite of his promises, Pinkerton appears to have backed away from the James case in mid-1875.

Chicago, May 11/75

My Dear Friend,

I have not seen you, but yet I cannot help calling you a friend, and one of those dear friends, whom, one can never have but once in life.

I have received your letter of the 7th inst. and was glad indeed to see it. Oh, how my heart bled, as I read in Dr. Bernard's letter tome, of the great thoughtfulness of a woman, and when you first heard the shot which told of your husband's death, you sent your daughters out of the room and destroyed the letters of mine, it showed careful forethought when it occurred to you that none other should know what your husband held in life, in death the proof died with him. I thank you and wish only that I was able to see you, and who knows but such an event may happen ere long.

I want to see you for as your husband has told me, you were one of the few women, that could live, and do just as you have done. I want to see you, to gaze into your eyes, because there must be feeling in them, and I know it would do to be true to you. Oh! how I've thought over Daniel Askew's murder, and hope the time will come when both you and I shall seek the same revenge, my own men have been slaughtered, as you know, both in Clay Co. and Monegau Springs; those men the Younger's and James' are red with my men's blood. I want to impress upon all the men in my company that they shall be avenged, and it must be so, we must take time however, we must be slow and sure, but as I said before, I hope I will be able to see, and thank you, and your friends, for all your many kindnesses to Rob. and Sam. and in fact there are other men, than those already mentioned.

I would like to ask you, as a favor, to bear up, for yourself and the sake of your children; great things have got to be done, and they shall be done until these men are utterly wiped out forever. What a sickening thought it is that Clay Co. or even Missouri, has to be populated with such murderers and thieves, but I ask you, My dear Mrs. Askew, have confidence and patience, and it will come all right in the end. I may assure you that I have not lost my confidence in H[ardwicke]. I have just heard from him, he tells me he has to be careful, but the dawn is beginning to appear and I have no doubt he speaks the truth, "behind the clouds the sun still shines". I think it will come out all right in the end, he has to be pretty quiet for a little time yet; bear a little time longer H[ardwicke] speaks to me of the noble traits that your husband had, he says as I do, that he was a martyr, and as a martyr, he shall bring forth strong men ere long—this must not be known to any one, keep it to yourself until things are safe.

Whenever there is anything I can do for you, let me know, and Oh! I say again do not give up to grief get over it and strive to live for Dan Askew's sake. Remember, you have got to live to see those murderers receive their penalty.

I have sent one of my volumes to Kearney. I have but no thought but that they will be looking into it, but it has nothing to tell, its simply a volume, and so I thought there was no harm in sending it.

I will get up the tombstone for Mr. Askew, if you could give me the date of birth, if not then I will say about such an age, murdered; if you could give me about what age when he died, then I could get on with all the rest. I know it, it is stereotyped [in?] my mind, and never can be effaced as long as reason remains.

Thank Dr. Bernard in my name for what he has done for you, and tell him I never can forget his kindness. When you can, write to me and tell me all you hear, and whenever there is anything you might want, fail not to write me and if it is in the power of man, you shall have it.

I shall send the tombstone as soon as it is got out, it will probably take one month to get ready. I know what will suit a man, who died a martyr. I shall send it as freight addressed to you. You may say you don't know who it came from, as we have never met, have it put in the graveyard, and if it be ever safe for me to come to Kearney, I shall go there and mix my tears with the ground in which your martyred husband lies.

> Ever Truly, Your Friend
> Allan Pinkerton

THE FOLLOWING letter was sent to Gov. C. H. Hardin of Missouri by Daniel Geary of Kansas City. It is in the governor's papers at the Missouri State Archives in Jefferson City and offers yet another viewpoint on the situation in Clay County.

> Kansas City, Mo.
> April 17th 1875.

To His Excellency
Gov. C. H. Hardin
Jefferson City, Mo:

Sir:

You have undoubtedly heard of the recent atrocious murder of Mr. Askew near the residence or former home of the notorious "James Boys" in Clay Co. Mo, a crime which if left unavenged by punishment of the guilty parties will forever remain a stigma on the people of that county. In connection with this matter I wish to say that my brother-in-law resides about two miles from the James place, is a widower with a large and extensive family, has an excellent farm, but no money, and has been repeatedly warned by these desperadoes or their friends to leave the county. He has paid no attention to these threats but since the attack on the house of the mother of these boys, all northern men especially, as well as those who have discountenanced or denounced the acts of these bandits will live in constant fear of assassination and undoubtedly many will meet that fate sooner or later, as these outlaws will believe that the parties who attacked the Samuels house were assisted by these law abiding people. Since that Mr. Brown (my brother-in-law) has recd. notice from one person who is supposed to posses absolute knowledge of the intentions of the marauders, and enjoys their confidence, and also from a citizen of Liberty advising him to leave the county at once or he would undoubtedly be killed. Also, on the night that Askew was killed he has every reason to believe, judging from the location and number of horse tracks and general appearance of his place that they had intended to kill him and his youngest son that night but failed of an opportunity; and now fears a more successful effort in the near future. He is a strictly law abiding man, takes no part in politics (I cannot say to which party he belongs, for that matter, I suppose it is immaterial, as freedom in such matters is the privilege of every man) but may have said things not calculated to flatter the James. The result of this condition of things is to cause himself and family great distress of mind, as he cannot sell his farm nor procure a livelihood for his family elsewhere. I presume there are other families similarly situated but they say nothing except to those in whose discretion they have the utmost confidence. Mr. Brown is of the opinion that if about five persons in that vicinity were driven out or removed from the county the James would have no place of resort, to secrete themselves, nor procure intelligence such as they wish. These persons possess their confidence, sympathize with them and he thinks actively assist and encourage their crimes. It is absolutely cruel to think that good honest industrious people are not permitted [to] pursue their avocations, but are to be slaughtered or driven from their homes into want and destitution by three or four men, and the Great State of Missouri cannot guarantee them protection. I have never heard of a parallel case in times of profound peace, and yet it is allowed to continue from year to year. I do not know that I can suggest a practicable remedy nor do I believe or charge that the authorities, whose duty it is to suppress lawlessness have been willfully remiss in their duty; but the fact is nolonous that murder and horse thievery is the normal condition of the county, & that many of the citizens sympathize with the criminals is well understood otherwise the perpetrators would be arrested and punished. It may be that the James are not guilty of all the crimes attributed to them, but they are guilty of some of these acts or they would [not] refuse to surrender to proper civil authority when guaranteed protection and a fair and impartial trial. If I might be permitted the boldness of a suggestion, Your Excellency, it could be this: issue a proclamation commanding them to surrender themselves to some proven civil authority, to be designated by Your Excellency, within a specified time, guaranteeing them protection & a fair and impartial trial for the crimes charged against them, and in case they fail or refuse to surrender as required, proclaim them outlaws and set a price on their heads. This method, it strikes me, will either cause them to surrender and prove their innocence or result in their speedy capture.

Pardon my boldness in thus addressing you but my feelings are entested in behalf of my friends whom I cannot believe would be sacrificed to appease the wrath of these bandits. The Hon G C Bingham [see Appendix D] is personally acquainted with the writer and will undoubtedly endorse my statements as their honest intentions and general purport. The state *must do something* to protect the innocent and law abiding from highway Robbers and murderers.

       Respectfully
       your obt Sevt
       Daniel Geary

Appendix D

The Report of Adj. Gen. George Caleb Bingham of Missouri Regarding the Raid on the James-Samuel Farm

Dear Sir; In pursuance of instructions received from you [Gov. Charles H. Hardin] on Friday last, I proceeded without delay to Clay county, to ascertain as far as possible the facts relating to the recent outrages perpetrated in said county upon the family of Mr. Samuel, the step-father of the notorious James brothers, and to co-operate with the authorities there in any proper effort to bring the perpetrators to justice.

Having no power to compel witnesses to testify under oath, I have been able to obtain but little information beyond what has already been given to the public through the press.

Mr. Samuel resides about 2½ miles east of Kearney, a small town 9 miles north of Liberty, and located on a branch of the Hannibal & St. Jo. Railroad, running from Kansas City to Cameron. On the night of Jan. 26th, between 12 and 2 o'clock, the residence of Mr. Samuel was approached by a party of men, the precise number thereof not known. A portion of these men stationed themselves behind an ice-house on the east side and in front of the dwelling, about fifty or sixty yards therefrom. Another portion went in the rear of the building, the same being in the form of the letter L, containing two rooms; the one farthest from the main building serving for a kitchen and sleeping room for negro servants. The entire building was a weather-boarded log structure, somewhat dilapidated by time. The party which approached the rear and west portion of the building set fire to the weather-boarding of the kitchen in three or four different places, and threw into the window thereof a hand grenade.

This instrument was composed of cast and wrought or malleable iron, strongly secured together and covered with a wrapping saturated with turpentine or oil. As it passed through the window and as also it lay on the floor it made a very brilliant light alarming the family who supposed the kitchen to be on fire and rushed in to extinguish the flames. Mr. Samuel seeing the burning instrument on the floor mistook it for a turpentine ball and attempted to kick it into the fireplace. Failing in this on account of its weight he seized a poker or a pair of iron tongs by means of which he succeeded in getting it into the fire-place. It immediately exploded with a report which was heard a distance of two or three miles. The part composed of cast iron broke into fragments and flew out with great force. One of the fragments shattered the right arm below the elbow of Mrs. Samuel, the mother of the James brothers, to an extent that made amputation necessary. Another entered the body of her little son Archy, wounding him mortally and causing his death in about four hours.

Mr. Samuel succeeded in putting out the fire in the weather-boarding, and aroused the surrounding neighbors with the cry of murder, which he continued to repeat until he was exhausted. Four pistol reports were heard by neighbors as they came toward the dwelling, but when they reached it the parties perpetrating the outrage had disappeared.

Who are the parties? This is a question which yet finds no answer, except in circumstances which do not seem sufficient for a complete solution of the mystery. On Monday, January 25, about half-past seven o'clock in the evening, an engine with only a caboose attached came down the road from the north and stopped in the woods about two miles north of Kearney. Several unknown men got off the caboose, which then continued south in the direction of Kansas City. About two or three o'clock in the morning, Tuesday, the same or similar engine and caboose came from the direction of Kansas City and stopped a considerable time at the place where the unknown men had been left after dark on the previous evening. The tracks of persons who were stationed behind the house and those who set fire to and threw the grenade into the kitchen, and which were found on the path of their retreat, were made of boots of a superior quality, quite different from those usually worn by farmers and farm hands in the surrounding country. In following the trail of the parties on their retreat, a pistol was found which is now in my possession. The pistol has marks upon it which would scarcely be seen unless sought for. And which, I have been credibly informed, are identically such as are known to be on the pistol of a well known band of detectives.

The bullet holes found in the fence on the east side of the dwelling, of which frequent mention has been made, do not indicate a conflict. If discharged from the direction of the ice-house, the Samuel's dwelling would have been out of their range, and it cannot be supposed that the James brothers, had they really been at home, would have left the dwelling to expose themselves openly to a superior force under cover. There are seven of these holes, and all within a space of eighteen inches or two feet. The neighbors who came to the house immediately after the alarm was given, all concur in the statement that but five reports were heard, one very loud and the other four subsequent thereto as such might be caused by discharges from pistols. Their impression is that this firing was for the purpose of keeping them at a distance until the assailants could make good their retreat. These bullet holes may be result of some previous target shooting with pistols.

A little blood was found in several places in the snow in the path of the assailants as they retreated from the dwelling, but not more than might be caused by an accidental scratch on the hand or bleeding at the nose. The parties who perpetrated the outrage doubtless approached the house on the belief that the James brothers were there, and set fire to it and threw in the grenade for the purpose of forcing them out and then shooting or capturing them; and on discovering that they had murdered an innocent lad and mutilated his mother, they deemed it prudent to retire and leave as little evidence by which they could be traced and identified as possible.

I could not learn from any reliable source that either of the James brothers had been in the area since last April. If they were in the house at the time they could only have escaped through the cowardice of those attempting their capture. I had a correspondence at some length with Mrs. Samuel, their mother. She has had the advantages of an early education, and seems to be endowed with a vigorous intellect and masculine will; but she could give no information bearing upon the object of my visit.

I am satisfied that nothing short of the inquisitorial power of a grand jury is likely to elicit such evidence as will lead to the identification of the parties engaged in a transaction the nature of which naturally permits them to resort to every possible method of concealment.

In the foregoing statement I have omitted to mention the names of citizens from whom I have obtained such information as it contains, believing it best for the ends of justice that they not now be given to the public. I am convinced that the people of Clay County would feel greatly relieved if the James brothers could be captured and brought to justice. Their notoriety as desperadoes and the impunity which has accompanied their reckless doings are regarded as a most serious injury both to the character and material interests of their county, charged as it has been with affording them cover and protection.

Respectfully, G. C. Bingham, Adjt. General.

Appendix E

The Amnesty Bill of 1875

THE AMNESTY BILL was introduced in the Missouri legislature on March 17, 1875, by Rep. Jefferson Jones of Calloway County. Apparently the wording was done with the assistance of editor John Newman Edwards. The measure failed to pass.

Whereas, by the 4th section of the 11th article of the Constitution of Missouri, all persons in the military service of the United States or who acted under the authority thereof in this state, are relieved from all civil liability and all criminal punishment for all acts done by them since the 1st day of January, A.D. 1861; and

Whereas, by the 12th section of the said 11th article of said Constitution provision is made by which, under certain circumstances, may be seized, transported to, indicted, tried and punished in distant counties, any Confederate under ban of despotic displeasure, thereby contravening the Constitution of the United States and every principle of enlightened humanity; and

Whereas, Such discrimination evinces a want of manly generosity and statesmanship on the part of the party imposing, and of courage and manhood on the part of the party submitting tamely thereto; and

Whereas, Under the outlawry pronounced against Jesse W. James, Frank James, Coleman Younger, James Younger and others, who gallantly periled their lives and their all in defense of their principles, they are of necessity made desperate, driven as they are from their fields of honest industry, from their friends, their families, their homes and their country, they can know no law but the law of self-preservation, nor can have no respect for and feel no allegiance to a government which forces them to the very acts it professes to deprecate, and then offers a bounty for their apprehension, and arms foreign mercenaries with the power to capture and kill them; and

Whereas, Believing these men too brave to be mean, too generous to be revengeful, too gallant and honorable to betray a friend or break a promise; and believing further that most, if not all the offenses with which they have been charged have been committed by others, and perhaps by those pretending to hunt them, or by their confederates; that their names are and have been used to divert suspicion from and thereby relieve the actual perpetrators; that the return of these men to their homes and friends would have the effect of greatly lessening crime in our state by turning public attention to the real criminals, and that common jus- tice, sound policy and true statesmanship alike demanded that amnesty should be extended to all alike of both parties for all acts done or charged to have been done during the war; therefore, be it

Resolved by the House of Representatives, the Senate concurring therein, that the Governor of the state be, and he is thereby requested to issue his proclamation notifying the said Jesse W. James, Frank James, Coleman Younger, and James Younger and others, that a full and complete amnesty and pardon will be granted them for all acts charged or committed by them during the late civil war, and inviting them peacefully to return to their respective homes in this state and there quietly to remain, submitting themselves to such proceedings as may be instituted against them by the courts for all offenses charged to have been committed since said war, promis- ing and guaranteeing to each of them full protection and a fair trial therein, and that full protection shall be given them from the time of their entrance into the state and his notice thereof under said proclamation and invitation.

Appendix F

Frank James's Stage Speeches

BELOW ARE the texts of two short speeches given by Frank James while touring with a summer stock company in 1904 or possibly earlier. Frank was criticized in the press and from the pulpit for going onstage and using his reputation as an outlaw to draw crowds to several turn-of-the-century melodramas. The original copies of these speeches are in the collection of Lee Pollock, of Princeton, Illinois, who graciously allowed me to reprint them here.

Ladies and Gentlemen:—A man's interests and surroundings are the key to his actions: and as is the man so is the nation.

Had General Washington been born on British soil, he might have thought it right to tax the American Colonies. But born a Virginian, he resisted that claim of Britain's, and dedicated his perseverance, bravery, and military Genius to the cause he thought just—because he thought he was an American and not an Englishman. It is safe to say that had General Grant been born in Virginia as was General Lee, of slave-holding people, who saw in the institution of slavery a benefit and safety to black people that they would not have possessed as freedmen, he would have done as Lee—carefully considered the situation, decided what was his duty, no matter what it would cost him in Military Rank and money—then linked his fortunes with his native state. And had General Lee been born in Ohio as was General Grant, where slavery was not known except as an institution of other states, he would have been the victor of Appomattox, who generously refused to accept his antagonist's sword, and gave to the naked and famished soldiers of the conquered army their horses to plow their bare and fenceless fields.

No stronger and purer motives actuated the great men of those great wars than the humblest soldier in the ranks, who at his officer's command walked into the cannon's mouth to die, or perhaps to live while comrades fell. But living or dead to remain unknown, though each in his way helped to gain the victory that brought renown to his commander.

It is easy to say a man should do this, or should have done that, but it is usually much easier to say wise things than to do them. With very few exceptions we all feel alike and do alike in moments of supreme trial; and before passing judgment upon another we should try to put ourselves in that one's place, and see the matter from his point of view.

Wrong begets wrong, though the teachings of the good have been against revenge ever since the coming of the Great Teacher. But a man does not think of the teachings of his boyhood when his blood is hot with the impetuosity of youth and the thought of wrong done him and the innocent of his kin. He is then like the lion whose lair has been invaded, his mate killed and his cubs captured or lying dead beside their dam. He goes out with hate in his heart to rob and ruin those who robbed and ruined him. We all go down to the level of the blood-seeking brute when wrong rankles our hearts, recking not the consequences, seeking only the sweetness of revenge. But this is not saying this course is right, and should be defended. I am only saying how we are; and how much that seems without excuse or warrant in a man's life is often brought about.

But we are not now in an age of war and devastation, but of peace and amity. Where once shrieked the cannon ball and shrapnel and whistled the minie, we hear the shriek and whistle of the engine—the agent of peace and prosperity. The men that once faced each other with gun and sword in hand, now meet with flowers in those same hands to lay upon the graves of comrades and foes alike. We are one country and one people now. The few differences that agitate us are not strong enough to divide us; and there is none who would have it otherwise.

Put yourself in his place. "Gently hear and kindly judge."

⚜

BELOW IS a shorter speech that Frank apparently used as an alternate to the monologue above.

An up country lawyer friend told me of a client he and his partner had, who greatly annoyed them with his too frequent visits to talk over his case; so much so that he became a nuisance. One day he came in, and to freeze him out the lawyers were very busy, and wrote away at their desks, paying no attention to him. After an hour or two, he coughed, and hummed a tune, to attract attention, to no avail. Finally, in utter despair, he got on his feet and said: "boys, when a man wants to what['s] he to say"? This is my fix at this moment. There is something I want to say, but what and how to say it is the rub. I am a believer in the Bible, but all of its truisms are not applicable under all circumstances. It tells us that from the abundance of the heart the mouth speaketh. Perhaps that was said with a condition, provided there is a head to a man to help form the words.

If I had adequate to the fullness of my heart this evening you would hear some eloquent utterances. But there is no gift of oratory always equal to the task of fully expressing emotions of sorrow and joy, and especially the sense of gratitude. These may be felt, and sometimes may be acted, but cannot be fully spoken.

If there has been one aspiration in the later years of my eventful life more irrepressible than another, it has been to so acquit myself in citizenship and fidelity to trust, however humble the calling or hard the conditions, that employers and friends might say of me: he has kept faith and merited public confidence. It is said that every man has his motto. Mine is the sentiment of the great actor and portrayer of the human heart—paraphrased:

> Not unto mortals is it given to command success;
> But I'll do more Sempronius, I'll deserve it.

This occasion, the presence of faces where the glad smile of friendship rests to cheer me, put new stars of hope in my sky. This will be one bright oasis in the weary march of life to be gratefully remembered; and it will be an inspiration to look hopefully to the future. This night I lift a single goblet, filled with the sparkling wine of life. To my friends I drink in love, to my enemies, if any, I drink forgetfulness.

⚜

THERE WAS also a third variant:

Ladies and Gentlemen,—

I do not doubt that some in this audience think I am better suited for a tragedy than a tragedian. I trust, however, that I may be indulged to say, that this feeling does not illustrate the fact that there is a vast difference between reputation and character.

While my unenviable reputation may account for my presence here to-night, much of it has as little foundation in truth as there is in me the quality of a good actor.

If there is one ambition in my heart, paramount to the desire to earn a competency for my wife and child, it is with the yearning to live long enough to convince the world that I am not as bad as I have been painted; for beneath the ugly caricatures unjustly given of me by the public press., I beg to assure you that there beats a heart of truth, kindness, love for my fellow man, and loyalty to society.

In only one trial in which I was ever brought before a tribunal of Justice, I was fairly and honorably acquitted. And as the law of the land, which all good citizens respect, declare every man to be innocent until proven, under the judicial process, to be guilty, may I not invoke the charitable consideration of all right-minded men and women in my struggle for an honest living, and for an honorable fame? I live in unbounded faith of the sense of fair play of the American people.

> "I dare do all that may become a man;
> Who does do more is none."

Appendix G

A Jesse James Filmography, 1908—95

SINCE 1908 the James story has been a Hollywood staple. Below is a listing of all known American films in which Jesse James appears as a character. They range from drama and adventure to comedy and even horror. There reportedly are some foreign-made Westerns that portray Jesse James, but I have not yet accessed this information. Film seems to have taken up where the dime novels left off, and the portrayal of Jesse James in the cinema is usually wildly inaccurate, from Roy Rogers's singing Jesse to Robert Duvall's psychotic Jesse. Perhaps the best portrayal of Frank James was by Henry Fonda, and one can only wonder after viewing *Once Upon a Time in the West* and his performance in *The Return of Frank James* what he could have done with a good script. Probably the most historically accurate film overall is *The Last Days of Frank and Jesse James*, but even this made-for-television opus has numerous shortcomings. Several of the early films have been lost. The earliest James picture for which prints are known to exist is *Jesse James Under the Black Flag*, a copy of which turned up in a barn and was restored in the 1980s. The late Humphrey Bogart is said to have dismissed the offer of a part in *The Bad Men of Missouri* with the statement, "Are you kidding?" The same could be said of most of these films.

1908   *The James Boys of Missouri* (Essenay Film Co., silent)

1911   *Jesse James*

1921   *Jesse James Under the Black Flag* (starring Jesse Edwards James as his father)

1922   *Jesse James as the Outlaw* (starring Jesse Edwards James as his father)

1927   *Jesse James* (starring Fred Thomson)

1939   *Days of Jesse James* (starring Don "Red" Barry as Jesse James, Michael Worth as Frank James, Roy Rogers as himself, and George "Gabby" Hayes as Gabby Whittaker)

1939   *Jesse James* (starring Tyrone Power as Jesse and Henry Fonda as Frank)

1940   *The Return of Frank James* (starring Henry Fonda as Frank James)

1941   *Jesse James at Bay* (starring Roy Rogers as Jesse James, "Gabby" Hayes, and Gale Storm)

        The Bad Men of Missouri (starring Alan Baxter as Jesse James)

1942   *The Remarkable Andrew* (starring Rod Cameron as Jesse James)

1946   *Badman's Territory* (starring Lawrence Tierney as Jesse James and Tom Tyler as Frank James)

1947   *Jesse James Rides Again* (starring Clayton Moore [the Lone Ranger] as Jesse James)

1948   *Adventures of Frank and Jesse James* (starring Clayton Moore)

1949   *I Shot Jesse James* (starring Reed Hadley as Jesse James and John Ireland as Bob Ford)

        The Fighting Man of the Plains (starring Dale Robertson as Jesse James)

1950   *The James Brothers of Missouri* (starring Keith Richards as Jesse James and Robert Bice as Frank James)

        Kansas Raiders (starring Audie Murphy as Jesse James and Richard Long as Frank James, with Tony Curtis in an early role as "Kit" Dalton)

1951   *The Great Missouri Raid* (starring McDonald Carey as Jesse and Wendell Corey as Frank James)

        The Best of the Badmen (starring Lawrence Tierney as Jesse and Tom Tyler as Frank James)

1953   *The Woman They Almost Lynched* (starring Ben Cooper as Jesse James and James Brown as Frank James)

        The Great Jesse James Raid (starring Willard Parker as Jesse James)

1954   *Jesse James vs. the Daltons* (starring Brett King as Jesse James)

        Jesse James' Women (starring Don "Red" Barry as Jesse James and Jack Buetel as Frank James)

1957   *The True Story of Jesse James* (starring Robert Wagner as Jesse James, Jeffrey Hunter as Frank James, Agnes Moorehead as Mrs. Samuel, and Hope Lange as Zee James)

        Hell's Crossroads (starring Henry Brandon as Jesse James and Douglas Kennedy as Frank James)

1959   *Alias Jesse James* (starring Wendell Corey as Jesse James, Jim Davis as Frank James, Bob Hope, Gary Cooper, Bing Crosby, James Arness, Gene Autry, Roy Rogers, Fess Parker, Ward Bond, et al.)

1960   *Young Jesse James* (starring Ray Stricklyn as Jesse James and Robert Dix as Frank James)

1965   *The Outlaws Is Coming* (starring Wayne Mack as Jesse James and the
        Three Stooges)

1966   *Jesse James Meets Frankenstein's Daughter* (starring John Lupton as Jesse
        James)

1969   *A Time for Dying* (starring Audie Murphey as Jesse James)

1972   *The Great Northfield Minnesota Raid* (starring Robert Duvall as Jesse
        James, John Pearce as Frank James, Elisha Cook Jr. as Bunker, and R. G.
        Armstrong as Clell Miller)

1980   *The Long Riders* (starring James Keach as Jesse James and Stacy Keach as
        Frank James)

1986   *The Last Days of Frank and Jesse James* (starring Kris Kristofferson as Jesse
        James and Johnny Cash as Frank James)

1995   *Frank and Jesse* (starring Rob Lowe as Jesse and Tom Paxton as Frank
        James)

Appendix H

Press Conference Regarding the 1995 Exhumation and Forensic Study of Jesse James

THIS IS an abridged version of the transcript of a press conference given by Prof. James Starrs at the Forty-eighth Annual Meeting of the American Academy of Forensic Sciences at the Opryland Hotel and Convention Center in Nashville, Tennessee, on February 23, 1996.

PROFESSOR STARRS: I'd like to make a comment first. Obviously you have seen the best of the best in the presentations here today in the young scientists in the forensic science community. I don't take credit for choosing well in choosing the members of this team. They are standouts that are such standouts that it's so easy to find them and it was immensely easy to convince them. In fact, very little convincing was required. So my hat's off, my hair's off, everything is off to all of you for the assistance you gave me and I think they all deserve a strong round of applause.

Now, the question is where we are at with respect to all the accumulation of the aggregate of all of the individual items provided by the scientists from each individual discipline. I think the chart in the largest dimensions speaks for itself, but I would like to make one additional observation.

Back in 1882 the *Saint Joseph Gazette* came out with a headline, special edition, in connection with the death of a person then thought to be Jesse James at Saint Joseph. The title of that article which has become well known among the Jesse James historians and others was titled "Jesse By Jehovah." There is some ambiguity with respect to that. I would think that the summary of the findings we have today is "Jesse By Science" and there may be some ambiguity in that as well, by which I mean the scientific process, as I said early on, is rarely, if ever, a process which brings us to a conclusion with apodictic certainty. We would all like to have that. We would all like to know what it means but—either way, that kind of absolute certainty, its indescribable certainty, is something that, indeed, most seasoned scientists even search for,

371

realizing that it is such a phantom quest. But so, we do not and cannot say that we have that in this case.

I'm not going to utilize in any of the other fields other than the field of molecular biology that you have heard descriptions of population statistics or any other kinds of statistics to simply say as the chart points out, that everything we have that indicates a direct relationship to Jesse James indicates a consistency with everything we analyzed having come from Jesse James. And that's how far we can go and it's as far as I am willing to go. There is nothing to exclude and everything to include.

Questions now. And any member of the team, by the way, is welcome to join in in the answering process obviously. I certainly do not feel comfortable doing the work myself, nor do I feel able to do so, nor do I feel able or comfortable to respond to any questions that there may be from members of the media. Are there any members of the media who dare to ask a question in public? They have been asking so many questions out of the limelights. It's your turn to be in the limelight. There's one. Gary Chilcote from the Saint Joseph Museum.

GARY CHILCOTE: The *Saint Joseph News Press*.

STARRS: The *Saint Joseph News Press*.

CHILCOTE: Right. So, in other words, are you saying this is Jesse James or maybe Jesse James?

STARRS: The term "maybe" is not a term I prefer to use. I don't want to change and have other terms thrown in. I am saying that everything that we have is consistent with the remains being those of Jesse James and I'm going to be locked in to the term " consistent with."

BOB WORLEY: Bob Worley, with KNPC in Kansas City. . . . What effect do you expect this to have on the claims of the various relatives to be his descendants?

STARRS: My experience in the field of historical investigations is that there are some people who are forever locked into their point of view regardless of what the findings may be. And I remember, for example, that Dr. Bill Maples in his work on the disappearance of Anastasia, one of the Romanoffs, and the reappearance of Anna Anderson in Virginia and the work that—the cooperative work of Dr. Stoneking in that matter proving again even beyond the limits that we have here, because they had other items to work with and there is a large— there are a large contingent of persons, even today, of scholarly credentials, who are of the strongly held view, permanent view, that they were wrong and that Anastasia was in fact Anna Anderson, and, of course, science told them quite the contrary. And I have seen this time and time again in historical investigations so that there are some mountains that not even Mohammad could move. And certainly in this respect, we're doing as much as we can do with the current technology.

GENE DENFREY: Gene Denfrey from the *Kearney Courier*. Professor, can you address the bullet hole in the wall at Saint Joseph as to its authenticity?

STARRS: Well, I think that the bullet hole in the wall in Saint Joseph's, as is described in the bulletin—the billboard as you enter Saint Joseph's, "Come See. Is it legendary now or is the bullet hole in the wall in the home." It goes back to the question of whether or not there was or was not an exit wound. I am not going to come forward and say exactly and precisely with any degree of even lesser than apodictive certainty that there was no exit wound. We are dealing with—we didn't have the full skeletal remains from the skull and— but I'd prefer to have Dr. Finnegan address that question if he wishes to do so. Mike, would you like to—

DR. FINNEGAN: Sure. One of the—in order to answer that question, one of the things in the forensic situation is that in order to come up with fairly concrete statements, we need all the information. While we successfully reconstructed the cranium and the larger parts of the skull, we're still missing much of the pieces of the face. If, in fact, our assessment of the trajectory of the projectile, based on the entrance wound, we suggest that the exit wound should have been up in the area of the boss of the frontal bone or the area we call the terrion. Those areas were completely reconstructed and there was no exit wound in that area. Having said that, in the area in the orbit of the eye, none of the pallet or plate bones in the eye orbit were present. And, in fact, we could be wrong on the trajectory and the trajectory might have exited lower in an area where in fact we could not adequately reconstruct it. So we can't be positive that there wasn't an exit wound, but certainly there was not an exit wound based on where the exit wound should have been once we analyzed the entrance wound. . . .

JOHN POPATONE: Dr. Starrs, John Popatone from WGAF-TV in Kansas City. I know you have made it clear that you can't say with absolute certainty that this is—your findings have proven that this is Jesse James, but I was wondering if I could pin you down a little more on what consistent means. For example, if we use legal standards today, if you were called into court with this evidence, could you say beyond a reasonable doubt that this is Jesse James or that the preponderance of evidence indicates that this is Jesse James?

STARRS: Well, the terminology of "consistent with" is quite consistently used in legal proceedings and is considered to be quite acceptable. It was the terminology that was used in connection with the identification of the firearms and the tracing those to Sacco and Venzetti in that famed case. That may not be a good case to cite of an example of its proper use, but nevertheless it has long roots in the legal field and it is eminently acceptable from other scientists in the legal field. There are a variety of other formulations such as in the case of forensic pathologists that come into court and describe the reasonable medical certainty they have, which is equivalent, in my view and in the legal view, to the statement of consistency between what is known and what was found. So that, in short, there are people on death row and many who have been executed based, in part, on "consistent with" statements and quite properly so. . . .

KELLY DORBIS: Kelly Dorbis, *Kansas City Star*. So, are you satisfied to a reasonable scientific certainty that the remains are Jesse James' or are you leaving the door open a crack?

STARRS: You're changing the terminology again from "consistent with," but I'll go out on the deep end—I have never done that before—and say I feel a reasonable degree of scientific certainty that we have the remains of Jesse James. [Applause] And now, I'll dare to plunge even deeper into this bottomless pit by saying Mike, do you agree?

DR. FINNEGAN: Professor, in part, I came here to drink your Guinness, but not to buy it for you. However I concur in that.

CARRAHER: In trying to explain the predicament that some of you find yourselves in, I am reminded about when we went to medical school years ago, there were a few gray hairs on my head here, that we talked about Koch's postulates. You take tubercle bacillus, grow it out in a jar, you inject it into the guinea pig, you prove unequivocally that you have satisfied Koch's postulates. This is the disease, tuberculosis. The American public has a difficult time understanding how the professional comes to the conclusion. And, fortunately, the legal system has helped us out because they say to a reasonable degree of medical certainty that this is the diagnosis. So, I think that even though this is painful to the American public, I think that the terminology the professor has used is the proper scientific terminology. . . .

JERRY HOPKINS: Jerry Hopkins with GLAV-TV. Given that there are some people in the audience who claim to be relatives, is it possible that mitochondrial DNA can be transmitted through females who are cousins? Would it hold true for the nuclear family?

STARRS: Thank you for taking the heat or the light off me. Dr. Stoneking, why don't you handle that? Maybe we can repeat the question.

HOPKINS: Would mitochondrial DNA hold true, would there be a pattern that would hold true for cousins as long as there was a female linkage?

DR. STONEKING: Yes, what I tried to make clear with the mitochondrial DNA evidence shows is that the skeletal remains that were exhumed from Mount Olivet Cemetery cannot be excluded as being those of a maternal relative of the individuals that are known to be the maternal relatives of Susan James. So that leaves, still leaves the possibility open that there would be some other individual besides Jesse James and still be a maternal relative.

HOPKINS: Were there any other relatives who could have been tested through the maternal lineage?

DR. STONEKING: I am not familiar enough with the lineage to know whether that's the case or not.

STARRS: Other questions? Gene Gentry.

GENE GENTRY: Would it be possible then for Jesse James, the Fords, or some of these other relatives, if it's a direct descendant from the female side to get, you know, some mitochondrial DNA test done on their blood?

STARRS: I take it that you're asking whether or not Dr. Stoneking is available and willing to do tests, continuing tests, on individuals who are willing to submit blood samples to him for the purposes of having him determine whether they would be included or excluded. I'm not going to impose that burden on him, but if he wants to take it on himself, it's entirely up to him.

DR. STONEKING: We certainly do this sort of analysis as a service for a fee, but certainly we would want to consult with the individual beforehand and make sure their mitochondrial DNA analysis would be informative and address the questions they are interested in. . . .

STARRS: Kelly Garbis, *Kansas City Star*.

KELLY GARBIS: Now, I'm a little confused. We talked about a lot of different bullets and calibers and guns. What was the caliber that killed him?

STARRS: What was the caliber that killed Jesse James?

GARBIS: And were there two or three bullets taken from the grave?

STARRS: John, do you want to come up here so everybody can hear the answer?

JOHN CAYTON: Well, the firearms evidence that we have, we recovered a bullet from the farm grave site in 1978 that was a .38 caliber with five line groove to the right. Projectile that was recovered in the Mount Olivet Cemetery in the exhumation was a .36 caliber round ball with a mark on the front of it that's consistent with a cap and ball revolver similar to the Colt 1851 Navy model. It has a compression ring around the front that indicates that it was loaded in that type of firearm. Other than those two projectiles and the beveling around the wound in the skull, we don't have any other firearms information as far as physical evidence. We have a .38 caliber hollow-based bullet and a .36 caliber round ball.

GARBIS: Do you think the .36, though, was the one that went into the skull? Was that the one that went into the skull?

CAYTON: No, I think—well, the .36 was found in the exhumation, I think they said in the area of where the ribs were, but they were of the right thorax area. Dr. Finnegan has a comment to make on this as well.

DR. FINNEGAN: If you remember in our talk, we suggested that the hole is about the
size of one which could have been produced by a .45 caliber. The wound itself
is right below my finger [points to plaster cast of the skull]. Obviously you can't
see the characteristics of the wound from the distance that you sit, but the
reason why I say it could be a .45 caliber are for the following reasons: We're
not exactly sure if a projectile goes through something before it hits the skull, it
may have flattened a little bit, it becomes larger. And so, it creates the hole
that we analyzed and is suggestive of a .45 caliber. It could in fact have been a
much smaller caliber. We're concerned that, with projectiles, they could hit
something and part of the projectile could be shaved away so that only a fragment of the original fire projectile goes into the skull or makes the wound, in
which case the hole might be very much smaller or irregular in some manner.
So, our estimate of a .45 caliber is just that, it's an estimate. We can't tell from
the wound what the caliber was. However, if size, shape to the extent that we
can look at it is suggestive of a .45 caliber.

⁂

SEE NOTE 11 for chapter 14 for excerpts from the accounts of the 1882 autopsy as
they were unofficially reported in the *Kansas City Daily Journal* and *Saint Louis
Globe-Democrat*.

⁂

ON MAY 20, 2000, amid a frenzied atmosphere, a team of forensic scientists from
South Texas State University struggled to exhume the remains of J. Frank Dalton
from Granbury Cemetery in Granbury, Texas. The event, spearheaded by Oklahoma used-car salesman Bud Hardcastle, had ample media buildup, and there was
great excitement when a burial vault was uncovered.

Professor James Starrs, back in Washington, D.C., was "exceedingly skeptical"
of the whole business, and reiterated that he felt the real Jesse James had been
unearthed in 1995. Nevertheless, he invited the Texas scientists to reevaluate his
team's tests and conclusions. "Notable people die like everyone else, but the myths
surrounding many of their deaths live on to confound both logic and science,"
Starrs commented in a letter to the *Washington Times*.

Several weeks later, it was announced with great chagrin that the wrong grave
had been opened. The error was attributed to the fact that in 1951 temporary
markers had been stolen and replace incorrectly. The remains unearthed in May
2000 were those of a one-armed man; Dalton had never lost an arm. Undeterred,
Hardcastle vowed to obtain another exhumation order.

Notes

CHAPTER 1: GADS HILL

1. *Saint Louis Daily Globe*, February 2, 1874; *Little Rock Daily Gazette*, February 2, 1874.
2. *Saint Louis Daily Globe*, February 2, 1874; *Little Rock Daily Gazette*, February 2, 1874; M. C. Eden, "Missouri's First Train Robbery: Gad's Hill, Wayne County, Mo, 31st January 1874," *English Westerners' Society Brand Book* 16, no. 2 (January 1974): 13–24 (cited hereafter as Eden). Some later accounts, chiefly feature articles and books from the twentieth century, erroneously have a railroad depot or station building at Gads Hill in 1874 when it only rated a freight platform.
3. *Saint Louis Daily Globe*, February 2, 1874; *Little Rock Daily Gazette*, February 2, 1874; Eden, 13–24; *Saint Louis Republican*, February 2, 1874. Another account of the robbery by Billy Farris in the *Kansas City Star* on October 28, 1978, is probably bogus at worst or wild exaggeration at best. Farris claimed to be waiting in a station building for his father, who was on the train, and later claimed to have waved the flag that brought the train to a halt. Conductor C. A. Alford, in the *Little Rock Daily Gazette* account, credits a "masked man" with this flag waving. According to the *Saint Louis Daily Globe* account, a state legislator was on board whose son was waiting at Gads Hill, but it gives no name. Farris also claimed the track was blocked with railroad ties. Not so, according to contemporary accounts, though this would be a feature of later robberies in the Kansas City–Independence area. The masks were possibly old flour sacks, although the *Republican* says, "The masks they wore were dirty looking rags tied on their faces." Conductor Alford, in the *Gazette*, described the outlaws as wearing "white cloth thrown over the head and shoulders, and a long white scarf wrapped around the neck and tied turban-like over the head." Hollywood portrayals often to the contrary, these bandits wanted their identities hidden.
4. *Saint Louis Daily Globe*, February 2, 1874; *Little Rock Daily Gazette*, February 2, 1874; Eden, 13–24; *Saint Louis Republican*, February 2, 1874. The main account here is from the *Daily Globe* interview with Alford, with similar details he provided to the *Gazette* after reaching Little Rock.
5. *Saint Louis Daily Globe*, February 2, 1874; *Little Rock Daily Gazette*, February 2, 1874; Eden, 13–24; *Saint Louis Republican*, February 2, 1874. The mail agent, named Martan, and the baggage master, Louis Constant, were taken without resistance, but the expressman briefly held a revolver on the robbers until it became obvious that

this was futile. The taking of a four-thousand-dollar parcel from the registered mail is cited in Eden, 16, which cites the *Little Rock Gazette*, October 9, 1966.

6. *Saint Louis Daily Globe*, February 2, 1874; *Little Rock Daily Gazette*, February 2, 1874; Eden, 13–24; *Saint Louis Republican*, February 2, 1874. Alford's account in both the *Gazette* and the *Daily Globe* makes no mention of the bandits examining hands. The brief account appears in the *Republican* without a source cited for this alleged incident. The list of passengers robbed may be incomplete, so it is hard to say. The *Republican* would later show something of an editorial tilt in sympathy with Frank James and the Democratic Party element that would come to his defense. See Patrick Pringle, *Stand and Deliver: Highwaymen from Robin Hood to Dick Turpin*, 21–22, 65, for allusions to "Gad's Hill" in Shakespeare and in history. Frank James, as will later be noted, had a fondness for quoting Shakespeare. See also Robert V. Bruce, *1877: Year of Violence*, 44–46 (cited hereafter as Bruce, *1877*). Conductors earned, on average, $2.78 a day, so Alford's fifty-dollar loss was significant.

7. *Saint Louis Daily Globe*, February 2, 1874; *Little Rock Daily Gazette*, February 2, 1874; Eden, 13–24; *Saint Louis Republican*, February 2, 1874. See also Edward L. Ayers, *The Promise of the New South: Life After Reconstruction*, 17, for information on the "ladies car" and a trip on the Louisville and Nashville Railroad. Mrs. Scott was reportedly from Pennsylvania, which may account in part for her being robbed. Regardless, it would appear that this incident was not quite the stuff of legend, and it would be discreetly omitted from accounts of the robbery that appeared in later books. See also John M. Taylor, *Garfield of Ohio*, 113.

8. *Saint Louis Daily Globe*, February 2, 1874; *Little Rock Daily Gazette*, February 2, 1874; Eden, 13–24; *Saint Louis Republican*, February 2, 1874. The total sum of around $6,080 assumes the amount taken from the registered mail is correct. With the additional $800 taken in Gads Hill, as well as the rifle, the sum would be closer to $7,000. At the very least, the day's events tallied more than $3,000 in loot. Alford gives at least a partial accounting of individual losses in his two interviews. But according to Eden, 16–17, Alford's account may not be complete. There is also some reason to believe the names of victims, in several instances, were misspelled. One list gives the victim's names as follows: Silas Ferry (Terry?), $7.50; C. D. Henry, $154.50; G. L. Dart, $30; Mr. Lincoln, $200; Mr. Merriam (Morran?), $200; O. S. Newell (sleeping car conductor), $20; W. A. McLanan (McClann? McClain?), a ring valued at $30 and a pin valued at $100 and $15; Alfred Butler, $50; "unknown man," $50. This does not include Alford and others named in the text. Eden, 16, also mentions a Col. J. H. Morley, chief engineer of the Cairo and Fulton Railroad, a passenger who is not listed among those robbed, though he had a confrontation with the bandits.

9. Eden, 17, cites the *Liberty (Mo.) Tribune* of February 8, 1874, as the source for the telegram transcript.

10. *Saint Louis Daily Globe*, February 2, 1874; *Little Rock Daily Gazette*, February 2, 1874; Eden, 13–24; *Saint Louis Republican*, February 2, 1874. Also, *Boonville (Mo.) Weekly Advertiser*, February 6, 1874. According to the article in the 1874 *Little Rock Gazette*, the bandits wanted "this affair reported correctly, and not be misrepresented, as we were by Stilson Hutchins, about the Malvern Hill affair." This

refers to a stage robbery between Malvern and Hot Springs, Arkansas, two weeks prior to Gads Hill.

11. *Little Rock Daily Gazette*, February 2, 1874; *Saint Louis Republican*, February 2, 1874.

12. *Saint Louis Dispatch*, February 10, 1874.

13. William A. Settle Jr., *Jesse James Was His Name*, 50–51 (cited hereafter as Settle). Settle's book is mandatory for anyone doing serious study of the James brothers. Marley Brant, in a telephone interview on October 17, 1994, in regard to Jim and Bob Younger, said, "Neither Bob nor Jim were notorious for robbery at the point of the Gads Hill robbery." Brant is author of *The Outlaw Youngers*.

CHAPTER 2: BACKGROUND TO BANDITRY

1. Settle, 6. W. Terry Martin, "Rev. Robert Sallee James, or Baptists, Books and Bandits," *James Farm Journal* 8, no. 3 (n.d., ca. 1990): 3–4 (cited hereafter as Martin). Martin Edward McGrane, *The James Farm: Its People, Their Lives and Their Times*, 6–7 (cited hereafter as McGrane, *James Farm*). Martin's account of Robert James's early education and career is very well researched and deserves to be reprinted.

2. Martin; *New York Graphic*, April 8, 1882; *Louisville Courier-Journal*, April 17, 1882. Basil Duke was also a brother-in-law of Confederate Brig. Gen. John Hunt Morgan. Duke later attained similar rank, taking over Morgan's old brigade after the latter's death in 1864. In 1867 he authored *A History of Morgan's Cavalry*. Georgetown, Kentucky, is often an overlooked aspect of the James story. Robert James had been sent to Georgetown by the trustees of a church in Russellville, Kentucky, according to Duke.

3. Martin, 3; McGrane, *James Farm*, 7; Settle, 6–7; *Kansas City Daily Journal*, April 6, 1882, for Frank James's birth information.

4. Martin, 3; Settle, 7.

5. Martin, 3; McGrane, *James Farm*, 7–8; Settle, 6–7; *Liberty (Mo.) Tribune*, October 25, 1850; Milton F. Perry, "Rev. Robert S. James' California Grave," *James Farm Journal* 5, no. 3 (September 1985). The Reverend James died in Hangtown on August 18, 1850, according to Perry. Martin claims the town was called "Rough and Ready" but gives no date. Perry states that the town burned in 1856, and the cemetery had wooden markers, all destroyed in the fire. Now called Placerville, Perry believed James was probably buried in the city cemetery there.

6. *Saint Louis Republican*, April 6, 1882, contains the description of Zerelda by Jesse Gloss, a director of the Bank of Shelbyville, Kentucky. Joan M. Beamis and William E. Pullen, *Background of a Bandit: The Ancestry of Jesse James*, 56–59 (cited hereafter as Beamis and Pullen), contains the most accurate genealogy of the family to date. The affair at Cole's Tavern reportedly involved Richard Taylor and John Gillespie on one side and Zerelda's grandfather, Richard Cole, and sons Amos and James on the other, though there is some confusion about the date of James Cole's death, as is discussed in the text. Zerelda reportedly disliked her stepfather, Robert Thomason, a widower with several children of his own, and this was reportedly the reason for her staying behind. If this was the case, she must have overcome her aversion later. Phillip W. Steele, *Jesse and*

Frank James: The Family History, 39–42 (cited hereafter as Steele, *Family History*), contains the reference to Cole's Tavern as "Sodom." "Saint Catherine's Female School," *James Farm Journal* 8, no. 3 (ca. 1990), contains a reprint of an article on the school from the *Catholic Advocate* of Bardstown, Kentucky, January 7, 1837, that says Zerelda attended from 1840 to 1841. A sampler that she embroidered at the school is on display at the James Farm Museum near Kearney, Missouri. See also "Zerelda James Samuel—A Profile," *James Farm Journal* 6, no. 2 (September 1986); Duke's comments are from the *Louisville Courier-Journal,* April 17, 1882.

7. Milton F. Perry, "Dr. Samuel Identified—At Last!" *James Farm Journal* 2, no. 1 (March 1984); "The Samuel Family," *James Farm Journal* 5 (3?), no. 5 (December 1985), has further information on Dr. Reuben Samuel from the research of Dr. Till M. Huston of Athens, Georgia, and apparently Perry's research in Clay County, Missouri, court records, where the prenuptial agreement was found. Steele, *Family History,* 43–45, gives the date September 25, 1855, for the Samuel wedding while Perry's earlier "Dr. Samuel Identified," says September 26, as does Homer Croy's *Jesse James Was My Neighbor,* 21 (cited hereafter as Croy, *James*). Steele's work must be used with caution. Croy claims the family of Reuben Samuel came from the area near Samuels Station, Kentucky, though the name of the town does not contain another *s*. See also Settle, 8–9.

8. "Wild Bill' Thomason," *James Farm Journal* 5, no. 5 (December 1985); Jim Cummins, *Jim Cummins' Book* (1988 rpt.) (cited hereafter as *Cummins' Book*), 21–25. Cummins gives an interesting account of Thomason and Frank's somewhat ironic practice of taking some of the family's slave children out for military drills with cornstalks for arms. Cummins's account is one of the few regarding the pre–Civil War years of the James brothers.

9. *Liberty (Mo.) Tribune,* October 26 and November 9, 1860; Gary G. Fuenfhausen, *A Guide to Historic Clay County, Missouri, Architectural Resources and other Historic Sites of the Civil War,* 15–16 (cited hereafter as Fuenfhausen).

10. Thomas L. Snead, "The First Year of the War in Missouri," *Battles and Leaders of the Civil War,* 1:262–64 (cited hereafter as Snead); Elmo Ingenthron, *Borderland Rebellion,* 35–37 (cited hereafter as Ingenthron); Fuenfhausen, 11, 72–73, 83–84; U.S. War Department, *The War of the Rebellion: A Compilation of the Official Records of the Union and Confederate Armies,* 1:649–50 (cited hereafter as OR).

11. *Liberty (Mo.) Tribune,* May 10, 1861; Snead, 264–65.

12. Snead, 263–73, contains a full account of the complexities of the political and military situation in Missouri; Ingenthron, 95, tells briefly of the formation of Gamble's provisional government in Missouri; *Columbia (Mo.) Herald,* September 24, 1897, gives a brief mention of Wilson's Creek by Frank James. See also Settle, 20; and Fuenfhausen, 72.

13. James A. Milligan, "The Siege of Lexington, Mo.," *Battles and Leaders of the Civil War,* 1:307–13; Hughes's account is in a footnote on p. 312. See also Snead, 270–73; Albert Castel, *General Sterling Price and the Civil War in the West,* 29, 50–56 (cited hereafter as *Price*); Settle, 20; William A. Albaugh III and Edward

Simmons, *Confederate Arms*, 168, concerning Price's army; William Garrett Piston and Thomas O. Sweeney, "Don't Give an Inch: The Missouri State Guard," *North & South 2*, no. 5 (June 1999): 10–26, offers one of the best overviews of the MSG.

14. Castel, *Price*, 54–56; Ingenthron, 101–2.

15. Settle, 18–20.

16. Ingenthron, 95–96.

17. Robert G. Hartje, *Van Dorn: Life and Times of a Confederate General*, 137–71; *Price*, 75–83.

18. *Cummins's Book*, 25; Settle, 20; *Liberty (Mo.) Tribune*, May 5, 1862; Frank Triplett, *The Life, Times and Treacherous Death of Jesse James*, 304–5 (cited hereafter as Triplett); *Saint Joseph (Mo.) Morning Herald*, April 6, 1882; Anon, *History of Clay and Platte Counties, Missouri*, 266–67 (cited hereafter as *History of Clay*); Edward E. Leslie, *The Devil Knows How to Ride: The True Story of William Clarke Quantrill and His Confederate Raiders*, 185 (cited hereafter as Leslie), is perhaps the most balanced and up-to-date account yet, although there are some facts, which will be noted elsewhere, that are questionable. See also Fuenfhausen, 86.

19. Michael Fellman, *Inside War: The Guerrilla Conflict in Missouri During the American Civil War*, 10–131 (cited hereafter as Fellman). This work, while slightly flawed by some geographical bloopers and the acceptance of the bogus memoir of "Kit" Dalton (a deserter from the Seventh Tennessee Cavalry named John Dalton [see James I. Robertson, "The War in Words," *Civil War Times Illustrated*, September 1987, 12]), is still a remarkably fine analysis of the war in Missouri and the factors that influenced it. Richard S. Brownlee's *Gray Ghosts of the Confederacy: Guerrilla Warfare in the West, 1861–1865*, 42–52, 142–79 (cited hereafter as Brownlee), is perhaps a more concise account of the situation in Missouri than Fellman provides. Brownlee uses a chronological rather than a topical framework. Both accounts are invaluable studies of the chaos that Missouri plunged into as the war progressed. The *Liberty (Mo.) Tribune*, June 26, 1863, is the source of the letter about conditions in northwest Clay County. See also Fuenfhausen, 21–22.

20. Settle, 22–23, cites the account of John McCorkle as evidence that Frank James was not at Prairie Grove in 1862. It is likely that Shelby and John Newman Edwards, his adjutant-biographer, were engaged in "Bourbon Democrat" politics of the 90-proof variety at the time of his 1883 interview, reprinted in Daniel O'Flaherty, *General Jo Shelby, Undefeated Rebel*, 366–69 (cited hereafter as O'Flaherty); Lurena (Lou) McCoy, "About the Fight at Richfield, Mo," *Confederate Veteran 20*, no. 9 (cited hereafter as McCoy), and information related to the author by the late Milton F. Perry. McCoy may have aided Frank in the escape by making an impression of the jail key in wax and having another cast and smuggled in to the prisoners. According to an old photograph, the jail was built like a house but with thick stone walls. It was still standing, in ruins, around the end of the nineteenth century. Brownlee, 159, gives an idea of what paroled Southern sympathizers faced. See also James A. Hamilton, "The Enrolled Missouri Militia: Its Creation and Controversial History," *Missouri Historical Review 69*, no. 4 (July 1975): 417–32; and Fuenfhausen, 20.

21. *Louisville Courier-Journal*, September 29, 1901, provides an interesting account of the Quantrill veterans reunion at Blue Springs, Missouri. Note that Frank James states he joined the guerrillas in May 1863, not 1862. Thus it's believed that Joseph Shelby's earlier statement about Frank James having saved him at Prairie Grove, Arkansas, was probably politically motivated.

22. Albert Castel, *William Clark Quantrill: His Life and Times*, 22–109 (cited hereafter as Castel, *Quantrill*). For other sources on Quantrill, see Ted P. Yeatman, "William Clarke Quantrill, 1837–1865," *Book of Days, 1987: An Encyclopedia of Information Sources on Historical Figures and Events*; and Brownlee, 62–63.

23. McCoy, 425–27; OR, 22, pt. 1, 335–36. The *Kansas City Journal*, May 30, 1863, reported all five men killed. This is not the case with the OR account. The *Journal* account is the basis for the version of the ambush given in Castel, *Quantrill*, 109, though it may be inaccurate. See also the *Annual Report of the Adjutant General of Missouri (1865)*, 204–6 (cited hereafter as *Adjutant General, Mo.—1865*), for background on the Twenty-fifth Missouri; Graffenstein belonged to Company B of the Twenty-fifth. *History of Clay*, 230, 235–36. Sessions belonged to Company K, Forty-eighth Enrolled Missouri Militia. Prior to the war he was almost lynched in Liberty by a mob that claimed he was an abolitionist but was saved by several proslavery men. Scott was a former Liberty saddler.

24. McCoy, 427; OR, 336.

25. File of Frank James, Union Provost Marshal File of Papers Relating to Individual Citizens, National Archives Microfilm Publication M345, Roll 142, War Department Collection of Confederate Records, Record Group 109, National Archives, Washington, D.C. (cited hereafter as Provost Marshal Papers). See also Brownlee, 30.

26. Joseph A. Dacus, *Illustrated Lives and Adventures of Frank and Jesse James and the Younger Brothers, The Noted Western Outlaws*, 167; John Newman Edwards, *Noted Guerrillas, or the Warfare of the Border*, 170–71 (cited hereafter as Edwards, *Guerrillas*); *Annual Report of the Adjutant General of Missouri for 1864*, 381. According to one account, Frank James was responsible for the capture of Birch, whose name is incorrectly spelled "Burch" in earlier accounts. According to the adjutant general's report, Birch was commissioned on December 28, 1862, and resigned on August 14, 1863. No account of the Plattsburg affair is to be found in the OR. Thomas Goodrich, in *Black Flag: Guerrilla Warfare on the Western Border, 1861–1865*, 71, gives an account by a newspaper editor from Plattsburg who claimed that the garrison was reduced to four or five muskets and their ammo. When the ammunition was exhausted, the troops surrendered. This account would tend to contradict Edwards, and while it is possible and perhaps even probable, it is unproven. Goodrich did not document his sources in this work.

27. Files of Lurena (Mrs. Moses) McCoy, Provost Marshal Papers, M345, Roll 181.

28. Ibid. Mrs. McCoy was apparently unaware of her sister's affidavit.

29. McCoy, 446–47. The story of Quantrill swapping a provost marshal for Mrs. McCoy has little basis in fact and is a means of explaining away what really happened. It appears to have been common practice to release female prisoners, especially those with children, after they took the Oath of Allegiance.

30. Edwards, *Guerrillas*, 171. Other information about Jesse's intelligence gathering and pro-guerrilla activities came from discussions with the late Milton F. Perry, who, prior to his death in 1991, researched the Civil War years of Jesse James.

31. Julian Street, "The Borderland," *Colliers*, September 14, 1914, gives a most interesting and overlooked account of the hanging of Samuel. Information is provided by Samuel's son, John T. Samuel, who was born on December 25, 1861. No doubt he heard the commotion, if he did not witness it, when the Missouri militiamen came to the James-Samuel farm in May 1863. He surely heard more about it from other members of the family over the years. See also *OR*, 22, pt. 1, 336, 993; and *Saint Joseph (Mo.) Morning Herald*, May 29, 1863. A Lieutenant Rogers's account in the *Herald* indicates that he belonged to the command of Captain Turney, who, according to the *OR* report of Captain Schmitz, was sent from Plattsburg to find the guerrillas. The *OR* list of unit designations identifies Turney's command as belonging to the Fifty-first Enrolled Missouri Militia (EMM). The *Herald* credits this group to Clinton County, but some Clay County militiamen of the Forty-eighth EMM appear to have been in the party as well, according to *History of Clay*, 229–30, 247, 267. Younger, of Company E, Forty-eighth EMM, may have commanded, but if so it appears to have been a pickup detachment, as at least one individual credited as being there, Alvis Dagley, belonged to Company F.

32. See *Kansas City Daily Journal*, April 6, 1882, for the account of William James. See also *History of Clay*, 267. Information about Bond and Dagley's role was supplied by Milton F. Perry, who was trying to locate service records for the pair, with the author's assistance. See Castel, *Quantrill*, 107–8, for Ramberlin hanging and Penick information; Edwards, *Guerrillas*, 171–72; and *Saint Joseph (Mo.) Morning Herald*, May 29, 1863, for the account of Lieutenant Rogers. The news account spells the name as "Turney" instead of "Tourney," a misspelling given in the *OR*. *History of Clay* gives the name J. W. Turney and his unit Company F, Fourth Provisional Regiment, EMM. Some units had more than one numerical designation. Leslie, 185–86, is in error concerning the hanging episode.

33. Files of Reuben and Zerelda Samuel, Provost Marshal Papers, M345, Roll 142. *Liberty (Mo.) Tribune*, December 15, 1893; Leslie, 185–86, is again in error. Dr. Samuel was paroled on June 24, 1863, not after July 6, as stated in Leslie.

34. Files of Reuben and Zerelda Samuel, Provost Marshal Papers, M345, Roll 142. *Liberty (Mo.) Tribune*, December 15, 1893.

35. *Liberty (Mo.) Tribune*, August 7, 1863. The article "Three Southern Gentlemen in Search of Their Rights" leaves readers wondering whether robbery, in this case, was in the eye of the beholder. The amount of money taken from Mitchell is subject to question. In the article it appears as "$1 25," with a space, possibly for a decimal point, which is later given in Castel, *Quantrill*, 120–21, as "$1.25" in a footnote. This fails to mention Mitchell's provost pass "to cross the plains." If he was indeed planning to head west via Leavenworth, $1.25 would seem to be a rather small sum to be carrying. Settle, 23, gives the sum as "$125," noting the missing decimal point but not the space.

36. According to Milton F. Perry, Jesse James apparently tried to join the guerrillas but was rejected as being too young. There is no solid indication of his being with

Quantrill at the subsequent raid on Lawrence, Kansas. Both Brownlee, 62, and Settle, 26, say that Jesse joined after Lawrence, Brownlee saying it happened in 1864 and Settle being somewhat less specific but admitting it was possibly in early summer of 1864. Artist and James-photo authority George Warfel related that he was told a different version of how Jesse lost his fingertip by Jo Frances James, granddaughter of the outlaw. In a telephone interview on April 17, 1994, Warfel said Jo Frances James said the incident happened at the farm before Jesse joined the guerrillas. The story is related in *Cummins' Book*, 55, and in Homer Croy, 30, as having happened a few weeks after joining the guerrillas in 1864. Warfel related that Jo Frances was emphatic that this version was in error, timewise. See *History of Clay*, 267, for source for Jesse and tobacco crop.

37. Thomas Goodrich, *Bloody Dawn: The Story of the Lawrence Massacre*, 30–35 (cited hereafter as Goodrich). Leslie, 5–29, gives a good picture of the role of Lawrence in the pre-1860 border strife and the character of the jayhawkers.

38. Goodrich, 59–60; Brownlee, 38–39; Leslie, 92–93.

39. Goodrich, 15, 33–34, 37–40, 52–55, 58–62, 66–69.

40. Goodrich, 20–26; Brownlee, 117–25. Marley Brant's *The Outlaw Youngers*, 23–34 (cited hereafter as Brant) is the best available account of the Youngers. Chapter 4 details the historical maze surrounding Henry Younger's death. See also "Thomas Ewing" in *Biographical Directory of the United States Congress, 1774–1989*, 979 (cited hereafter as *Biographical Directory-Congress*). Leslie, 194–98, has done an excellent job in reconstructing the events leading to the prison disaster.

41. Brownlee, 110–27; Castel, *Quantrill*, 122–43. See Thomas Elsey Connelley, *Quantrill and the Border Wars*, 317–85 (cited hereafter as Connelley), for a detailed account of the raid itself. Connelley has excellent primary sources, and many are cited at length throughout the book. But his book is highly biased. Similarly, Edwards's *Guerrillas* must be used with caution and crosschecked with other sources where possible. Edwards repeats "war stories" of the guerrillas, who were probably prone to exaggeration. For example, Edwards (194) states that Jesse James was at Lawrence, when he probably wasn't (see previous note 36). Still, as will be seen, Edwards's work contains some details that may provide a missing piece to the puzzle. Leslie, 32–34, gives a sound evaluation of the above authors. See also 92–93, 201–41, for an account of the raid. I have chosen to omit a blow-by-blow discussion as it is covered in detail in other works.

42. Connelley, 360, 384–85, relates how some of the raiders showed unfired revolvers to one resident and said how they had come "to burn and destroy, but not to kill." See also Leslie, 223, 237.

43. Wiley Britton, *The Civil War on the Border*, 2:139–43 (cited hereafter as Britton); Leslie, 236, 254–56.

44. Charles R. Mink, "General Orders No. 11: The Forced Evacuation of Civilians During the Civil War," *Military Affairs* (December 1970): 132–36, is an excellent scholarly account of the history and impact of the order. See also Brownlee, 125–27; Goodrich, 152–69; Castel, *Quantrill*, 144–48; and Leslie, 257–67.

45. Britton, 209–15. See also *OR*, 22, pt. 1, 457–61, for the report of Confederate Brig. Gen. Douglas H. Cooper regarding Honey Springs. See also Alvin M. Josephy, *The

Civil War in the American West, 371–72 (cited hereafter as Josephy); Albert Castel, "Jim Lane of Kansas," *Civil War Times Illustrated* 12, no. 1 (April 1973): 27 (cited hereafter as Castel, "Lane"). According to one soldier from Kansas, Blunt possessed "a worse reputation than even Lane himself." Blunt reportedly took financial kickbacks for army contracts with the posts under his command, some of which found its way back to Senator Lane.

46. Britton, 215–16.
47. OR, 22, pt. 1, 691, 695; Connelley, 422–24.
48. OR, 22, pt. 1, 698–99; Connelley, 424–25.
49. OR, 22, pt. 1, 688–701; Connelley, 425–30; Brownlee, 128–29; Britton, 216–21.
50. Britton, 218–25; Josephy, 372–74, 381–83; OR 22, pt. 1, 692, 696–98; see 22, pt. 2, 666, for the removal order by Schofield. Josephy appears to be in error regarding the date and sequence of events surrounding Blunt's removal. Blunt would confront Price during the Confederates' raid into Missouri and Kansas the following fall. He managed to salvage some of his military reputation before the war ended with the battle at Westport (now part of Kansas City), Missouri.
51. OR, 22, pt. 1, 700–701; 26, pt. 2, 339; Britton, 224–25; Leslie, 281, 294–95. Leslie theorizes that Quantrill was elected "colonel" of the combined guerrilla bands just prior to the march south, but this was never officially recognized by Confederate authorities.
52. Thomas C. Reynolds Papers, Library of Congress, letter book, 14, 171–73, 175.
53. OR, 53, 907.
54. OR, 26, pt. 2, 348.
55. Ibid., 383.
56. Brownlee, 137–39; Brant, 54–55; Castel, *Quantrill*, 157–59; Connelley, 435–47. The woman Anderson lived with was Bush Hunt. Leslie, 189, gives the name Bush Smith and says a marriage license was found in Texas several years ago.
57. OR, 34, pt. 2, 853, 945, 957–58, 1107; 34, pt. 3, 742–43, 746–47; Leslie, 295–301.
58. Connelley, 449–50; Castel, *Quantrill*, 169–72.
59. *Cummins' Book*, 34, 54–55; Edwards, *Guerrillas*, 364; information about Dagley and Bond was provided by Milton F. Perry while I was doing research for him at the National Archives (see previous note 32). Edwards's account credits the James brothers with the Bond affair, but *History of Clay*, 247, credits the other four guerrillas while remaining noticeably silent about the two recruits who killed Dagley (called "Dailey"). The county history is probably more accurate than Edwards here, but both accounts are given for the record. The *Kansas City Star*, October 12, 1898, contains an interesting 1897 interview with Zerelda Samuel at the farm. She calls Bond "Bain," but is obviously referring to Brantley Bond.
60. Harry Soltysiak, "Anarchy in Missouri," *Civil War Times Illustrated* 24, no. 8 (December 1985): 31–32 (hereafter cited as Soltysiak); Fuenfhausen, 22–23.
61. Soltysiak, 33; Eugene D. Genovese, *"Slavery Ordained by God": The Southern Slaveholders' View of Biblical History and Modern Politics*, 7–30. See also *Christian History* 11, no. 1 (1992) for an exhaustive special issue, *Christianity and the Civil War*. The *Kansas City (Mo.) Western Journal of Commerce*, August 15, 1863, reprinted the sermon of Rev. George Miller for August 6: "We consider all complicity with this

rebellion highly criminal in the sight of God, and opposition to it not only a civil but a religious duty, for the faithful discharge of which we have to answer at the bar of God."

62. Connelley, 269, 278–79; OR, 41, pt. 2, 75–77; History of Clay, 248–52. Though it has been said that Anderson was Jesse's guerrilla mentor, in fact he was only in contact with Anderson during a period of about a month. Jesse James learned the guerrilla trade from Anderson's lieutenants: Taylor, Shepherd, and Clement. See also Leslie, 314; Hale, Quantrill, 149, concerning Taylor's wounding; Cummins' Book, 43, for the proposed Iowa raid. The Kansas City Star, October 12, 1898, contains an interview with Mrs. Samuel, who also mentions the proposed raid. According to her account it was Quantrill, not Todd, whom Taylor was planning the raid with. Is it possible that Taylor's "accidental" wounding by another guerrilla was part of a power struggle going on within the guerrilla band? The idea for a raid on Des Moines sounds a bit more like Quantrill. Todd never followed through with it, if in fact he was the other person involved. For whatever reason, Taylor made himself scarce for the remainder of the conflict.

63. Liberty (Mo.) Tribune, August 19, 1937; Milton F. Perry to Ted P. Yeatman, February 24, 1986, author's papers. Perry identifies the farmer as George Heisinger and states that he has seen three accounts relating to the story from 1885, 1912, and the account given here from 1937. He believed that this was the way Jesse's chest wound actually occurred. Perry, who finished a manuscript about Jesse James's Civil War experiences before his death in 1991, had the following to say: "All accounts of the battle of Flat Rock, where Jesse was supposed to have been wounded, can be traced to Edwards's book [Noted Guerrillas]. I wouldn't put it beneath Edwards to make Jesse's wounding more glamorous than [having it occur] while stealing a saddle. In 1875 Jesse was a glamorous figure, and Edwards wouldn't hesitate to puff him up. Shouse grew up about a mile southeast of the James farm and played with the boys." Leslie, 315, gives August 15, 1864, as the date of Jesse's wounding by "a pistol ball" in a fight with militia in Carroll County. This appears to be in error, though a county history is cited as the source. The account of Dr. Ridge shared here, taken with what Jesse told Shouse, makes Leslie's account unlikely.

64. The Kansas City Star, June 30, 1902, contains an account by Dr. Ridge concerning his treatment of Jesse James in 1864. As of this writing, the exact date of his wounding is uncertain, though Settle, 27, states that it was August 12 or 13.

65. Files of Reuben and Zerelda Samuel, Provost Marshal Papers, M345, Roll 142. Despite the disclaimer that they were not related, this may have been Reuben's cousin Edward M., the elector for Bell in 1860. I found a number of letters from E. M. Samuel, on bank stationery, in other files, while searching provost marshal records on microfilm. Samuel apparently was heavily involved as an informant. A bad report from Samuel regarding a person's loyalty could result in a person's being arrested, or worse. The observations about Dr. Samuel are noteworthy regarding the James brothers, and makes it interesting to speculate what might have happened had their father, Robert James, survived.

66. Goodrich, 174–76; Leslie, 316–17; *Columbia (Mo.) Herald*, September 24, 1897; *Kansas City (Mo.) Daily Journal*, April 4, 1882.

67. Donald R. Hale, *They Called Him Bloody Bill*, 39–47 (cited hereafter as Hale, *Bloody Bill*); Brownlee, 216–18. Hale used the centennial issue of the *Centralia (Mo.) Fireside Guard*, June 6, 1957, containing thirty years of research on the massacre by local historian Edgar T. Rodemyer, who collected many eyewitness accounts.

68. Hale, *Bloody Bill*, 47–57; Brownlee, 216–20. *Adjutant General-Missouri-1865*, 258–61, contains information on the Thirty-ninth Missouri. Company A, raised in the Kirksville area, seems to have suffered most. Companies G (Shelbyville area) and H (from the Hannibal, Canton, and Waterloo areas) suffered no apparent loss of officers. Capt. Adam Theiss of Company H was apparently in charge of the troops left behind in Centralia and escaped with a number of his command. The *Columbia (Mo.) Herald*, September 24, 1897, contains an interview with Frank James and his "recollection" of events. Leslie, 322, says that Frank was seen on the train in Centralia that morning. This is entirely possible.

69. Hale, *Bloody Bill*, 47–57; Brownlee, 218–20; *Cummins' Book*, 51. Most accounts have Jesse present at Centralia, killing Johnson. Cummins and Frank James did not get along well in later years, though this may not totally account for Cummins's questioning who killed Johnson. In a melee like this it was probably just as Cummins explained it—"a general mixup"; OR, 41, pt. 1, 440, contains the report of Lt. Col. Daniel M. Draper of the Ninth Missouri State Militia Cavalry. Leslie, 328, estimates the dead at 149.

70. Brownlee, 223–25; Castel, *Price*, 204–5, 222–23, 226–27. OR, 41, pt. 1, 632, contains Price's account of his orders to the guerrilla leaders and what they did or didn't accomplish. See John Newman Edwards, *Shelby and His Men*, 471, for Thomas Reynolds's quote on the situation at Price's headquarters.

71. Brownlee, 226–27; Leslie, 334–35, on Todd's death.

72. Hale, *Bloody Bill*, 75–81; Castel, *Quantrill*, 198–99; Britton, 540–46. "Major Cox, Who Slew Bill Anderson, Dies," *James Farm Journal* 8, no. 4–9, no. 1 (1991), is a reprint of an undated obituary notice with much information about Cox. According to Britton, who appears to have gotten his account from Cox, Anderson's bridle, scalps and all, was sent to Missouri Adjutant General Gray. One can imagine his reaction upon receipt of this unique war trophy. See also Fellman, 188–89, 214, 255, 297, 301, for further particulars of body mutilation during the war in Missouri and the psychological rationale of such acts. *The History of Daviess County, Missouri*, 210–11, 218 (cited hereafter as *History of Daviess*), lists Cox as a private in Company D of the "Oregon Battalion" of Missouri volunteers who camped on the later site of Fort Kearney, Nebraska. Though Cox's obituary mentions his being an Indian fighter against the Sioux, it is uncertain that he saw anything more than routine camp and patrol duty during this period. He doubtless had a chance to speak to some genuine frontiersmen at this time and perhaps learned Indian-fighting tactics from them, much as Frank learned from Wild Bill Thomason. Cox is listed in this work as being in charge of a detachment of the First MSM Cavalry with the Fifty-first EMM under Maj. John Grimes. No mention is made of the Thirty-third EMM, however. See note

32 for problems encountered with EMM unit designations, and see Leslie, 337–38, 478, for an account of the affair. Cox had resigned a Missouri Militia commission in 1862, following a bout of typhoid fever. He was leading the militia as a civilian at the request of Brig. Gen. James Craig. Cox was afterward recommissioned and promoted to lieutenant colonel. According to Leslie, Craig was given the war trophies, not Gray. See also Ruth Coder Fitzgerald, "Clell and Ed Miller—Members of the James Gang," *Quarterly of the National Association for Outlaw and Lawman History, Inc.* 15, no. 3 (July-September 1991): 29 (cited hereafter as Fitzgerald, "Miller"); and Albert Castel and Thomas Goodrich, *Bloody Bill Anderson: The Short, Savage Life of a Civil War Guerrilla,* 124–30, notes that previously Cox had worked for Russell, Majors, and Waddell, a freighting business, where he came into contact with frontiersmen like Kit Carson. Castel and Goodrich observe that some of Cox's militia were armed with revolvers and that these men were sent in pursuit—no prisoners were taken.

CHAPTER 3: LONG RIDE TO DESTINY

1. *OR,* ser. 2, vol. 7, 302. The detective who signed with the initials "E.F.H." was reporting to a Col. J. P. Sanderson. It is odd that a woman from this area of Missouri would have the money for a junket to Kentucky and then decide to return to the war-ravaged border area. It is probable that she was on a scouting mission, bankrolled by Quantrill, or by Confederate agents in Missouri. See also Donald R. Hale, *We Rode with Quantrill,* 112–21 (cited hereafter as Hale, *Quantrill*), for an account of Kate King-Clarke. Hale says Quantrill and King-Clarke were married. Connelley, 60, 282, 451, paints a more negative picture of Kate, but his book is notoriously biased, as has been mentioned.

2. *Cummins' Book,* 51–52. Edwards, *Guerrillas,* 383–84, gives the story of the rendezvous at Mrs. Wigginton's with the date of December 4. John McCorkle, *Three Years with Quantrill,* 128–29 (cited hereafter as McCorkle), states that Quantrill started out for Illinois and Ohio first but was stopped and turned back by ice along the Missouri. This story is at odds with that given by Edwards, who says Quantrill did not turn back, but encountered the ice at Saline City and decided to go south. Edwards says Quantrill crossed the Lamine River then crossed the Missouri Pacific Railroad eight miles west of Tipton, marching southeast between Cole Camp and Florence. While Edwards may be faulted for some things, he is often right concerning Quantrill's line of march, with a few matters for debate that will be noted later. The accounts of the guerrillas are often confusing, and Edwards probably did as best he could to bring some order to the chaos when he wrote his book. Historians do themselves a disservice in totally ignoring Edwards as a source.

3. *OR,* 41, pt. 1, 984, 1008, 1094; Connelley, 458; McCorkle, 129–30. The *OR*'s report gives Quantrill's alias as "Clark," though he appears to have used the name "Moses" as well. It is assumed that he used Clark as his name at Tuscumbia.

4. McCorkle, 130–31; Edwards, *Guerrillas,* 387–88; Ingenthron, 269–70; Eunice Pennington to Ted Yeatman, February 11, 1992, author's papers. The exact route is open to question. McCorkle states that they followed the Current River while

Edwards gives the route via Salem to present-day Mountain View and Thomasville. According to Ozark historian Pennington: "There were trails along the rivers, generally on both sides. . . . It was, in the first place, a way of travel that saved a person from getting lost and starving for water . . . these woods at that time were filled with huge tall trees with very little ground brush or cover as we see today. Horseback riders could travel about anywhere with great speed except for the extremely high hills and steep valleys. . . . The old Bellview and Pocahontas road was in use and was used by both North and Southern armies. It broke off from Big Pike Creek south at Poca Hollow between Van Buren and Fremont and was a direct route south into Arkansas and points beyond Pocahontas." This route is near the Current River, mentioned by McCorkle, and had been used by Confederate raider M. Jeff Thompson in a foray from Pocahontas in December 1862.

5. Connelley, 456–58, gives a variety of versions of the story that Quantrill fed his men. Castel, *Quantrill*, 201–2, dismisses the story of Quantrill planning to kill Lincoln, but in light of some further research it deserves a reexamination. *Cummins' Book*, 52, states that personality conflicts were responsible for the split. McCorkle, 132, states that the group left Quantrill at the home of a "Colonel Morrison" farther down on the ridge, toward Memphis. Edwards, *Guerrillas*, 387–88, identifies the home of a "Charles Morrison" as the sometimes headquarters of a "Major Morrison Boswell," who was "in the secret service of the Confederate government . . . operating with two score or more of scouts." Edwards was sometimes off with names and often tended to "gild the lily" in his writing, but it has been theorized that a plot to capture or eliminate Lincoln may have been hatched in the Confederate government during 1864–65. This thesis is explained at length in William A. Tidwell, James O. Hall, and David W. Gaddy, *Come Retribution: The Confederate Secret Service and the Assassination of Lincoln*, and in the sequel, William A. Tidwell, *April '65: Confederate Covert Action in the American Civil War* (see vii–xiv, 1–13, 52–53, 160–96). Quantrill's possible connection to this scenario and to the Confederate strategy for 1865 may be worthy of further study. It is possible that "Major Boswell" is the "Minor Major" alluded to in *Come Retribution*, 164–67, who had organized a group to sabotage steamboats along the Mississippi. The group seems to have had strong ties to Missouri, both politically and personnel-wise; Leslie, 344, states that Olliver "Oll'" Shepherd commanded the group that went to Texas, which is probably incorrect. Settle, 30, 206, citing Edwards, *Guerrillas*, 327–33, and Castel, *Quantrill*, gives George Shepherd as the leader, as does *Cummins' Book*, 52, and Jim Cummins was there.

6. McCorkle, 132–36; Robert H. Fristoe, Military Service Record, Eighth Kentucky Mounted Infantry, National Archives Microfilm Publication M319, Roll 125. Edwards, *Guerrillas*, 389–90, gives a story of Quantrill coming in conflict with the commander at Paris, who tried to retain his men, but this story is open to question in light of McCorkle's statements. Interestingly, it would seem that Paris was the rendezvous point for some sort of special operation. See Telegrams Received, Department of Kentucky, R.G. 393, pt. 1, Entry 2174 (vol. 22–16 DKY), 173, National Archives, Washington, D.C. In a telegram from Bvt. Brig. Gen. E. H. Murray, Bowling Green, Kentucky, to Capt. J. Bates Dickson, A.A.G. of the

Department, dated May 6, 1865, there is a cryptic mention of a "force that captured the Cumberland" being "about annihilated. They were mostly officers of the Army of Northern Virginia Banded together to operate in Ky." Seven men had reportedly been killed by a detachment of the Seventeenth Kentucky Cavalry under the command of a Colonel Johnson, who was told by one of the dying officers that "there were several Cos. organizing near Paris, Tenn. to come over." In other words, the Confederates at Paris were somehow also involved in this operation, whatever it was. It seems curious indeed that Quantrill was bumping into people with ties to what appear to be Confederate covert operations.

7. Files of Reuben and Zerelda Samuel, Provost Marshal Papers, M345, Roll 142; Special Orders No. 9, January 9, 1865, Records of the Adjutant General's Office, R.G. 94, Entry 44, Orders and Circulars 325, Special Orders, Department of the Missouri, 1865, National Archives, Washington, D.C. (cited hereafter as Special Orders No. 9).

8. Special Orders No. 9. The "Mrs. Cummings" may have been the mother or a relative of guerrilla Jim Cummins. Mrs. McCoy is the woman whose earlier contrition toward Federal authorities, mentioned in chapter 2, had apparently lost its luster. Also named are Kemp M. Woods, Wesley Martin, John Ecton, Mrs. James H. Ford, Mrs. Sarah Roupe (?), Mrs. George Taylor, and a Mrs. Searce. The order was to be "carried into effect" by Brig. Gen. Clinton B. Fisk, who shortly after the war helped to found Fisk University in Nashville, Tennessee. The order was given by Maj. Gen. Grenville Dodge, who later worked as chief engineer of the Union Pacific Railroad during the construction of the first transcontinental railway.

9. Emmitt C. Hoctor, "Rusticating in Nebraska: 1862–1882," *Quarterly for the National Association for Outlaw and Lawman History* 17, no. 3 (April-June 1993). Hoctor's article contains some interesting information on the Cole family in Nebraska. A cousin, Anjalina Cole, was married to David Plasters, sheriff of Nemaha County from 1866 to 1876. This is north of Rulo, in another county, however. Nebraska City is about fifty to sixty miles north of Rulo. Monroe W. Neihardt reportedly took the photo of Jesse and one of Frank. The photo of Jesse, or at least a sketch of it, has been seen by the author, but not the one of Frank. Hoctor gives a story of Zerelda teaching in Burt County, Nebraska, in 1862, but this conflicts with known events and records. Burt County is some distance from Rulo. Emmitt C. Hoctor, in "Safe Retreat Found," *Quarterly for the National Association for Outlaw and Lawman History* 15, no. 4 (October-December 1991), states that there were cousins who were "lawmen and judges" in Nemaha County, which is twenty-five miles north of Rulo. The Coles settled there in 1852 and had spread into several other counties in Nebraska.

10. OR, 48, pt. 1, 458–59. General Orders No. 7 was issued January 8, 1865, the day before the order banishing the family. See also Frederick S. Calhoun, *The Lawmen: United States Marshals and their Deputies, 1789–1989*, 106–7 (cited hereafter as Calhoun, *Lawmen*). In cases where real property (land) was confiscated, the U.S. marshals took "all the right, title, interest, and estate," giving notice to the people on the property of the seizure. Normally only the title would be seized, not the land itself.

11. McCorkle, 136. The *Louisville Courier-Journal*, April 29, 1874, contains an account that claims Quantrill's band crossed at Eddyville. McCorkle's account of the death of "Old Charley" at Canton is in conflict with other accounts. The various newspapers were full of stories of the impending collapse of the Confederacy, and it is possible that some members of the group considered going back to Paris rather than chance the trek to Virginia and Maryland on what may have seemed a suicide mission. See Leslie, 364, 482, on the death of "Old Charley" prior to Quantrill's last fight, with documentation by Connelley.

12. L. L. Valentine, "Sue Mundy of Kentucky: Part 1," *Register of the Kentucky Historical Society* 62, no. 3 (July 1964): 179–83 (cited hereafter as Valentine, "Mundy, pt. 1"). Valentine's article is one of the best on the origins and nature of the guerrilla war in Kentucky and of the case of "Sue Mundy" in particular. The sensational "Sue Mundy" stories were a journalistic fiction featuring a long-haired female guerrilla who was outsmarting the military authorities. The series was created by *Louisville Daily Journal* editor George D. Prentice (a Union Democrat) in an effort to goad General Burbridge and Unionist Republicans in Kentucky as well as to sell newspapers. The guerrilla activities of "Sue Mundy" were actually based primarily (though not exclusively) on those of Marcellus Jerome Clarke, a long-haired, twenty-year-old raider who had formerly served under John Hunt Morgan.

13. Ibid., 183, 185, 197; Lowell H. Harrison, *The Civil War in Kentucky*, 75–78.

14. Col. H. M. Buckley to Brig. Gen. Edward Hobson, January 15, 1865, Regimental Letter Book, Fifty-fourth Kentucky Infantry, R.G. 94, National Archives, Washington, D.C.

15. McCorkle, 137–38; Edwards, *Guerrillas*, 391–92. The author has chosen the number of men as six, given in McCorkle's account, though this may be approximate. Essentially, the accounts in Edwards and McCorkle seem to match in the general particulars. Edwards seems to have the geography of their probable route down plausibly. The only other account, in the *Louisville Courier-Journal*, April 29, 1874, is similar to that of Edwards and appears to have been based on the account of a former guerrilla. Edwards, in this case, makes more sense than Connelley and for the most part can be corroborated independently.

16. Connelley, 460. OR, 49, pt. 1, 657–58, gives the full particulars of the Hartford affair. Edwards, *Guerrillas*, 392–95, credits Frank James with the killing of Barnett. Edwards was sometimes inaccurate with unit designations, and the regiments named here were not checked by the author.

17. McCorkle, 139. See Hale, *Quantrill*, 141–42, for the account of Allen Parmer, taken from the *Kansas City Post*, August 21, 1909. See also the *Louisville Courier-Journal*, April 29, 1874, and Edwards, *Guerrillas*, 395–97. The date of the Houstonville affair is given as the day before the subsequent action at Danville, which can be dated via the OR. The *Louisville Daily Democrat*, January 31, 1865, identifies the man killed as a fellow named Cunningham. Parmer identified him as a Major Houston. Leslie, 352, gives the name as "Lt. G. F. Cunningham, late of the Thirteenth Kentucky Cavalry."

18. OR, 49, pt. 1, 17–18; McCorkle, 139–40; Connelley, 463–64, footnote 10. Sylvester Akers relates the story of the encounter with Bridgewater's men, which

would seem to fit somewhat into the account by McCorkle. McCorkle's story of the mother begging for the life of her officer-son seems a bit melodramatic, though. Both the Akers and McCorkle accounts sound like "war stories" in light of the OR accounts and an account in the *Louisville Daily Democrat*, January 31, 1865, which mentions no body of Federal troops near town. The *Democrat* article claims that several guerrillas had attended school at Danville before the war but were from Missouri. See also the *Report of the Adjutant General of the State of Kentucky* 2, 1861–1866, 792–93 (cited hereafter as *Adjutant General-Ky.*), for information on Bridgewater's Company. Another source is an undated newspaper article from 1927, "Men Led By Frank and Jesse James Killed During Skirmish in Mercer," probably from a Harrodsburg, Kentucky, newspaper obtained from the Milton F. Perry, who probably acquired it from a historical-society file in Kentucky. The article recalls Frank James's visit to the Harrodsburg area in July 1897. In this account Quantrill's men were "on their way to Washington to capture the government." While the article confuses Stanford with Danville, it mentions that the guerrillas "got in a spree, which led to the officers getting wise as to their identity and were followed when they rode out." This seems to fit with Akers's account and with that in McCorkle. Still, it does not explain why Quantrill would divide his command in the face of an approaching enemy, and thus is suspect. Saying that Union forces backed down would tend to take some of the sting out of the defeat when told to admiring women and youngsters in later years. Leslie, 351–52, says a Colonel Weatherford rode from Houstonville to Stanford to alert Bridgewater, who arrived after the guerrillas had left.

19. John Bridgewater, Pension Record #764.241, R.G. 94, National Archives, Washington, D.C. Bridgewater, who was a lieutenant at the time of the fights with Quantrill, was denied a pension in 1894 for his Civil War service, as his unit was in state rather than federal service. His file contains the quotes mentioned in a deposition, as well as citations from the OR, 39, pt. 1, 120, 273, concerning activity against Morgan's command in 1864. See also *Adjutant General-Ky.*, 2:292–93, which states that Company A "was originally raised as an independent Company of Scouts attached to the secret service," when formed in 1864. This probably meant acting incognito as scouts or spies against Morgan and any guerrilla bands, with later expansion as a state guard unit.

20. Edwards, *Guerrillas*, 401. This account must, as has been said, be read with caution concerning details. Edwards omits Jim Younger's name from the list of those captured, which may or may not be in error. He gives the number of those present at the house as eleven, which might be the case if Renick, from another squad, is counted among the casualties. Edwards gives the most detailed picture of all books on the Kentucky campaign but his details must be independently verified. McCorkle, 140–43, gives Jim Younger as a prisoner. This may well be the best account of the fight that is available. Castel, *Quantrill*, 204–5, mentions Younger's capture, probably drawing from McCorkle's account. OR, 49, pt. 1, 18, 615–16, states that Quantrill's force at Danville was estimated at around thirty-five. Some of his men may have deserted along the way, if earlier accounts are accurate. Three squads of around twelve men would seem to fit. The bodies of the four men killed were buried in Oakland

Methodist Church Cemetery then moved about 1897–98 to the Confederate lot at Spring Hill Cemetery in an unknown area, perhaps Harrodsburg, Kentucky, or even Saint Louis. The Harrodsburg newspaper, *The Sayings*, July 2(?), 1897, gives an account of Frank James's visit with Kit Chinn and raises the possibility that Frank would return in August to remove the bodies to Saint Louis. An unidentified Harrodsburg newspaper clipping, "Frank James," July 7, 1897, says, based on an interview with Frank, that the fight took place "near Oakland church." It further states: "When Quantrill left Missouri his intention was to go into Maryland. He crossed the Mississippi . . . and worked his way into Kentucky and having no guide got into confusion and suffered many dangers and privations." Thomas Selby Watson, *The Silent Riders*, 32 (cited hereafter as Watson), references the article from the *Louisville Courier-Journal*, April 29, 1874, which gives an account of the escape and agrees with McCorkle on Jim Younger's capture near Harrodsburg. The *Louisville Daily Democrat*, January 31, 1865, gives an account of Bridgewater's men arriving at Danville just after the guerrillas had left and says the guerrillas lost two killed outright, with four wounded and five or six captured. Leslie, 352–53, has a guerrilla named Tom Evans kept at Lexington under suspicion of killing Cunningham until released after the war. Connelley, 463, has a Bill Robinson hanged for allegedly killing Cunningham.

21. *OR*, 49, pt. 1, 18, 625–26, 634–35; McCorkle, 143–45; Edwards, *Guerrillas*, 409–15. Edwards specifically names Marion as the guerrilla leader on this raid, which is often attributed to Marcellus Jerome Clarke, alias Sue Mundy. See Valentine, "Mundy, pt. 1," 177, 199, 201–3. Valentine makes the point that it was apparently Marion, not Clarke-Mundy, who led the raid on Midway and Georgetown. On page 203, in footnote 125, he mentions that a historical marker was erected at Midway, giving credit for leading the raid to Clarke-Mundy, who may have been miles away at the time. The account in Edwards fails to mention Clarke-Mundy and probably indicates that it was indeed Marion who was responsible, as Clarke-Mundy attempted to show through testimony at his trial. This brings to mind a story about another historical marker error, in Tennessee, which was brought to the attention of a local official. "It can't be wrong. It's cast in bronze," was his incredulous reply.

22. McCorkle, 145, mentions a Saunders family and a widow named Cooper he had known in Jackson County, Missouri, who had been banished as a result of General Ewing's order. Edwards, *Guerrillas*, 417–23, contains a wildly exaggerated account of the fight at Bradfordsville, though he seems to have the geography down correctly. See also *OR*, 49, pt. 1, 35–36, 673–75, and compare the Federal reports with Edwards to understand why his book is considered unreliable for the facts of an engagement. It would have been embarrassing to admit that Quantrill's men were fighting disabled troops with any difficulty.

23. Edwards, *Guerrillas*, 423–24; *OR*, 49, pt. 1, 35–36, 684. According to Edwards, Jim Younger was wounded and captured in this fight. If so, it was for the second time. It is possible that Younger was captured later. Leslie, 355–56, has Quantrill probably escaping on his horse, Old Charley.

24. *OR*, 46, pt. 2, 724, for Stanton telegram to Hancock. This would tend to support the contention that Quantrill had somehow been ordered to this area. He may have been expected at any time, but failed to show, and somehow word of his potential

presence leaked out. Interestingly, just prior to this telegram, guerrillas under Jesse McNeil captured Gens. George Crook and Benjamin Kelley at Cumberland, Maryland, northwest of Hancock's location in Virginia. These were men of guerrilla leader Gilmore's former command (he'd been captured). See *OR*, vol. 49, pt. 1, 788–89, vol. 49, pt. 2, 406, for an account of Hickman and West Tennessee activities. Connelley, 462–65, says the leader at Hickman may have been Clarke-Mundy. He then quotes in full Quantrill's bastardized version of Byron, dated February 26, 1865. Quantrill's band was apparently even more shaken by this defeat, which is omitted in most guerrilla memoirs. Frank James, in a wild story told in New Orleans to a reporter for the *Cincinnati Enquirer* that was reprinted in the *Liberty (Mo.) Advance* on May 18, 1894, related a tale about stealing a mule during the campaign, only placing it at Columbia, Tennessee, and with Jesse *east* of the Mississippi. If there's even a grain of truth to this account it may only be very loosely based on difficulties encountered after Houstonville when Frank reportedly stole one mule and the herd followed. For more on the Lincoln kidnapping-assassination plot, see William B. Feis et al., "The Lincoln Assassination: Do The Pieces Fit?" *North & South* 2, no. 4 (April 1999): 26–34. This is a round-table discussion of the thesis propounded in *Come Retribution* and *April '65* by Tidwell, Hall, and Gaddy.

25. L. L. Valentine, "Sue Mundy of Kentucky: Part II," *Register of the Kentucky Historical Society* 62, no. 4 (October 1964): 278–305 (cited hereafter as Valentine, "Mundy, pt. 2"). This source gives the remainder of the Mundy story, which touches only briefly on Quantrill's command, if at all. It does paint a good picture of operations against the guerrillas, of which more will be said elsewhere. John M. Palmer, *Personal Recollections of John M. Palmer: The Story of an Earnest Life*, 226, 267 (cited hereafter as Palmer, *Life*), states that he took command on February 18, 1865.

26. Valentine, "Mundy, pt. 2," 281; *Adjutant General-Ky.*, 198–99, 316–17.

27. Connelley, 467–70; Watson, 28–30, 44–49; Edward L. Terrill (*sic*), Service Record, First Kentucky Infantry, M319, Roll 79, Seventh Kentucky Cavalry, M319, Roll 43, Ninth Kentucky Mtd. Infantry, M319, Roll 135, R.G. 109, National Archives, Washington, D.C. Terrell enlisted in the First Kentucky on June 1, 1861, at Owensboro, Kentucky, and was discharged on May 19, 1862. He was in the hospital for rheumatism. An Edward "Terrill" was enlisted in the Seventh Kentucky Cavalry by Col. Basil Duke, classmate of Robert James, on August 27, 1862, at Hartsville, Tennessee. He was listed as having deserted his command on September 7, 1862, during a raid at Lexington, Kentucky. An Ed Terrill was also in the Ninth Kentucky, another unit under Morgan, date of enlistment not given, first shown on rolls in March 1863. He was captured near McMinnville, Tennessee, on April 11 [10?], 1863. Ed Terrell probably belonged to the Seventh Kentucky, as the signature on the parole papers for the man in the Ninth Kentucky doesn't match that of a known Terrell letter, according to Watson, 46. Terrell is thought to have served in Tennessee under John Hunt Morgan. See the *Louisville Daily Democrat*, February 1, 1865. The *Louisville Courier-Journal*, December 14, 1868, carried a minibiography-obituary of Terrell. It mentions that Terrell deserted from Morgan during Bragg's invasion of Kentucky in 1862, as did "Terrill" of the Seventh Kentucky. Leslie, 344–45, claims he never found a variant spelling of Terrell's name in Confederate

service records. But they are indeed there, as cited above. Using a signature from a letter dated January 6, 1865, Watson says the spelling is Terrell. The name is often found spelled with an *i* in military records and correspondence, however.

28. John M. Palmer telegram to Terrill (*sic*), April 11, 1865, R.G. 393, Dept. of Kentucky, Telegrams Sent, Entry 2169 (vol. 12 Kentucky), 168; Capt. J. Bates Dickson, letter to D. W. Lindsay, Adj. Gen. of Kentucky [April 1865], R.G. 393, Entry 2164, Dept. of Kentucky, Letters Sent, vol. 3, 59; Palmer, *Life*, 267–68.

29. *OR*, 39, pt. 1, 511–12. Connelley, 465, 471–78, contains James Wakefield's account of Quantrill's last fight. O. L. Joyner, "Quantrill's Death Verified," *Confederate Veteran* 19, no. 6 (June 1911): 285, contains an interview with Frank James on the alleged visit to his fallen leader. Frank mentions a Mrs. Nev (Harriet) Ross, a refugee from Jackson County, Missouri, whose son served with the Missouri guerrillas, as having visited Quantrill in Louisville. People from western Missouri apparently had deep family roots in the Nelson-Spencer County area. This probably accounts for the Missouri guerrillas being on better behavior than in other areas where they had campaigned. McCorkle, 145–55, relates that there were relatives of some of the guerrillas in the area. McCorkle surrendered after he learned of Lee's capitulation and went to New Castle, Kentucky; others left before Quantrill was wounded, as well. See Watson, 44, 51–63, for what may be the most exhaustive account of the Wakefield fight and its aftermath. Watson includes a roster of Terrell's men on page 44, a list that is omitted in Connelley, which was taken from a paymaster file in the National Archives. There were twenty-eight enlisted scouts, plus the officers listed in Connelley, 470. The enlisted men made $20 per month. Terrell made $50, and his lieutenants, John Thompson and Horace Allen, made $35 and $30, respectively. Enlisted men were: Thomas Wilson, Anderson Terrell, George Trumbo, Joseph Taylor, Charles Taylor, Elias Stohl, Henry Smith, Benjamin Stevens, John Rogers, Albert Ross, John Middleton, John Langford (who probably shot Quantrill in the spine), Benjamin Kirkpatrick, John Johnson, Thomas Johnson, Warren Hacker, Talton Embry, Robert Edwards, Franklin Dougherty, Sylvester Cheatham, Lev Cotton, William Cook, Joseph Cook, Andrew Cook, Gilbert M. Brooks, Albert Bowman, William Bloom, and Scott Anschutz. Terrell may have shot off one of Quantrill's fingers in the fight. Reportedly Terrell's men were armed with both pistols and Spencer repeating carbines at the time of the fight. Thomas Coleman Younger, *The Story of Cole Younger, By Himself*, 54 (cited hereafter as Younger), relates that Jim Younger was captured in the Wakefield fight and was in the military prison at Alton, Illinois, until released in the fall of 1865. Richard Glasscock, who had escaped from prison in Louisville, was killed in the Wakefield fight, but it is uncertain, even with Cole's statement, whether Jim Younger was recaptured here or in the Houstonville fight of February 9, 1865, or at another time. See also Leslie, 361–68.

30. Edwards, *Guerrillas*, 331–32. The militiaman is identified by the name Harkness, but Edwards didn't always get the names right. That he would cite Jesse James, whom he normally portrayed in a more positive light, as an accessory to such a killing, says much. See also Kingsville, Missouri, Papers (C 3516), "The Kingsville Massacre," Western Historical Manuscript Collection, University of Missouri-Columbia. This account states that a prisoner of the guerrillas had his throat slit at their camp on the

aptly named Louse Run, in Cass County, on May 6, 1865, the night prior to the
Kingsville affair. George Scholl to Fletch Taylor, November 2, 1911, transcript in my
papers, claims that 144 guerrillas left Sherman on March 5, 1865, and departed
Mount Pleasant on April 6.

31. *OR*, 48, pt. 2, 286 (cited hereafter as *OR*, 48–2).
32. Ibid., 200–201, 211–12, 214–15, 269–70, 296, 322–25, 500, 785. See also Patrick
    Brophy's letter and map sent to Ted Yeatman, October 31, 1994, concerning
    Third Wisconsin posts in Vernon County, Missouri. Also see *Compiled Records
    Showing Service of Military Units in Voluntary Union Organizations*, National
    Archives Microfilm Publication M594, Roll 197; Chandler P. Chapman, *Roster of
    Wisconsin Volunteers: War of the Rebellion*, 126–51 (cited hereafter as *Wisconsin
    Volunteers*). The regiment was reorganized early in 1865. New Company F (the
    same as old Company F) was stationed at Fort Insley, probably at Douglas Ford, on
    the Marmiton River, northeast of the present community of Deerfield. New Com-
    pany H (old Company C) was at Fort McKean, Kansas, right along the state line
    on the West Fork Drywood Creek. New Company I (old Company D) was at Fort
    Hamer, probably at Lambert Ford of Drywood Creek, due north of where the
    creek crosses the present County Highway HH. New Company K was at Fort
    Curtis, at the site of old Balltown in 1865, southeast of the present community of
    Metz. Service Record of John M. Bernard, Company M, Third Wisconsin Cavalry,
    Record Group 94, National Archives, Washington, D.C.
33. Service Record of Clayton E. Rogers, Company B, Fiftieth Wisconsin Infantry,
    Record Group 94, National Archives, Washington, D.C.; Lance J. Herdegen, "The
    Lieutenant Who Arrested a General," *Gettysburg Magazine* 4 (January 1991):
    25–32 (cited hereafter as Herdegen, "Lieutenant"). This article is perhaps the best
    overall account of Rogers's service and life, and it has a particularly good account of
    his role in the battle of Gettysburg, at least as interesting as some of the exploits of
    the James brothers but not within the scope of the present book. After his arrest,
    General Rowley was hustled off to command a mustering point for army draftees in
    Portland, Maine. The court-martial, in April 1864, found him guilty of drunken-
    ness at Gettysburg, among other things, but political connections apparently pre-
    served his rank. He spent the remainder of his service riding a desk to glory as
    commander of the Department of the Monongahela in western Pennsylvania.
34. *OR*, 48–2, 342; Edwards, *Guerrillas*, 332–33; *Kansas City Daily Journal of Com-
    merce*, May 10, 11, 1865; John Hoyt Williams, *A Great and Shining Road: The Epic
    Story of the Transcontinental Railroad*, 263–68 (cited hereafter as Williams,
    Railroad). The Union Pacific apparently changed officers before its completion;
    Kingsville, Missouri, Papers, (C 3516), Western Historical Manuscript Collec-
    tion, University of Missouri-Columbia. The killed and wounded at Kingsville are
    listed as follows: James Paul, Walter Burris, Will Duncan, L. C. Duncan, Sam
    Duncan, Abner Ryan, William Johnson, and David Givens, along with four
    unnamed railroad workers. Leroy Duncan is called "Deacon" in the news account.
35. *Kansas City Daily Journal of Commerce*, May 13, 1865; *OR*, 48–2, 342, 352–53.
36. *OR*, 48–2, 408–9. George Scholl to Fletch Taylor, November 2, 1911, transcript
    in my papers, claimed that one hundred or more Federal troops were concentrated

at the crossroads and did not follow the guerrillas into the brush. This may be a confused memory of the fight of May 15. Likely he dimly recalled the troop concentrations at the crossings of the Missouri and confused it with the group from the Third Wisconsin that happened to be at the crossroads.

37. Ibid., 408–11.

38. Ibid., 421–22, 431.

39. Ibid., 470; Edwards, *Guerrillas*, 332–33.

40. *OR*, 48–2, 470; Edwards, *Guerrillas*, 333–34. The account in Edwards appears to be a typical "war story" related by a former guerrilla.

41. *Liberty (Mo.) Tribune*, August 19, 1937. Settle, 206, gives a brief summation on Judge Shouse as a source. Shouse was repeating the story as related to him by Jesse James.

42. *Wisconsin Volunteers*, 134–36, 150–51; Service Record of John J. Jones, Companies D and I, Third Wisconsin Cavalry, Record Group 94, National Archives, Washington, D.C.; Service Record of John Jones, Company B, Third Wisconsin Cavalry, Record Group 94, National Archives, Washington, D.C.; Regimental Letter Book, Third Wisconsin Cavalry, Record Group 94, National Archives, Washington, D.C. On 23 and 104 are letters dated March 26 and April 14, 1865, from headquarters in Little Rock, Arkansas, concerning John Jones of Company B, who is the only other John Jones in the regiment. John J. Jones from Wales, of Company I, is most likely the man who shot Jesse James since the other Jones was with that part of the regiment in Arkansas. See Ted Yeatman, "Jesse James' Surrender," *Old West* 31, no. 1 (Fall 1994): 14–19; and Summary Statements of Quarterly Returns of Ordnance and Ordnance Stores on Hand in Regular and Volunteer Army Organizations, National Archives Microfilm Publication M1281, Roll 3. The service record of John J. Jones says that he purchased his "Colts revolver" on being mustered out of the regiment. Ordnance records of June 30, 1864, the last of record, show Jones's unit armed with twenty-five .52-caliber Cosmopolitan carbines and no revolvers. The .36-caliber ball could have been from a privately owned revolver belonging to Jones or from one issued after the quarterly ordnance report at the end of 1864. Or it could have come from a gun used by one of the Johnson County EMM, if indeed they were present. Information on the bullet was given to the author on August 14, 1995, by Derek Regensburger, research assistant for Professor James Starrs, who conducted the exhumation of the grave of Jesse James on July 17–18, 1995. As the force sent to Lexington was an ad hoc group, with apparently some companies of the Third not having side arms at the end of 1864, it is possible that they might have received other revolvers in 1865. I erred in giving the arms of old Company D of the Third Wisconsin, on 18. The *Kansas City Times*, August 14, 1965, repeats an earlier interview with Jim Cummins. Given Arch Clement's reputation and earlier actions, it is not likely that he was returning from surrender negotiations, as related in Edwards, *Guerrillas*, 333–36. The *Saint Louis Republican*, April 27, 1882, gives an account stating that the Federals allegedly had sent a company out, on orders of Captain Rogers, to meet with the guerrillas. While it is possible that some might have been awaiting a reply to Clement's note of May 11, 1865, it seems unlikely.

43. Robertus Love, *The Rise and Fall of Jesse James*, 438–39 (cited hereafter as Love), gives Cummins's 1902 account. Cummins said they received assurances *after* the fight that they could surrender. See Jim Cummins, *Jim Cummins the Guerrilla*, 49–50. The *Saint Louis Republican*, April 27, 1882, gives an account of Jesse taking the oath at the Virginia Hotel. The *Saint Louis Dispatch*, November 22, 1873, contains John N. Edwards's interview with Jesse James concerning the surrender. See also the Roll of Confederate Soldiers Taking the Amnesty Oath, Lexington, Missouri, Record Group 109, National Archives, Washington, D.C.; and Robert Barr Smith, "The James Boys Go to War," *Civil War Times Illustrated* 32, no. 6 (January-February 1990): 60; "The Untold West: Outlaws, Rebels and Rogues," Modern Times Film Co., 1993, is a documentary, first shown on TBS and later released by TBS on home video, that contains an interview with a prominent authority on the myth of the Old West who contends that the guerrillas were not allowed to surrender. *Kansas City Daily Journal*, May 23, 1865. The various pseudo-historical works are discussed in Appendix A, "The Jesse James of Legend." Leslie, 377, 484, questions whether Jesse actually surrendered. In all probability he did.

44. Jesse Edwards James, *Jesse James, My Father*, 54 (cited hereafter as James, *Father*). Jesse Edwards James confuses the dates and apparently used Edwards as a source, but he also has much information based on family lore, probably including details about Rogers and Jones. See also *Saint Louis Dispatch*, November 22, 1873.

45. OR, 48–2, 545–46, 738, 785, 872; Charles W. Porter, Company F, Third Wisconsin Cavalry, diary, entry of June 6, 1865, Wisconsin Historical Society, Madison, Wisconsin. On May 13, 1865, Porter noted "a shooting affray" at Leavenworth between Doc Jennison and a Major Anthony in which the jayhawker colonel was wounded in the thigh. Excerpts from the diary have been reprinted, on a limited basis, by the Bushwhacker Museum in Nevada, Missouri. See also Herdegen, "Lieutenant," 31–32. Rogers returned to Wisconsin, where he served a brief term as sheriff of Vernon County and later worked for the North Wisconsin Lumber Company in Hayward. He was active in the Wisconsin Grand Army of the Republic and was a deacon in the Congregational Church. His death on April 30, 1900, was "the genuine sorrow of the people," with schools and lumber mills closing out of respect. Frederick Weyerhauser, the timber tycoon, was one of his pallbearers. In many early "histories" of the James brothers, Rogers was misidentified and relegated to oblivion. A thirty-two-year-old captain, he became "liberal old Major J. B. Rogers, a U.S. regular army officer" in Frank Triplett's *The Life, Times and Treacherous Death of Jesse James* (1882), and "Major J. W. Rodgers" in Edwards, *Guerrillas* (1877).

46. Circular No. 3, Headquarters, Dept. of Kentucky, April 29, 1865, Regimental Order Book, Fifty-fourth Kentucky Mounted Infantry, Record Group 94, National Archives, Washington, D.C.

47. Maj. Gen. George H. Thomas to Maj. Gen. John M. Palmer, telegram of May 1, 1865 (forwarded May 2, 1865), Telegrams Sent, 160, Entry 2169, Dept. of Kentucky, Record Group 393, National Archives, Washington, D.C. Telegram to Capt. Terrell from Maj. Gen. John M. Palmer, May 2, 1865, 159. Maj. Gen. John M. Palmer to commanding officer, Emminence, Kentucky, telegram of May 10, 1865, 168. Connelley, 481–82, gives an account from the *Louisville Daily Courier*,

May 14, 1865, which states that Terrell got orders to report back to Louisville shortly after he struck the trail of the guerrillas who were thought to be "One-Arm" Berry's group. Leslie, 363. It's possible that the slaying of farmer Hercules Walker by Terrell's men, which was getting unfavorable press coverage, was in part responsible for the recall.

48. Capt. E. B. Harlan to Maj. Gen. John M. Palmer, telegram of May 18, 1865, 172. Maj. Gen. John M. Palmer to Capt. E. B. Harlan, telegram of May 18, 1865, Telegrams Received, Entry 2174, Dept. of Kentucky, Record Group 393, National Archives, Washington, D.C.

49. United States v. Samuel O. Berry, Alias "One-Arm" Berry, citizen, January 1866, Case MM 3528, Records of the Office of the Judge Advocate General, Record Group 153, National Archives, Washington, D.C. (cited hereafter as Berry Trial). The transcript of this obscure case is the best primary source on the events leading to the surrender of the remaining members of Quantrill's guerrillas in Kentucky. See also Palmer, *Life*, 268–69, which stated that Henry Porter, Quantrill's successor, came in and proposed surrender terms. If so, it is not mentioned elsewhere. As will be seen, Palmer's memory is subject to question. See also Robert I. Alotta, *Civil War Justice: Union Army Executions Under Lincoln*, 30–32, for cases of rape by Federal soldiers as addressed by Union military courts. Cases were prosecuted swiftly and forcefully, with an average three-day lag between sentence and execution, the shortest of all crimes studied, including murder, mutiny, desertion, robbery, theft, and treason. Only twenty-two executions for rape were recorded for Union soldiers in this study. See also Thomas P. Lowry, *The Story the Soldiers Wouldn't Tell: Sex in the Civil War*, 123–31, for further attitudes toward rape and rapists during the war.

50. Berry Trial; Edwards, *Guerrillas*, 443–46; McCorkle, 156–57.

51. Berry Trial; Cyrus J. Wilson to Maj. Gen. John M. Palmer, June 5, 1865, 195, Telegrams Received, Entry 2174, Dept. of Kentucky, Record Group 393, National Archives, Washington, D.C. M. B. Morton, "Error in Regard to 'One-Arm' Berry," *Confederate Veteran* 20 (1912): 221. Berry was eventually arrested, tried before a military commission in January 1866 on a laundry list of charges, and sentenced to hang. Palmer, in his infinite mercy, saw to it that Berry was shipped off to prison at Auburn, New York, to serve a ten-year sentence, reportedly in solitary confinement (he "never saw the light of day" again, according to his brother), only seven of which were completed at the time of his death. See also Ezra Warner, *Generals in Blue: Lives of Union Commanders*, 115–16 (cited hereafter as Warner, *Generals in Blue*), and Valentine, "Mundy, pt. 2," 304–6. Ironically, the commission that tried Berry was headed by Bvt. Maj. Gen. Jefferson C. Davis, who in 1862 had shot his former commander, Gen. William Nelson, in a quarrel at the Galt House in Louisville. Davis was never tried for his own obvious murder of Nelson, due to the political string-pulling of Gov. Oliver Morton of Indiana. However, Davis was never promoted above his rank in the volunteers. Palmer undoubtedly knew of Davis's killing Nelson and may have considered the sentence he handed down as hypocritical. See Palmer, *Life*, 273–76, where he credits the commutation of the death sentence of one Jim Davis, "a worse man than Berry," as his motivation. This may have been only part of the story.

52. Berry Trial; see also, Col. S. F. Johnson to Bvt. Maj. Gen. Stephen G. Burbridge, February 7, 1865, 414, Telegrams Received, Entry 2174, District of Kentucky, Record Group 393, National Archives, Washington, D.C. Palmer probably was not aware of the telegram sent from the headquarters of the Seventeenth Kentucky Cavalry at Russellville, possibly regarding something that happened around Hopkinsville. It said, "Sir, on the twenty-ninth last month Capt. Bridgewater captured lot of guerillas under Capt. Clarke. These men murdered several citizens in this vicinity. I want to handle them if you will allow me to do so. I send full particulars by mail." These details were not found in National Archives. It is possible that this could refer to the work of stragglers from Quantrill's group. There was apparently a steady attrition rate, exclusive of the fighting, among the members of Quantrill's band. Russellville is a good distance from the line of march that the group took, unless Johnson means the Hopkinsville area. It is probable that there were additional unreported killings that went unaccounted in Edwards and other sources on Quantrill in Kentucky.

53. Connelley, 478–79; McGrane, 30; Alex James, Parole Certificate, photographic copy in author's collection; Berry Trial; *Adjutant General—Kentucky,* 540; Letters Sent, Entry 2164, Department of Kentucky, Record Group 393, National Archives, Washington, D.C. A search of formal correspondence coming out of Palmer's Headquarters failed to locate any record of a letter to the president regarding a pardon. Perhaps it was merely a list, with Palmer's endorsement on one side, and whether it actually got out to Washington and/or was lost amid the piles of paperwork of a disbanding Union army is as yet uncertain. It is also possible that this request was deliberately withheld. Pardon Petitions and Related Papers Submitted in Response to President Andrew Johnson's Amnesty Proclamations of May 29, 1865, National Archives Microfilm Publication M1003, Roll 36, shows no record of a pardon applied for or granted. Also checked were House Executive Document No. 31, 39th Cong., 2d sess., serial 1289; House Executive Document No. 116, 39th Cong., 2d sess., serial 1293; House Executive Document No. 32, 40th Cong., 1st sess., serial 1311, which lists persons pardoned under Johnson's first amnesty proclamation. "Alexander" or "Alex." James does not appear in any of the lists and neither do the names of other guerrillas who surrendered at Samuels Depot. See also Capt. E. B. Harlan to Lt. Glasgow, Kentucky, May 29, 1865, Telegrams Sent, 177, Entry 2169, Department of Kentucky, Record Group 393, National Archives, Washington, D.C.: "Paroled rebel prisoners are allowed to retain their private property but not allowed to carry arms." The surrender terms were rather unique for the men of Quantrill's band.

54. O. L. Joyner, "Quantrill's Death Verified," *Confederate Veteran* 19, no. 6 (June 1911): 285; Watson, 64; Hale, *Quantrill,* 68–75. See also Leslie, 406–40, for perhaps the best account of the strange journey of Quantrill's remains. Scott secretly retained some of the bones, which eventually made their way into the hands of the Kansas Historical Society in Topeka. They were taken to Missouri and buried in the Confederate Cemetery at Higginsville in October 1992 with full military honors. The skull, also retained by Scott, was given to his son after unsuccessful attempts to sell it. It was used in initiation rites by a fraternity until the 1940s, and after briefly surfacing again at a banquet given for fraternity alumni in 1960 was given to the Dover, Ohio, Historical Society in 1972.

55. Special Orders No. 80, May 24, 1865, 11-1865, E-2178, Special Orders, Department of Kentucky, Record Group 393, National Archives, Washington, D.C.; *Louisville Daily Democrat,* September 6, 8, 1865. Watson, 65, cites August 25 as the date of Johnson's death. I choose to believe the date of August 27 given in the *Democrat.* Leslie, 367–68, says that Terrell's group was mustered out of service on May 13, but this is not what the record indicates. It happened on May 24, just after the saloon incident and the capture of Froman and his guerrilla companions.

56. Watson, 65–66; *Louisville Courier-Journal,* December 14, 1868. See also Castel, *Quantrill,* 212. An oft-used source, Castel is in error in saying that Quantrill outlived Terrell. Evidence simply does not bear this out. To Watson must go the credit for first tracking Terrell's activities after the war. Leslie, 388–91, deserves the honor of tracking down Terrell's death.

CHAPTER 4: THE OUTLAWS OF MISSOURI

1. *Saint Louis Dispatch,* November 22, 1873.
2. *History of Clay,* 268; *Boonville (Mo.) Weekly Advertiser,* November 16, 1900. Jesse was probably given opiates to dull the pain, which would account for his listless condition.
3. Ibid. *Kansas City Daily Journal,* April 4, 1882. By one unconfirmed account, Jesse also may have been wounded in the leg or thigh in the fight outside Lexington with the Third Wisconsin Cavalry. In most accounts the lung wound is the only one mentioned, however.
4. *Kansas City Daily Journal,* April 4, 1882, regarding Dagley and Frank in Nelson County; Beamis and Pullen, 13, 75; *Saint Louis Weekly Missouri Republican,* April 13, 1882, regarding visitation to Logan County; *Saint Louis Dispatch,* November 22, 1873; J. A. Murray to Col. N. S. Andrews, Comdg. Post, Bowling Green, Kentucky, October 30, 1865, R.G, 393, Department of Kentucky, Letters Received, Entry 2173, National Archives, Washington, D.C.
5. Warner, *Generals in Blue,* 54–55; Fellman, 231–42.
6. Robert J. Wybrow, "'Ravenous Monsters of Society': The Early Exploits of the James Gang," *English Westerners' Society Brand Book* 27, no. 2 (Summer 1990): 4 (cited hereafter as Wybrow, "Monsters"). This is undoubtedly the best account of the early robberies.
7. Ernest Lisle Reedstrom, "Of Mines and Men," *Wild West* 6, no. 5 (February 1994): 37; Files of Reuben and Zerelda Samuel, Provost Marshal Papers, M345, Roll 142.
8. Wybrow, "Monsters," 4–5; Settle, 33–34; *Cummins' Book,* 60, regarding the caged birds comment. Wybrow, "Monsters," 22–23, questions whether this comment was ever made. Love, 59–71, says that many people believed Arch Clement was responsible since Jesse still had to drain pus from his lung wound each day and Frank was allegedly still in Kentucky at the time. See also Fuenfhausen, 43.
9. Wybrow, "Monsters," 6–8. *History of Clay,* 233, 261, lists Bird as county tax assessor from 1863 to 1864.
10. Wybrow, "Monsters," 7–8. *Cummins' Book,* 60, credits Bud Pence and Frank James with obtaining the two sacks used in the robbery. Brant, 71–76, 325, 340, gives an

intriguing thesis, based on a reported manuscript by the mistress of Bob Younger, that Jesse thought up the idea for the robbery on his sickbed and passed it on to Cole Younger and other former guerrillas via his brother, Frank. The plan was worked out from there. Unfortunately, the manuscript, by one "Maggie," is in private hands as of this writing, and its authenticity was not confirmed at press time. This account does seem to somewhat dovetail into a story handed down in the James family and presented in fictional form in James R. Ross, *I, Jesse James*, 56–70, though in that version Jesse is a participant in the holdup. James R. Ross to Ted Yeatman, May 19, 1993, author's notes for pages to papers, contains the following statement: "The story of how Jesse came up with the idea of robbery of the Liberty Bank. It is as stated in my book. Behind what is stated is what was told to Jesse Jr. by 'Uncle Ben' (what Jesse Jr. and the rest of that generation and my mother called Frank James). Also, told by Zerelda to my grandfather. . . . I don't know who on earth would have known of this better than Frank James and Zerelda Samuel. Of course nothing could be stated or admitted until after Frank's death."

11. *Kansas City Weekly Journal of Commerce*, June 23, 1866; Wybrow, "Monsters," 8. The *Journal* makes no mention of Perry's escape, but Wybrow mentions his recapture in September 1866, and his possible death at the hands of James M. Devers, later accused of participation in the Richmond, Missouri, robbery. Perry's ultimate fate is unresolved.

12. Fellman, 235. On March 15, 1866, the mayor of Lawrence, fearing attack, requested military protection in the wake of reports from spies that another raid was imminent. Gen. Grenville Dodge, at Fort Leavenworth, Kansas, took these stories seriously, fearing that the disaffected would link up with Indian tribes he was then campaigning against. He sent an infantry company to Lawrence just in case. See Castel, "Lane," 28; and Albert Castel, *A Frontier State at War: Kansas, 1861–1865*, 232.

13. Wybrow, "Monsters," 9–10.

14. Martha Kohl, "Enforcing a Vision of Community: The Role of the Test Oath in Missouri's Reconstruction," *Civil War History* 40, no. 4 (December 1994): 292–307 (cited hereafter as Kohl, "Oath").

15. *Liberty (Mo.) Tribune*, November 2, 1866. This is typical editorial hyperbole of nineteenth-century Missouri journalism, but the right to vote was taken more seriously than it is today, and the denial of franchise, a situation also accorded to felons, women, and blacks, was generally deemed a slap at one's character and manly honor in a society that put heavy emphasis on those traits. See also Kohl, "Oath," 296–98; and *The World Almanac for 1868*, 98, for election statistics for Missouri.

16. *Liberty (Mo.) Tribune*, November 2, 1866; William E. Parrish, *Missouri under Radical Rule, 1865–1870*, 76–105 (cited hereafter as Parrish). Chapter 5 gives an excellent overview of the 1866 election and the use of U.S. troops in Missouri to guard polls, etc., instead of the politicized Missouri Militia. The militia had first been proposed in early 1866 to aid local radical sheriffs. See James M. Jones et al. to Maj. Gen. William Hoffman, Comdg. Post, Fort Leavenworth, Kansas, November 7, 1866, Letters Received, Entry 2593, Department of the Missouri, Record Group 393, National Archives, Washington, D.C. Sheriff Jones here may or may not have been

the same James Jones mentioned in *History of Clay*, 206, who with E. M. Samuel, of bank provost notoriety, and others, "were forced to flee" the Clay County area during Price's move on Lexington in 1861, "under the penalty of being 'put out of the way.'" Jones, Samuel, and compatriots fled to the Unionist settlement of Mirabile, in Caldwell County, until Price's retreat allowed them to return.

17. *Liberty (Mo.) Tribune*, November 9, 1866. Lest this sound too far-fetched, see Kohl, "Oath," 293–98, for radical leaders' quotes to similar effect. This story ultimately gets twisted and turned on its head in fiction and film, with the evil railroad trying to obtain land at cut-rate prices by driving out the agrarian locals. Some have tended to regard this perceived threat undergirding the James story as (if not a threat in fact) "legend," "melodramatic fiction," or "folklore." It deserves more serious consideration in the historical realm. See *History of Clay*, 449; and Settle, 36. Murder was a real possibility that local Unionists had to live with. Earlier, in September, Richard Sloan, a member of Company A, Sixth Missouri State Militia Cavalry, who two years earlier had been a party to the hanging of seventy-year-old David L. Ferrill, was himself gunned down near Centerville, by unknown parties. Ferrill had two sons in the Confederate army, and his grandson, Red Monkus, reportedly was a former bushwhacker who was suspected of participating in the Liberty bank heist.

18. *Saint Louis Republican*, April 7, 1882; *Kansas City Journal*, April 6, 1882.

19. William A. Pinkerton, *Train Robberies, Train Robbers, and "Holdup" Men*, 18 (cited hereafter as Pinkerton, *"Holdup" Men*); Jim Cummins, *Jim Cummins the Guerrilla*, 17. Cummins denounces Pinkerton and claims that Frank James was not arrested. It is interesting to note that he ascribes this only to Frank and makes no mention of Jesse in relation to this affair. Rickards was reportedly sheriff from late 1866 to 1868, and a deputy before this. *History of Clay*, 919, has Lucas appointed circuit judge in Platte County in July 1867. See also *Saint Louis Dispatch*, November 22, 1873; *Saint Louis Republican*, March 28, 1874; Settle, 53–54, 210 nn. 33, 34. There is an apocryphal story related to the effect that Jesse had a bloody gun battle at the family homestead on the evening of February 18, 1867, with five militiamen trying to capture or kill him. Surprisingly, for a county with a newspaper like the *Liberty (Mo.) Tribune* with its radical-baiting editorials, there is no mention of this episode in the local press. Furthermore, Frank's son would later claim that the story had no basis in fact. A similar story is related about a gun battle between Frank James and a posse hunting horse thieves (or Federal soldiers, depending on the version) at Brandenburg, Kentucky, just after his surrender (or in 1866, depending on the version) in which Frank is wounded and kills or wounds those after him, depending on the account, but somehow escapes, wounded either in the mouth or the hip. Frank's son, Robert, again, doubted the story.

20. Wybrow, "Monsters," 11; Scott Derks, ed., *The Value of a Dollar: Prices and Incomes in the United States, 1860–1989*, 2. A good rule of thumb when figuring the approximate take in any one robbery, in today's dollars, is to multiply the amount by ten.

21. Wybrow, "Monsters," 11–13; Settle, 35–37.

22. Wybrow, "Monsters," 13–14; Settle, 37; *Cummins' Book*, 61–62, provides information on the Samuels connection with the Pence boys. See also *The World Almanac*

for 1868, 90–91. Nelson County went heavily for McClellan over Lincoln in the 1864 election by a staggering 858 to 17. It is well to consider the political leanings of the various counties, both in Kentucky and Missouri in the late 1860s, or at least the election results. Party partisanship would exert a great influence on the situation. The status of the former guerrilla-bandits had become highly politicized in the sometimes extremely rancorous state and the local politics of the era.

23. *Saint Louis Dispatch*, November 22, 1873; B. F. Byrd Jr., "Dr. Paul Eve, 1806–1877," *Send for a Doctor: Paragraphs from Nashville History, 1974–75*, 110–20; Gunther E. Rothenberg, *The Art of War in the Age of Napoleon*, 228–36. Dr. Dominique Jean Larrey, chief surgeon under Napoleon, was a major innovator in field surgery during the Napoleonic Wars and was responsible for the adoption of the ambulance in the French army to evacuate the wounded.

24. *Saint Louis Dispatch*, November 22, 1873; Settle, 54; *Louisville Courier-Journal*, April 10, 1882. According to an interview with George Hite Jr., a cousin of the James boys, Jesse James was at the Hite place, near Adairville, at the time of the Russellville robbery. This may have been prior to the robbery, instead, but this is uncertain. "He was sick at the time at our house," according to Hite, still suffering from the lung wound, apparently.

25. Wybrow, "Monsters," 15–17; Tom Marshall, "Russellville Robbery Only One Since James Boys Raid" (hereafter cited as Marshall, "Russellville Robbery") (uncited news clipping, possibly Louisville, Kentucky, or Nashville, Tennessee, paper, September 30, 1934), gives information on the history of the bank. Edward Coffman, *The Story of Logan County*, 237, indicates that the bank was reorganized by Nimrod Long in 1863 while the county was under Federal occupation. This would indicate that, as in Liberty, the bank was associated with the Union element in the community.

26. Wybrow, "Monsters," 15–17; Marshall, "Russellville Robbery"; *Louisville Daily Journal*, March 23, 1868; Settle, 96–97. This may have been Cole Younger's initiation into outlawry. He had captured, with another man, two horse thieves, turning them in at the old jail in Independence in January 1868, an event that is verified by a period news account. Apparently he was recruited into the raid by his brother-in-law, John Jarrette, who was accompanying George and Oll Shepherd back to Kentucky to rob the bank. *Louisville Courier-Journal*, April 10, 1882. Oll Shepherd reportedly shot and pistol-whipped Long during the robbery.

27. Wybrow, "Monsters," 15–17; Marshall, "Russellville Robbery"; *Louisville Daily Journal*, March 23, 1868; Settle, 96–97; *Louisville Daily Journal*, March 21, 28, 1868.

28. Wybrow, "Monsters," 17–18; *Louisville Daily Journal*, March 28, 1868. A wanted poster from the bank offered a five-thousand-dollar reward "for the arrest of the five Robbers." Sheriff Rickards of Clay County, Missouri, identified several of the bandits. A copy of this reward poster, with Rickards's comments, was reprinted in recent years by the Jesse James Bank Museum in Liberty, Missouri. See also the *Louisville Courier-Journal*, April 10, 1882. George Shepherd's sentence was reportedly light in view of "strong sectional sentiment in the county." See also note 25.

29. *Saint Louis Dispatch*, November 22, 1873; Settle, 54–55. Marshall, "Russellville Robbery," provides information on Nimrod Long. Banker Long was apparently

not terribly bad off after the robbery, judging by the giant obelisk that marks his grave. Brant, 85, also gives information regarding Long and the father of the James boys. See the *Louisville Courier-Journal*, April 6, 1882, for Cole Younger's account of Jesse's lung wound, also the *Kansas City Journal*, April 6, 1882.

30. *Kansas City Star*, April 11, 1874; *Saint Louis Republican*, April 7, 1882; *Kansas City Journal*, April 6, 1882; *History of Clay*, 451–52.

31. *Saint Louis Globe-Democrat*, October 17, 1942, for interview with Edward Clingan; Wybrow, "Monsters," 18–21.

32. Ibid. *Kansas City Times*, December 16, 1869.

33. *Kansas City Star*, August 2, 1925, for interview with William Thomason; *Annual Report of the Adjutant General of Missouri for 1864*, 357; *Kansas City Times*, December 16, 1869; Steele, *Family History*, 80.

34. *Kansas City Times*, December 16, 1869.

35. *Kansas City Star*, August 2, 1925; Settle, 39, 41; Gov. Joseph W. McClurg to Sheriff of Jackson County, Missouri, telegram of December 24, 1869, Manuscript 557, State Historical Society of Missouri, Columbia, Missouri.

36. *Liberty (Mo.) Tribune*, June 24, July 15, 22, 1870, reprinting features from the *Kansas City Times*; *History of Daviess*, 494–500; Richard Patterson, *Historical Atlas of the Outlaw West*, 82. The title is a bit misleading; this is a very handy and useful reference work of sites associated with Western outlaws, with an early state-territorial map at the start of each chapter. See also Pinkerton, *"Holdup" Men*, 13; and Settle, 40.

37. *Liberty (Mo.) Tribune*, June 24, July 15, 22, 1870.

38. *Saint Louis Republican*, April 7, 1882; *Liberty (Mo.) Tribune*, July 22, 1870.

39. *Kansas City Star*, August 2, 1925.

40. Ibid. *Saint Louis Dispatch*, November 22, 1873. This story has been questioned by some historians in the past, but appears to be confirmed by William Thomason's account in the *Star*. He identifies his brother Oscar as having been involved, whereas the Edwards account gives "Deputy Sheriff Thomason." See also Love, 106–8, which relates a version told by Plunk Murray, a former guerrilla under Anderson.

41. Settle, 43, 208, n. 2. Clell Dean's son explained to Settle in 1945 that his father believed the man who interrupted him was Frank James. James D. Horan, *Desperate Men: Revelations from the Sealed Pinkerton Files*, 60–62 (cited hereafter as Horan, *Desperate Men*), is apparently based on clipping files kept by the Pinkertons, not actual reports of investigations (despite its sensational title). Horan's quotations of alleged dialogue are open to question.

42. Pinkerton, *"Holdup" Men*, 22.

43. *Richmond (Mo.) Conservator*, July 8, 1871, reprinting from the *Kansas City Times*; Settle, 43–44; Fitzgerald, "Miller," 29–31.

44. Arthur M. Schlesinger, ed., *The Almanac of American History*, 314–20 (cited hereafter as Schlesinger). Tweed was connected with the Tammany Hall political machine and a Democrat. Gould used (quite literally) his connections with the Grant administration to gain information and set the stage for his attempt on the gold market. It was an age when bad apples, regardless of party affiliation, would find common cause in the quest of the almighty dollar. See also John Steele Gordon, *The*

Scarlet Woman of Wall Street: Jay Gould, Jim Fisk, Cornelius Vanderbilt, the Erie Rail-road Wars, and the Birth of Wall Street, for an account of Gould's earlier career and connections with the "Tweed Ring."

45. *Louisville Courier-Journal,* May 1, 2, 1872; *Saint Louis Dispatch,* November 22, 1873, Jesse James would later claim that he and Frank were in Lafayette County at this time and rode over to meet with Gen. Jo Shelby, who he said had been on the same train stopped by the mob at Holden.

46. *Louisville Courier-Journal,* May 1, 2, 1872.

47. Ibid.; Robert J. Wybrow, "The James Gang in Kentucky: A Tale of Murder and Robbery in the Blue Grass State," *English Westerners' Society Brand Book* 15, no. 12 (January 1973): 25–28 (cited hereafter as Wybrow, "Kentucky"). The "Lowery gang" was actually a corruption of "Lowry." In February and March 1872, journalist George A. Townsend wrote a sensational series about the Lowrys, a band of Lumbee Indians in Robeson County, North Carolina, for the *New York Herald.* For a comparison of the James and Lowry stories see Richard Slotkin, *Gunfighter Nation: The Myth of the Gunfighter in Twentieth-Century America,* 129–39. This attempt to foist the blame on the Lowry gang was preposterous, but it illustrates the strange sense of humor that would run throughout the story.

48. Wybrow, "Kentucky," 27.

49. *Kansas City Times,* September 27, 1872; Settle, 44–45; James William Buel, *The Border Bandits,* 78. A reporter for the *Kansas City Journal* at the time, Buel claimed the girl was actually trampled by one of the horses of the robbers, not accidentally shot. Information on Bess Wallace Truman was given to the author by the late Milton F. Perry, who was also formerly curator at the Truman Library and Museum for many years and knew the Trumans well.

50. *Kansas City Times,* September 27, 1872; Settle, 44–45; James William Buel, *The Border Bandits,* 78: Settle, 16, 41; Martin McGrane, "Press Agent for Outlaws," *Rural Missouri,* February 1980, 4–5; Albert Castel, foreword to Edwards, *Guerrillas.* Edwards was born on January 4, 1839, in or near Front Royal, Virginia, and moved to the Lexington, Missouri, area with his family in the mid-1850s. He began working for the *Lexington Expositor* and ultimately became editor. Though he lacked formal education, he was a voracious reader of authors like Victor Hugo and Sir Walter Scott. See also Parrish, 303–4, for an example of related Missouri political guff. For example, before the 1870 state elections, Clay County Democrats courted new black voters for a week before the election with entertainment and political harangues. Local demagogues told assembled blacks that the rival Republicans planned to tax each black male above the age of eighteen to the tune of fifty dollars. Failure to pay would result in arrest and two years in prison. As a result, the county's blacks defected to the Democrats.

51. *Kansas City Times,* September 29, 1872; Settle 45–46, 130, 158; Herbert Hendin and Ann Pollinger Haas, *Wounds of War: The Psychological Aftermath of Combat in Vietnam,* 133–59. This is a very insightful study. There are striking parallels between Vietnam combat vets and the ex-guerrillas who served under Quantrill and Anderson. Unfortunately this aspect has been overlooked in other works about the Missouri guerrillas or the James and Younger brothers. In fairness, many works on the

guerrillas or outlaws were written prior to the Vietnam War, when post-traumatic stress disorder became a subject for study. Edwards seems to have been aware of the situation, partly from his own experiences under Shelby in Mexico, if not in Missouri. His drinking may have been a symptom of his own problems in this regard. However Edwards tries to put a spin on the predicament, one can read between the lines. See also Eric T. Dean Jr., "'We Will All Be Lost and Destroyed': Post Traumatic Stress Disorder and the Civil War," *Civil War History* 37, no. 2 (June 1991): 138–53, which notes an overall increase in the postwar crime rate and incarceration of ex-soldiers in the North. It backs up the aforementioned Vietnam study with similar cases, even citing as a consequence outlaw activity in Missouri (page 149). Dean expands on this in *Shook Over Hell: Post-Traumatic Stress, Vietnam and the Civil War,* 59–63, 91–113. See also *Kansas City Daily Journal of Commerce,* September 27, 1872.

52. *Kansas City Times,* October 5, 1872.

53. Schlesinger, 322–25; Williams, *Railroad,* 269–87, on the Credit Mobilier investigation.

54. O'Flaherty, 368, quotes from an interview with Shelby in the *Kansas City Journal* during the spring of 1883. The *Saint Louis Dispatch,* November 22, 1873, gives a version in which Jesse says the near lynching occurred in November 1872.

55. Settle, 47–48. The *New York Times,* July 23, 26, 1873, for the best accounts of the Adair robbery, drawn from the *Davenport (Iowa) Gazette,* etc. See also Richard Patterson, *The Train Robbery Era: An Encyclopedic History,* 2–3, 20, 86 (cited hereafter as Patterson, *Train*). Compare the robbery at Adair, Iowa, with those at Briscoe Station and Franklin, Kentucky, October 11 and November 8, 1866, respectively. Writers in other works about train robbers (Harry Sinclair Drago, *Road Agents and Train Robbers,* 171–72; Paul I. Wellman, *A Dynasty of Western Outlaws,* 85–86) have suggested that the gang somehow learned the idea of train robbery from someone with the Reno gang, but the Renos didn't rob trains by wrecking them. This was a technique used in Kentucky both during and after the war. As Patterson shows in his excellent work, train robbery was not just confined to the Trans-Mississippi and Trans-Appalachian West but also occurred along the East Coast. Patterson deserves credit for using the *New York Times* articles above instead of blindly following earlier accounts. Walter T. Durham, *Rebellion Revisited: A History of Sumner County, Tennessee, from 1861 to 1870,* 287, gives a local tradition that the James brothers visited Sumner County after the war and possibly knew Ellis Harper, a guerrilla who operated along the Tennessee-Kentucky line. Harper used similar train-wrecking tactics during the war. Durham cites a period article in which Harper is "accompanied by a man named James." This also might have been another person of that name. Patterson, *Train,* 20, lists a man named John James, of Allen County, Kentucky, as a suspect in the Briscoe Station robbery. Allen County borders on the northeast half of Sumner County.

56. Settle, 48, 50–56; *Saint Louis Dispatch,* November 22, 1873. Edwards also gives the fantastic story of Jesse and Frank James's alleged involvement in a fight with Jennison's jayhawkers at Cabin Creek in Indian Territory on November 22, 1864. In fact, they had yet to leave Missouri with Quantrill. "Terrible Quintette" is a mixture of mundane fact and outrageous fiction, along with some genuinely verifiable

escapades. Some of the yarns may well have been spun by the outlaws, with polishing by Edwards. An example is the tale of the melodramatic-sounding "Brotherhood of Death," which was supposedly responsible for the killing of Sheets at Gallatin. The tale of Cole Younger testing out an Enfield rifle-musket on a row of Union army prisoners also has its apparent origin here. Despite the fabrications, some of the more mundane material seems legitimate, and other stories, like that of Oscar Thomason's meeting Jesse on the trail, are independently verifiable.

57. Schlesinger, 324–25. See Eric Foner, *Reconstruction: America's Unfinished Revolution, 1863–1877*, 512–63 (cited hereafter as Foner, *Reconstruction*), for a background on the causes and effects of the 1873 Panic.

58. See *Little Rock Arkansas Daily Gazette*, January 18, 1874, for the best account of the robbery. See also Settle, 49–50; Love, 129–32; *Tennesseans in the Civil War: A Military History of Confederate and Union Units with Available Rosters of Personnel*, part 2, 113, lists a G. K. Crump, in Company K, Twenty-first–Twenty-second Tennessee Cavalry, raised in west Tennessee and serving mostly there and in northern Mississippi. This is most likely the same man, with the middle initial being a clerical error, either by the army or the newspaper. The newspaper version is given here in this text, though it could be either; *Tennesseans in the Civil War*, part 1, 102–4, gives a history of the unit, which served largely under Nathan Bedford Forrest. The mention of a telegram to the *Saint Louis Democrat* indicates how media conscious at least one of the robbers was, and this act of grace was probably meant to sway public opinion.

CHAPTER 5: TO CAPTURE THE JAMES BOYS

1. Frank Morn, "'*The Eye That Never Sleeps*': A History of the Pinkerton National Detective Agency, 17–52 (cited hereafter as Morn); James D. Horan, *The Pinkertons: A Detective Dynasty That Made History*, 2–151 (cited hereafter as Horan, *Pinkerton*). Of these two books Morn's is the most scholarly and best documented. While Horan's account too often falls down on documentation, it nevertheless contains some interesting material. Morn's work, out of print and difficult to obtain at this writing, deserves a reissue and is a must for the study of the Pinkerton Agency and pioneer detective work in America. See also Patterson, *Train*, 185–86; and George William Brown, *Baltimore and the Nineteenth of April, 1861*, 11–19, 120–37, contesting the existence of a plot to kill Lincoln in 1861. The latter pages are an appendix on the alleged plot taken from Col. Ward H. Lammon's *Life of Abraham Lincoln*. Lammon was a friend of Lincoln, and his observations are worthy of note.

2. Morn, 53–67; Horan, *Pinkerton*, 150–79; Patterson, *Train*, 185–86, 207–9.

3. Morn, 53–67; Wayne G. Broehl Jr., *The Molly Maguires*, 143–44 (cited hereafter as Broehl). This work is one of the best on Pinkerton operations in the mid-1870s. See also Kevin Kenney, *Making Sense of the Molly Maguires*, probably the most thorough examination of this particular case to date.

4. Settle, 49, 69; *Adjutant General, Mo.—1865*, 780. *New York World*, March 28, 1874, gives the names of Pinkerton's employers in the case and their tracking of the gang.

5. Jack Barth et al., *Roadside America*, 49. Burden won his case against Hornsby and was awarded fifty dollars for his trouble.

6. *Nashville (Tenn.) Morning World*, April 28, 1882, giving a story from the *Saint Louis Democrat.*

7. *Saint Louis Republican*, February 2, March 13, and 20, 1874, February 4, 1875. The *Republican* article of February 2 reported a man being taken to a Pullman car and forced to strip by bandits searching for a "secret mark," probably a tattoo, identifying Pinkerton agents. Whicher's body was identified by a tattoo, as mentioned in the article of March 13. Undoubtedly the detective met a reception similar to that which greeted George Vest, either before or at the farm, and the gun and tattoo gave him away. *New York World*, March 28, 1874. Whicher was a native of Des Moines, Iowa, who shipped out of New York as a boy but was forced to seek a new career after breaking his ankle in 1871. *History of Clay*, 206, 334. O. P. Moss was accused in the *World* of being in league with the James boys, or at least this rumor floated about Liberty. There was an O. P. Moss who commanded a company in the Mexican War; however, both he and E. M. Samuel were loyal Unionists and had to flee in 1861 on the approach of Price's State Guard. The *World* somehow had him a classmate of the James boys who had "served in the rebel army with them." Pinkerton, *"Holdup" Men*, 24, indicates that the area where Whicher was found was at or near the place where Robert Pinkerton had given up his search after Corydon. Settle, 59–60, gives an interesting account of the affair but incorrectly gives Whicher's name as John, not Joseph, as taken from his tombstone in Chicago and William Pinkerton's account. This error is often repeated because of the general reliability of Settle's book. Eden, 19–20, gives a brief account of the Whicher affair based on a *Liberty (Mo.) Tribune* article that gives the ferry's name as "Owen's Landing." This may well be another name for Blue Mills Ferry. I had a conversation in 1983 with Nashville musician Gordon Terry, who reportedly owned a gun used by Jesse James in the killing of Whicher. It was said to be a cartridge conversion of a cap-and-ball Colt revolver. The gun was reportedly given to brother-in-law Allen Parmer and was obtained from a member of that family. The *Saint Louis Republican* of March 13, 1874, reported that the bullets removed from the corpse were all "dragoon size," or .44 caliber. The *Chicago Tribune*, December 24, 1879, reported that Dory Fox, a former guerrilla, was arrested in Kansas and jailed in Kansas City and charged with the killing of Whicher. The trial was set for January 12, 1880, with Fox pleading not guilty to the charge. The *Tribune* reported that there was "good evidence" of Fox's guilt, but failed to elaborate. The Fox case deserves further research. *Violent Kin!* 4 (October 1989), states that Jim Anderson was later killed by George Shepherd. Edwards, *Guerrillas*, 460, placed this incident in Texas. This may have been in Sherman circa 1875. Brownlee, 242–43. Anderson's friend, Arch Clement, was killed in an ambush by Missouri Militia on December 13, 1866, in Lexington, Missouri. Clement had never formally surrendered but came into town to enroll for militia duty as something of a joke. Maj. Bacon Montgomery failed to see the humor. He ordered his arrest, resulting in a shootout in the City Hotel bar. Escaping on horseback, Clement was shot down. See Fuenfhausen, 24–25, on Moss.

8. Brant, 61–144, 340. Based on Pinkerton correspondence, it would appear that Wright's real name was in fact Boyle. It is given as Wright in Brant's account. The story of Jesse planning the raids, and Cole's participation in the Liberty heist, came

from the so-called Maggie account, which is of unconfirmed authenticity as of this writing, and was used by Brant in her book. See chapter 4, note 9 for further discussion. The account of fencing the bonds came from a statement made by Cole to Harry Hoffman; Wilbur A. Zink, *The Roscoe Gun Battle: The Younger Brothers vs. Pinkerton Detectives*, 1–28; *New York World*, March 28, 1874; *Saint Louis Republican*, March 20, 1874; Settle, 60–61; *World Almanac for 1868*, 98, showing election results in Cass County; Marley Brant, *The Families of Charles Lee and Henry Washington Younger: A Genealogical Sketch*, 1–39, for background on the Younger family. An aunt of the brothers, Adeline Lee Younger, married Lewis Dalton and was mother of the notorious Dalton brothers. The Daltons are sometimes erroneously said to be cousins of the James brothers, in some poorly researched books and articles, when they were in fact cousins of the Youngers. Grandfather Fristoe, somewhat ironically, was said to be the grandnephew of Chief Justice John Marshall of the U.S. Supreme Court.

9. *Saint Louis Republican*, March 21, 24, December 24, 1874. See Settle, 62–67, for a very insightful discussion of the political impact of the James-Younger gang's outlawry. *Kansas City Times*, May 24, 1874; Wendell H. Stephenson, "Samuel Clark Pomeroy," *Dictionary of American Biography*, 8:54–55. Just a few months previous the notorious "Pomeroy scandal" had occurred in Kansas. U.S. Senator Pomeroy was accused of buying his position and bribing the Kansas legislature, who elected members of the Senate at that point in history. State Sen. A. M. York stated that Pomeroy offered him eight thousand dollars for his vote in 1873. Pomeroy, who had held office since 1861, countered that he had given money to York to establish a bank. The affair ended his effective political career. Pomeroy is spoofed as the character of Senator Dilworthy in Mark Twain's novel *The Gilded Age*. See Fuenfhausen, 24, for information on the Clay County courthouse.

10. Allan Pinkerton to George Bangs, April 17, 1874, Pinkerton's National Detective Agency Papers, Library of Congress, Washington, D.C. (cited hereafter as Pinkerton Papers).

11. *Kansas City Daily Journal*, April 6, 1882, for account of William James; Stella Frances James, *In the Shadow of Jesse James*, 31–33, 122–25 (cited hereafter as Stella James). This is one of the best accounts of the James family and deserves a place in the library of any serious student of the James story; Settle, 69–70.

12. *Saint Louis Dispatch*, June 7, 1874. The information in the *Dispatch*, Edwards's paper, was apparently intended to throw detectives off the mark. It mentioned a honeymoon in Mexico. Zee apparently stayed with relatives in the Kearney area into early May, when she departed by train for a rendezvous with Jesse at the home of Allen and Susan James Parmer at Sherman, Texas. The couple moved briefly to Dallas sometime in September, returning to the Kansas City area at the end of the year; Harry A. Soltysiak, "The Pinkerton Bomb," *American History Illustrated* 27, no. 2, May-June 1992, 54, with reference to the *Saint Louis Democrat* editorial.

13. Allan Pinkerton to George Bangs, May 12, 1874, Pinkerton Papers.

14. Brant, 134, mentions the possibility that Boyle may have been an ex-Confederate, based on newspaper accounts; Settle, 52; William A. Pinkerton to Dan O'Connor, chief detective, Saint Louis Police, July 2, 1874, State Archives, State Historical

Society of Missouri, Columbia, Mo. Pinkerton may have been as concerned that Boyle might know too much for comfort about agency operations in Missouri. As will be seen, the Saint Louis police would be looked upon as rivals, and may well have been seen in that light, at least potentially, at the time of this letter. In any event, there were earlier suspicions about Boyle's competence and character beyond this, at least in the mind of Allan Pinkerton.

15. File of Samuel Ralston, Provost Marshal Papers, M345, Roll 224. This contains two letters to Gen. James Law, for October 2 and 6, 1861, regarding soldiers who had taken slaves, a wagon, buggy, and horses from his property: "I am a Mason, as are you, and my wife, who will hand you this note is a Heroine of Jessie." No other items are to be found in this file. Paul I. Wellman, "The Girl Who Eloped with Frank James," *Kansas City Star,* July 16, 1944, is unreliable in its early history of the Ralston family and alleged involvement in the war. Wellman, a journalist who later wrote *A Dynasty of Western Outlaws*, mercifully omitted this from the aforementioned book. He uses highly suspect information supplied by a neighbor, John Barnhill, who claimed that Samuel Ralston had served under Gen. Jo Shelby during the war. Hattie E. Poppine, *Census of 1860 Population Schedules for Jackson County, Missouri,* 197, lists Samuel Ralston as fifty years old and his son Samuel Jr. as age ten. Another son, probably from an earlier marriage, is John, age twenty-two, a law student. Ralston's real estate was valued at $15,700 and his personal property at $9,000. Consolidated Index to Compiled Service Records of Confederate Soldiers, M253, Roll 393, National Archives, Washington, D.C., shows neither a Samuel nor a John Ralston serving in a Missouri Confederate unit during the war. The Barnhill story is typical of the myth-making that has accompanied the James story for so many years. Stella James, 132. A note by Milton F. Perry states that the family was expelled under Order No. 11, but there is no record pro or con on this in the provost marshal file. It is entirely possible. Perry also states that Sam Ralston never served in the military and that various guerrillas, including Frank James, congregated about the house at times during the war. The *Storm Lake (Iowa) Pilot* of August 17, 1881, reprinted an intriguing story from the *Omaha Republican* relating that Sam was a Unionist "and had served in the Union army" and had moved to Omaha where he worked in freighting. This allusion to army service may be a reference to some stint in the militia. The story also claims that "sympathizers of the lost cause made it so unpleasant [for the Ralstons]" in Missouri. The *Kansas City Times* of January 6, 1899, gives an obituary for Sam Ralston that says he "took no part in the civil war, with the exception of a fight at Rock Creek, a few miles distant from this city. In that fight he was wounded." Most probably Ralston lived at his farm near Independence at least until the time of Order No. 11. He may have served briefly with the EMM. Rock Creek was a small engagement in 1861 not far from Ralston's home. The move to Omaha removed him and his family from the war zone. *The History of Jackson County, Missouri...,* 469, notes that Ralston was wounded at Rock Creek, June 13, 1861. Whether he was a spectator or participant is uncertain. Saint Amand, Jeannette Cox, comp., *Pitt County Gravestone Records,* 3:84. Ralston had earlier lived in North Carolina, where he erected a gravestone in memory of his uncle and namesake, Sam Ralston, who had been forced into exile from Ireland after involvement in the abortive rebellion of 1798 against the

British, a fact noted on the marker. The stone, erected in Pitt County's ironically named "Yankee Hall Cemetery," can be seen to this day with the epitaph: "His Foibles are Lost in the Contemplation That He was an Honest Man." Such could hardly have been said of his son-in-law, a fact that probably galled Sam Ralston no end, especially when posses began making regular visits later on. The old Ralston home is now a bed and breakfast.

16. Stella James, 132–33; Settle, 91–92. There are a number of alleged accounts of how Frank and Annie met in various books and feature articles; it is difficult to determine their accuracy. It apparently was a surprise to the family that she had eloped with Frank, and various tales that she had been forbidden to see him are suspect. In all likelihood the family wasn't aware of her interest. It is probable that the relationship developed while Annie was away teaching school at Little Santa Fe, on the old Santa Fe Trail near the Kansas line. Annie and Frank apparently shared an interest in literature and horses. *Kansas City Star*, July 6, 1944. The wedding was apparently reported as being at Independence, Missouri; Leavenworth, Kansas; and Omaha, Nebraska, the latter place being cited as correct. Frank apparently used his full name on the marriage license, Alexander Franklin James, according to this account. As has been mentioned, there were relatives on the Cole side of the family in Nebraska. Frank and Annie only spent a brief time in Omaha, fearing possible detection.

17. *Lexington (Mo.) Caucasian* quoted in the *Saint Louis Republican*, September 2, 1874. Mattie's name, as given in the article, is spelled Hamlett, with two *t*'s, while it is sometimes spelled Hamlet, as it is in Settle, 71–72. I have chosen to use the newspaper spelling; Brownlee, 256, lists a "Jesse Hamet," who served under Anderson and who drowned in 1864.

18. *Lexington Register*, August 31, 1874, quoted in Settle, 72, and *Kansas City Times*, September 1, 1874.

19. *Saint Louis Republican*, September 9, 1874.

20. Settle, 72–73; *Kansas City Times*, September 9, 1874.

21. Settle, 73–74; C. C. Rainwater to Charles P. Johnson, September 3, 1874, State Archives, State Historical Society of Missouri, Columbia, Missouri.

22. Settle, 66–67; *Saint Louis Republican*, September 25, 1874. Schurz repeated his charges against the Democrats several days later in Kansas City. It is ironic that Schurz was a Liberal Republican, the faction the Democrats had backed in the 1872 election for president. Now Schurz was tarred in the Democratic press with the Radical Republican stigma, the branch of the party that he himself attacked in his Saint Louis speech.

23. David Thelen, *Paths of Resistance: Tradition and Dignity in Industrializing Missouri*, 62–70 (cited hereafter as Thelen). This is a thought-provoking analysis of Missouri in the fifty years following the Civil War from a socioeconomic viewpoint. To Thelen must go the credit for uncovering information relating to railroad bond issues that others writing about the James story have apparently overlooked.

24. *Carrollton (Mo.) Journal*, reprinted in the *Lexington (Mo.) Caucasian*, September 19, 1874; *Lexington Caucasian*, December 12, 1874; Thelen, 69–70; Samuel L. Clemens and Charles D. Warner, *The Gilded Age*. The title for this novel was later

used to name the post–Civil War era as well. Undoubtedly this novel was circulating among Missouri readers, having been published in 1873. Such chapters as "Harry and Philip Go West to Lay Out a Railroad," "Model Railroad Engineer: Survey to Stone's Landing," "Stone's Landing Becomes the City of Napoleon—On Paper," and "How Appropriation Bills Are Carried," must have both amused and enraged concerned readers in the Show-Me State. In some ways the book seems strangely relevant to the present, if one reads carefully. Senator Dilworthy was drawn from the character of Sen. Samuel Clarke Pomeroy of Kansas, a colleague of Jim Lane's, who apparently bribed members of the Kansas state legislature to obtain his reelection to the U.S. Senate in 1873, senators not being popularly elected at that time (see note 9, this chapter). The affair created a sensation, with Pomeroy accusing his accuser in a Senate investigation that tended to whitewash the matter. His career in politics was ended, nevertheless, with the exception of a brief run for president in 1884 on the Prohibition Party ticket.

25. *Saint Louis Republican*, December 9, 10, 11, 12, 14, 15, 1872. Another man, Harrison Buckland, was with Purtee in his Muncie, Kansas, store at the time of the robbery and was taken prisoner as well. At the same time as the Muncie affair the robbery of the Tishomingo Savings Bank at Corinth, Mississippi, was also attributed to the gang. Those robbers were thought to be from Texas. One was apparently caught trying to cross the Mississippi River near Helena, Arkansas. Others were chased to the vicinity of Sand Mountain, Alabama. It was probably not the James gang, however. Marley Brant, in a telephone interview on January 27, 1992, speculated that Frank and Jesse James, Cole and Bob Younger, and Clell Miller were involved in the Muncie robbery with the assistance of Bud McDaniel and Bill Ryan. The latter two were allegedly out to rob the train when the gang just happened by. It's rather difficult to say with certainty just who was involved. The author personally questions Bill Ryan's involvement in this 1874 event as he apparently first joined the gang in 1879. Only five bandits were mentioned in the news accounts, and it is assumed they were the James and Younger brothers and either Bud McDaniel or Clell Miller (probably McDaniel). *Saint Louis Republican* in the *Boonville (Mo.) Weekly Advertiser*, July 9, 1875, gives an account of McDaniel's demise. *Violent Kin!* 4 (October 1989): 3, offers a synopsis of his life. McDaniel's was apparently wounded somewhere west of Lawrence and died on June 29, 1875.

26. Allan Pinkerton to P. H. Woodward, letter of December 15, 1874, Pinkerton Papers. "Patrick Henry Woodward" in *The National Cyclopedia of American Biography*, 25:348–49, contains a good biography of Pinkerton's contact at the Post Office Department. Woodward, a native of Connecticut, was born in 1833 and attended Yale University and Harvard Law School; he was admitted to the Connecticut Bar in 1859. In 1862 he joined the editorial staff of the *Hartford Courant* but left in 1865 to help reorganize, with the title of special agent, the postal service in Georgia. He was eventually put in charge of the Railway Mail Service in the states south of the Ohio River. In this post he pioneered the sorting and distribution of mail on moving trains, making for faster delivery. Woodward was made chief special agent in 1874 but resigned in 1876 when Postmaster General Jewell left office. His book, *Guarding the*

Mails; or The Secret Service of the Post Office Department, appeared in that year. Basically his book is an account of the exploits of other agents. It would appear that, despite this tome, the James-Younger gang was too much for the post office to handle; thus the Pinkertons were retained. Regretfully, but understandably, no mention of the attempts to capture the James or Younger brothers is made in this work. Most of the work of the agents was against relatively nonviolent con artists and purveyors of pornography who used the mails.

27. See *History of Clay*, 336–39, for a biography of Hardwicke. Hardwicke's father, Phillip, also took part in some Indian campaigns, commanding a company in the early 1800s. Like the father of the James boys, Phillip Hardwicke died returning from the California gold rush. See David Lavender, *Bent's Fort*, 118, for the story of Hardwicke's uncle, Josiah Gregg, and his shooting match with Comanche Indians. W. J. Ghent, "Josiah Gregg," *Dictionary of American Biography*, 4:597–98; Allan Pinkerton, letter to Samuel Hardwicke, December 28, 1874, Pinkerton Papers.

28. Allan Pinkerton letter to Samuel Hardwicke, December 28, 1874. Broehl, 238–42, contains an interesting sidelight to the Reno lynching alluded to in Pinkerton's letter to Hardwicke. Evidently one of Pinkerton's former agents had attempted to blackmail him for collusion with the vigilantes. Professor Broehl states that circumstantial evidence pointed to the agent's having cooperated with local vigilantes, and the letter to Hardwicke would tend to bolster this supposition. Broehl also contends that Allan Pinkerton's public posture was sometimes at odds with his personal actions and his motivation for them.

29. Entry #1152, December 30, 1874, Register of Letters Received, 1863–1906 6, Records of Rock Island Arsenal, National Archives—Great Lakes Region, Chicago, Illinois. Found by western historian Fred Egloff in 1991, this, along with information revealed in the letter to Samuel Hardwicke, is the "smoking gun" regarding the identity of "Robert" and the origin of materials used to damage the Samuel house. Egloff was unable to find the actual letter, as correspondence from this period had been lost or destroyed. The Pinkertons' employment by the post office was probably the reason they were able to receive aid from the U.S. Army.

30. Broehl, 194, gives some brief biographical data on Robert J. Linden. Fred R. Egloff, "The Greek Fire Bomb," *True West* 39, no. 10 (October 1992): 24 (cited hereafter as Egloff, "Bomb"), describes Linden's involvement in the case. Egloff, interestingly, notes that city directories for Chicago between 1874 and 1876 list his occupation first as "police" and later as "collector." Apparently his employment by the Pinkertons was publicly concealed.

31. Paul Andrew Hutton, *Phil Sheridan and His Army*, 17, 20–21, 201–5; Moritz Busch, *Bismarck: Some Secret Pages of His History*, 2:127–28. Sheridan held the French responsible for the "Mexican adventure" of Emperor Maximilian at the time of the Civil War, in violation of the Monroe Doctrine. See Jeffrey Wert, *From Winchester to Cedar Creek: The Shenandoah Campaign of 1864*, 143–45, 157–60, for an account of Sheridan's destruction in the Shenandoah Valley, which had its own area dubbed the Burnt District. One cannot help but wonder if somehow the Pinkertons' use of incendiary material was not Sheridan's idea. Certainly the methodology was his, regardless of whose idea it ultimately was. Thomas H. S. Hamersley, *Complete Regular*

Army Register of the United States: For One Hundred Years, 1770–1879, 439, gives a brief synopsis of Flagler's military career. He was brevetted to the rank of captain and later major for "gallant and meritorious service" at the battle of New Berne, North Carolina, and at the siege of Fort Macon, North Carolina, in March and April 1862, respectively. At Fort Macon he was in charge of the siege mortars that brought the garrison to surrender. He was brevetted lieutenant colonel in March 1865 for his overall Civil War service. According to Civil War historian Brian Pohanka, Daniel Flagler served on the staff of Maj. Gen. Joseph Hooker during Hooker's tenure as commander of the Army of the Potomac in 1863. Pinkerton seems to have had difficulty with Flagler's name, calling him "Gallagger" in his letter. See William R. Trotter, *Ironclads and Columbiads: The Civil War in North Carolina—The Coast*, 136, 139–41, 143–45, for an account of Flagler's activity at Fort Macon.

CHAPTER 6: THE HUNTERS AND THE HUNTED

1. *Journal of the State Senate of Missouri, Regular Session 28th General Assembly* (1875), 21–23; Thelen, 66–70. Thomas Jefferson Younger, uncle of the Younger brothers, was elected to the Saint Clair county court primarily because he was their uncle, around 1878. The locals, who had destroyed the tax records one night in December 1877, apparently figured that he would not be in sympathy with the railroads. Eventually some county judges were elected on their opposition to paying railroad bonds. Memory of militia depredations during the war, as well as resistance to paying bonded debt, probably made many think twice about funding a state militia at this time. Woodson, it will be remembered, had served as inspector general of the Missouri State Militia during the war, and that connection certainly didn't generate support from ex-Confederates for his militia proposal. A little banditry by the James-Younger gang was preferable to what had gone on with the militia during the 1860s.
2. *Boonville (Mo.) Weekly Eagle*, September 11, 1874.
3. *Journal of the House of Representatives of the Regular Session of the 28th General Assembly of the State of Missouri* (1875), 99–101.
4. *Liberty (Mo.) Advance*, February 11, 1875, contains the report of Adj. Gen. George Caleb Bingham, who reached no conclusion on the number of men leaving the train. See also the *Saint Louis Republican*, January 29, February 1, 2, 4, 1875. The February 1 article claims there were eight men on the train leaving the farm. The January 29 article states that the tracks of seven horses were found. The story of February 2 states that "seven or eight men got off" near Kearney, based on a railroad conductor's information. The article of February 4 is a reprint of a *Chicago Tribune* feature that states four men got off the train.
5. Allan Pinkerton to P. H. Woodward, January 27, 1875, Pinkerton Papers. While it may be debated whether Pinkerton was actually present at the raid, this letter is written as though he were an eyewitness. One must recall that Pinkerton had expressed a resolve to be in on the final showdown in his April 17, 1875, letter to George Bangs. The train bearing the raiders arrived in Illinois on January 26, and it is conceivable that a letter was sent immediately. Pinkerton's later indictment for murder further indicates his probable presence. The *Saint Louis Republican* of

February 4, 1875, reprints an article saying some of the detectives were spotted at Ottumwa, Illinois, on January 26. One frequently repeated story claims that William Pinkerton took part in the raid, and this has been included in several accounts of the bombing. The *Saint Louis Globe-Democrat*, July 4, 1802, repeats an interview with Luther James, cousin of the outlaws, who said he didn't believe this to be the case. James knew William Pinkerton, who told him that one of the bomb throwers was dead and buried in Lawrence, Kansas, his hometown.

6. *Saint Louis Republican*, January 29, February 1, 4, 1875; *Kansas City Times*, January 28, 1875; *Liberty (Mo.) Advance*, February 11, 1875; Robert J. Wybrow, "A Night of Blood," *English Westerner's Society Brand Book* 16, no. 4 (January 1974): 25–27 (cited hereafter as Wybrow, "Night"); Egloff, "Bomb," 24, 26. Milton F. Perry related to me that during the restoration of the James cabin in the late 1970s, charred portions of the outside logs from the Pinkerton attack were found.

7. *Liberty (Mo.) Advance*, February 11, 1875; *Saint Louis Republican*, January 29, 1875, reprinting the *Kansas City Times* article of January 27 with the coroner's report.

8. *Saint Louis Republican*, February 1, 4, 1875. The train also was reportedly spotted at Brookfield, Missouri, earlier in the day. See also note 5.

9. See the *Saint Louis Republican*, February 2, 1875, for the legal ramifications.

10. *Kansas City Journal of Commerce*, January 29, 1875, reprinting Edwards's earlier editorial from the *Saint Louis Dispatch*. The sometimes incoherent logic of this piece may indicate that Edwards was drinking at the time he wrote it. Certainly he was quite angry and overwrought. The *Journal*, a staunch Republican organ, was probably reprinting this out of condescending ridicule. Edwards certainly approaches self-parody in some parts of his diatribe.

11. Rose Fulton Cramer, *Wayne County, Missouri*, 240, cites the *Patterson (Mo.) Times*, September 10, 1874, for the source of the Reed confession. In an interview reprinted in the *Nashville Daily World* on April 22, 1882, Jesse's widow claimed that Jesse was indeed involved in the Gads Hill affair but not in the Malvern stage robbery. Settle, 118, points to the recovery of a watch taken from John A. Burbank at Malvern after Jesse was killed, strongly pointing to his involvement in that robbery. It could be that Reed simply wanted the notoriety or felt that he could deflect some of the blame from the James brothers. What is curious, however, is the telegram given to the Gads Hill robbery victims to send to the *Saint Louis Dispatch*, a signal that would have aroused strong suspicions in the direction of the James and Younger brothers. It was either extreme bravado on their part, with a bit of stupidity, or perhaps it was Reed and friends trying to shift the blame to the James-Younger gang. See also *Violent Kin!* 4 (October 1989): 6; and Bill O'Neal, *Encyclopedia of Western Outlaws*, 260–61, for brief biographies of Reed. Some information in O'Neal may be questionable. Neither source agrees on the date of Reed's birth.

12. *Saint Louis Republican*, February 2, 4, 1875. The February 4 article reports that Jesse had gone to Jackson County on Monday to visit friends. See *History of Clay*, 143–44, 207, 334–36, for biographical material on Groom. Note: The author wishes to correct an error in his "Allan Pinkerton and the Raid on Castle James," *True West* 39, no. 10 (October 29, 1992): 18–21, indicating that Sheriff Groom was involved in the Pinkerton raid. This was partly the result of a feature concerning a story passed down

about a badge owned by Edward Davis of Liberty, Missouri. See Jim Dullenty, "Bombing of the James Home: New Proof the Pinkertons Did It," *True West* 30, no. 1 (January 1983): 20–21. Supposedly, six deputies were assigned to help the Pinkertons, but reports show that only around seven horses and a similar number of men were present during the raid. It appeared earlier that the December 28, 1874, letter from Pinkerton to Samuel Hardwicke may have alluded to Groom. These letters, taken off microfilm, were partly illegible. A subsequent examination of the original copies has made transcription necessary. The man thought to be Groom was apparently a man named Towne, associated with the Hannibal and Saint Joseph Railroad. In new light, Davis's story appears questionable, at best. Davis has the detectives getting off at Liberty where they are joined by deputies, something that didn't happen. This was probably a total Pinkerton operation. Pinkerton would have been suspicious of local authorities, given their record in the past, and the untried Groom would have been even more suspect, given his affidavit about Jesse and his Confederate service. Possibly Davis was a member of the later posse assembled by Groom, but this is hard to determine at the time of publication. Newspaper reporters ferreted out a good bit of information after the raid, including reports of suspicious telegrams to the Pinkertons from Hardwicke and the detectives working for the U.S. Post Office Department. If Groom did lend out his men, there was a phenomenal cover-up afterward. Even such a cover-up does not explain away the error about the detectives' arriving at Liberty on their train. It seems more likely that if the sheriff or his men had been involved, a larger force probably would have participated, using tactics akin to his own raid of August 29. The raid of January 25–26 looks more to be the handiwork of the detectives, using too few men and an ill-conceived plan of action, with revenge as partial motivation. One doubts that Groom would have gone along with the plan to burn the Samuel home. In any event, this book supersedes my *True West* feature of October 1992 regarding the Pinkerton raid.

13. *Saint Louis Republican,* January 29, 30, February 2, 1875; *Kansas City Times,* January 29, 30, 1875; Steele, *Family History,* 72–76.

14. Settle, 78–79; *Saint Louis Republican,* February 1, 3, 4, 1875; *Liberty Advance,* February 11, 1875.

15. *Saint Louis Republican,* February 3, 4, 1875. The *Chicago Tribune* feature was reprinted on February 4. Both papers turned up interesting information that Bingham's censored report did not mention.

16. *Liberty Advance,* February 11, 1875. See also Wybrow, "Night," 28, and Settle, 79, for background on Bingham's report.

17. *Liberty Advance,* February 11, 1875; Egloff, "Bomb," 24–27. Egloff's piece is the most complete analysis to date of what the Pinkertons probably threw in the house. See also Ned Brandt, *The Man Who Tried to Burn New York,* 64–65, 95–105, 118–19, for an example of how Greek fire was used in an attempt to burn New York City during the Civil War. The substance was described as a mix of phosphor in a bisulfide of carbon that was to ignite on exposure to the air. Harry A. Soltysiak, "The Pinkerton Bomb," *American History Illustrated,* 27, no. 2 (May-June 1992): 55, contains an interesting account of the 1992 recovery of a portion of the shell that had been stolen from a display at the James farm in the late 1970s. Mention is also made in

Horan (*Pinkerton*, 199–202) that the device was referred to as a flare shell, ostensibly intended simply to illuminate the interior of the house. This last work is flawed with poor documentation and should be used with great care. Attempts to verify some citations revealed extreme carelessness in the notes. Some sources were found not to exist as cited or to exist at all. The account of the raid is questionable, as written. The account of "Doctor" Munford, who allegedly rode with the raiders, is suspect because it says they proceeded to Union Station, in Kansas City, after the raid, when in fact they hightailed it back to Illinois. Horan's account of the alleged telegraph messenger on page 199 is similarly open to question (see note 12). Horan, a journalist, should have been capable of much better work; his work on the raid is all but worthless except to document apologia for the Pinkertons. His account of the Pinkerton activities to catch the James boys is chronologically jumbled in many places. Similar work may be found in Horan, *Desperate Men*, 88–93, minus documentation. The statement on page 92 about Frank James's saying there was no bomb is very questionable. See Settle, 198–99, for a further critique.

18. "George McQueen" [Allan Pinkerton?] to Sam [Hardwicke], February 16, 1875, Pinkerton Papers.

19. Ibid. See also *History of Clay*, 288, 339. Hardwicke was a pioneer Mason in Clay County and very active in that organization. He was the first commander of the Liberty Commandry, no. 6, Knights Templar.

20. "E.J.A." [Allan Pinkerton?] to an unknown recipient, February 26, 1875, Pinkerton Papers.

21. Clay County Circuit Court, File No. 449, Liberty, Missouri.

22. Ibid.; Jack Wymore, telephone interview of September 2, 1991. Wymore and Milton F. Perry both mentioned to me a letter, now in private hands, from Jesse James to his stepfather, Reuben Samuel, arguing that Hardwicke should be indicted as well. Certainly Jesse's telegraphic communications in code were common knowledge. M. Cody Wright, archivist, Illinois State Archives, to Fred Egloff, January 11, 1995 (copy in my papers). Wright had searched RS 103.87 Executive Section—Requisitions from other states, RS 103.88 Executive Section—Petitions for Requisitions to the Governor, and RS 101.17 Governor's Correspondence (John Beveridge, 1873–77), and reported, "No records were found relating to a request for assistance in delivering up Mr. Pinkerton and/or Mr. Linden to the state of Missouri in 1875." Wybrow, "Night," 28, concluded that no attempt was made for extradition. See also Ronald D. Rotunda, *Professional Responsibility*, 10–12, 53–57, for a discussion of legal ethics, historically, and how it would apply to a similar case today. In the nineteenth century there were no formal restraints on legal conduct nationally. These came, largely, in the first decades of the twentieth century. An attorney following Hardwicke's path today would probably be subject to disciplinary action.

23. Settle, 80–84. Carl W. Breihan, *Saga of Jesse James*, 70, contains illustrations of the requisition from Kansas and the Missouri arrest warrant. *Saint Louis Republican*, February 2, 1875, relates charges pending against the James boys.

24. *Carrollton Journal* in the *Saint Louis Republican*, April 8, 1875. The press reported that Miller was the uncle of Whitsett's wife, but I have been unable to confirm this connection.

25. John Nicholson, partial transcript of tape interview with Milton F. Perry, N.D, author's papers.

26. *Liberty (Mo.) Tribune*, April 16, 1875.

27. *Saint Louis Republican*, April 17, 18, 1875. Askew lived on a farm to the east of the Samuel place. The author was unable to determine at the time of this writing how long Askew had resided there. Census records were of no help. It is entirely possible that, if Askew lived there during the war, he had some role in informing on the Samuel family. At any event, his Radical Republican sympathies probably made for trying relations later, and the Pinkerton raid may have been the culmination of that tension. Sheriff Groom and his deputies openly told at least one reporter that they felt the killing was the work of Frank and Jesse James. Jesse was reported to have crossed the Missouri at Blue Mills Ferry after the shooting of Askew, being recognized by his horse, "a fine mare."

28. Allan Pinkerton to Dr. J. C. Bernard, April 16, 1875, Pinkerton Papers.

29. Allan Pinkerton to Adeline Askew, May 11, 1875, Pinkerton Papers. Mrs. Askew was also given a copy of Pinkerton's latest ghostwritten book, *The Expressman and the Detective* (1875), concerning a pre–Civil War case. Pinkerton was a tireless self-promoter, which is perhaps one reason his agency is remembered today. For a discussion of this literary aspect of Pinkerton's life in relation to the James legend (see pp. 224–25 of the text). The promised tombstone must have been replaced at some point in this century. Milton F. Perry told me that the current tombstone on Askew's grave appeared to be of a later vintage. Looking at the weathered examples of agents' tombstones in the Pinkerton plot at Graceland Cemetery in Chicago, it becomes apparent that the detective chief was certainly thrifty.

30. Settle, 80; Broehl, 194–95, 237–42, 245–48, 252–55, 264–66, 327–29, 351–53, 357–62. Broehl's work is one of the best on the Molly Maguire case and the Pinkerton involvement. The pages noted are particularly relevant regarding Linden or questionable activity by the Pinkertons, notably in the organization of vigilantes. See also Morn, 69–109, for an analysis of some of the agency's methods; pages 77–78 give two cases of agents, one case involving son Robert Pinkerton. The agents were arrested for acting beyond the bounds of the law in Boston and New York. Morn's work is required reading for anyone seriously interested in the history of the agency. Philip S. Foner, *History of the Labor Movement in the United States*, 1:455–64, 474, presents a thought-provoking case to the effect that the Molly Maguire affair was actually an effort at union-busting by railroad-coal baron Franklin B. Gowan. Coming in the wake of the "Long Strike" of 1875, it was an attempt to quash the Ancient Order of Hibernians, a fraternal organization that aided Irish miners. According to Foner, the mine owners had employed vigilante groups to terrorize miners involved with union activity during the late 1860s and early 1870s, with inevitable retaliation and murders committed by both sides. Those men eventually hanged were convicted on questionable testimony and were "mainly leading intellegent men whose direction gave strength to the resistance of the miners."

31. Settle, 80; Broehl, 194–95, 237–42, 245–48, 252–55, 264–66, 327–29, 351–53, 357–62. The *Saint Louis Globe-Democrat*, February 19, 1885, reported: "Under the statutes the State can take but two continuances on its own motion, the defendant

being entitled, when the third continuance is asked for, to an acquittal without trial." This same law helped Frank James in the later Otterville train robbery case, where two continuances had been given.

32. Stella James, 66, declared that Zerelda would sometimes take with her friends posing as relatives. She would also gather up groups of people to take along on her pass. How much this eventually cost the Hannibal and Saint Joseph cannot be estimated, but it must have ultimately rivaled the take in several of the gang's railroad heists. This generosity on the part of the mother of the James boys no doubt made the "Robin Hood" legend more believable in later years.

CHAPTER 7: THE HUNTINGTON RAID

1. Settle, 85–86; *Chicago Times* in *Kansas City Times*, May 5, 1875; *Saint Louis Republican*, April 20, 1875; John S. Groom to Charles Harding [Hardin], State Archives, State Historical Society of Missouri, Columbia, Missouri (Groom was careless in spelling Gov. Hardin's name). *History of Clay*, 263, mentions that 1875 was called the "grasshopper year" as swarms of Rocky Mountain locusts ravaged the county in May: "Entire fields . . . were devoured in a few hours." In the fall there were good crops to replace those lost. Thelen, 15, recounts how Governor Hardin called for a day of fasting and prayer on May 17, 1875. The insects eventually veered north into Iowa. This situation probably affected the attempted sale of the James-Samuel farm.

2. Dee Brown, *Year of the Century: 1876* (cited hereafter as Brown, *Century*), 83–91. The Whiskey Ring case would drag into 1876. Schlesinger, 329, contains a synopsis of the scandal.

3. *Nashville Morning World*, April 22, 1882, includes an interview with Zee James. Apparently she left the Sherman, Texas, area for Dallas in September 1874 after things became "too hot." This would coincide with increased detective activity following the Lexington stage robbery and might have been the result of a Pinkerton investigation in the area. Zee claimed she was the cousin of Susan James Parmer, which indeed she was. The *Chicago Tribune* in the *Saint Louis Republican*, February 4, 1875, mentions Jesse's being in the Kearney, Missouri, area around the time of the Pinkerton raid because of "the illness of his wife." If this is the case, it could have been morning sickness on Zee's part. In the interview, Zee appears to be fully aware of her husband's activity as a bandit, not trying to cover the fact. Croy, *James*, 283–84, gives the site of the first James residence as 606 Boscobel Street based on oral history interviews. This agrees with contemporary accounts. The *Nashville Banner* in *Saint Louis Republican*, April 21, 1882, gives an account by Dr. W. M. Vertrees and his son John that incorrectly states the family lived at this site for two years. In the *World* interview, Zee James said that they moved in the fall of 1875, a date that is doubtlessly correct. The *Nashville American*, April 19, 1882, gives an abbreviated account.

4. *Nashville Banner* in *Saint Louis Republican*, April 21, 1882; *Nashville American*, April 19, 1882. The *Banner* account erroneously has Jesse and Zee living on Boscobel Street for two years, when in fact it was probably less than a year. This story is repeated in other books and articles, as a result.

5. *Louisville Courier-Journal,* April 10, 1882.
6. *Louisville Courier-Journal,* June 22, 1875; *Nashville Republican Banner,* July 11, 1875. Jesse claimed that Frank had left for California ahead of him, in late January 1868, leaving New York on January 26 by ship, on the "U.S. mail line of steamers." *Liberty (Mo.) Tribune,* July 23, 1875, ran an item from the *Richmond (Mo.) Conservator* expressing disbelief in the authenticity of the letter "as Jesse James knows how to write as well as spell, having had the advantages of a good country education." In answer the *Tribune* editor stated, "We don't know about the letter in question, but if the editor of the *Conservator* will come to Liberty, he can see several specimens of Jesse's letters that contain more bad spelling than the one in question, and penmanship as bad as the spelling." I believe this and other letters published in Nashville are probably genuine, though whether they were actually written from Missouri is another question. They probably were forwarded from there to throw off the Pinkertons, whom Jesse was stalking in Chicago at some point. See also Robert J. Wybrow, "From the Pen of a Noble Robber," *English Westerner's Society Brand Book* 24, no. 2 (Summer 1987): 11, 13, 21 (cited hereafter as Wybrow, "Pen"). Wybrow says that correspondence to Governor Hardin no longer exists. According to one letter, Jesse was forwarding mail.
7. *Nashville Republican Banner,* July 28, 1875. Pinkerton was probably not involved. He was certainly never mentioned in the indictment, though his father, Allan, was.
8. *Nashville Republican Banner,* August 8, 1875. Jesse's wife was probably sending him the notices in the Nashville press that he was responding to. The *Banner* was apparently a Democratic paper, despite its name. Tennessee had been redeemed by the Democrats some years previous, and Nashville has been a Democratic Party stronghold for generations since. Starting in February 1862, Nashville had undergone a particularly long and harsh occupation by Union forces, complete with secret police, arbitrary imprisonment without trial, and confiscation and/or destruction of property. There was still a small army garrison at Ash Barracks in north Nashville on the site of the present Buena Vista School, though it was withdrawn in 1877. Jesse mentions that Sheriff Patton of Clay County was related to Gen. Benjamin F. Cheatham, a former corps commander in the Army of Tennessee and a political figure of some note in the Nashville area both before and after the war.
9. Wybrow, "Pen," 11–13. On page 11 Wybrow quotes private correspondence that was written in late May 1875 but was not published until 1882. In it Jesse mentions letters being forwarded and sent from Kansas City. Wybrow believes the letter was probably sent to Sheriff Groom or some other lawman that he felt on good terms with. Jesse mentions multiple mail drops, starting out of Kansas City with his sister-in-law. Allan Pinkerton was obviously not the only one to use this tactic. The original letter appeared in the *Sedalia (Mo.) Democrat* on May 20, 1882. Settle, 87, is unclear as to whether Keene or Webb was the true name.
10. Robert J. Wybrow, "The James Gang in West Virginia: The Huntington Bank Robbery, 1875," *Portraits in Gunsmoke* (English Westerners' Special Publication No. 4, 1972), 66–73 (cited hereafter as Wybrow, "West Virginia"). See also Joseph Platania, "Riding High in Huntington," *Huntington Quarterly* (Winter 1990): 37 (cited hereafter as Platania); *Huntington Advertiser,* August 10, 1903. Frank James later

claimed that he was in Saint Joseph, Missouri, when Clell Miller was mistaken for him. Knowing Frank's credibility rating, it is just as likely as not that he was at Huntington, but the mention of Miller is given for consideration. While the matter will never be known conclusively, the author suspects that the bandit described later with the "long nose" was probably Frank; Clell Miller had a short nose. See also *The West Virginia Heritage Encyclopedia*, Supplemental Series, 10–11:385, 14:90–91, for information regarding a story that the gang allegedly passed up the robbery of the Bank of Princeton, West Virginia, which kept deposits in a horsehair trunk. Wybrow's account is based on the confession of Tom Webb in the *Huntington Advertiser* of December 16, 1875, which apparently contradicts this story geographically. The gang probably moved by rail at first, starting in the northern panhandle and moving southward, never getting into the area of the state where Princeton lies, near the Virginia line. See the *Louisville Courier-Journal*, October 21, 1875, for information on Webb. According to the *Huntington Advertiser*, October 28, 1875, Webb was born in Pike County, Illinois, on December 18, 1849, and allegedly served two years in the Confederate army. James M. Prichard, "Missouri Outlaws Raid in West Virginia," *Wild West* 11, no. 4 (December 1998): 51–52 (cited hereafter as Prichard). I believe Webb was possibly named Matt Brock and had seen service with the guerrillas in Missouri during the war. Brock was reportedly the brother-in-law of Jim Reed, first husband of Belle Starr and an outlaw of some repute in his own right.

11. *The West Virginia Heritage Encyclopedia*, 11:2414–16, Supplemental Series, 10–11:240–41; Stuart Dagett, "Collis Potter Huntington," *Dictionary of American Biography*, 5:408–11 (cited hereafter as Dagett); "The Emmons Family" in *First Families of Huntington*, 12; *Huntington Advertiser* (?), February 21, 1909, concerning banks in the area. The copy of the newspaper furnished to me is not attributed by name and might be vol. 1, no. 34, of another local paper, thus the question mark.

12. See Dagett, 408–11, regarding Huntington's personality and character. Williams, *Railroad*, 275–87, says one of Huntington's congressional friends was Rep. Thomas T. Crittenden of Missouri. See also *New York Sun*, December 29, 30, 1883, for some *very* revealing correspondence between Huntington and David D. Colton of the Central Pacific; and Denis Drabelle, "The Devil's Lexicographer," *Washington Post Book World* 26, no. 3 (January 28, 1995): 4, for a review of *Ambrose Bierce: Alone in Bad Company*, by Roy Morris Jr. In the mid-1890s Bierce was sent to Washington by newspaper mogul William Randolph Hearst to cover the story of Huntington's efforts to gain congressional forgiveness on seventy-five million dollars the Central Pacific owed the U.S. Treasury. Apparently Huntington tried to bribe Bierce, and Bierce said his price was the above amount paid to the U.S. Treasury. When the story created a sensation, Huntington's supporters distanced themselves and Congress voted against the measure. W. A. Swanberg, *Citizen Hearst*, 49–50, reports how Hearst's *San Francisco Examiner* hounded the big four (Huntington, Mark Hopkins, Charles Crocker, and Leland Stanford). In 1888, while pleading how poor the railroad was, in order to obtain forgiveness for government loans, the *Examiner* (August 4, 1888) pointed out that Huntington partner Leland Stanford had endowed a university to the tune of thirty million dollars, bought his wife a one-hundred-thousand-dollar necklace, and spent millions on estates, racehorses, and art. Bierce

would sometimes refer in print to Huntington's partner as "£eland $tanford" or "$tealand £andford." See also *The Big Four*, by Oscar Lewis; and *Huntington Advertiser* (?), February 21, 1909, concerning the targeted Adams Express package.

13. Don Tony Macri, "The Great Huntington Bank Robbery," *Hearthstone* 6 (1981): 33–34 (cited hereafter as Macri); Wybrow, "West Virginia," 67, 72–73; *Louisville Courier-Journal*, September 15, 16, 1875. The September 16 issue carried a letter, dated September 11, from bank president Russel, who, along with his cashier, identified Cole Younger from a photo sent by Louisville detective Delos T. "Yankee" Bligh. The letter stated: "We have shown the picture of Cole Younger to a number of parties who saw the parties who robbed our bank, and find that all who saw and talked with him recognize the picture as his. . . . Our cashier . . . also recognized it as one of the men who held the pistol in his face." Webb was also identified, after his capture, as the man who sprang over the counter. The *Nashville Daily American*, September 8, 1875, carried an account of the robbery from the *Cincinnati Gazette*. See also *Huntington Advertiser* (?), February 21, 1909, June 19, 1921. The 1921 article has an interview with Henry Clay Wentz, Isaac Crump's son-in-law, who witnessed the arrival of Frank and Cole in 1875. He places the outlaws first at the Reese farm. The 1909 article has a different version of who stayed where, claiming that McDaniel and Webb lodged at the house of Backus Bowen at Buffalo Shoals, in Wayne County. The bandits had a rendezvous for lunch at the home of James Barbour, a farmer who lived on Camp Creek five miles south of town. These 1909 details are not found in contemporary reports and are open to question. Some of the information in this article appears to be from Webb's confession, but part could as well be from bad memory or local folklore.

14. Wybrow, "West Virginia," 67–68; Macri, 34–35; Platania, 37–38; *Louisville Courier-Journal*, September 15, 16, 1875, giving the route of pursuit; Prichard, 49–50.

15. *Louisville Courier-Journal*, September 16, 17, 21, 25, 1875. Contemporary news accounts state that the Dillon brothers were armed with revolvers and that three citizens were mistaken at first for gang members. Love, 171–73, has them armed with old muskets loaded with lead slugs. No source is given. Love also fails to mention the mistaken identity of the men viewing the body in the coffin, preferring to end the story with the outlaws coming back to view their comrade's corpse and possibly to seek revenge. The gang members were probably long gone when McDaniel died. While recently reprinted by a major university press, Love's work should be consulted with great care. The stories in Love have been repeated in other works by other authors. Prichard, 50–51, says William Dillon reportedly served under Bridgewater during the war.

16. Melville O. Birney, "Captain Bligh, 'Toughest Fly-Cop in the Country'" (publication uncertain—may be *Louisville Courier-Journal Magazine*), January 23, 1958, copy in my files; Jim Reed, "You Didn't Mess with Captain Bligh" (publication and date uncertain, Louisville magazine ca. 1960s–1980s), copy in author's files; Thomas Selby Watson, "The Day Jesse Turned Yankee Bligh Around," *Real West* 18, no. 134 (1973): 26–30, copy in author's files. The information about Shepherd's incarceration in and removal from Nashville came from a *Louisville Courier-Journal* article ca. August-September 1868, quoted in Watson. Reed sug-

gests that Sir Arthur Conan Doyle may have been influenced by Bligh in his creation of Sherlock Holmes as the result of Bligh's work in the Bank of England case. See Edwin Finch, "Yankee Bligh Blighted," undated and unattributed feature clipping, which relates that Bligh ran into Jesse at the J.M.&I. R.R. depot, and a message to Bligh came via post card from Baltimore; Croy, *James*, 156–57, 287, relates the same essential story and post card attributed to Baltimore, the source being an article in the *Louisville Courier-Journal Magazine*, May 16, 1937, by Joe Hart. Hart, however, says that the post card came from Indianapolis. Croy says the post card was, at the time of his book (1949), in a scrapbook at the Louisville City Hall. I have not seen this post card. Undated and unattributed obituary notices for Delos Thurman Bligh, Louisville, Kentucky, ca. March 2, 1890, copies in author's files.

17. Wybrow, "West Virginia," 71–72; *Louisville Courier-Journal*, October 21, 1875; *Huntington Advertiser*, December 16, 1875; *Cookeville (Tenn.) Citizen*, May 21, 1963, January 26, 1965. A column, "Lore and Legends of the Upper Cumberland," by E. G. Rogers, recalls stories of "Jesse James" in the area. One concerns an alleged stop made with one Robert Martin who lived on "the old army road leading from Overton County into Kentucky." Overton borders Fentress County, where Webb was caught. This could be only folklore, but it's also possible that this is a recollection of the retreat of the gang members from Kentucky. The Walton Road, which dated from pioneer times, was the main route between Nashville and Knoxville, running approximately where US 70 North is now. This would have been the most direct route back to Nashville. Prichard, 52, says a package containing only a piece of black crepe was sent to McDaniel's lady friend in Missouri, from Wilsonville, in Spencer County, on September 18. This might tend to indicate an alternate route of escape via Nelson and Spencer Counties.

18. *Nashville Daily World*, April 22, 1882, carries the account of Zee James. Love, 272–76, recalls the story told him by Samuel Allender of Saint Louis, as related to him by Frank James. See also *Wood's Baltimore City Directory . . . 1876*, 307. Jesse used the same alias in Nashville and was listed as a laborer in the 1881 Nashville city directory. A check of Baltimore directories, before and after, fails to show another John Howard with this occupation. Jesse was normally consistent with his Howard alias over the years while Frank's alias in Baltimore is unknown. While I cannot say with total certainty that Jesse lived on Burrows Court, it is highly probable.

CHAPTER 8: THE ROAD TO NORTHfiELD

1. *Nashville Daily World*, April 22, 1882. Zee's account implied that these men recognized by Jesse were important state officials, many of whom were apparently on hand for the opening of the Centennial. *Harpers Weekly*, July 15, 1876, includes the interview with Fukui Makoto, commissioner from Japan to the exposition. Brown, *Century*, 112–37, contains an excellent account of the Centennial.

2. *Saint Louis Republican*, August 17, 1876, reprint of *Kansas City Times* article; Stella James, 134. In an appendix, Milton F. Perry quotes from what appears to be a newspaper interview with Ralston, in which Ralston states that Frank arrived in the

morning and had breakfast with the family. Perry cites a *Kansas City Times* article, with no date given. Essentially it is the same basic story, with the exception of Frank being invited for breakfast. Sam Ralston was left in an Irish furor, regardless. Poppine, Jackson County 1860 Census, 197, gives Ralston's age and nationality. Homer Croy's book does not relate this episode.

3. *Saint Louis Republican*, August 13, 1876.

4. Brant, 161–65, 329, 339–40. Brant credits her source as being, primarily, certain letters of Jim Younger, and an account by "Maggie," which this author has not had a chance to examine.

5. *Saint Louis Republican*, August 13, 1876.

6. Ibid., July 9, 1876, for an account by eyewitnesses. Settle, 88, 215, credits the account of the preacher to the *Boonville Daily Advertiser* and the *Weekly Advertiser* following the robbery. For some reason this is not mentioned in the accounts given by witnesses for the *Saint Louis Republican*.

7. *Saint Louis Republican*, August 10, 13, 1876.

8. *Saint Louis Republican*, July 18, 26, August 8, 18, 1876. The possibility that Tom Webb was a McKean or McKeehan has not been explored and deserves further research. This outlaw's life is relatively obscure, as are those of many gang members.

9. *Saint Louis Republican*, August 4, 5, 6, 10, 11, 13, 17, 18, 1876; Settle, 89–91; Marley Brant: "Bruce Younger: The Man, the Myth, and the Mummy," *True West* 36, no. 3 (March 1989): 37–39, is the most complete account of the life of the uncle of the Younger brothers. Brant speculates that "Younger's Bend" may have been named by Belle for Bruce, not Cole Younger. Bruce's sister, Adeline, was the mother of the notorious Dalton brothers. Bruce's mummified corpse was found in a cave in the Guadalupe Mountains of New Mexico in the late 1800s. One newspaper account has the mummy being sent to a Boston "museum." The disposition of his remains is still something of a mystery. Younger, 72–73, gives his own account of Belle but fails to mention Uncle Bruce. See *Violent Kin* 4 (October 1989), for Kerry's sentence.

10. Settle, 90–92; *Saint Louis Republican*, August 12–31, 1876.

11. *Saint Louis Republican*, August 10, 13, 1876; Schlesinger, 331–33. See Edwin Emerson, *A History of the Nineteenth Century, Year by Year*, 3:1558–60, for a brief account of the troubles in Bosnia. See also Foner, *Reconstruction*, 567–69.

12. Brant, *Youngers*, 165–71. According to Brant, Stiles was from Monticello, Minnesota, and did his horse stealing around Saint Paul. Maggie Lee, ed., *Defeat of the Jesse James Gang: Small Town Routs Notorious Outlaws in the Northfield Bank Raid*, 5 (cited hereafter as Lee, *Northfield*). A tabloid released by the *Northfield News* in 1981 is one of the best publications on the raid and contains much primary source information. According to historian Ron Hunt, Stiles had been a surveyor for Dodge County, adjacent to Rice County, where Northfield is located. Some accounts have the gang in Minnesota in early July, but this is highly questionable. See the *Saint Louis Republican*, August 18, 1876.

13. Lee, *Northfield*, 4–6; Annette Atkins, *Harvest of Grief: Grasshopper Plagues and Public Assistance in Minnesota, 1873–1878*, 1–15, 24–27, 128–31; Atkins is the best book on this obscure episode in American history. Laura Ingalls Wilder also wrote of the locust plagues in her book *On the Banks of Plum Creek*.

14. *The Northfield Bank Raid*, 27–32. This booklet is another publication of the *Northfield News*, dating from 1933; no author or editor is identified. John W. Pullen, *The Twentieth Maine: A Volunteer Regiment in the Civil War*, 1–3, 14–17, 34–39, 52–53, 130, 133, 170, 285. Pullen credits Ames's leadership and discipline in molding the regiment.

15. Rod Gragg, *Confederate Goliath: The Battle of Fort Fisher*, 37–53, 109, 133, 141, 145, 169–73, 184–85, 197, 209–14, 222, 227.

16. Ibid., 39, 265–68. After the war Ames apparently became embroiled in a controversy regarding his conduct at Fort Fisher. See Shelby Foote, *The Civil War, A Narrative: Fort Sumter to Perryvillle*, 534–35. Albert D. Kirwan, ed., *The Confederacy*, 142–48, contains a letter written by Alexander Walker, a political prisoner under Butler, to Jefferson Davis. Though perhaps subject to bias, it gives an excellent perspective on the regard many Southerners, particularly from New Orleans, had for Butler, both before and after the war. Richard Nelson Current, *Those Terrible Carpetbaggers: A Reinterpretation*, 306–27, does an interesting job of debunking the myth of the carpetbagger in this work. In Foner, *Reconstruction*, 558–63, footnote 85 on 559 is of particular interest. Ames was later vilified in John F. Kennedy's book *Profiles in Courage*, oddly enough. An attempt to clear the record by Ames's great-grandson, author George Plimpton, appeared in the December 18, 1980, issue of the *New York Review of Books*.

17. *Younger*, 77. This small book must be used with caution, as it contains many falsehoods and much apologia. However, in light of how the gang appears to have targeted certain banks, it seems that the bank at Northfield would be a logical choice, for the reason given.

18. *Saint Paul and Minneapolis Pioneer-Press and Tribune*, September 8, 1876; Lee, *Northfield*, 5–9; George Huntington, *Robber and Hero: The Story of the Northfield Bank Raid*, 5–24 (cited hereafter as Huntington). The exact chronology of events as they happened at Northfield is sometimes difficult to sort out. Because witnesses recalled events differently, Huntington was obliged to tell the story in an approximate fashion. I have done likewise. Huntington identified the bandits from identifications made later of those gang members who were killed or captured. Brant, *Youngers*, 170–77, gives her conjecture as to the movements of the gang prior to Northfield and their actions during the robbery. Note that an alleged account of the raid, supposedly a transcription of a letter from Jim Younger, in the possession of Wilbur Zink, has the gang arriving in Minnesota on horseback in two separate groups and meeting at Dundas for the first time just prior to the raid. As this document is apparently not in Jim Younger's handwriting it is difficult to verify its authenticity. W. C. Heilbron, *Convict Life at the Minnesota State Prison*, 132 (cited hereafter as Heilbron), contains a section in which the author interviewed Cole Younger. I have used certain quotes from this account that seem to agree with other versions of the raid. Some portions are suspect, however. Cole credits his brother Bob and Stiles with scouting the bank. Considering Bob's involvement, and Stiles's knowledge, this could be so. Brant, citing a local news account, says it was scouted by Frank and Jesse James.

19. Heilbron, 136–39; Huntington, 23–37; Lee, *Northfield*, 9–13. According to Harry Hoffman, quoted in Lee, Bob Younger rode behind Cole. Huntington also claims

it was Bob. Heilbron, in an earlier account, has Cole saying it was Pitts. Brant, *Youngers*, 182–83, has Bob rescued and Pitts covering the retreat.

20. *Saint Paul Pioneer-Press*, August 20, 1993. Some contend that Gustavson was "stewed as usual" at the time of the raid while others contest this. See also Lee, *Northfield*, 11–12.

CHAPTER 9: THE GETAWAY

1. Blanche Butler Ames, comp., *Chronicles from the Nineteenth Century: Family Letters of Blanche Butler and Adelbert Ames*, 2:403–6 (cited hereafter as Ames); Lee, *Northfield*, 9, 14–16; Brant, *Youngers*, 187–89; Huntington, 47–56; *Saint Paul and Minneapolis Pioneer-Press and Tribune*, September 8, 10, 12–14, 1876.

2. *Saint Paul and Minneapolis Pioneer-Press and Tribune*, September 10, 13, 14, 1876; *New York Times*, September 8, 1876.

3. Brant, *Youngers*, 192–94; Huntington, 57–59; Lee, *Northfield*, 16–17; *Saint Paul and Minneapolis Pioneer-Press and Tribune*, September 14, 1876. There are varying versions of the gang's split-up given in all the accounts. My account is an approximation. The *Saint Louis Globe-Democrat*, December 5, 1876, contains an interesting account from the *Sedalia (Mo.) Bazoo* of a man who reportedly was in a posse that trailed the James boys from Mankato into southwest Minnesota. It contains a good bit of detail not found elsewhere.

4. S. D. Webster, *The Webster Journal*, July 17, 31, 1930. The account by T. L. Voight's son is given here, and there is information about Oscar Sorbel, who died on July 11, 1930, and was a local veterinarian in later life. Sorbel's family was Norwegian. *Sioux Falls (S.D.) Argus-Leader*, undated clipping of article, ca. June-December 1924, by J. A. Derome, "Webster Man Gives His Story of James-Younger Raid; Was First to Tell of Gang's Hiding Place." This little-known and overlooked article gives the account of Oscar Sorbel. It was apparently prompted by a series about the raid that appeared in the paper from March 22 to June 4, 1924. Huntington, 62–71, names Capt. W. W. Murphy, Sheriff James Glispin, T. L. Voight, B. M. Rice, G. A. Bradford, C. A. Pomeroy, and S. J. Severson as the men who went into the woods after the Youngers and who shared the reward with Sorbel, incorrectly identified as Oscar Suborn. Huntington seems to miss the involvement of others in the capture of the Youngers and has been used as a prime source for information on the raid since his work appeared in 1895. On pages 91–100, Huntington also gives biographical information on the seven men. Brant, *Youngers*, 195–200, gives an account of the capture and further background on the seven as well as Pitts. Brant also takes note of the involvement of others in the posse. Heilbron, 144, has Cole Younger's mention of the numbers involved. Earlier versions of the capture were written without taking into the picture the Sorbel and Younger accounts. It has not been my purpose here to attempt a blow-by-blow reconstruction of the capture. Again, some accounts vary, but two things appear clear: that a number of other individuals, besides the seven who took the Youngers into custody, were involved in the capture, and that, given Sorbel's account, the shootout took longer than generally credited. Captain Murphy, Sheriff Glispin, the other five, and Sorbel, shared in the reward, as did several of the

outpost guards who watched the bandits. Others probably never received a cent. According to one account Sorbel and the seven men received $235 each and the outpost guards $100 each. The reward money could have been a motive for Glispin, Murphy, et al. to downplay the role of the others or the duration of the gun battle involving a larger posse. Having gone into the woods first and taken the Youngers into custody, they could claim that this entitled them to the reward and give Oscar, and the folks who watched the Younger party while he was gone, a share because of their role. Love, 223–42, gives an interesting and rather detailed account of the capture that is unfortunately marred by fictional dialogue. Love notes that others were involved in the capture and gives some idea of the maneuvering that took place between the posse and the outlaws.

5. *Saint Louis Globe-Democrat,* December 5, 1876; *Sioux Falls (S.D.) Argus-Leader,* April 5, 12, 19, 26, May 3, 10, 1924. The *Argus-Leader* articles are valuable sources of previously overlooked primary-source information concerning the escape of the James brothers from the Luverne, Minnesota, area through South Dakota and into northwest Iowa. The author speculates that the pair escaped into Nebraska, but this point may be open to debate. A number of people were still living in 1924 who had memories of this affair, and they sent their accounts to J. A. Derome for his series. The feature articles also shook loose the little-known account by Oscar Sorbel, previously cited. Huntington, 58–61, gives a rather sketchy account of the escape of the James boys. See also Lee, *Northfield,* 17–18. An account, based on a story by G. W. Hunt, editor of the *Sioux City Democrat,* says he aided the brothers in escaping downriver in exchange for the story. Given the sensational journalism of the times and the lack of scruples some had in getting a story, this claim is possible but is subject to question. The account in Lee, taken from another account credited to Homer Croy, has it that Mrs. Mann lived in Kingsley, Iowa, a good twenty or more miles from Sioux City. The *Saint Louis Globe-Democrat,* October 16, 1876, carried a brief account of the experience by Dr. Mosher. The contemporary *Globe-Democrat* account says it was James Station, about eight miles northeast of Sioux City.

6. Ames, 425; Brant, *Youngers,* 200–201, 203–13; Huntington, 73–76; Lee, *Northfield,* 19–21; *Sioux Falls (S.D.) Argus-Leader,* April 5, 1873; William Holtz, "Bankrobbers, Burkers, and Bodysnatchers: Jesse James and the Medical School," *Michigan Quarterly Review* 6, no. 2 (Spring 1967): 90–98; telephone interview with Jack Wymore, Liberty, Missouri, September 2, 1991, regarding Hardwicke's role in obtaining the body and an interview Wymore had with Samuel Hardwicke's son, Norton. Most accounts claim that Wheeler kept the skeleton of Miller, and there is some general confusion over this. Possibly both bodies were in a skeletal state by the time Hardwicke arrived on the scene and Wheeler pulled a switch. Another possibility is that Wheeler gave back Miller's remains and simply told people that Stiles's skeleton was Miller's. Whatever the case, Hardwicke got back in the good graces of Mrs. Samuel, and the Miller family was grateful. See Nancy B. Samuelson, "How the James Boys Fled the Disaster at Northfield and the Capture of 'Frank James,'" *WOLA (Western Outlaw and Lawman Assn.) Journal* (Spring-Summer 1993): 9 (cited hereafter as Samuelson, "James Boys"). It appears from a letter by Hardwicke, written on December 23, 1876, that he was not involved with anything related to the James

gang until the end of 1876. Samuelson reprints this and several other letters in her article. It seems more likely that he entered the picture sometime in the last half of 1876. By this time the corpses would probably have been dissected and would have been in a skeletal state. It would have been easier to pull a switch, if such were done, in this sort of situation, unless teeth were missing and the skull examined by relatives or others who knew of this. At the same time, none of Wheeler's later patients would have been able to tell a skeleton of Stiles from a skeleton of Miller and were repeating what they were told. Another story has it that the remains of Miller were displayed at a carnival, but the Michigan account indicates that both Stiles and Miller were shipped to Michigan, which was probably the case. Homer Croy, *Last of the Great Outlaws: The Story of Cole Younger*, 97–99 (cited hereafter as Croy, *Younger*), gives the source of the story about Pitts's skeleton as Dr. Henry Hoyt's book, *Frontier Doctor*. Hoyt would have a later connection with Jesse James.

7. Samuelson, "James Boys," 7–8. Samuelson quotes in full text the letter from James McDonough to Governor Hardin, October 13, 1876. *Saint Louis Globe-Democrat*, October 15, 16, 17, 18, 1876. Sergeant Boland reported that the house of Dr. Noland was guarded during the evenings and that the roads leading to the house were picketed during the daytime. It is possible that, somehow hearing of Goodwin and his wound, the James boys, and/or their relatives and friends, concocted a setup to fool the overzealous lawmen. It would have been easy to plant the information and get some of the local loafers from the Crackerneck area south of Independence, Missouri, in on the plot. Interestingly, Zerelda Samuel, mother of the James boys, had something of a reputation as a prankster. See Stella James, 57–63, for examples and compare with the Goodwin episode. The *Kansas City Times* article and editorial are quoted in the *Globe-Democrat* of October 18, 1876.

8. *Saint Louis Globe-Democrat*, October 19, 1876. The Saint Louis police were in the process of having Dr. Mosher, who had reportedly treated Frank's wound as Frank and Jesse fled across Iowa, come down to identify the prisoner at the time of Goodwin's release. Hobbs Kerry stated, on seeing a photograph of Goodwin, that it was not Frank James. Undoubtedly the Saint Louis police commissioners had some further "words" with Chief McDonough. It was reported that Goodwin might sue the police department for false arrest.

9. *Saint Louis Globe-Democrat*, October 18, 1876.

10. *New York World*, November 22, 1876; Lally Weymouth, *America in 1876: The Way We Were*, 120–31; Foner, *Reconstruction*, 565–77. Public morality in high places left much to be desired during the period, and it wasn't just banks and trains that were being robbed.

11. *Saint Louis Globe-Democrat*, November 25, 26, 1876.

12. *Saint Louis Republican*, November 27, 1876; *Saint Louis Globe-Democrat*, November 29, 30, 1876; Lee, *Northfield*, 20–22; Settle, 93–94.

CHAPTER 10: ALIAS WOODSON AND HOWARD

1. *Saint Louis Globe-Democrat*, December 19, 1876; Thomas A. Bailey, *The American Pageant: A History of the Republic*, 495–98; Phillip S. Foner, *The Great Labor Uprising*

of 1877, 15 (cited hereafter as Foner, *1877*). Foner gives a good account of the power of the railroads and the "robber barons." Pennsylvania Railroad's Thomas Scott even provided his private railroad car to Hayes to take him from Ohio to Washington, D.C., for the inauguration. The best overall account of the "Compromise of 1877" is to be found in C. Vann Woodward, *Reunion and Reaction; The Compromise of 1877 and the End of Reconstruction*. See also Mark Wahlgren Summers, *The Era of Good Stealings*, 274–306 (cited hereafter as Summers), for some of the latest scholarship on the election and an eye-opening look at period corruption. See Settle, 101; Jack Wymore, Liberty, Missouri, telephone interview, September 2, 1991. Wymore had seen a portion of a diary allegedly in Jesse's handwriting, giving his location from December 1876 to March 1877. The first entries are in Benton County, Arkansas; Little River County; Paris, Texas; and eventually the Sherman, Texas, area for a visit with his sister. The authenticity of the diary is unverified. Lee, *Northfield*, 18, has a later quote from Frank, taken from the *Milwaukee Journal*, to the effect that both he and Jesse went to the Hite place in Kentucky.

2. See Samuelson, "James Boys," 9, for the full text of Hardwicke's letter. It has been previously claimed that the detectives had no good photograph to go from, but there is reportedly a photograph, allegedly of Frank and Jesse James, that apparently was discovered by the Pinkertons. See the photo in Phillip W. Steele with George Warfel, *The Many Faces of Jesse James*, 81; while this photo does bear a similarity, it is not of Jesse or Frank. As the photo alluded to by Hardwicke is only of one person, it is likely that the picture identified in Northfield was different.

3. For details on the strike of 1877, see Foner, *1877*, 7–35, 44–54, 74–77, 102–29, 210–29 231–80; Bruce, *1877*, 9–58, 101–14, 253–89, 308–21; David T. Burbank, *Reign of the Rabble: The Saint Louis General Strike of 1877*, 1–7, 48–53, 168–69, 174–205. The troops in Saint Louis were under the command of Col. Jefferson C. Davis, the same officer who had headed the military commission that had tried "One-Arm" Berry in 1866. Allan Pinkerton, *Strikers, Communists, Tramps and Detectives*, ix–xii, 13–24. Pinkerton's book states, "Ever since the great strikes of '77, my agencies have been busily employed by great railways, manufacturing, and other corporations, for the purpose of bringing the leaders and instigators of the dark deeds of those days to the punishment they so richly deserve. Hundreds have been punished. Hundreds more will be punished." In those days "punishment" often meant blacklisting individuals from employment. The preface to Pinkerton's book sounds as though it was actually written by, or at least dictated directly by, Allan Pinkerton, because it uses some of the same phrases found in his earlier correspondence.

4. Cummins, *Cummins' Book*, 105, It is probable that the James families left for Tennessee during the strike and arrived in Tennessee sometime in August 1877. Tyler Burns apparently left them somewhere near the Tennessee-Kentucky line and returned to Missouri.

5. *Saint Louis Post-Dispatch*, June 24, 1923; Lydia D. Corbitt, *History of Plant Community*, 1; Lydia D. Corbitt, *Denver, Tennessee Remembered*, 1, 4, 6–7.

6. *Saint Louis Post-Dispatch*, June 24, 1923. This is one of the best accounts of Jesse's residence in Humphreys County. It relies on interviews with people who knew him there who were still alive in 1923.

7. *Nashville Daily American*, October 10, 1882; *Nashville Banner*, October 10, 1882; Love, 256–57, 260–61.

8. *Waverly (Tenn.) Democrat-Sentinel*, August 9, 1934; Settle, 132. According to a story passed down through the James family, Zee nursed Annie's baby, Robert, just after the death of her twins. Robert was born in February 1878. The exact date of the twins' birth is uncertain. In a letter from Mrs. Jill K. Garrett, dated July 19, 1975, I was directed to the cemetery at the Link place, where I found no evidence of any hand-carved stones marking the graves. The stones were in fact boulders, according to Garrett. Other stones seemed to have appeared near the grave around 1963, one of which bore the date 1842 or 1847. Garrett, who was an authority on Humphreys County history and cemeteries, was adamant that she did not recall any carved stones when she visited the site. Her family had lived on the farm adjacent to the Link place at the time the "Howards" lived there. *Nashville Tennessean*, April 8, 1979, carried Elmer Hinton's column confirming Jill Garrett's account of the stones: "I don't recall whether there were any carved stones at the place or not, but as I remember there were only field boulders at the graves of what was said to be the twins." Hinton visited the cemetery prior to 1963. The stones in question appear in a photo in Carl Breihan's *The Escapades of Frank and Jesse James*, 148. Breihan related to me that this photo came into his possession around 1963.

9. *Nashville Daily American*, October 10, 1882; *Nashville Banner*, October 10, 1882; Davidson County, Tennessee, First Circuit Court, Minute Book 10, 1878, for April 5, 1878, Metro Courthouse, Nashville, Tennessee.

10. *Nashville Daily American*, October 10, 1882; *Nashville Banner*, October 10, 1882; Davidson County, Tennessee, First Circuit Court, Minute Book 10, 1878, for April 5, 1878, Metro Courthouse, Nashville, Tennessee. Interview with Stanley F. Horn, August 3, 1975. Horn related a story told to him by a member of the Walton family; Croy, *James*, 138–39, cites Horn as a source.

11. *Nashville Daily American*, August 2, 1902. In the 1902 account Young meets Frank at a country store; it does not mention the smithing, and the argument apparently started over a horse trade. Frank gave his version in an 1882 interview. Croy, *James*, 141, 282, repeats the same story; his source was Horn also.

12. Settle, 132; Croy, *James*, 139.

13. Love, 258–59; *Nashville Daily American*, April 21, 1884. Taylor mentions the yellow-fever outbreak of 1878 in West Tennessee in his testimony at Frank's 1884 trial. There were also outbreaks of malaria. Jill Knight Garrett, *A History of Humphreys County, Tennessee*, 163 (cited hereafter as Garrett), mentions that Jesse collapsed while waiting to vote in an election there. This could be a symptom of malaria. Malaria was a problem in the Tennessee River area until TVA projects eliminated the malaria-bearing species of the insect in the late 1930s and early 1940s. See the *Saint Louis Post-Dispatch*, June 24, 1923.

14. Information about Jesse's disguising horses with shoe polish was related to me by Sherry Link of Nashville, Tennessee. See also *Saint Louis Post-Dispatch*, June 24, 1923; and Garrett, 163.

15. Service Record of Ennis Morrow Cooley, Napier's Battalion, RG 109, M 268, Roll 82, National Archives, Washington, D.C. Cooley enlisted in Company E, Napier's

Battalion, on December 11, 1862, "for 3 years or the war" at Waverly. Nana Cooley, interview, Nashville, Tennessee, August 25, 1984. The dialogue given is a quote related by Nana Cooley, passed down in a story about Jesse and the cattle swindle. Cooley was the daughter of James T. Cooley, who lost his education money in the swindle, sort of in counterpoint to the fabled "widow story" (which alleged that Jesse paid the mortgage on a widow's farm and then stole the money back shortly after the banker had collected it). Cooley was able to attend medical school, but his education was delayed. Cooley told the author that the amount was $1,000, but other sources have it as $500 or $900. Ennis Morrow Cooley served under Forrest and was in the battle of Parker's Crossroads in December 1862. Kate Jackson, affidavit, July 13, 1979, re: Wade and Kessler stockyard: Jesse reportedly used the alias of "Mr. Young" in the deal. This was the only time I found that Jesse handled a significant herd of cattle. Kate Jackson's father worked for Wade and Kessler. *Saint Louis Post-Dispatch*, June 24, 1923; Garrett, 163; Davidson County, Tennessee, First Circuit Court, Minute Book 10, 1878, for September 11, 1878, Metro Courthouse, Nashville, Tennessee; Love, 266–67. Koger gives his account of the 1878 Tennessee State Fair. H. G. Crickmore, comp., *Krick's Guide to the Turf, 1878*, 114–15; Amy Owens, "Mr. Howard's Horses," *The Blood-Horse*, January 2, 1988, 54–55.

16. *Saint Louis Post-Dispatch*, June 24, 1923.
17. John Davis Howard [Jesse James] to Henry Warren, January 12, 1879. The copy I received was provided by Lee Pollock, Princeton, Illinois.
18. Garrett, 163; *Nashville World*, April 25, 1882, reprinting an article from the *Waverly (Tenn.) Journal*. As far as I know there are no copies of the *Journal* presently in existence from this time period. See also the *Saint Louis Republican*, April 22, 1882. Jesse reportedly was willing to make a settlement of $300 on $900 worth of stock, but Cooley said he would have "all or nothing." He received the latter. I was fortunate in being able to interview and tape Nana Cooley before her death regarding the swindle. Apparently the suit was brought in Humphreys County Court. All the records for that time period were lost in a fire. No record could be found in court records in Davidson County. Apparently the case went to the Tennessee Supreme Court but had not been heard at the time of Jesse's death. Cooley was able to fill in some details, in particular that Jesse paid with a bad check and that the money was to be used for her father's medical education at the Nashville College of Surgeons. Without the information she provided, this part of the history would have been lost, as has happened to much of the James story over the years. Most Tennessee court records are, at best, docket entries.

CHAPTER 11: BACK ON THE OUTLAW TRAIL

1. Croy, *James*, 140, 144; *Nashville Daily American*, April 19, 1882. Garrett, 163–65, includes transcripts of the letters sent by Jesse to Henry Warren. These letters, until a few years ago, were in the possession of Warren's descendants. They were later sold to Lee Pollock; H. G. Crickmore, *Krick's Guide to the Turf, 1879–1880*, 11, 14; *Nashville Banner*, April 3, 1933. In this interview, Mary James Barr, daughter of Jesse, says that half brother John Samuel joined the brothers at the Smith place.

2. *Nashville Daily American*, October 12, 1882.

3. *Nashville Daily American*, April 20, 1882. This sounds like a scene out of a Western, but it happened in Nashville.

4. Henry F. Hoyt, *Frontier Doctor*, 183–85, 481–86; Richard Patterson, "Jesse James Meets Billy the Kid: Fact or Fantasy," *True West* 30, no. 1 (October 1992): 39–43. There has been some contention over the years as to whether Jesse actually went to New Mexico. Patterson makes a case for it happening, and I concur. Hoyt was later chief surgeon of the U.S. Army around the turn of the century. See also Robert M. Utley, *Billy the Kid: A Short and Violent Life*, 124, 247–48.

5. Hoyt, *Frontier Doctor*, 183–85, 481–86. See also Patterson, "Jesse James Meets Billy the Kid"; Utley, *Billy the Kid*.

6. Larry D. Ball, *The United States Marshals of New Mexico and Arizona Territories, 1846–1912*, 95–97; Howard Bryan, *Wildest of the Wild West: True Tales of a Frontier Town on the Santa Fe Trail*, 97–123. For information about the Thompson brothers and others in Colorado and Wyoming, see Settle, 102; John Lord, *Frontier Dust*, 72–78; Agnes Spring, *The Cheyenne and Black Hills Stage and Express Routes*, 200–201, 254–55, 284–85; *Richmond (Mo.) Democrat*, December 6, 1879; *Saint Louis Republican*, November 10, 1879. The *Chicago Semi-Weekly Inter Ocean*, November 20, 1879, has two men going under the names Tom Smith and Bill Green who were suspected of being the James brothers in Colorado. See also William B. Secrest, *I Buried Hickok: The Memoirs of White Eye Anderson*, 167–78, for more malarkey about the "James boys" robbing stages in Colorado. These heists sound like either the work of an impostor or of someone spinning a tall tale about them. John Lord, "Close Encounter with the James Gang," *Tombstone Epitaph National Edition* 7, no. 12 (December 1980): 18–19, has more on the Thompson brothers.

7. Information about Jesse and the Mocker barrel factory was supplied by Ralph Ganis, who has been researching the photograph in question. Ganis has pieced together an interesting, though circumstantial, case that Jesse was probably involved in some way with Andrew Moorman "Mome" Diggs and Merriman Little, of Union County, North Carolina. Both Diggs and Little were thought to have been involved in bootlegging and counterfeiting operations, and there is some reason to think that they may also have been involved in a bank robbery at Corinth, Mississippi, on December 7, 1874. Ganis's research is ongoing. It is hoped that his work will shed some light on the nineteenth-century underworld milieu in the Southeast following the war and that area's likely connections to the James and Younger brothers.

8. *Saint Louis Republican*, October 10, 11, 13, 1879. The October 2, 1881, issue carried Bassham's testimony in the Glendale trial of Bill Ryan. See the *Independence (Mo.) Examiner*, October 11, 1940, for an account by Phil McCarty. See also George Miller, *The Trial of Frank James for Murder*, 283–88 (cited hereafter as Miller); *Saint Louis Globe-Democrat*, October 10, 11, 1879; Gerard S. Petrone, *Judgment at Gallatin: The Trial of Frank James*, 56 (cited hereafter as Petrone).

9. *Saint Louis Republican*, October 10, 11, 13, 1879, October 2, 1881; Miller, 287–88; *Saint Louis Globe-Democrat*, October 10, 11, 1879.

10. Settle, 103–5; *Saint Louis Republican*, October 10, 1879; *Cummins' Book*, 80–81.

11. H. G. Crickmore, *Krick's Guide to the Turf, 1879–1880*, 198–203; William Preston Mangum, "Frank and Jesse James Raced Horses Between their Holdups," *Quarterly of the National Association and Center for Outlaw and Lawman History* 13, no. 2 (Fall 1988). The *Saint Louis Republican*, April 22, 1882, reported: "A Gentleman of this city [Nashville] whom James owed a gambling debt of $60 has a letter stating that his (James') wife had gotten on to his sporting, and would not let him have a dollar with which to gamble." The man was later given a gold watch in compensation. See *Nashville American*, October 9, 1882; *Nashville Banner*, June 22, 1930.

12. *Nashville American*, October 9, 1882; *Nashville Tennessean*, February 27, 1939; *Cummins' Book*, 86–87.

13. Settle, 104, 108–9, 116; *Cummins' Book*, 86–87; information from Miller family tradition related to me by Lee Pollock, Princeton, Illinois, who heard this from one of Miller's relatives; *Liberty (Mo.) Tribune*, April 21, 1882. Fitzgerald, "Miller," 35–36, indicates Miller had an inheritance from his father. Miller, according to family tradition, only planned to stay in the gang until he could get enough money together to move farther west and buy a farm. An inheritance would have made continued work with the gang unnecessary. Fitzgerald is the best account of the lives of Ed and Clell Miller. See also Croy, *James*, 160.

14. H. H. Crittenden, comp., *The Crittenden Memoirs*, 161–62 (cited hereafter as Crittenden); Jeffrey Michael Duff, Kentucky Department of Libraries and Archives, letter to Ted P. Yeatman, July 14, 1983, author's papers, regarding prison records pertaining to Clarence Rutherford. He was a married twenty-six-year-old laborer with a common school education. Rutherford was given a life sentence for murder by the Logan County Circuit Court during its November 1879 term and was received at the old Kentucky penitentiary at Frankfort on January 7, 1881. Rutherford was discharged by commutation, pardoned August 4, 1883. If other records exist, this case would bear additional investigation for any possible connection to Jesse James in the murder case.

15. Miller, 290–92; *Louisville Courier-Journal*, May 16, 1937, for Vial account; C. Walker Gollar, "The Mammoth Cave Stagecoach Robbery and the Effectiveness of the Kentucky Judicial System in the 1880s," *The Filson Club History Quarterly* 69, no. 4 (October 1995): 347–51 (cited hereafter as Gollar); *Nashville Daily American*, September 5, 1880; *Nashville Banner*, September 6, 1880; *Murfreesboro (Tenn.) Rutherford Courier*, February 25, 1941, reprinting a Louisville news account from September 1880; Wybrow, "Kentucky," 30–32, gives accounts of the take at between $882 and $1,920; Ted P. Yeatman, *Jesse James and Bill Ryan at Nashville*, 7–8, 14 (cited hereafter as Yeatman, *Nashville*), I estimated the total take based on newspaper accounts and other information on hand in 1980. On reexamination I find some question as to whether Jesse or Bill Ryan offered the passengers the whiskey. It could well be that the news accounts garbled this as they garbled the amount taken. It appears, however, that the main bandit who did the talking was probably Jesse, that both outlaws had been drinking, and that Jesse was the one who put the bottle down and had the men take a drink. There is

one more reason to believe this bandit was Jesse. Bill Ryan, according to a deposition by Alex Smith in the 1881 Muscle Shoals robbery case (see chapter 13, note 7, later in this volume), spoke with a pronounced Irish brogue, something that probably would not have gone unnoticed for someone trying to pass himself off as a Kentucky moonshiner. There is no mention of this accent at the stage robbery. Some accounts say the preacher was black. Little Hope Baptist Church got its name from Little Hope Hill. It was said that when it rained the road here became so slippery there was little hope of going down or up; thus the name. Crittenden, 158, gives an account by George Hite Jr., who's quoted as saying, "Ryan tod me that *they* made a negro preacher who was on the stage drink some whiskey with *them*. They laughed a good deal, over some of the incidents. They always talked about their robberies, and used to laugh considerable over them" (italics added). Note that Ryan was not speaking in the singular here. J. Winston Coleman, *Stage-Coach Days in the Bluegrass: Being an Account of Stage-Coach Travel and Tavern Days in Lexington and Central Kentucky, 1800–1900*, 251–54; "Knott, James Proctor," *Dictionary of American Biography*, 5:470. Knott was born near Raywick, Marion County, Kentucky, in 1830. He moved to Missouri in 1850 and studied law there, later rising to the post of attorney general in 1860. While a Southern sympathizer, he opposed secession. He was imprisoned in 1862 by Union authorities for refusing to take the Oath of Allegiance. He returned to Kentucky and began practicing law there in 1863, and served in the U.S. House of Representatives from the Fourth District during 1867–71 and 1875–83. It was in the course of this last period that Knott was one of the House managers of the impeachment of Secretary of War W. W. Belknap, charged for corruption in the appointment of military post sutlers. Jesse certainly must have heard of Knott by reputation, if he read the papers and knew anyone in Lebanon, as he claimed he did. For more on the Belknap scandal see Summers, 133–34, 180, 183–85, 259, 261–63.

16. Gollar, 351–53; Robert M. Ireland, *The County in Kentucky History*, 40ff. According to Ireland, corruption was rampant among county law enforcement officers. Some were known to fabricate a crime in order to get paid for arresting the alleged criminal. It was in this environment, as we will see later, that the James boys could move with ease.

17. Miller, 292–93; Otto A. Rothert, *A History of Muhlenburg County*, 387–88; Wybrow, "Kentucky," 31–32. George Dovey later went on to become president of a National League baseball club in Boston, Massachusetts, from 1906 until his death in 1909.

CHAPTER 12: LAST HIGHWAYMEN OF THE NATCHEZ TRACE

1. Settle, 182–87. J. A. Dacus, *Annals of the Great Strikes in the United States*, 366–75, contains some very good bashing of the robber barons and others. Dacus tended to side with Edwards, to some extent, though not quite in the same romanticized haze. James William Buel, *The Border Bandits*, 64–68 (cited hereafter as Buel, *Border Bandits*), a chapter entitled "The Mysterious Hiding Place in Jackson County" is pure hogwash. Interestingly, the copy of this pulp history that I

acquired came from Fulton County, Pennsylvania, and it just so happens that there is a tale in those parts of a cave where Jesse James allegedly hid, even though he probably never stepped anywhere closer to the county in his life than Baltimore or Philadelphia. I believe Buel's is probably the first account of an alleged cave hideout; his readers were probably responsible for spawning more versions over the years across many parts of the country. The term "fakelore" was coined by folklorist Richard M. Dorson to differentiate between genuine folklore, or lore of the people, and something that has an identifiable source, be it a book, television, film, or advertising. An example of fakelore is the story of Paul Bunyan and his blue ox Babe. It was conceived as an advertising campaign by the lumber industry in the 1930s and 1940s. Stella James, 73, for Frank's comment on the cave stories. Fred Egloff, "Lawmen and Gunmen: A Contrasting View of Old West Peace Officers in Kansas and Texas," *Journal of the West* 34, no. 1 (January 1995): 19–26, makes some interesting points concerning the matter of violence in the Old West: "Violence in the Old West was often greatly exaggerated. A relative lack of violence is what gave rise to the enormous notoriety accorded to events that shattered that calm. . . . The average citizen and his property were often very secure." Frontier violence had more appeal to readers than peace did. In turn, the writers of numerous pulp stories of a mythical West churned out various episodes of mayhem in order to sell their product. This created the distorted image we have of the Old West today. One can see this in reading newspaper accounts of the James gang. A bank robbery that today might only play on the local eleven o'clock news would get national media attention in the press in that day. Egloff points out that in the film *Tombstone*, the original script called for only thirty seconds of gunplay (as actually occurred) during the OK Corral sequence. But the shootout was significantly lengthened for the sake of sensation. One of the best exposés of the "image" of the Western gunman is seen in Clint Eastwood's classic *The Unforgiven*, in particular the scene in which lawman Gene Hackman straightens out a dime novelist's misconceptions of a past "gunfight" involving "English Bob," played by Richard Harris.

2. Census Roll, 1880, Davidson County, Tennessee, Part 31, 23d District, page 2, microfilm in Tennessee State Library and Archives, Nashville, Tennessee. The census records cited were taken June 1–2, 1880, by Charles M. Cantrell and show the James families at the Hyde place under their aliases. Ben J. Woodson is listed as age 40, a farmer, born in Maryland, father and mother from Maryland. His wife Fanny, age 27, also from Maryland, both parents from Maryland, their son is listed as Rob, age 2, born in Tennessee. Jesse is listed as Geo. D. Howard, brother-in-law, age 32, also a farmer, both parents from Maryland, wife Josie, age 29, from Maryland, parents from same. Children listed as Charles, age 4, and Mary, age 1, both born in Tennessee; *Nashville Daily American*, October 9, 1882; *Nashville Banner*, June 22, 1930; Buel, *Border Bandits*, 140, 237–40, mainly a chapter dealing with Bassham's confession. See also, *Kansas City Journal*, November 7, 1880.

3. *Cummins' Book*, 69–89. Cummins's rambling account sometimes mixes up the chronology of events, as occurs when he relates a story about the train robbers Evans and Sontag in California, which must have occurred in the early 1890s, if it

actually occurred at all. Generally speaking, Cummins's account fairly well fits with that of Frank James, with certain exceptions. Cummins liked to make himself out as a tough talker, and Frank painted him as a coward. Cummins probably saw that it was time to leave Nashville if he didn't want to get killed by Jesse or others, or wasn't of a mind to take on Jesse and potentially everyone else in order to avenge Ed Miller. He could probably sense that something was wrong, if Jesse was baiting Frank, who was trying to go straight, and pulling a gun on Liddil. *Nashville Daily American*, October 9, 1882; *Chattanooga News*, April 7, 1933, for Killough account. The *Nashville Morning World,* May 11, 1882, published a letter from Zee James to A. F. Speed, another boarder at Mrs. Kent's. I was able, with the use of old fire insurance maps and city directories, to determine that the boarding house was under a portion of the present Tennessee Performing Arts Center. The move to Mrs. Kent's seems to coincide with Jesse's appearance with Bill Ryan and Dick Liddil, along with a prowler at the Eastman place, and of course Ryan's drinking. Frank probably realized that Jim Cummins had little cause to attract attention or get involved in any schemes with Jesse. Ryan and Liddil were another matter.

4. *Nashville Daily American,* October 9, 1882; Miller, 24, 36, 294–96. *Cummins' Book,* 89, states that upon Cummins's return to Missouri he was offered five thousand dollars if he would surrender to Sheriff Timberlake of Clay County and help him capture Frank and Jesse. Cummins reportedly declined the offer then went into hiding in Kansas. The amount seems rather excessive for Clay County to have offered, but this may have had something to do with Governor Crittenden's later reward offer that summer. W. Stanley Hoole, *The James Boys Rode South,* 19–23, suggests that Ryan was scouting Muscle Shoals, Alabama, as a prospective holdup site. Obviously some advance work went into the next robbery. It's possible that they may have picked up on the idea in conversation with Norris while they visited him in Selma. Norris, a contractor, may have mentioned the canal project. The image of a large payroll probably lured them to Muscle Shoals. Though Hoole says the trip was made in March, it probably occurred in February, after Cummins ran off. A trip to Selma would have gotten Frank and Jesse far enough away, should Cummins have sought to betray them. Frank was most certainly in Nashville in March, trying to keep a rather high profile, as can be seen from reliable sources. The testimony of his Nashville friends was decisive in his acquittal in 1884 when he was tried for alleged conspiracy in the Muscle Shoals robbery.

5. James, *Father,* 5–6. Judging from the age of Jesse Jr. and his description of the location, it seems probable that this incident occurred in February 1881 at 903 Woodland Street, which is also on a corner. Jesse's absence at the time would be explained by his trip to Selma. There is a listing for John D. Howard, laborer, in the 1881 *Nashville City Directory,* at 903 Woodland Street. See also *Nashville Daily American,* April 19, 1882, for Jesse's connection with this site. It is the same alias and occupation that Jesse is believed to have used in Baltimore, and, like Baltimore, it turns up only for this year. Jesse was living in the county before this. *Chattanooga News,* April 7, 1933; R. C. Vardell, statement of January 20, 1979, to Steve Eng, Nashville, Tennessee, copy in my papers, concerning 711 Fatherland Street; *Nashville Tennessean,* May 13, September 19, 1948. I believe Jesse moved

from 903 Woodland Street to 711 Fatherland Street. Frank is known to have lived at 814 Fatherland in the last month or so of his stay in Tennessee. There is an oral account in the Vardell family related to R. C. Vardell by his grandfather, William C. Vardell, who lived at 709 Fatherland, that Jesse lived next door and was known as Mr. Howard, a grain dealer. The Vardell family only lived at 709 Fatherland for about two years prior to the James family's departure. Most likely 711 Fatherland was the last house rented by Jesse before he left Nashville.

6. See *Nashville Daily American*, April 19–26, 1884, for a rough transcript of the testimony given at the Muscle Shoals trial. Miller, 295–96. Liddil tried to implicate Frank in the Muscle Shoals robbery to give himself bargaining power with the authorities. Unless some solid citizens of Nashville, including at least one officer of the law, perjured themselves in providing Frank with alibis, this is highly unlikely. I have tried to use Liddil's confession where it appears relevant and can be corroborated. Thomas Peden, deposition, September 21, 1881; Daniel Comer, deposition, June 16, 1881, concerning the Muscle Shoals robbery. Records of the Chief of Engineers, Unregistered Letters, Reports, Histories, Regulations and other Records, 1817–94; RG 77, Bulky File 348, Box 17, National Archives, Washington, D.C. All records from this primary source are hereafter cited as "Bulky File." This is one of the best sources for information on the case and has been overlooked by scholars for well over a century. It consists of depositions and correspondence sent to the chief of engineers about the robbery. Daniel Comer's report is particularly useful in tracing the gang's route along portions of the old Natchez Trace. The James gang was the last of the old-time horseback robbers to use the trace to perpetrate a heist— some forty-five to fifty years after the breakup of John A. Murrell's activity there. For Murrell's activities, see James Lal Penick, *The Great Western Land Pirate: John A. Murrell in Legend and History*. Criminal activity that went on along the trace during its heyday would make an interesting study. Much that has been written to date lacks the substance of Penick's work. The typical work rattles off stories about the Harpes, Sam Mason, Murrell, et al., with the same depth of research that has gone into pulp histories of the James gang.

7. Alexander G. Smith, deposition, May 7, 1881; John Berendsen, deposition, September 20, 1881; John Springer, deposition, September 20, 1881; all concerning the Muscle Shoals robbery, "Bulky File." Smith was probably under suspicion, if only briefly, as being in complicity with the robbers. This explains his comments to Springer about being a "ruined man." It would appear that his movements to and from Florence and the camp had become somewhat routine. At a given day of the month he would go to town and get the money, like clockwork. Having accurate information allowed the gang to plan an affair like the payroll heist at Muscle Shoals, probably one of the only robberies they pulled that came off on schedule. More commonly they were making a shot in the dark based on a rumor, as was the case at the Dovey Mines, when the robbery netted only thirteen dollars and a gold watch. Any doubts about Smith would have vanished with the capture of Bill Ryan and part of the payroll. See Miller, 128, for a description of Wood Hite.

8. Daniel Comer, deposition, June 16, 1881, Muscle Shoals Robbery, "Bulky File." Comer may have belonged to Forrest's Cavalry, and a man named Daniel Comer

served in the Twenty-second Tennessee (Nixon's) Cavalry in 1864–65 from nearby Lawrence County. See Service Record of Daniel Comer, Twenty-second Tenn. (Nixon's) Cavalry, RG 109, M268, roll 79, National Archives, Washington, D.C.; Maj. W. R. King, letters to Chief of Engineers, March 14, June 2, 1881, RG 77, National Archives, Washington, D.C. Comer was paid five dollars a day, "to include all traveling expenses," as a "scout" for the Corps of Engineers for twenty-one days in March and April. Four other scouts were also hired for a total of thirty-one days in April. Who these men were and where they went is not stated.

9. *Nashville Daily American*, April 20–22, 1884.

10. *Nashville Banner*, March 26, 1881; *Nashville Daily American*, April 1, 1881; Miller, 36. These are the best primary source accounts of Ryan's capture. See also Ted P. Yeatman, *Nashville*, 8, 13. The latter page includes a discussion of the accounts of Homer Croy and Carl Breihan. Croy, for example, in *Jesse James*, 152, has Ryan lugging around "$1,300 in gold." While Ryan did apparently get the gold when the split occurred, according to the Smith deposition, "Bulky File," he was also carrying a lot of paper money, by Nashville accounts, when he was searched.

CHAPTER 13: THE JAMES BOYS ON THE RUN

1. *Nashville Banner*, March 26, 28, 30, 1881; *Nashville American*, March 29, 1881, April 20, 1884.

2. *Nashville American*, April 21, 222, 1884; Miller, 98–99, 134.

3. *Nashville American*, October 9, 1882, April 20, 1884; Miller, 25–27, 36–37, 50, 126–27, 136–37. The story of the stolen horses is related by both Frank James and Dick Liddil, so it is probably true. It appears that the gang's reputation as horse thieves has been sorely underestimated if Liddil's account has any truth to it.

4. *Nashville Banner*, March 28, 30, 1881; *Nashville American*, March 29, 1881. Clawson denied knowing Ryan. In all probability Jesse had scribbled a note to his uncle, George Hite, on a piece of scrap paper with Clawson's name on it. Nevertheless, it was careless.

5. *Nashville Banner*, March 30, 1881; *Nashville American*, April 1, 1881; Smith deposition, "Bulky File."

6. Maj. W. R. King, telegram to Chief of Engineers, April 14, 1881, Adjutant General's Office, Letters Received, RG 94, M689, Roll 24, Letter # 2715; Miller, 126–27; Harry James Brown and Frederick D. Williams, ed., *The Diary of James A. Garfield*, 4:572–75; David Y. Thomas, "Stephen Wallace Dorsey," *Dictionary of American Biography*, 3:387. Dorsey was indicted for conspiring to defraud the U.S. government in the Star Route case, but was acquitted in two rather sensational trials. Although it is not mentioned in his biographical entry, Dorsey was involved in the conflict over the Maxwell land grant in Colfax County, New Mexico, during the 1880s. See also Morris Taylor, *O. P. McMains and the Maxwell Land Grant Conflict*, for more on this. See H. Wayne Morgan, *From Hayes to McKinley: National Party Politics, 1877–1896*, 156–58, and Schlesinger, 348–49, for more on the Star Route Frauds. Wayne MacVeagh to the President, April 16, 1881, Adjutant General's Office, Letters Received, RG 94, M689, Roll 24, Letter # 2715.

Also in this file is the text of the Posse Comitatus Act as distributed through the
army in 1878. Maj. H. W. C. Furman, "Restrictions Upon the Army Imposed by
the Posse Comitatus Act," *Military Law Review, vols. 1–10, Selected Reprint*,
339–83, gives a good overview of the act but fails to pick up on some of the other
nuances for its adoption. Rep. William Kimmel of Maryland, one of those pushing
the bill, had seen the Democratic Party almost suppressed by Union army bayonets
during the Civil War. Knott's wartime imprisonment in Missouri is not mentioned
either. Both Kimmel and Knott did not directly mention their experiences during
the war in the debates, but it is hard to believe it was far from their minds as they
pushed the legislation through Congress. The allusions used in the debates were
very carefully picked. One was the reminder of Oliver Cromwell's army deposing
Parliament after the English Civil War in the 1600s. As many serving in both
houses of Congress were Union veterans, the use of the English Civil War as an
example carefully sidestepped what could easily have became a very partisan issue.
Biographical Directory-Congress, 206–9, 979, 1310: Kimmel was a delegate to the
1864 Democratic convention and an unsuccessful candidate for Congress in that
year from Maryland. Interestingly, Thomas Ewing, author of Order #11, was also a
member of Congress, and as a Democrat, he voted with Knott and Kimmel for the
Posse Comitatus Act. For text of the debates see *Congressional Record*, Reel 107,
45th Congress, 2d Session, 1877–78, 3578–89, 3844–55, 4240–49, 4294–305,
4686; James P. O'Shaughnessy, "The Posse Comitatus Act: Reconstruction Politics Reconsidered," *American Criminal Law Review* 13, no. 4 (Spring 1976):
703–35. Robert M. Utley, *High Noon in Lincoln: Violence on the Western Frontier*,
76–77, 84, 86, 114, 117, 130, covers the Lincoln County War in New Mexico and
the use of U.S. troops there. See also Larry D. Ball, "The United States Army and
the Big Springs, Nebraska, Train Robbery of 1877," *Journal of The West* 34, no. 1
(January 1995): 34–45, for a case where the army formed a posse to pursue the
Sam Bass gang prior to the adoption of the act. See also Clayton D. Laurie, "Fill-
ing the Breach: Military Aid to the Civil Power in the Trans-Mississippi West,"
Western Historical Quarterly 25, no. 2 (Summer 1994): 149–62; and Larry D. Ball,
"The United States Army as Constabulary on the Northern Plains," *Great Plains
Quarterly* 13, no. 1 (Winter 1993): 21–32.

7. Miller, 37, 51; Maj. W. R. King to Marshal R. H. Crittenden, May 23, 1881; G. W.
Hunter to Det. William P. Watson, May 19, 1881, Marshal R. H. Crittenden to
Maj. W. R. King, May 23 [?], 1881, Records of the Chief of Engineers, RG 77,
National Archives, Washington, D.C. See Calhoun, *Lawmen*, 121–42, 155–57.
Calhoun's book is perhaps the best overview of the U.S. Marshals Service to date.
Stephen Creswell, *Mormons and Cowboys, Moonshiners and Klansmen: Federal Law
Enforcement in the South and West, 1870–1893*, 140–80, 207–14, 223–25, 234,
240–44, 256–58, gives another, more specialized study that is also quite good.

8. Alvin Fay Harlow, *Weep No More My Lady*, 256–66. No date is given for this
encounter, but I assume it happened in late May 1881. Some court testimony has
the gang clear of Kentucky by this time, but the testimony is rather vague and
contradictory and thus is suspect. See Miller, 37, 51, 137. In his testimony Liddil
indicated that a plan for a robbery was made in late April or early May, and then

in late May or early June, two different times. Frank declined to answer the question, "Were you at peace in Nelson County?" during his trial at Gallatin, Missouri. See *Biographical Directory—Congress*, 1287–88, for information on Johnson.

9. Miller, 50–51, 128–29, 137. Maj. W. R. King to Chief of Engineers, June 2, 1881, RG 77, National Archives, Washington, D.C.; Court Minutes, Davidson County Criminal Court, Division I, January–July 1881, Metro Court House, Nashville, Tennessee; Case History of Bill Ryan, #1359, Pinkerton's Inc.; Extradition requisition for William Ryan, June 4, 1881, papers of Gov. Alvin Hawkins, Tennessee State Library and Archives, Nashville, Tennessee.

10. Robert Todd Lincoln to Wayne MacVeagh, Attorney General, June 14, 1881, U.S. Department of Justice—Source Chronological File—War Department, RG 60, June 1881, National Archives, Washington, D.C.; S. F. Phillips to Robert T. Lincoln, Secretary of War, June 21, 1881, Letters Sent by the Department of Justice to Executive Officers and to Members of Congress, 1871–1904, M702, Roll 10 (vol. J), November 27, 1880–November 21, 1881, National Archives, Washington, D.C.; S. F. Phillips, letter to George M. Thomas, U.S. Attorney, Louisville, Kentucky, June 21, 1881, Letters Sent by the Department of Justice: Instructions to U.S. Attorneys and Marshals, 1867–1904, M701, Roll 11 (vol. L), June 6, 1881–June 17, 1882, National Archives, Washington, D.C.; S. F. Phillips, letter to James A. Warder, U.S. Attorney, Nashville, Tenn., June 21, 1881, Letters Sent by the Department of Justice: Instructions to U.S. Attorneys and Marshals, 1867–1904, M701, Roll 11 (vol. L), June 6, 1881–June 17, 1882, National Archives, Washington, D.C.; James A. Warder to Wayne MacVeagh, Attorney General, June 26, 1881, Letters Received by the Department of Justice from the State of Tennessee, 1871–1884, M1471, Roll 3, National Archives, Washington, D.C.; Wayne MacVeagh to W. H. Smith, U.S. Attorney, Montgomery, Alabama, July 6, 1881, Letters Sent by the Department of Justice: Instructions to U.S. Attorneys and Marshals, 1867–1904, M701, Roll 11 (vol. L), June 6, 1881–June 17, 1882, National Archives, Washington, D.C.; J. H. Ross telegram to Wayne MacVeagh, Attorney General, July 15, 1881, Letters Received by the Department of Justice from the State of Alabama, 1871–1884, M1356, Roll 2, National Archives, Washington, D.C.; Wayne MacVeagh to J. H. Ross, U.S. Marshal, July 18, 1881, Letters Sent by the Department of Justice: Instructions to U.S. Attorneys and Marshals, 1867–1904, M701, Roll 11 (vol. L), June 6, 1881–June 17, 1882, National Archives, Washington, D.C.

11. Settle 107–10; Brant, *James*, 210–11; Miller, 39–41, 45–46, 141, 307–8; Stella James, 6–7, 110–13; Petrone, 56–66; *Saint Louis Republican*, July 17, 21, 1881, April 13, 1882; *Saint Louis Weekly Republican*, April 13, 1882; *Washington Post*, March 19, 1899. Frank James would later claim he had gone to Texas and had not been in northwestern Missouri. Liddil would use his testimony against Frank as leverage for immunity from prosecution. Both had reasons to give less-than-honest testimony. In exchange for his release from prison, where he was dying of tuberculosis, Clarence Hite, Frank's first cousin, later gave a confession naming Frank as one of the robbers. While the possibility remains that Hite might have agreed to say anything to die a free man, it's just as likely that he was telling the truth. Jesse's

widow, in an interview published in the *Saint Louis Republican* on April 13, 1882, mentions Frank being in Kansas City in September. Frank denied being anywhere closer than Saint Louis, and attorneys apparently did not question Zee about the matter later in court. Sorting through this hodgepodge of facts, lies, and half-truths, it is difficult to reconstruct events of this period with any degree of certainty. Just when the gang arrived in Missouri is a matter of question. Was it in April, or May, or June? Detective George Hunter, as mentioned in note 8 above, thought there was reason to suspect they were still in Kentucky in late May. Liddil claimed he and others had done considerable horse stealing, which may well have been the case. He also claimed, to Acting Attorney General John Phillips, that Frank had told Jesse there would be no killing. Jesse shot the conductor in order to pull the band together with a possible murder charge hanging over all of them. Liddil later gave a different version in court. Harry C. Hoffman, "On Woodland Avenue," *James Farm Journal* 8, no. 1, ca. 1989–90, 2–3 (cited hereafter as Hoffman, "Woodland"), is an account of Hoffman's first connections with the James family, taken from a copy at the Missouri State Museum, Jefferson City, Missouri.

12. Settle, 106–7, 187–89; Stella James, 115–16. Williams, *Railroad*, 278, has Crittenden acting in collusion with Huntington to quash some unfavorable railroad legislation while in Congress. "Crittenden, Thomas Theodore," *Dictionary of American Biography*, 4:550; *Saint Louis Republican*, July 20, 21, 27, 1881, April 10, 11, 1882; *Saint Louis Weekly Republican*, April 13, 1882 (a weekly edition of the daily paper of the same name); D. W. Stevens, "The James Boys in Minnesota," *The Five Cent Wide Awake Library* 1, no. 479, March 8, 1882. "Stevens" was a pen name for John R. Musick, an attorney from Kirksville, Missouri, who would have done better, in a literary sense, sticking to legal briefs. In a financial sense, he apparently made off better than Jesse did, leaving a large estate. Linda Reed, "The Pulp Heroics of a Bandit King," *Quarterly of the National Association and Center for Outlaw and Lawman History* 5, no. 4 (July 1980): 9–12. According to Reed, *The Train Robbers* was released on June 27, 1881. Reed's is perhaps the best article on the dime novels. Her 1978 master's thesis at the University of Texas-Austin was "Frank Tousey's Jesse James: Bandit King of the Dime Novels."

13. Miller, 45–46, 300–302, 313–19; *Saint Louis Republican*, September 8–12, 18, 1881. Frank apparently stayed out of the way as the result of the killings at Winston. Jesse carried a Colt .45 and a Smith and Wesson .44 plus a double-barreled breechloading shotgun. Clarence Hite had a .44 Remington and a Winchester. Frank had his .44 Remingtons and a Winchester, and Liddil had two Colt .45s and a shotgun like Jesse's. Charlie Ford and Wood Hite were only armed with pistols, a Remington and Smith and Wesson .44 for the former, and a .44 Smith and Wesson and Colt .45 for the latter.

14. Miller, 302, 318–19, 331; *Saint Louis Republican*, September 9–18, 1881; Settle, 111–13.

15. Settle, 113–14; Miller, 338–43; *Saint Louis Republican*, September 28–30, October 2, 10, 16, 1881; William H. Wallace, *Speeches and Writings of Wm. H. Wallace, with Autobiography*, 263–79 (cited hereafter as Wallace); James Horan, *The Authentic Wild West: The Lawmen*, 75–101.

16. Miller, 130–31, 302–3, 320–22, 343; *Saint Louis Republican*, September 30, 1881, April 6, 13, October 9, 1882; Wallace, 283; Crittenden, 152–62. The gang reportedly intended to rob a train at Muldraugh's Hill, but the plan fell through because some gang members wouldn't come along. Just what was going on in Kentucky was unclear. Croy, *James*, 159, 288, has Jesse cutting his name in a window at Bardstown on October 18, 1881, with a diamond ring. The pane reportedly existed in 1948 and was seen by Croy in Louisville. Other sources, including the confessions of Clarence Hite and Dick Liddil, contradict the story of his returning to Kentucky after the Blue Cut robbery. If Congressman Ben Johnson's story, explained in note 8, indeed occurred later than the spring of 1881, it would have had to be around this time. Still, there is no other corroboration by others in the gang that Jesse came to Kentucky in October.

17. John Fitch, *Annals of the Army of the Cumberland*, 539–42; Marmaduke Beckwith Morton, *Kentuckians Are Different*, 268–70; Carl Breihan, *The Man Who Shot Jesse James*, 254 (cited hereafter as Breihan, *Man Who Shot*); *Saint Louis Republican*, May 4, 1882; Settle, 168; Crittenden, 152–62. According to another account, it was Jesse who was having an unauthorized liaison. Breihan gives an account, apparently from sources around the time of the trial of Bob Ford for the killing of Wood Hite in October 1882, to the effect that it was Liddil having an affair with Sarah Hite. It is inexplicable that Wood and Clarence Hite would follow Jesse if he had been the culprit. Liddil's being Sarah Hite's paramour would explain much of Wood Hite's antagonism.

18. Crittenden, 152–62; *Saint Louis Republican*, April 8, 1882; Breihan, *Man Who Shot*, 241–54; Miller, 62–68, 303–4. Settle, 116, says that Hite and Liddil were both rivals for the affection of Martha Bolton. The story of the money allegedly stolen, while perhaps part of the equation, was probably not all of it.

CHAPTER 14: AN END AND A BEGINNING

1. Miller, 131–33; William Preston Mangum, "Frank James' Secret Travels Authenticated," *Quarterly of the National Association and Center for Outlaw and Lawman History* 9, no. 4 (Spring 1985): 16; *Lynchburg News*, June 23, 1903, February 20, 1915.

2. *Saint Louis Republican*, April 6, 10, 1882; *Saint Louis Weekly Republican*, April 13, 1882; Breihan, *Man Who Shot*, 18–22; James Williamson, *Mosby's Rangers*, 316–24, 478; *Saint Joseph (Mo.) Daily Gazette*, April 5, 1882; Hugh C. Keen and Horace Mewbern, *43rd Battalion Virginia Cavalry: Mosby's Command*, 319; *Violent Kin* 4 (October 1989); *Cummins' Book*, 87.

3. *Saint Joseph Daily Gazette*, April 5, 1882; *Saint Louis Republican*, April 7, 1882; *Saint Louis Weekly Republican*, April 13, 1882; Breihan, *Man Who Shot*, 45–63.

4. *Saint Louis Republican*, April 13, 1882; Saint Joseph *Daily Gazette*, April 5, 1882; *Saint Louis Weekly Republican*, April 13, 1882; Hoffman, "Woodland," 2–3.

5. *New York Daily Herald*, April 4, 6, 8, 1882; Miller, 133.

6. *Saint Louis Weekly Republican*, April 13, 1882; *Saint Joseph Daily Gazette*, April 5, 1882; *Saint Louis Republican*, April 6, 7, 9, 12, 18, 1882; *Sedalia (Mo.) Daily Democrat*, April 13, 1882; *Nashville Morning World*, May 3, 11, 31, 1882; *Faribault (Minn.) Democrat*, April 21, May 12, 1882.

7. Rupert Hunt-Davis, ed., *The Letters of Oscar Wilde*, 112–15; *Saint Louis Republican* April 29, 1882. James E. Fulton, Wilde's advance agent, bilked W. R. Carey of Kansas City, Missouri, of five hundred dollars allegedly invested in the Wilde tour. Fulton then departed with the proceeds from Wilde's Kansas City lecture on the English Renaissance. He was arrested in Saint Louis. Marshal Cornelius Murphy, who had searched in vain for Jesse James in 1881, escorted Fulton back to Jackson County.

8. Gollar, 356–65; *Saint Joseph Gazette*, April 5, 1882.

9. *Saint Louis Republican*, April 6, 8, 9, 1882; Wallace, 280–82.

10. *Saint Louis Republican*, April 8, 10, 18, 19, 21, 22, 1882; *Saint Louis Weekly Republican*, April 13, 1882.

11. *Louisville Courier-Journal*, April 8, 1882; Settle, 192–93; Triplett, ix–xxxvii, 244–77; *Saint Louis Republican*, April 21, 29, May 5, 1882; *Nashville Morning World*, May 11, 1882; *Saint Louis Weekly Republican*, April 13, 1882. The *Kansas City Daily Journal* of April 7, 1882, contains an account of the autopsy performed on the evening of Monday, April 3, by coroner J. W. Hedden, who was assisted by Dr. George C. Catlett, Dr. Jacob Geiger, and a Dr. Hoyt. The cap to the skull was removed and sawed through to get at the brain. "It was found that the bullet had entered the lower part of the occipital bone on the right of the median line, and had taken a course slightly upwards and to the left. The ball did not pass through the head as first stated, and it was found partly imbeded in the bone. The scalp not being punctured at all. The ball was lodged at the junction of the suture which divides the occipital, parietal and temporal bones of the left side. The occipital bone was very much shattered, the whole continuity of the cranium being broken up. The cerebellum was found crushed and mangled terribly, large pieces of bone having been carried with the brain by the bullet in its progress." The article "Jesse James' Brain," *James Farm Journal* 12, no. 1 (April 1995), contains a reprint of an undated clipping from The *Saint Joseph Herald*, ca. 1892, repeating a feature from the *Saint Louis Globe-Democrat:* "There in a jar on a shelf, in a glass office case, was the bandit's brain, the spot where the bullet had entered being easily distinguished by the effusion of blood." The writer said, "The doctor who pointed it out to me was a personal friend, and he laughed slyly when I asked how he accomplished it. He invited me to go in where Jesse lay dead in his coffin, and as I looked at his face I endeavored to discover the marks of the scalpel, but in vain. When we were out of the room I asked him how the brain was removed without leaving a trace of the knife, and he then told me that the scalp had been cut across the back part of the head and drawn forward over the brow, leaving the skull exposed to the action of the saw. The top of the skull was carefully sawed and the brain was removed. The scalp was then drawn back into its place over the cap of the skull, and when Mrs. Samuels next gazed upon the pale face of her son his appearance was not altered in the least, but his brain was in a glass jar." See also Appendix H.

12. *New York Times*, May 31, June 1, 2, 1882; Petrone, 25–30; *Kansas City Times*, October 6, 1882; Triplett, 283–85; *Atchison (Kans.) Daily Globe*, October 9, 1882; *Nashville Banner*, October 9, 1882; John Newman Edwards to Frank James, October 26, 1882 (copy in my papers); *Louisville Courier-Journal*, October 7, 1882; *Saint*

Louis Republican, April 12, 14, 18, 25, 1882; *Saint Louis Weekly Republican*, April 13, 1882; *Nashville Morning World*, May 11, 1882.

13. Settle, 136–48; William H. Wallace, *Speeches and Writings of Wm. H. Wallace, With Autobiography*, 263–95; Petrone, 51–187, presents a blow-by-blow account of the trial and is written with a definite bias. The matter of Liddil's self-interest in aiding the prosecutor perhaps needs further attention. There was sufficient reasonable doubt raised in the course of the trial concerning Frank's guilt, and the jury returned a verdict accordingly. See also George F. Miller, ed., *The Trial of Frank James for Murder*, for an abridged transcript of the trial. Miller omits most of the summary arguments given at the trial. Other details can be found in an undated newspaper clipping from the *Kansas City Times* containing Philips's obituary, author's papers. *Adjutant General, Mo.—1865*, 498–500, contains a brief history by Philips of the Seventh Missouri State Militia Cavalry from 1861 to 1863. More detailed accounts of the militia's activities can be found in various reports reprinted in several volumes of the *OR*.

14. *Nashville American*, April 18–26, 1884; John Newman Edwards to Frank James, October 2, 1883; November 10, 1883; October 20, 24, 1884; copies in author's papers; Frank James to Annie James, copy in author's papers. Settle, 144–59; Foner, *Reconstruction*, 300, 331, 342, 349, 439, 441, for background on Smith. It is likely that the defense team had some idea in advance of the evidence against Frank. In the "Bulky File" containing the depositions collected by the Corps of Engineers in the Muscle Shoals case is a mailing label indicating that the file was at one time forwarded to Congressman William C. Oates of Alabama. On July 2, 1863, Oates served as colonel of the Fifteenth Alabama Infantry that attacked Col. Joshua Lawrence Chamberlain's Twentieth Maine on Little Round Top at Gettysburg. Oates's congressional district was in another part of the state, but he was involved with the Democratic Party machinery in Alabama as well as Confederate veterans groups. See also Robert Desty, ed., *The Federal Reporter: Cases Argued and Determined in the Circuit and District Courts of the United States*, 18 (November 1883–February 1884): 853–59, for *In re James*. See *Saint Louis Globe-Democrat*, February 19, 20, 23, 1885; *Saint Louis Republican*, February 19, 20, 21, 23, 1885.

15. Patrick Brophy, *Bushwhackers of the Border: The Civil War Period in Western Missouri*, 48; *Omaha Daily Bee*, August 2, 1887. See also John F. Philips to Frank James, June 1, 1887, copy in author's papers; Prichard, "Missouri Outlaws," 51, for Webb's release in 1883. See Settle, 162, for Bob Younger's death. See also *Jefferson City (Mo.) Daily Tribune*, April 16, August 17, 1889, for Bill Ryan's release. *Cummins' Book*, 73–74, mentions Cummins's encountering Ryan in California in the early 1890s. John N. Reynolds, *The Twin Hells: A Thrilling Narrative of Life in the Kansas and Missouri Penitentiaries*, 308–9, offers an interesting picture of convict life and mentions that Ryan was a model prisoner. Jennie Edwards, *John N. Edwards: Biography, Memoirs, Reminiscences and Recollections*, 24–32, 196–208. See James D. Horan, *The Authentic Wild West: The Outlaws*, 134, for Liddil's death in 1901. Breihan, *Man Who Shot*, 238–40, 255–96. Breihan claims that Liddil died in Cincinnati in 1893 (p. 259), but I believe Horan is probably closer to the right year. The site of Liddil's death is uncertain, although it most likely was in the

eastern half of the country. See Bryan, *Wildest*, 200–207, for Ford and Liddil in Las Vegas, New Mexico.

16. Stella James, 8–11; Chuck Rabas, *Jack "Quail Hunter" Kennedy*, 1–14; Jeff Burton, "John F. Kennedy of Missouri and to His Circle of Train Robbers, Part I," *English Westerners' Tally Sheet* 26, no. 3 (April 1980): 29–38; Patterson, *Train*, 121–23; *Kansas City Star*, September 25, 26, October 1, 2, 12, 13, 16, 17, 18, 19, 22, 25, 26, 1898, February 7, 23–28, March 1, 1899; *Kansas City World*, February 23, 1899, mentions Pendergast being in the courtroom on duty; James, *Father*, 111–85; Ted P. Yeatman, *Nashville*, 11–12; William M. Reddig, *Tom's Town: Kansas City and the Pendergast Legend*, 62–65; Lawrence H. Larsen and Nancy J. Hulston, *Pendergast!* 29–31. The county prosecutor, James A. Reed, had been elected the previous November; his campaign was bankrolled chiefly by the saloon and gambling interests headed by Pendergast, who had also created one of the most notorious political machines in the country. His brother, Deputy County Marshal Tom Pendergast, guarded young Jesse in court. Brother Tom was also heavily involved in ballot-box stuffing, which on election days involved his rounding up the homeless to vote early and often for the machine candidates. Long lines of transients served as well to discourage opposition voters. At the time of Jesse Jr.'s arrest, a scandal had broken regarding the troops who were being mustered in the area for service in Cuba and the Philippines—they were quickly registered to vote as soon as they were quartered near town. Later Jesse Jr. was briefly involved in a Democratic splinter group that sought to oppose the Pendergast machine. County prosecutor Reed was later sent to Washington as a U.S. senator, and though a Democrat in name, he was notable for his opposition to the League of Nations. The James case was one of only two that Reed lost as county prosecutor.

17. Settle, 163–64; Stella James, 42, 125–26; *Kansas City Journal*, November 15, 1900; *New York Herald*, March 4, 1900; *Kansas City Journal*, November 15, 1900; *Omaha Daily Bee*, August 20, 1885; "Mrs. Jesse James Devout Worker in Revival," *James Farm Journal* 5, no. 5 (March 1988): 2; Stella James, 42, 125–26. John F. Philips to Frank James, June 21, 1899, copy in my papers; William Ward's *Jesse James, Gentleman, or The Hold-Up of the Mammoth Cave Stage* is an example of a later pulp novel overuses poetic license; "Harry Truman and the Jameses," *James Farm Journal* 2, no. 2 (August 1984): 1, contains information by Milton F. Perry recollected from a conversation with President Truman; Bob Hayman and Arne, "Books About Old West Outlaws Still Fascinate Readers," *Antique Week* (Eastern ed.) March 7, 1994, 6, 15, repeats the McDonald ghostwriting story; James R. Ross to Ted P. Yeatman, October 28, 1994, my papers, explains: "As to A. B. McDonald having ghostwritten 'Jesse James, My Father,' this is absolutely untrue. Daddy [Jesse E. James] wrote the book and so stated to me on numerous occasions. . . . I might add that after he wrote the book, he went to law school, graduating Summa Cum Laude." See also *Kansas City Star*, October 12, 1898; January 3, 6, October 25, 1901. The October 12, 1898, issue contains the comment by Mrs. Samuel on dime novels. See *New York Sun*, February 21, 1901; Ernest Kirschen, *Catfish and Crystal: The Story of St. Louis, U.S.A.*, 306–29, which includes an interesting account of Ed Butler's career as a political boss. Butler recalled that once the Democrats hired his men to throw

an election as far away as Indiana, but this long-distance ballot cramming was an exception. While Frank was in Saint Louis, the Republicans won the city elections of 1895 and 1897 with Butler's help. The *New York Sun* article treads lightly but implies that was Frank's allegedly "protecting" the polls in either 1895 or 1897.

CHAPTER 15: OUTLAWS OF THE SAWDUST TRAIL

1. *Saint Louis Republican*, November 10, 1901.
2. *Kansas City Star*, February 10, 11, 1902. See also Kenny, *Molly Maguires*, 155, 176–77. Shenandoah, Pennsylvania, was the center of Molly Maguire activity in which Pinkerton agent Robert J. Linden had played a notable role after being shifted off the James case. Obviously the Wild West theatrical promoters were anxious to cash in on the anti-Pinkerton sentiment that pervaded in this region of Pennsylvania.
3. E. Lisle Reedstrom, "The Cole Younger and Frank James Wild West Show," *True West* 39, no. 10 (October 1992): 28–32 (cited hereafter as Reedstrom, "Wild West"); Howard Roberts Lamar, *The Far Southwest, 1846–1912: A Territorial History*, 137, 142, 144–47, 150, 151, 162, 164, 166, 186, 193, 273, 288, 290, 490. Elkins was known to some as "Smooth Steve" Elkins. See Robert M. Utley, *High Noon in Lincoln County: Violence on the Western Frontier*, 24–37, for more on the Santa Fe Ring.
4. *Memphis Commercial-Appeal*, May 25–26, 1903.
5. Robert H. Cartmell, diary, Robert H. Cartmell Papers, Tennessee State Library and Archives, Nashville, Tennessee.
6. *Nashville American*, June 1, 8, 1903.
7. *Columbia (Tenn.) Daily Herald*, June 9, 1909.
8. *Nashville American*, June 8, 14, 1903; Frank James to John Trotwood Moore, June 21, 1903, John Trotwood Moore Papers, Tennessee State Library and Archives, Nashville, Tennessee.
9. *Chattanooga Daily Times*, June 13, 1903; *Chattanooga News*, June 12–13, 1903.
10. *Knoxville (Tenn.) Sentinel*, June 15, 1903.
11. Ibid. *Knoxville (Tenn.) Daily Journal and Tribune*, June 15, 1903.
12. *Morristown (Tenn.) Gazette*, June 10, 1903. A check of Johnson City and Bristol newspapers indicated that nothing outstanding was reported in the press there during the show's visits.
13. *Lynchburg (Va.) News*, June 21, 23, 1903, February 20, 1915.
14. Cole Younger to John Trotwood Moore, June 28, 1903, John Trotwood Moore Papers, Tennessee State Library and Archives, Nashville, Tennessee. Access to Moore's correspondence with Cole Younger was at one time restricted. Whether true or not, there was some speculation that members of the family may have been embarrassed by Moore's connection with Cole Younger. There was also some correspondence with Lizzie Daniels about Cole. Moore was born in 1858 in Marion, Alabama, and used the name Trotwood, taken from Dickens's *David Copperfield*, first as a pen name and later as his adopted middle name. The information about Cole's connection to Lizzie Daniels and Moore was supplied to the author by Marley Brant; Reedstrom, "Wild West," 37.

15. *Washington Post*, July 3, 1903.
16. *Baltimore American*, July 3–4, 1903. Oddly, the newspaper made no mention of Frank's former residence in Baltimore.
17. Cole Younger to John Trotwood Moore, June 28, 1903, John Trotwood Moore Papers, Tennessee State Library and Archives, Nashville, Tennessee. Cole gave the following show route to Moore: July 4, York, Pennsylvania; July 6, Lancaster; July 7, Harrisburg; July 8, Lewiston; July 9, Tyrone; July 10, Hollidaysburg; July 11, Phillipsburg; July 13, Clearfield; July 14, Punxsutawney; July 15, DuBoise; July 16, Ridgeway; July 17, Kane; July 18, Warren; July 20, Erie; Reedstrom, "Wild West," 37.
18. *Huntington (W.V.) Advertiser*, August 1, 3, 10, 11, 1903.
19. *Maryville (Mo.) Nodaway Forum*, September 3, 1903; *Maryville (Mo.) Tribune*, September 3, 1903. The *Tribune* claimed that the grifters, who were selling seats for the show, "reached over the borderland of graft into outright crookedness." See also Reedstrom "Wild West," 37–38.
20. *Kansas City Journal*, August 21, 1904; *Kansas City Star*, November 2, 1904; Settle, 164. The information about Hadley was supplied by Settle to me. Hadley was Roosevelt's floor manager at the 1912 Republican convention but supported Taft after TR bolted the GOP to set up the Progressive, or "Bull Moose," Party. See Love, 419–22. Frank did manage to pen a note to the president, telling him he was a man after his own heart. *Phoenix (Ariz.) Republic*, September 20, 1992, reprinting an article from the *Saint Petersburg (Fla.) Times*, carried journalist Margo Hammond's suggestion that "Eastern working class readers [of dime novels] . . . saw in the defiance of Jesse James . . . echoes of their own battles."
21. *Kansas City Star*, November 22, 1904. See also speeches by Frank James, copies in my papers from Lee Pollock Collection, Princeton, Illinois. See Appendix F for full transcripts.
22. Undated and unattributed Butte, Montana, newspaper clipping, ca. 1904–5, giving the Galland incident in an article, "City For Sensations," and the review of Frank's acting, copy in author's collection. The troupe subsequently appeared at Anaconda and Missoula, Montana, and then went to Spokane [Washington?].
23. Undated and unattributed news clipping, "Kindly Frank James and Beautiful Wife Recalled in Oklahoma Town," copy in author's collection; Settle, 164. Frank apparently owned a town lot in Darrow, Oklahoma, purchased December 16, 1904, for seventy-five dollars from the Guthrie, Fairview, and Western Railroad. A copy of a certificate for payment is in the author's collection. The ultimate disposition of this property is not known.
24. Croy, *Younger*, 137–39, 169; Croy, *James*, 213–14.
25. *Kansas City Times*, March 23, 1909. Cummins and Frank James had a rather cool relationship at best. It had been alleged that Cummins, not Frank, had been involved in the Winston robbery, and this led in part to Cummins's life on the run for more than two decades. See *Cummins' Book*, 106–9, and Love, 430–46, for background on the rift between Frank and Cummins; Hale, *Quantrill*, 81, gives the date of Cummins's death as July 9, 1929. He was eighty-two years old. See also *Cummins' Book*, 93–106, for more on Cummins as scout and deputy and his return to Missouri.

26. *Kansas City Post*, November 5, 1909, September 20, 22, 1910, September 17, 1911. The *Post* gave the story treatment in rather sensational tabloid style. The domestic difficulties are completely overlooked in Stella James's posthumous memoir, *In The Shadow of Jesse James*, 87–91. Other than this omission, this is perhaps the best account of the lives of the family members after the turn of the century. Stella and Jesse had four children: Lucille Martha (1900–1988), Josephine Frances (1902–64), Jessie Estelle (1906–87), and Ethel Rose (1908–91).

27. Stella James, 62–66, 73, 129–31. See the *Nashville Banner*, April 4, 1927, for the story of the cabin section taken to Hot Springs. I had several conversations with Milton F. Perry, who before his death had tried unsuccessfully to find what had become of the cabin section. John Allen Gable, *The Bull Moose Years: Theodore Roosevelt and the Progressive Party*, 126–31. Joseph L. Gardner, *Departing Glory: Theodore Roosevelt as Ex-President*, 270–79, contains the best account of the assassination attempt. Frank James to Col. Theodore Roosevelt, telegram transcript, October 15, 1912, copy in my collection; Elbert Martin to Frank James, October 19, 1912, copy in my collection. According to Milton Perry, the Roosevelt campaign staff apparently somewhat soft-pedaled their reply to Frank. His offer to raise a bodyguard could have been a political double-edged sword. It is not mentioned in any of the Roosevelt biographies.

28. Julian Street, "The Borderland," *Collier's Weekly*, September 26, 1914. Street's article gives an interesting glimpse of Frank James just prior to his death and contains some valuable information. His account of the hanging of Dr. Samuel in 1863, cited elsewhere, is particularly valuable, as it corroborates other accounts. But on other topics, Frank dodged issues right and left. The author asked, in regard to Dan Askew, the neighbor living next to the James-Samuel farm before the disastrous raid in 1875, "I should have thought he would have been afraid to harbor a Pinkerton Man," to which Frank replied, "You'd have thought so, wouldn't you?" See Settle, 164–65; *Nashville Tennessean*, April 9, 1939, for the quote by Frank's widow.

29. Brant, *Younger*, 312–16; Breihan, *Complete and Authentic Life*, 149–53.

30. Stella James, 92–98, 136–38. The film was actually in two parts, *Jesse James Under the Black Flag* was part 1, and *Jesse James as the Outlaw* was part 2.

31. Ibid., 96–98; Ted P. Yeatman, "The Guns of Jesse James," *Old West* 33, no. 1 (Fall 1996): 21–22. James R. Ross to Ted P. Yeatman, June 22, 1995, my collection, containing information regarding the Supreme Court brief and the comments by Chief Justice Hughes. Apparently the original document disappeared in one of several moves, but Judge Ross recalled from memory the comments. Settle, 177; Glenn Shirley, "Fred Thomson," *True West* 32, no. 8 (1985). Frank would have sorely disapproved of his nephew's involvement in this picture. In the opening Civil War sequence Jesse is portrayed as a spy who is saved from capture by Zerelda Mimms, a woman from up north who is stranded on the plantation of her "uncle," Frederick Slade. After the war Jesse is informed by "Parson Bill" that his mother was maimed by Union radicals, and he goes on the warpath. While this cinematic "Jesse" robs trains, bank robberies are not in his line. Escaping an attempt to capture him by arch traitor Bob Ford and posse, "Jesse" rides into the sunset with Zee after being married by good old Parson Bill. Silent film star Fred

Thomson had quite a following, and this obviously accounts for much of the film's success. The picture grossed at least $1.2 million.

32. *Nashville Banner*, April 4, 1933; Stella James, 43–46; Croy, *James*, xii.

CHAPTER 16: THE RESURRECTION OF JESSE JAMES

1. Settle, 170; Stella James, 99–103, 138–39. Stella James's account is probably the best version describing the John James hoax.

2. *Washington Post*, July 28, 1914; *New York World* in *Boonville (Mo.) Weekly Advertiser*, August 21, 1914; Settle, 169; Ramon Adams, *Burs Under The Saddle*, 281–83; idem, *More Burs Under the Saddle*, 158–61; Ted Yeatman, "Missouri Spuriana: Books and Booklets By and About James Gang Impostors," *Show-Me Libraries* 34, no. 8 (May 1983): 29–30 (cited hereafter as Yeatman, "Spuriana"). Joe Vaughn may well have been Quantrill veteran Joe Vaughn, suffering the effects of dementia. Whoever he was, he was not the real Frank James. The two books by Ramon Adams are must reading for anyone interested in books promoting the various impostor claims.

3. Settle, 169–70.

4. *Nashville Banner*, August 16, 1974.

5. David Smith to Ted P. Yeatman, August 20, 1999, my papers; George Warfel to Ted P. Yeatman, October 24, 1994, my papers. Information on the house and cabin construction that had been given to Warfel was valuable during the restoration of the site in the late 1970s.

6. *Nashville Banner*, April 9, 1939; *Kansas City Star*, July 6, 1944. George Warfel said that Frank's widow would go into her room whenever he visited the farm.

7. James R. Ross to Ted P. Yeatman, May 19, 1993, author's papers. Ross relates the involvement of his mother, Jo Frances James Ross, in the project. Nora Johnson, *Flashback: Nora Johnson on Nunnally Johnson*, 11, 69, 71–74; William R. Meyer, *The Making of the Great Westerns*, 56–75; Ken Weiss and Ed Goodgold, *To Be Continued . . .* , 269–70, for information on "Jesse James Rides Again." This serial is remarkable for the number of sharp objects used against Jesse.

8. Steve Eng, "The Great Outlaw Hoax," *True West* 33, no. 2 (February 1986): 17–18 (cited hereafter as Eng, "Hoax"). Eng's is one of the best accounts of the hoax available. James D. Horan and Paul Sann, *Pictorial History of the Wild West*, 244. Horan calls the gang led by Jennings "a pale imitation of the real thing" and gives a brief history. Patterson, *Train*, 117–18, gives a more detailed account of Jennings's life. At a meeting of the Western Writers of America at Branson, Missouri, in the mid-1980s, I had a chance to speak to Paul Bailey of Claremont, California. It appears that sometime in the 1940s or 1950s, Bailey, who edited and published books on the Old West, negotiated with Jennings for his autobiography. The book was about to go to press when Bailey received a phone call notifying him that another publisher had exclusive rights to Jennings's life story, based an a previous book by the Oklahoma old-timer. Al Jennings was certainly a great rogue, if a poor excuse for an outlaw.

9. Eng, "Hoax," 18; Stella James, Letter to Harry Hoffman, August 26, 1948, Missouri State Museum, Jefferson City, Missouri. The correspondence of Jesse Jr.'s old friend

sheds considerable new light on the hoax as it affected the James family. The files of the State Museum contain a collection of letters from Hoffman to Curator Donald M. Johnson, including some material from Stella James.

10. Eng, "Hoax, 18–19; *Nashville Tennessean*, September 17, 1948; *Clarksville (Tenn.) Leaf-Chronicle*, September 27, 1948; Yeatman, "Spuriana," 30; Nancy B. Samuelson to Ted P. Yeatman, March 16, 1993, author's papers. Just who Dalton really was may never be certain. According to Dalton family historian Nancy B. Samuelson, he was probably a member of a Texas branch of the Dalton family that moved from Tennessee to Texas. Possibly he was a "black sheep" in the lineage of the family of Marcus Lafayette Dalton, a rancher who was killed by Indians. J. Frank Dalton is known to have been involved in the wildcat oil-well business, as were some of Marcus Dalton's sons; Carl Breihan, "Alias Jesse James, Part 1," *Real West* (January 1971): 22–27, 68–69 (cited hereafter as Breihan, "Alias, pt. 1"). Breihan's two-part series is one of the best exposés of Dalton. William Marvel, "The Great Impostors," *Blue and Gray Magazine* 8, no. 3 (February 1991): 32–33, gives a good rundown on the many "last" veterans of the Civil War and is a masterful exposé.

11. Carl Breihan, "Alias Jesse James, Conclusion," *Real West* (February 1971): 50, 73; Harry Hoffman to Donald M. Johnson, Missouri State Museum, Jefferson City, Missouri.

12. Breihan, "Alias, pt. 1," 22–26; Ola Everhard, "My Experiences with Jesse James, Alias J. Frank Dalton" in Rudy Turilli, *I Knew Jesse James* (pages unnumbered); Eng, "Hoax," 19–20.

13. *Nashville Banner*, December 23, 1949, March 11, 1950; *Nashville Tennessean*, March 11, 1950; *Saint Louis Post-Dispatch*, March 13, 1950; *Franklin County Tribune (Union, Mo.)*, March 17, 1950; Breihan, "Alias, pt. 1," 22, for the UP feature; Henry J. Walker, *Jesse James, The Outlaw*, 133, 145–46. Walker's book is valuable primarily as a record of Dalton's yarns recalled separately from the works of Orvus Lee Howk–"Jesse James III." Walker observed Dalton while visiting the caverns on three different trips and swallowed the blather. Steele, *Family*, 49; *South Western Reporter*, 2d ser., 473:757–63 (cited hereafter as 473 S.W. 2d 757).

14. Yeatman, "Spuriana," 30–31; Eng, "Hoax," 21. My information on films comes from my research for James Starrs.

15. Eng, "Hoax," 21; Steele, *Family*, 46–47; *Los Angeles Times*, November 17, 1983; *Nashville Tennessean*, March 16, 1984; *Poplar Bluff Daily American Republic*, March 25, 1991, January 10, 1993; Irving Wallace and David Wallachinsky, *The People's Almanac, #2*, 516–17; 473 S.W. 2d 757.

16. *Dallas Morning News*, September 28, 1992, July 12, 1995.

17. Emmett C. Hoctor, "Jesse James Revisited," *Wild West* 7, no. 1 (June 1994): 42–49.

18. Author's recollections; AP feature, "Scientists Want to Dig Up Jesse James," June 27, 1995; American Bar Association, *Presidential Showcase Program: The Trial of Jesse James—High Tech Meets the Wild West*, August 4, 1996, Tab 1, "Motion to Exhume the Body of Jesse James" (no page numbers).

19. *Washington Post*, July 9, 1995; *Poplar Bluff (Mo.) Daily American Republic*, July 7, 1995; *Friends of the James Farm Journal* 12, no. 2 (Fall 1995): 1, 4; *Saint Louis Post-Dispatch*, July 16, 1995.

20. Blaine Harden, "Jesse James: Dead and Alive," *Washington Post Magazine*, November 19, 1995, 19–21, 24–27, 34–39 (cited hereafter as Harden, "James"). Harden's article is must reading for both the story of the exhumation and a description of the colorful Starrs. *Kearney (Mo.) Courier*, "Probing a Mystery," 14–24 (cited hereafter as *Courier*, "Mystery"). This is a collection of articles from the Kearney newspaper reprinted in a special publication. *Saint Louis Post-Dispatch*, July, 16, 18, 19, 1995; *Poplar Bluff (Mo.) Daily American Republic*, July 18, 20, 1995; *USA Today*, July 19, 1995.

21. *Courier*, "Mystery," 26–27, 32–36, 38–44; *Poplar Bluff (Mo.) Daily American Republic*, October 22, 29, 1995; *Saint Louis Post-Dispatch*, October 29, 1995; *Friends of the James Farm Journal* 12, no. 3 (Winter 1995): 1–2.

22. *Courier*, "Mystery," 50–53; *Saint Louis Post-Dispatch*, February 24, 1996; *Kansas City Star*, February 24, 1996; Bob Holladay, "Tracking the Outlaw Bloodline," *Nashville Scene*, February 29, 1996; Harden, "James," 20, with an account of two other Jesse James survival claims, besides those of Dalton, that surfaced prior to or during the exhumation; observations of the author at Nashville on February 22–23, 1996. Ross is a retired judge of the Superior Court of Orange County, California; Harden, "James," 20. Both Simmons and Crawford were present at the Kearney exhumation. Curiously, Randy Schneider and Vincel Simmons, *Jesse James: The Real Story, Book 1* (unfortunately the pages are not numbered), appears to make the case that Jacob Benjamin Gerlt (who died in 1950 and was buried near Sedalia, Missouri) is the same person as J. Frank Dalton (who died in August 1951 and was buried in Granbury, Texas); see the sections "My Year with Jesse James," by Joe Wood, and "The Final Resting Place of Jesse James and His Wife Zerelda."

23. Anne Dingus, "Body of Evidence," *Texas Monthly* (August 1997): 22–24; Greg Lalire, "Beyond Jesse's DNA," *Wild West* 11, no. 4 (December 1998): 6. Reportedly there are photos that have been matched to those of Jesse by an "expert." Photographic identification of individuals, either from another photo or from life, has its limitations; see Jurgen Thorwald, *The Century of the Detective*, 65–74, 93–95. In the early part of this century there was the case of Adolf Beck in Britain, whose arrest was based on his resemblance to a known criminal in a photograph. This criminal had identical Bertillon measurements, i.e., measurements of the features of the man's head, to the man in question. Fortunately, the real criminal was captured. It was then discovered that the two men could have been doubles except that fingerprints, which were then coming into use, showed they were actually two very different people. Similarly, two identical men were incarcerated at Leavenworth Penitentiary, ca. 1903, further demonstrating the shortcomings of the Bertillon system. It was soon after these episodes that the Bertillon system fell into disrepute for criminal identification and was replaced by fingerprint identification. DNA identification can be even more precise—and lasting. Betty Dorsett Duke, *Jesse James Lived and Died in Texas*, 41–44, 49, 204, questions the DNA evidence of the 1995 James exhumation, claiming that the tooth used was of doubtful provenance. Her argument was refuted by Michael Finnegan, "Forensic Analysis of Osseus Material Excavated at the James Site, Clay County, Missouri," in *Human Identification: Case Studies in Forensic Anthropology*, ed. Jane E. Buikstra, 380–91,

which appeared in 1984. Finnegan discusses the teeth and other material found in the grave; he also worked on the 1995 exhumation and study. Apparently Duke was unaware of this study and its documentation of the 1978 excavation of the first gravesite at the James farm. It is possible that some of these later "Jesse James" candidates—Gerlt, Courtney, etc.—were at one time in their lives involved in some sort of criminal enterprise that was confused later with that of the original James gang. It may also be suggested that a connection with the James gang was fabricated by these impostors in their latter years to make their past more acceptable to other family members. Duke's book makes reference to James and Bill Wilkerson, associated with Courtney, as "known" members of the James gang. In all my years of research, I have never encountered these names in connection with the gang. There were two Quantrill veterans named Wilkerson who were suspected in the 1866 Liberty bank robbery; however, no one by that name was suspected in any of the robberies committed after the December 1869 Gallatin bank holdup, which marked the first robbery formally attributed to either Frank or Jesse James. In any event, just as now, there were any number of people named James and Bill Wilkerson, and it is difficult to say that these men were the same as the Liberty suspects.

24. Eric Hobsbawm, *Bandits*, 51. This book must be considered a classic and is a "must read" for anyone interested in legendary outlaws. Hobsbawm draws on bandit scholarship from around the world, proving such legends are not just an American phenomenon. There are other bandits who "never died" scattered across the globe; the noble outlaw is an archetype found in other cultures and ages. It is interesting to note that the various James impostors, and notably J. Frank Dalton, tried to model their yarns on the legendary Jesse James. Some of these tales have the touch of the dime novel or the B-movie serial. Undoubtedly they were trying to rope in the gullible dime-novel readers who bought and read these stories as factual. The equivalent practice today would be to get one's news from the grocery-store tabloids.

APPENDIX H

1. Based on reports in the *Fort Worth Star-Telegram*, May 30, 2000; the *Dallas Morning News*, May 31 and June 30, 2000; and the *Washington Times*, June 2, 2000.

Selected Bibliography

NOTE: Full citations of articles, interviews, and manuscript collections appear in the endnotes.

BOOKS AND BOOKLETS

Adams, Ramon F. *Burs Under the Saddle*. Norman: University of Oklahoma Press, 1964.

———. *More Burs under the Saddle*. Norman: University of Oklahoma Press, 1979.

———. *Six-Guns and Saddle Leather*. Norman: University of Oklahoma Press, 1954.

Albaugh, William A., III, and Edward Simmons. *Confederate Arms*. New York: Bonanza Books, 1957.

Alotta, Robert I. *Civil War Justice: Union Army Executions under Lincoln*. Shippensburg, Pa.: White Mane Publishing Co., 1989.

American Bar Association. *Presidential Showcase Program: The Trial of Jesse James—High Tech Meets the Wild West*. Chicago: American Bar Association, 1996.

Ames, Blanche Butler, comp. *Chronicles from the Nineteenth Century: Family Letters of Blanche Butler and Adelbert Ames*. Clinton, Mass.: Privately printed, 1957.

Annual Report of the Adjutant General of Missouri for 1864. Jefferson City, Mo.: W. A. Curry, 1864.

Appler, Augustus C. *The Younger Brothers: The Life, Character and Daring Exploits of the Youngers, The Notorious Bandits Who Rode with Jesse James and William Clarke Quantrill*. 1876. Reprint, New York: Frederick Fell, 1955.

Argall, Phyllis. *The Truth about Jesse James*. Sullivan, Mo.: Lester B. Dill and Rudy Turilli, 1953.

Atkins, Annette. *Harvest of Grief: Grasshopper Plagues and Public Assistance in Minnesota, 1873–1878*. Saint Paul: Minnesota Historical Society Press, 1984.

Ayers, Edward L. *The Promise of the New South: Life after Reconstruction*. New York: Oxford University Press, 1992.

Bailey, Thomas. *The American Pageant: A History of the Republic*. Boston: Little, Brown, 1962.

Ball, Larry D. *The United States Marshals of New Mexico and Arizona Territories, 1846–1912*. Albuquerque: University of New Mexico Press, 1992.

Barth, Jack et al. *Roadside America*. New York: Simon & Schuster, 1986.

Beamis, Joan M., and William E. Pullen. *Background of a Bandit: The Ancestry of Jesse James*. Liberty, Mo.: Jesse James Publishers, 1981.

Biographical Directory of the United States Congress, 1774–1989. Washington, D.C.: Government Printing Office, 1989.

Bradley, R. T., ed. *The Outlaws of the Border, or The Lives of Frank and Jesse James*. Saint Louis: J. W. Marsh, 1882.

Brandt, Nat. *The Man Who Tried to Burn New York*. 1986. Reprint, New York: Berkley, 1990.

Brant, Marley. *The Families of Charles Lee and Henry Washington Younger: A Genealogical Sketch*. Burbank, Calif.: privately printed, 1986.

————. *Jesse James: The Man and the Myth*. New York: Berkley Books, 1998.

————. *The Outlaw Youngers: A Confederate Brotherhood*. Lanham, Md.: Madison Books, 1992.

Breihan, Carl W. *The Complete and Authentic Life of Jesse James*. New York: Frederick Fell, 1953.

————. *The Day Jesse James Was Killed*. 1961. Reprint, New York: Signet, 1979.

————. *The Escapades of Frank and Jesse James*. New York: Frederick Fell, 1974.

————. *The Man Who Shot Jesse James*. New York: A. S. Barnes, 1979.

————. *Saga of Jesse James*. Caldwell, Idaho: Caxton, 1991.

————. *The Younger Brothers*. San Antonio: Naylor, 1961.

Britton, Wiley. *The Civil War on the Border*. New York: G. P. Putnam's Sons, 1899.

Broehl, Wayne G., Jr. *The Molly Maguires*. Cambridge: Harvard University Press, 1964.

Brophy, Patrick, ed. *Bushwhackers of the Border: The Civil War Period in Western Missouri*. Nevada, Mo.: Vernon County Historical Society, 1980.

————, ed. *"Found No Bushwhackers": The 1864 Diary of Sgt. James P. Mallery, Co. A, Third Wisconsin Cavalry, Stationed at Balltown, Mo*. Nevada, Mo.: Vernon County Historical Society, 1988.

Brown, Dee. *Year of the Century: 1876*. New York: Scribner, 1976.

Brown, George William. *Baltimore and the Nineteenth of April 1861*. 1887. Reprint, Baltimore: Maclay, 1982.

Brown, Harry James, and Frederick D. Williams, eds. *The Diary of James A. Garfield*, Vol. 4, 1878–1881. East Lansing: Michigan State University, 1967–81.

Brownlee, Richard S. *Gray Ghosts of the Confederacy: Guerrilla Warfare in the West, 1861–1863*. Baton Rouge: Louisiana State University Press, 1958.

Bruce, Robert V. *1877: Year of Violence*. Indianapolis: Bobbs-Merrill, 1959.

Bryan, Howard. *Wildest of the Wild West: True Tales of a Frontier Town on the Santa Fe Trail*. Santa Fe, N.M.: Clear Light Publishers, 1988.

Buel, James William. *The Border Outlaws and The Border Bandits*. 1882. Reprint, Harrisburg, Pa.: National Historical Society, 1994.

Buikstra, Jane E., and Ted Rathbun, eds. *Human Identification: Case Studies in Forensic Anthropology*. Springfield, Ill.: Thomas, 1984.

Burbank, David T. *Reign of the Rabble: The St. Louis General Strike of 1877*. New York: A. M. Kelley, 1966.

Burns, Frank. *Davidson County*. Memphis, Tenn.: Memphis State University Press, 1989.

Busch, Moritz. *Bismarck: Some Secret Pages of His History*. New York: Macmillan, 1898.

Calhoun, Frederick S. *The Lawmen: United States Marshals and Their Deputies, 1789–1889*. 1989. Reprint, New York: Penguin Books, 1991.

Castel, Albert E. *A Frontier State at War: Kansas, 1861–1865*. Ithaca, N.Y.: Cornell University Press, 1958.

————. *General Sterling Price and the Civil War in the West*. Baton Rouge: Louisiana State University Press, 1968.

————. *William Clarke Quantrill: His Life and Times*. New York: Frederick Fell, 1962.

————, and Thomas Goodrich. *Bloody Bill Anderson: The Short Savage Life of a Civil War Guerrilla*. Mechanicsburg, Pa.: Stackpole, 1998.

Chandler, Chapman P. *Roster of Wisconsin Volunteers: War of the Rebellion*. Madison, Wis.: Democrat Printing Co., 1886.

Clemens, Samuel L., and Charles D. Warner. *The Gilded Age*. 1874. Reprint, New York: Doubleday, 1964.

Coffman, Edward. *The Story of Logan County*. Nashville, Tenn.: Parthenon Press, 1962.

Coleman, John Winston. *Stage Coach Days in the Bluegrass*. Louisville, Ky.: Standard Press, 1935.

Comstock, Jim, ed. *West Virginia Heritage Encyclopedia*. Richwood, W.V.: Comstock, 1974.

Connelley, William Elsey. *Quantrill and the Border Wars*. 1910. Reprint, New York: Pageant Book Co., 1956.

Corbitt, Lydia D. *Denver, Tennessee, Remembered*. Waverly, Tenn.: Privately printed, 1986.

————. *History of Plant Community*, N.p.p.: Privately printed, 1976.

Cramer, Rose Fulton. *Wayne County, Missouri*. Cape Girardeau, Mo.: Ramfire Press, 1972.

Cresswell, Stephen. *Mormons and Cowboys, Moonshiners and Klansmen: Federal Law Enforcement in the South and West, 1870–1893*. Tuscaloosa: University of Alabama Press, 1991.

Crickmore, Henry G., comp. *Krick's Guide to the Turf, 1878–80*. New York: H. G. Crickmore, 1878–81.

Crittenden, Henry Huston, comp. *The Crittenden Memoirs*. New York: Putnam, 1936.

Croy, Homer. *Jesse James Was My Neighbor*. New York: Duell, Sloan and Pierce, 1949.

————. *Last of the Great Outlaws*. 1956. Reprint, New York: Signet, 1958.

Cummins, Jim. *Jim Cummins' Book.* 1903. Reprint, Provo, Utah: Triton Press, 1988.

————. *Jim Cummins the Guerrilla.* Excelsior Springs, Mo.: Daily Journal, 1908.

Current, Richard Nelson. *Those Terrible Carpetbaggers: A Reinterpretation.* New York: Oxford University Press, 1988.

Dalton, Kit [John W.?]. *Under the Black Flag.* Memphis, Tenn.: Lockard Publishing Co., 1914.

Dacus, Joseph A. *Annals of the Great Strikes in the United States.* Chicago: L. T. Palmer and Co., 1877.

————. *Illustrated Lives and Adventures of Frank and Jesse James.* Saint Louis: N. D. Thompson and Co., 1882.

Dean, Eric T. *Shook Over Hell: Post Traumatic Stress, Vietnam, and the Civil War.* Cambridge, Mass.: Harvard University Press, 1997.

Derks, Scott, ed. *The Value of a Dollar: Prices and Incomes in the United States, 1860–1989.* Detroit: Gale, 1994.

Desty, Robert, ed. *The Federal Reporter: Cases Argued and Determined in the Circuit and District Courts of the United States, Vol. 18, November 1883–February 1884.* Saint Paul, Minn.: West Publishing, 1884.

Dibble, Roy Floyd. *Strenuous Americans.* New York: Boni and Liveright, 1923.

Donald, Jay. *Outlaws of the Border.* Philadelphia: Douglas Brothers, 1882.

Drago, Harry Sinclair. *Outlaws on Horseback: The History of the Organized Bands of Bank and Train Robbers Who Terrorized the Prairie Towns of Missouri, Kansas, Indian Territory, and Oklahoma for Half a Century.* New York: Dodd, Mead, 1964.

————. *Road Agents and Train Robbers: Half a Century of Western Banditry.* New York: Dodd, Mead, 1973.

Duke, Betty Dorsett. *Jesse James Lived and Died in Texas.* Austin, Tex.: Eakin Press, 1998.

Durham, Walter T. *Rebellion Revisited: A History of Sumner County, Tennessee, From 1861 to 1870.* Franklin, Tenn.: Hillsboro Press, 1999.

Edwards, Jennie, comp. *John Newman Edwards: Biography, Memoirs, Reminiscinces, and Recollections, including Shelby's Expedition to Mexico.* Kansas City: Privately printed, 1889.

Edwards, John Newman. *Noted Guerrillas, or the Warfare of the Border.* 1877. Reprint, Dayton, Ohio: Morningside Press, 1976.

————. *Shelby and His Men.* Cincinnati: Miami Printing and Publishing Co., 1867.

Emerson, Edwin. *A History of the Nineteenth Century, Year by Year, Vol. 3.* New York: P. E. Collier and Son, 1902.

Fellman, Michael. *Inside War: The Guerrilla Conflict in Missouri During the American Civil War.* New York: Oxford University Press, 1989.

Feunfhausen, Gary G. *A Guide to Historic Clay County, Missouri: Architectural Resources and Other Historic Sites of the Civil War, Also Exploits of John C. Calhoun "Coon" Thornton, a Clay County Confederate Officer.* Kansas City, Mo.: Little Dixie Publications, 1996.

Fitch, John. *Annals of the Army of the Cumberland: Comprising Biographies, Descriptions of Departments, Accounts of Expeditions, Skirmishes and Battles; Also It's Police Record of Spies, Smugglers, and Prominant Rebel Emmissaries, together with anecdotes, Incidents, Poetry, Reminiscences, etc., and Official Reports of the Battle of Stone[s] River and the Chickamauga Campaign.* Philadelphia: J. B. Lippincott, 1864.

Foner, Eric. *Reconstruction: America's Unfinished Revolution, 1863–1877.* New York: Harper & Row, 1988.

Foner, Philip S. *The Great Labor Uprising of 1877.* New York: Monad Press, 1977.

————. *History of the Labor Movement in the United States, Vol. 1.* New York: International Publishers, 1975.

Foote, Shelby. *The Civil War, A Narrative: Fort Sumter to Perryville.* New York: Random House, 1958.

Gable, John Allen. *The Bull Moose Years: Theodore Roosevelt and the Progressive Party.* Port Washington, N.Y.: Kennikat Press, 1978.

Gardner, Joseph L. *Departing Glory: Theodore Roosevelt as Ex-President.* New York: Scribner, 1973.

Garrett, Jill Knight. *A History of Humphreys County.* Columbia, Tenn.: Privately printed, 1963.

Genovese, Eugene D. *"Slavery Ordained By God": The Southern Slaveholders' View of Biblical History and Modern Politics.* Gettysburg, Pa.: Gettysburg College, 1985.

Goodrich, Thomas. *Black Flag: Guerrilla Warfare on the Western Border, 1861–1865.* Bloomington: Indiana University Press, 1995.

————. *Bloody Dawn: The Story of the Lawrence Massacre.* Kent, Ohio: Kent State University Press, 1992.

Gordon, John Steele. *The Scarlet Woman of Wall Street: Jay Gould, Jim Fisk, Cornelius Vanderbilt, the Erie Railroad Wars and the Birth of Wall Street.* New York: Weidenfield and Nicholson, 1988.

Gragg, Rod. *Confederate Goliath: The Battle of Fort Fisher.* New York: HarperCollins, 1991.

Hale, Donald R. *They Called Him Bloody Bill: The Badman Who Taught Jesse James Outlawry.* Clinton, Mo.: The Printery, 1975.

————. *"We Rode with Quantrill": Quantrill and the Guerrilla War as Told by the Men and Women Who Were with Him.* N.p.p.: n.p., 1975.

Hall, Frank O., and Lindsay H. Whitten. *Jesse James Rides Again.* Lawton, Okla.: LaHoma Publishing Co., 1948.

Hammersley, Thomas H. S. *Complete Regular Army Register of the United States: For One Hundred Years, 1779–1879.* Washington, D.C.: T. H. S. Hammersley, 1880.

Harlow, Alvin F. *"Weep No More, My Lady."* New York: McGraw-Hill, 1942.

Harrison, Lowell H. *The Civil War in Kentucky.* Lexington: University of Kentucky Press, 1975.

Hartje, Robert S. *Van Dorn: Life and Times of a Confederate General.* Nashville, Tenn.: Vanderbilt University Press, 1967.

Heilbron, W. C. *Convict Life at the Minnesota State Prison, Stillwater, Minnesota*. Saint Paul: W. C. Heilbron, 1909.

Hendin, Herbert, and Ann Pollinger Haas. *Wounds of War: The Psychological Aftermath of Combat in Vietnam*. New York: Basic Books, 1984.

History of Clay and Platte County, Missouri. Saint Louis: National Historical Co., 1885.

History of Daviess County, Missouri. Kansas City: Bidsall and Dean, 1882.

The History of Jackson County, Missouri. 1881. Reprint, Cape Girardeau, Mo.: Ramfire Press, 1966.

Hobsbawm, Eric J. *Bandits*. New York: Pantheon Books, 1981.

Hoole, Stanley. *The James Boys Rode South*. Tuscaloosa, Ala.: Privately printed, 1955.

Horan, James D. *The Authentic Wild West: The Lawmen*. New York: Crown, 1980.

————. *The Authentic Wild West: The Outlaws*. New York: Crown, 1977.

————. *Desperate Men: Revelations from the Sealed Pinkerton Files*. Garden City, N.Y.: Doubleday, 1962.

————. *The Pinkertons: The Detective Dynasty that Made History*. New York: Bonanza Books, 1967.

————, and Paul Sann. *Pictorial History of the Old West*. New York: Crown, 1954.

Hoyt, Henry F. *Frontier Doctor*. Boston: Houghton Mifflin, 1929.

Hunt-Davis, Rupert, ed. *The Letters of Oscar Wilde*. New York: Harcourt, Brace and World, 1962.

Huntington, George. *Robber and Hero: The Story of the Northfield Bank Raid*. 1895. Reprint, Saint Paul: Minnesota Historical Society Press, 1986.

Hutton, Paul Andrew. *Phil Sheridan and His Army*. Lincoln: University of Nebraska Press, 1985.

Ingenthron, Elmo. *Borderland Rebellion*. Branson, Mo.: Ozarks Mountaineer, 1980.

Ireland, Robert M. *The County in Kentucky History*. N.p.p.: n.p., n.d.

James, Jesse Edwards. *Jesse James, My Father*. 1906. Reprint, Cleveland, Ohio: Arthur Westbrook Co., 1906.

James, Stella Frances. *In the Shadow of Jesse James*. Edited by Milton F. Perry. Thousand Oaks, Calif.: Revolver Press, 1990.

Johnson, Nora. *Flashback: Nora Johnson on Nunnally Johnson*. Garden City, N.Y.: Doubleday, 1979.

Josephy, Alvin M. *The Civil War in the American West*. New York: Knopf, 1991.

Keen, Hugh C., and Horace Mewbern. *Forty-third Battalion Virginia Cavalry: Mosby's Command*. Lynchburg, Va.: H. E. Howard Co., 1993.

Kenny, Kevin. *Making Sense of the Molly Maguires*. New York: Oxford University Press, 1998.

Kirchten, Ernest. *Catfish and Crystal: The Story of St. Louis, U.S.A.* Garden City, N.Y.: Doubleday, 1960.

Kirwan, Albert D., ed. *The Confederacy*. New York: Meridian Books, 1959.

Lamar, Howard Roberts. *The Far Southwest, 1846–1912: A Territorial History.* New Haven: Yale University Press, 1966.

Larsen, Lawrence H., and Nancy J. Hulston. *Pendergast!* Columbia: University of Missouri Press, 1997.

Lee, Maggie, ed. *Defeat of the Jesse James Gang: Small Town Routs Notorious Outlaws in the Northfield Bank Raid.* Northfield, Minn.: Northfield News, 1981.

Leslie, Edward E. *The Devil Knows How to Ride: The True Story of William Clarke Quantrill and His Confederate Raiders.* New York: Random House, 1996.

Lord, John. *Frontier Dust.* Hartford, Conn.: Edwin Valentine Mitchell, 1926.

Love, Robertus. *The Rise and Fall of Jesse James.* 1926. Reprint, Lincoln: University of Nebraska Press, 1990.

Lowry, Thomas P. *The Story the Soldiers Wouldn't Tell: Sex in the Civil War.* Mechanicsburg, Pa.: Stackpole, 1994.

McCorkle, John. *Three Years with Quantrill: A True Story Told by His Scout, John McCorkle.* 1914. Reprint, Norman: University of Oklahoma Press, 1992.

McGrane, Martin Edward. *The James Farm: Its People, Their Lives and Their Times.* Pierre, S.D.: Caleb Perkins Press, 1982.

Meyer, William R. *The Making of the Great Westerns.* New Rochelle, N.Y.: Arlington House, 1979.

Miller, George F., ed. and comp. *The Trial of Frank James for Murder.* 1898. Reprint, New York: Jingle Bob–Crown, 1977.

Monaghan, Jay. *The Civil War on the Western Border.* Boston: Little and Brown, 1958.

Morgan, H. Wayne. *From Hayes to McKinley: National Party Politics, 1877–1896.* Syracuse, N.Y.: Syracuse University Press, 1969.

Morn, Frank. *"The Eye That Never Sleeps": A History of the Pinkerton National Detective Agency.* Bloomington: Indiana University Press, 1982.

Morton, Marmaduke Beckwith. *Kentuckians Are Different.* Louisville, Ky.: Standard Press, 1938.

Nashville City Directory—1881. Nashville, Tenn.: Tavel, Eastman and Howell [?], 1881.

O'Flaherty, Daniel. *General Jo Shelby: Undefeated Rebel.* Chapel Hill: University of North Carolina Press, 1954.

O'Neal, Bill. *Encyclopedia of Western Gunfighters.* Norman: University of Oklahoma Press, 1979.

Otero, Miguel Antonio. *My Life on the Frontier, 1864–1882.* New York: Press of the Pioneers, 1935.

Palmer, John M. *Personal Recollections of John M. Palmer: The Story of an Earnest Life.* Cincinatti: R. Clarke Co., 1901.

Parrish, William E. *Missouri under Radical Rule, 1865–1870.* Columbia: University of Missouri Press, 1965.

———. *The Train Robbery Era: An Encyclopedic History.* Boulder, Colo.: Pruett Publishing Co., 1991.

Patterson, Richard. *Historical Atlas of the Outlaw West.* Boulder, Colo.: Johnson Books, 1985.

Penick, James Lal. *The Great Western Land Pirate: John A. Murrell in Legend and History.* Columbia: University of Missouri Press, 1981.

Petrone, Gerard S. *Judgement at Gallatin: The Trial of Frank James.* Lubbock: Texas Tech University Press, 1998.

Pinkerton, Allan. *The Expressman and the Detective.* 1874. Reprint, New York: Arno Press, 1976.

———. *Strikers, Tramps, Communists and Detectives.* 1878. Reprint, New York: Arno Press, 1969.

Pinkerton, William A. *Train Robberies, Train Robbers, and "Holdup" Men.* 1907. Reprint, New York: Arno Press, 1974.

Poppine, Harttie E. *Census of 1860 Population Schedules of Jackson County, Missouri.* Kansas City, Mo.: Privately printed, 1964.

Probing a Mystery. Kearney, Mo.: Kearney Courier, 1996.

Pringle, Patrick. *Stand and Deliver: Highwaymen from Robin Hood to Dick Turpin.* New York: Dorset Press, 1991.

Pullen, John W. *The Twentieth Maine: A Volunteer Regiment in the Civil War.* Philadelphia: Lippincott, 1957.

Rabas, Chuck. *Jack "Quail Hunter" Kennedy.* Independence, Mo.: Joanne C. Eakin, 1996.

Reddig, William M. *Tom's Town: Kansas City and the Pendergast Legend.* Philadelphia: J. B. Lippincott, 1947.

Report of the Adjutant General of the State of Kentucky, 1861–1866. Frankfort, Ky.: Kentucky Yeoman Office, 1866–67.

Reynolds, John N. *The Twin Hells: A Thrilling Narrative of Life in the Kansas and Missouri Penitentiaries.* Atcheson, Kans.: Bee Publishing Co., 1890.

Ross, James R. *I Jesse James.* Thousand Oaks, Calif.: Dragon Books, 1989.

Rothenberg, Gunther E. *The Art of War in the Age of Napoleon.* Bloomington: Indiana University Press, 1978.

Rothert, Otto A. *A History of Muhlenberg County.* Louisville, Ky.: J. P. Morton and Co., 1913.

Rotunda, Ronald D. *Professional Responsibility.* Saint Paul, Minn.: West Publishing, 1992.

St. Amand, Jeannette Cox, comp. *Pitt County Gravestone Records, Vol. 3.* Wilmington, N.C.: St. Amand, 1960–65.

Schlesinger, Arthur M., Jr., gen. ed. *The Almanac of American History.* New York: Bramhall House, 1986.

Schneider, Randy, and Vincel Simmons. *Jesse James: The Real Story, Book 1.* Mountain Home, Ark.: Ozark Life, 1994.

Secrest, William B. *I Buried Hickock: The Memoirs of White Eye Anderson.* College Station, Tex.: Creative Publishing Co., 1980.

Send for a Doctor: Paragraphs from Nashville History, 1874–1975. Nashville: Public Library of Nashville and Davidson County, Nashville Room, 1975.

Settle, William A., Jr. *Jesse James Was His Name: Or, Fact and Fiction Concerning the Careers of the Notorious James Brothers of Missouri*. Columbia: University of Missorui Press, 1966.

Slotkin, Richard. *Gunfighter Nation: The Myth of the Gunfighter in Twentieth Century America*. New York: Harper Perennial, 1993.

Smith, Sarah B. *Historic Nelson County*. Louisville, Ky.: Gateway Press, 1971.

South Western Reporter, 2d ser., vol. 473. Saint Paul, Minn.: West Publishing, 1972.

Spring, Agnes. *The Cheyenne and Black Hills Stage and Express Routes*. Glendale, Calif.: A. H. Clark and Co., 1949.

Steele, Phillip W. *Jesse and Frank James: The Family History*. Gretna, La.: Pelican Publishing Co., 1987.

———, with George Warfel. *The Many Faces of Jesse James*. Gretna, La.: Pelican Publishing Co., 1995.

Summers, Mark Wahlgren. *The Era of Good Stealings*. New York: Oxford University Press, 1993.

Swanburg, W. A. *Citizen Hearst*. New York: Scribner, 1961.

Taylor, John M. *Garfield of Ohio*. New York: Norton, 1970.

Taylor, Morris. *O. P. McMains and the Maxwell Land Grant Conflict*. Tucson: University of Arizona Press, 1979.

Tennessee Civil War Centennial Commission. *Tennesseans in the Civil War: A Military History of Confederate and Union Units, with Available Rosters of Personnel, Part 2*. Nashville: Tennessee Civil War Centennial Commission, 1964.

Thelen, David. *Paths of Resistance: Tradition and Dignity in Industrializing Missouri*. New York: Oxford University Press, 1986.

Thorwald, Jurgen. *The Century of the Detective*. New York: Harcourt, Brace & World, 1965.

Tidwell. William A. *April '65: Confederate Covert Action in the American Civil War*. Kent, Ohio: Kent State University Press, 1995.

———, James O. Hall, and David W. Gaddy. *Come Retribution: The Confederate Secret Service and the Assassination of Lincoln*. Jackson: University Press of Mississippi, 1988.

Triplett, Frank. *The Life, Times and Treacherous Death of Jesse James*. Edited by Joseph Snell. 1882. Reprint, New York: Promontory Press, 1970.

Trotter, William R. *Ironclads and Columbiads: The Civil War in North Carolina—The Coast*. Winston-Salem, N.C.: J. F. Blair, 1989.

Turilli, Rudy. *I Knew Jesse James*. Stanton, Mo.: Privately printed, 1966.

U.S. War Department. *The War of the Rebellion: A Compilation of Official Records of the Union and Confederate Armies*. 128 vols. Washington, D.C.: Government Printing Office, 1880–1901.

Utley, Robert M. *Billy the Kid: A Short and Violent Life*. Lincoln: University of Nebraska Press, 1989.

————. *High Noon in Lincoln: Violence on the Western Frontier*. Albuquerque: University of New Mexico Press, 1987.

Walker, Henry J. *Jesse James, the Outlaw*. Des Moines, Iowa: Wallace-Homestead Co., 1961.

Wallace, Irving, and David Wallachinsky, eds. *The People's Almanac, no. 2*. New York: Morrow, 1978.

Wallace, William H. *Speeches and Writings of William H. Wallace, with Autobiography*. Kansas City, Mo.: Western Baptist Publishing Co., 1914.

Ward, William. *Jesse James, Gentleman; or the Hold-up of the Mammoth Cave Stage*. Cleveland, Ohio: Arthur Westbrook, 1908.

Warner, Ezra. *Generals in Blue: Lives of Union Commanders*. Baton Rouge: Lousiana State University Press, 1964.

Watson, Thomas Shelby. *The Silent Riders*. Louisville, Ky.: Beechmont Press, 1971.

Weiss, Ken, and Ed Goodgold. *To Be Continued . . .* New York: Crown Publishers, 1972.

Weymouth, Lally. *America in 1876: The Way We Were*. New York: Random House, 1976.

Wellman, Paul I. *A Dynasty of Western Outlaws*. Garden City, N.Y.: Doubleday, 1961.

Wert, Jeffrey. *From Winchester to Cedar Creek: The Shenandoah Campaign of 1864*. Carlisle, Pa. : South Mountain Press, 1987.

Williams, John Hoyt. *A Great and Shining Road: The Epic Story of the Transcontinental Railroad*. New York: Times Books, 1988.

Williamson, James Joseph. *Mosby's Rangers: A Record of the Operations of the Forty-third Battalion Virginia Cavalry from Its Organization to the Surrender, From the Diary of a Private, Aupplemented and Verified with Official Reports of Federal Officers and also of Mosby: With Personal Reminiscences, Sketches of Skirmishes, Battles and Bivouacs, Dashing Raids and Daring Adventures, Scenes and Incidents in the History of Mosby's Command . . . Muster Rolls, Occupation, and Present Whereabouts of Surviving Members*. 1896. Reprint, Alexandria, Va.: Time-Life, 1982.

Woodward, C. Vann. *Reunion and Reaction: The Compromise of 1877 and the End of Reconstruction*. Boston: Little, Brown, 1951

Woodward, Patrick Henry. *Guarding the Mails; or The Secret Service of the Post Office Department*. Hartford, Conn.: Winter & Co., 1886.

Woods' Baltimore City Directory, 1876. Baltimore: John W. Woods, 1876.

World Almanac for 1868. New York: Press Publishing, 1868.

Yeatman, Ted P. *Jesse James and Bill Ryan at Nashville*. Nashville, Tenn.: Depot Press, 1981, 1982.

Younger, Thomas Coleman. *The Story of Cole Younger, By Himself*. 1903. Reprint, Provo, Utah: Triton Press, 1988.

Zink, Wilbur A. *The Roscoe Gun Battle: The Younger Brothers vs. The Pinkerton Detectives*. Appleton City, Mo.: Democrat Publishing Co., 1967, 1982.

NEWSPAPERS

Atcheson (Kans.) Daily Globe
Baltimore American
Booneville (Mo.) Weekly Advertiser
Booneville (Mo.) Weekly Eagle
Centralia (Mo.) Fireside Guard
Chattanooga Daily Times
Chattanooga News
Chicago Semi-Weekly Inter-Ocean
Chicago Tribune
Clarksville (Tenn.) Leaf-Chronicle
Columbia (Mo.) Daily Herald
Cookeville (Tenn.) Citizen
Dallas Morning News
Faribault (Minn.) Democrat
Harrodsburg (Ky.) Sayings
Huntington (W.V.) Advertiser
Independence (Mo.) Examiner
Jefferson City (Mo.) Daily Tribune
Kansas City Daily Journal
Kansas City Daily Journal of Commerce
Kansas City Journal
Kansas City Post
Kansas City Star
Kansas City Times
Kansas City Weekly Journal of Commerce
Kansas City World
Kearney (Mo.) Courier
Knoxville Daily Journal and Tribune
Knoxville Sentinel
Lexington (Mo.) Caucasian
Lexington (Mo.) Register
Liberty (Mo.) Advance
Liberty (Mo.) Tribune
Little Rock (Ark.) Daily Gazette
Louisville Courier-Journal
Louisville Daily Courier
Louisville Daily Democrat
Louisville Daily Journal
Lynchburg (Va.) News

Maryville (Mo.) Tribune
Maryville (Mo.) Nodaway Forum
Memphis Commercial-Appeal
Morristown (Tenn.) Gazette
Murfreesboro (Tenn.) Rutherford Courier
Nashville Banner
Nashville Daily American
Nashville Morning World
Nashville Republican Banner
Nashville Scene
Nashville Tennessean
New York Daily Herald
New York Graphic
New York Herald
New York Sun
New York Times
New York World
Omaha (Neb.) Daily Bee
Poplar Bluff (Mo.) Daily American Republic
Richmond (Mo.) Daily Democrat
Saint Joseph (Mo.) Daily Gazette
Saint Joseph (Mo.) Morning Herald
Saint Louis Daily Globe
Saint Louis Dispatch
Saint Louis Globe-Democrat
Saint Louis Post-Dispatch
Saint Louis Republican
Saint Louis Weekly Republican
Saint Paul Pioneer-Press
Saint Paul–Minneapolis Pioneer-Press and
     Tribune
Sedalia (Mo.) Daily Democrat
Sioux Falls (S.D.) Argus-Leader
Storm Lake (Iowa) Pilot
Union (Mo.) Frankin Country Tribune
Washington Post
Waverly (Tenn.) Democrat-Sentinel
Waverly (Tenn.) Journal
Webster (S.D.) Journal

Index